# History of the Parish of Wraysbury, Ankerwycke Priory, and Magna Charta Island; with the history of Horton, and the town of Colnbrook, Bucks.

Gordon Gyll

*History of the Parish of Wraysbury, Ankerwycke Priory, and Magna Charta Island; with the history of Horton, and the town of Colnbrook, Bucks.*
Gyll, Gordon
British Library, Historical Print Editions
British Library
1861]
4°.
10350.f.11.

## The BiblioLife Network

This project was made possible in part by the BiblioLife Network (BLN), a project aimed at addressing some of the huge challenges facing book preservationists around the world. The BLN includes libraries, library networks, archives, subject matter experts, online communities and library service providers. We believe every book ever published should be available as a high-quality print reproduction; printed on- demand anywhere in the world. This insures the ongoing accessibility of the content and helps generate sustainable revenue for the libraries and organizations that work to preserve these important materials.

The following book is in the "public domain" and represents an authentic reproduction of the text as printed by the original publisher. While we have attempted to accurately maintain the integrity of the original work, there are sometimes problems with the original book or micro-film from which the books were digitized. This can result in minor errors in reproduction. Possible imperfections include missing and blurred pages, poor pictures, markings and other reproduction issues beyond our control. Because this work is culturally important, we have made it available as part of our commitment to protecting, preserving, and promoting the world's literature.

## GUIDE TO FOLD-OUTS, MAPS and OVERSIZED IMAGES

In an online database, page images do not need to conform to the size restrictions found in a printed book. When converting these images back into a printed bound book, the page sizes are standardized in ways that maintain the detail of the original. For large images, such as fold-out maps, the original page image is split into two or more pages.

Guidelines used to determine the split of oversize pages:

- Some images are split vertically; large images require vertical and horizontal splits.
- For horizontal splits, the content is split left to right.
- For vertical splits, the content is split from top to bottom.
- For both vertical and horizontal splits, the image is processed from top left to bottom right.

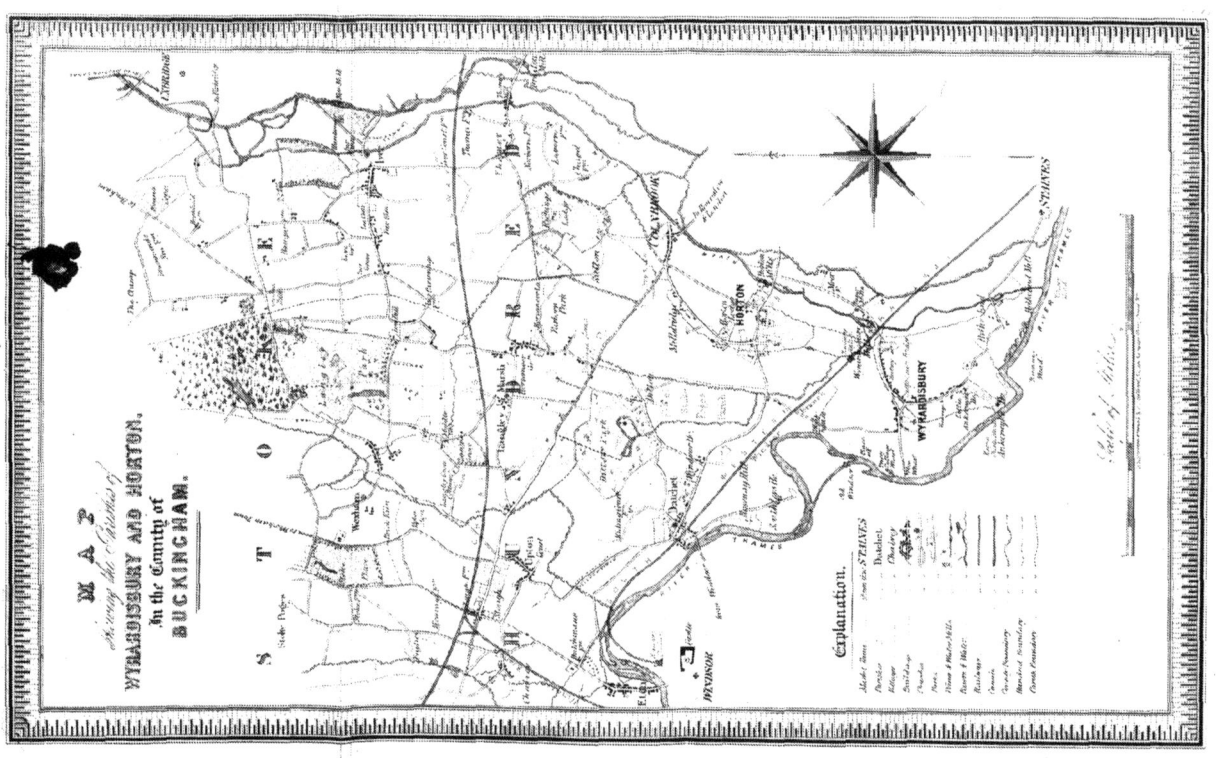

# HISTORY

## OF THE PARISH OF

## WRAYSBURY, ANKERWYCKE PRIORY,

AND

## MAGNA CHARTA ISLAND;

WITH THE

## HISTORY OF HORTON,

AND THE TOWN OF

## COLNBROOK, BUCKS.

BY

GORDON WILLOUGHBY JAMES GYLL, Esq.,

OF

WRAYSBURY.

LONDON:
HENRY G. BOHN, YORK STREET, COVENT GARDEN.
MDCCCLXII.

# DEDICATION.

## TO
## FIELD-MARSHAL HIS ROYAL HIGHNESS THE PRINCE ALBERT
### OF SAXE COBURG GOTHA AND PRINCE CONSORT,

In testimony of the admiration of public and private virtues which exalt a national character and impart additional splendour to the highest position—

The Work, comprising a History of the Parish of Wraysbury, once a feudal possession of the ancient Kings of England, who resided at Old Windsor, and formerly an integral part of the Crown lands, with the adjacent Parish of Horton, the Town and Township of Colnbrook, is respectfully dedicated by his obedient and humble servant,

THE AUTHOR.

# LIST OF SUBSCRIBERS.

### Dedicated by Permission to His Royal Highness the Prince Consort.

His Grace the Duke of Buccleuch, K.G.
His Grace the Duke of Wellington, K.G.
Earl of Orford.
Earl of Orkney.
Lord Boston.
Lord Camoys.
Lord Chesham.
Lord Llanover.
Lord Taunton.
Viscountess Gort.
Lady Garvagh.
Countess de Roulhée, Thorpe Lee, Egham.
Lady Sophia Tower, Huntsmore Lodge, Iver.
Dowager Lady Bowyer Smijth, Thorpe Lee.
Lady Otway, Portman Square.
Lady Atkinson, Portman Square.
Lady Rolt, Great Cumberland Place.
Lady Gyll, Feltham, Middlesex.
The Hon. Colonel Hood, Cumberland Lodge.
Hon. W. G. Cavendish, M.P., Latimer, Chesham.
Right Hon. Benjamin Disraeli, M.P., Hughendon Manor.
Right Hon. Milner Gibson, M.P.
David Robertson, Esq., M.P., Ladykirk, Lord-Lieutenant of Berwickshire.

Sir John de Beauvoir, Bart.
Sir William Call, Bart.
Sir John Cathcart, Bart., Englefield Green.
Lieut.-General Sir William Colebrooke, C.B., Datchet
Lieut.-Colonel Sir Claude de Crespigny, Bart.
Sir Charles Forbes, Bart., Castle Now, Aberdeenshire.
Sir John Gibbons, Bart., Stanwell.
Sir James Hamilton, Bart., Portman Square.
Sir Charles Hamilton, Bart.
Sir Fitz Roy Kelly, M.P., The Chantry, Suffolk.
Sir John Neeld, Bart., Grittleton, Wilts.
Sir George Otway, Bart., Portman Square.
Major-General Sir Travell Phillips, Kt., Senior United Service Club.
Sir Peter Van Notten Pole, Bart.
Sir Seymour Sadler, Kt., Carlton Chambers.
Sir William Bowyer Smijth, Bart., Hill Hall, Essex.
Sir Gardiner Wilkinson, Kt.
Sir William Yardley, Kt., Horton House.
Sir Charles George Young, Kt. Garter.

The Hon. and Very Rev. the Dean of Windsor.
The Hon. and Rev. Charles Courtenay, Canon of Windsor.
Dr. Hawtrey, Provost of Eton.
Admiral Evans, Englefield Green.
Lieut.-General Scott, Thorpe Lee, Egham.
Major-General Wood, Littleton, Middlesex.
Lieut.-Colonel Thomas Tulloch, Senior United Service Club.
Lieut.-Colonel Ruggles Brise, Spain Hall, Essex.
Lieut.-Colonel Charles Murray, Whitton Park, Hounslow.
Colonel Sissmore, Datchet.
Lieut.-Colonel William Watson, Great Cumberland Place.
Lieut.-Colonel Henry Salwey, Runnimede Park, Egham.
Captain William Morris, R.N.
Captain Maw, R.N., Ashford.
Major Edward Jodrell, Bayfield Hall, Norfolk.
Major Walsh, Datchet.
Captain Ives, Norwich.
Captain Richard Weyland, Woodrising, Norfolk.
Captain Shelton, Wraysbury.
Lieutenant Fleming George Gyll, Royal Artillery.
Frederick Dundas, Esq., M.P., Hanover Square.
Beaumont Coles, Esq., M.P., Portman Square.

Aldane, Messrs., Wraysbury.
Arabin, Mrs.
Arden, Joseph, Esq., Cavendish Square.
Ashford, William, Esq., Petersham, Surrey.
Ashby, Mr Charles, Staines.
Ashby, Mr. Frederick, Staines.
Auldjo, Thomas, Esq., Rutland Gate, Hyde Park.
Beaumont, John, Esq., Wimbledon.
Bennet, Rev. Leigh, Thorpe, Surrey.
Bonnell, James Harvey, Esq., Pelham Place, Old Windsor.
Bonnet, Mrs., Wraysbury. (4 copies.)
Boultbee, Rev. Richard Moore, Iver.
Browne, John Bathurst Graver, Esq., Morley Hall, Norfolk.
Buckland, Mr. Francis, Wraysbury.
Buckland, Mr. Thomas William, Wraysbury.
Buller, Mrs. Charles, Devonshire.
Bullock, Rev. Walter, Falkborne Hall, Essex.

## LIST OF SUBSCRIBERS.

Burton, Mrs., Gloucester Place.
Bury, Edgar, Esq.

Chichester, Robert Bruce, Esq.
Clayton, Oscar, Esq., M.D., Cavendish Square.
Clifford, Wm., Esq., Magna Charta Isle, Wraysbury.
Colegrave, Mrs. Frances.
Cooper, Wm., Esq., Carlton Chambers, Regent Street.
Covey, Rev. Charles, Alderton, near Cheltenham.
Coxwell, Charles, Esq., Malvern, Worcestershire.

Dobinson, William, Esq., Thorpe Lee, Surrey.
Dodd, George, Esq., Grosvenor Place.

Eliot, Rev. William, Eton.
Ellison, G. T., Esq., Upper Seymour Street.
Elwes, T. Elton Harvey, Esq., Stoke College, Suffolk.

Foote, Rev. G., Horton Rectory.
Fladgate, Mr., Yeoveny, Middlesex.

Gardiner, Mrs., Brighton.
Gardiner, Samuel, Esq., Combe Lodge, Oxon.
Goldie, Rev. Charles D., Colnbrook.
Goodrich, Francis, Esq., Wraysbury.
Goodyear, George, Esq., Gloucester.
Gowing, Mrs. Charles.
Greatorex, W. A., Esq., Horton.
Groom, Mr. William, Horton.
Gwatkin, Frederick, Esq., Twickenham.
Gyll, Brooke Hamilton, Wraysbury House.
Gyll, Hamilton Flemying Campbell, Ryde.
Gyll, Bellenden Charles John, Ryde.

Harcourt, George Simon, Esq., Ankerwycke, Wraysbury.
Harris, Mr. Thomas P., Staines.
Harrison, George, Esq., College of Arms.
Haslewood, Mrs., Sussex Terrace.
Hawtrey, Rev. Stephen, Eton.
Hayne, Seale, Esq., Dartmouth.
Hickman, Mr., Colnbrook.
Holgate, Mr., Staines.
Houblon, John Archer, Esq., Hollingbury, Harlow, Essex.
Hunter, Richard, Esq., Lincoln's Inn.

Ibotson, Messrs., Wraysbury.
Innis, Mrs., Ryde, Isle of Wight.

Jennings, Richard, Esq., Portland Place.
Jennings, William, Esq., Victoria Street.
Jordan, Mr. Samuel, Wraysbury.

Joyce, Charles, Esq., Englefield Green.
Ladell, and Ibotson, Messrs., Wraysbury.
Leigh, Boughton, Esq., Brownsover Hall, Warwickshire.
Little, Capt., Onslow Square, Brompton.
Lennard, Henry, Esq., Great Cumberland Place.
Lucas, George, Esq., Newport Pagnell, Bucks.

Macnamara, ——, Esq.
Meeking, Charles, Esq., Richings Park, Iver.

Neville, Rev. Seymour, Wraysbury.

Oliveira, Benj., Esq., Hyde Park Street, Hyde Park.

Painter, William, Esq., Belgrave Square.
Parkin, Rev. Charles, Lenham, Kent.
Paterson, George, Esq., Poyle House, Colnbrook.
Paxton, Archibald, Esq., Cholderton, Wilts.
Paxton, Rev. Archibald, Otterden, Kent.
Pearl, Dr. Windsor, M.D.
Platt, Samuel, Esq., Wimbledon.
Prinsep, Charles, Esq., St. George's Place, Eccleston Square.
Pullin, Mr. Henry, Horton.
Pullin, Mr. Stephen, Horton.
Pullin, Mr. James, Wraysbury.

Richardson, Charles, Esq., Bruton Street.
Rogers, Richard R. Coxwell, Esq., Dowdeswell Court, Gloucestershire.
Rudge, Nouaille, Esq., Harley Street.

Scholefield, Cotterill, Esq., Ankerwycke, Wraysbury.
Schuckford, James, Esq., Feltham, Middlesex.
Slocock, Mr. Samuel, Wraysbury.
Small, Mr. James, Colnbrook.
Smijth, Rev. Alfred Bowyer, Attlebro', Norfolk.
Stephens, Mr., Horton.
Stokes, Rev. J., Staines.
Sturges, Misses, Datchet.

Thackeray, Miss, Old Windsor.
Tharpe, Joseph, Esq., Chippenham, Cambridge.
Tower, Christopher, Esq., Huntsmore Lodge, Iver.
Tudor, Henry, Esq., Brighton.
Tupp, George, Esq., Cedars, Horton.
Tyrrell, Edward, Esq., Berkyn Manor House, Horton.

Watson, Edward Temple, Esq., Horton.
West, Rev. H., Wraysbury.
Windham, Rev. Crole, Rutland Gate, Hyde Park.
Wood, Albert, Esq., College of Arms.
Wrench, Henry, Esq., Old Windsor.
Wright, John, Esq., Kelvedon, Essex.

# CONTENTS.

| | PAGE |
|---|---|
| Map of the Locality. | |
| Ditto, a Profile of the River Thames from Boulter's Lock to Mortlake. | |
| Title Page. | |
| List of Subscribers. | |
| Dedication to the Prince Consort. | |
| Introduction to the History. | |
| On the County and Locality | 1 |
| Descent of the Manor | 3 |
| Pedigrees of Montfitchet, Bolebec | 6 |
| Ditto of Plaiz and Howard | 6 |
| Ditto of Windham and Norris | 6 |
| Ditto of De Vere, Howard, Smijth | 7 |
| Ditto of Walden | 9 |
| Ditto of Burnel | 13 |
| Ditto of Paulet | 15 |
| Ditto of Fray | 16 |
| Ditto of Norris | 17 |
| Ditto of Sharrow and King | 19 |
| Ditto of Pyncheon | 21 |
| Ditto of Sandford and Brome, Dorington | 22 |
| Ditto of Lee, Conyers, Jodrell, Nourse, Weyland | 23 |
| Ditto of Blagrove | 24 |
| Smaller Manors in Wraysbury | 25 |
| Ankerwycke Priory | 26 |
| Pedigree of Spenser | 29 |
| Prioresses of Ankerwycke | 30 |
| Computation of their Expenses and Administration | 31 |
| Lands and Possessions of Ankerwycke Priory | 32 |
| Ecclesiastical Value temp. Henry VIII. | 33 |
| Mansion on the site of the Nunnery | 34 |
| Biography of Sir Thomas Smith, Kt. | 37 |
| Pedigree of Smijth | 41 |
| Ditto of Salter | 43 |
| Ditto of Harcourt, of Ankerwycke | 45 |
| Ankerwycke House | 46 |
| Park and Gardens of ditto | 47 |
| Magna Charta Island | 50 |
| Place Farm and Remingham Manor | 55 |
| Pedigree of Stonor, Brecknock, and Walshe | 59 |
| Ditto of Tower and Hale | 62 |
| Ditto of Oxenbridge | 64 |
| The Manor House Place Farm | 64 |
| Old Windsor Ferry | 65 |
| Welly House | 67 |
| Pedigree of Montagu and Scott, and Dukes of Buccleugh | 69 |
| Pedigree of Trumball | 71 |

| | PAGE |
|---|---|
| Paper Mill on the Colne | 71 |
| Minor Holdings in the Parish | 75 |
| Pedigree of Gould | 75 |
| Pedigree of Hassel | 77 |
| Ditto of Irby, Lord Boston, and De Crespigny and Drake | 78 |
| Mill Bridge over the Colne, near Horton | 79 |
| Suspension Bridge and Post Office | 80 |
| Pedigree of Neville and Southwell | 82 |
| Ditto of Urwin and Nicholls | 83 |
| Hythe End Bridge | 84 |
| Farms at Hythe End | 85 |
| Pedigree of Powel and Ringer | 86 |
| Hythe End Mill and Ferry | 86 |
| Pedigree of Kederminster | 89 |
| Ditto of Flower, Viscount Ashbrook | 91 |
| Wraysbury House | 91 |
| Lessees of the Rectory and College Lands | 93 |
| Pedigree of Carleton | 95 |
| Continuation of Lessees of College Lands | 95 |
| Pedigree of Gyll | 99 |
| Pedigree of Flemyng, Earl of Wigtoun | 101 |
| Pedigree of Howard, Wyndham and Smijth | 102 |
| Ecclesiastical History and Statistics | 103 |
| Rectors and Vicars of Wraysbury | 106 |
| Churchyard and Monumental Inscriptions | 108 |
| Wraysbury Church and Monuments | 113 |
| The Chancel of Wraysbury | 118 |
| Day and Sunday Schools | 124 |
| Pedigree of Gyll, of co. Northampton | 125 |
| Charities | 127 |
| Parish Register | 128 |
| Gyll and Wright Charity | 133 |
| Charities and Gifts to the Church | 133 |
| Alms Houses | 134 |
| Clothing Club | 135 |
| Churchwardens of Wraysbury Parish | 135 |
| Proprietors of Lands in Wraysbury | 136 |
| Ditto Freeholders in 1861 | 136 |
| Names of Holders of Lands with acreage, according to the Award Maps of 1798 and 1803 | 137 |
| Parish Overseers' Accounts | 137 |
| Parish Rates from 1744 | 140 |
| Churchwardens' Accounts | 141 |
| Miscellaneous Names of Gentry who have held property in Wraysbury | 143 |
| Names of Literary and distinguished Characters | 145 |
| Proprietary according to the Award Map | 145 |

## CONTENTS.

| | PAGE |
|---|---|
| Houses and their Proprietors | 146 |
| Gentry who have rented Houses in Wraysbury | 146 |
| Tenants of Ankerwycke House | 147 |
| Names of some Old Inhabitants of the Parish | 147 |
| Ditto of Persons rated in 1734 | 147 |
| Ditto of Electors in 1861 | 148 |
| Agricultural Affairs | 148 |
| Agricultural Statistics | 149 |
| Miscellaneous Matter with the Civil Government of the Parish | 152 |
| Fines and Deeds relative to Wraysbury | 154 |
| Reference to the Map of the Parish of Wraysbury, surveyed in 1845 | 160 |
| Abstract of the Commissioners' Award relative to the enclosure of Wraysbury Parish | 167 |
| Wraysbury Tithe Apportionment | 168 |
| Value of Rent Charge for 1843 | 168 |
| Data for Wraysbury Tithe Commutation | 171 |
| Rectorial Tithes received | 171 |
| Wraysbury Court Rolls | 172 |
| Court Rolls of the Manor of Yeoveny, Staines | 181 |
| Extracts from Staines' Parish Registers | 186 |
| Appendix | 187 |
| Wraysbury Volunteers | 187 |
| Petition of Jone Tanner relative to Walter Stonor, Esq. | 187 |
| Some Monumental Inscriptions to the Gyll family, of co. Herts | 188 |
| A Scotch Service of Return as heir of line to B. H. Gyll, Esq. | 190 |
| An omission relative to Wraysbury Manor appertaining to Lords Hungerford and Molyns | 191 |
| Additional Notes | 191* |

### HORTON.

| | PAGE |
|---|---|
| Introduction | 193 |
| The Soil | 194 |
| The Parish | 195 |
| The Mills | 198 |
| Descent of the Manor | 200 |
| Pedigree of Gaynsford and Whethill | 205 |
| Ditto of Brudenell | 206 |
| Ditto of Windsor | 208 |
| Ditto of Digby | 209 |
| Ditto of Knyvett | 212 |
| Ditto of Bulstrode and Croke | 217 |
| Ditto of Scawen, Blunt, and Atkinson | 223 |
| Manor House, formerly Place House, now Horton House | 224 |

| | PAGE |
|---|---|
| Pedigree of Brierwood | 227 |
| Ditto of Williams | 228 |
| Pedigree of Aubrey and Carter | 229 |
| Ditto of Gosset and Creuse | 230 |
| Notice of lesser Proprietary of lands in Horton | 230 |
| Pedigree of Salter, Peters, Nichols and Slocombe | 233 |
| Ditto of Hearne | 233 |
| Ditto of Bowser | 234 |
| Ditto of Blount | 234 |
| Berkyn Manor House | 234 |
| Pedigree of Tyrrell | 236 |
| Biographical Notice of Milton | 237 |
| The Church | 242 |
| The Churchyard | 247 |
| Plague Burial Statistics | 250 |
| Ecclesiastical Matters | 251 |
| Rectory House | 252 |
| Rectors | 253 |
| Charities | 254 |
| Churchwardens | 256 |
| Parish Register Extracts | 257 |
| Baptisms | 257 |
| Marriages | 260 |
| Burials | 261 |
| Contingent matter | 265 |

### COLNBROOK.

| | PAGE |
|---|---|
| Description of the Town | 267 |
| Inns of Colnbrook | 270 |
| Pedigree of Buckingham | 273 |
| Proprietary in Colnbrook | 273 |
| Pedigree of Pitt | 274 |
| Ditto of Shorter | 275 |
| Early Account of Colnbrook | 276 |
| Pedigree of Wigod | 276 |
| Ditto of Apsley and Bathurst | 281 |
| Corporation of Colnbrook | 281 |
| Miscellaneous matter, with the Civil Government of the Township | 283 |
| Pedigree of Goade | 284 |
| On the Chapel and Chapelries | 287 |
| Pedigree of Meale | 289 |
| The Church of St. Thomas the Apostle | 290 |
| List of the Chapelwardens | 291 |
| Railway | 293 |
| Horton and Colnbrook Fines and Recoveries | 295 |
| Public Records | 303 |
| Index | 305 |

# INTRODUCTION TO THE HISTORY OF WRAYSBURY, HORTON AND COLNBROOK.

It was in the year 1846 that the author of the histories of these parishes, and especially that of the parish of Wraysbury, was invited by Dr. Lipscomb, the eminent topographer of the county of Buckingham, for which he had issued proposals in 1829, to furnish any facts he might possess, either directly interesting or bearing relation to the locality.

Having concurred in this suggestion, the author supplied what with other matter now appears in this work; but thinking more might be gleaned, and that a yet ampler account of a place distinguished for some considerations, and especially as being (in reference to the event shewing the locality to be among the interesting of our island) the very village in which the liberties of England were ratified at Magna Charta Isle in 1215—a fact not less momentous or less worthy to be recorded than that which eventuated on the spot where the Battle of Hastings was fought in 1066, which laid the Saxon power in the dust—the author of this epitome of the parishes herein described was induced to cull additional materials for the accompanying histories; and these, for which he has need of indulgence, he submits to the candour of the public, with the assurance that what he communicates is derived from the most authentic sources within his reach, and what he has written he purposed to write without claim to descriptive or rhetorical delineations, but in all simplicity.

One pleasing motive for choosing this subject and making the collection has been gratitude to a place with which his family has been connected since the 17th century, and what we spontaneously choose, we think is eligible and fit by its proper excellencies and appendages to awaken zeal, which is a constant incentive of love or duty.

The historian we know should not dare to report the thing that is not, neither is there anything he should not dare to tell; and the author trusts he can vouch for all he advances. And as in architecture the porticos and entries of a building have their symmetrical proportions, so the preamble of a speech or a history should be in ratio to the importance of the subject; hence little is required for a succinct history in point of introduction.

Topography is a kind of literature peculiar to our nation, for in no foreign country is this species of composition known, and even antiquity recognises no such medium of local intelligence. It deals only with geography and wider and more pretending history, and indeed we must admit that even our purely topographical specimens are of no earlier origin than the 16th century.

Our first essayist in this department of specific history was Dugdale, whose History of the County of Warwick was published in 1656, and the County of Hertford soon followed from the able hand of Chauncey. These specimens in a new career excited admiration and zeal, the parent of progress and improvement.

It is the duty of the topographer, within certain restrictions, to furnish full, vivid and authentic records of the essential features of a parish, its natural products above and beneath the earth's superficies.

## INTRODUCTION.

Again artificial objects, which may be termed indigenous, with biographies and genuine anecdotes of persons of "mark and likelihood," joined to notices of phenomena, peculiar to the locality, for what is local is often national, are to be admitted and described as either attractive or useful.

County histories and especially fragmentary parts of shires are not so much perused, because interests are considered too *local*; hence they are inferred to be generally compiled only by the humble diligence of those unaspiring antiquarians who employ their time in merely collecting armorial *insignia*, in poring over parish registers, in transcribing lapidary inscriptions, or detailing anecdotes of some who may have towered above the common mark, of referring to histories of the obscure and such like; and although such memoirs are meant for and are addressed to what Swift called *Prince Posterity*, they are not always delivered according to the *direction*.

However undervalued such materials may be, yet these subsidiary aids to topography, if properly digested, may become works of entertainment and even of general concern, for they comprise delineations of ancient and modern arts, customs, usages, &c.; and these brief chronicles of the spot, with letters of private individuals and traditions, constitute interesting and essential evidences, to be sought and recorded.

In modern times private documents are disclosed with more generosity than heretofore, when knowledge and the inlets to it, like freemasonry, were withheld, and instruments, legal and private, deeds and muniments containing family and public records, were guarded by wardens and authorised officials, as if they were preserved only silently to disintegrate piecemeal, and were sedulously withheld from inspection through ignorance or jealousy.

Access is now accorded sufficiently to stimulate the student or laborious indagator, to satisfy the veteran critic, and to disclose the *arcana* of chest and closet.

Hence topography begins now to fulfil its mission, and to assume a literary *status* in dignity and utility equipollent to history, which is precept and philosophy teaching by examples.

Considering that originally Wraysbury belonged in specialty to the Saxon Sovereigns, who dwelt at Old Windsor prior to the settlement of the Royal court at New Windsor, and that the fields herein were the hunting-grounds of monarchs, and that subsequently many of the Queens of England had a *quota* of their marriage settlements made on Wraysbury lands, which was an *appanage* to the Crown (*abban* in Saxon implies property given in marriage), besides being the residence of individuals of the first eminence, the author thought, and he trusts not very distant from the boundaries of reason and verisimilitude, that there was "ample room and verge enough" to trace in an extended disquisition the story and characteristics of this portion of the shire of Bucks contained within the Chilterns, an estate of the Crown passing from east to west through the middle of the county, whose Stewardship is a nominal office with a salary of 20s, which if conferred on any Member of the lower House of Parliament the representative vacates his seat.

These two parishes, though small in geographical area, are replete with historical interest in a county notable for such associations, as well as for the bright cluster of its poets, some native and to the county bred, some sojourners only; and for its great agricultural repute, its natural fertility, and the success of art as applied to the vegetative properties of the earth.

Long after the Royal Court had repaired to Windsor, the area of this then wild locality was appropriated to hunting purposes by the Sovereign owners of its soil.

The parish was in the Crown, and leases of land were granted, while temporal advantages either for money, services, or esteem were conferred by Sovereigns on favourites or others until the dawn of the Reformation, when the Priory itself was assumed by the nation, in common with all conventual institutions, and so the land passed into the tenure of divers individuals of merit, chivalry, or learned renown at the will of the reigning potentate.

Nor was it until the spirit-stirring epoch of King Charles I. that any section of this parish was alienated from the Crown; subsequently to which time it succumbed to its fate, while commercial but opulent individuals were constituted the proprietary in this same village, once consecrated to Royalty.

At this period much of the national possessions were conveyed by grants to subjects, a political prelude to removing from the hands of the Royal owners the Crown lands, for which a money indemnity was accepted.

This latter scheme was matured on the accession of King George III. in 1760, when a fixed sum in lieu of the civil list revenues was voted by Parliament, and now the Crown lands constitute items peculiar to themselves, and are carried to the Exchequer accounts like other taxes or imposts.

Several imperial properties remained, as the Stannaries in Cornwall, with private possessions, there being a marked distinction between hereditary and Crown revenues. These comprise the relics of the ancient patrimony of the Crown intended to maintain the dignity and punctually defray the expenses of the Executive Government, public credit being the true basis of political power.

Formerly our native Sovereigns, as on the Continent, were supported from the soil, and not by the system of revenue which has been so effectually organised in modern times.

Manufactures were in their infancy, and although corn laws existed, cereal transactions were unimportant, yet has England in her exuberance been an exporting country. Of metallic money there was little in currency, and imposts were few; but gradually a means of supplying necessities by taxation was adopted, and from this date may be assigned the alienation of hereditary revenues.

The chief residue of the possessions were what are termed Crown lands, consisting of parks, forests, chases, manors, fisheries, and royalties, with exclusive estates, church livings, fee-farm rents, lighthouse dues, coal, tin, and copper mines, &c.

William of Normandy possessed lands and revenues of some half million sterling annually, and to ascertain the relative value we should multiply by 10 or even 12 times—a gross net revenue very insignificant in contrast with our present amount of near 80 millions sterling, the largest sum yet raised, which has ever found its way into the Exchequer, without the aid of loans to swell our national debt, which is enormous and larger than that of many foreign kingdoms; but the American Republic is building up a debt by civil war and hostile factions which may eventually touch the colossal dimensions of England's obligations, the heritage and growth of all our wars since the advent of the Orange dynasty. America consists of 33 Confederate States, and the slave-holding States cannot well co-exist with the free-soil States—perhaps an amicable disjunction as well on the plea of *politics* as on *area of land* would be most politic. The United States in square miles are large enough for *several distinct* Republics.

From the period of the demise of Norman William the territorial income of England declined, or made small definite progress, until the reign of King Henry VIII., when by the unexpected sequestration of religious houses and territory the revenue augmented.

The national resources *temp.* Elizabeth were estimated at no more than £500,000 *per annum*, of which £132,000 was the produce of Crown estates, kept intact until the days of the Commonwealth, when some two millions sterling in value of lands were alienated.

In remote times Sovereigns were seldom equal to resist the solicitations of pressing courtiers or influential magnates, hence hereditary Crown estates were often impoliticly leased at *nominal* rents.

Another great transference of these Royal properties ensued upon the accession of William of Orange to these realms, whose liberal profusion extended to his supporters in Parliament, as well as to his personal friends and abettors, some of whom had accompanied him from Holland, as the Bentinck family, on which was conferred the county of Denbigh, in Wales, almost in its entirety.

In the reign of Queen Ann a preliminary compact was established between Sovereign and people, and an annual civil list of £700,000 was granted in commutation for the soil and other revenues hitherto enjoyed by her predecessors; and the act suggests that it was to defray part of the governmental expenses, and to lessen the burdens on the subject by means of preservation and improvement in the Crown lands; this scheme was brought to ripeness under our third George.

Public returns shew the average receipts from Crown lands in both kingdoms, from 1793 and 1829, to be £560,000 annually, and it is in the Woods and Forests to superintend and collect this revenue, and to dispose of it on objects of public utility.

Davenant, in his treatise on the lands of England, estimates the common rights of the Crown at 300,000 acres, while the total produce of all lands at the disposal of the Crown, not considered to be under the control of Parliament, from the accession of King George III. to that of his son and successor, in 60 years, was £12,705,461. 11s 7d. See Parliamentary Papers, No. 1, Sessions 1820.

It may be that this *precis* of the Crown revenues, of which Wraysbury was once an important part (where, as on the dependencies of Venice, Queens had their dower), is too diffuse, yet it furnishes a value of what these royal fontinels of income were, placed in apposition with present times.

History is the most popular species of writing, and adapts itself to every capacity, so I have endeavoured to trace the descent of the Manor of Wraysbury, and to give the names and some account of the lessees under the Crown, and to interweave all points of interest which have occurred in the parish since mention has been made of it in story.

In the time of Edward the Confessor, A.D. 1041, Wraysbury was in the tenure of a Thane whose name is not transmitted, neither is his exact rank given, for this order of society was divided into Regis, Mediocres, and Minores, or the lowest freeholders, a title which became extinct after the accession of Norman William.

Thane was an appellation of honour equipollent with our Earl, as Thane of Glammis and Cawdor. But in the time of the Conqueror we are certain of the proprietor, and that the lands were then in the gift of King William, who bestowed them *in capite* on a *relative* and follower and knight in arms, Robert de Gernon; and this village he held with many other demesnes of wide extent, whose centre was at Mountfitchet in Essex.

After the Conquest this iron son of Mars and minion of Fortune dispensed his guerdons prodigally to his associates, some of whom were even those whom the antique Romans stigmatised as the *fæces populi*, the dregs of society, men who wanted nothing but money and virtue; while some, let us hope the majority, shone brilliant in ancestry or prowess under his invading standard, whose personal conduct and courage were commensurate with exigencies, and who neither relied on, nor were content with a false glitter of unsubstantial glory.

After the extinction of the male line of Montfitchet, have been specified in detail the successors to their estates here, until the epoch of the middle and *dark* ages, "the reign of night and nothing," when all Europe fell into a long sleep of inanity and degradation for almost a *thousand* years.

The public records have disclosed to whom the reigning Sovereigns temporarily granted the hamlet of Wraysbury, with Langley and Cippenham, and the names of the several grantees have been enumerated in the descent of the Manor.

The chapter on Magna Charta Island gives a summary of all that can now be recovered, and it is hoped that it will constitute an interesting *resumé*, although details might have been expanded had it consisted with the character of this work.

The author has expatiated on local topics, and has been more full on Ankerwycke Priory with its possessions, and circumstances relative to the rise and fall of conventual institutes of Great

Britain, with a detail of the lives of some eminent in adversity and prosperity—for the history of such men, as well as that of former generations, are lessons to posterity, that we may glance back on the receding vista of events and be admonished.

Wherever it has been practical, and to illustrate the parochial history, appropriate genealogies have been inserted, and if they are not always *rigidly* faithful, it may be that pedigrees which have not been transmitted through visitations are liable to error—one of a similar baptismal name may be mistaken for another, while misprisions in names and times arise from several families having the same appellations, which involve heralds and genealogists in entangling complications; yet elucidations are approximated by giving the exact places of births, burials or unions, as well as references to legal documents in sustentation of genuine descents. Heraldic visitations, from which source genealogists derive so much assistance, were first suggested and adopted in the reign of King Henry IV., and they were repeated, but at no stated periods, until the beginning of the last century, when these useful perambulations were abandoned, as had been *post-mortem* Inquisitions, on the accession of King Charles II. The discontinuance of these auxiliaries to genealogical information were a decided loss to all engaged in such pursuits.

The smaller manors in the parishes under consideration have been investigated, and their claims set forth and descents recorded with as much accuracy as the means of verification would allow.

Glebe lands and the great tithes are held here under the Chapter of Windsor, and it has been shewn how that property, with the advowson, came into possession as a free gift of King Edward III. to the Chapter, effected through an exchange with St. Peters of Gloucester, and it has been noted when the alteration from a rectorial to a vicarial cure took place, with the enumeration of the lessees of the College lands and tithes from an early period in the 16th century. This is accompanied with the most authentic list of Rectors and Vicars, their appointments, resignations and deaths from 1219 to our day.

Extracts from what remains of the Parish Registers are superadded. Charities to the parish and donatives to the Church, with the names of the benefactors, have been supplied, that none should be defrauded of praise and the undying gratitude due as tributary to real benevolence.

What is recorded relative to the Churchwardens from 1734, and their accounts, may prove interesting, as noting the rise and depression of rates.

To these are annexed the names of the present, as well as the earlier proprietary in Wraysbury, with a list of all who have been of eminence in their epochs, whether in literature, politics, in public offices, or arts, or in that cultivated taste which is the perfection of humanity joined to true religion and virtue.

A summary of agricultural references is subjoined, whilst the last paper, which is of documentary importance, reveals the names of all who have conveyed and bought lands, tenements, &c. in the two villages and town of Colnbrook from the earliest date of deeds, fines, recoveries, &c.; very useful *addenda* to such a work, and of *unique* application, for commonly the fines only which bear reference to *specific* places under consideration are inserted in topographical narratives; but to enhance the value of these histories and to rouse the curiosity and interest of the public *every* transfer of land has been detailed which our national depositories reveal, opening the long avenues of the past to all curious or devoted to analogous pursuits.

It had not been originally the project of the author to extend his inquiries beyond the parish of Wraysbury, but hoping it might prove serviceable to the vicinity, and gratifying to some who affect such investigations to annex a history of Horton and Colnbrook, he has ventured to incorporate them in this publication; and although he feels he may not have done justice, such as an abler historian or one of *happier* industry had done, yet he trusts to have added considerably and usefully to the fragmentary accounts which alone are extant of this division of the county.

The same scheme and order have been adopted in detailing the examinations of both—the one a village peculiarly rural, honoured by the presence (as well as being the habitation for some years of his important life) of the great Epic Bard of England, John Milton—one, with the exception of Shakespere, whose name is above every name in literature, who gave to his countrymen, besides some accurate and exquisite pieces of poetry composed at Horton, the noblest poem that genius conducted by art could produce—one whose great renown reaches, if it does not transcend that of those epic poets who have embalmed the regions of their nativity, Greece and Rome, by a divine energy of intellect, and whose fame can only perish with the civilization of a world daily producing new marvels for posterity.

The other locality which comes within the sphere of our historical periphery is a town, Coln-brook, heretofore of some significance and antiquity, singularly enough *twice* elevated to the rank of a borough town, but from which proud eminence it fell either by neglect or some unknown eventuality, or by the confusion of the civil wars of King Charles I., similar to those of the Roses in the heavy times of York and Lancaster, which shook England to its core, and akin to France in the whirlwind of the French Revolution, an act retrogressive to freedom's cause in every age and clime.

The author had been in quest and found and has printed a novelty in this kind of composition, a *congeries* of interesting records of fines and recoveries, receding to the time of King John, coeval with Magna Charta, which he has faithfully and at considerable *personal* trouble (the manuscripts being very deteriorated, and often almost illegible), extracted from our public records with his own hand, having no coadjutor for this or any other part of this work—without vanity he may say *meâ unius operâ* (by my own labour) he has transcribed all acts of conveyance, purchase and exchange, treasured in our public repository of deeds: in fact he has been almost unassisted throughout the work.

In addition to many important manuals for summaries of deeds and rolls, &c. he has himself consulted wills at the Prerogative Office as far back as 1383, the date of the *first* testament at that invaluable and extensive repertory; with all evidences to corroborate facts, identify links in pedigrees, and illuminating what was obscure by endeavouring to exhaust the subject under consideration.

Maps have been added—one, that portion of the Ordnance Survey which appertains to the locality, and one a *profile* of the Thames from Maidenhead Bridge to Mortlake, likely to be available to topographers or anglers, although the date of the map recedes to the year 1770.

With deference, therefore, he submits the compendious, but imperfect, accounts of these interesting localities to the ingenuousness of the public, fortified with a proud assurance in his integrity of purpose, and in the hopeful conviction that his researches have supplied something more and better to the slender topographical knowledge of the places he undertook to illustrate in an occasionally discursive work—a work elaborated, albeit the offspring of inadvertence and human infirmity—but which must be considered historical rather than agricultural, geological, or delineative; and as the author does not pretend to deep philosophical inferences, so he hopes he shall not be charged with superfluous details, his object being a local history of the places *pure et simple*.

And lastly, the author proffers his unfeigned thanks to the Prince Consort for graciously permitting him to dedicate to His Royal Highness the results of his diligence in the history of these unpretending localities, especially Wraysbury, adjacent to Windsor, and among the most ancient of the feudal possessions of the English Crown; a village which the Prince occasionally deigns to visit with its neighbour, Horton, and on whose Agricultural association His Royal Highness has been pleased to bestow tokens of his munificence and condescension.

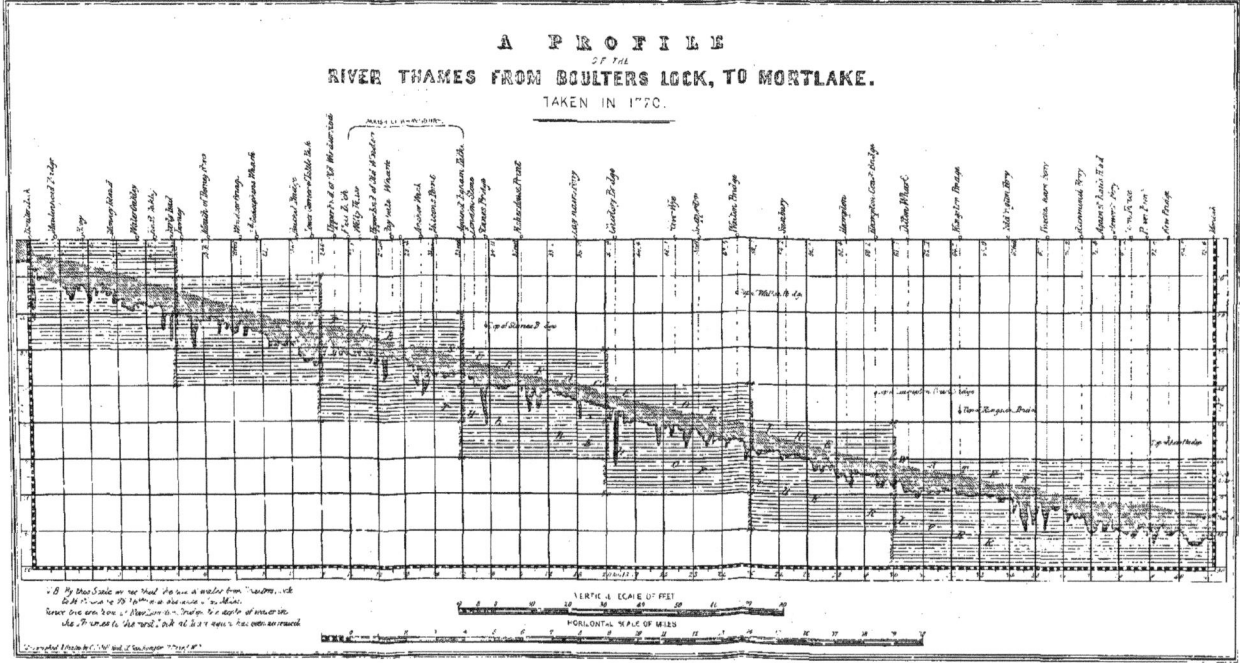

# HISTORY OF WRAYSBURY.

## ON THE COUNTY AND LOCALITY.

Wyrardisbury, or Wraysbury, in the county of Buckingham, the hundred of Stoke, the deanery of Burnham, and the diocese of Oxford, is situated three miles south of Colnbrook, and within one mile of Horton village, joining Staines, four from Windsor, and about twenty miles from London by the road. It is at the extremity of the shire, and at points of junction with Middlesex, Berkshire, and Surrey, lying on the left bank of the Thames, being adjacent to Langley Marsh on the north, which is contiguous to Horton and to the township of Colnbrook on the north-east, with Upton, Slough, Windsor, and Datchet to the north-west.

This proper name, like others, has passed through various transmutations, as appears in records by the Muse of History's pen, although now its orthography and pronunciation coincide. It seems in these utilitarian times extravagant to pronounce Wyrardisbury, Wraysbury, yet not more so than to make Cholmondeley to glide into Chumley, or Utoxeter into Uxeter. Still such anomalies exist, much to the mirth of our light neighbours the French, who allege that we pronounce nothing as it is spelt, and we may return the *badinage* with safety. I have seen the name of Leighton written fifty-five different ways, and Grittleton, the seat of Sir John Neeld, Bart., has been spelt twenty-two ways, which would seem to require the aid of the work called "Reading made Easy by means of the Phonetic Alphabet."

This place is written in Domesday Book *Wireisberie*, and its derivation is from Wier a dam, and burg or bury. This is apparent from the description given of the Thames at Old Windsor, so early as Edward the Confessor, A.D. 1041, the last of the Saxon line who ruled in England, and died 1066, at which period there were *piscaria*, sluices, and fish markets, fish garths and fisheries in the locality. This name is written diversely—Wyresdebyri, Wiredesbury, Wyrardesbury, Wardesbury, Wraisbury—in a deed of gift by Christiana de Mariscis to the Priory of Ankerwyk, 29 E. 1, 1300, and Wyredysbury in the grant 31 H. 8, 1540, to Lord Wyndsore; and although the orthography has fluctuated in every century, the pronunciation has been uniform, as the modern sound now is, Wraysbury and Wresbury. Das Wehr in German is the Weir, or Wehrdam, in Anglo-Saxon Pæn. Wær-wâr, wahren to keep. Hence we have many names, as Warham Norfolk, Wær-ham, Ware-ham Dorset.

From its contiguity to Windsor, and from the tradition at least that "Place farm" here was the hunting-box of King John, we have, primâ facie, perhaps good foundation for belief that this village was once a portion of the hunting-grounds when the Saxon kings resided at Old Windsor. This has been the diversion of savage and civilized life, for there is in hunting an all absorbing whirl of idea produced by the rapid changes of sensation, hence it becomes a willing refuge to all; the hunter, driving with perseverance over bush and brake, leaves no leisure for other cares than his own—and the waste ground in this parish, immediately opposite the site of the Palace, constituted a fit area for this still peculiarly English and manly recreation.

Wyndsor is a corruption of Wynd-shore, and it is cited in the charter of Edw. Confessor, who gave it to Westminster—"To the honor of Almighty God I have given for a portion and perpetual inheritance for the use of the servants of God, *Windleshore*, with its *appurts*," and the Charter says, By the constitution and favour of the Venerable Abbot of Westminster I have agreed for Windleshore for the King's use, the place appearing proper and convenient for royal retirement on account of the river and its nearness to the forest (ferestæ-feræ) for hunting, &c., in exchange for which I have given Wokendune and Feringes—It appears that then there were here 100 *hagæ* or houses, whereof twenty-two were free from tax, the rest paying 30s.—CAMDEN'S BRIT. vol. I. p. 151.

It is not agreed how long the Saxon kings dwelt at Old Windsor, but on the erection of the splendid palace at New Windsor, on the summit of a hill commanding so vast an expanse of country, and the subjected plains, they abandoned Old Windsor, except for purposes of *venation*, and finally the Saxon residence disappeared. So that we may now say, old things are passed away—"etiam periere ruinæ." But New Windsor dates from the time of Norman William, although the works were not achieved till King Henry I. invited *cunning* workmen from Normandy in 1110, as Solomon had engaged such from Hiram, King of Tyre, for Jerusalem, which became the joy of the whole earth, and was a triumph of genius and art.

The Thames, however, was a source of amusement, and fishing with weirs and nets had been taught to the aborigines of Britain by Bishop Wilfred in 678; and this art by supplying them necessaries rendered their minds tractable to moral and religious instructions, which accomplished ulterior conversions.

William II. succeeded to his father, and history records that in the ninth of his reign, 1095, he celebrated the festival of Whitsuntide at *Windsor*, and the following year he kept Christmas there, and in 1097 he also held Easter there; but whether these festivals were observed at the Castle of Windsor, or at the Saxon Palace in Old Windsor, is not ascertained.

He was devoted to the chase, and of it was so tenacious that he imprisoned 50 *persons* of the first rank under pretext of killing deer, and they not only bought dearly their liberty, but suffered the ordeal of fire. Henry I. during the building of the Castle certainly resided at Old Windsor, and a removal to the Castle is assigned to the year 1163, which was solemnised at Whitsuntide, when Henry II. went thither with his wife Matilda, a lady whose taste, learning, and munificence have been duly celebrated. It was this sovereign who, on the loss of his son William by shipwreck, is reported never to have smiled again.

John Brocas (from the Brocas at Eton, which name is derived from broca, a brook) was appointed by King Edward III. 25, 1351, to survey the works of Windsor Castle, while William de Wyckham was made Surveyor-General to the king's works at *both* the Windsors, 30th of his reign, 1356; to effect which workmen were sent by various counties. At its completion, in 1374, the Order of the Garter was instituted, and met there for the first time 23rd April, 1349.—Pyne's History of Royal Residences.

The manor of Old Windsor passed into a variety of hands on lease under the Crown, by the service of finding a man with lance and dart to attend the royal army. In the Nomina Villarum the lordship was in Oliver de Burdens, 1316. At the Norman survey there were eight manors in the Crown in Bucks, and two royal palaces in the county. Few manors belonged to the Church, and there was no religious house in Bucks at the period of the Conquest.

Cippenham is called the palace of the Mercian kings, and so continued till *temp*. Henry III., as the foundation charter of Burnham Abbey confirms.

In 1377, the poll-tax made for this shire enumerates the population then at 24,672.

The name of Wraysbury is not mentioned in any Roman itinerary, but it appears that the direct road from Calley or Calleva, near Reading, ran to Bath from London, and that *Pontes* was either at or near Wraysbury, on the peninsula formed between the Colne river and the Thames, some twenty miles from the centre of London, where the Bath and Salisbury roads united at Runimede, at the west end of Egham. But Camden was of opinion that the *Pontes* of Antoninus' itinerary was at Colnbrook.

In Domesday Book (a work instituted to discover every man's fee and to fix his homage, began 1080 and finished 1086; and a tax of 6s. was raised on every ploughland to defray expenses for compiling it), Vol. I. p. 149, is recorded to whom the lands in this village belonged, and that they were the property of Edward Confessor, with the manor, but were let to a Thane or Baron (a title abolished at the Conquest), and the worth computed at £22 annual value. It may have been estimated at a high rate, for in his reign a sore famine oppressed the land, wheat rising to 60 pennies, or 15s. a quarter, equal to £7. 10s. of our money, exceeding the dearth of Queen Elizabeth's reign, when a quarter of wheat sold for £4.

It, says the book, answered for 25 ploughs (se defendebat). There are 5 hides in the demesne, besides 2 ploughs and 32 villains, with 18 bordars with 15 ploughs, and 18 ploughs may yet be made. Later we find Robert Gernon, a relative of William the Conqueror, holding the manor in capite, and the worth estimated at £20, which would, at 11 to one, be about £220; but this during the middle ages averaged only 8 to 1, taking grain for the standard. It consisted of 25 carucates of land (carruca, plough), or as much land as one team could plough in the year. In the demesne 5 hides—12 carucates made 1 hide—and this hide was the measure of land *temp.* Edward Confessor, and the carucate was that to which it was reduced *temp.* William I. There were also 7 servants and 2 mills of 40s. rent, and 5 carucates of pasture and hay for the use of the cattle, which belonged to the manor house (ad animalia curiæ), and pannage enough to feed 500 swine, 4 fisheries and weirs, worth £1. 7s. 4d.

These possessions were held by Thanes (denan, to serve), similar to Knights' fees, or tenures *in capite*. The practice of entail is found in these times, and even gavelkind existed. The term folksland fell by degrees into disuse, which gave place to the term *terra Regis*, or crown land, till at last the entire soil of England became *demesne* land of the King, held under him by feudal tenure. Property was once divided into almeden, or public property, and allodium, or private property. An allod could only be alienated by consent of the family, and was only hereditary in the male line. The term feudal is fe- od-, fe is the same as *vieh*, means cattle—pecus—pecunia; od means estate.

## DESCENT OF THE MANOR.

This Manor was the especial donative of the Conqueror to his blood relation, Robert Gernon, who held it as part of his barony, of which the head was at Stansted Mountfitchet, in Essex, a parish of some 3000 acres, united with Stansted Abbots, in Herts, containing 2470 acres. Here a castle was built on a hill artificially raised for its foundation, and so his descendants dropping the patronymic of Gernon assumed the appellative Montfitchet, which they retained till the extinction of the male succession in Sir Richard de Montfitchet. He sold his wardenship of the forest of Essex in 1267 to Thomas de Clare, and died in 1268, when his sisters became his co-heirs. Forest Verderers were officers to prevent trespasses on vert or venison-food, and for care of deer or game.

There is extant a book of records styled *Testa de Neville*, a name given to two ancient volumes, supposed to have been compiled between the reigns of King Edward II. and Edward III.; they have been printed by order of the House of Commons, and their chief use is to ascertain the principal proprietary throughout the land, and the tenures by which they held. In this compilation Sir Richard de Montfitchet is stated to have holden *Langele cum Waredesbur'* of the King in capite, which pertained to the Barony of Stansted, so there was no exaction of military service.—Testa de Nevil, p. 246. The historian of Bucks asserts that he owed no military service in this county, hence he is not noticed in the Liber Niger, or Liber Ruber, under Bucks. There are three books in the Exchequer with epithet *niger*, containing descriptions of this nature, that is, the distribution of lands divided among the vassals of William, who imposed on them the obligation of supplying the Crown with a certain number of knights specified in the enfeoffment. These lands were termed *fees*, and the number of such at that time was more than 60,000, of which the clergy held 28,000.

The extent of two carucates, or some 100 acres, went to each knight's fee, of the value of £5, but in the time of William III., 600 years later, it was raised by statute to £50; and in order to ascertain precisely what lands were held mediately or immediately of the king or lord, inquisitions were established, and at the death of the lord an exact return was rendered to the Crown. They began *temp*. Henry III., and they continued till 20 Charles II., when there was an intermission of the business of the court, and subsequently the court was abolished with the Star Chamber, as too despotic, and in fact circumstances outgrew their necessity. These inquisitions form a most valuable *succedaneum* to the genealogist where claims to a barony or earldom by tenure is sought, but the proof of ancient demesne still rests in Domesday Survey as the evidence most unexceptionable.

Domesday Book is supposed to have been completed in 1086, and it was printed by Act of Parliament in 1783, since which time Sir Henry Ellis, in 1833, has published a volume of general introduction to it with a glossary. The Conqueror divided such parts of England as did not belong to the Church or himself into 700 baronies, or great fiefs, and these he dispensed to his marauding followers, many of whom wanted nothing but money and virtue; and their issue became magnates in the land. These were again subdivided into 60,215 knights' fees, and the Normans had them all, for some generations elapsed before a solitary Saxon family obtained rank as barons. Some 35 peers out of 249 noblemen claimed descent beyond the Conquest; 49 prior to 1100, 29 prior to 1200, 32 prior to 1300, 26 prior to 1400, 17 prior to 1500, 26 prior to 1600, and 30 but little prior to 1700, according to an abstract of the printed peerage. Among the Scotch the house of Mar seemed to be the only one who could derive from very remote antiquity. The family of Flemyng, Earls of Wigtoun, show an unexceptionable traduction as early settlers from Flanders in the twelfth century, and were ennobled in 1281. Of the 25 barons (to whom the kingdom was assigned at the time of Magna Charta,) who swore by their souls, the King disposing, not *one* male descendant is known to be alive.—See under Magna Charta Island.

Richard de Montfitchet held Langley and *Wraysbury* of the King, paying hidage 37s., and *de sectâ*, or suit, 5s., *temp*. Henry III. Richard de Gernon, in 1112, gave to St. Peter's of Gloster several donations, and it may be that the Wraysbury Rectory came to that monastery through him, of which I shall write under the Church. This monastery was founded in 680, and was rich at all times; *temp*. Edw. III. 1343, its value was £287. 18s. 7d. annually, and at the dissolution, *temp*. Henry VIII. it was worth £2000 per annum. Adam Staunton was prior of St. Peter's at Gloster in 1349, when Wraysbury was transferred to St. George's, Windsor.

In 1281, part of this property of Wraysbury was given by the Crown, or rather leased, to Christiana de Mariscis, with Langley, to hold during pleasure at a fee farm rent of £110 per annum, as usufructuary, and it was ordered to Richard de Holebrok, sen., that Christiana should have it with lands, oxen, studs of horses, carts, cows, &c., and that Holebrok should be responsible for the rent. This is found in the *Originalia* rolls, which are estreats transmitted from the Court of

Chancery of all grants of the Crown where any rent is reserved, salary payable or service to be performed, which estreats begin 20 Henry III. 1237, and continued to a late period.

By what right the Sovereign took away this Manor to give it to a tenant, and no blood to Sir Richard de Montfitchet, does not appear; but as it was held *in capite* there might be some power inherent in the Crown to justify a seizure either by escheat or lapse, (reversion to the King, being ultimate lord of the soil, lands returned to him as grantor), which took place during the minority of Ralph de Plaiz, who died in 1268, without heirs, and is described as cousin and heir of Aveline Montfitchet, although the estate was claimed by Isabel Countess of Oxford, daughter of Hugh de Bolebec by Margaret, sister and co-heir of Sir Richard Montfitchet, as heir of Ralph. This Hugh (2 John, 1200) founded Medmenham Abbey, the same that was afterwards annexed to a cell in Woburn, Beds., and realised £23. 17s. 2d. per annum.

However, the King's claim was virtually retained till 1447, when a grant, or rather lease, of these crown lands was made to Sir John Fray, who was appointed Chief Baron of the Exchequer, 1436. A deed, however, recorded in the Parliamentary rolls, assigns these lands to Eton College, but it was a fugitive grant. The family of Fitz Other had Eton, and it passed to the Hodenges, Huntercumbs, and Scudamores, then to the Lovels, of whom it was acquired by Edward IV., though the college was founded in 1440. King Edward I. gave the escheat of the Manor of Langley cum Wraysbury, which belonged once to Edmund his brother, and Aveline his wife, now deceased, to the heirs of Aveline, with all precepts.—Rot. Orig. p. 22.

For the clearer understanding relative to the descent, I have subjoined a pedigree of Montfitchet, with collaterals comprising those of De Plaiz and De Vere, and Baron Norris, of Rycote, a member of whose house had a grant of Ankerwycke Priory, and in the diverging branches will be found that of Howard Duke of Norfolk, whose daughter and heir intermarried with the Wyndhams, whose property came by heirship to Sir Edward Bowyer Smijth.—See Ped. of Smijth.

The Plaiz family certainly succeeded here, for Richard de Plaiz was cousin and heir of John de Lancaster, who died 1334, without heir; and though Dr. Lipscomb asserts that no discovery could be made to whom these lands descended after the *extinction* of the male line of Montfitchet, yet did they devolve to Richard de Plaiz, who died 1360, thence to his daughter Margery, who married Sir John Howard, and so to his granddaughter Elizabeth, who espoused John de Vere, twelfth Earl of Oxon, and he being beheaded as a Lancastrian in 1461, his property was confiscated, and the Wraysbury part fell to the Crown, with his other lands, &c.; and that is another reason why Elizabeth, widow of Edward IV., held them in dower, some lands taking a royal title, as *Queen's Mead*, even to this day.

In the book styled Nomina Villarum, Harl. MS. 6281, Wraysbury is not mentioned, coming under Langley *Muffichet*. It is a book of the cities, boroughs, villages and hundreds, their names, and who were lords of every manor throughout all the counties of England, from 1316 to 1559. These places, with Cyppenham, were in Manu Regis. Eton and Langley were in the lordship of Thomas Hodong. Six places are only cited in this work as being in the Hundred of Stoke.

Some of these lands were sold by John de Lancaster to John de Vere, son of Robert third Earl of Oxon, and the De Veres also enjoyed portions of the Mountfitchet estates in Essex.

The pedigree given of this house shews how the De Veres held and transmitted to Jane, daughter of John de Vere, who died 1512. She married Sir John Norris, and his grandson John re-appears in Wraysbury from the grant to him of Ankerwycke in 1537. The descent and collaterals are more fully disclosed in the genealogy.

* Subsequently part of the old Montfitchet estate in Essex came to John Gyll, of Wydial, Herts, by virtue of the will of his father-in-law, George Canon, who made purchases there in 1509, 1513, and 1534.—See Fines.

# PEDIGREE OF MONTFITCHET IN ALLIANCE WITH FITZWALTER, BOLEBECK, PLAIZ, DE VERE, HOWARD, WYNDHAM, AND SMIJTH.

**Arms of Montfitchet.** — G. 3 chevrons, O. a label of as many points. Az.

**Arms of Plaiz** — a lion ramp. pass. guardant.

---

**ROBERT DE GERNON**, a. = **ROHAIS**. Norman, held Wraysbury in capite, 1066.—Dugdale.

**RICHARD FITZ GILBERT**, Justiciary of England.

**WILLIAM** took name of Montfitchet, and held = **MARGARET**. lands in Wraysbury. 25 H. I. 1125.

**GILBERT**, Earl of Clare. =

**ROBERT.** =

**GILBERT**, Earl of Pembroke. =

**SIR GILBERT MONTFITCHET**, founded Abbey = **AVELINE**. of Stratford, Essex, and Ankerwyke Priory, 3 H. II. 1157; and in 12 H. II. held 48 knights fees, and in 14 H. II. he paid £31. 10s.

**WALTER FITZ ROBERT**, Marshal of the Army of God and Holy Church.

**RICHARD STRONGBOW**, went to Ireland, d. 1176.

**RICHARD DE MONTFITCHET**, Forester of Essex, = **MELLICENT**, living 1211. and 1201, High Sheriff of Essex and Herts, died 5 John, 1203. the wardship of her son given to Rog. de Lacy.

**AVELINE.** = **WILLIAM DE FORTIBUS**, Earl of Albemarle, starved to death in the Levant, 1241.

**SIR RICHARD DE MONTFITCHET**, one of the 25 barons of K. John chosen to govern England. Prisoner at battle of Lincoln, 1217. High Sheriff of Essex, 1242. Lands in Wraysbury, &c. in capite. d. 1268. sp.

sold by Matthew Paris to be a woman of wonderful beauty. d. 1239.

**GEOFFERY DE SAY.** = d. 1214.

**PHILIPPA**, d. and coh. = **HUGH DE PLAIZ**, d. 1186; of Wraysbury.

**WALTER** or **HUGH DE BOLEBEC**; d. 1186; of Wraysbury.

**MARGERY**, eld. dau. and event. co-heir of her brother; living 8 John, 1207.

**BEATRIX DE SAY**, divorced 24 H. 3, 1240.

= 1st H. **HUGH DE NEVILLE.**

**ALICE** m. Ingelram de Percy, 46 H. III. 1261, sp.

**AVELINE** d. & eventual heir, m. 6 July, 1269, d. 10 Nov. foll.

= **PRINCE EDMUND**, E. of Lancaster, 2d son of H. 3, d. 10 Nov. 1296.

**THOMAS**, heir of his father. æt. 7, in 1259, sp.

**WILLIAM DE F.** = **ISABEL**, d. of Baldwin de Redvers, Earl of Albemarle, d. 1255. Countess of Devon, d. 1293.

**HUGH**, ob. s. p. 1207.

**WALTER**, ob. 1262.

**CONSTANCE**, m. Elias de Beauchamp.

**THEOPHENIA.** =

**HUGH** =

**ISABEL**, ob. 1245.

= **ROBERT DE VERE**, 3rd Earl of Oxford, ob. 1221.

**RICHARD DE PLAIZ**, nephew and heir of Richard de Montfitchet, escheat 1274, by which a division between the issue of Hugh Bolebec, William de Fortibus, and Ric. de Plaiz; æt. 44 in 1267.

**HUGH**, ob. 1263.

**NICHOLAS CORBET**, of Salop.

**MARGERY**, d. and heir, gave her poss. in Wraysbury to Ralph de Grimsthorp.

**MARGERY CORBET** got part of estates.

**WM.** Lord of Grimsthorp.

**RALPH.**

**ALICE**, d. & h. sold Wraysbury to Robt. Burnel, & enfeoffed Giles de Baddesmere, who enfeoffed Robt. Burnel, Bp. of Bath & Wells.

**WALTER DE HUNTERCOMBE**, of Oxon, d. 1312, sp.

**HUGH DE LA VAL.** m. 1273, d. 1302.

= **MAUDE**, d. and co-h. æt. 12, in 1261, gave prop. to sister Margery, who enfeoffed Robert Burnel, d. 1281, and John de Lancaster, was consin and heir in 1208.

**PHILIPPA** sold her Wraysbury prop. to Rbt. Burnel, Bp. of Bath and Wells, d. 1293.

= **ROGER DE LANCASTER** d. 1290, Baron of Kendal.

**GILES** d. 1302, Dugdale's Bar.

**RICHD. DE PLAIZ**, æt. 6 in 1303, d. 1327.

**Dau.** =

**ANNORA** joining in sale.

= **JOHN DE LANCASTER**, heir to aunt Maud de la Val. Sold estates to John son of Robt. de Vere, 3d E. of Oxon ; died 1334, sp.

**RICHARD DE P.** cousin and h. of Jo. de Lancaster, all the other issue of Montfitchet being extinct; æt. in 1334, d. 1360.

= **SIR ROBERT HOWARD** d. 1388.

= **MARGARET**, d. of Robt. 3rd Lord Scales of Wydial, Herts.

**SIR JOHN**, æt. 18 in 1360, d. 1388.

**MARGERY**, d. and h. = **SIR JOHN HOWARD**, died 1381 d. 1437.

= **ALICE**, d. of Sir Wm. Tendring of Suffolk, d. 1426.

**SIR JOHN HOWARD**

**SIR ROBERT HOWARD,**

## PEDIGREES OF VERE, NORWODE, HOWARD, ETC.

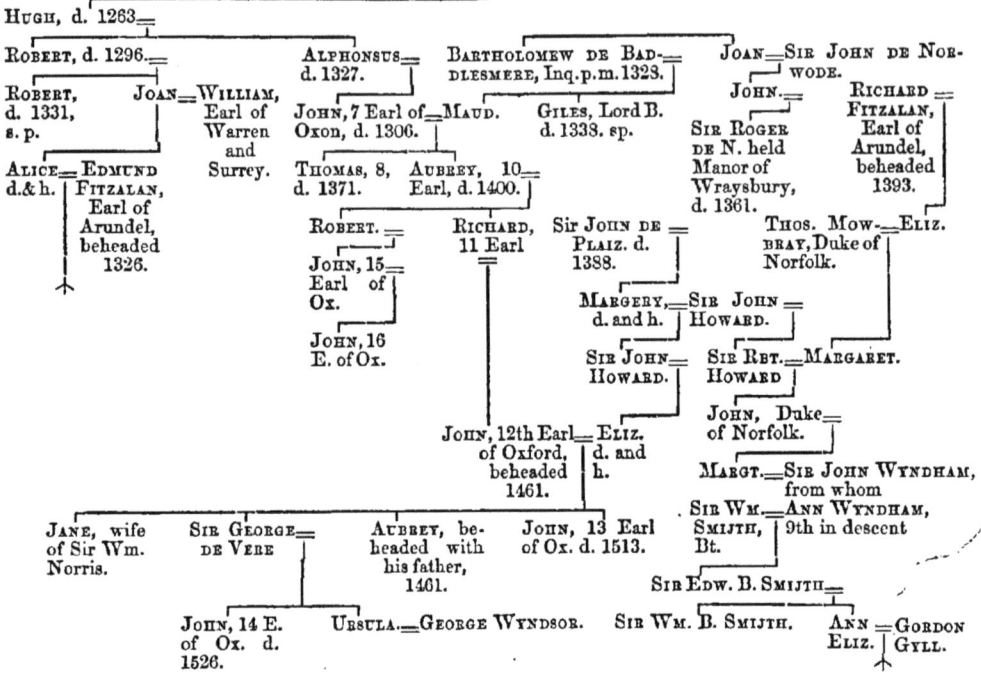

I therefore pass to others of the proprietary here, first mentioning Sir Roger de Norwode, connected with the Baddlesmeres, who had intermarried with De Vere.

From this period small holders were introduced, and many manors were recognized as offshoots from the parent demesnes, and the sovereign rewarded the services of friends by temporary grants here, or with leases for definite periods. But the superior holders were Burnel and Christiana de Mariscis.

The manor of Langley was commonly united to Wraysbury, and took its name from Mariscis, or Maries, and the connection of the churches is coeval with the Conquest, Langley being a church of ease to the mother church. The profits being small the king united these two parishes in the leases, and a commission was given to Christiana to enter on and enjoy the lease, for which she was to pay £110 per annum; the deed dates at Westminster, and we shewed how Richard de Holbrok was steward for the rent—(page 4.)

Rot. Orig. 28 E. I. 1299, for a fine of 50s. were granted to Ralph, son of Wm. le Ken, six acres of land, &c., in Langley near Windsor, to be held to himself and the heirs of Christiana de Mariscis for life, and after his decease to said Christiana and her heirs for ever by the service of 2s. rent; this goes to confirm the opinion that in earlier times there were several manors, where the possessors cannot be regularly deduced through the long succession of centuries which intervened between the period when K. Henry II. was feudal lord. He did not succeed to the Montfitchets, as Dr. Lipscomb avers, one of whom, Sir Richard de Montfitchet, founded the Priory or Nunnery of Ankerwycke, and to it gave certain circumjacent lands in fee, which were held of the nunnery at the time of the dissolution of religious houses in 1537.

There were several of the Le Ken family in England, coevals and of some distinction. One, Matilda of Abingdon, in 1223; and in 41 Henry III. 1257, Pat. Rolls, there is a deed between Peter le Ken and Michael de Mozam and his wife, about property in Welisford, Berks; and Agnes le Ken of county Beds, temp. K. John.

This Ralph le Ken had a grant of land in Wraysbury with the consent of Christiana, who had conceded lands to one John Hamond, in villenage, 28 March, 1299. Persons employed in servitude within a manor were styled villeins, as belonging to the lord of the soil, and though they are said to hold as of the will of the lord, it was agreeable to the custom of the manor. These customs were enrolled and admissions recorded and witnessed by the steward, hence tenants by Copy of Court roll, and the tenure is a copyhold.

On Sunday before Philip and James the Apostle, 1 May, 1300, an *inquisitio ad quod damnum* was held, and a precept obtained about Langley and Wraysbury, in which some concession was made by Christiana to Ralph, son of Wm. le Ken, who had applied for the lands held by Hamond, and a surrender was made to Christiana because Hamond was too *poor* to hold them. This inquisition was held at Egham; a transcript dated 21 Nov. 28 Edw. I. 1300, but the original in the Record Office dates from York, 23 June, 28 Edw. I. 1299. It was indispensable to have these judicial inquiries to protect the rights of the crown revenues from injury or encroachment, and they contain a variety of intelligence,—for on an information laid a jury assembled to determine if damage directly or collaterally would ensue—hence the term *ad quod damnum*. They date from Edw. II. to 38 Hen. VI. 1460, and are most useful to the antiquarian and genealogist.

We here infer how Christiana was already a proprietor in the village, and when Le Ken entered it. In 1312, 6 Edw. II., that king granted to Roger de Norwode, with other manors, that of Cippenham, with the hamlet of Eton, and the manors of Langley and Wraysbury, to hold during pleasure.

Langley was not separately surveyed in Domesday Book, being included in Wraysbury, and was part of the Gernon holdings styled parcel of the Barony of Stansted Montfitchet, and so this place was united in spiritual marriage to Wraysbury until 1855, when the incumbent Mr. Champnes died vicar here, since which time it has been a vicarage by itself.

Sundry of the patronymic of Norwode resided in this county, and in 1257 there is a deed between William de Noting and William de Norwode, about *tents* at Clifton—Pat. Rolls. It seems that the ancestor of Roger de Norwode, John Norwode, who was summoned to Parliament 8 June, 1294, and whose inquisition was taken 1284, left a son John, who went with Edward I. to Scotland. He married Joane, sister of Bartholomew Lord Baddlesmere, and at the age of 31 he died, being succeeded by his grandson and heir Sir Roger, the same who had tenure of land *here* during pleasure. Dying 5 November, 1361, the king regranted the lands to another. The genealogy directs us to the alliances between Norwode, De Vere, De Plaiz—for Hugh de Plaiz married Beatrice, and Sir Roger de Norwode married Joanna daughter of Sir Geffrey de Say, and she dying in 1404, after her son John Norwode, subsequently the honours and wealth of this baronial house declined upon daughters (tomber en quenouille, as the French law hath it), and Barley of Herts and Norton of Kent obtained them—hence we hear no more of them in Wraysbury, though they are entered in the visitation of Bucks, 1566. There is an ancient brass in the Isle of Sheppey, Kent, to the memory of Sir John de Northwode and his lady, 1330.

The next important personage was Sir Humphrey de Walden, Steward of King Edward II., and styled *Senescallum regium Castrorum*. He had a beneficiary interest here, the deed citing Cippenham, Langley with the hamlet of Wraysbury comprising the usual adjuncts; he constituted Humphrey auditor of the revenues thereof, Rot. Orig. 13 Edward II. 1320, as the abbreviation shews, which are transcriptions *in extenso* of the originals yet preserved.

It is most likely that at the death of Sir Humphrey in 1331, the grant was resumed by the Crown, but we find that his connection with the parish came through John de Lancaster, whose manor he also held, Matching, Essex, under the Lord of Stansted Montfitchet.

Sir Humphrey de Walden, who was High Sheriff of Herts, 1348, and his brother's (Roger) issue became distinguished in the shire of Essex. He was twice appointed by the King to lands in Wraysbury, and continued his Seneschal till 1324—doubtless a lucrative service, and one which obtained in all royal and very great houses—

"Marshall'd feast
Served up in hall with sewers and seneschals,
The skill of artifice or office mean."—*Par. Lost, IX.* 38.

These three offices were held by gentry of rank and power. The marshal placed the guests according to their rank; the sewer or *asseoir* preceded the viands and arranged them on the table; while the seneschal was the household steward — synonymous with High Steward of the King's household.

In Scotland the Earl Marischal was one of the principal nobles of the realm, and the Stewarts, who ascended the Scottish throne, were originally only *Stewards;* yet, like the Mayors of the Palace in France, they mounted the royal seat and wielded the imperial sceptre. Some titles are hereditary in families, as Butler, Marischal, &c.—the latter, always in the Keith family, is now in the Crown.

## PEDIGREE OF DE WALDEN.

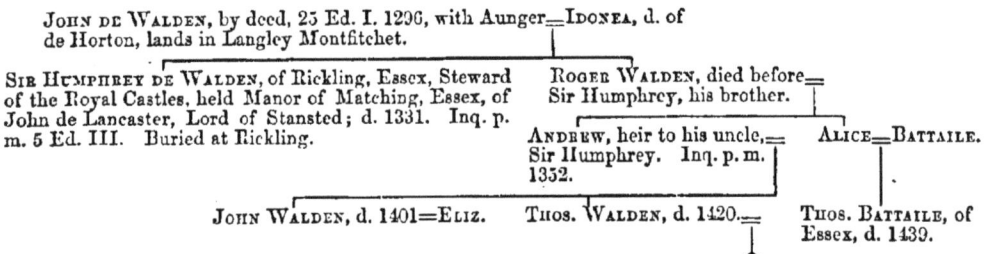

There was a Roger Walden (Hasted's Kent, Vol. IV.) who subsequently rose to be Bishop of London, 1404, Lord Treasurer and one of the trustees for the Crown. He was also Archbishop of Canterbury, 1397, and died 2 November, 1406. Another family of this name were large proprietors at Erith, in Kent, descended from John Walden, 1350, which ended in Sir Lionel Walden, Kt. of Cambridge, who died 1719, without issue male. See Hasted's Kent.

In the year 1323 we find Humfry de Walden again appointed, with one Richard Ikene, *joint seneschal* to the manors of Wraysbury, &c. and in addition to the manors of Fulmer and Bolecroft *ats Bulstrode,* in Hedgerly, Bucks. The family of Bulstrode of this place is first found here in 1338, as possessors in Datchet. They settled in Hedgerly in 1473. In 1324, there is a new appointment to Richard Ikene alone, and he was associated with another usufructuary in Richard de

Wynferthing, and they had the same manors under the same limitations. Rot. Orig. 13, 17, 18, Edward II.

The name of Ikene is most uncommon, but Richard was a celebrity of his day, or he had not been Seneschal or Steward of the Castle in 1323, and he was twice nominated to the appointment and to these manors; but his tenure was no more than three years duration, ending by death or supercession—and his associate Wynferthing enjoys a name as singular and unique in England. I find one Hugh de Wynferthing gave to the Priory of St. Martin, Dover, lands, &c., in Gussestone: and he had some right over Buckland, Barkway, &c., temp. Edward III., as an *ad quod damnum* deed discloses, and in it there is a citation of a loss he sustained in these words, "H'ver 'tota blada sua per tempestatem destructa,"—that is, his corn and hay, &c., were destroyed by an unusual tempest.

It seems as if all the most curious patronymics were constringed into a mass, and that in this village too, for we find the next proprietor here was John de Shobenangre, to whom King Edward III. committed the custody of his manors of Cippenham, Langley Marsh, and Wraysbury, to hold *durante bene placito*, as the Roll. Orig. 20 Edward II. 1326, declares. He had also the manor of Wycombe, Bucks., at the rent of £62 per annum, temp. Edward III.

The probability is that these functionaries or lessees of the Crown had but a temporary interest in the locality, and, like absentees, rarely visited the sources of their incomes, either granted by lease or *bought*, for most things may be had at *their true worth*, and few times have been when *omnia venalia sunt* was not of daily occurrence in every civilized community.

In the following reign, that is, 49 Edward III., 1376, rolls disclose that the King of his great bounty committed to Robert le Smyth the custody of the manor of Wyrardesbury to hold for 10 consecutive years at the rent of £44. The frequency of this name has prevented me identifying him with any of this old patronymic, a name as old as names may be, dating from Adam.

The next occupant here, as tenant of royalty, nominated in 1377 by Edward III., is Henry atte Water, and this for good services rendered—*Hostiarum aulæ*—that is, what he did and expended on the chapels. Hence to him was assigned the custody of the manor of Wraysbury for the term of 10 years, paying £44. per annum, the exact sum his predecessor paid, and probably he succeeded to him on death, resignation, or a new appointment. A Bishop Atwater died 1520. There was a family of this name famous in Lenham, Kent; one Mary, the wife of Robert Honeywood, she died 1620, at the mature age of 93, leaving 16 children, 114 grandchildren, and 367 lawful descendants of her body—a singular instance of fecundity. See hereafter about Esther, wife of Sir Thomas Temple, of Stowe, Bart., under pedigree of Sandys.

I have past in review the parties who seem to have been only temporary lessees, and not to interrupt the current of this history, I shall resume inquiry about those who were the real proprietary in fee. So I revert to an old inhabitant in Robert Burnel, who was Archdeacon of Buckingham and Rector of Wraysbury, which latter appointment he resigned in 1219, having been presented to it by the Abbot and Convent of Gloster, to whom the rectory then belonged (page 4); and this was in the palmy days of Sir Richard de Montfitchet. This prelate was a relative of the famous Robert Burnel, and to illustrate the history I append a pedigree, in consideration of the extent of his holdings here, and the long tenure he had of them and the benefits which accrued to the Priory of Ankerwycke through this family.

The sterling founder of it in Wraysbury was the Bp. of Bath and Wells, Robert Burnel, son of Philip Burnel, who died 1249, and both blood relations to the Robert who resigned the rectory in 1219.

This ecclesiastic was of high renown and of unequivocal character for piety, and his life in brief is set forth in the third volume of Foss's Judges of England, and Hartshorne's Archæological Journal. He was a man of erudition, great suavity of disposition, honour, and integrity, and his fame is characterized—" Regi tam utilis, plebi affabilis, omnibus amabilis, vix nostris temporibus illi similis invenietur." This inherent and practical goodness secured him the confidence of his sovereign, Edward I., who raised him from being Archdeacon of York to be Chancellor, which honour he held for 18 years. He was also Lord Treasurer of the realm, and on 23 January, 1274, he was made Bishop of Bath and Wells, and so continued till his death, which happened at Berwick on Tweed, 25 Oct. 1292. He had been Archbishop of Canterbury, which election was annulled by the Pope—and Philip, (son of his brother Hugh, then dead also,) was his heir, who soon followed his uncle, in 1294, leaving by Maud, daughter of Richard Earl of Arundel, a daughter Maud, who married John de Handlo. His son Nicholas took the surname of Burnel, a practice known in early times, when a large heirship was inherited. There is an ancient brass in memory of Richard Lord Burnel, 1382. The Burnels are among the oldest families in Salop—a Sir William, a follower of the Conqueror, dying in 1087, leaving issue, from whom these were direct and diverging branches. There were intermarriages with the Corbets and the Bromes, who settled in Wraysbury, one of whom, Mary Brome, married William Gyll, Esq. (Pedigree of Brome.)

According to recorded evidence the Bishop of Bath and Wells was desirous of fortifying his hands in Wraysbury, for Philippa, daughter of Hugh de Bolebec, and wife of Roger de Lancaster, sold part of the inherited property, and with it the Wraysbury portion, to this dignitary of the Church; and the sisters and coheirs, viz. Margery, wife of Nicholas Corbet, a Salop family, with whom some relationship existed, for Sir William Burnel, an ancestor, had married a Petronella Corbet, obtained a share of the property of her younger sister Maud, wife of Hugh de la Val, and having sold it, that her sister Margery had enfeoffed Bishop Burnel with it. The same is affirmed of Alice, another coheir of Hugh de Bolebec, that she had also enfeoffed the Bishop with her interests in Wraysbury, while some subsidiary or collateral interests were purchased of the De Vere family, one of whom had espoused Isabel, daughter of Hugh de Bolebec, and Margaret, sister of Sir Richard de Montfitchet. Hence the Bishop became owner of all the proprietary rights here, except what had devolved on the De Plaiz family; which goes to illustrate the descent of the manorial and other privileges.

Christiana de Mariscis played an important part in the destinies of Wraysbury. This name is found in various disguises in England, all arising from property in or by *marches*—Langley Marsh, Morres, Mores—for such surnames began with the nobility in 1200, and the genealogy of this house has been collected and published by Col. Hervé de Montmorency Mores, 4to. Paris edition, which points Christiana out as wife of William de Mauriscis, who died 1284, 'descendant of one Geoffrey, whose biography indicates its rise and misfortunes. This Christiana is not to be confounded with another of the same name, wife of Geoffrey de Mauriscis, and daughter of Walter de Bidlesford, Baron de Bray, who was brother of Jordan, father of William, the husband of our Christiana, who was daughter and heir of Robert de Burnel, Lord of Balbriggan, near Dublin. Indeed, this family was very influential in Ireland, as Geoffrey was Viceroy there, and dying, 1245, left a son, Sir William, who was executed with sixteen others for an attempt on the life of King Henry III. A deed, Pat. Rolls, 18 Hen. III. 1234, makes William, son of Jordan, proprietor of the Isle of Lundy, on the Devonshire coast, and to this very isle did one William de Morisco fly, another descendant, after attempting the life of King Henry VIII.

The earliest mention of Christiana, the future proprietor of so much of our village, is to be found in a deed, 34 Hen. III. 1249, which states she was then an orphan, and under age, and that the custody of her marriage was given to one Ellon de Genera.

This practice was a frightful source of evil, for the right of disposing of heirs and heiresses was bought and sold, and sometimes money was given to be allowed *not* to marry the party to whom the victim was assigned. In the second year of John, 1200, the widow of one Ralph Cornhill gave the king 200 marks (which at 13s 4d each would be £133. 6s 8d, or in relative value as to times, some £1300), three palfreys, and other valuables, *not* to marry Godfrey de Louvaine; whilst he, Godfrey, sent to the king a more *sterling* bribe, in the shape of 400 marks, that she *might* be constrained to marry him. The *oblata* rolls contain accounts of these offerings and free gifts to the king from every great personage for some favours; in fact, this potent power, which makes and breaks religions, "solders close impossibilities and makes them kiss," prevailed in the earlier and *simpler* ages. This privilege of obtaining heirs began at the Norman Conquest, and it was not wholly extinguished until the cessation of inquisitions, temp. Charles II. At what period Christiana married is left to conjecture. In 1281 she appears to have a license from Edward I. to hold the manor of Langley and Wraysbury during pleasure, at a fee farm rent of £110, or about £1000 per annum. Rex dilect. sibi Christiana de Mariscis salutem. The grant gave a right to hew down twelve oaks, "optas ad *maeremium* ad quasdem operationes quas infra Prioratum de Ankerwyke fieri faciatis."—Teste Rege ap. Cantuar. 17 June. Close Rolls, 30 Edward I. 1302.

In these times the rents of the Crown were casual or certain; the latter consisting of fee farm, castleguard, &c.; the casual were in fines, issues, amerciaments, &c., accounts of which were kept in what is known as the Pipe roll, which originated temp. Henry II., and the series is a most complete record, for on its membranes are found not only fiscal affairs, but transactions and names of all people of mark and their families. There is also a perfect list of sheriffs of counties, which have been of great use in establishing genealogies and illustrating topography.

Rot. 15, Edw. I., Carta de Maydenheth facta Christiane de Mariscis de omnibus terris et ten' cum pert in Maydenheth, &c. This is recapitulated in another short record, No. 2 Roll, abbrev. placitorum Berks, p. 217.

We find in a Pat. Roll deed, No. 42. 37 Hen. III. 1253, styled exemplification of a record that Christiana de Mariscis held the manor of Bastington (Basildon), Berks, of the king by the service of one knight's fee and a half, at the rent of four marks, and that the service was of Robert de Burnel, and that the king conceded to said Robert (her father) in fee sundry lands and rents in Salop. She was second wife of William, Lord Montemarisco, daughter of Robert de Burnel and Margaret, who remarried Richard Plunket, Lord of Bathregan, who was dead in 1338, and was grandfather of Sir Christopher Plunket, first Baron Dunsany. Lodge's Peerage, Vol. III. p. 163.

In a deed, 1280, this lady held largely in Ireland, which recapitulates the *Wardesbury* property, with Langley. Other similar deeds date 1282, 1300, 1306.

At page 8 there is an account of an *ad quod damnum* inquisition, 1299, relative to John Hamond of Wraysbury, and William le Ken, and in 1284 there is a letter written by Christiana on the exemplification of the deed, 37 Hen. III. 1253. There is also a *quitclaim*, which she brought in inheritance, for *homage* which Christiana made to Robert de Burnel for this same Bastington manor, which belonged to her father. Homage is service paid and fealty professed to a superior lord, and consisted in homage, fealty, and investiture; and Ducange enumerates 98 *varieties* of the last, as the duties of the vassal commenced on the completion of investiture; on this followed the rights of relief, fines on alienation, escheats, aids, wardship and marriage, &c. But these badges of servitude are now abolished, and enfranchisements of lands are compellable on application. In the Parliamentary writs, Vol. I. p. 727, it is stated she held lands in Northamptonshire to the amount of £20 yearly, and she is summoned under the general writ to perform military service, 7 July, 1297.

This Lady Christiana was alive in 1306, but whether she married again, or the Inquisitio post mortem is lost, I know not, for I find no *positive* record of her death. Her son John was 30 years old in 1283, so if his mother was married in 1250 it would tally with the custody and marriage of her by Ellen de Genera in 1249. There is in 1282 a warrant whereby the king, Edward I. seeks against Peter le Botiler and Aveline his wife, about the moiety of the manor of Bastenden which was *terra Normannorum*. They call to warrant *Christiana*, who came bodily into court, and said that King Henry III., father of Edward I., gave and demised this manor to Robert de Gynes, and that he demised it to Peter Dansy, called also Peter de Anesyn, and that Richard, his nephew and heir, gave that same manor to Christiana de Mariscis, who recites a deed of 1240, and another deed of Robert de Gynes. Christiana came again into court and admitted that she held the right of Robert de Burnel, Bishop of Bath and Wells, rendering four marks annually to Robert de Gynes.

The last deeds I have to quote, that a *precis* of her history may be known, are an *ad quod damnum* inquisition, temp. Edward II., in which she is styled of Langley Montfitchet, while another deed states she holds the manor of Overston, Northamptonshire, to which I have adverted. This very manor afterwards belonged to Sir Thomas Smijth, Knt., of Ankerwyke, who died 1577; and upliftable from this estate he gave to Queen's College, Cambridge, where he was educated, a rent charge of £12. 7s 4d per annum. This came ultimately to Laurence Scott, son of William Scott, by Ann, daughter of John Smijth, who died 1558, elder brother of Sir Thomas Smijth, and it reverted to Sir William Smijth, who sold it, 1631. Bridges' Northamptonshire, Vol. I. pp. 455—459.

The gift of this Christiana to Ankerwyke Priory will come under that section of the history.

## PEDIGREE OF BURNEL.

Sir Robert Burnel, of Acton Burnel, Salop, ob. 15 Nov. 1087, buried at Buildewas, Salop. Dugdale's Baronage, Vol. II. p. 60.

Arms: Lion ramp. S. crowned O. within a bordure Az.

Sir John Burnel, ob. 11 Dec. 1107=

Sir Hugh Burnel, ob. 12 May, 1142.=Sir Roger, ob. 1145.

Sir William, ob. 1211.=Isabel, d. of — Longespé.    Robert de Burnel, Archdeacon of Bucks and Rector of Wraysbury, resigned 1219.

Sir Hugh,=Petronella, d. of — Cheney.    Sir Robert Burnel,=Margaret, d. of    =Richard Plunket, Lord of Bathregan, dead in 1338, from whom Sir Christopher Plunket, Baron Dunsany.
ob. 1242.    dead before 1249.

Sir Robert, ob. 1269.=    Sir William. Sir Philip. both drowned, 6 Nov. 1282.    Christiana, d.&h.=William de Mauriscis, ob. 1284.
ob. cir. 1306.

Philip Burnel, ob. 1282. Rot. Script. Escheat 10 Edw. I. 1282.

William Bur-=Ducia, d. of, living 36 H. III.
nel, ob. v. p. 1282.

Hugh, was dead in 1292.

Robert Burnel, Chancellor of England, 21 Sept.1274, which he held for 18 years; 1275, Bp. of Bath and Wells; Abp. of Canterbury,1278,which appointment was annulled by the Pope; ob. at Berwick, 25 Oct.1292, buried at Wells. He bought Wraysbury lands, page 11.

Joan=De St. Michael.
Bartholomew de St. Michael

William Burnel, did homage for his father's lands, 31 Hen. III. his father being an outlaw, and died the following year, 36 Hen.III.

Philip, nephew and heir of his uncle Bp. of Bath and Wells, æt. 25 in 1292, had livery of Stansted Montfitchet; ob. 1294; held lands in Essex of the heirs of Rich. de Montfitchet.=

Edward Burnel, cus-=Aliva, d. of Hugh le Despenser, who held lands in Wraysbury.
tody given to John de Drokensfield, æt. 12 in 1294, ob. sp. 1315.

John=Maud, eventual heir,=John de Handlo, ob. 1346.
Lovel. æt. 24 in 1315.

Nicholas, took name of Burnel, ob. 1382.=

Sir Hugh, ob. 1420, when the Barony fell in abeyance.

The next gift to this parish is found in orig. de anno RR Edward III. xxiii. 1350, by which Richard of Gloucester, heir of Isabel de Duton, gave to his Majesty in full right 1 messuage and 17 acres of land, and one acre of meadow, and 3s rent, about £1. 10s in Wraysbury; and there is a warrant ratifying this donative to royalty. This Richard may be connected with Hugh le Despenser, Jun., of whom the Prioresses of Ankerwyk complained for disseising the nunnery of 30 acres of land and 29 of meadow in Datchet, of which more hereafter. Can this 17 acres of land be the same 18 acres still held by the Church as a gift, and the name of the donor lost?

Whether there were any other intermediate lessees to whom the Sovereign granted leases here, between the dates 1326 and 1461, I have not detected, but the Parliamentary rolls shew that in the last year a grant was made to Richard Wylly, one of the yeomen of the crown, to the office of keeper of the park of Langley Marsh for life with Wraysbury, which grant was excepted out of any resumption by the King. In the grant to Sir William Paulet there was a saving to Richard Wylly, and nothing in the act was to be *prejudiciable* to him or others, " yomen of the crowne nor noon of theym,"—being of our letters patent of 6d by the day for the fee of the crown. Provided also that Richard Wylly have the office of kepyng of the *Palice* called the Princes Paleis at Westminster of letters patent for time of his life for the kepyng of our beddes and clothes there and for term of his life of kepyng of our park of Langley Marreys in our Counte of Buk'.

This Richard Wylly is classed with twenty-eight others, yeomen of the crown—and I believe he built Welly or Wylly-house in Wraysbury of which under that head. There is a village of this name in the County of Bucks, and I find his widow Matilda was lady of the manor of Southal, Middlesex, and that Courts were held there in her name in 1473.

He is styled Yeoman of the Crown, which was a Military Corps, and preceded the Yeomanry of the Guard in 1485, called Yeomen Hangers, from their superintendence of *hangings and tapestries* of the royal apartments, and yeomen *bed-goers*, from their taking charge of beds during the royal removals. They use to carry up the royal dinners also, and obtained the name *Beefeaters* (buffet a cupboard or sideboard); and they now line the palace on Court and Levee days, their Captain being *ex officio* member of the Privy Council. They are divided into Lieutenant, Ensign, and four Exempts or Exons—from the French *exempts des gardes du Corps*. The word yeoman is the German *Gemein*, common—not raised to the rank of gentility. The corps of Gentlemen at Arms was formerly styled Band of Gentlemen Pensioners. This name was changed, 17th March, 1834, by King William IV., to Honourable Corps of Gentlemen at Arms. A famous yeoman, temp. Elizabeth 4, founded a hospital, and in the days of Elizabeth a descendant of the Sir William Paulet, of whom hereafter, a Sir Anthony Paulet, was captain of the Yeoman Guard, while Sir Walter Raleigh held it in 1587. The pension in 1509 was 70 marks a man—each mark being 13s 4d, or £46. 13s 4d, or at eight times present value, £373. 6s 8d.

The same act assured to Richard Willy from a resumption of grants, one which embodied also a grant to William Paulet by letters patent, 4 July, 1461, of the office of *Tailor* of the Wardrobe, at 12d a day (equal to 10s per day at ten times value) out of the issues, profits, farms, and revenues of the Manor of Langley Marsh, &c., which estate, with Wraysbury, among the many grants, Vol. V., Patent rolls, page 627, formed part of the dower of Elizabeth, wife of King Edward IV., widow of Sir John Grey, who was killed at the battle of Bernard's-heath; and the widow applying to King Edward, the yielding sovereign became enamoured, and made her his wife in 1464. He died in 1483, and she outlived him nine years, and was buried at Windsor. This was the first alliance in the right line of Plantagenet, from William the Norman, that was contracted with a *commoner*, for Elizabeth was daughter of Sir Richard Woodville, and of this marriage came Elizabeth, in whose person was blended the warring Houses of York and Lancaster. The confiscation of these lands in part, and partly the hereditary right in them enabled sovereigns to dower their Queens in Wraysbury. This manor was assigned by Henry VII. in dower to Queen Catherine of Aragon upon her marriage to Prince Arthur his eldest son, in 1501, who died the following year without issue. And in her widowhood, when subsequently about to be married to Henry VIII., that monarch by patent, 10th June, 1509, regranted the manor in satisfaction of dower to the same lady, under the title of Princess of Wales. She was divorced in 1533. One of the early rolls of the manor, 26 Henry VIII. does not state who was Lord in 1535, but that prerogative was in Queen Catherine, whose demise did not take place till 1538.

Let us advert now to William Pault or Paulet, and the high function of royal *tailor* of the Great Wardrobe; which office, I presume, corresponds to the Mistress of the Robes with queens and princesses. It was an office of some antiquity and dignity. Privileges were conferred on the holder, *temp.* Henry VI., which were confirmed by his successors; for James I. not only enlarged them, but ordained that this office should be a corporation or body politic at the salary of £2000 per annum. Subordinate were a comptroller, a patent clerk, and other servants of the Crown; but the establishment was abolished in 1782 by Act of Parliament, and the duties were transferred to the Lord Chamberlain.

In a resumption of a grant with a new disposal of it are the words that this act be *not prejudicial* to William Paulet, &c., and it is dated 23rd March 1463, giving him "the office of tailour in oure grete warderobe from the first of our reign, together with our levery and clothing, to be perceyved yerely by the hands of the keper of oure seid warderobe," Vol. V. p. 540; and again, 7 and 8 Edward IV. he is called "sergeant tailour at 100s. by the yere, and an hous by him within the cite of London hired." There are other grants to him in the counties of Somerset and Dorset. By another grant, 15 Edward IV. 1473, a reservation to the same William Pault, our *tailour*, by letters patent, 6th March, 6 Edward IV., receiving 12d. a day, and for his house £6. by the year, to be paid by the hands of the Shirref of the same. From William Paulet, of Melcomb, Somerset, Serjeant-at-law, sprung Sir William Paulet, created Earl of Wiltshire. One of this patronymic was Lord Treasurer of England for twenty years, and attained the age of ninety-seven, and died 1572, having lived during the reigns of nine sovereigns, and his posterity numbered about 100 at his death.

As this family was of pre-eminence here as well as in England, I append a pedigree, because connections with it appear in the course of the work.

## PEDIGREE OF PAULET.

Sir John Paulet, ob. 1378=

  Sir John Paulet, ob. 1447=

    Sir Thomas Paulet=      William Paulet, of Somersetshire, Serjeant-at-Law, to whom Wraysbury, &c. was leased, from whom sprang the extinct ducal house of Bolton, and Sir William Paulet, Baron Basing, Earl and Marquis of Wiltshire, d. 1572, æt. 97, had the Great Seal delivered to him in 1547.

      John Paulet, of Gotehurst, Somerset=

        Sir Thomas=

          Sir William Paulet=

            Sir Amias Paulet, ob. 1538=

              Sir Hugh Paulet=

Sir Amias Paulet, ambassador to France, d. 1558=      Edward Paulet=

Catherine, dau. of Henry, Lord Norris=Sir Anthony, d. 1600    George=Elizabeth.

Sir John Paulet, created Baron Poulett 1627,=
    died 1649.

During some intermediate period, a benefit in Wraysbury was conferred on a man of eminence, Sir John Fray, Baron of the Exchequer, in 1436; he may not have had specific property in fee, but merely usufructuary. A celebrity in his time, and M.P. for Herts, 1420. In the recapitulation of his property, Inq. p. mort. 1 July, 1460, he seems to have held of Stansted Montfitchet, Essex. His will is dated 22 March, 1457, and proved 23 July, 1461, in which he cites his sister Catherine and his then two unmarried daughters, Agnes and Katherine. His eldest daughter, Margaret, married Sir John Leynham, or Plomer, grocer, in London, who built, 21 Edw. IV., a *cantaria*, or chantry, to sing masses for the souls of the founders. His daughter Elizabeth was the wife of Sir Thomas Waldegrave, who is executor to his will, and he dying, 1500, she remarried Sir William Say, who died 1529 (page 8). Alice married Henry Tracy of Glostershire.

By the marriage of Sir John Fray with Agnes, daughter of John Danvers of Oxon, connected with the Bulstrodes, she became acquainted with the Say family, of whom mention is made in this book, and she remarried Sir John Say, who died 1478. The son of this Sir John Say, viz. Sir William Say, who deceased 1529, married Elizabeth, daughter of Sir John Fray—all related to Beatrix Say, wife of Hugh de Plaiz, lord here, through Philippa, sister and coheir of Sir Richard de Montfitchet. Sir William Say and Sir William Essex, and Elizabeth his wife, buy the moiety of the manor of Ayot Montfitchet, Herts, with the advowson by fine, 23 Hen. VII. 1507.

| Sir John Fray held lands in Wraysbury, Baron of Exchequer 1436, Inq. p.m. 1st July 1460. | = Agnes, dau. of John Danvers of Oxon, obiit 1478. | Sir John Say, of Herts, Under Treasurer of England, ob.1478. | = Elizabeth, dau. of Laurence Cheney of Bucks, ob. 25 Sept. 1473. | Frederick Tylney. |
|---|---|---|---|---|
| Agnes, married Sir Geoffrey | Margaret, married Sir John Plomer, ob. sp. | Catherine, married Sir Humphry Stafford. She ob.1487. | Alice, married Henry Tracy of Gloster. | Sir Thomas Waldegrave, ob. 1500. = Elizabeth, æt. 20 in 1461. = Sir William Say, ob. 1529. |

A deed is dated 10th April, 37 Henry VI. 1457, and it relates also to a grant of the Wraysbury Manor to the College of Eton, under the then provostship of William Westbury, who had been appointed 1447, and who died 1477. It cites another deed, 4th March, 25 Hen. VI. 1446, in which it states that John Fray held Wraysbury Manor with Langley Marsh for life, and that after his decease it was to devolve to Eton College, the deed being executed while the Parliament was held at Bury St. Edmunds. Eton and Langley were under the lordship of Thomas Hodong in 1316, according to the Nomina Villarum.

The next persons who followed in the manor appear to be Sir David Brecknock and John Brecknock, Esq. his nephew.—Martin's Index, under *Wraysbury*. John Brecknock was Sheriff of Bucks for 1440.

The deed alluding to them carries date 4th March, 32 Hen. VI. 1453, from the feast of St. Michael for ten years to come. By the present letters patent the College of Eton had Wraysbury Manor to farm, &c. 29th November, 36 Hen. VI. 1457.

I have alluded to this under Place Farm, where the Stonor family dwelt, which they probably obtained through the Brecknocks, as the intermarriage with them is found in the pedigree. Margaret Brecknock, late wife of Daniel or David Brecknock, Esq., grants to Sibilla, late wife of Robert Brecknock, all her right in property at Datchet, Stoke Poges, Cippenham, and in Staines parish. Calend. Close Rolls, 14 Edw. IV. 1475. This family possessed Hardwick manor, near Aylesbury, in 1460, which was sold, 1542, to the Lees, as well as the manor of Sanderton, which John Brecknock sold, 1474, to Sir John Leynham ats Plomer, who married Sir John Fray's daughter, and she sold it in 1481 to Moreton, Archbishop of Canterbury, 1486.

We now approach the stormy and unquiet times of King Henry VIII., and if coevals could cite a thousand heavy days passed in the wars of York and Lancaster, posterity too could quote the sanguinary doings enacted by the rude, imperious monarch, whose name for political violence, as well as that for superstition and persecution in his daughter Mary, are synonymes in England, what time tyranny cowed the commonalty, and when oppressions made wise men mad. But the blood of the martyrs proved the seed of the Church, "so full of dismal terror was the time." About the year 1530, doubts arose relative to theological questions, and it occurred to King Henry VIII., ratified by advices of his council, that it was necessary to shake the power of the Pope, who exacted money as well as obedience, neither of which concurred with the ideas of bluff Harry, who found that the Popes would never want pence as long as they could wield pens. The ecclesiastical lands were alienated in England, and as there was a nunnery in Wraysbury it shared the same fate, of which more under Ankerwycke Priory.*

Suffice to say, that with the transference of the religious houses came also much of a divided territorial interest, and in 1536 the family of Norris, well known in this county, obtained a temporary settlement in Wraysbury.

## PEDIGREE OF NORRIS OF WRAYSBURY.

John Norris, of Bray, Berks, Edward III.

Roger Norris

Sir William Norris

Sir John Norris, d. 1466—Alice, dau. of Richard Sherbroke of Yattendon.

Sir William Norris of Yattendon—Jane, dau. of John Vere, Earl of Oxford. See page 7.

Sir Edward Norris        Sir Henry Norris, beheaded 1537

Sir John Norris, grant of Ankerwycke 1537.        Sir Henry Norris, created Baron Rycot 1572.

This conveyance of land was succeeded by another, and that to the ancient family of Windsor, of whom I have treated largely under Horton, the lordship of which, with Stanwell, was in that house anterior to the Conquest, and remained till it was *forcibly* wrenched from them by Henry VIII. who bore no contradiction, was of a strong will, and what he willed he did. Andrews, created Lord Windsor of Bradenham in 1539, was the noble who first held sway here in Wraysbury. It is uncertain if he gave the ecclesiastical lands or the bridge lands, but his son William succeeded here and died in 1558, whose daughter Elizabeth married Sir William Paulet, Marquis of Winchester. He possessed lands here and in Boveney, &c. which he surrendered *inter alia* to King Henry VIII. who thereupon granted an exchange in Stoke Pogis, which had been part of the possessions of the monastery of St. Mary Overy, Southwark, and which had come into the King's hands.—Rot. Pat. 34 Hen. VIII. test. 17 Ap.

* The last lessee of Ankerwycke Priory, anterior to the dissolution of the Nunnery, was Sir Walter Stonor, Kt. To whom, styled our well beloved, we give to farm our manor of Wyrardesbury, with all lands, &c. excepting what belonged to Joane, late Queen (Jane Seymour, who died in 1537), for twenty-one years, paying £13. 6s. 8d., he keeping the houses and edifices in repair, for which a *grossum mæremium* was allowed (p. 12). He was to furnish housebote, hedgebote, fyrebote, heybote, ploughbote, cartebote, &c. The deed is dated 20th March 1534, at Westminster. I have supplied details of Sir Walter Stonor, with a pedigree, under Place Farm, where he had his principal residence; also of Lord Windsor, to whom King Henry VIII. granted the Priory, 4th August 1540, which reverted to the Crown, and was re-granted, 6th August 1550, to Sir Thomas Smyth, Kt. under the description and account of the Priory, &c.

It does not appear that any of the lessees of the Crown, whose lands they held with the site of the manor, enjoyed manorial rights. Neither Sir Walter Stonor, Lord Windsor, nor Sir Thomas Smyth held courts, which shews that the privilege centred in the Crown.

Henry Bulstrode is the next person of distinction who held property and influence here, of whom I have treated under Horton, where he was Lord of the Manor; but he, by patent 24th April 1616, had a right of *free warren* in Wraysbury and Horton, with several purchases, one 9 Charles I. 1627, of John Reede. A warren is any enfranchised district enclosed or open, and subject to common law as well as forest or chase.

This manor, whose tenure was coeval with the Norman age, continued in the Crown until the dark days of Charles I., when the times were out of joint and stern necessity compelled its alienation to sustain the royal cause. Hence Wraysbury lands became obnoxious to a common fate, and the Sovereigns, lords paramount, were compelled to alienate, while the grantee was one John Sharowe, citizen and merchant tailor of the metropolis. The purchase money was £617. 16s. 1¼d. by deed dated 1627. To him, his heirs and assigns in fee, the entire manor, with all the waste land lying near Culvett Mill, that is, Wraysbury Green, subsequently enclosed in 1799, and this mill was then in the tenure of Edward Bulstrode, gentleman; and all the lands styled Eton Green, with the increased rent since 1622, and all such perquisites of the manor, &c. as were parcel of the possessions of Joane, late Queen of England (Jane Seymour), excepting certain regalian rights and the site of the manor of Wraysbury, with Queen's Mead, woods, pastures, &c. and all the rights of the church, advowson, &c. The manor was held as that of East Greenwich, so called to distinguish it from West Greenwich or Deptford, which manor remained part of the royal demesnes till the death of Charles in 1648, when it became the property of the State; and in 1649 an ordinance was passed for the crown lands, in which the honour and manor of Greenwich, with many others, were reserved to its own use.

Wraysbury was held in common soccage, not in capite or by Knight's service, at the yearly rent of £39. 16s 10½d. This was a temporary arrangement, or only formal, as Sharowe is now styled Lord of the Manor in the Court Rolls, and to the manor he joined the ecclesiastical lease. He retained the purchase only one year, for by indenture, 26 November, 1627, he re-conveyed the manor with all its privileges to Henry Bulstrode, Esq., of Horton. He was associated with Isaac Pennington of Chalfont, Constable of the Tower, and one of the Council of State to Oliver Cromwell. This latter gentleman was eventually condemned to perpetual incarceration, and was a prisoner in the very fortress which he had once commanded. He it was who introduced Elwood the Quaker to Milton the poet, at whose suggestion Paradise Regained was added to his former epic. The life of Pennington, as once of our parish in power and esteem, is singular. In 1671 he was imprisoned at Reading, having been in Aylesbury Gaol in 1666. He died, 8th August, 1679, ætat. 63, and his remains were brought from Kent, where he expired, and were conveyed to Jordan's Quaker-burial-ground near Chalfont. He was a man of learning and piety, being also the author of virtuous and multifarious publications, and was coeval with George Fox, by whose preaching he was converted to Quakerism. Of him some account John Pennington his son has published. His ancestors had purchased lands in Chalfont in 1559, and he was connected with the Fleetwood family; William Penn married Guglielma Maria Springett, daughter of Mary, wife of Isaac Pennington her first husband. This Isaac Pennington was of Fishmongers' Hall, and Lord Mayor of London in 1643; and the celebrated William Penn gave testimony to his worth and abilities.

Other parties in this comprehensive deed of alienation of the Manor of Wraysbury were Alexander Croke of Chilton and Francis Croke of London, members of the ancient house of Studley

Priory, Oxon. Another person who appears in these transactions is James Parkes, senior, who was an adherent of Pennington, and who wrote his biography. His daughter Mary Parkes married John Sharowe, who died in 1634, and then became the wife of Sir Andrew King, also Lord of Wraysbury, whose decease took place in 1659. Another name in this sort of *omnibus* conveyance was Mr. Crowder, and through him we find descendants in 1734 in Ralph and John Crowder, who were joint-tenants of the paper-mills with William Pearson.

It appears also by deed, 14 June, 1628, that the site of the manor of Wraysbury, with Queen's Mead, &c. were granted in fee to Edward Ditchfield, John Highlord, and others, citizens and trustees for the City of London, in consideration of the sum of £12,496. 6s 6d. A clause is introduced, relative to what had been demised by the Crown to Sir William Smijth, Kt.; and 28th June, 1631, the City of London disposed of certain property here to William Trumball, Esq. and George Clay, Esq.; but the *manor* seems to have been *bonâ fide* in the tenure of the Sharowe and Parkes families; for by deed, 18th October, 1641, they united in transferring it to Andrew King, Gentleman, in a conveyance, which looks like a transcript of previous sales. It was thus enrolled, 22nd February, 1641.

This Andrew King (was son of Ambrose King who came from Salop or Wales) was a merchant-tailor of London, and continued in his immunities and rights till he yielded to fate in 1659. He was a considerable landed-proprietor here as the fines evince. Of him Nicholas Pinchon bought in 1653, and this property the latter reconveyed to John Sibley of Wraysbury.

After the death of Andrew King in 1659, to whose effects administration was taken out, but which instrument is lost, the manor descended to his son, subsequently knighted, 9th June, 1660, by name of Sir Andrew King, and he lived at Ankerwycke House, having intermarried with the widow of his friend and co-merchant-tailor, viz., Mary, once wife of John Sharowe, and daughter of James Parkes, buried at Wraysbury, 17th August, 1641. The Knight dwelt in the parish some twenty years, and may have been interred here, could but records be found; his will was proved 21st March, 1679, and he died issueless. He put his estates in trust to William Oakley of Salop his cousin, Thomas Powney, John Needham, and Thomas Edwards, Gentleman of London, for sale, for the benefit of his nephew Nathaniel, son of his brother of the same name, who had predeceased him some years. And thus this family removed wholly from our parish, when the trustees sold to Mr. Lee.

### SHAROWE IN ALLIANCE WITH KING.

JOHN SHAROWE, of Ashby, Yorksh.=ANN dau. of —— POPE.   AMBROSE KING, from Wales.
visn. London, 1634.

ANDREW KING, Lord of the Manor, 1612, adm. July, 1659.

JOHN SHAROWE, City and Merchant-tailor, Lord of the Manor of Wraysbury, 1627, Inq. p. m. 1 May, 1634. No will in Prer. Office. = MARY dau. of James Parkes, whose son was buried at Wraysbury, 17 Aug. 1641. = SIR ANDREW KING, Lord of Wraysbury Manor, 1659. married about 1636, knighted 9 June, 1660, will proved 21 March, 1679, ob. sp.

NATHANIEL KING, of Pentrynant, Co. Montgomery, will proved 15 May, 1672. = ALICE, dau. of extrix. 1672.   dau. m. Thos. Sharowe. He ob. 1648, s.p.

JAMES SHAROWE, of the Middle Temple.   WILLIAM SHAROWE, Merchant Tailor, 1642.   JOSEPH SHAROWE.   RACHEL, buried at Wraysbury, 7 Sept. 1641.   MARY.   THOS. SHAROWE, m. dau. of Andrew King. Will proved 4 March, 1648, sp.   NATHANIEL KING, heir to his uncle, Sir A. King.   ANDREW.   MARY.   MARTHA.

The manor of Wraysbury was in the market about fourteen years only, when a gentleman by name John Lee of London, merchant, and a cadet branch of that of Salop, who had made divers purchases in the vicinity, and especially that of Ankerwycke Purnish of the Smijth family in 1652;

and another in 1657 of Anne West in Horton, which was followed by two more lands investments in Colnbroke and Langly in 1679, set his eyes on Ankerwycke Priory, and this was conveyed to him by indenture, dated 10th August, 1685, in which deed it is asserted that he had recently acquired the manor.

I shall have occasion to advert to Mr. Lee again under Ankerwycke, which perhaps will palliate a digression here relative to the Pynchon family, who held possession for some time, and were also lessees of the college land with Wraysbury House.

William Pynchon was a gentleman of a distinguished family, raised to the honour of Baronets, and originally from Essex, as the subjoined pedigree will shew. He was a very pious man, and a literary celebrity too, and composed a work styled "The meritorious Prince of our Redemption;" not much known now, but of some significance in its day, and for which he received a very *common* reward, either for sense or extravagance—*persecution*. He quitted Wraysbury, and embarked for Connecticut in America, and there he abided till 1656, when it would appear that he sighed for Old England with a burning *maladie de pays*.

This induced and even forced him home; for though man desires to wander, and has his wish indulged, yet as the bent tree springs back to its form of growth, he is pursued by a *nostalgia*, having a double aspiration after an unknown future and the unforgotten past, which preserves in him an exclusive attachment to the present by a beautiful and touching instinct—

> "And the small, quiet hamlet where he dwelt,
> Was one of that complexion which seems made
> For those who their mortality have felt."—CHILDE HAROLD, C. iv. 32.

A fragment of the old parish register proves that he was interred here 7th November, 1662, and in the same year his son John bought of Edward Bulstrode lands in Wraysbury, Michaelmas, 14 Charles II. 1662. This same John Pynchon, of Springfield, England, by fine, Michaelmas 1686, sells certain property in Wraysbury to John Topham, Esq. lessee of Wraysbury House and the College lands, in 1679. He was also admitted customary tenant of Wraysbury on the surrender of William White of London, goldsmith, 20th December 1686; and on the 12th December 1687 he again surrendered to Richard Fryer. One Henry Pinchon was also customary tenant of Yeoveny in 1686; and this was surrendered to Richard Fryar, and through his son Peter Fryar it came to Elizabeth, widow of Benjamin Hassell, Esq. in 1703; and so by descent to Brooke H. Gyll, Esq.

I find Pinchon here in 1653, when Nicholas Pinchon bought lands of Andrew King, Esq., and by another deed of cotemporaneous date he also buys Wraysbury lands of John Bland, Esq.

The last record we have of the Pynchons in our parish is 1686, as above recited, when they repaired again to America; and I believe no one connected with them, or with the parish, heard of the name of Pynchon till the author of this work received a communication, 18th October 1856, from Thomas Ruggles Pynchon, making inquiries about his family; for which purpose he stated that he had personally visited Wraysbury. He asserts that his immediate predecessor, William Pynchon, had first emigrated to New England in 1630, and was one of the principal projectors of the colonization of that country, and among the first settlers in the great valley of Connecticut, where he built a house called Springfield, after the family residence in Essex, where he and his relatives have since dwelt. It is a fact that he published his "Meritorious Prince" in America, and that persecution there was the proximate cause which made him take refuge in Old England. This occurred about 1655, and that he again established himself in Wraysbury, and in it expired in 1662.

Mr. Pynchon alleged that his ancestor had bought confiscated lands here belonging to the Crown, which were rented at the Restoration, and that there were many letters dated from

Wraysbury, from which it is collected that he was an intimate friend of Sir Harry Vane, junior, ancestor of the Dukes of Cleveland; and that a packet of epistles written to him by Sir Harry Vane had been in the possession of his family, concerning the difficulties in New England, similar to those experienced under him (Sir Harry) when Governor of Massachusetts. Mr. Pynchon solicited all reliable information about the family and the village, to publish it in America, where he is a Professor at Trinity College, Hartford, Connecticut. They intermarried with the family of Ruggles of Essex, and every male descendant has since borne that appellative. The writer supplied what he knew, and thus terminates this digression with a Pedigree of Pynchon; while that of Bulstrode, in alliance with Croke and Empson, will be given under Horton.

## PEDIGREE OF PYNCHON.

Arms: Per bend A. and S. three roundles within a bordure engrailed counterchanged.

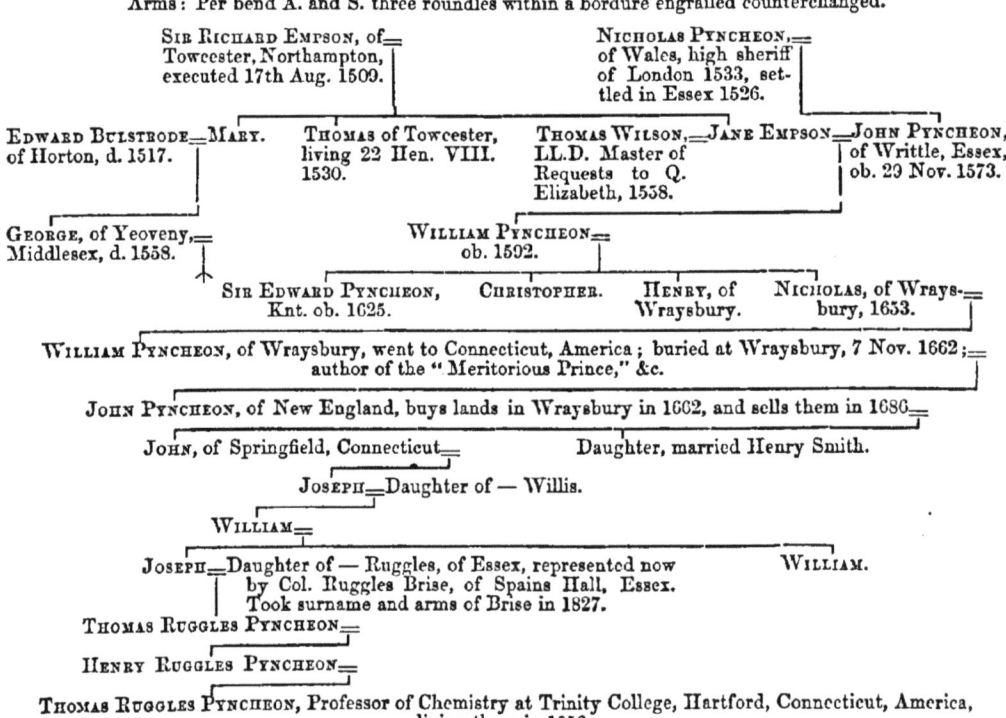

Thomas Ruggles Pynchon, Professor of Chemistry at Trinity College, Hartford, Connecticut, America, living there in 1856.

I will recapitulate here the property bought by the Bulstrodes, who had been early connected with Wraysbury as well as Horton, and they seem to have bought Horton House of Robert Hall, 17 Charles I. 1640, and the manor of Wraysbury, 26th Nov. 1627, of John Sharowe. In 1632 there is a fine between Thomas Bowry, yeoman of the parish, and Dorothy his wife, with Henry and Thomas Bulstrode, relative to messuages and lands in Horton; and here in the following year, 1633, a transference of land in a deed of Philip Smyth and Henry Bulstrode, his brother-in-law; also one between John Evans and the same Henry Bulstrode about three closes in Wraysbury.

By a fine, Easter 1657, Richard West and Edward Bulstrode, and Mildred his wife, lands in this place, with free fishing, &c.; in 1658, John Powney buys land of John Sandford, Gent. in Langley; and in 1671, a similar instrument between William Sandford, Esq. and Thomas

Bulstrode; and in Hilary Term of the same year, Thomas Bowry buys property of Thomas Bulstrode, who died in 1676.

The marriage of Edward Bulstrode with Mildred, daughter of George Brome, Esq. of Ashford, introduces the latter into this parish; and here I shall cite a fine, 1647, between George Brome, Esq. Robert Hall of Horton, and William Sandford, Esq.; and Robert Brome buys in Wraysbury three messuages, two mills, six gardens, and some forty acres of land of Edward Bulstrode and his wife Mildred. Edward Bulstrode held lands in Yeoveny in 1691, from which time these names totally disappear from Wraysbury and Horton; but a descendant may be recognised in Richard Brome, Gent. who sells property to John Green, in Denham, Bucks, in 1767. The William Sandford had a son, John Sandford, of Bishop Stortford, Herts, who had a daughter Cordelia, who married John Brome in 1713. A branch of this family, originally from Salop, is found in John Brome, Esq. of Ludlow, whose eldest daughter and coheir Mary married William Gyll of Wraysbury House. (See Pedigree of Gyll.)

### PEDIGREE OF SANDFORD AND BROME.

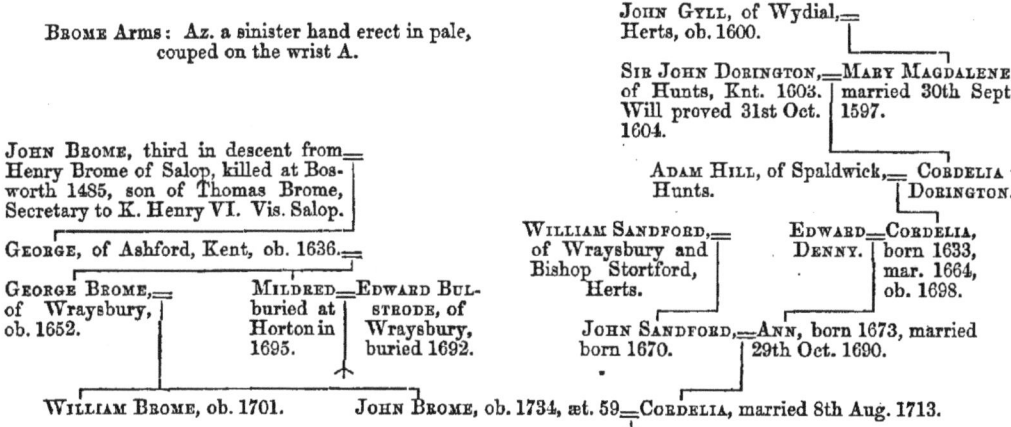

I now revert to the next successive Lord of the Manor in Wraysbury, viz. John Lee, Esq. of London, merchant. The indenture, dated 9th July, and enrolled the same day, 1652, shews that Thomas Smyth, Esq. of Horeham Hall, Essex, sells to John Lee, Esq. of London, for £3700, all that manor and lordship called Ankerwycke Purnish, with the site and demesnes thereof, formerly belonging to Ankerwycke Priory, &c.

In 1657, as before shewn, Mr. Lee buys property in Horton; and in 1678 he added thereto in Colnbrook and Langley a property bought for £2600 of Thomas Berenger, son of Richard Berenger, whose widow also held Wraysbury lands. This fostered a desire for a further and ampler investment; and in a recital of the settlement of his possessions of Ankerwycke, by deed dated 14th January 1678, he adverts to this property. The manorial rights and the Priory were conveyed to John Lee the son, by indenture dated 10th August 1685. John Lee the elder died, and his will is dated 11th August 1675, and proved by his son John, 10th August 1682, who was of the Middle Temple; and there are extant deeds by him of the same purport executed in 1685 and 1687. I do not find that he added much to the original purchase from the heirs of Sir Andrew King; and as I shall again refer to him under Ankerwycke, I shall record a pedigree and the death of this last male proprietor in his line, which took place in 1704 without issue. He left Mary, his widow, lady of the manor, who continued to hold courts here till her death in 1725. Her maiden name was

Morse, of London. The property had been settled on the issue of her only sister, Elizabeth, who died in 1713, and who was the second wife of Sir Philip Harcourt, Knt. who deceased 1688.

I have, through the liberality of George Simon Harcourt, Esq. examined the Wraysbury Court Rolls, which are contained in four books, the earliest date being 14th Oct. 1725, when Philip Harcourt, grandson of Elizabeth, daughter of John Lee, and wife of Sir Philip Harcourt, Knt. was lord here; and I very much regret that the ancient Court Rolls, which are in existence from a very early date, were not open for inspection.

Histories would be but imperfectly written if the proprietary possessing such valuable information did not extend their courtesy to historiographers; nor should they peevishly decline to render service to literature by burying family muniments in old boxes, and so withhold them from publication, and prevent the securing of the contents of those records which neglect is often hastening to decay.

## PEDIGREE OF LEE, CONYERS, JODRELL, NOURSE, AND WEYLAND.

LEE Arms: G. a fesse componée O. and Az. between 8 billets A.

THOMAS LEE, of Cotton, Salop, thirteenth in descent from Hugo de Lega. Visitation Salop. = DOROTHY, dau. of Richard Otley, of Petley.

JOHN LEE, of London, merchant, bought Ankerwycke Purnish in 1653 of Sir Thomas Smijth; will dat. 11th Aug. 1675, and proved 10th Aug. 1682, died 1682, æt. 82. = MARY, dau. of — Pollard, married 1627, living 1675.

RICHARD LEE = RICHARD LEE, 1678.

LANCELOT LEE = THOMAS LEE, of Cotton, Salop.

HANNAH. MARY.

GEORGE LEE, of Stoke Milbro', Salop, d. 22nd Sept. æt. 33. = CECILY, d. and heiress of Rob. Goodwin, of Sussex, d. 24th June, 1664, æt. 21.

JOHN LEE bought manor of Wraysbury 1685; will dated 20th Feb. 1697, and proved 26th Aug. 1704, sp. = MARY, dau. of Richard Morse, Lady of the Manor till her death, 13th Ap. 1725, æt. 69.

ELIZABETH, d. & eventual heir, settlm. 1674, 24 Dec. d. 17th Aug. 1713; will proved 3rd Sept. foll. = SIR PHILIP HARCOURT, M.P. for Oxford, d. 30th March 1688, æt. 51.

ANN, d. of Sir William Waller, Knt. of Bucks, d. 1664.

MARY, dau. and heir, æt. 17 in 1680, married 16th January 1686. = JOHN CONYERS, æt. 27 in 1680, of the Middle Temple, d. 1722.

*a quo* GEORGE SIMON HARCOURT. Ped. of H.

*a quo* Earl of Harcourt.

JOHN CONYERS, of Essex, d. 1742.

RICHARD WARNER = ELIZABETH, dau. of Edw. Lombe, of Norfolk.

PAUL JODRELL ob. 1744.

ANN = FRANCIS NOURSE.

JOHN CONYERS = HANNAH.

ELIZABETH, d. 1794. = PAUL JODRELL, d. 1751.

GILBERT JODRELL, of Ankerwycke House, d. 1772.

JUDITH m. 1739, d. 1750. = JOHN NOURSE, of Wood Eaton, Oxford, d. 1774.

SARAH, married at Wraysbury 6th Oct. 1763. = ROBERT CHILD.

ELIZABETH NOURSE d. 1822. = JOHN WEYLAND, of Wood Eaton, d. 1825.

SARAH CHILD, married 1782 = JOHN, Earl of Westmoreland.

RICHARD P. JODRELL

HENRY JODRELL, d. 1814, sp. = JOANE, d. 1855.

CECILY LETITIA = SIR EDWARD B. SMIJTH, Bart. d. 1850.

EDWARD JODRELL, d. 1852.

SIR RICHARD P. JODRELL, Bart. d. 1861.

EDWARD JODRELL, of Bayfield Hall, Norfolk. = ADELA MONKTON.

ANN ELIZABETH = GORDON GYLL, of Wraysbury.

SIR WM. B. SMIJTH, Bart.

On the death of Mrs. Lee, Philip Harcourt succeeded, and in him the manorial lordship continued till 1759; and as he died without heirs of his body, he was followed by his brother John, who married Margaret Irene, daughter of John Sarney, Esq., whose fate it was to have three husbands. Her second, Molyneux, Lord Shuldham, Admiral of the Blue, deceased in 1798, when she re-married, July 1805, with John Mead, Earl of Clanwilliam, who died 3rd September following. The Lady repaired to Germany, and died also, 22nd February, 1811. Her husband John Harcourt, at his decease in 1785, left several male children, the eldest, John Simon Harcourt, inheriting the Ankerwycke Estates, but not by fee-entail. This enabled the possessor John Harcourt to alienate by suffering a *recovery*, when the manor, with the Priory of Ankerwycke, was announced for sale. The recovery fine is dated, Trinity Term, 1794, Admiral Cornwaite Ommaney v. William Johnson—the manor of Wraysbury, with 10 messuages, 4 dovecots, 20 gardens, 300 acres of land, 100 acres of meadow, 100 acres of pasture, 50 acres of wood, 200 acres of furze and heath, common of pasture, free-fishing, liberty of foldage, Courts Leet and Baron, view of frankpledge, &c. in Wraysbury and Horton. The vouchee in the deed is John Simon Harcourt, Esq.

This manor came into the hands of Mr. Lee in 1685, and in 1794 his heir, through a sister, alienated it—and the purchaser was John Blagrove, Esq., of Cardiff Hall, Jamaica, an opulent merchant there. He had dwelt previously at Little Ankerwycke, and secured at the public sale there much that was essential to his domestic comfort; adding divers pieces of property to the manor, and he continued to dwell there till his death, 9th April, 1824, aged 70 years. By his last will, 3rd February, 1824, the manor was in the hands, and invested in the names of John Bradshaw, Hugh Parkin, and Augustus Hill Bradshaw, Esquires—as trustees for his daughters and co-heirs, 1828.

## PEDIGREE OF BLAGROVE.

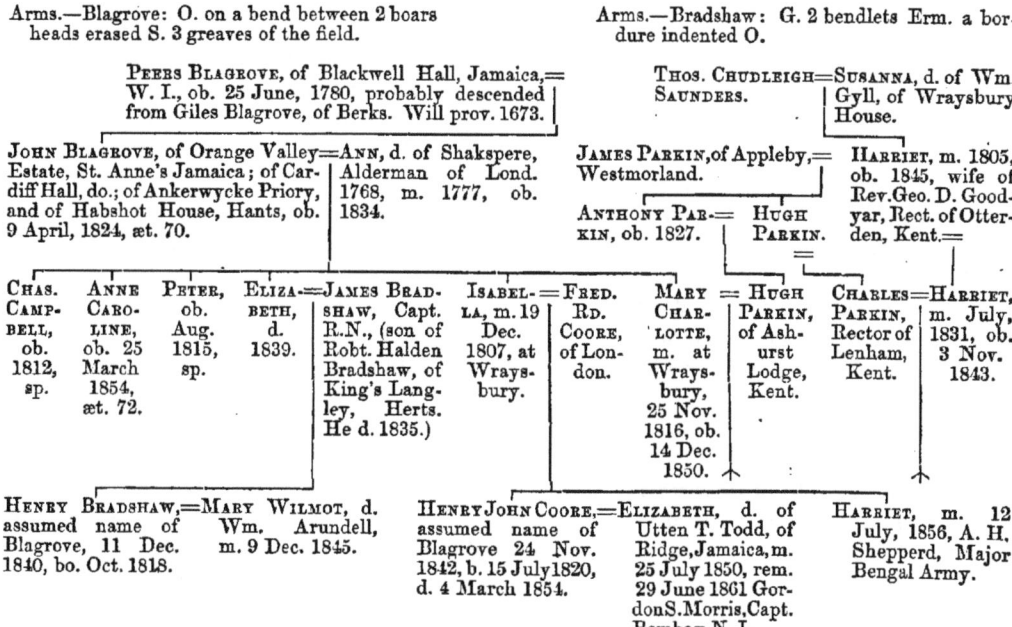

The first general Court Baron and Court of Survey of John Blagrove, Esq., Lord of the Manor of Wraysbury, was entered in the Court Rolls, 14th Feb. 47 George III. 1807, while the first General

Court Baron in which the names of Bradshaw, &c. are introduced, is dated 6th June, 1828, as Lord of the Manor of Wraysbury.

This entry is followed by another, "the special Customary Court of George Simon Harcourt, Esq., Lord of the Manor, 2 Nov. 1829;" since which period the alienated estates have been again brought into the house of Harcourt. Mr. Harcourt purchased also divers pieces of land in this parish belonging to the coheirs of Mr. Blagrove and others, and having become undoubted proprietor (see deed, Easter 1828, John Lake, Gent. *v.* John Williams, for sundry acres of land and common of pasture, in which George S. Harcourt, Esq. is vouchee), he was made Deputy Lieutenant and was elected M.P. for the county, and is again Lord of the Manor, and the male representative of a family whose lineage deduces from ancestors anterior to the Norman Conquest, a succinct pedigree of which will be entered under Ankerwycke Priory.

## SMALLER MANORS IN WRAYSBURY.

There are sundry manors within this small parish, but whether there were any which are now absorbed in the only two remaining manors, is doubtful; it is not improbable that in earlier times several distinct manors existed, whose possessors cannot be deduced through the long succession of ages which have intervened between the period when the Montfitchets were Lords here by whom the Priory of Ankerwycke was founded, and to which the chief estates seem to have belonged until the dissolution of religious houses in 1537. These minor manors, each *imperium in imperio*, constitute a feature in our parochial histories, and courts were uniformly held to recognise and sustain their rights. Few title deeds are of such antiquity as Court Rolls of copyhold and ancient demesnes. A deed must be shewn of at least 60 years to confirm a title to an estate or landed possession; this is not the case on the transfer of manors, the Court Rolls of which being public documents, and in the nature of public property, are generally preserved with care, and are remitted to each successor in the manor—some of which date as early as 1272, 1 Edw. I.

But manors are really coeval with our Saxon constitution substantially, though our jurists consider them of Norman institution, when every Lord held immediately of the Crown. His manor was styled a Barony, and himself the *Lord and Baron;* hence there was a jurisdiction and a Court Baron, and the people employed were called Villeins, and were transferred with the property, as in Russia now, unless the Emperor breaks their bonds in sunder this 1861.

At the period of Domesday, 1088, the manors immediately subordinate to the Crown numbered about 1422: those of the Lords 2720, divided among nine persons; the largest holder being the Earle of Moretaine, who possessed 793 manors.

Lamborde, in his Kent, denies there ever were bondmen or villeins in that shire; neither were they bounden by copy nor customary tenure. These tenures, though rare in Kent, yet have existed there with the law of gavelkind. So some may think, with Shakspere, in addition to its physical beauties, that

> Kent in the Commentaries Cæsar writ,
> Was deemed the pleasant place of all the isle.

These copy rolls or transcripts of them are occasionally found very perfect. The names of the Lords of the Manor throughout the counties of England from 1316 to 1559, are in the British Museum, and there is a transcript of the Book called Nomina Villarum, (page 5).

The parish of Wraysbury, as to its locality, has been already described. According to the last survey its area was 1656 acres, previously set at 1610 statute acres in 1831. Its shape is amorphous, a kind of *trapezium.* The Thames circumscribes it on the south and west, although there be some few acres of Old Windsor (about 13) in the parish circuit, and also some part of the parish, some seven or eight acres, on the right bank of the Thames at Egham, occasioned probably by an irruption of the water in past ages.

The north of it is bounded by a line which now runs nearly parallel with the railroad, and on the east a ditch or brook divides it from Staines parish and Middlesex county. Its circumference is about four and a half miles, and it is watered by the Colne, which disembogues into the Thames by two divergent branches at Hythe End and at Staines. It is not unlike the figure of South America, having two unequal excrescences on both sides, and it tapers down to a point on the Lammas land, which abuts on Staines town. Here four counties almost meet in convergent junction—a rare occurrence in England. It is a sequestered village, once a hamlet, and very flat, but the position of which in a nook at the extreme verge of the shire, contiguous to the heights of Cooper's Hill, receives and radiates their beauty.

The recognized manors then are those of the manor of Wraysbury, formerly held as of the honor of Windsor (Ankerwycke Purnish is in Surrey), the manor of Remingham and Cokke, and the Rectorial manor. It is not unlikely there was a small manor at Hythe End.

By the 39 Geo. III. 1799, an act for enclosing the common fields within the parish and manor of Wraysbury, it is stated in the preamble that John Simon Harcourt, Esq., is Lord of the Manor and proprietor of part of the lands directed to be inclosed. That the Dean and Canons of Windsor are Lords of the Manor of the Rectory, and owners of the Rectory impropriate and entitled to the glebe belonging to the Rectory; but Mr. Gyll is lay impropriator and lay Rector of the great tithes under them, who reserve in their own hands the patronage of the Vicarage, and also their manor of the Rectory, which is noticed and recognised in the Commissioners award in the inclosure of the parish.

## ANKERWYCKE PRIORY.

The manor is said to belong to the Priory, probably comprised in the original endowment, but since 1537 the Priory and manor have gone together.

The derivation of this name is Anchoret's wick or wyke (wick, wig, vîk, a bay—viega, biegen, to bend or bow—vigen, Sles-wig, &c.), on which was an Abbey or Priory, containing monks, nuns, or anchorets, or people mewed up in walls, who had receded from the practical duties of life—$\dot{\alpha}\nu\alpha\chi\omega\rho\eta\tau\dot{\eta}\varsigma$—a Greek word implying secession.

The *ancren* rule is of the 13th century. Ancren, anker, ancress, are all synonymes for anchorite—$\dot{\alpha}\pi o\ \tau o\tilde{v}\ \dot{\alpha}\nu\alpha\chi\omega\rho\epsilon\iota\nu$. The anchorites of the East are mentioned in the Council of Trullo, 692, and that of Frankfort in 787; and they all legislated for devotees termed *recluses*, and were divided into *inclusi* and *inclusæ*—the former enclosed in a cell only opened by a Bishop's order, termed *Anker*-house or *anker*-hold. Some lived in wooden houses in churchyards, under the eaves of the church. The *anchoretæ conclusi* were civilly dead, and there were canons drawn up for these *solitaires* or *melancholy* children of superstition, an anomaly in Christianity, for the most acceptable hymn that can be paid to the Creator is one of joy and thankfulness—while to enjoy is to obey.

Anker-houses had two apartments, one for the lady and one for the maid. There were three windows or *thurles*, or apertures. The parlour window (parler) was assigned for conversation, having a black curtain with a white cross thereon. It was a violation of the rules for the *professed* to go abroad; but this was disregarded, and the poor prisoners, "who were taught to merit heaven by making earth a hell," were glad to find some erratic being who, from mill, market or smithy, brought news to dissipate or qualify their accumulated *ennui*. Monks were divided into two classes, *Cœnobites*, who lived under a regular discipline, and *Anachorets*, who indulged their unsocial independent fanaticism—and they derive their appellation from their practice of grazing in the fields with the common herds, like Nebuchadnezzar, and affecting to resemble beasts, and they even passed days without food and years without speaking. One Simon Stylites, the very *quintessence of insanity*, undertook in his frenzy to accomplish an aërial penance, and so ascended a column of some 60 feet in altitude, and there he lived, resisting the alternations of temperature for 30 years. He ended his celestial life on the summit of the pillar, A.D. 451, and gradually defaced God's image in man by destroying all sensibility of mind and body. A cruel and unfeeling temper has distinguished monks in every age and clime, exciting the pity and contempt of philosophers Pagan and Christian, vitiating the faculties of man by the corruption of truth, by credulity and superstition, which almost extinguished the light of philosophy and science for ten centuries. So this dark millennium is a blank in human history.

On the bank of the Thames, in the south-western section of the village, nearly at its centre, stood a small nunnery, the ruins of which at the present day are next to nothing. This religious house was founded by Sir Gilbert Montfitchet, conjointly with his son Sir Richard, about the reign of K. Henry II. who began his regnal career in 1154. Perhaps it was conceived in a goodly spirit, to propitiate heaven for deeds done in the days of flesh, or it may be from sheer superstition, yet was it dedicated to St. Mary Magdalen, and the order was to be that of St. Benedict, a recluse who abjured society, and, mole-like, lived under ground, founding this order, and *graciously* giving them rules of his composing. He died in 547 of the year of grace, and his life is written by Gregory the Great, who, to give *à plomb* to his biography, has marred all probability by a concatenation of most extravagant miracles. The Benedictine monasteries pervaded all Europe through the instrumentality of St. Dunstan.

Tradition talks, as it is wont to talk, preposterously—that a bough was conveyed by a dove from Ankerwycke to Germany, and being planted there in a convent garden, a slip of it was transferred to Spain, there to be venerated by the priestly superstitious and their satellites as of divine virtue.

When the founder of the nunnery "shuffled off his mortal coil" is not ascertained, but his coadjutor's death, Sir Richard Montfitchet, is supposed to have happened about 1203. The Order was not neglected here, for Sir Richard, in 1256, 41 Hen. III. obtained from that king a charter confirming the several donations of land which had been made to the nunnery, and among the rest certain lands in the parish of Wraysbury held by the Lady Abbess in her own right. The Priory of Bermondsey was possessed of the tithes of Stikelton, Greenford, Middlesex, and this year, 25 Hen. III. 1241, the brotherhood compounded with them with the Priory of Ankerwycke at 8s. a year, as we find in the Chronicle of Bermondsey. This estate was given by Nicholas de Farnham to Ankerwycke Priory previous to the confirmation of the Charter of 41 Hen. III. 1256. The Stickleton manor was held under the Bohuns.

Dugdale's Monasticon, Vol. iv. p. 229, asserts that Hugh, Abbot of Chertsey in 1107, was one of the benefactors to Ankerwycke, whose names are inserted in the Charter 41 Hen. III. 1256. This (Chertsey) was a rich abbey, being one of the mitred abbeys, and the Abbot one of 29 who held of the King by barony. The year 1256 was that which preceded the death of Sir Richard Montfitchet, and he may have been urged by his confessor to enact deeds of alms, and leave an odour of sanctity to be followed by the godly in the village of Wraysbury.

The Benedictine nuns had priories at Ankerwycke, Little Marlow, Mursley or St. Margarets at Ivinghoe; and history alleges that Richard King of the Romans, brother of our King Henry III., and who died 1271, in 1265, founded an abbey of Benedictine nuns at Burnham, which was endowed with the manors of Burnham, Cippenham, Stoke, Bulstrode. In the days of Henry VIII. the value was £51. 2s 4¼d. This property, temp. William I. was in the possession of Walter Fitz Other.

What class the intermediates to this priory were we have no means of ascertaining, but it is not improbable that benefactors, as well as the adjacent lands, were tributary to the good offices. There were certainly Chartularies of this religious house, of one of which Thomas Hearne the antiquary makes mention in a work, 9 July, 1732, as being then in the possession of Mr. Philip Harcourt.

Ankerwycke was not taxed in the valuation of Pope Nicholas, who was elevated to the *miscalled* chair of St. Peter in 1288 (for no authority proves that Apostle was ever *bodily* in Rome), except as to the property in Egham; and I find an inquisition post mortem, 9 Edw. I. 1280, relative to the Prioress of Ankerwycke, in which property or rental was derived from Egham, and some possessions are rather obscurely defined by *platea vasta* in that parish. Egham was so called from Ege—edge, and ham—home.

This convent had also friends in the neighbourhood, who took a lively interest in the *poor nuns* here, as a charitable gentleman, Ralph Jocelyn, 51 Hen. III. 1267, gave certain rents in the parish of Stanwell, to the annual amount of 12s (about £7 of our money) to the Prior and Convent of Ankerwycke.

Another Son of Charity in the same place, by name William Passevant, in 1285 gave also 50 acres of land in Stanwell, held under Richard de Wyndsore, to this our priory (escheat 13 Edw. I. No. 115), and if we add thereto the lands opposite on Englefield Green, styled Ankerwyk Pernerhs (Purnish), this religious house was not destitute of worldly support.

A few years prior to this donation it seems by deed, 10 Edw. I. 1281, that the king granted this manor of Wraysbury with *appurtenances* to Christiana de Mauriscis, but whether from benevolence to the lady or for the good services of her husband, William de Mauriscis, is not recorded. It probably came through her father, Robert de Burnel. By an inquis. p. mortem, 29 Edw. I., 1302, taken at the decease of the said Christiana, her property here is cited, for in the same year she paid a fine of 40s to the bishop for license to give a certain tenement to the Prioress and Nuns of Ankerwycke. "Pro monialibus de Ankerwyk, 1 virgate of land, 1 messuage, &c.," in which the two parishes of Wardesbury and Langley manors are cited, and one stream of water, on the Thames, abutting on Ankerwyk in Wardesbury parish.

Between the years 1245 and 1304, a pious gift of three virgates of land, with *appurtenants* in Takeleia (Takeley, Essex, a parish of 3110 acres) was received from William, son of Helia, by the good Prioress Letia. This Takely had been the estate of Robert Gernon of Wraysbury, temp. William I.

After the death of Christiana de Mariscis, King Edward II. granted these manors to others, as we have seen under the manorial history, the grantees living rarely on the spot, so that some neglect may have been the cause, that in the days of King Edward III., the Prioress and Convent, calling themselves *Poor Nuns* of Ankerwyk, petitioned the legislature in 1295, on account of their having been disseised by the famous Sire Hugh le Despenser the elder, a peer of the realm, and deriving its patronymic from the office of Dispenser of the Household and Sovereign in bygone days, like Botiler and Mareschale (page 9). This Baron was created Earl of Winchester in 1322, and was decapitated in 1326 for a traitor. He was accused of seducing the King Edward II., and oppressing the State; by the orders of the Queen he was drawn on a hurdle through the streets of Hereford on St. Andrew's Eve, and was beheaded on a gallows 50 feet high, and his head was fixed on London Bridge. The accusation against him here was, that he had seized 30 acres of land, and 29 acres of meadow-land in Datchet, and of the profits of £100 sterling (some £1200 of our day) praying restitution. This apparent wrong continued till his death in 1326, Rot. Parl. Vol. ii. p. 406, and Monast. Angl. Vol. iv. p. 231. Whether the *poor* nuns recovered the claims, or what further proceedings ensued, if any, appear not; but the allegations may not have been substantiated, or else even-handed justice refused to do her duty, for no mention is made of the possessions in the ecclesiastical valuations, temp. Henry VIII. They may have had some indemnity from the young king, Richard II., who began his career in 1377, and was, as history avers, a generous benefactor to the Priory of Ankerwycke.

As the Despensers were large proprietors in this place and Datchet, and were connected with the Earl of Gloucester, from whom benefits were received by the nuns, it may not be irrelevant to advert to the origin and family of these magnates.

By deed, 1250, Richard de Gloster, heir of Isabel de Duton, gave to King Edward III. a messuage and 17 acres of land arable, with some meadow-land, and 3s rent in Wraysbury, which was duly ratified and registered. Geoffrey de Mauriscis (between whom and William de Wendleshore there is a fine in Horton and Wraysbury, 8 Hen. III. 1223), and who died 1272, had married Christiana, daughter of Walter de Riddlesford. They had a daughter Emmeline, who was wife of Maurice Fitzgerald, whose daughter Julienne married, 1276, Thomas de Clare, youngest son of Richard Earl of Gloster. Gilbert de Clare died in 1313, leaving his sisters his heirs, of whom Aliana the eldest married Hugh le Despenser, thought to have been the next Earl of Gloster in right of his wife, because 19 Edw. II., 1326, he is summoned only as Hugh le Despenser, jun., and this was the Parliament before his execution, 9th October, 1326.

Thomas de Spenser had the sentence of banishment reversed, which had been passed against his grandfather in 1321—and was created Earl of Gloster; which Hugh le Despenser was a man of considerable opulence, holding 59 lordships, with flocks and herds, and *mirabile dictu*, a library. His destiny was to adhere to Richard II., and to end his life on a scaffold in 1400, when the Earldom fell into abeyance. His son Richard may be the Richard de Gloster (heir of Isabel de Duton), who died sp. m.; and hence his daughter Isabel became sole heir, and was united to Richard Beauchamp Earl of Worcester, who again left Elizabeth daughter and heir, the wife of Edward Neville, younger son of Ralph Earl of Westmoreland.

Froissart's Chronicle records the execution of the two Spensers, father and son. "Sir Hugh Spencer the elder was about xc. yeres of age, executed in October 1326, in the sight of his son, and previous to execution was barbarously mutilated. After this, Sir Hugh Spenser junior was captured, mutilated, and executed, at the instance of the Earl of Kent and Earl Mortimer, who soon after suffered precisely the same indignities with execution in 1329."

### PEDIGREE OF SPENCER.

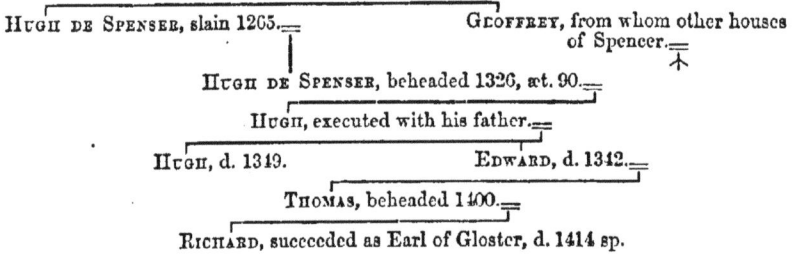

Prior to the dissolution of religious houses in 1535, a Court was established under the title of Court of Augmentation of the Revenues of the Crown, to determine differences relative to lands, possessions, &c.; and in this depository are kept the records concerning all monastic estates. The Court was dissolved, and on its re-establishment was annexed to the Exchequer in 1554, from which time it took the name of Augmentation Office, and in it are grants, fee farm rents, escheat rolls, surveys of manors, original deeds, charters and evidences belonging to the dissolved religious institutions.

An impression of the common seal of this nunnery is here preserved, and there is another representation affixed to a deed, 54 Hen. III., 1270. It indicates a rude building, with a cross at either end of its roof, with a pointed cupola in the centre, representing a modern barn, having these words around it—SIGILL. ECCLE. SCE MARIE MAG DE ANKWIC.

In the Monasticon, also, is a third impression, appendant to an instrument in the British Museum, marked L. F. C. x. 7, citing an agreement, beginning in the usual form, "Hæc est finalis Concordia inter Letiam Priorissam de Ankerwyc et William filium Helie de tribus virgatis terræ cum pertinentibus in Takeleia"—of which we have made mention.

Edward the Confessor was said to be the first Sovereign in England who put his seal to a charter; but subsequent discoveries of Anglo-Saxon seals warrant an earlier date—viz. 850.

Coats of arms are found on seals appended to wills, deeds, &c. enabling genealogists to classify families. Specimens of hereditary armorial bearings appeared on the shields of adventurers, *temp.* Hen. II., but it was not till after the holy wars that these cognizances became general. At the time of Edward I. the statute of Exon ordains the coroner's jury to certify with their respective seals. Ancient charters and evidences were only sealed, and not signed; and every shape and colour of wax was adopted, though red ultimately prevailed. The devices were arbitrary—as flowers, birds, crescents, Agnus Dei, &c.; and during the thirteenth and fourteenth centuries medieval seals attained their highest artistic excellence, and antique intaglios were used on personal seals during the middle ages.

The Pope's instruments issuing from the Roman Chancery were termed Bulls, from *bulla,* a seal, which really derives from *bullion,* or silver, hanging to them—bulls not being confined to Popes. The bull of Clement VII.—confirming the title of Defender of the Faith to Henry VIII.— had a seal with gold appended.

## PRIORESSES OF ANKERWYCKE.

It may not be out of place here to record the names of those who have been Prioresses, which have been preserved since the thirteenth century.

Emma, died 1236; Celestia, elected 1239; Joan de Roan or Rotomago, elected 1241; Juliana, 1245; while Letia occurs in the reign of Henry III. as the lady who gratefully received the land of William, son of Helia,—of which mention is made.

Allowing about half a century between her predecessor and Alice de Stanford in 1304, we record the next Prioress as Joan de Oxon in 1326. Joan Godman follows in 1384, to whom succeeded Maude Bache, 30th August 1391, 13 Richard II. in whose reign a donative was received from the Crown.

One Elizabeth Golope is next in order, 1400, and her successor is found in Margery Kirby, whose election is fixed in 1443. Margaret Pert died in 1478, and Alice Spendlow presented 24th October 1478, probably of the family of this name in the county of Lincoln. The only Prioress who resigned was Alice Worcester, to be followed by the election, 26th October 1526, of Magdalen Downes, the last of the long file of dead Prioresses who were declined to dust. She survived the dissolution of 1538, and her name is recorded in a receipt for a pension of 100s. or about £60 per annum for her temporalities.

According to Tanner, the veracious antiquary, in his "Notitia Monastica," Bishop of St. Asaph, who died in 1735, whose work was republished in 1744, there were but five religious houses remaining at the date of the dissolution of this priory, whose estate then amounted to £28 a year, as says Leland, the eminent antiquary, dignified by Henry VIII. with a commission in 1533, laying commands on him to search after England's antiquities in cathedrals, priories, &c. in which quest he spent six years. He died in 1552, leaving accumulations which are admitted to be a national treasure.

In the records of these days, the Priory of Ankerwycke was worth £32. 0s. 2d. which John Speed the historian, whose Chronicle was said to be the largest and best hitherto extant, makes £45. 14s. 4d.

Money was paid into the Exchequer by weight; and it has increased thirty times in value since the Conquest, a pound then being three times the quantity at present and ten times its value in purchasing commodities; so that this £44 would be equivalent to £457. 3s. 4d. However, the word "value" has at least two different meanings, sometimes expressing the utility of a particular object, and sometimes the power of purchasing goods which the possession of that object conveys; hence one is called value in use, and the other value in exchange.

Land was sold prior to the Conquest for a shilling an acre, and a pound sterling was divided into twenty shillings. The value of money *temp.* Henry II. and III. did not vary, but the interest was fifty per cent. The Jews, who were the usurers, often paid in *teeth* or *persecution* in those humane times, as well as in money; and history says that in 1243 a talliage was laid on them of 60,000 marks—a sum nearly equal to the whole yearly revenue of the Crown. At the time of the monastic dissolutions, the standard of money was that of the preceding reign, Henry VII. when silver was at £1. 17s. 6d. a pound, which, Hume remarks, makes the treasure of Henry VII. to be nearly three millions of our money.

*Computation of the Administration temp. Henry VIII. Abstract Roll, 28 H. 8—15. Augmentation Office. Priory of the Nuns of Ankerwycke.*

| Co. Bucks— | £. | s. | d. | Co. Middlesex— | £. | s. | d. |
|---|---|---|---|---|---|---|---|
| Fyndstede Parva | 0 | 7 | 0 | Greneford Manor | 4 | 0 | 0 |
| Great Fyndstede Great field | 1 | 6 | 8 | Stanwell Park Manor | 3 | 6 | 8 |
| Ditto Old Meadow | 1 | 6 | 8 | Staynes, land | 1 | 11 | 10 |
| Ankerwycke Fishery | 2 | 0 | 0 | Surrey—Parnyshe in Egham Manor | 3 | 11 | 0 |
| Tynset (Tinsey), pasture land | 1 | 0 | 0 | Co. Berks—Windsor, lands | 0 | 14 | 10 |
| Lay Mede | 0 | 8 | 0 | Co. Essex—Bassingborne,* Takeley, rents | 1 | 0 | 0 |
| Cambehurst, land | 0 | 13 | 0 | City of London—Land, rents in Camsvyk strete, St. Bridget parish | 11 | 6 | 8 |
| Himlett Gate, ditto | 0 | 13 | 4 | | | | |
| Horton, rent of land | 0 | 5 | 10 | Co. Bucks—Ankerwick Lords land | 6 | 9 | 4 |
| Alderburne Manor | 3 | 6 | 8 | | | | |
| Hardington and Heys, land | 1 | 5 | 0 | | £44 | 12 | 6 |

The family of Crofte seems known here. Sir James Crofte requested Queen Elizabeth to grant to Edward Wymarke, Esq. six acres of land, two of wood, &c. in Langley Marsh and Iver, called the Rayles, &c. in the occupation of William Windsor, Esq. formerly part of the possessions of Ankerwycke Priory, to him and heirs, by the fealty and at the rent of 2s. per annum, 25th February, 29 Eliz. 1583.

* This Bassingborne property was bought in 1528 by George Canon, Esq. and others for £200. It is near Takeley; and it descended to his son-in-law, John Gyll, Esq. of Wydial, Herts. George Gyll bought some of the Stansted Montfitchet estates in 1553; whilst, in 1517, George Canon had preceded him in purchases in that locality—all of which came to John Gyll in 1534. The latter buys land there in 1537, 29 Hen. VIII.

The town and college of Eton had something to do with Ankerwycke before it became the nursery of our legislators and statesmen, founded by Henry VI. for seventy indigent scholars, who were to swear they had not £3. 6s. a year. College annual revenues computed now at £10,000, arising from manors, estates, &c. Thirty-seven livings, are vested in the Provost and seven fellows. Besides foundation scholars, there are oppidans, or town scholars, who pay for education.

LANDS AND POSSESSIONS OF ANKERWYCKE PRIORY, AUNKERWYK.

Ankerwike Prioratus Monalium Lincolniensis Diocesis Gilbertus et Ricardus Muntfitchet Milites, Fundatores.

This is a Charter of Hen. III. confirming the donatives to the nuns of Ankerwike, date 16th August, 41 Hen. III, 1256.

The gift of Gilbert de Muntfichet, all the lands styled Ankerwyk, &c. and totam *assartam exaratum* (woodland cleared from forest or waste, and cultivated, and made fit for pasture), quod Ricardus de Bruer tenuit.

5 acres of meadow in Wyresdebyri—totam terram de Alerburn cum pertinentibus.

The gift of Richard de Muntfitchet and Aveline his wife, the meadow called Wymede. Moreland and the meadow which a certain Gocelin held in the village. Also the gift of Richard, a certain isle in the Thames called *Tyng-Eyt* (Tynsey), with appurtenants. Also the gift of said Richard, son of Richard Muntfitchet, one messuage, half a virgate of land, and a certain (gurgitem) or stream of water with appurtenants, which one Thomas le Newe had here.

Half a hide of land and 5 acres with appurtenants in Pernerhs (Purnysh), the gift of Ralph son of Mathew. 10 acres of land, 30 acres of grain with appurtenants in Herpenfield.

The gift of Grunwin of Trottesworth, an acre of land in Egham.

Gift of Geoffrey of Middelton, all the land which one Aylmer held here. The gift of Robert de Myddelton 13 acres in this parish. Gift of Henry son of Henry de Middelton, a croft called Tutescroft here. Fines Horton 1256.

The gift of Ralph Pike, one acre of land here.

Gift of Aylene (Helen) de Maneghedene and William, son and heir of the same, some woodland called longam leyam, curtam leyam (open way or wood). Hardwyn's croft near La defens Agn, and a croft near terram Briencii in Maneghedene.

Of the gift of Richard Anglicus (English) 15s rent in the parish.

The gift of Albreth de Basingburn 20s rent with appurtenants in Takeley, Essex.

The gift of Walter Brun 50s rent with appurtenants in London.

The gift of Martin de Capella certain assarta (clear woodland) in Allerburne.

The gift of Master Nicholas de Farnham a messuage, octies viginti, 8 times 20 or 160 acres of land, 1½ acre of meadow, 20s rent, and the service of the sixth part of a Knight's fee with appurtenants in Greneford.

The gift of Walter le Fraunkeleyn, 25 acres of land, 2s and 18 pennies rent in Greneford.

The gift of Alice de Oppenhore 6s 8d rent in Horton.

The gift of John Pillessedisse, 11s rent in Dodesdene.

Ditto that of Geoffrey, son of Henry, 11s 11d in Henlegh (Henley).

Ditto that of the Chaplain Simon, son of Richard de Burnham, a messuage in Windsor.

Ditto that of John de sancto Phileberto, 14s 10d in Old Windsor.

Ditto of John, 2s 4d in Prestewyk.

Ditto of William de Papworth, 5s rent in Papworth (Cambridge),

This confirmation was given at Chester and ratified by ten witnesses, one of whom was King Henry III., styled William de Valencia (nostri fratris), Roger Bigod Earl Marshal of England, and Hugh de Vere Earl of Oxford.

Tanner gives the following references concerning the Priory from the public records.

26 Hen III., 1241. License for the entry of sixty pigs into Windsor Forest without pannage.

Patent Rolls. 35 Hen. III., 1250. For ten mills belonging to the king in Windsor Park.

Close Rolls. 51 Hen. III., 1266. Concerning lands and tenements in Stanwell.

Patent Rolls. 10 Edw. I., 1281. About imparking 100 acres of waste in Egware within Windsor Forest.

Patent Rolls. 29 Edw. I., 1300. Concerning lands in Stanwell.

Patent Rolls. 40 Edw. III., 1366. Concerning certain rents in Staines.

Patent Rolls. 6 Ric. II., 1382. Allows the Prioress of Ankerwycke in perpetuity a certain rate of pannage (that is waste of hedges on which cattle feed, or money paid for it in a forest), viz., each year in wood, within Windsor Park and without, 60 swine "ad pessonam (mast or acorns) et pasturam quietos de pannagio et herbagiveis concessis."—Per. 26 Hen. III., 1241. This seems to be the deed above recited.

Patent Rolls. 3 Hen. V., 1415.

Receipt into the Treasury. 6 Hen. VI., 1427.

Receipt into the Treasury. 7 Hen. VI., 1428.

Patent Rolls. 12 Hen. VI., 1433.

Patent Rolls. 13 Hen. VI., 1434.

Close Rolls. 21 Hen. VI., 1442. About rents and tenements in the Parish of St. Bridget, London.

Patent Rolls. 8 Edw. IV., 1468.

*Ecclesiastical value, temp. Henry VIII. Transcript of return, 26 Hen. VIII. 15 . First-fruits Office. Priory or House of the blessed Mary Magdalene of Ankerwyk, where Alicia Worcester is Prioress.*

| Value in temporals in Co. Bucks. | £ | s. | d. |
|---|---|---|---|
| *Ankerwyk.* | | | |
| Value of the land remaining in the hands of the Priory per annum | 4 | 13 | 4 |
| *Wyrardesbury.* | | | |
| Value in rents and farms per annum | 5 | 6 | 8 |
| *Horton.* | | | |
| do. do. | 1 | 17 | 11 |
| *Alderburne.* | | | |
| Value in lands | 3 | 6 | 8 |
| | 15 | 4 | 7 |
| Co. *Middlesex.* | | | |
| *Hunsloo and Drayton.* | | | |
| Value in rents and farms | 1 | 5 | 0 |
| *Greneford.* | | | |
| Value in the manor farms | 4 | 0 | 10 |
| *Stanwall.* | | | |
| do. do. | 3 | 6 | 8 |
| *Stanes.* | | | |
| do. do. | 2 | 3 | 10 |
| | 10 | 16 | 4 |

| Co. *Surrey.* | £ | s. | d. |
|---|---|---|---|
| *Purnish.* | | | |
| Value in rents and manor farms | 5 | 2 | 6 |
| Co. *Barkshire.* | | | |
| *Wyndesore.* | | | |
| Value of rents and farms | 0 | 18 | 9 |
| Co. *Essex.* | | | |
| *Takeley.* | | | |
| Value in rents and farms | 1 | 0 | 0 |
| City *of London.* | | | |
| Value in rents and diocese tenements | 9 | 6 | 8 |
| Perquisites in common years | 0 | 16 | 2 |
| By sale of wood do. | 1 | 13 | 4 |
| Fines and 10ths do. | 0 | 6 | 8 |
| Summary of temporalities | 45 | 5 | 0 |
| *Spiritualities in Co. Bucks.* | | | |
| Certain tenths | 0 | 9 | 4 |
| Total sum of land and possessions of Priory of Ankerwyk per annum | £45 | 14 | 4 |

*What disbursements are made at the Priory.*

*In temporalities.*

| Rents paid. | £ | s. | d. |
|---|---|---|---|
| To Chertsey Abbey for rents paid | 1 | 3 | 6 |
| Do. Priory St. John, Jerusalem, and for lands and tenements in Fleet Street | 2 | 0 | 0 |
| Do. to Abbey of Westminster for tenements in Fleet Street, London | 0 | 4 | 0 |
|  | 3 | 7 | 6 |

| *Fees official.* | £ | s. | d |
|---|---|---|---|
| To Lord Windsor, seneschal of the monastery | 1 | 0 | 0 |
| To William Carter, bailiff, do. | 3 | 6 | 8 |
|  | 7 | 14 | 2 |

*Spiritual Salaries.*

| | £ | s. | d |
|---|---|---|---|
| For a chaplain to do duty at the will of the Prioress, within the monastery before the nuns | 6 | 0 | 0 |
| Total outgoings | 13 | 14 | 2 |
| Clear value | 22 | 0 | 2 |
| 10th part to the King | 3 | 4 | 0¼ |

There were 3182 Monasteries of all religions, besides Friars' houses, valued at £140,784. 19s. 3d. which at ten times the present value would be £1,407,849. 12s. 6d.

## MANSION ON THE SITE OF THE NUNNERY, CALLED ANKERWYCKE HOUSE.

The mansion here erected was either built by Andrew Lord Windsor, or by Sir Thomas Smijth, Kt. The hall had been mentioned as long standing, although, according to Browne Willis, the ancient structure had been so entirely demolished that no part of the original was traceable in his time—yet there is a very large fragment which, from its appearance, must be coeval with the Priory, and probably was erected on the *debris*.

These conventual buildings are returned as wholly ruinous in the report of the Commissioners in the days of Henry VIII. which took place on the suppression of the remaining monasteries by Act of Parliament in 1538, and pensions were assigned to the inmates varying from 100 marks, or £66. 13s 6d, to a smaller stipend; and hence, instead of entombing themselves alive, and "singing faint hymns to the cold fruitless moon," many returned home or lived independently. To such a height of social disorder had these miscalled places of devotion arose, that by statute of Henry V. 1414, alien priories had been suppressed, and 142 of them were dissolved, the *precursor* movement of dissolution by bluff Harry; and it is a matter of history that the ancient Councils were often convened to regulate and correct the *morals* of the clergy as well as to decide on controversial points. To stay rapacity, the statute of mortmain was passed in 1279, for the prevention of the *utter absorption* of all lay property. This was, however, inefficient, the large fish broke through the net, and another statute was imposed. The clergy held *one fifth* of all England, no insignificant patrimony, unequally distributed among 400 or 500 monasteries. This instigated a visitation of the professed as well as the secular clergy, in 1523, and Wolsey alleges as the ground for this suppression, the *great wickedness* that prevailed therein; and he suppressed some 40 of them, which gradually prepared men's minds for further reductions of the houses, and the wealth accumulated by fraud and shameless intimidations. The fraudulent possessors "cried these dreadful summoners grace," so a number of abbots made surrender, and the smaller convents were abolished by Act of Parliament, to the number of 376, and their estates were vested in the Crown. In one year 57 surrenders were made—37 being monasteries, 20 nunneries, and 12 Parliamentary abbeys. The preamble of the Act 27 Henry VIII. 1536, recapitulates the evil ways of the delinquents and what had impelled condign punishment, while many remembered the *comminations* in the Bull of Innocent VIII. who died 1492—for this monastic discipline could not be reconciled with a reasonable system of religion or public utility. Necessity and public convenience have no law superior to them.

A large proportion of conventual revenues arose out of parochial tithes diverted from the legitimate object of maintaining the incumbent, to swell the pomp of some remote abbot. King Henry purposed to make 18 new bishopricks, of which only six were created, and a Bill for that end was read *three* times in one day in the Lords, while other projects he had conceived became abortive—as a seminary for statesmen, &c. Yet England has to rejoice at the scheme of violence, for no nation can flourish under a system which casts a blight on spiritual and temporal concerns. Our Poor Law is a good equivalent for monkish alms, a law suggested by that of 27 Hen. VIII. 1535, to make a collection in every parish for the indigent.

Sir Henry Norris and Sir John Norris were great warriors, *Martis pulli*, men of the sword, " great in a charge, which is of the sword, and in a retreat, which is the shield of war."

This priory had scarcely devolved into royal hands before it was demised to John Norris by deed, 28 Hen. VIII. 1537, for 21 years, and this was the first alienation since 1155 to a private individual, but it soon reverted to the Crown from this recipient of royal favour. The gentleman died 21st Oct. 1563, without issue, whilst his brother, of the body guard of King Henry VIII. was beheaded in 1537, ancestor of Baron Norris of Rycote, Oxon. (see page 17).

Henry Norris, his brother, had a grant of Langley manor for his life in 1524, and in 5 Edw. VI. the Duke of Somerset gave Parlaunt Park there to Sir Thomas Heneage, of Lincoln. The same grant was renewed, 7 Eliz. 1565, to John Duke of Northumberland. Latterly this manor passed by marriage to Sir John Parsons, who married a Kidderminster, and he sold it to the Seymours.

In 1538 the devoted nunnery of Ankerwycke, then estimated at £40 or £50 per annum, was bestowed on Bisham Abbey, and on the dissolution of that monastery in 1540, the king gave it to Andrew Lord Windsor, and he died in 1543. It was a rich monastery, set at £285. 11s, clear yearly value, equivalent to £2855. 10s of our money. This opulent fraternity was further enriched with the lands of Chertsey and the dissolved priories of Ankerwycke, Little Martin, and Medmenham, changing its establishment to an abbot and 18 monks of the Benedictine order. At the next crash this cherished monastery, among the last surviving, met the usual fate, whose worth was £661. 14s 9d, or some £6707. 6s, and King Edward granted the site of it to his father's repudiated wife, Ann of Cleves, who surrendered it in 1553, when it was bestowed on Sir Philip Hoby, to whose nephew, Sir Edward Hoby, Queen Elizabeth paid a visit in 1592. This Sir Philip Hoby was connected with Wraysbury, and died 1558, having married Elizabeth eventual heir of her brother, John Stonor, children of Sir Walter Stonor, of Place Farm, in our village. They are buried in our church, with memorial brasses, and will be mentioned again in this history.

A deed appears which recapitulates the grant bearing date 4th August, 1540, whereby Andrews Lord Windsor of Burnham, cr. 1529, obtained the house and site of the Priory of Ankerwycke, with certain lands containing 88½ acres, and the tithes for 21 years at the rent of £6. 9s 4d, or £64. 13s 4d, and the lease dated 27th April, 1542, reports that the king had demised to him 18½ acres of lands in Queen's mead, once belonging to the Priory, for 21 years at the rent of £1. 6s 8d, and that in consideration of £1050, or £10,500, paid by Lord Windsor, His Majesty granted to him all the property so leased, together with the church of the Priory, and all lands without and within the precincts or circuit of the Priory, and also all those pools, waters, and fisheries being in the river Thames from the passage called Ankerwycke Ferry to Old Windsor and elsewhere, &c. (which pools Thomas Edwards and William Domley hold), with lands, &c., in Wraysbury, parcel of the Priory property. By the terms of this grant the estate was limited to Andrews Lord Windsor for life, then to Edward and Thomas his sons; then to William Windsor, his heir; then to the other sons in tail male; then to Lord Windsor in fee by the 20th part of a knight's fee, paying yearly £2. 9s. 6d, or £24. 15s.

This property continued with the Lord till his death in 1543, and then to his son William, who died in 1558. Margaret, daughter of William de Windsore, took the veil, and was a nun at

Ankerwycke, temp. Edw. I. Originalia, 31 Hen. VIII. 1540, 4th August, Rex concessit Andreæ Domino Wyndesore reversionem scitus nuper Prioratus de Ankerwycke et terræ in Wyrardysbury, in Com. Bucks. ac manœria de Alderbourne, etc., Greneford park in Stanwell et Parnyshe nuper Prioratu spectand: ac omnia messuagia, etc., in Wyrardysbury, etc., infra parochiam de Egham, etc.

Monasteries and nunneries in this reign were as transferable as they had been permanent; hence Ankerwycke soon found another proprietor and occupant, for it came again to the Crown in an exchange, and an original deed of conveyance on vellum is in the hands of the author of this History, a transcript from the one in the Augmentation Office, whose date is 17th July, 4 Edw. VI. 1550. It states that, in consideration of £414. 10s. 4d. equal to £4141. 13s. 4d. and a conveyance of other property, the King, Edward VI. granted to Sir Thomas Smyth and Elizabeth his wife (daughter of William Karkek of Devonshire, who was probably buried at Wraysbury, as she died 3rd August 1553, which was before the purchase of Hill Hall was effected), and their issues and assigns for ever, the site of the late Priory of Ankerwycke and the manor of Ankerwycke Purnish, which is at the foot of Cooper's Hill, opposite to Great Ankerwycke, with appurtenances in Surrey formerly parcel of the Priory, &c. with certain lands in Werardisbury, Westdrewe, Purnish, and Egham, which Lord Windsor had sold to King Henry VIII. to be holden *in capite* of the fortieth part of a knight's fee, paying a fee-farm rent of £1. 16s. 8d. per annum.

The manor and lands were renewed to Sir Thomas Smyth in 1555, and again in 1571; for in a deed, 13 Elizabeth, he holds the house of Ankerwycke for thirty years, and another renewal took place in 1593 for thirty more years. Besides this, Sir Thomas had an annuity of £200 a year from the Crown. The Priory was converted into a family mansion, and the conventual part was pulled down, and on its foundation was enlarged or erected by Sir Thomas the house in which he and his family resided. Here it was that he received Dr. John Taylor, the deprived Bishop of Lincoln, who was fellow in the same college at Cambridge as Sir Thomas, and had been master there, which office he resigned in 1546, on account of the incessant differences between him and the fellows. He sought an asylum, which was generously conceded, and in 1553 the Bishop died at Ankerwycke: the loss of the parish registers prevent our knowing if he were interred at Wraysbury, which is highly probable. Sir Thomas found this residence pleasant from its natural qualities and its contiguity to Windsor, whither he went for interviews with the King or Queen, whose faithful minister and counsellor he did not cease to be till death put a term to his existence, at Mount Haut, in 1577. This fine house of palatial dimensions at Theydon Mount, in a parish of some 1700 acres, and on its loveliest site is Monthaut or Hill Hall, built on the summit of the elevation, commanding the subjected plain and a view of St. Paul's Cathedral: it was purchased by Sir Thomas, 3 Philip and Mary, 1554-5, of the daughters and coheirs of Sir John Hampden, who had died in 1553.

There is a very copious inventory of all the furniture in Ankerwycke (see Lipscombe, vol. iv.), whereby the size of the mansion may be computed, as appears by a ledger still at Hill Hall, dated 27th September 1569. The initials of himself and wife are on the linen, dated 1542, 48, 49, 52, and the furniture in the bed-chamber assigned to his father John Smyth, who died *circa* 1556, and the contents of his father's chest. One chamber is styled My Lorde's Chamber—Duke of Somerset. The high gallery called Cole's Chamber, the Chamberlayne's ditto, and that known as the Great Guest's Chamber, the Hall and the Great Parlour, and the Chappel, wherein were vestments and an *albe* for a priest, a Bible, and a *payer* of virginalls, used for organs. The Matted Chamber and the Inner ditto, the Wardrobe, and the Lodge.

This interesting inventory of a gentleman's furniture at this period is subscribed, "Ankerwycke and Farms. Tho. Hurst, Bailiff there, 28 Sept. 1562."

There was also a Library of Books—a rare possession; the same as are recapitulated in Strype's "Life of Sir Thomas Smyth," "Books found in my studie the IX Ap. 1576, and the XVIII yere of Queene Elizabethe." They consist of a very varied collection, comprising law, divinity, physic, history, &c. in the learned tongues, with some French and Italian; the number about 400 to 500 volumes. His fondness of books reinforced in him the observation, "that, without them, God is silent, justice dormant, physic at a stand, philosophy lame, letters dumb, and all things involved in darkness."

## BIOGRAPHY OF SIR THOMAS SMYTH.

It may not be irrelevant to give a *précis* of the life of this accomplished scholar, statesman and gentleman, whose name reflects honour and credit on England as well as on this parish, where he loved to dwell, at a distance from the cares of politics and strife, and remote from "fumum et opes strepitum que Romæ."

Sir Thomas Smyth was a native of Saffron Walden in Essex, and Strype who wrote his Life, speaks of him as the best scholar of his time, an admirable philosopher, orator, linguist and moralist. He was born in 1512, but he was not the eldest son of John Smyth of the same place and his wife Agnes Charnock of an old house in Lancashire, whom he married about 1509. They are both mentioned in the will of John Nicholl of Saffron, in 1515.* John Smyth was born in the reign of Edward V. or Richard III.; was sheriff of Essex and Herts in 1531 and 1538; and, when treasurer of Walden, he joined with William Strachey, junior, to erect alms-houses, by deed dated 18th February 1550, to be called "King Edward's Alms-houses." He purchased the Guild of Walden for £531. 14s 11d, and the school was advanced to a royal foundation; and he obtained from Barker, Garter principal king of arms, a coat of arms, 12th March 1545-6.

Thomas was put to the public school at Saffron, and soon betrayed promise of eminence which years matured, and in time, through gratitude, he procured his school to be advanced to a royal foundation, with emoluments from Willingate Spane, in Essex, for its support. At the age of fifteen he was transferred to Queen's College, Cambridge; and the University choosing him Greek Professor, he read lectures, and with Sir John Cheeke he altered the pronunciation of the Greek language, as taught by modern Greeks. In 1538 he became University Orator; and such was his renown, that Gabriel Harvey, a relative, says the name of his college was like to be changed from Queen's to Smyth's College. Dr. Harvey died in 1630, æt. eighty-five, having written a poem, "Smythus Valdinatus (of Walden) sive Musarum lachrymæ pro obitu clarissimi Tho. Smyth Equitis," published in 1578. Smyth now travelled to Paris, and graduated at Padua in Italy, and returning to Cambridge in 1542 he was made D.C.L.; became tutor to Edmund de Vere, twelfth Earl of Oxon, a nobleman appointed in 1586 to sit in judgment on Mary Queen of Scots—a man of a chivalrous spirit and a wit, being held for the first writer of comedy in his day; and, to add to his notoriety, he became a *petit-maître*, of whom it is said he was the first to introduce perfumes and embroidered gloves, a pair of which he presented to Elizabeth, which so delighted the vain queen that she had her portrait painted ostentatiously with her hands enveloped in gloves.

A more important destiny now forced Smyth to advance Protestantism, inclining to truth only as it is set forth in Holy Writ, and not disfigured by tradition and trumpery. He was appointed

* "Item, I bequeath unto John Smyth for to be true to my soul health xls. in money and a black gown of xiiis. iiijd., and to Agness his wife for to buy with a black gown xs. Item I bequeath unto John Nicolls and John Smyth to each of them viiid, for each noble (6s 8d) that they shall gather of my debts after my decease." John Smyth was joint executor with John and George Nicolls, his sons. He also witnessed the will of John Nicolls, the son, as John Smyth, *Senior*, which shews he was not dead on 9th Sept. 1553, so he lived to see his son settled at Hill Hall. His will is not to be found in London or Essex.

King's Professor of civil law and Chancellor to the Bishop of Ely, with the benefice of Leverington, Cambridgeshire, being a *lay* brother: this preferment he resigned in 1549. His next step was an appointment in the family of the Duke of Somerset, which essentially contributed to his promotion, being uncle and governor to King Edward VI. under whose reign Smyth became a courtier. Unluckily, his patron was environed by envious men, and by them he fell more than by his own misdeeds, being executed in 1552-3; but Smyth had been made Master of the Requests by him—an office for advancing the suits of needy men, and for being overseer of justice towards them. To this appointment his next rise was Steward of the Stannaries, and for this he was well adapted, being an excellent metallurgist and chemist, in which attractive science he dabbled to his own pecuniary loss. Smyth had now become a man of recognised worth and learning, and on the 27th December 1547 he was nominated Provost of Eton College, where there is a very handsome portrait of him at the Provost's residence, given by Lady Bowyer Smijth, widow of Sir Edward B. Smijth, Bart. lineal descendant of George, brother of Sir Thomas Smyth. He was Lay Dean of Carlisle, having been only in deacon's orders; and at last he attained the summit of his wishes, being knighted, 1st October 1549, and made Secretary of State. He resided in Chanon Row, Westminster, where the Commissioners met in 1558, to consult for the reformation of religion, and to compile the Book of Common Prayer, chiefly prepared by Smyth.

The day before he became Secretary of State he married, 15th April, 1549; and receiving money with his wife Elizabeth, daughter of William Karkek, (whose Will is in the Prerogative Office, proved 4th April, 1849) he bought of the Commissioners for the Chantry the College of Derby for £33 per annum; and was appointed guardian of her brother Ralph Karkek while at Paris, as the indenture, 20th April, 1551, evinces, allowing £8 in hand and £8 yearly for two years for his maintenance. This Lady died 1553; and as Sir Thomas then resided at Ankerwycke, her body may have found its last resting-place in Wraysbury, for he had not yet purchased his Hill Hall estate, which came through his next wife Philippa, daughter of John Wilford of Kent, and widow of Sir John Hampden, who died in 1553 without issue male. This marriage took place 23rd July, 1554, and she had a life-interest in the property, and the reversion of it was bought by Sir Thomas, 3 Philip and Mary, 1555. One of the daughters and co-heirs of Sir John Hampden was Ann wife of William Paulet, connected with the William Paulet who had the manor of Wraysbury in 1460 (page 15).

Of this wife it was that Secretary Cecil (afterwards Lord Burleigh) spake when in 1565, Smyth having been Ambassador in France, (to which honour he was during life three times accredited), and earnestly desiring him to come home, Cecil wrote him word that his wife should either speak or send to the notorious Earl of Leicester, that he would despatch Mr. Thomas Hoby, whom the Queen had determined to send Ambassador in his room, but delayed it. This gentleman was half-brother of Sir Philip Hoby, who had married Elizabeth, daughter and heir of Sir Walter Stonor, Knt. of Place Farm in this parish (page 17). She was buried here in 1560, as will appear under church affairs.

Troubles environed him, for he had been imprisoned in the Tower with the Duke of Somerset, and State affairs had their discomforts. Nevertheless he was appointed Ambassador to Brussels in 1548, for in the same year we find in the Book of Auditors' declarations of issue, "To George Smyth, for his charges coming and going in post with letters from Mr. Secretary Smyth and the Commissioners with the Regent of Flanders, £10 in 1548." His coadjutor here was Thomas Chamberlayn, his brother-in-law, who had married Ann, sister of his first wife, daughter of William Carkek. One of Smyth's letter to the Duke of Somerset, Lord Protector, is dated from Brussels, 19th July, 1548. About this time he was consulted on the teston (tête) coinage and other monies under consultation to be redressed, and his letter decided the question: and the teston coin was forbidden to be issued, and William Sharrington of the Mint was convicted of fraud and robbery.

He was engaged in religious controversies, taking cognizance of the examination of Bishop Bonner—the scourge of Protestantism—and by the defection of friends he was deprived of his office of Secretary of State in 1549, and with eight more was committed to the Tower on the disgrace of Somerset; and 15th September, 1550, Mr. William Cecil was appointed in the room of Mr. Wotton, who had succeeded Sir Thomas in that office.

Being summoned witness in the great trial of Gardiner Bishop of Winchester, Smyth conducted himself with such Christian moderation, that it was of ultimate benefit to him in the days of Mary's persecutions.

The year 1551 found him Secretary of State again, when he was appointed Ambassador to France, concerning a match for Elizabeth, eldest daughter of Henry II. King of France, who subsequently married Philip II. of Spain. Persecution and bigotry now ruled the land, and he again forfeited all his employments, but was allowed £100 a year to maintain him, and was imperatively charged not to quit the kingdom; so he passed his time at Ankerwycke, and in memory of his escape from the fiery tyranny, when it was overpassed, he changed his crest, or rather added another crest, a Salamander in the centre of flames. He propitiated all parties, while he witnessed the Spanish marriage, in which two remorseless bigots were united in person, as well as for the temporary overthrow of true religion—the loss of Calais, and the realm reduced to almost unparalleled persecution by Mary, fostered by Philip.

On the return of Queen Elizabeth, Sir Thomas was recalled to office and confidence in public and religious matters as the Commission, dated 23rd December, 1558, confirms. The nation wished the Queen to marry, hence Smyth wrote a pamphlet with eloquence and wit in a dialogue between one who desired a marriage and one who did not, while a third person suggested and patronised a marriage with a Briton only. This was followed by a work on the Commonwealth in 1565; Strype says it was not published till 1621, but there has been found an earlier edition in 1581; it was and is a work much appreciated.

It was in the hopes of some that Calais, surrendered in the last reign, might be recovered, and it weighed greatly on the heart of many, remembering that we took it from the French in 1347, and lost it in Mary's reign in 1558. So Smyth was sent with Sir Henry Norris (page 17) in 1566, to demand the restitution of Calais; but luckily it was unavailing, or we had never been at ease with France.

His next desire was to obtain the Chancellorship of the Duchy of Lancaster, but here an adroit politician and warrior, Sir Ralph Sadleir, superseded him, and Smyth was constrained "to spend the four next years among *turfs*, wishing the Queen no worse counsellor than he." But on Cecil's elevation to the Barony of Burleigh in 1571, Sir Thomas was readmitted to the Council; and in 1572 again went Ambassador to France, to treat *inter alia* of the marriage with the Duke D'Alençon, which match going off the Queen indemnified Smyth with the Chancellorship of the Order of the Garter, 21st April, 1572. St. George was chosen a great tutelary saint by the Normans, and under his name King Edward III. instituted the order, and the title of Chancellor was adopted by the Church, and became half an ecclesiastical and half a lay office.

This year he was readmitted Secretary of State, an office entrusted to him twenty-four years before; the chief impediment to the D'Alençon match was the almost-unparalleled and inhuman massacre of St. Bartholomew, 24th August, 1572, on the anniversary of which day even Voltaire was wont always to put on mourning.

During his sojourn at Ankerwycke, which he quitted because he was obnoxious to rheums and colds, as being low and waterish, he frequently passed to Windsor, there to transact important business relative to England and Scotland; and he also procured a colony to be sent to Ireland by patent, 11th November, 1571, to subdue this country for the establishment of the colony in the Ardes, of which Sir Thomas was to be Lieutenant-General: and had the scheme succeeded, his wealth and territorial accession had been enormous, and perhaps at last he would have covered his head with a coronet. He was armed by Government with great powers, but casualties befell him, and he lost this territory assigned to him by a royal patent, which his heirs tried to retrieve; which loss was occasioned by the usurpation of James, son of Rev. Hans Hamilton, a branch of the ducal house of that name. The last attempt to recover it in 1660 failed, on its being alleged that the covenants were broken, and that King James I. became again seized of the territory *in jure coronæ*, and the Hamiltons, Viscounts of Clanboye, subdivided it.

We now bring to a close this narrative of the life of so worthy a man, and a long resident in Wraysbury. When Ambassador in France in 1564 he had experienced a most searching illness, which shattered his constitution, and nearly terminated his being, but on a sudden it abated; yet was he not framed in the prodigality of nature to be able to rejoice in the madness of superfluous health. Latterly he became a valetudinarian, which carking care and losses, to which all exalted or low are subject, superinduced. The *diagnoses* of disorders were not then known, or the appliances to arrest and modify them understood as in our more experienced times, when the material and physical phenomena are studied in their true relations—for we essay to do by implements and effect what used to be done by the eye or by induction—with a stethoscope, and instruments of incalculable virtue to trace progress or mark the source of error.

The subject of this biographical sketch resigned himself, knowing that the sequel is the will of the Author of life; and to yield up his days he retired or confined himself to Hill Hall, where he trusted to leave his sickness or his life. He now drifted into a consumption, or kind of atrophy, or marasmus, and on the 12th August, 1577, he expired in his sixty-sixth year, and was buried with considerable pomp, and he lies under a most noble monument in Theydon Mount Church, on the north-side of the chancel. He is represented in an effigy by a statue of marble lying on his right-side in armour, a loose robe about him, with the arms of the Knighthood of the Garter upon the left arm of the robe, denoting him to have been Chancellor of the order. Over him on the highest part of the monument is his coat-armour, with some Latin lines around it, and under the coat his motto—*Quâ pote lucet;* also some lines about physical science, his desire to know the divine mysteries, the secrets of Providence, the frame of this world, the motions of the heavens, and properties of planets, with all created entities. He left behind him his wife Philippa, who followed him to the secret house of death, 20th June, 1578.

Sir Thomas was of a fair sandy complexion, a forked beard, the fashion of the age; and his picture represents him with a round cap on his head, and in a doctor's gown (D.C.L.); a great ruby on his forefinger set in a signet-ring, his left hand resting on a large globe of his own construction.

His will was proved 15th August, 1577, by his next brother George Smyth, who died intestate 1584 at Ankerwycke; and by it he gave his library of some thousand volumes chiefly to Queen's College, Cambridge; and also to the college he gave £12. 7s 4d, rent charge, from his Overston estate in Northton (page 13), £4 for a lecture in Mathematics, and £4 for one in Geometry, and £4. 7s 4d for two Scholarships, preferring his own kindred, and 20s to a yearly commemoration.

In addition to his political life, for he died as principal Secretary of State to Queen Elizabeth, his correspondence was voluminous, and maintained with the *élite* of the age. He died honoured and lamented, having lived long enough for nature and for glory, while the works he has left behind are an illustrious monument to the memory of an active and useful existence.

## PEDIGREE OF SMIJTH OF ANKERWYCKE AND HILL HALL, ESSEX.

SMIJTH Arms: S. a fesse dancetté A. billettée, between three lioncels ramp. guar. of the second, an altar O. flaming ppr.

JOHN SMITH, probably the one cited in the Churchwardens' Account at Saffron Walden, 1417.

WILLIAM KARKEK, will proved 1549, grant of arms 1530.

JOHN SMITH, born about 1480, high sheriff of Essex 1531 and 1536, witnesses will of John Nicholls 1555, ob. abt. 1556-7. = AGNES, daughter of — Charnock, mar. about 1508, living 1515.

RALPH KARKEK, of Devon.

CHRISTIAN, ux. John, son of Sir Wm. Brown, Lord Mayor of London, 1513.

ANN, married Sir Thomas Chamberlayn.

ELIZABETH, m.15 Ap.1549, d.3 Aug.1553, buried at Wraysbury.

SIR THOMAS SMYTH, born 28 March 1512, knighted 1 Oct. 1549, grant of Ankerwycke 1550, of Hill Hall, Essex, ob. 12 August 1577.

= PHILIPPA, d. of John Wilford, of Kent, m. 23 July 1554, ob. June 1578.

= SIR JOHN HAMPDEN, Kt. of Co. Bucks, and Hill Hall, Essex, ob. 1553.

JOHN SMITH, b. 1510, will prov. 16 Feb. 1558. = ELIZABETH, dau. of —

GEORGE SMYTH, of Ankerwycke, buried at Wraysbury, admin. to effects by wife Isabella 9 Mar. 1584. = ISABELLA, dau. of —, d. 1584, administration by sons James and Edward Smyth.

ALICE, m. John Nicholls of Saffron Walden, buried 26 Feb. 1570.

JOAN, m. A. Wood, of Kent. He d.1557. She d.1585, rem. Th. Petit, of Greenstead.

WILLIAM SMYTH, ob.23 Jan. 1577, sp. = JANE CAWODE, mar. 25 Oct.1574.

JOHN = DAU.

ANN = WILLIAM SCOTT.

LAURENCE SCOTT held lands in Northton, which reverted to Sir William Smyth in 1631.

EDWARD CONWAY, Lord Conway, ob. 1631. = BRIDGET, dau. of Thos. Fleetwood, of the Vache, Bucks, ob. 1633. = SIR WILLIAM SMYTH, of Ankerwycke, knighted 1603, ob. 12 Dec. 1626, æt. 76.

HELEGONWAY, mar. settl. 9 April 1627, ob. 1630. = SIR WILLIAM SMYTH, of Ankerwycke, ob. March 1631-2. = ANN, dau. of Edward Croft, m.1631, ob.1675, remar. Sir Wm. Salter.

JOHANNA, dau. of Sir Edw. Altham, of Essex, m. 1632, ob. 1658. = SIR THOS. SMITH, b. 1602, of Ankerwycke, sold it 1652, and Place Farm 1651, cr. Bt. 1661, d. 5 May 1668.

EDWARD SMYTH, buried 24 Jan. 1651-2, sp.

SIR EDWARD SMIJTH, ob. 1713, æt. 77. = JANE, dau. of Peter Vandeput, ob. 1720.

SIR EDWARD SMIJTH, of ditto, ob. Aug. 1744. = ANN, dau. of Sir Charles Hedges, Judge of the Court of Admiralty, ob. 18 Oct. 1719.

SIR EDWARD SMIJTH, of ditto, ob. 1760, æt. 50, sp. = ELIZABETH, dau. of Thomas Johnson, of Mylton Bryant, Beds, ob. 1770.

SIR CHAS. SMIJTH, h. sheriff of Essex 1761, ob. 1773, æt. 61, sp.

SIR WILLIAM SMIJTH, of ditto, Rector of Theydon, ob. 1777, æt. 57. = ABIGAIL, dau. of Andrew Wood of Salop, ob. 1787, æt. 71.

SIR WILLIAM SMIJTH, of ditto, Colonel West Essex Militia, ob. 1 May 1823, æt. 78. = ANN, dau. and heir of John Wyndham, of Norfolk, m. 22 March 1779, ob. 20 Dec. 1815. Page 7.

SIR EDWARD BOWYER SMIJTH, 10th Bart. assumed name of Bowyer 10 June 1839, ob. 15 Aug. 1850, æt. 65. = LETITIA CECILY, dau. of John Weyland, of Wood Eaton, Oxon, and Woodrising, Norfolk, m. 23 May 1813.

JOSEPH SMIJTH, assumed name of Wyndham in 1823, ob. 3 Feb. 1857, æt. 64. = CATHERINE, dau. of John Trotter, m. 10 Aug. 1824.

CAROLINE, m. 29 May 1817, Augustus James Champion de Crespigny = SIR CLAUDE DE CRESPIGNY, Bart.

SIR WM. B. SMIJTH, Bart. of ditto, M.P. for So. Essex 1852. = MARIANNE FRANCES, d. of Sir Hen. Meux, Bt. m. 2 April 1839.

ALFRED JOHN B. SMIJTH, Rector of Attleboro', Norfolk. = MARY CONSTANTIA ROLT, d. of Gen. Sir John Rolt, K.C.B. m. 17 June 1847.

CICELY ABIGAIL, m. Henry Bullock, of Essex, d. 1859; 2ndly, 1861, EdgarBury

ANN ELIZABETH, m. 1839 Gordon Gyll, of Wraysbury. See page 7.

ADELA MONKTON, m. 1843 Major Jodrell. See page 23.

MARIANNE WEYLAND, m. 1847 Colonel Ruggles Brise of Spains Hall, Essex. See page 21.

WM. B. SMIJTH, born 1840.

EDWARD DE GREY SMIJTH, b. 1846.

CECILY.

ALFRED JOHN SMIJTH, b. 1850.

CLEMENT WEYLAND, b. 1851.

EDMUND CASWELL, b. 1853.

Three Daus.

G

As the elder brother of Sir Thomas Smyth, viz. John Smyth, had predeceased him in 1558, and left a son William who would have been the heir to his father and his uncle, but who died also in 1576 without issue male, the youngest brother of Sir Thomas, viz. George Smyth, succeeded him in Ankerwycke, and he disposed of all estates to this brother, a recapitulation of which is made in the Inq. p. m. of Sir Thomas, taken 26th November, 1578, in which the Wraysbury property is detailed. It is probable that George remained at Hill Hall until the return of his son William from Ireland in 1580, being a Colonel in the Army; afterwards he gave that inheritance to his son, and withdrew to Ankerwycke, where he died, as appears by his administration granted 9th March, 1584, while another was granted 31st March following to the effects of his widow Isabella; and as they were not interred in the family-vault at Theydon, it is to be inferred they were also buried at Wraysbury, where they resided and expired.

It is certain that the next resident here was Sir William Smyth, Knt., born in 1550. He was early in life an officer in the army, and followed the wars in Ireland till he was thirty years old, and went to Spain. Knighted 7th May 1603, and Member of Parliament for Aylesbury 1603; he was of great figure and service in the county.

There are many deeds extant shewing his right to buy and sell, and the interest he took here. He died 12th December, 1626, leaving by Bridget his wife, a daughter of Thomas Fleetwood of the Vache, Bucks, several children. According to Cole's escheat (but it seems a mistake) she remarried with Edward Viscount Conway, Secretary of State in 1626, and dying in 1633, was buried at Theydon with her first husband under a most sumptuous monument of marble. Her family is of considerable antiquity in this county, the name of her paternal estates styled *Vache*, from a French family of that appellation, *temp.* Edward I., which a female brought to the Greys, and hence it devolved on the Fleetwoods, one of whose descendants intermarried with Thomas Milton, son of Christopher, the brother of John Milton the Poet, who resided at Chalfont, St. Giles. See under Horton. A member of this family, Elizabeth Fleetwood of Amersham, married at Wraysbury 5th November 1746, John Jervis White, Esq., of St. James's, Westminster.

The next occupant in Ankerwycke Priory was Sir William Smyth, son and heir of the last of both names. He was knighted, being Sheriff of Bucks, 1631, and was an officer in the army. His career was short, and his marriage-settlement, dated 9 April, 1627, shews us that he espoused Helegonway daughter of the same Lord Conway by his first wife, to whom his mother was united *en secondes noces*. This Lady died in childbed in 1630; and the following year he remarried Ann daughter of Edward Croft, Esq., one of the Ladies of the Chamber to Helegonway, his former spouse. This marriage was the speedy precursor of his death, for that followed at the age of thirty-two in 1632, leaving by his will, dated 5th May 1631, the property and mansion of Ankerwycke to his widow Dame Anne for four years, in which estate she was also jointured. She did not carry her weeds long, for we find her wedding Sir William Salter of Iver, and they both resided at Ankerwycke immediately, as the parish registers shew the baptisms of two of their children in 1633 and 1634.

Sir William Smijth paid to the collection, raised in the Privy Seal in Bucks, £120; and left a son William who lived to manhood, and served as a Volunteer under Prince Rupert, during whose minority the great Ardes estate in Belfast, Ireland, was utterly lost to the family (p. 40). He died in 1651, unmarried, so the estates here and in Essex devolved on his uncle Thomas, who was raised to a Baronetcy, 28th November, 1661. He it was who disposed of Place Farm in 1652, and the Priory being in lease to the Salters caused a severance of the Bucks from the Essex possessions. Nothing remarkable occurred at the Priory, but an entry in the Parish Registers of St. Andrew's, Holborn.*

---

* Says that Ann a child and daughter of John Harris, serving-man of Ankerwycke, and of Elizabeth his wife, was hurried along London streets from parish to parish to the upper end of Holborn, being crushed by the crowd, and was buried out of widow Roberts' house in Holborn, 19 March, 1633.

## HISTORY OF WRAYSBURY.

We now come to new inmates of the Priory, for a lease of it was granted to the Salters, in addition to the bequest which left four years of it to Dame Ann, now wife of Sir William Salter, Kt. How long exactly he continued to rent it is not known, but he retired again to Iver, and was there buried in 1643, while his widow, Ann, did not yield up her existence for more than thirty years after, and found a last resting place in the Salter vault at Iver, 29th February, 1675-6. His first wife, Mary, was daughter of Thomas Sherland, of Suffolk, and her effigy is in Iver Church, rising in her shroud from her coffin, a work of art much admired.

The family of Salter was of some significance in this county, and their chief possessions lay in and around Iver; they bought property also at Horton and Wraysbury. They descend from William Salter of Richings Park, whose death there in 1606 caused his son, Sir Edward Salter, knighted 1621, to succeed. He had been Carver in Ordinary to King James I. in 1608, and also to King Charles I., and dying in 1646 a very old man—near a century—he transmitted to his son William, (who married the widow of Sir William Smijth) the court office of Carver also—one of some antiquity in foreign realms, for in Germany the Count Palatine was Imperial Carver or Server, or Lord High Steward, and bore the globe of empire at the coronation, and placed the first dish on the table. All very great magnates had a carver in their palaces and mansions. With princes this office was exercised on stated days, when they took their repast in public—and there is a curious picture in Hampton Court of the King and Queen of Bohemia dining in public, and a monkey leaping on the *Gentleman Carver*, scratches his head, while the obedient functionary complacently continues his *cutting* operations.

Several of the Salters rented the Priory, and one Nicholas resided here in 1684, says Browne Willis. He was Sheriff of the county 1687, and Christopher Salter of Stoke Poges, in 1810, was also High Sheriff of Bucks. See more of Salter under Colnbrook.

### PEDIGREE OF SALTER.

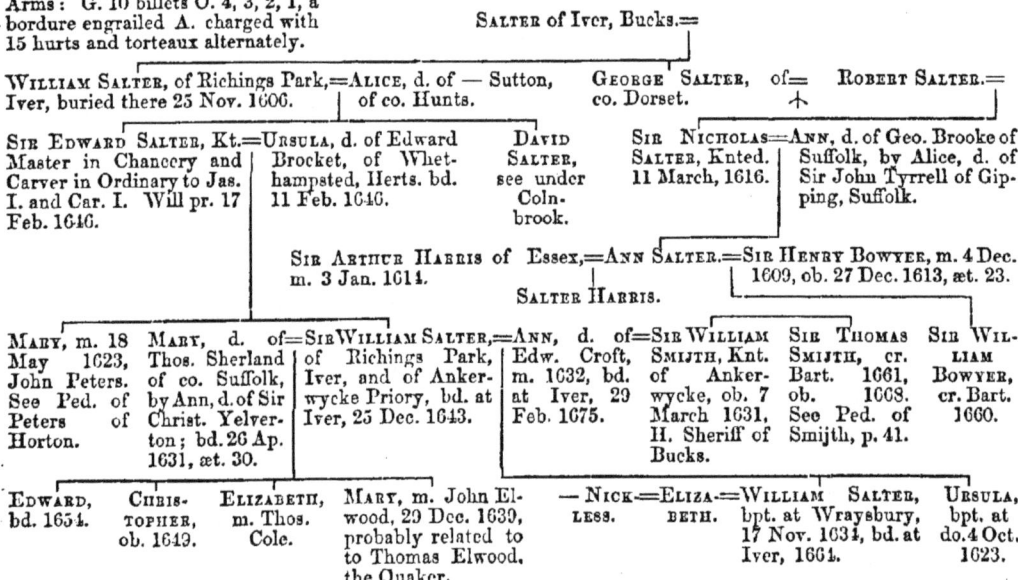

Under the descent of the manor I have shewn how the family of King came to Wraysbury, and it is not improbable that Andrew King, who died Lord of the Manor, lived here till 1659; he was followed by his son, Sir Andrew King, who married Mary, widow of John Sharowe, who died lord of the manor in 1634. On the death of this knight in 1679, it is likely that Nicholas Salter rented the Priory, as he was tenant of it in the year 1684, and he was followed by John Lee, Esq., who added the property in 1685 to what had been previously bought in 1652, by indenture 17th July, of Thomas Smyth, Esq., who may have been forced to dispose of his outlying estates in Wraysbury (for he dwelt latterly at Hill Hall) to liquidate a charge of £8000 levied on him as a *malignant* in the sharp times of the republic.

In the Court Roll there is an entry or presentment, 15 April, 1653, viz., The homage, who upon their oath say and on the oaths of Richard Terry, Thomas Harrison and Stephen Day, that the lands which belonged to Ankerwycke Priory are as mentioned, &c., stating that the river of Thames and fishery which belongeth to Ankerwycke, which is a little above Mr. Smith's house of Old Windsor on the north side, and on the west side beginning at an elm in Padnett, and so leading down the river to the lower end of Caphill—which presentment was made on the occasion of the purchase by Mr. Lee of Thomas Smijth, Esq., of Hill Hall.

From this time the Priory was in the hands of the Lees, and so continued till the death of Mary, widow of John Lee the younger, in 1725. The manor of Ankerwycke having been added to that of Purnishe, and both enjoyed by one proprietor. There is a confirmation of the purchase by John Lee from the executors of Sir Andrew King, Kt. in deeds dated severally 1671, 1685, and 1687. The elder Mr. Lee enjoyed the Priory but three years, as he died in 1682, but his son John had tenure of it till 1704, and this in his will, with a codicil, 26th August, 1704, he leaves to Mary his wife, daughter of Richard Morse of London, and she was lady of the manor and of the Priory till her decease in 1725; leaving no issue this mansion passed with certain estates to Mary, sister of John Lee, junior, in 1674, the wife of Sir Philip Harcourt, the direct ancestor of the Earls of Harcourt, through Simon Harcourt, a most eminent jurisconsult who became Lord Chancellor in 1710, and whose patent of nobility dates 3rd September, 1711. In 1721 he was elevated to a Viscounty, and he died in 1727, one of the most eloquent and accomplished lawyers and politicians of his epoch. It was to his only son Simon that Pope in 1720 wrote his short yet feeling epitaph of eight lines, to be seen on his monument at Stanton Harcourt, Oxon. The Chancellor had no monument erected to him at Stanton Harcourt, for he had so lived as not to stand in *need* of such memorials, and he who would familiarize himself with this noble occupant of the woolsack, must peruse his life, written in 70 glowing pages by the late Lord Chancellor Campbell. His grandson of the same baptismal name succeeded, and was further exalted to the dignity of Earl in 1749: he was accidentally killed in 1777 by falling into a well. The last Earl Harcourt died in 1830, and with him the honours became extinct, while the Vernon family, with which there was an intermarriage have assumed the patronymic of Harcourt in addition to their own. George Simon Harcourt, Esq., of Ankerwycke, is the sole remaining male heir of his name and family in England, whose genealogy can be traced for 100 decades of years, possessing landed estates in most English counties, and everywhere holding appointments of trust and honour. There are few more historic names than in this knightly and lordly house—one of the oldest brasses extant is to memorialize Sir Richard Harcourt, 1293. Michael Harcourt was M.P. for Bucks in 1593, and died 1597, leaving Winifred, a daughter, married 12th October 1565 to Sir Anthony Greneway of Dinton, Bucks; and in the year 1834, George Simon Harcourt was High Sheriff of the county, and subsequently M.P. for Bucks in 1837, as colleague with the Marquis of Chandos, since Duke of Buckingham. The diverging branches of Harcourt are not given, as they are fully detailed in Lipscomb's Bucks, from Bernard the Dane who assisted Rollo in the conquest of Normandy, the antecessor of a puissant race of statesmen and heroes.

## PEDIGREE OF HARCOURT OF ANKERWYCKE.

Arms: G. two bars O.

Sir Simon Harcourt, of Stanton (18th in descent from Bernard the Dane, 896), ob. 1547.=

Sir John Harcourt, ob. 1566.=

Simon Harcourt, ob. 1577. — Michael, M.P.1593, ob. 1597. — Edward=Dau. of Thos. Windsor, of Bucks. — Thos. Essex of Lamborn, Berks.=m.1594, ob. 1627. — Alice=Sir George Gyll, of Wydial, Herts, ob. 1619.

Sir Walter, ob. 1639.=

Robert=Frances, dau. of Jeffrey de Vere, son of John, 5th Earl of Oxford. — Jane=Sir William Essex, taken prisoner at Edge Hill, 1642, and died soon after.

Sir Simon, knighted 1627, Governor of Dublin Castle, slain 1643.=Ann, dau. of William, Lord Paget of Beaudesert. — Sir Wm. Waller, of Osterly Park. — Vere Harcourt, ob. 1683.=

Ann, dau. of Sir Wm. Waller, m. 1660, ob. 1661.=Sir Philip Harcourt, d. 1683. — Elizabeth, da. of John Lee of Ankerwycke, m. 1674, ob. 1713. Page 23. — 1. Elizabeth, dau. of Sir Richard Anderson.=Simon Harcourt, of Pendley, Herts, ob. 1724. =2. Elizabeth, da. and heir of Geo. Morse, of the co. Gloucester, d. 1708. P. 23. =3. Mary, dau. of Sir Philip Harcourt, relict of Thos. Ringer.

Sir Simon Harcourt, Lord Chancellor 1710, Viset. Harcourt 1721, ob. 1727.=Rebecca, dau. of Rev. Thos. Clarke, ob. 1687. =2nd wife, Elizabeth, dau. of — Phillips, m. 9 July 1696. — Philip, ob. 1709.=Elizabeth, da. & heir of Timothy Woodroff, ob. 1728. — Mary, widow of Thos. Ringer.=Simon Harcourt, ob. 1724. — Ann, mar. Thos. Powell — Elizabeth, ob. 1715.=Richard, ob. 1728. — Henry, ob. 1743.=

Richard= m. 1756.

Henry, only son. — Elizabeth Sophia, d. 1846.=Charles Amadis d'Harcourt, Colonel in the French army, d. 1831.

William Bernard Harcourt, d. 1847=

Simon Harcourt, ob. 1720.=Elizabeth, d. of John Evelyn, of Surrey, ob. 1760. — Philip Harcourt, of Ankerwycke, ob. 1759. sp.=Sarah, dau. of Henry Hall, of Essex, settlements 1728. — Lee Harcourt, ob. 1726 sp. — John Harcourt, of Ankerwycke, ob. 1785.=Margaret Irene, dau. of John Sarney, m. 7th Aug. 1771, ob. 22nd Feb. 1811. — Molyneux, Lord Shuldham, Adml. of the Blue, ob. 1798.=JohnMead, Earl of Clanwilliam, m. July 1805, ob. 3 Sept. 1805.

Simon, created Earl of Harcourt, 1749, ob. 1777.=Rebecca, dau. of Ch. le Bass, m. 1733, ob. 1765.

George Simon Harcourt, 2nd Earl of Harcourt, ob. 1809 sp. — William Harcourt, Earl of Harcourt, ob. 1830 sp. — John Simon Harcourt, of ditto, born 14th Dec. 1772, ob. 21st Feb. 1810.=Elizabeth Dale, dau. of Major Henniker, niece of John, Lord Henniker, m. 7th Dec. 1800, ob. 10 May 1811. — George Wm. Richard Harcourt, Maj.-Gen. Governor of St. Croix, ob. 12th Dec. 1812 sp.

Jessy, 2nd dau. of John Rolls, of the Henre, Monmouthshire, m. 24th June 1833, ob. 1842.=George Simon Harcourt, High Sheriff of Bucks 1834, M.P. for ditto, born 25th Feb. 1807.=Gertrude Charlotte, only child of Geo. Lucas, of Newport Pagnell, Bucks, m. 16th June 1846.

John Simon Chandos, b. 28th Sept. 1835. — Three sons, died young. — Anne Philippa, m. 17th Oct. 1860 — Mansfield, son of Thos. Mansfield, of Donegal, Ireland. — Mary, ob. 1848. — Gertrude Danby. — Otto Simon Henry, born 1849. — Grace Isabel Rolle. — Cyril Baldwin, b. 1851. — Albert Alexander, b. 1852.

William Fleming, b. 1853. — Agnes Matilda. — Longueville Bridges Harry, b. 1857. — Eliz. Alice

## ANKERWYCKE HOUSE.

It is much to be regretted that we have no drawings of the old Priory, although we know the exact position and spot on which the Priory stood. It is said to be a *small* nunnery in old deeds, but in the lapse of time as the solitary and melancholy system of life prevailed, more claimants for protection arose or devotees to asceticism solicited asylum in these houses, to destroy the blossom of life in superstition, one day of virtuous activity being worth years of such futile retirement.

The area of the building doubtless increased which contained the "Poor Nuns of Ankerwycke," and which covered a space from the existing ruins to the banks of the Thames. There are remnants left of the old House called the Old Hall, nearly smothered in brambles, yet with wild roses and such flowers, as give charm and fragrance to the revered relics. What is left is of stone, and two arches still exist through which the park may be seen. One arch is covered, and the other a pointed arch but smaller is open. Above them are two square windows, and adjacent to the lancet arch (early English), with a sort of stone hood overhanging, are other square windows, looking parkward, in dilapidation. Another moiety of the ruins, overshadowed with large trees facing the Thames, is a great object of interest to all travellers and archæologists. One square window is very perfect with oval arches and a pointed archdoor, with some other windows, left as skeletons to denote what the architecture was, as in comparative anatomy, a tooth or bone leads the inquirer to discriminate and detect the symmetry and nature of the extinct animal. It had doubtless all the accommodation of a noble building with its "jutty, frieze, buttress, and *coigne*" (ancona or elbow) of vantage.

No doubt all was upreared on the *debris* of the Priory, but about what period the building was taken down and on which little Ankerwycke arose is not known. The latter is mentioned in the rate-book of 1734, and we have a *facsimile* of the house as it was in 1803, the precursor of that now occupying the ground, but not the same spot.

It is said that the then building being in a dilapidated state and requiring extensive repairs, it was determined by the proprietor, Mr. Blagrove, to remove it, and substitute the one now known as Ankerwycke House, a commodious rather than an elegant mansion, standing on low ground near the course of the Thames, and a small branch of the Colne, an affluent to the main-stream.

Little Ankerwicke, styled New House in the Rate-Books, was built about 1730, and has been tenanted by very many persons to whom it has been leased by the Harcourts.

Mr. Cornelius Townsend, connected with the Marquis of that name,* lived here in 1749, and he was succeeded by Mr. George Barne in 1765, son of John Barne, citizen of London, and an Italian merchant, who died 1683. But the longest tenant was Gilbert Jodrell, Esq., son of Paul Jodrell of Lewknor, Oxon., whose daughter Sarah married in Wraysbury, 1763, Robert Child, Esq. Mr. Jodrell held property in the county, in Hambledon parish, in 1745, with John Vernon, Esq. The rate-book assesses him in 1750, and so till his death in 1772, when his widow Ann, daughter of Samuel Vanderplanck, whom he married in 1747, resided here till 1774. Her successor was Sir Edwin Wynn, Bart. 1774, followed by Thomas Bates Rous, Esq., M. P. for Worcester, who died 1800, sp. Admiral Molyneux, Lord Shuldham, dwelt at Ankerwycke, and died in 1798, second son of Rev. Samuel Shuldham. His Lordship had married Margaret Irene, widow of John Harcourt of this place, who died 1785. The Lady died 1811, having been widow of Earl Clanwilliam—her third husband, who died two months after marriage in 1803.

The next occupant was a gentleman of notoriety in his day, though he did not tower much above the ordinary level, Mr. John Crickett, Proctor and Marshal of the High Court of Admiralty,

---

* Admiral Isaac Townshend of Thorpe ob. 1765, and his son Charles J. ob. 1764.

one well recollected in the annals of conviviality, who kept the house warm for many years. He was Master of the Stationers' Company, and died 30th August, 1811, ætat seventy-six, probably son of or related to Charles Alexander Crickett, Member of Parliament for Ipswich, a proctor and banker in Essex, who died 1803.

The successor here was a Lady King of the Kingsborough family for a brief period, as Mr. Blagrove resided here in 1803 previous to his pulling down the house which, with the priory, he bought by public auction in 1804. The present residence has since undergone few alterations exteriorly, but every comfort which taste and means can combine have been found in a building, honourably tenanted by Mr. G. S. Harcourt, and now by Mr. Cottrill Scholefield, whose father and brother for many Parliaments have represented Birmingham. After the death of Mr. Blagrove in 1824, who caused the new mansion to be built in which he lived twenty years, this house was inhabited by his son-in-law, Hugh Parkin, Esq., for four years, exercising all the rites of hospitality. In 1829 the purchaser, George Simon Harcourt, Esq., came to reside. Several intermediate tenants have rented it—Elizabeth, Countess of Norbury, widow of Hector John second Earl of Norbury, and only child of William Brabazon, Esq.; Lord Charles Beauclerk, fourth son of William, eighth Duke of St. Albans; Captain William Brooke, R.N.; and in 1850 Felix Pryor, Esq., who left it in 1854.*

The mansion though not extensive is large enough for a considerable family. The roof is on an incline and not flat. It is an oblong building coated with white cement, of two stories high, having ten windows in the upper or chamber-floor, and it is entered by a portico of four doric columns which conducts into the Grand Hall, a spacious room, containing a billiard-table, and adorned with pikes and various kinds of large and small armoury. There are dining and drawing-rooms, two galleries, a library having the Harcourt arms and quarterings splendidly emblazoned over the mantel-piece of oak, with iron-steps from the window to the lawn, boudoir and saloon. The staircase of stone is very handsome, light, and spacious, conducting to twelve bed-rooms with dressing-rooms, school and bath rooms; and there is above a long gallery, enlivened by portraits, called the corridor or picture-gallery. The back part of the mansion faces the Thames, some streamlets of which, or tributaries from the Colne, ascend to the house, around which are handsome net wire-fences imparting a picturesque appearance. The offices are most convenient, with a brew-house and a laundry, and all apartments for social and domestic use, a servants' hall, dairy and larder, &c. The stables are capacious containing space for many carriages, with stables, boxes, &c.; and annexed, at a convenient distance, is a farm-house with a machine-house.

The mansion is now and has been since 1855 in the occupation of Mr. Cottrill Scholefield, and he is an excellent tenant and a worthy successor to the former indwellers of the ancient priory, dispensing hospitality to friends and comfort to the needy.

## PARK AND GARDENS OF ANKERWYCKE.

The pleasure grounds are filled with flowers, fragrant and of every hue; and to these are added a kitchen-garden and a flower-garden between lofty walls, surcharged with every fruit which grows in our climate; there are extensive hot-houses and green-houses containing exotic and native plants, with all that is necessary and superfluous.

"The well-tilled earth proclaims the fertile mould,
The reddening apple ripens here to gold."

The original designation of park is *parcus* or parcellus honoris vel manerii—the parish, as pertaining to an honor or manor. Parks are almost indispensable to a stately mansion.

* On the 14th May, 1855, the proprietor caused an auction to be set up here, by which all the goods and furniture in the house and grounds were sold, realising some £3000.

The acreage of this entire park is some eighty acres, and a good soil, the general character of which is gravel and black loam: all this with piscatory appliances for the Thames, a convenient fishing-box, gardener's cottage, &c., contribute to make this locality the *sejour* of happiness and health.

Before the entrance door of the mansion and near a large tree is a colossal stone-figure of Hercules strangling Antæus on a plot of ground arrayed with flowers. The spot is salubrious, although adjacent to the stream from which there are large basins of water diverging and traversing the grounds and woods. The canals are virtually outlets against any unusual superflux of water to which the river is periodically subject. Yet this does not disturb the sanitary state of the site, no miasma arising from pools often productive of intermittent fever or ague, the type of disease, operating according to the idiosyncrasy of constitution and realising the curse of Caliban,

"All the infections that the Sun sucks up from bogs, fens, flats, and pools."

The park is judiciously interspersed with lofty trees of various kinds, and clumps charmingly disposed with every attention to its natural beauties, consisting of the softer cast of landscape. If the bolder crag and deep dell be wanting, these are compensated by the richly enamelled meadow and highly cultivated plain on the banks of the Thames, while Windsor Castle bursts in all its majesty, "distance lending enchantment to the view."

There were some remarkable plane trees, of which the only remaining one is at 4 feet from the ground, 11 feet in girth, and covers with its spreading branches a diameter of 30 feet, its height being 80 feet,—and is computed to contain at least six loads of clear timber.

There also remained a few years ago three willows of the red and white or Huntingdon kind, the trunk of one measured 20 feet in circumference, a splendid ruin of its former grandeur.

Under a wide-spreading yew tradition reports that King Henry VIII. made an appointment with Anne Boleyn, whom he privately married at Dartford Priory, 25th January 1533, which reputed circumstance inspired the muse of William Thomas Fitzgerald, Esq., who in 1807 wrote these commemorative lines—

> "What scenes have passed since first this ancient yew,
> In all the strength of youthful beauty grew.
> Here patriot Barons might have musing stood,
> And planned the Charter for their country's good—
> And here perhaps from Runnimede retired,
> The haughty John with secret vengeance fired
> Might curse the day which saw his weakness yield,
> Extorted rights in yonder tented field.
> Here too the tyrant Harry felt love's flame,
> And sighing breathed his Anna Boleyn's name,
> Beneath the shelter of this yew-tree's shade
> The royal lover wooed the ill-starred maid.
> And yet that neck round which he fondly hung
> To hear the thrilling accents of her tongue,
> That lovely breast on which his head reclined,
> Formed to have humanised his savage mind,
> Were doomed to bleed beneath the tyrant's steel,
> Whose selfish heart might doat, but could not feel.
> O had the yew its direst venom shed
> Upon the cruel Harry's guilty head,
> Ere England's sons with shuddering grief had seen
> A slaughtered victim in their beauteous Queen."

After a union of only three years, on the 19th May 1536, beauty and innocence were immolated. The first instance of a judicial queen-murder in England, and on the next day, 20th May, King Henry married Jane Seymour, that Queen who was dowered in Wraysbury (p. 18), dying in childbed of Edward VI. in 1537.

If an educated king murdered his queen, was it surprising that a violent uneducated rabble should sacrifice the Queen of France in the fever of revolution—when "France got drunk with blood to vomit crime," fatal to the cause of freedom in every age and clime?

This remarkable yew is one of the noblest ornaments of the park, by admeasurement at four feet from the ground it is 29 feet in girth, while the diameter of the out-spread branches in 78 feet. It is perfectly healthy, boughs and foliage vigorous, although it may have the weight of some ten centuries on its head, probably coeval with King Egbert.

Yew trees are of long adoption in most countries and churchyards, to defend the edifice from winds, and to furnish bows by a statute, 35 Edw. I. 1307; but as the tree is rather knotty and liable to snap, our old bow-staves were procured from the continent, and a good foreign bow was worth 6s 8d—or about £4, while a bow of English wood was only valued at 2s—or about £1. 4s.

These grounds boast also of a cedar-tree which, like the yew, is amongst the most hardy and long-lived of evergreens. Since the discovery of the Californian woods these trees have been found of incredible bulk, altitude, and age in a region where nature displays an ever-new magnificence.

The author of this history, while in Mexico in 1832, visited Chapultepec near the capital, and measured a prodigious cedar of 40 or 50 feet in circumference; in Lebanon some are reported to be 100 feet in girth. Humboldt mentions a tree in Oaxaca in Mexico of 112 feet in the waist at 4 feet from the ground; and travellers assert, that in California there are trees varying from 300 to 400 feet in altitude, 30 feet in diameter, and 80 feet in circumference.

It may not be out of place, whilst on the interesting subject of the Ankerwycke trees, to remind the reader of the vast Indian vegetable productions in the banyan tree, the lateral branches of which send down shoots which take root, "and daughters grow about the mother-tree," forming a grove. A tree in Nearchus' days, B.C. 300, is said to have covered five acres.

The situation of Ankerwycke, albeit it is on a level, is watered by the Thames, which takes a long bend from Milson's point round the wood, and continues its course in a straight line to the Weir at the Angler's Rest. It is enlivened by fishermen with pliant rod and dancing cork, while snowy swans and downy cygnets drift majestically along the transparent flood.

Opposite is the screen of hills known as Cooper's Hill, on which, says Pope in his Windsor Forest, the Muses dance,—
"On Cooper's-hill eternal wreaths shall grow,
While lasts the mountain, or while Thames shall flow."

These elevations are composed of sand and gravel, a ridge of the Bagshot sand stretching to the north-west, and rising abruptly from the plashy meadows. Beds of this formation consist in part of loose siliceous sand, or sandstones composing the Bagshot or other heaths, and are styled upper marine formations, containing shells. The term gravel is applied often to different materials—a mixture of sand and stones angular and rounded, drift period, glacial period, and boulder formation are all terms of this kind. This range, an object of great beauty from the village of Wraysbury, descends from Englefield Green, on the summit of which, as well as on St. Ann's Hill at Chertsey, whose elevation is 250 feet, there is a noble panoramic area little inferior to the Devil's Dike view near Brighton, which suggested to Denham the poet the often-cited lines in his celebrated descriptive poem on the Thames published in 1643.

This bard was not a native here, but only resident, like many others, making Bucks a nest of singing-birds, for Spenser was an occasional resident, as well as Milton, Waller, Gray, and Cowper. The grandfather of Denham, one John a goldsmith, lies buried in Thorpe Chancel. He died 1583, ætat. 54, whilst his son, Sir John Denham, Knt., Chief Baron of the Exchequer, deceased in 1638, and caused the alms-houses on West Hill, Egham, to be built in 1624.

> "Who strives to mount Parnassus' hill,
> And thence poetic laurels bring—
> Must first acquire due force and skill,
> Must fly with swan's or eagle's wing."

Hence this hill is the local Parnassus, and it is sacred to the poet, on whose death in 1688 it was deemed honourable to inter his remains in the holy precincts of Westminster Abbey, near the grave of Spenser.

The poet's mother, Cicely, was daughter of Anthony Bond of Rusham Thorpe, whose father, John Bond, was Clerk of the Household to King Henry VIII, and Joane, daughter of — Clarke of Egham.

On the summit of Cooper's Hill, on the western side, is a stately structure heretofore the property of the Harcourts of Ankerwycke, known as Ankerwycke Purnish, an estate granted to the nuns of the same place in the reign of King Stephen by Hugh Abbot of Chertsey, and now the property of Sir John Cathcart, Bart. (page 27.)

The Coopers' Company have property at Egham, with alms-houses and school founded by Mr. Henry Stroode in 1703, a very ancient and opulent company dating from 1501; although not one of the twelve great city companies it ranks among the minor companies, of which there are ninety-one in London. Mr. George Hopkins, Mr. John Garrett, and Mr. George Taylor were masters here, curates at Wraysbury, and all received testimonials.

Before quitting Ankerwycke Park let us advert to a neat white house in the park styled Ankerwycke Cottage, now in the occupancy of Mr. Burckhardt of the Post Office, London, related to the celebrated traveller in Nubia, who died in the fulfilment of his engagements in 1817—like his brave predecessor Mungo Park. Here resided Mr. Samuel Jordan for thirteen years, until his removal to Place Farm in 1855. The land is rented by Mr. Slocock of Wraysbury, and the house is situated in an extensive orchard of some ten acres, through which a passage is made to gain Magna Charta island. There is also a path on the right conducting to the church at the end of this orchard, across the enamelled meadows.

This house and eight acres of land once belonged to the Buckland family, and was known as Woodhill, being tenanted by Mr. Griffith, and the land was exchanged by Mr. Blagrove.

## MAGNA CHARTA ISLAND.

The inhabitants of Wraysbury may well be proud of this distinction, for on this very island, now annexed to the mainland, if trust can be reposed in story and in Matthew Paris the Chronicler, the liberties of England were ratified—an event as important to England as was the Battle of Hastings—the one depriving Britons of the liberties and soil, the other confirming them in those liberties which had been the stem and root of all the rest.

This deed and resolution were of as great importance in those days politically as was the Reformation three centuries later to the moral and religious improvement of the whole community.

England rose in one case from political non-entity, and in the other from religious humiliation. Had it not so been we had been probably at this very time a third or fourth-rate power, while despotism and superstition, "like mischief in all its horrid shapes and forms combined, had stalked wide-wasting o'er the affrighted land." Foes to human happiness there have been who hate freedom by whatever means achieved or by whatever institutions secured. It is the object of their implacable hatred; they hate it with the malevolence of fiends who tremble while they are obliged to adore, for they quiver by instinct at the sound of the name. Such was John. Matthew Paris remarks, "Rex vires suas Baronum viribus impares intelligens sine difficultate leges subscriptas et libertates concessit, et charta sua hunc in modum confirmavit."

It was to repress and end such a tyranny that the scenes on Runnimede took place, and an island was found and selected in the then humble hamlet of Wraysbury, since immortalised by the event, a spot sacred to British freedom on which was signed on the 25th June 1215, the ever-famous Magna Charta.—*Laus Deo.*

No column has been erected to perpetuate the event, but in anticipation Akenside the poet framed some appropriate lines to discover the integrity of purpose and hope.

This island, to which no specific name was given anterior to the event, containing between two and three acres, was until 1834 a narrow slip of land on the left bank of the Bucks shore or ripe of the Thames within Wraysbury parish, as are all the eyots on the stream contiguous to the demesnes of Ankerwycke.

The proprietor has filled up the channel of the river towards the western extremity of the islet, and has attached it to the main land, not only to protect the isle, but the spot consecrated to our national honour. Some may however wish it had not changed its insular position. The junction of the island to the land is effected by a bridge—not arched, of about eight feet long. The sides of the banks are stoutly boarded here as well as half up the isle.

Runnimede is on the opposite or Surrey side of the water, a hamlet in the parish of Egham, where, in 1215 the confederated Barons having got King John in their power, the monarch, whom mild persuasion could not engage to do the work of fear, at length terrified, "for present fears were less than horrible imaginings," yielded to the just demand of his subjects, who, under pretext of securing his person from the fury of the multitude, conveyed him to this part of the possessions of the Ankerwycke nuns, where he signed the instrument of their deliverance from a yoke that had become intolerable. On the same day the Forest Charter was signed, and on the fourth day at the same place was signed the writ or precept by which twelve knights were to be elected to each county.

As if commemorative of some remarkable occurrence there now exist four large walnut-trees, a little mangled by *Boreas*, which, from their apparent age, may be surmised to be coeval with the Charta signature. They seem to have formed part of a circle, the exact position of which has been rendered more evident by the discovery of two others in the bed of the river, having their roots in the bank, when the present building was in process of erection to mark the great conjuncture.

In exploring the ruins of the Priory, as well as on Magna Charta Isle and other parts of the estate, many curious coins of different reigns have been recovered, and in the body of the river or mud one of some antiquity was found which is in the possession of the owner of the isle; and on each successive digging bones of animals and antlers are disinterred. The island is subject to serious inundations, and in 1861 the water rose five feet, nearly invading the dwelling-house, forcing the gardener to move in a boat across the isolated spot. There are some good trees on it—alders, willows, ash, chesnut, and evergreen oaks. Contiguous to this is another island of some three acres in area, all coming under the generic name of eyots.

There was an ancient causeway on the south side of Runnimede, constructed *temp.* Henry III. by a merchant named Thomas de Henford or Oxenford, for the safe conveyance of his wool—the staple of England, and for other precious merchandize; and of such value and utility was this causeway, that it was kept in repair at the public cost, being no charge on the parish or indwellers. He also built a bridge across the Thames at Staines. See Escheats, 24 Edward III. doubtless of surpassing utility when ferries supplied the want of bridges.

The house on the island has been much improved and augmented also by Mr. William Clifford, who went to reside in it in 1857. There is a drawing-room, and the Baron's Chamber—now a dining-room, and there are six bed-chambers above. The ferry which transported passengers to and from the opposite Runnimede shore is now discontinued.

The doors and windows of the Cottage are all arched and of a castellated style on a building of stone, square blocks of chalk and freestone, which are said to have been brought from Marlow Church. The interior of the Fisherman's Cottage is very interesting, in which a book was kept to record the names of visitors, and in the centre is a large stone, known as the Charter Stone, on which the signing or sealing of the written instrument is affirmed to have been executed. The stone is an octagon of about three feet in diameter, and is fixed in a handsomely carved and strong frame of oak. It bears this inscription, achieved with an enthusiasm commensurate with the event.

"Be it remembered that on this island, 25th June 1215, John, King of England, signed Magna Charta; and in the year 1834, this building was erected in commemoration of that great and important event by George Simon Harcourt, Esq. Lord of the Manor, and then High Sheriff of the County."

Of course this allegation as to the *very stone*, at such a distance of time, must be held apocryphal: there is an old oaken table, once in Place Farm, now at Wraysbury House, of which the same is predicated.

History alleges with verisimilitude that the Charter was concluded on the isle, but that the *actual* ratification or re-writing of it was done at Westminster, where such enactments were executed, as the act and deed and concession of a monarch to a grateful people.

Adjacent on the Ankerwycke side are still left five walnut trees, two being very antique from the brush of time, which augment and impart a grandeur and solemnity to the spot. Through these giants of the earth Ankerwycke is clearly discerned, photographs of which have been taken, as well as of every object of interest, by Mr. Scholefield, to whom the writer is indebted for specimens.

The Barons' Room is fitted up with a series of the cognizances of those who were in array at Runnimede, and in the centre are the arms of John, and adjacent appear those of Harcourt.

Of the twenty-five Barons who signed this instrument of delivery from a servile yoke, *three* only could write, the rest making the usual substitute—a cross. This expedient is said to owe its *origin* to Withred, King of Kent, who was himself ignorant of the manual science of writing; but modern investigation shews that this distinctive sign and badge of Christianity was used by early Christians. The names of the twenty-five Runnymede Barons are—Earl of Albemarle; William de Aubenie; Hugh de Bigod; Roger Bigod, Earl of Norfolk; Earl of Clare; Gilbert de Clare, Constable of Chester; Gilbert Delaval; George Delaval; John Fitz-Robert; Robert Fitz-Walter, Earl of Gloster; William de Huntingfield, Earl of Hereford; William de Lanvalay; William Malet; William Mareschal, junior; Roger de Mombezon; William de Mowbray; Roger de Montfitchet of Wraysbury; Richard de Perci; Robert de Ros; Geoffrey de Say; Robert de Vere, Earl of Oxford; Eustace de Vesci.

All or most of these names are found in the Roll of *Battle Abbey*, the earliest reputed record of the Normans, kept by the monks there. The abbot was mitred and was invested with large powers, while the Grand Charter exempted the brethren of Battle from episcopal jurisdiction. The table, containing some 630 names of those who accompanied the Conqueror, was suspended in the abbey, among which is found that of Harcourt, ancestor of the owner of Magna Charta Island. But neither archæologists nor genealogists repose implicit confidence in the preserved list; for monks felt no indelible qualms of conscience at occasional interpolations to propitiate favour or gratify pride.

Under the graceful slopes of Cooper's Hill, containing some 160 acres of meadow land, and about two miles from Egham Hythe to Milson's Point at Ankerwycke, lies an almost flat plain, called Runnimede, Runingermund, Runingemede, whose derivation is doubtful, but by some is said to be the meadow of *Runes*, or magical charms—the field of mystery and the field of council—if it be not more probable from the ever-running waters, where, in the month of June 1215, the feudal troops of the English Barons covered both mead and hill. The mead was bounded by two others, styled Long Mead and Yard Mead, where the troops lay, and both were open from Egham to Old Windsor. Here the Primate Langton passed John and the indignant Peers preparatory to the signing of the deed—the nucleus of our political strength, and secret of our greatness.

With the exception of the 20th day of the same month, King John resided at Windsor from the 10th to the 26th of June; but every day between Monday, 15th, and Tuesday, 23rd, this potentate attended a conference at Runnimede, and returned to Windsor Castle at night. The Charter was signed (and that very day was also signed the Charta de Foresta) "Juratum, &c. bonâ fide et sine malo ingenio observabimus, testibus supradictis et multis aliis data per manum nostram in prato quod vocatur *Runingemede*, inter Stanes et Windleshores, decimo quinto die Junii anno regni nostri septimo decimo." Hence it is inferred that the signature did not take place on the eyot, but on the very mead. Matthew Paris, an English historian and a Benedictine monk, who died in 1259, and so contemporaneous, recites that a treaty of peace was signed here; and one author has "prope villam de Stanes juxta flumen Thamisiæ in quâdam insulâ," &c.

It is said that this identical instrument was lost, and that Sir Robert Cotton found it in his *tailor's* hands ready to be cut up, with the numerous seals attached to it. There is a facsimile published: on the top are five large seals, that of the King in the centre; at the base of the instrument is one large seal, by the sides of which are twelve seals, smaller in size and round; while on either side of the deed are twelve seals, on the usual shields of the time, thus: ▽. He rescued the precious document from the sacrilegious hands of the knight of the needle, and it is now deposited with the Cottonian MSS. in the British Museum. It is nearly three feet long by two feet wide, with the arms and seals of the Barons elaborately emblazoned in gold and colours. The Cottonian Library was founded by Sir R. Cotton, who died in 1631; and this was hastened by the loss of his library, the fruit of forty years' experience and inquiry, so as to justify the appellation of the English Vatican.

The *Charta* ordained that all privileges and immunities extorted from the King should be extended by the Barons to their inferior vassals, the Barons obliging the King to deliver London and the Tower to their sole custody until the execution of the articles in the Charter, for which purposes twenty-five of them were nominated Conservators of the public liberty, and to them obedience was sworn. This acquiescence lasted only till John, instigated by the demon of mischief, Pope Innocent III. issued a bull abrogating the Charter, trusting to avenge himself on the Barons, who were constrained to invoke Lewis, son of Philip, King of France, to offer him the British crown. In addition to treason, the Pope fastened the *brand of heresy* on the Barons—a common *expedient* to frighten the timid, according to Matthew Paris, whose Chronicles were finished in 1269; "a man," says Fuller, "who seldom kisseth the Pope's toe but to *bite* it."

In September 1217, King Henry III. after the death of John in 1216, with the Earl Marshal and Pandulf the legate, met on this *same isle* Lewis of France with the Barons, who solicited him to accept England with her destinies. Hence Magna Charta was signed, the bulwark of English liberties; since confirmed by thirty Acts of Parliament. So we enjoy juries and other rights, the best inheritance of Englishmen; although, historically, we owe the debt of juries to Alfred in 870.

Runnimede, the spot of this eventful scene, is now traversed by horse and foot, and on its smooth green surface once a year are horse races, where the beauteous and gay flock to witness the fleet contest for the 100 guinea plate given by King William IV. who revived these meetings. In the days of King James I. Newmarket was used for races; and *temp.* Charles II. Datchet Mead was converted to that national purpose. They were called Bell-courses, a bell being the prize; now judiciously commuted into plate of exquisite workmanship, or money.

Perhaps it would not be judicious to terminate this succinct history of Ankerwycke without adverting to a trial of some military operations which took place here in 1853. The proposed intent was to throw a *pontoon* bridge across the Thames at that portion of the water opposite Runnimede, and that an attack was to be made upon Ankerwycke. The company who came to inspect the manœuvres was amply rewarded by one of the most interesting and brilliant spectacles. The enemy occupied a strong position on the north side of the Thames, their front secured by the river and their rear protected by an orchard on the Ankerwycke estate. The forces marched to the attack in three divisions; Sir Richard England's brigade descended from Englefield Green, over Cooper's Hill, while other regiments moved off by the wood in their rear towards the Egham road, and the 4th Dragoons by the Staines road, forming the advanced guard consisting of the Royal Artillery and pontoon train. The column under the Duke of Cambridge proceeded along the Egham road to Runnimede. The troops ultimately crossed the river and invaded Ankerwycke Park, and for some time rested on the lawn, where men and cattle were refreshed by the hospitality of Mr. Felix Pryor, then tenant of the mansion, who also provided a splendid luncheon in marquees for the officers and their friends.

A singular accident occurred as the field batteries were crossing the pontoon bridge, a horse drawing a 9-pounder became restive, and the limber and gun went into the water, dragging with them the six horses and several of the Sappers and Miners; one man nearly perished, and two horses were drowned, while four were brought safe to land in an exhausted condition. The gun and limber were hauled up out of 15 feet water; had it been at the bend of the river, termed in old maps Milson's point, where the depth is 70 feet, there had been small chance of recovery.

The extreme beauty and fitness of the spot selected for this splendid exercise of troops and experiment, was admitted, and when the locality was peopled by thousands of spectators, and emblazoned by the pride, pomp and circumstance of mimic war, in the person of 10,000 troops, the moving panorama presented to the eye was of a most exciting character—a living picture, to dazzle, instruct and delight.

The present made by Felix Pryor, Esq., to Mr. Jordan, a tenant at Ankerwycke, on the occasion, should not be pretermitted—a silver cup weighing 4 lb. 10 oz., value 20 guineas. July 27, 1853. Presented by Felix Pryor, Esq. to Mr. Samuel Jordan of Wraysbury, to commemorate the event of Her Majesty's troops, under the command of Lieut.-Gen. Lord Seaton, from the encampment at Chobham, Surrey, passing over the Thames on the pontoon bridge, on the occasion of their visiting the grounds of Ankerwycke.

From the scene of war *in procinct*, it were a pity and omission not to record another reunion within the precincts of time-honoured Ankerwycke.

The 20th August, 1859, witnessed another sight, in connection with the Windsor and Eton Literary, Scientific and Mechanics' Institute. The house and grounds are now in the occupation of Cottrill Scholefield, Esq., who very liberally placed the park at the disposal of the members, and the sum of £3½ was collected at the entrance.

The programme opened with a cricket match in one innings, between the members of the Egham and the Windsor and Eton Literary Institute. After the game a dinner took place in the tent, 150 persons sitting down; Mr. Vansittart, M.P. for Windsor, occupying the chair. Buffo singers enlivened the repast, plays were performed and gymnastics enacted, and in a Maypole dance by 12 youths, as much proficiency was exhibited as in the dance of Sir Roger de Coverley by experienced sons of Terpsichore—the Muse of dancing. Nor was there wanting the Creole Minstrel singers, while a very choice selection of music was played by the band of the 1st Life Guards. Archery, trap and base ball, were included in the diversions on the firm-set land, as well as boat racing on the pellucid flood, a cup being presented to each of the rowers of the winning boats. The event passed off without accident, although a heavily laden platform gave way and made some of the sons of curiosity and sport bite the dust.

In 1860, 17th August, a similar festivity was renewed in the Park, a spot devoted to pastime, and consecrated by hospitality, whose reward is gratitude, of which the possessor can never be deprived. Having surveyed these spots dear to liberal Britons, we must join with Dr. Johnson, "far from us be such frigid philosophy as may conduct us indifferent and unmoved over any ground which has been dignified by bravery, wisdom, or virtue. He is little to be envied whose patriotism would not gain force upon the plain of Marathon," or whose zeal would not effervesce upon the fields of Runnymede.

## PLACE FARM AND REMINGHAM MANOR.

So called because it was the principal farm of the village. By tradition it is called also King John's hunting lodge, where royalty was wont to fish and hawk, ride and run with hound and horn, what time all this village seems to have been one uninterrupted sporting ground, when Old Windsor was the residence of the Saxon kings; and doubtless the amusement of which K. Henry II. was so enamoured, sporting, and on whose account King John signed the Forest Charter simultaneously with Magna Charta, gives a certain verisimilitude to the tradition. The forest laws were then equivalent to our game laws, and though the supporters of them were very tenacious, some distinctions of *feræ naturæ* were recognized. There is an interesting work published called "Perambulations and Proceedings relating to the Forests, from 10 John, 1208, to the end of the reign of K. Edward III. 1377," and to enforce these statutes the Justices in Eyre (itinere) were sent round, who held pleas of the *forest*, as well as common and criminal pleas.

It has been found expedient to keep up these game enactments, the law of trespass alone being insufficient to protect this species of property. Although the exclusive right to game does not rest on the same basis as that of property—for mankind will not be so easily persuaded that taking game is quite so criminal as filching a purse—yet are these laws fruitful sources of crime and immorality, filling jails with delinquents. Prior to the time of Charles II. there was no qualification act to kill game. In this county of Bucks, in 1845, of 539 persons committed, 196 were for offences against the game laws. Despite the poaching, of which there is so much complaint, and of bad seasons also, the increase of game is amazing; in 1859, a newspaper detailed an account of a *battue*, in which 5700 head of game was killed, half of which was pheasants, in five days' sport. Recently, in 1860, a new law of game licence has been enacted.

These grounds were adapted to hawking, a sport known in England *temp.* Ethelbert, 760, when he wrote to Germany for a brace of falcons; and latterly, *temp.* James I., Sir James Monson, gave £1000 for a *cast* of hawks. The office of Grand Falconer is still in the St. Alban family. There were *mews* for hawks, as kennels or inclosures for dogs; the King's mews at Charing Cross was for this purpose, King Henry VIII. converted them into stables, and so stables were termed *Mews*. The name derives from mue, or the process of shedding feathers at moulting, in falconer's language.

Place Farm was once a manor house, called in old deeds, public and private, the site of the *manor* formerly the property of the Crown, to which it was annexed as of the Honour of Windsor, and the manor is styled of Remingham and Cokke, extending then over parts of Wraysbury, Langley, Datchet and Old Windsor, and it went with such part of the Ankerwycke property as was reserved in the Crown lands, but whether co-ordinate, or subordinate, or distinct, is not determinable in consequence of very long disuse, and it is probable that the eyots on the river became parcel of the property in right of this manor.

The first deed I have seen which bears directly on this manor, is to be found in the Abbreviation Rolls, Vol. II. p. 310. 43 Edw. III. 1369, in which that king granted a lease to John Jourdelay (probably ancestor of Thomas Jourdelay, of Eton, in 1456), and Thomas Remenham of Wraysbury, and with it the park of Langley, which seems to have been thrown in as a makeweight in Wraysbury Crown leases, with Cippenham. I shall translate the deed from the original Norman French—

The King grants and lets on lease to John Jourdelay and Thomas Remenhan of Wyrardesbury, the house of his manor of do. Bucks, viz., an antique hall and a cowshed covered with straw, and a grange covered with tiles, with gardens adjoining and 237 acres and one rood of arable land, 16 acres 3 roods and 7 perches of pasture, &c., lying in *Radelahen Eyt*; 14 acres and 10 do. in *Warneslade*; 10 acres and 7 perches, and in *Grosmere* 1 acre and 3 roods together, with one piece of indifferent and dry meadow called the Westmede, containing 15 acres, &c., to have and to hold for the term of 30 years, at the rent of £8. 10s, the said tenants keeping all in repair, and to have reasonable *Housbote* (provision) within the park of Langele Mareys. This deed is among those named in law language de redisseis—Redisseisinis.

The family of Remenham is of antiquity in these parts. In 1289 John de Remenham and his wife held lands and a mill in Wraysbury, and again in 1291 he appears in a deed with John de Halle, one Wexford, and his wife, about lands and rents in Horton. This same John has also dealings with Hugh de Remenham about some Horton property, and subsequently John de Remenham, junior, is found in a deed, 1343, with Walter Rabbe, regarding a messuage, rents, and a mill in Wraysbury and Horton. An endowed chantry at Hillingdon was styled Rabbe's Chantry; some lands paid a chaplain to pray for the soul of Walter Rabbe. Escheat 46 Edw. III. 1372. In 1548 it was valued at £5. 3s 6d per annum. It is remarkable how few fines are extant for Wraysbury or Horton between 1400 and 1500.

The tenant of Place Farm, Thomas Remenham, in 1369, was son of John de Remenham, junior, but the next proprietors on record were John Pollard, Gent. and John Ball, Gent., the former a family of some note here. In 38 Henry III. 1255, a writ had been directed to John Pollard, the King's escheator, to give pledges about a certain meadow in Datchet, which one Ralph de Neketon, the King's M.D., held to farm of Henry de Pinkenie, late deceased. He died 1254, seised of the Barony of Wedon, Northamptonshire, and lands in Essex and Bucks. In the Placita Rolls, co. Bucks. 15 Richard II. 1391, there is an account of a claim made by Thomas Butiller, Custodian of the Free Chapel of Windsor, and the College, against William Creedy, Roger Creedy, and others, for certain tithes of wood from Iver and Wraysbury.

There is a deed of fine in which John Pollard is the querent and Sir Walter Stonor deforciant. By a recovery deed Trin. 29 Henry VIII. 1537, Sir Walter Stonor and Margaret his wife, sell the manor of Remenham and Cokke, and Dytton, with appurtenances, 40 messuages, 500 acres of land,

100 meadow, 200 pasture, 100 wood, 300 furze, plain and briar, and 40s. rent, in *Warerdesbury*, Langle Mareys, Horton, Stoke and Datchet.

There is a recapitulation of a deed about this property which went to Stonor for life, then to Walter Welshe and Elizabeth Lady Compton (widow of Sir William Compton), his wife, and daughter of Sir Walter Stonor. Should Mr. Welshe die issueless, then to his wife Elizabeth for life, and if she died sp. then to Sibilla, daughter of David Brecknock, and after her decease to John Brecknock, all related in blood to the Stonors. See page 16.

This shews that Place Farm was in the tenure of the Stonors, and his only son, John Stonor, was buried in Wraysbury chancel in 1512. In a deed without date, temp. Henry VII. appears in the proceedings of the Duchy of Lancaster, a complaint of one Ione Tanner, a Wraysbury tenant, who brought an action against Walter Stonor, Gent., for that he had illegally prosecuted her on a charge of high treason, and for false imprisonment of her husband Thomas Tanner, of this parish, in the Marshalsea Prison, and she declares all parties wholly free from the accusation. The result of the action I do not know, but Sir Walter was a man of trust and honour, and held the responsible appointment of Lieutenant of the Tower, for which he had £100 a year, and so it was his duty to address himself to all addicted to treasonable practices or political pravity.

"Petition of Ione Tanner—To the Kyng our Soveyn Lo... Hen. VII.—wiffe of Thoms Tanner of y⁰ lordschip of Wyrardesbur' co. Bucks. wʰ Walter Stoner of the same Countie, Gentilma, hath of long tyme hadde to ferme." Speaks of decay within the last 25 years, and then about fines, &c., to the *valure* of CC marks, which were to be divided among the tenantry,—"wherfor the seid Walter Stonner, peevyng color thus made be the seid Thos. Tanner and other of yʳ tenants for yoʳ emprovemēt hath of his cruell mynde made labor to indite theym in foreyn counteis and with thretyngs, &c., grevosly trowbillyd them—forced tenants to surmyse treason on the seid Tho. Tanner my husbond that he shuld speke obprobrious words against yʳ Heynes be the space of a quartʳ of a yer passid, the whiche thing as God knoweth he never dide nor thochte and yt I take God to my gage. He hath now sedicosli causid my seid husband to be comitted into yʳ prison of yᵉ Marshalse." She requests an examination of the *premisses* "for the forther trewth therin to be knowen, and yʳ seid orator shall evmor prey for the psuacō (preservation) of yʳ Grace long to induere. Indorsed, Committitur cᵃ mrō Hemson et mrō Southewell. John Ednam." Sir Richard Empson was Chancellor of the Duchy of Lancaster from 21 Henry VII. 1505, to about 1509.

We have adverted to the fact that Sir Walter Stonor was lord of the manor of Wraysbury under the descent of it, page 17.

It seems that the first lease of 21 years had terminated with the Crown, for we find by deed dated 20th March, 24 Henry VIII. 1533, the site of this manor of Wraysbury, with certain demesnes, park, &c. with Queen's Meade *als* New Mead, excepting woods and wards formerly parcel of the possessions of Joane (Seymour, page 18) Queen of England, were leased for 21 years more to Sir William Stonor, Knt.,* paying yearly £13. 6s 8d, all which advantages, with his freeholds here on the decease of his son John in 1512, sp. to his only daughter and heir Elizabeth, married to Sir Philip Hoby, Knt. (page 35), formerly wife of Walter Walshe of Elmely, Worcester, who was of the Privy Council to King Henry VIII. From this gentleman and his wife Elizabeth Stonor, descended in the fifth degree William Walshe, who died in 1708, and of whom Pope speaks in so

---

* The Patent Rolls date this lease at Westminster, 20th March, 24 Hen. VIII. 1533; he keeping houses and edifices in repair, for which he was allowed *grossum mæremium* (any sort of timber fit for building) to keep up housebote, hedgebote, fyrebote, heybote, ploughbote and cartebote. Page 17.

I

flattering terms, as being his patron, who urged him to poetry and authorship, in these words, "and knowing Walshe would tell me I could write."

By an inquest on Sir Walter Stonor, 25th June, 1551, he died 8th October, 1550, and his will is dated 25th August 1549, wherein he mentions his third wife, Elizabeth, then surviving, daughter of Geffrey Chambers, of London, whose marriage settlements were dated 3rd September, 1547.

The lands descended to his daughter and heir Elizabeth, widow of Sir Philip Hoby, Knt., who by his will left her all his interests in *Wresbury*, furniture, plate, &c., and cites her children Walter Walshe, Margaret and Frances. The will is dated 1st May, 1550, and proved 2nd July following; states there is £4000 due to the sisters by their brother Walter; makes Sir William Cecil, (afterwards Lord Burleigh), and Sir Richard Blount, executors. A second administration was taken subsequently, 12th Dec. 1597, by Sir William Cecil, or in his name.

Elizabeth, daughter and heir of Sir William Stonor, and widow of W. Walshe, continued to reside here (the Oxon estates devolving on her uncle by primogenial right), and here was buried by the side of her only brother, 25th August, 1560. Her son, Walter Walshe, survived her only till 25th February, 1561, when he was deposited in the vault under the Communion table in Wraysbury chancel, and his son Sir William Walshe had the Wraysbury property in addition to that at Abberley, county Worcester.

Here I insert some deeds. February 1611, an indenture between Sir William Walshe, Kt. and Ambrose Aldridge, of Wraysbury, the former selling to the latter the manor of Remingham and Cow. This deed (in the possession of the writer of these memoirs, with many others relative to Wraysbury) is much mutilated by ancient contusion and the brush of time, so that the writing is scarcely legible. The name of Sir William Smijth is cited in the instrument, and the autograph of Sir William Walshe is neatly executed, in the presence of Robert Cornwall and Henry Aldridge.

By another deed, 23rd Oct. 1613, it appears that Ambrose Aldridge, of *Wyrardesburie*, Bucks, Yeoman, did sell, and bargain, and enfeoff, and convey to Felix Wilson (the same who was lord of the manor in Horton, and held the advowson in 1618—the lawyer) all that manor known by the name of Remingham and Cow, and the capital messuage called *Place*, for the sum of £500. There is mention made of a bond of £650 in the Court of Chancery, which was to be enrolled in the names of Felix Wilson and Richard Dod. In this deed are cited the names of Dame Elizabeth Walshe, who died 1560, and Sir William Walshe with that of Sir William Smyth, Kt., of Monthaut, Essex. Signed John Wilson.

There is a deed of this Felix Wilson, which gives 10s. to the King and Ambrose Aldridge, and Emma his wife, for 6 acres of meadow, 5 pasture, with appurtenants in Wraysbury, 1618. This is followed by another deed, 29th Nov. 1613, wherein a sum of £300 is mentioned between Sir William Walshe, of Abberley, Worcester, and Ambrose Aldridge, of Langley Marsh, Yeoman, in which Aldridge is bound for £80. The signature is confirmatory of the transaction by Aldridge, and to it is also appended an autograph of Sir William Smyth, Kt., of Ankerwycke, in neat caligraphy.

27th Oct. 1617.—Some difficulty arises about this property, because Mr. Ambrose Aldridge left the village, and is now styled of Chesham, Bucks, and sells for £140 a certain close and lands and pasture grounds, by name *Johannes*, containing six acres, near Ankerwycke, between the mead of Sir William Smyth called *Reddings*, and another called *Day Meade* and the common called *Johannes*' Green, lately occupied by Richard Moore. The signature of Aldridge is again inscribed, and at the back of it are found the names of Thomas Mathew, Richard Dod, William Page, John Stonor, Lazarus Grove.

## PEDIGREE OF STONOR AND BRECKNOCK.

Arms of STONOR: Az. 2 bars doncetté O. a chief of the last.
Arms of WALSHE: A. a fess between 3 martlets S.

SIR JOHN STONOR=Dau. of Lord Lisle.

SIR JOHN or RICHARD STONOR=MARGARET, dau. and heir of Sir John Harnhull, of Co. Gloucester.

SIR JOHN STONOR, 34 Edward III. 1361=MAUD, dau. of — Fitzlewis.

SIR JOHN, ob. 1361=Dau. of John Wenard of Cornwall.

SIR EDWARD, ob. 1382=Dau. of Bevill of Ulton.

EDMUND HAMPDEN,=JANE, dau. of Sir=SIR RALPH,=— dau. of James Butler, of Bucks, ob. 1420. Robert Belknap ob. 1395. 2nd Earl of Ormond.

THOMAS STONOR, ob. 1430=ALICE, dau. and h. of Sir John Kirby, Kt.

JOAN or ALICE, natural=THOMAS, ob. 1474.     SIR DAVID BRECK-=ROBERT BRECK-=SIBILLA.
dau. of Sir John de la     NOCK, of Wraysbury.    NOCK. Lysons'
Pole, Duke of Suffolk.         Bucks, p. 627.

SIR WM. STONOR,=ANN, dau. and    JOHN STONOR,=    THOS. STONOR,=ISABEL,    JOHN BRECKNOCK,=
knighted 1477.    co-heir of John    ancestor of    of Blount Court, dau. &    living and had in-
   Neville, Marq.    Lord Camoys.    Oxon. heir.    terest in Wrays-
   Montacute.          bury.

         JOHN, 1537.    SIBILLA.

ANN=SIR ADRIAN   MARY.=JOHN   HENRY=MAR-   MARGA-=SIR WALTER=ELIZABETH,   JOHN =MARGA-
FORTESCUE    STONOR    GERY,    RET, d. of   STONOR, of    dau. of   WALSHE.   RET, da.
son of Sir       da. of    Nicholas   ditto, Ox. and    Geoffrey   See   of Sir
John For-       Wm.    Foliot, of   Place Farm,    Chambers,   Nash's   John
tescue, be-       Love-    Worcester.    Wyrardis-    settl. dated   Worcester,   Blount.
headed       lace,       bury, knight.    3 Sep. 1517,   vol. i.
1539.       of       1513, ob. 8    who rem.
      Hen-       Aug. 1550,    Sir Edward
      ley.       will dated    Griffin, of
            1549, inq. p. m.    Northton.
            25 June 1551.

                                                                                     =WM. HOBY=

MARGA-=THOMAS,   JOHN STONOR,   1. h. SIR WM.=ELIZABETH,= 2. h. WALTER =3. h. SIR PHILIP   SIR THOMAS
RET,    Lord    son and heir,   COMPTON, of   dau. and heir   WALSHE,   HOBY, Kt. ob.   HOBY, d. 1566,
dau. &   Went-    ob. sp. 29 Aug.   Co. Gloster.   ob. 25 Aug.   of Wrays-   31 May 1558,   succeeded Sir
heir.    worth,    1512, buried    ob. 30 May   1560, buried   bury, privy   admin. by Sir   Thos. Smyth
   ob. 5th    Wraysbury    1528, Chan-   Wraysbury.   councillor   Wm. Cecil &   as Ambassa-
   Ed. VI.    Chancel.    cellor of Ire-     to K. Hen. 8,   Sir Richard   dor to France,
         land, a quo     sheriff of   Blount 12   m. Elizabeth,
         Marquis of     Worcester   Dec. 1597.   dau. of Sir An-
         Northampton.     1535.     thony Cook, of
                        Essex. p. 38.*

                                                                             FRANCES.

WALTER =DOROTHY, dau.=RICHARD SHEL-   MARGARET,=SIR JNO. CHEEKE,   MARY=SIR WM.=MILDRED,†
WALSHE,   of Richard Hill,   LEY, of Sussex,   ob. 30 Nov.   Greek Professor   CHEEKE,   CECIL,   dau. of Sir
of ditto,   Serjeant of the   ob. 1594. Of this   1616, æt. 84.   with Sir Thomas   m. 154-,   Lord   Anthony
ob. 25 Feb.   Cellar to Hen. 8,   family was P. B.   m. 1546.   Smyth at Cam-   ob. ditto.   Burleigh,   Cooke,
1561.    ob. 4 June 1600.   Shelley the poet,     bridge, ob. 1557,     ob. 1598.   m. 1546.
      who died 1822.     æt. 43, p. 37.

                 GEORGE BOARD, of Sussex.=                              * At Bisham is this entry:—"Mar-
                                                                    ried, 23rd Dec. 1574, the Right Hon.
SIR WM. WALSHE,=ELIZABETH BOARD,   TIMOTHEA=WALTER WALSHE,      Lord John Russel and the renowned
of ditto, ob. 1622.   ob. 20 Dec. 1618.   BOARD.   ob. 1613.      Lady Elizabeth Hoby."
                                                                    † This lady had great erudition,
JOSEPH WALSHE, ob. 1682.=    WILLIAM WALSHE=ELIZABETH, dau. of        and wrote some handsome epitaphs
                                       Sir George Blount.                   in *Latin* : one on the death of a much
WILLIAM WALSHE, the critic, ob. 1708.                                            revered man, Thos. Noble, who died
                                                                        in 1567; and one on her husband,
                                                                        which inscription is on his monument
                                                                        in Bisham Church.

From this time the names of Stonor and Walshe disappear from the manor of Remingham. There was also a manor of this name near Henley-on-Thames, which *temp.* Henry VI. belonged to the family of Ernestfort and Montforts. Lord Lovelace died seised of it in 1634. He married Catherine, daughter of George Gyll, of Wydial, Herts; as inserted in the pedigree. The barony of Camoys was granted in 1839 to Thomas Stonor, as senior co-heir of Hugh the last Lord Camoys, who died issueless in 1426, when his two sisters became his heirs, between whose descendants and representatives the barony was in abeyance. The first of this name was Ralph de Camois, a Baron by tenure, who died 43 Henry III. 1258.

The reversion of that estate was granted by patent of the Crown, 23rd March 1544, to Sir Thomas Smyth of Ankerwycke and his heirs and assigns for thirty years, beginning from 1563, at the same rents and with the same clauses of exception as in the lease of his predecessor, in consideration of a surrender made by Sir Thomas to Queen Elizabeth of £31. 19s. 4d. due to him for services done whilst ambassador in France. It is not unlikely that, as the reversion was to take effect from 1563, and the anticipatory grant was made in 1544, Sir Thomas made arrangements with Dame Elizabeth Hoby to let him take immediate possession of Place Farm. If it was not so, the lease of Stonor almost expired with his grandson Walter Walshe in 1562, from which time we may date the advent of the Smyths as connected with Place Farm and the Remingham Manor. Some adjustment was certainly made, because we find by another deed, 20th February 1574, that Queen Elizabeth grants to Sir Thomas Smyth, her principal Secretary of State, a further extension of the original lease of the lands stipulated and described, and of the site of the manor of Wraysbury, for thirty more years, commencing Michaelmas 1593. This lease the Secretary did not live to see expire, though he died *Secretary of State*, his useful life ending in 1577; so his brother, George Smyth, came to Ankerwycke, resided, and died *there* in 1584. His son and heir succeeded him, and he again renewed the lease by patent of King James I. 21st March 1605, with the identical covenants and contingencies, for forty more years, beginning from the date of the patent.

As the writer possesses certain original parchment deeds relative to this parish, with which the Smyths are concerned, to illustrate the history he will insert them here.

One dated 10th March 1629, is an indenture of lease between Dame Bridget (daughter of Thomas Fleetwood, of the Vache, Bucks, page 42), and widow of Sir William Smyth, Knt. and William Childe, of Wraysbury, who leases Remingham, and Cow, and house, &c. for £103 per annum. It appears that these two lawyers, Felix Wilson and Richard Dod, had bought or had this property assigned to them by Ambrose Aldridge of Wraysbury. The names of John and Felix Wilson are on the deed of 1629. This was the last deed she executed here, for she died in 1633, having remarried Edward, Viscount Conway. In the State Paper Office, 21st November 1626, the vicarage of Wraysbury was conferred on Ellis Beverley, at the instance of Edward Lord Conway, Secretary of State, by the Chapter of Windsor. In the will of Lord Conway, proved 12th November 1631, he mentions a wife *Catherine* and a daughter Mary; so it may be a mistake in Coles' Escheats that he remarried Bridget, widow of Sir William Smyth.

About this period King Charles I. was in want of money, and a refractoriness in Parliament to vote loans, give aids or supplemental contingencies, benevolences, &c. induced the Sovereign to have recourse to the sale of Crown lands to repay money borrowed. So in his need the straitened Majesty of England fixed his eye on our village, and by deed 14th June 1628, *inter alia*, the site of Wraysbury Manor, with Queen's Mead, &c. were granted to Edward Ditchfield and others for £12,496. 6s. 6d. a clause being inserted which exempted all lands and agreements made to Sir William Smyth, Knt. This seems to have taken effect; for a new deed was drawn, whereby the

City of London again disposed of this property, 28th June 1631, to William Trumball, Esq. George Clay, &c. This gave rise to subdivision in the Crown demesnes, and the proprietary of Wraysbury became extensive, and to them I shall advert.

The Smijths retained their property in this section of the village until Thomas Smijth, Esq. was raised to a Baronetcy in 1661, succeeding on the death of his nephew Edward Smijth without issue in 1651 to all the Essex and Bucks estates. I have before adverted to the fact of this gentleman being mulcted in the sum of £8000 as a *malignant*, which meant one evilly disposed towards the new order of things; and to compound for the alienation of his estates perhaps he sold his outlying lands at Wraysbury, and went permanently to live at Hill Hall, bought in 1554. Hence the Place Farm and Remingham Manor with its dependencies, eyots on the Thames, were sold by deed 11th February 1651 to Richard Hale, Citizen of London, for £1960; which deed the writer possesses, with the autograph of Sir Thomas Smijth, witnessed by his brother-in-law John Altham, whose sister Joane Sir Thomas had married. On it is the name of Robert Yarway, servant or steward of his Wraysbury property, and that of William Warne, *servant* to the said servant. Hence the Place Farm and other lands hereabouts departed from the hands of the Smijths after a tenure of more than a century, dating from the first patented-grant in 1550.

We now come to a new proprietor in the family of Hale of Windsor: I believe previously of Datchet, where Maurice Hale dwelt. There is a Maurice Hale mentioned in the Patent Rolls, 12 Eliz. 1569. John Hale and Maurice Hale of Datchet were living in 1586, the latter having a grant of the ferry and passage at Datchet in that year. In 1661, Recovery fine, 43 Eliz. Thomas Nelson, Gent., sells land, &c. in Datchet to Thomas Hale.

Richard Hale and Elizabeth his wife were the purchasers from the Smijths, and Thomas Hale, senior, buys lands here in Wraysbury of George Penyman in 1671. By fine Trin. 1672, this property, then occupied by Ann Bernard, was conveyed by Mr. Hale and his grandson, Dr. Richard Hale, to Robert Baker, Citizen of London, in which deed appear the names of Richard Hale of Beckingham, Kent, and Richard his son and Elizabeth *uxor*, and John Sorrell, junior, of Much Waltham, Essex (Mr. Sorrell is called cousin in the will of Richard Hale, 1727), to levy a *fine of recognoisance de droit* and sixty acres of land in Wraysbury, Langley, and Salt Hill, with some Essex property.

Again, by indenture 21st September 1683 of lease and release, between John Slocombe of Colnbrook, Mercer, and Richard Hale of New Windsor, for and in consideration of £40 he did sell a close called Peter's close, occupied by William Hearne and Shadrach Child, abutting on Welly Lane, near the land of Dr. Trumball.—(See Pedigree of Peters under Horton.)

Dr. Richard Hale was an eminent M.D. in London, and bequeathed by his will, 20th November 1727 and proved 1st October 1728, the sum of £450 to the Royal College of Physicians of which he was a member, to buy books, having previously given £50 with other endowments for the advance of science. He was a publicist, and contributed tracts in the philosophical transactions. He also gave £500 to a charity-school in Windsor.

On his decease in 1728, ætat. 58, he bequeathed these lands with *appurtenants* to his nephew Thomas Tower, Esq., of Huntsmore Lodge, Iver, second son of Christopher Tower, Esq., who had married his sister Elizabeth Hale. This same gentleman had bought Huntsmore Lodge in 1696, now a mansion of taste and beauty, seated in a park distinguished for symmetry and graceful disposition of timber, in the possession of Christopher Tower, Esq., some time Member of Parliament for the County of Bucks, a lineal descendant; and to this estate is added that of Weald Hall, Essex, which was inherited from Thomas Tower, Esq., who made the purchase of it in 1745, all which properties have continued in the Tower family, with the exception of Place Farm and the Remingham Manor. In the Court Rolls of Wraysbury is the admission of Thomas Tower, Esq., 19th November 1724, on the surrender of Thomas Potter, citizen and *hippiatrus* (farrier) who came before Mary Lee, lady of the manor. The recapitulation is of 30 acres, 40 acres of meadow, 40 acres of pasture, &c., with oziers in Wraysbury; and in 1743 Thomas Tower, Esq. surrendered 45 acres in the occupation of William Weyland, and some land between, to Lady Salter and Gilbert Urwin, Gent.; also some land surrendered by Thomas Potter to the use of Sir Philip Hall of Upton, Knt., and Thomas Powell, Esq. of the Six Clerks' Office. Indenture tripartite 17th October 1728 between Philip Harcourt, Esq. and Henry Hall, Esq. and Sarah, daughter of Sir Henry Hall (Pedigree of Harcourt, p. 45), and John Wiseman, Esq. and Thomas Tower, Esq. On the surrender of Thomas Tower, Esq. in 1768, Harcourt Powell, Esq. was admitted on the Court Rolls.

## PEDIGREE OF TOWER AND HALE.

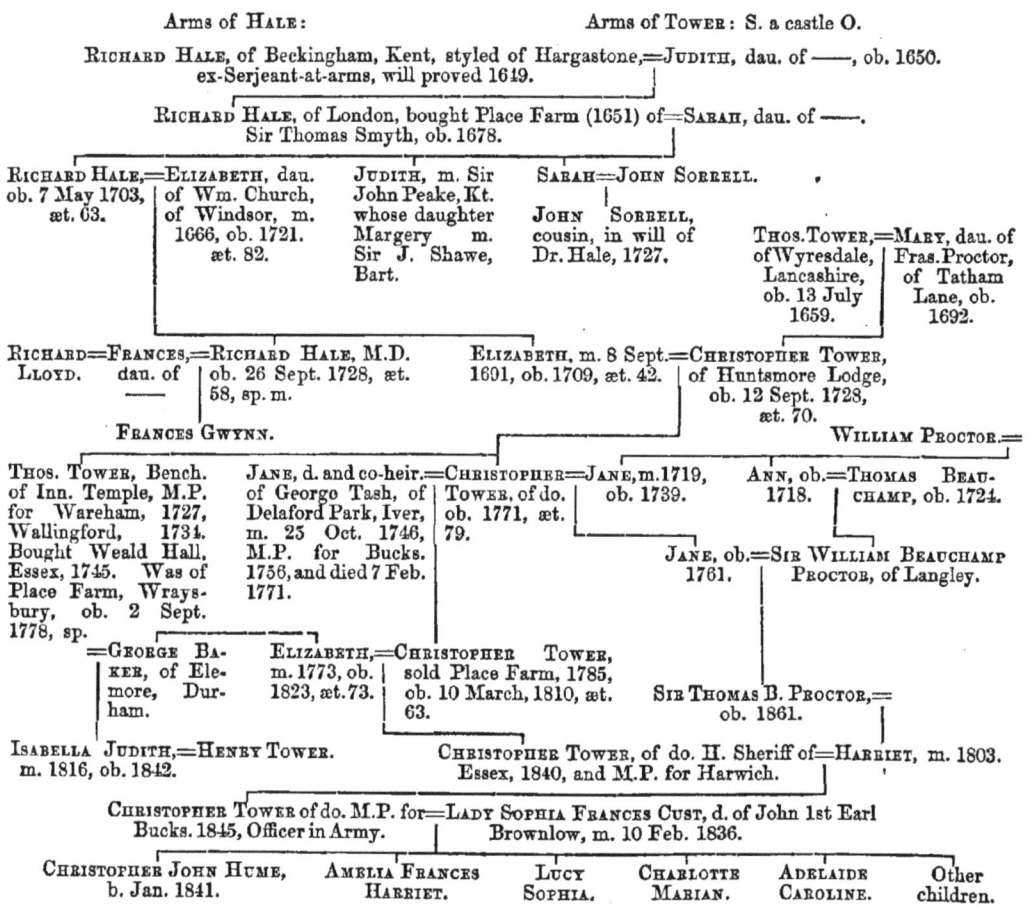

There is also a licence, 1747, to demise the Bridge Lands, Wraysbury, to Thomas Tower, Esq. and others for 21 years. In an indenture tripartite 18th January 1779, there is a detail of lands and rents at Huntsmore, Iver, and an indenture about the Manor of Farnham and divers lands in Essex and Herts belonging to the Tower family; and in 1825 there was a sale in which Christopher Tower, Esq. was vouchee, whereby the manors of Remingham and Cow (that part of it which is in Langley Marsh), viz. 50 messuages, 50 gardens, 1000 acres of land, 500 acres of meadow, 200 acres of pasture, 50 acres of oziers, and 30 acres of land covered with waste, and 2 separate fisheries in Iver, Thorney and Langley Marsh, were offered.

Thomas Tower, Esq. died in 1778 without issue, and as his nephew Christopher Tower was his heir, he alienated this estate 21st October 1785 to William Gyll, Esq. of Wraysbury House, in whose descendants it still remains.

As we have now brought the Remingham Manor to its present possessor, before we describe Place Farm it may not be uninteresting to interweave here, as an episode, what relates to a family named Oxenbridge who held lands in this section of Wraysbury, some account of which is to be found in the Chancery proceedings, temp. Elizabeth.

It appears that Robert Oxenbridge had a suit against Rev. William Day, Dean of Windsor, in 1572, and who had been Provost of Eton in 1561 and died 1596. This Mr. Day had a daughter Rachel married to Robert Barker, and so connected with the Bulstrodes. This suit was for the discovery of a will and claim under the same for divers lands in Old Windsor and *Waresdsbury*, Bucks, which the Plaintiff claims as heir under certain limitations stated in the will of John Oxenbridge, Clerk, sometime a Canon of Windsor.

The deed bears date 27th June, 1587, in which Robert Oxenbridge complains that John Oxenbridge died seised of property in Old Windsor, in Sunninghill, and certain lands, tents, and hereditaments in *Warerdsbury*, with lands also in Richmond; and that the said John Oxenbridge had died 14 Henry VIII. 1532, and made his will in writing, and that it was not a *nuncupative* will —but as plaintiff had no copy he could not assign an exact date to it. But he believes he devised the same to William Oxenbridge and his heirs lawful, and in default to the first male child born to Margaret Hothorne, &c., whom failing to Robert (son of Sir Goddard Oxenbridge) father of Robert Oxenbridge the plaintiff. Soon after the making of this testament the said John Oxenbridge died, and so did William Oxenbridge son of Sir Goddard, and issue of said Margaret Howthorne. Hence Robert Oxenbridge the plaintiff claimed to have the will or a copy of it, which he declares Dr. William Day will not give, and that he *sedulously* hinders him from seeing it, by ordering his officers not to let him look at the registry of Wills.

The answer of Dr. William Day, dated 3rd July 1587, denies the statement, and alleges that search had been made for it, and that neither entry nor original were in the catalogue or registry of wills, but promises a copy of it if one should be found—(signature) Wm. Daije.

The granddaughter of Sir Robert Oxenbridge the plaintiff, viz., Elizabeth, married Edward Woodward of Upton Park, Squire of the Chamber to King James I.; and Sir Robert Oxenbridge resided at Southampton, and died 1616. The Woodwards intermarried with the Bulstrodes. See Pedigree.

As there is neither fine nor recovery of whom or when John Oxenbridge obtained the above mentioned lands in Wraysbury, I presume they came by inheritance or bequest.

John was sixth son of Robert Oxenbridge of Brede, Hants, who died in 1487; he was brought up an ecclesiastic. By his father's will his son Thomas, Serjeant-at-law, was devisee of the residue of his estates, and was to pay John his brother, the clerk, ten marks per annum till he should obtain a benefice worth £10 a year. Thomas died 1497, leaving the *clerk* his crimson gown furred with martens. This John founded a chantry at Windsor, and he was made a canon there; and in 1504 was presented by the Abbey-Convent of Ramsey, Hunts, to the living of Shillingdon, Beds. It appears that *the lost* will was found, for in it the canon gives money to his nieces, daughters of Sir Goddard Oxenbridge his brother, who died 1531. See Sussex Archæological Collections, Vol. viii. p. 230.

## PEDIGREE OF OXENBRIDGE.

Arms: G. Lion ramp. A. within a bordure Vert. charged with 8 escallops O.

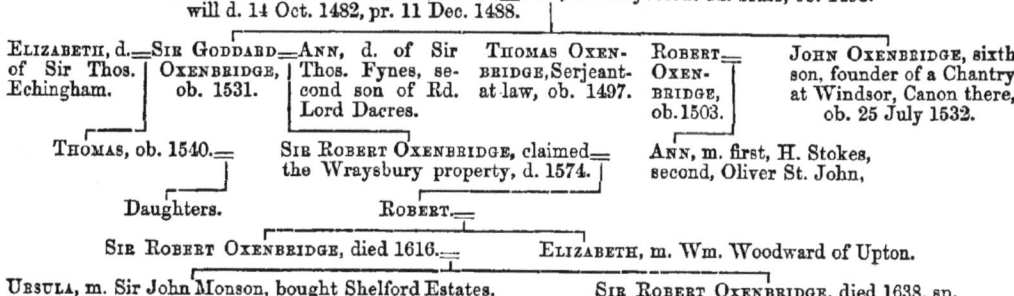

## THE MANOR HOUSE, PLACE FARM.

By tradition, an oral account from age to age, and which embalms broken facts, this House is styled the Hunting Lodge of King John (p. 55), and that the Sovereigns who dwelt at Old Windsor may have had some similar building on this side of the stream is very probable. How late the regal proprietors continued to sport in Wraysbury, is not ascertained, but the name of King John seems familiarised here, as it is also in Colnbrook, where his house is reported to stand at this day. In this mansion dwelt the Stonor family, temp. Henry VII.; and it was doubtless of goodly proportions, as ruins are found in the orchard abutting on the Thames, towards which it may have had an appropriate façade. It was always subject to inundations, and once in about a quarter of a century the waters almost reach the farm-house, now a fragment, and an humble building, very different from the architecture which prevailed in a house of its pretensions centuries ago, then an ornament to the parish and the silver Thames, on whose verdant banks it stood in dignified isolation. As a proof of its antiquity and the quality of the indwellers the windows exhibit stained glasses containing the armorial cognisances of Stonor—the same arms and quarterings in brass as are on the Stonor monument in the chancel of Wraysbury Church, viz.: A fesse between three martlets S. Walshe, quartering A. chevron between three roses G. Wyard. Az. two bars dancetté, and a chief O. Stonor. Three roses G. Harnhull. On a bend Az. three mullets of the field, Wenard. Az. six lioncels rampant A. on a canton O. a mullet G. Kirkby. Az. on a fesse between three leopards faces O. an annulet, Delapole. A chevron between three lions gambs erased S. Brecknock. A fesse checqué ——. Barry Az. and O. ——. G. a saltire vair between four mullets, Hill. These are on the bedroom windows, first floor. The other glasses were probably bedizened with *insignia*.

The House itself is but a fragment of the antique mansion, and it is at least as old as the 15th century, with its primitive windows and curious gables, and peculiar doorway, very low, with seats on either side. It seems in its caducity, rather bent with age and the hastening process of time. The rooms also are very low, huge timbers and some grotesque carving, badly distributed, and very inconvenient for modern necessities and expectations, cramped, cribbed and confined.

The fact is, whatever veneration we may cherish for the "King's hunting lodge" we regret to see drooping almost to decay, such buildings should be replaced by one of commodiousness, for a good farm deserves a good homestead, which with good roads are productive of and ancillary to good husbandry.

It is surrounded by an extensive set of barns, and heretofore some very noble walnut-trees adorned the locality, especially at the back, where three of the finest of that kind of tree had flourished for centuries—of prodigious altitude, and twenty-four feet in girth at three feet from the ground, which were injudiciously cut down in 1855, as it is not hyperbolical to surmise they may have been coeval with our Edwards, or have been planted at the corresponding period with those walnuts (page 51) which embedded in the river formed a circle, and if not quite contemporaneous with the signing of Magna Charta were little posterior to that conjuncture.

It is asserted that an underground passage has been detected leading under the Thames: our ancestors were fond of such retreats, although they were not achieved with quite the engineering skill which marks the Thames Tunnel. Several such passages have been found at Windsor Castle, and evidences of similar refuges are not unknown in antique castles all over the kingdom, where craft strove to counteract violence.

The last deed of purchase was effected by indenture 21st October 1785, between Christopher Tower, Esq., son of Christopher Tower, Esq., of Huntsmore Lodge, Iver, who sells the Manor of Remingham and Cow (Cokke), and Place Farm with appurtenances to William Gyll, Esq. of Wraysbury House for £3150, with certain lands containing 130 acres, &c., Ferry House from Fleetditch above Welly House, with oziers and eyots, &c., now in the occupation of Thomas Haynes. Annexed to this purchase is a deed about lands in Datchet, Langley Marsh, with Peter's Close, &c.

The farm was for some years in the tenure of the yeoman family of Groom, as an indenture 1st May 1822, between George and William Groom, farmers, evinces (citing a lease of 1807) with Mary Gyll, widow.

This lease was subsequently surrendered 25th April 1822, when an auction took place, (that compendious means of disposing of goods, introduced into England in 1700,) which realised £402. 10s 9d; and again under a distress some £446 was taken, which produced in all £738. 13s 2d, under Mr. James Stephens the auctioneer from Staines.

There are two maps of Place Farm, one which belonged to Mr. Tower in 1753, and one to Mr. Gyll in 1787. The farm is in the tenancy of an esteemed yeoman, Mr. Samuel Jordan, an agriculturist of experience, perfectly efficient and cognisant in the mysteries of the soil. He had tenanted Ankerwycke Farm for many years (p. 50), and reaped and merited the praise and high regard of his neighbours.

## OLD WINDSOR FERRY.

There can be little doubt of there having been a ferry from Old Windsor to Wraysbury since the Saxon days, what time the kings crossed the stream to reach their hunting grounds; and that the waters yielding fish after their kind caused appropriate weirs to be constructed, which gave the name Wiers-burg, or Wraysbury, as noticed before, page 1. The eels are said to be excellent, and formerly salmon appeared, but the last captured here was in 1820, and weighed about four pounds. In Scotland some have been taken of nearly 60 pounds weight.

But whether the tortuous flood has kept an even course, is of doubt; for if Cæsar were to return with a full reminiscence of his debarkation on our shores, and survey the current of the Thames, he would not be able distinctly to say where the intrepid islanders gave the legions so warm a reception. This part of the Thames has deflected, and the depth, some 6 to 12 feet only, and in other places five times that profundity, must have varied in ages. The length of the Thames from point to point, where it enters Wraysbury above Welly House, to where it quits the parish, is about four miles, the bottom of it generally gravel and the water pellucid, and fishermen do not complain that it is destitute of the finny tribe. The Thames eel being proverbial, and very superior to lampreys, of a surfeit of which King Henry II. died, according to the *gastronomic* records.

There was also a punt from the Bells of Ouseley to the wharf on our side, and there must have been a common traject which traded to Hythe End. I have heard of only one fatal accident at the Old Windsor ferry, which took place some 40 years or more ago.

The pools, waters and fisheries at the passage styled Ankerwycke ferry, were in the hands of Thomas Edwards and William Domby when the Priory was granted to Lord Windsor in 1540, and in the next century we find an indenture, 24th May 1603, between Thomas Edwards of Horton, and Elizabeth his wife, and William Walshe, Esq., of Abberley, county Worcester, that the latter gives to Edwards £85, whereby he enfeoffed, bargained and sold all that messuage with a garden adjoining, in Wraysbury parish, known by the name of Ferry House, with some arable land lying on the south side, and an acre of land abutting on the Thames, called Wyrardesburye ferry, comprising all that water and free fishing on the *Temis* (Thames), from a certain *corrett* or *ileland*, &c. Appended to this deed is the signature of Thomas Edwards, and on the back the date 9th June, 1603, when Mr. Walshe took possession of the said house and ferry.

The ferry passed, on the subsequent sale of Remingham, &c., with the islands held with Place Farm. I have inserted conveyances of it in 1611, 1613, and the deed of 1629 between Dame Bridget Smijth and William Childe, hence I conclude this ferry and house became parcel of the Smijth estate, and so continued till it was aliened by them to Mr. Hale.

Who the intermediate tenants were, if any, is not seen, but in a deed dated 10th Feb. 1699, Richard Cobham has this ferry on lease, and he sells his interest to John Mitchell, but the parchment is so damaged that the writer could not entirely decypher the contents. R. Cobham affixes his *marke* on the parchment.

It is probable that the last tenant continued in the ferry house and attended to the fishery until he was superseded by one Benning or Bennet, whose widow continued here and took Thomas Haynes into her service, and he, Haynes, was tenant in 1785. After his death in 1817, his son William Haynes carried it on, and married the daughter of Richard Styles, who kept the Bells of Ouseley for 43 years. He, Styles, had succeeded one Friend, and he succeeded J. Pinnock, who it is said came from Owlesbury in Hants, which word was contracted into *Ouseley*, hence the name of the Five Bells Inn. Daniel Sills, brother to Richard Sills, tenanted Hythe End farm for years under his landlord Mr. Gyll, and his daughter Mary, the last of the stock, is yet alive at a very advanced age. Haynes died in 1854, aged 76, a very poor fisherman.

Sir Hyde Parker, Bart., in association with the Thames Company for the preservation of the waters, from the Thames in Berks to below the Thames at Hampton, with Mr. Greenwood, now, 1861, occupy on lease the ferry, with some lands contiguous. The stream is geographically known as the Windsor Gulls, or shallows, and above it is styled Welly Gulls, which was at the point of Welly ditch, and accidents have occurred here and barks have foundered, yet it is not in the memory of man to have heard the " cry of the swimmer in his agony." The situation is picturesque in summer, and the waters are enlivened by light craft and swans, though I believe that the Companies do not mount so high on *upping* festivities—a notch which is still made on the upper mandible of the bird—once of so great consideration that unless worth five marks, according to the sumptuary laws, no one could keep a swan. They were unknown in England until brought by King Richard I. from Cyprus. They all belong to the Crown or the Vintners and Dyers Companies.

The Court of Conservancy of the Thames, over which the Lord Mayor of London presides, is within the counties of Middlesex, Surrey, Kent and Essex; and the City jurisdiction extends from Yantlet Creek, Kent, to Staines. A little above the Colne ditch, on the margin of the Thames, is the boundary stone marking the limit of the jurisdiction of the City of London over the western portion of the river, and on a moulding round the upper part of the stone is inscribed "God preserve the City of London, 1280."

## WELLY HOUSE.

From the Manor House I proceed to another house, which now exists no longer. It was once used as a wharf and a beer house, before the Bells of Ouseley were established. It had been a farm house of considerable solidity, with a good garden attached to it, and which was standing some 30 years ago, and now scarce a fragment remains of what was formerly a handsome villa by the Thames, for it stood not 20 yards from the stream, and was known as Welly House.

This mansion, I presume, or one on the same site, was erected by a former opulent proprietor here, Sir Richard Willy, of whom mention has been made (page 14). He had a grant from King Edward IV., in 1460, of the office of Keeper of the Park of Langley Marsh for life, with Wraysbury, and was one of the yeomen of the Crown. It is not improbable that during his sojourn here, and the necessity as yeoman of being frequently near the royal person, that he chose this spot for a mansion; and I regret to say, that though I have searched diligently for his will to corroborate my suggestions, and that of his wife Dame Matilda, I have not been successful. I find his widow was lady of the manor of Southal and Norwood, Surrey, in 1473; nor can I detect anything of his family, although there is a village of that name in this shire, whence he may have come. It is not impossible but search may be made for this once responsible grantee in Wraysbury, and I add the names of some with whom he may be connected. Milo Willey was incumbent of Streatham, Surrey, to which he was inducted in 1513, and another Willey was rector of Guilford in 1330. There is a hamlet of Willey near Croydon, and John Wyllye, of Walton on Thames, Clerk, held the manor of Moorhall, Herts, temp. Edward II. which he conveyed to Sir Edward Kendal and Elizabeth *uxor*.

The eyots on the Thames at Welly Gulls or shallows were parcel of the Remingham Manor, and a ferry existed called Horse-Line Territt, where a towing path to Welly Ditch is still traceable. These islets are frequent on the water, eyt is isle—cy, found in Guerns-ey, Orkn-ey, and is the Norse for island. The names of the five eyts here belonging to Place Farm estate are, Home, Kitchen, Stop, Ferry Close, Horse-Line Territt. The last is much diminished in size, to about a quarter of an acre on the Windsor bank, nearly opposite to where Welly House stood; and if the line of demarcation be not distinctly established, even this will crumble away and fall to the Crown, to whom the side belongs, lately tenanted by Messrs. Torrington, Cheal, Cantrell. And no wonder the little eyts should be absorbed by the two moist elements—air and water, when the hollows of the high banks perpetually cave in, and add to the bottom of the river what is lost from its ripe, and to which the ferryman often calls attention.

The last tenant in Welly House was one Richard Shanks a bricklayer, and it was then occupied by two families. In 1734 Shadrach Child pays rates £2. 8s 8d for it, and in 1731 £1. 1s, which he rented with Place Farm till his death in 1781. In 1743 Thomas Child paid rates 5s 9d, and 1746 another Shadrach Child did the same. He was succeeded by —— White, a widow, in 1750, and then by one Burt.

There are several ozier beds on the Wraysbury banks to Ankerwycke, where the Thames makes a bend. It is to be observed that here a piece of Old Windsor belonging to Mr. Thompson is thrown on to the Wraysbury side, about twelve or thirteen acres—ozier beds, bound by a streamlet from the Thames, forming a boundary between the parishes—and it is not improbable that the Thames once went round this portion of the ground when the survey took place, and the limits of the adjacent parishes were determined in the days of King Edgar—10th century—for parochial districts were recognised by the laws made in his time.

As the same thing has occurred at Hythe End, and the amount of acreage nearly the same—about thirteen acres abutting on Egham parish, it is a reasonable conjecture that a deviation of the course of waters has taken place, and that the pieces of land which are in different parishes were once on different sides.

This spot commands an engaging view of Cooper's Hill and Old Windsor, St. Leonard's Hill, &c. This saint was tutelary patron of Windsor Forest and its purlieus.

Beaumont Lodge forms a fine feature in its elevation, originally styled Bowman's Lodge; and once the residence of Warren Hastings, who sold it to a Mr. Griffith, from whom it passed to Lord Ashbrook. At his death it was tenanted by his son-in-law Henry, son and heir of Sir Henry Every, Bart., who predeceased his father in 1855, leaving a son, Sir Henry Flower Every, tenth Bart. See Pedigree of Flower.

It was announced for sale, and in 1854 it was bought by private contract; and this noble mansion is now converted into a Jesuits' College, the first Romanist establishment that has had foundation or tenure here since the dissolution of the Priory of Ankerwycke.

In Rocque's map, one of authority in topographical matters, the house was built by Lord Weymouth, who died in 1705. It then passed to the Duchess of Kent, then to the Duke of Roxburgh, who bought it for his son Lord Beaumont, who altered the name.

An agreeably situated house at Old Windsor belonging to Mr. Thompson is rented by Henry Wrench, Esq., and at the extremity of the grounds flows the pellucid Thames. There is the old manor house called the Hermitage, now inhabited by the widow of the Rev. George Isherwood, late late Lord of the Manor of Old Windsor. Opposite to this house, between it and the Thames, is a fine row of lime trees, adjacent to the romantically situated church and cemetery. This place of mortal deposit contains monuments of some curiosity, many of which are shrouded in rank nettles. We will enumerate that of Frances, widow of the famous Richard Brinsley Sheridan, whose efforts in Parliament and at the trial of Warren Hastings " shook the Senate and fulmined o'er the land."

Contiguous to the Sheridan sepulchre is that of *Perdita*, or Mrs. Mary Robinson, an ingenious poetess and actress, the *chère amie* of King George IV. This name was assigned to her from her acting Perdita in the Winter's Tale. She became acquainted with the Prince of Wales in 1781, through her having been previously abandoned by a young and profligate husband, and on her the Prince settled an annuity for life, and then to her daughter Maria Elizabeth Robinson, who died in 1818.

Mrs. Robinson left the history of her intercourse with the Prince, written at a season when the heart deals with sincerity in distress; and she addressed some lines, inserted in the Annual Register, breathing a pensive spirit of tenderness, affection, and regret, entitled lines to him who will *understand* them.

There is also a monument to a poor shepherd, Thomas Pope, who died in 1832, aged ninety-six years, and was followed by his wife Phœbe in 1843, aged ninety years.

Contiguous to the Thames are several villas in Old Windsor, and one of peculiar note is the property of Miss Thackeray (only child of Dr. George Thackeray, D.D., Provost of King's College,

Cambridge, who died in 1850), which, from a small house, has been converted into a residence of just pretensions, and whose grounds are often enlivened with *al fresco* entertainments, and all the accompaniments of British hospitality towards those of her own sphere, while charity to the humble is never wanting.

At the extreme end of the village, near the Datchet Road, intersected by the railway, there lies on the right a farm which has been for more than a century in the hands of the Buccleugh family, and still by inheritance it belongs to Walter Francis Duke of Buccleugh of Ditton. It is precisely at the junction of three parishes—Wraysbury, Horton, and Datchet. The lands of the Duke in the village are few, and are interspersed with those of Mr. Gyll. Across the road there are four cottages in the tenure of the Gyll family, adjacent to college land of Windsor. The ducal possessions continue unbroken to Ditton Park, once the estate of Lord Beaulieu, the residence of the family of Montagu; and until her death in 1859 here resided Margaret daughter of Archibald, first Lord Douglas, and widow in 1845 of Henry James Scott, Lord Montagu, second son of Henry third Duke of Buccleugh, who deceased in 1812. He married in 1767 Lady Elizabeth daughter and heir of George Brudenell, fourth Earl of Cardigan, who assumed the surname and arms of Montagu in 1766, and was created Duke of Montagu, and died 1790. I find them rated in Wraysbury parish books, 1752. The dukedom became extinct in 1749 in the right line, so it descended to daughters.

One of this family was Edward Wortley Montagu, son of Sidney second son of Edward Lord Montagu, the heroic Earl of Sandwich, who, when his ship was on fire in a battle with the Dutch, leaped into the sea and perished, 28th May 1672. Edward Wortley married, 1712, the famous Lady Mary Wortley, whose eccentricities and letters are so well known. She was daughter of Evelyn Pierrepoint Duke of Kingston, and died in 1762, æt. 72.—The friend and companion of Pope, and of Sir William Trumball of our village.

## PEDIGREE OF MONTAGU AND SCOTT.

4thly. 1 and 4, France and England; 2, Scotland; 3, Ireland debruised by a baton Sinister A; 2 and 3, on a bend Az, a mullet of six points between two crescents of the field.—SCOTT.

JOHN MONTAGU, second Duke of Montagu,=MARY, dau. and co-heir of John Duke of
ob. 1749, sp. m. of Wraysbury. | Marlborough, ob. 1751.

WM. MONTAGU,=ISABELLA,=EDWARD | LADY MARY,=GEORGE BRUDENELL, 4th Earl of | ROBERT, | THOMAS,
2nd Duke of  m. 1743.  Earl of | 3rd dau. and | Cardigan, (assumed name and arms | *a quo*, | cr. Earl
Manchester.        Beaulieu. | coheir of do., | of Montagu,) cr. Duke of Montagu | Earls of | of Ayles-
d. sp. 1739.        d. sp. 1802. | ob. 1775. | 1766, and Baron Montagu in 1786, | Cardigan. | bury.
                                              with remainder to grandson, ob.
                                              1790.

CHARLES WILLIAM HENRY, 3rd=LADY ELIZABETH BRUDENELL,   JOHN MONTAGU, cr. Baron Montagu,
Duke of Buccleugh, ob. 1812. | m. 1767, ob. 1828.          1762, ob. 1770, sp.

HENRY JAMES SCOTT, 3rd Lord=JANE MARGARET, dau. of Archibald 1st Lord  CHARLES WILLIAM HENRY,=
Montagu, born 1776, ob. 1845. | Douglas, m. 1804, ob. 10th Jan. 1859. æt. 80. Duke of Buccleugh, ob. 1819. |

4 daughters and coheirs.        WILLIAM FRANCIS of Ditton Park and Wraysbury,
                                Bucks, 5th Duke of Buccleugh, born 1806.

In most parishes there are small proprietors, and Wraysbury is not too large to be in the possession of one individual in a country of enormous wealth, where poverty is said to be *infamous* by Sidney Smith. To recapitulate some large landholders we cite the names of the Marquis of Breadalbane in Scotland, who can ride 100 miles in his own territory; and the Duke of Sutherland in the same kingdom holds land from sea to sea. In England another Duke, that of Devonshire, owns 96,000 acres in Derbyshire; while the Duke of Richmond has 40,000 acres at Goodwood, and 300,000 at Gordon Castle, Scotland. The circumference of the estates of the Duke of Norfolk in Sussex is 15 miles.

It is asserted, that in 1786 the whole soil of England was held by only 250 owners, corporations and proprietors; and in 1822 by only 32,000 proprietary. Such broad estates are found in a narrow land of 37,000,000 acres. The entire empire of Great Britain, comprising foreign possessions, is 8,000,000 square miles, and a population of nearly 200,000,000.

How extensive or what the confines were of the Trumball property in Wraysbury we have no map to determine, but what was left descended to the Marquis of Downshire, who in 1803 sold the lands to which he became entitled in right of his wife Mary, created Baroness Sandys of Ombersley in 1802. In 1767 Martin Sandys and Mary *uxor* unite to sell a portion of their property in this village in the names of Francis and Christopher Hargrave—recovery.

The Trumballs were distinguished in their day, and rose from small beginnings; for I believe the Thomas Trumball, fishmonger, in 1537, was the progenitor of William Trumball who bought lands in Wraysbury in 1631. He was Agent and Envoy for King James I. to the Archduke Albert of Brussels from 1609 to 1625; and these lands he bequeathed in 1635 to his only son of both names, who was also parent of several sons and daughters.

The eldest, William, born 1638, afterwards knighted in 1684, signalised himself in diplomacy and literature, and was the fast friend of Pope, Lady M. Wortley Montagu, and St. John. He became Secretary of State, and is known by his large collection of letters, minutes, memoirs, and negociations and correspondence which widely ranged over literary and political matters. He was nominated Clerk of the Signet, and accompanied Lord Dartmouth to Tangiers. In 1685 he was appointed Envoy Extraordinary to France where he expostulated against the *inhumanity* of the persecution of Protestants by the relentless Louis XIV.—by some called the *Great*. This brought on his recall from a Court where bigotry and malignity strove for mastery, both, like controversy, *scabies ecclesiæ*. His merit was appreciated, and he was accredited Ambassador to the Porte, and before he embarked the Turkey Company presented him with a gold vase worth £60. On his return he was raised to a Lord of the Treasury, principal Secretary of State, and Member of Parliament for Oxford University. He it was who said to King William III., "Do not send embassies to Italy, but a *fleet* to the Mediterranean—for nothing save coercion can bring a jesuitical government into subordination to humanity." In the evening of his days his purpose was *vacare literis*, and at his instance Pope, whom he patronised, translated the Iliad, while the Swan of Thames has eulogised him in an appropriate epitaph. Dryden has also accorded to him condign praise in the postscript to his Virgil. This useful diplomatist expired 14th December 1716; the nation admitted his high administrative qualities, while this parish is proud to own him as one of the worthiest of its proprietary.

He left a son William who enjoyed the Wraysbury estate for 44 years, and died in 1760 (which is noticed in the Court Rolls), leaving by his wife Mary, daughter and coheir of Montagu Viscount Blundell of Ireland, an only daughter and heir Mary, to whom the Wraysbury property descended. She married in the year of her father's decease with the Hon. Colonel Martyn Sandys, son of Samuel created Lord Sandys of Ombersley in 1743. Her husband left in 1768 an only child Mary, who, on the 29th June 1786, became wife of Arthur Hill second Marquis of Downshire.

Soon after her husband's death in 1801, the Wraysbury lands were set to auction, and Thomas Williams, Esq. of Horton became chief purchaser,—and in his descendants they remained. The Marquis of Downshire and Mr. Williams and others by the award were entitled to depasture the waste. The Lady Sandys died in 1836 leaving two sons.

In 1769, on the death of Mary widow of Colonel Sandys, William Sandys son and heir is admitted on the Court Rolls; and in 1787, on the death of William Trumball Sandys, Mary wife of Arthur Hill Lord Fairford, sister and heir of William Trumball Sandys, is admitted, and the following year she surrenders to uses.—Lord Fairford is represented by Robert Mackason his attorney. This latter was subsequently a proprietor of land in Wraysbury. Another Court Rolls entry in 1801 admits the Marchioness of Downshire for life on the death of her husband, and cites the surrender of lands and the homage presented 3rd June 1788.

In 1831 Mary Marchioness of Downshire, Baroness Sandys, and Arthur Blundell Sandys Trumball Marquis of Downshire—indenture cited 29th November 1800; and Thomas Williams, Esq. and Pascoe Grenfell, Esq. for £450; the house of Ambrose Adkins—Fine £40.

## PEDIGREE OF TRUMBALL.

Arms: A. 3 bulls' heads erased S. breathing fire ppr.

WILLIAM TRUMBALL, of Craven, York.=ELIZABETH, dau. of — Brogden, of York.

WILLIAM TRUMBALL, bought lands in Wraysbury in=DEBORAH, dau. of Walter Downes, of Kent. 1631, Agent and Envoy to K. James I., ob. 1635.

ELIZABETH dau. of=WILLIAM TRUMBALL=MARGARET, d. of Richard George Rodolph. | of do., ob. | Lybb, of Oxon.

ELIZABETH, d. of Sir Charles=SIR WILLIAM TRUMBALL, of Eastham=LADY JUDITH, 2nd d. of Henry Alexander Cottrell, Kt., ob. 1704, 8 July. sted, Berks, Knighted 1684, Secretary 4th Earl of Stirling, m. Oct. 1706, of State do., ob. 14 Dec. 1716. died 1690. See a will, 1743, Prer. Office.

WILLIAM TRUMBALL, only child=MARY, dau. and coh. of Montagu of do., ob. 24 April 1760, will | Viscount Blundell of Ireland, cr. prov. 4 May following. | Peer 1720.

\* SAMUEL SANDYS, cr. Lord Ombersley, 1743, ob. 1770, 6th in descent from Edwin Sandys, Abp. of York, who died 1588.

MARY TRUMBALL, only child,=HON. COL. MARTYN m. 1760, ob. 1770. | SANDYS, ob. 1768.

ARTHUR HILL, 2nd Marquis of Downshire, ob. 1801.=MARY, dau. and heir of Baroness Sandys of Ombersley, 1802, m. 29 June 1786, ob. 1836.

ARTHUR Marquis of Downshire, sold Wraysbury Estates 1802. = ARTHUR MOYSES WILLIAM, Lord Sandys, Col., b. 1792, ob. 19 July 1860, æt. 68, unm.

\* Hester, daughter of Myles Sandys, born at Latimer, 1569, was parent and stock of 700 persons, whom she lived to see descended from her to the 4th generation. Her own children were 14 in number. See page 10. She married Sir Thomas Temple, Kt., of Stowe, Bucks; one of her sons was Sir Purbeck Temple. See Horton fines, 1668.

## PAPER MILL ON THE COLNE.

Colonel Williams owns the Paper Mill, in addition to some 300 acres of land in this parish, which abut on those of Mr. Harcourt and Mr. Gyll. Mr. James Pullin rents nearly all the land belonging to Colonel Williams, and dwells in the house known as Church Farm, which from its neat appearance is an ornament to that section of our village. The improvements began here under his predecessor, Mr. Stevens, his father-in-law, formerly of Horton, a most worthy yeoman and tenant of the Williams' family for many years at Horton, until he removed to this farm at Wraysbury. This mill is at the extreme limit of the parish where it unites with Horton, and is in the tenure of Messrs. Ibotson and Ladell, who also hold the Hythe End paper mill as their own in fee. This mill has found various occupants, the last being Mr. George Glasscott, who retired in 1841, after which the mill was leased to Messrs. Percy, Richard, and Thomas Ibotson—brothers, in

1844, at the rent of £600 per annum. They dissolved partnership, and one of the brothers confined himself to the paper mill at Poyle near Horton. The mill is conducted with all the skill due to modern invention, comprising patent steam-engines, &c. at a very great outlay, the patentees being the lessees of the mill, and the *plant* and machinery their own. There are spacious rooms fitted with apparatus for pressing paper, rending rags with steam power, drying, patent strainers, bleaching machines, steam guages, presses, slate cisterns, very perfect, such as taste and experience suggest, while the parish is greatly benefited by the employment of nearly a hundred hands: the proportion between the sexes is about sixty women to thirty-five or forty men. Some men earn £2. a week.

The quality of paper is the higher class of printing-paper for books, newspapers and charts, plate-printing, drawing paper, and for the more expensive sort of paper hangings. The business is conducted with great precaution, and for half a century there has been no fatal accident before the one in 1861, when the superintendant from London was caught by the machinery and crushed to death.

The lower mill at Hythe End is a freehold of the firm, and is worked in conjunction with the Colne Mill, for the manufacture of millboards, where steam and water combine for propulsion. Here are some twenty-five men and boys employed and a few women; both mills are at work throughout the year, day and night, save Sundays.

These mills are recognised as being of long standing in the parish, and are suitably situated on the Colne; it may be that the mention of a mill existing in Wraysbury so early as William I. means this *very one*, for it is remarkable that wherever a mill is mentioned in Domesday Book it is still subsisting. They belonged to the Lords of the Manor, and tenants were permitted to grind only at the lord's mill. *Water* mills is a Roman invention, but the production of the same effects by wind dates only from the 7th century. This is the one known in old records as Culvett Mill, but no records state who were the owners in centuries past, or even the intermediate possessors; but before the present owner's ancestor, Mr. Owen Williams, they were either in the sole hands of Pascoe Grenfell, Esq., of Taplow, Bucks, who died 1838, or his associates, and we find them uniformly rated in the parish books, which unfortunately do not reach beyond 1734, at which period Wm. Pearson, according to the Court Rolls in 1744, was owner with John Crowder. In 1725 John Leader, of Wraysbury, was a paper-maker here, who died 1731, as well as James Meeres. The next proprietor appears to be Henry Bullock, of Poyle, entered on Court Rolls 1746, who possessed property in this parish, and was dead in 1760, leaving a son John Bullock, while the last of his family, Henry Bullock, was interred in Horton in 1840, æt. 70. A rate was paid for them by the widow Crowder in 1761, for Mr. Bullock, but I do not know if they were then corn, iron, or any other mills.

The mill was entered in 1772 as an iron mill, and was in the tenancy of Jukes Colson, paying £1. 16s, and in 1777 the Gnoll Company held the copper mill with the river on the common. A gentleman, by name Mackworth, had property here, and Sir Herbert Mackworth, of Gnoll Castle, Glamorganshire, died 1791, leaving a son Sir Robert, who died in 1794. The Gnoll Company may have been introduced here by this family. Thomas Williams, Esq. of Horton bought these mills in 1790 of the Gnoll Company, and they now belong to Colonel Williams, M. P. for Marlow, Bucks.

The mills have been turned to various uses—corn, paper, iron, silk, snuff, &c. They were leased for some twelve years to Messrs. George and Thomas Glasscott, who were brass-founders in London, and who used them for metal mills. They were closed entirely in 1820, and now they are applied solely to the manufacture of paper, in which they greatly excell.

The earliest fact I have found relating to them is, that Henry Bulstrode, Esq. held them in 1627. In 1758 William Pearson was proprietor; he held lands at Yeoveny Staines, and his will is dated 5th January, 1760, leaving his property to his widow Elizabeth, then to his nieces, Mary and Ann

Aldridge, and his nephew John Aldridge. Subsequently, in 1775, Sarah, widow of William Pearson, was admitted customary tenant with her son James Pearson, but I do not know if they had any interest in the mill. Thomas was son of William Pearson, whose will is dated 18th March, 1763, making William Gyll, Esq. trustee for his Wraysbury property; and he surrenders in 1791 to William Augustus Towsey, son and heir of Susannah, wife of Charles Towsey, of Wantage, Berks, daughter and devisee of William Pearson, of Horton.

Thomas Williams, Esq. who was a lawyer, and a Mr. — Hughes discovered mineral mines in Wales, and these mines were worked with a Mr. John Dawes, a banker in Pall Mall, who provided the funds. Mr. Pascoe Grenfell had an agency under Mr. Williams, who subsequently purchased the mills, and his brother Mr. William Grenfell likewise was connected with the mill schemes. These gentlemen were natives of Cornwall. Mr. William Grenfell of Taplow, at his death left two sons, and Mr. Pascoe Grenfell settled at Taplow, and was returned M.P. for Marlow, 1807, 12, 18, and died 23rd Jan. 1838, æt. 76. Mr. Richard Barwick of Wraysbury, was for many years clerk at these mills, which he informs me were closed in 1820, when it was attempted to transfer them to the Temple Mills, Marlow. The Paris Copper Mine Mills are at Grenfield, county Flint. For further account of the family of Williams and the Pedigree, the reader is referred to Horton.

On 17th June, 1857, the paper-mill, by the kind permission of Mr. Richard Ibotson, was lent for a subscription concert in aid of the funds for purchasing a church organ. The building is capable of containing from 200 to 300 persons. Mr. John Holcombe, the Curate, with the Vicar, was instrumental in this procedure. This worthy tenant of the mills, Mr. Ibotson, was buried in Wraysbury churchyard, 27th March, 1858, and to mark his well deserved popularity the funeral was attended by a very large concourse of people as well from his own mill as from that of his brother's mill at Poyle.

As the subject of the paper duties has given rise to much discussion, and a bill for their repeal was rejected by the upper branch of the legislature in 1860, but carried in 1861, we may advert as succinctly as possible to the interesting question as to the material of paper, and the custom and excise duties on it. These excises were fixed in 1733; prior to that time they were all farmed. Improvement in the manufacture of paper is one of the greatest social benefits, and it enters largely into all commerce, the *great civiliser* of nations, and paper itself is the emblem of those of mean extraction who by art and industry attain a high preferment. The size to which it has been extended is a marvel among arts and crafts. For in 1830, in Derbyshire, one sheet of paper was extended to 13,800 feet, and 4 feet in width—and is a good substitute for the papyrus of old, too expensive and too rare for modern accommodation. Ours is made from linen rags and cotton, though it may be made from almost anything; there are about 150 sources from which good material may be obtained for the manufacture of paper; and every day seems to improve the fabric, because steam has superseded hands, and labouring machines are substitutes for many millions of individuals. A certain German, Sir John Spielman, who died 1626, and once jeweller to Queen Elizabeth, erected a paper-mill in 1558, and obtained a license for 10 years "for the gathering of alle maner of linnen raggs, scrolles or scrappes of p'chment, lether shredds, and chippings of cordes, and oulde fishinge nettes necessarie for the making of all or anie sort of white wrighting paper, and forbidding all other p'sons for the making of paper for the space of tenn yeres next." This curious docquet of license is dated 31st February, 1558, and is in Harl. MSS. 2296. This is said to be the *first paper* mill in England, and was erected at Dartford, Kent.

The imported amount of rags is incredible—32 million lbs., and the export is 20 million lbs. of paper—and more than half the paper made is from rags. The value exported of paper is £800,000,

L

and imported rags to the amount of more than one-fourth of that amount. Foreign rags were subject in 1860 to an export duty varying from £9. to £12. per ton, which is unfair to British industry and enterprise; but France will not as yet permit free trade in rags, so we propose a differential duty; yet the goodness of our commodity defies duties, for success must depend on the produce of the best article. Paper making should be encouraged, as it gives additional *smoothness* to verse and a *new face* to the literature of the country. *Our chief want is not materials—but knowledge, enterprise, and machinery.*

This digression may be excused or palliated in favour of a village where paper-making is of the finest quality, and has been carried on at its mills for a long series of years, and the firm of Ibotson and Ladell occupies a just reputation for the perfect production of that on which all business is conducted and letters written. What we do on paper the Babylonians did on bricks, and on them even *Exchequer bills* have been found in the recent Assyrian excavations, which passed for *coin* to pay Government taxes; while the Romans used papyrus, of which use was continued to be made in the 11th century; for Mabillon, the Benedictine monk, known for his "Lives of the Saints," and who died in 1707, asserts that so late as the 11th century the Papal bulls were written on papyrus. By a return made to Parliament in 1861 of the number of paper-mills at work in Great Britain from 1838 to 1860—the total in 1838 was 525, and in 1860 the total was 384.

There seems to have been many mills erected on the Colne stream, but Coltnett mill was the principal one, and this was the old Coltnett mill on the Horton side of Wraysbury.

The Colne, "whose dark stream his flowery islands lave," is formed by the junction of several affluents, uniting in the parish of North Mims, Herts, and so to London Colney, until it is increased by the Ver waters, whose name is absorbed in the Colne, and thus it continues till it divides the counties of Middlesex and Bucks, running through Wraysbury for a mile and six furlongs. Its name is recognised in Colnbrook, where there is a bridge connecting four channels of the stream. This stream having reached our parish enters it at the north directly from Horton, to get to which there is a wooden bridge, opposite the mill, of ordinary construction; and after various sinuosities the moist element proceeds to Hythe End, and there enters the Thames, while another branch of it passes through Staines and there disembogues into the same waters.

The bed is not deep, about 10 feet at the mill-tail, and varying from 3 to 6 feet down the stream. It is gravelly and would not be destitute of the finny tribe were care taken to prevent poaching and unduly lashing the waters, for at both the mills trout are to be found, the fluid clear, save when some chemical mixture or chloride is thrown in from the mill, which does not, however, apparently affect the fish generally. People in the vicinity of fisheries lament over the decline, and organise local associations for checking the evil. In the time of Magna Charta the free run of salmon was provided for—and this stream is under a similar protection, as is the Thames also for certain distances.

Every 20 years the stream is obnoxious to a prodigious overflow, from rain, melting of ice and snow, and stopping dams, and though a preventive cannot be found, yet it may be qualified by cleansing the ditches and keeping good banks to them. The submersion does not hurt the soil, as the deposit improves grass in colour and fertility, and clothes it with the luxuriance of vegetation, and it does not emit much miasma, nor is ague or any disease prevalent in the village, and our bills of mortality testify that the angel of health presides here. In 1809 was a great rising of the waters which flooded the locality, and washed down the oak paling at Wraysbury House.

The old road to Horton before the bridge was made, 1798 or 1800, at the time of the inclosure, passed by the mill where lately stood some fine and lofty poplars beautifying the path, since cut

HISTORY OF WRAYSBURY.                                                                75

down, and it continued its course along the right bank of the Colne to Horton, passing by Deep Lake Common to the house of Mr. Derby on Welly Common. A brook divided Horton from Wraysbury Common or Green, which terminated at Hythe End.

The old road is closed by a gate, and formerly some of the parishioners had keys to enter through, if they pleased, to use the park for riding or walking to Horton. The entire of the property here belongs to Colonel Williams, distant about a mile in a straight line to the village. The ditches are wide, and are filled with water cresses, of which the London salesman annually gets profit. At the back of the mill there is a very large black Italian poplar tree of near 80 feet altitude, by the cottages, near the ditch boundary of the two parishes, which joins the Colne.

## MINOR HOLDINGS IN THE PARISH.

The waste land or what was the Common, known as Wraysbury Green, prior to 1799 extended to Hythe End, and anciently many small proprietors had property hereabouts, but none quite defined.

By indenture, dated 24 Sept. 1611, Henry Bowrie held sections of land between those of Richard Reeve and William Peters, called Coltnet Mead, and adjacent to that of Anthony Still and William Peters, and in sundry deeds allusion is made to the mill and Coltnet's farm, which may be so called from the Colne, or a person of that appellation.

In this division of the parish is a piece of land about 10 acres, called Gill's Close, No. 298 on the map, in the possession of the Palmer family of Hounslow; Arthur Palmer was churchwarden in 1778 and 1781, and Thomas Palmer and John P. and Margaret ux. were vouchees to a sale in 1819 of 20 acres of land, 20 meadow, 20 pasture, and 8 of common, &c. here. Part of this was taken for the railway, and I suppose it to be the same which was bought, fine Trin. 1693, by Ambrose Adkins of Elisha Gill, probably the Elisha who married 6 July, 1724, Margaret Sheppey, if not his son; John Gill, his son, is rated in 1734. The name occurs again in Alfred Gill, who married in 1835.

There is a tract of land termed Ostnet Meadow in *Wresbury*, which I conjecture lay on the side of the parish adjacent to Horton, and it was disposed of by John Andrew of Burnham, Bucks, yeoman, to John Balnet of Horton, yeoman, by deed dated 8th Oct. 24 Hen. VIII. 1533, and in 1560, George Edwards buys land here in Horton of Henry Balnett.

## PEDIGREE OF GOULD.

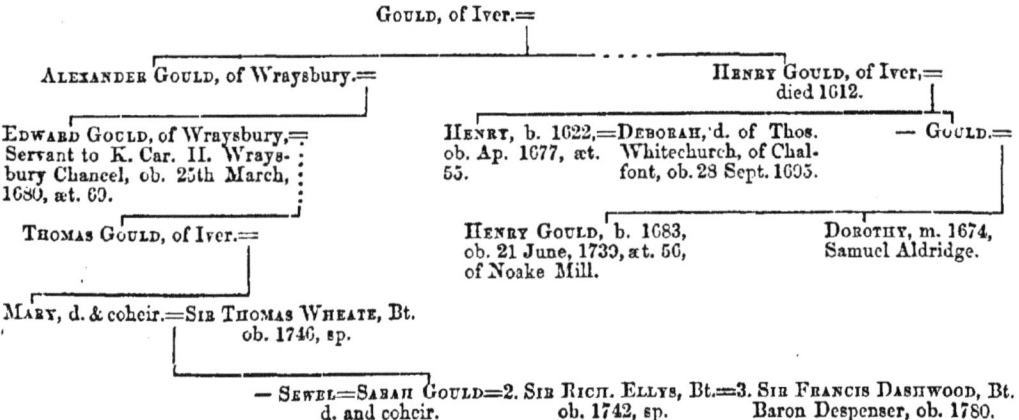

A century later the family of Gould, of Iver, held property in our parish, though I have not been able to identify the exact parts. They may have been residents only and lessees, but they were people of distinction, as the monument in the church testifies, by saying he, Edward Gould, was servant of King Charles II. and son of Alexander Gould, Esq. of Wraysbury, and departed this world in 1680. This family are very old proprietors in the county, and may be descended from Nicholas Gould and Amy *ux.* temp. Henry VI., for the family of Gould was among the names returned by the Commissioners, 14 Henry VI. 1433. The name of Gould appears late in the registers, but all in the lower grades of life. It is only a variety of Wald, Wold—meaning wood.

The family of Bowry seem to be coeval with Queen Elizabeth here, although the first dates on record are 1607 and 1611. A branch lived at Horton, where I find an entry in 1647 of the name. They held strips of property in most parts of the village, but they do not rise above the level of yeomen, and Henry Bowrie is styled husbandman, and as he could not write he affixes his mark. Francis Bowry was living here in 1632, and by his wife Dorothy he left a son, Thomas Bowry, and he one also, Francis, born 1648. He married a daughter of — Edwards, and she was buried in one of the aisles of Wraysbury Church in 1692, æt. 49; he survived till 1726. There were many of this family in Horton early in the 17th century, and continued till our time in Wraysbury, the last of whom was a day labourer. Their names are very frequent on the Court Rolls of Wraysbury from 1725, Edmund being admitted this year by the will of his grandfather, Francis Bowry. In 1739 Dinah Bowry was admitted on the will of her father Edmund Bowry, and Edmund Bowry, Jun. came to Court, and cites a deed poll, 8 Nov. 1738, of Thomas Virgo and Mary *ux.* daughter of Edmund Bowry, son of Francis Bowry, and in 1748 Francis Bowry surrenders to Matthew Palmer of Ditton, yeoman, and a sum of £51. 5s is paid.

In 1758 a presentment states that Francis Bowry of Horton held Brome's Corner, and there felled and carried off 80 trees without license of the Lord. After 1768 the name disappears from the Court Rolls, but not from the parochial registers.

Many old names, either fallen into oblivion or into decay, occur in our investigation of the parish records. Henry Gibbons, on the surrender of Robert Lewin, became copyholder in Wraysbury, 10th May, 1663; both these families were among the small holders. Robert Lewin was admitted 20th April, 1627, when John Sharowe, Esq. was Lord of the Manor, and John Peters surrendered to Robert Lewin; and one yet older is found in the Ledgold family, some of whom were Horton people. Richard and William Ledgold, of Echelford, Middlesex, were admitted customary tenants here 11th Oct. 1608, and in 1626 and 1638 tenants in Yeoveny, and 11th Oct. 1614, John Hellen was admitted as tenant of the messuage styled Gospits and other lands, on the surrender of Ralph Helpesley and William Greene; and on 20th Jan. 1617 these Rolls admit William, nephew and heir of John Hellen, while Cecily, widow of John Hellen, was customary tenant of 17 acres of land, &c. and had license of letting, with 2 acres at Fox Hill, Wraysbury, which had been relinquished by William Hellen.

In 1626 James Haynes and John Pultock were tenants here, descendants of William Pultock, living at Horton, 1571. In 1669 we find Richard Fryar, Gent. owing suit and service to the Lord of Yeoveny Manor, and in 1695 he was a copyholder in Wraysbury. There is an indenture, 10th Jan. 1695, between Frances, widow of Richard Fryar, deceased, Peter Fryar their son, and William Peake of St. George's, London, and Susan his wife, daughter of Richard Fryar, and Edward Coleman of London, and Edward Belitha of London, who married Sarah, daughter of Richard Fryar, for the sum of £214. 10s, and for the sum of £351. 10s paid by Belitha to Edward Coleman, for debts of said Peter Fryar, &c. for the farm called Coltnetts, with barns, stables, buildings, gardens, &c. in the occupation of Henry Fisse and Thomas Snape, also a pittle (little inclosure) behind the said Coltnett farm, beyond Wraysbury Moor, with a parcel of ground called Hore's lease in Horton.

This is followed by another deed 25th December, 1696, between Frances Fryar and Elizabeth, widow of Benjamin Hassel, Esq., deceased, whereby Elizabeth Hassel buys of Edward Belitha, of Kingston, with lands and messuages, a farm styled Coltnetts for £1100, and the deed is enrolled 18th February, 1697. Elizabeth Hassel administers to Cockman's land in Yeoveny, she being assignee awarded in re Peter Fryar, 1703—of which land she died seised in 1712, and John Hassel, her son, succeeded—and in 1719 Robert Prowse Hassel, son of John Hassel, takes up his admission 14th October.

John Hassel, however, bought by fine, Hilary 1696, of the same parties 2 messuages, 2 gardens, 2 orchards, 26 acres land, 17 acres meadow, 12 acres pasture, with appurtenants in Wraysbury, which first introduced Hassel to the parish.

## PEDIGREE OF HASSEL.

Hassel Arms: Vert. 3 adders erect A. Prowse: S. 3 lions rampt. A.

Nicholas Hassel, Deuxhill, Salop, living 1603.=Jane, dau. of —

Robert Prowse, of Tiverton, visn. Devon, 1565.

Thomas Hassel, of do. bpt. there 9 Sept. 1603, and was dead in 1638. =Dau. of — m. circ. 1624.

John, bp. here 1605=

Hugh=

Robert

Richard Prowse,=Hannah, dau. of — Waring. License, May, 1665. will pr. 22 June, 1706.

Benjamin Hassel,=Elizabeth, dau. of — b. 1626, of Merchant Taylors' Co. 1638. Became lessee of Wraysbury House and College lands, 20 June 1700, adm. by son John H. 3 Dec. 1714.

Timothy, b. at Chetton 28th March, 1710.

John Prowse, of Tiverton, will pr. 19 Aug. 1712.

Ann, m. Rd. Cock, of Tiverton, Devon.

Elizabeth, m.=John Hassel, of Wraysbury House, and Croydon, Surrey, will pr. 23 Dec. 1718. license 1 Oct. 1694, heir of her brother John.

— Rowland, of Newbury, Berks.=

John Hutton=— Dau. of Rowland.

John Rowland, of Wraysbury House, will prov. 3 Jan. 1745, ob. sp. 27 Jan. 1744.

Robert Prowse Hassel, b. 1696 of=Elizabeth, m. 1728, ob. 9 June do. ob. 2 April 1760, æt. 64, will 1773, æt. 80, will pr. 15 June fol. pr. 16 Ap. fol. by Wm. Gyll.

John Hutton, of London, ob. 14 Feb. 1764, æt. 70, sp. adm. 3 March fol. by Wm. Gyll.

William=Elizabeth Gyll, of Hassel, b. Wraysbury 1729, m. 4 House. Oct. 1751, ob. 29 Jun. 1769, æt. 39.

Mary, m. 24 Feb. 1759, Wm. Barbaroux, ob. Mar. 1774. He ob. 19 July 1799, sp.

Margaret, m. John Stracey, of Lond. He ob. 1794. She ob. 1761.

Jane, bpt. at Wraysbury, 20 Ap. 1734, m. 14 Dec. 1758, ob. 30. March, 1796.

Sir Abraham Pitches, knightd. 1782, in which year he was high sheriff of Surrey, ob. 10 Ap. 1792, æt. 72.

Sarah, bpt. at Wraysbury, 1737, ob. 1738.

Jane, m. 29 Sept. 1779, b. 19 March, 1817, ux. Lt.-Col. Wm. Boyce, ob. 1808.=

Peggy, m. 1780, George, Earl of Coventry.

Penelope, m. 1783, Sir Robt. Sheffield, Bart.

Julia, m. 1799, Rev. Wm. Jolliffe. =

Amelia, m. Sir Ed. Banks.

Sir W. G. H. Joliffe, Bart.

Henry Pitches Boyce, ob. 21 Aug. 1858, æt. 71.=Amelia Sophia, dau. of Geo. 3d Duke of Marlborough, ob. 1829, æt. 43.

Edward Belitha, Esq. was a small proprietor here, and he also sells in 1701 property in Langley Marsh to Thomas Robins, and he bought an estate at Kingston, Surrey, of Nathaniel Rous, Esq.,

1694. His son William Belitha, was High Sheriff of Surrey in 1720, marrying Mary, daughter of Samuel Hancock, 12th August, 1712. Their daughter Ann, ob. 1714, æt. 33, married Sir Swinnerton Dyer, who died 1736; and, again, his daughter Ann married, 1735, the famous Paul Whitehead, the poet laureate, who received with her in dower £10,000. He was a very virulent controversialist, and, like Churchill, of wit and poetry enough to be a sarcastic bard. In 1760 William Gyll, Esq. bought a messuage belonging to Coltnetts farm beyond Wraysbury Moor for £4000, and in 1768 another messuage, &c. in the same place.

As I shall have occasion to advert to the family of Hassel again under the Rectory, I have added the pedigree. Those whose curiosity may lead further I refer to Omerod's Cheshire, Vol. ii. p. 159; Visitation, Cheshire, 1588. Suffice to say this was an offshoot of an ancient house, the first in the genealogy being Henry, Lord of Hatishall or Hassel, in Cheshire, whose grandson Richard, living 1343, was the stem of a numerous family, whose diverging branches repaired to the adjacent county, where we find Nicholas Hassel, of Deuxhill, Chetton, Salop, temp. Elizabeth.

In most villages there are gentry as well as yeomen who own *strips* of land, and it would be impossible to enumerate all, where exchanges are so frequent, but under the specific list of miscellaneous names of many who have been landed proprietors here, those of Lord Braybroke and Lord Boston are found. The former being connected with the Rev. Seymour Neville, who is Vicar here, and also a landed proprietor, a pedigree has been inserted, and we here avail ourselves of the occasion to append a few descents of the ancient house of Irby, Lord Boston, in connection with Smijth (page 41) and De Crespigny.

The names of His Majesty George III. and his daughter, the Princess Augusta, are among those who were minor holders of land in our village.

## PEDIGREE OF IRBY, LORD BOSTON.

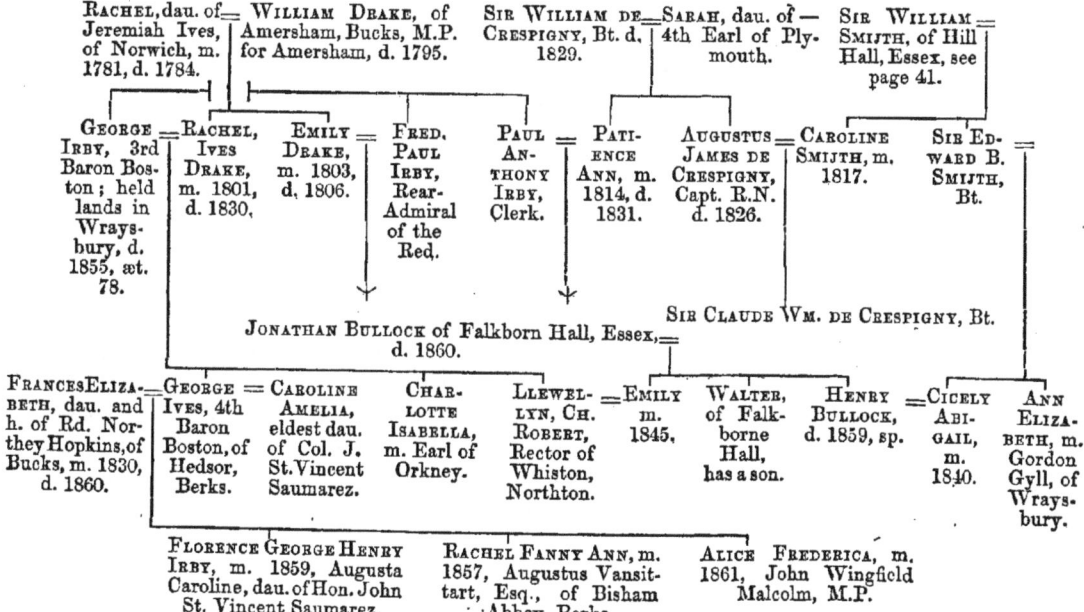

## MILL-BRIDGE OVER THE COLNE, NEAR HORTON.

By the award of 1798, the mill-bridge was to be kept in repair by the owner of the mill in consideration of the land assigned to him. The herbage on the roads to be enjoyed by the owners of adjoining lands, and no trees were to be planted less than 50 yards asunder. The repairs of the three drains, viz. Horton, Wraysbury Green, and Queen's Mead, to be effected by the surveyors of the roads, and a great public gravel pit to be digged by surveyors, &c. The particulars of the rights reserved to the inhabitants over 8 yards on each side of the river are in the 26th item of the award, and the 8 yards are to be delineated by dotted lines on the plan. This is to be extended to Hythe End along the banks of the water.

The parish runs across here by a very handsome black Italian poplar tree of 70 to 80 feet high. The boundary passes into and down the Colne water nearly at the mill-head, and doubling back by the mill residence, it crosses Mr. Gyll's field and so runs parallel with the railroad, which it traverses, and again re-crosses it, terminating in Fleet ditch, which pursues its course into the Thames near where Welly House used to stand.

Advancing from the wooden bridge (or bow, for anciently they were so called, as Stratford-le-Bow, the first stone bridge in England being thrown over the Lea, temp. Wm. I.) we reach the village. This bridge was repaired in 1853, and prior to the inclosure there was no public bridge, a ferry being used. The bridges generally are under the Bridge Trust Act, by which there is a fund to sustain them in repair. We now ascend the railway bridge, and the road has been considerably raised by the Company, and on the left side there is a new station on the right bank of the Colne river, the old station being abandoned for traffic, the station-master's house alone remaining. This looks very well and will be a great advantage to the Horton inhabitants, who come here generally for travelling purposes. The new station was opened April, 1861; and while the expense of the Company has been heavy, the time occupied in making the banks, new road and levels, station, &c. has been two years, and a pity it is that the suggestion did not arise before the land was bought for the old station and the apparatus supplied. The great objection to the old station was the mass of water through which passengers had in winter to pass in carriages, &c. The road now enters for the new station by Mr. Gyll's orchard gate, and it is an admitted benefit to all who come hither, and the eye will be gladdened with verdure, if the banks are judiciously planted, as before the change.

Formerly the road was on a level with the House known as Whitehall, a white stuccoed residence adorned with some 20 umbrageous and lofty elm-trees, not truncated and lopped as usual, which so disfigures the trees and country. The Whitehall House is a freehold of the paper-mill, but some part of the buildings and land adjacent belong to Mr. Gyll.

Proceeding, we quit Wraysbury House to the left (of which under its own chapter), we pass the Paper-maker's Beer house, and then to the Green Man public house or inn, a little beyond the farm held by Mr. Slocock, but bought in 1829 of the Bucklands by Mr. Harcourt. The farm-house is one of some antiquity as its architecture pourtrays, and once the property of Robert Style, a substantial yeoman; parts of it may be coeval with Wraysbury House, while Bowry's barn claims like antiquity, perhaps a *pendant* to the farm-house long ago taken down, styled Longbridge Farm, so called from its adjacency to the long foot bridge of some 90 feet; the precursor of the Suspension-bridge, which farm was formerly owned by Mr. Thomas Buckland the elder, and who died there in

1809. He removed thither from Wraysbury House farm, which he occupied in 1784; the same which is now tenanted by his son Wm. Thomas Buckland, a yeoman and a worthy man, useful and excellent in all the duties of life, and no less famed for an agriculturist than land gauger and auctioneer. He presides in his own chapel, a Baptist one, where he preaches fearlessly the revelations of his Heavenly Master, and enforces his doctrine by a strict moral and religious life. This service he has faithfully fulfilled for 35 years: he has visited the sick, and read to them, and succoured them in their spiritual necessity, when the clergyman, non-resident, has been absent, and this without fee or reward, feeling that the pleasure he had in doing it paid itself; laying up for himself a treasure which neither moth nor rust can corrupt.

Longbridge Farm was pulled down in 1809 or 10 by Mr. Virgo Buckland, the executor of Mr. Thomas Buckland, when the two farms were united.

## SUSPENSION BRIDGE AND POST OFFICE.

For many years this village was impeached, and the impeachment was valid, for having few good houses: but a change has come over the spirit of the inhabitants, and the combined influence of the New Road and the Railroad has induced the proprietors to rear better buildings, and improve the old ones; and this amelioration rescues the spot from obloquy and obscurity. A bishop, I have heard, used to say, "*Where* is Wraysbury, I can scarce find it on the map," and indeed few but itinerants then visited the place. It is a pleasing fact that the locality is now taking its place with others of the more prominent villages, and boasting as much or more in cleanliness and utility. The roads are good, the houses smart, and the bridges are kept in sound repair, with improving commerce.

There is a long, but intercepted row, of buildings from Bowry's barn to the Post Office, one of which is the Baptist Chapel, on which is inscribed " Providence Chapel, 1830," whose chief minister is Mr. William Thomas Buckland—near which is an old ivy-clad house, much improved in 1861, the property of the Buckland family, styled Ivy House, lately tenanted by Captain William Shelton. It constitutes a picturesque object at the corner of the road opposite to a grocer's shop, once the site of Longbridge Farm, and where the Post Office was established in 1847, an accommodation highly appreciated by the parishioners. The average rate of letters sent to the Post Office is about forty daily for transmission, and the number received about ten less. A post-cart passes from Windsor through Datchet to Wraysbury every evening at seven o'clock to collect letters: before this social benefit was established in 1850 the letters were left at Staines or Colnbrook, and a messenger was despatched to receive them. Quick communication of epistles and business letters, with *education* to the people, have done more good "than pen or tongue can give expressure to." Our penny-post system is about to be established in all advanced nations, swelling the sum of civilisation and felicity. The privilege of franking began in 1660, and ended 2 & 3 Victoria, when the present uniform rate of postage was adopted; and in 1860 the incredible number of letters, "speeding intercourse," transmitted by post was 550 millions.

The necessity of improving the communication between Staines and Slough had long been felt, whilst the changes effected in this part of the country by the formation of the Great Western Railroad, and the immense increase of travellers through the vicinity, with the great inconvenience experienced from the overflowing of the water of the rivers Thames and Colne, and the interruption of intercourse during the winter months prevented many residing in distant sections of the parish from attending divine service, or the market-towns, unless conveyed by boats or travelling a circuitous route, the road, being sometimes for weeks together three feet under water, rendered an improved mode of communication absolutely imperative. The funds however requisite for such an undertaking not being obtained, it was suggested by Mr. Buckland and Mr. Harcourt to construct on a higher level, and to raise where necessary a new line of road here, which should at all times be secure from floods. This latter gentleman generously gave some land, and advanced funds to induce others to follow his example, and assist in this utilitarian suggestion.

The old bridge, known as Long Bridge (adjacent to the residence of Thomas Buckland after his removal from Wraysbury House Farm in 1809), being dilapidated by time, corrosion, and traffic, in August 1832 a bridge for foot passengers, 90 feet long and 4 feet wide, was erected by voluntary subscription. In laying the foundation of the piers of the bridge, the workmen, digging through a stratum of peat immediately above the gravel on which the piers are erected, discovered several horse-shoes, which appeared of the date of Henry VI.'s reign; but nothing was found elucidatory of the period of their formation, or whether buried in the peat, or lost on the road beside it. It is conjectured that in this place was an ancient ford. Notwithstanding the great length of time they must have remained deposited, the hammer-marks of the smith were quite perfect, from which circumstance it has been inferred, that peat does not produce the like oxydising effects upon iron which is common in other soils.

This bridge being of little use, it was removed by the Bridge Trust Committee; and in 1842 the present elegant and ingeniously constructed fabric was erected by Mr. Dredge, Civil Engineer of Bath, at the expense of some £500 paid by Mr. Harcourt, on a much improved and entirely original plan of which he has the merit of being the inventor and patentee.

The new bridge is 200 feet long and 17 feet wide, has for its centre-span 100 feet, and was erected in the short space of one month from the laying of the foundation-stone of the first pier; the road over it being elevated several feet above the highest rise of the water, a dry and commodious passage has been formed uninterrupted by the greatest floods. On each of the four piers of the bridge at the base is engraven—"This bridge was built at the sole expense of George Simon Harcourt, Esq. T. Dredge, Patentee." In Dr. Lipscomb's history of the county there are particulars elucidating the construction of the bridge, perhaps one of the most appropriate boons ever conferred by a single individual on the village, which was done at some sacrifice: but good actions are the most acceptable sacrifices.

These bridges though light in make will bear a considerable load and pressure, and this one has been obnoxious to great weight and increase of traffic, yet it stands the assaults very well with occasional repairs of timber, for the machinery has withstood the demand made on its apparatus. The greatest triumph achieved in these bridges is over the Menai Straits, begun by Telford in 1818 and finished in 1825. The Britannia tubular bridge was constructed by Stephenson, and was finished in 1850. These light bridges are much used in parks.

The bank leading to and from the bridge has been raised, and it unites with the level of the old road towards the George Inn. This inn is of old date here, and is most creditably conducted. At it the village feasts are given, and the biennial agricultural meeting is held here under a canvas-tent of suitable proportions. In 1731 an entry in the Court Rolls says, the jurors appoint 25th October for *staking* day, and the meeting to be held at nine o'clock in the morning at the George Inn, on pain of 1s forfeit for non-attendance. Before the vestry-room was annexed to the church the parish-vestries were convened at the George Inn.

Adjoining the road is the residence of the vicar of the parish, Mr. Seymour Neville, who has converted an indifferent house into one where taste and usefulness are blended. It forms a very pleasing feature in the village, with stables and a garden suitable to the spot. Mr. Neville owns some freehold land immediately around it, which extending to the church is adjacent to that belonging to Colonel Williams.

## PEDIGREE OF NEVILLE.

Arms of NEVILLE :—G on a Saltire, O a rose seeded and barbed ppr.

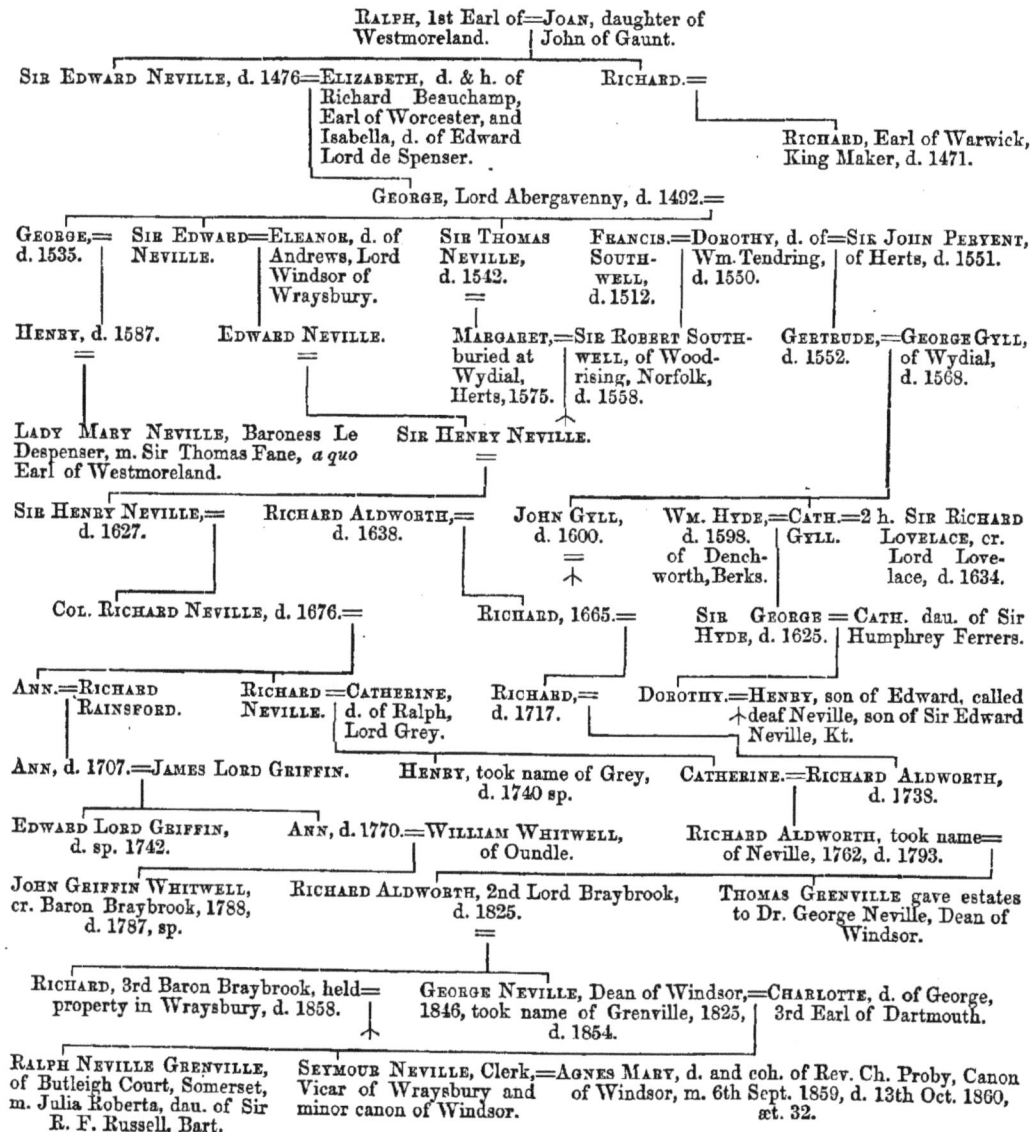

The appellation of Aldworth is of antiquity in the County of Berks, the family no doubt taking it from the parish of that name there.

Richard Aldworth held the manor of Garford Reading in 1547. Thomas Aldworth was Mayor of Reading at the same time, and M.P. for the borough 1558. Several have been mayors, and one, Richard Aldworth, died in his mayoralty in 1593. Richard Aldworth, husband of Catherine, daughter of Richard Neville, was the immediate ancestor. A pedigree of Neville is here introduced as members of this family have owned property in the village.

The new house just completed, belonging to Captain Shelton (son of William Shelton, Esq.) who formerly lived in Ivy Cottage, stands in an open space of four acres, which was bought in 1859; it commands a handsome view of Windsor Castle, Datchet, &c. reaching far into Middlesex. It is at the back of the George Inn; the house is square, built of brick, and large enough for a moderate sized family, evincing at once the taste of the projector and the skill of the architect. It is a great ornament to the parish, and it will be very serviceable. The land in this division of the village has frequently exchanged hands: it was sold by Mr. Harcourt, who obtained it from the trustees of Mr. Blagrove.

It may have been part of the lands held by the Urwins early in the last century, who were admitted at a Court held for this manor, 7th December, 1674. These lands were obtained of Thomas Mathews, and he bought them of James Parkes, Esq., 38 acres of heriotable lands, &c.; at that *writing* two heriots were due to the Lord of the best living or dead goods.

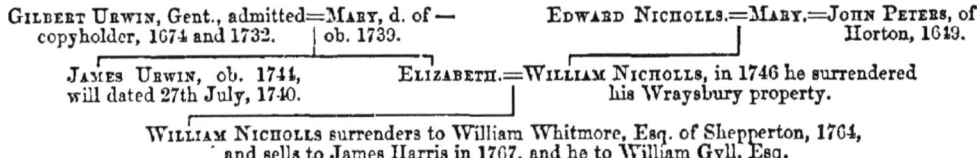

GILBERT URWIN, Gent., admitted=MARY, d. of —      EDWARD NICHOLLS.=MARY.=JOHN PETERS, of
copyholder, 1674 and 1732.    ob. 1739.                                               Horton, 1649.

JAMES URWIN, ob. 1744,        ELIZABETH.=WILLIAM NICHOLLS, in 1746 he surrendered
will dated 27th July, 1740.                              his Wraysbury property.

WILLIAM NICHOLLS surrenders to William Whitmore, Esq. of Shepperton, 1764,
and sells to James Harris in 1767, and he to William Gyll, Esq.

The fair which used to be held on the Common, or Wraysbury Green, in 1799, on a parcel of ground allotted for it, is now kept opposite the George Inn on a Friday in Whitsuntide, pursuant to ancient custom; time has shorn it of its glories, and it is like the trees of the locality, stunted and almost bare of foliage. However, it constitutes a variety, and an element of happiness and utility in the sequestered hamlet, while the show of some pottery and Sheffield ware, with an occasional monkey or wild beast, make up the sum of rural festivities.

Adjacent to the lock-up house, little used, much to the credit of the village, which if it does not tower above the common mark in morality, is not a bad average, is a house belonging to the parish, heretofore the Poor-house, now used and rented for the school, of which mention will be made under that head. The houses rented by Mr. Clarke the carpenter, comprise four cottages, his house and shop, and a blacksmith's shop, with some land in the rear, all belonging to the Gyll family. Another large house, receding from the road which leads to Hythe End, is the freehold of the Clark family, formerly of Wraysbury, now converted into residences for four families, and once belonged to Josiah Monnery, on whose death in 1819 his brother William Monnery was admitted a copyholder. He was a glover and hosier in the Borough, London. There are several good cottages contiguous, especially those lately built near the Post Office; and on the opposite side of the road is land in the tenure of Mr. Slocock, whose practical knowledge of farming is duly appreciated by the parishioners and his landlord, Mr. Harcourt, who sees in the well-being of his tenantry and the improved condition of his lands the best results for himself and for his country.

## HYTHE END BRIDGE.

Returning to the Suspension Bridge, which we again cross, we re-enter on the new road for which public necessity loudly called, and in the suggestion as well as in the consummation of which we owe Mr. Harcourt a debt of acknowledgment. The old road ran nearly parallel with the new one from this bridge to Hythe End, contiguous to ditches, whose frequent inundations prevented or impeded transit, and at night not unaccompanied by contingent peril. The alteration of the road has been of inestimable value in comfort and traffic, its course being continued to the Lammas Gate which divides Staines from Wraysbury, a distance of some half a mile. This road also was raised by Mr. Harcourt at the time of the making of the new road at his own cost, from a sum of money due to him by the parish of £242. 18s 7d. In fact the improvement in beauty and elevation of ground, and goodness of surface, is much to be appreciated, for with slight exceptions at Hythe End under some trees on the Staines side of the bridge no water lies, so that foot passengers may now walk dry with very moderately-soled integuments for the feet.

The time taken for the survey of the road and its completion was about a year, and at an expense of £1000, about £70 of which was raised from subscription in the parish, at which time some alterations were made in the ownership of the soil: equivalents being given.

The new road was opened in 1843, but it was not marked by any meeting to celebrate its inauguration. The entire length of it from Bowry's Barn to Colne Bridge is nearly 2 miles, and from Colne Bridge to Lammas Gate or County Bridge, called Wooden's Gate, some half a mile.

We must not omit to mention a very neat red brick cottage built in 1845 on copyhold land of Windsor, where once a small house belonging to Mr. Trout, or Tout—stood, (James Trout admitted 1765), by Mr. Francis Buckland, a substantial yeoman, and son of Mr. Thomas Buckland, formerly of Longbridge farm, which stood on the site of the present post-office; another ivy-mantled house, adorned with pottery in the front garden, is tenanted by Mr. Thomas Buckland, who holds the Hythe End farm as tenant under Mr. Gyll, and also assists his father, or is partner with him, in his business as auctioneer at Windsor.

This brings us to the quarter of the village known as Hythe End. Hythe is equivalent to head, the *d* being written d and sounded *th*—Maiden-hythe—Queen-hythe.

Here is a bifurcation of roads, the one conducting to the hythe or haven, and the other pursues the route to the termination of our parochial limits. There is nothing particular to be noted, except the road leading to the paper mill, until we reach Lammas Gate, where the ditch severs the Shires.

As this was the only road from Staines to Wraysbury, there must have been either a punt or ferry or a bridge, and we find mention of bridges here as early as the time of Christiana de Mariscis, and the bridge fund confirms the fact in later times. At the period when Ankerwycke House was rented by Mr. Jodrell in 1750 until his death in 1772, there was a bridge, but which tradition says either he built, or contributed to build. In Ireland a distich runs that a certain gentleman "of his great *bounty*, built a bridge at the *expense* of the county." But several bridges have spanned this body of the Colne. The necessity for a new one arose, and after due deliberation, which is the child of wisdom, the existing bridge was completed in 1852, a useful and ornamental means for transit over the sometimes angry Colne, which kisses the banks and moistens the adjacent meadows, planted with the water-loving willow, a very handsome tree if left to nature, and indigenous to the soil here, and found in such number and usefulness that it is termed *Wraysbury Oak*. This bridge was finished at the cost of £260, raised by rate and subscription. It is on piles and has no arches, the base and surface being horizontal, very strongly constructed with four stout iron bars to prevent danger of falling over on either side. It has small piers of brick at each end, which are covered with a white roman cement. The depth of the water here is not considerable, for on the bridge the bottom may be seen, and adjacent to it are spacious beds of osiers, which belong to Messrs. Ibotson & Co., who also own here about 8 acres of freehold land, bought of Mr. Ashby, with the paper-mill.

## FARMS AT HYTHE END.

The principal farm here is possessed by Mr. Harcourt, of some 200 acres of land, with a homestead, &c., and this was a portion of the old family estate. It came however to Thomas Powell, Esq. who married about 1760, Ann, daughter of Sir Philip Harcourt and Elizabeth his wife, who obtained it in marriage, at his death in 1761, and it devolved on his son, Harcourt Powell, Esq., of London, lawyer, who strictly entailed it by will, proved 1782. It has returned however to the owners of Ankerwycke, by purchase from the Blagroves, and was rented by Mr. James Pullen, who in 1852 removed to Church farm near the church, belonging to Colonel Williams.

Under the tenancy of Mr. Mark Westaway, the homestead in August 1857 narrowly escaped entire consumption by fire, when much farm produce was destroyed. Flames first issued from the barn, containing a small quantity of corn: about 30 loads of straw, and numerous implements of husbandry were soon in a blaze; two haystacks of 50 loads were ignited and burnt, with the cart-shed in which were three loaded waggons of wheat with valuable farming apparatus. A hayrick of 75 loads, a stump of old hay, about 16 loads, and a rick of prime old hay of some 55 loads, with the stabling for four horses, and the tackle. But the dwelling house was saved by pulling down a thatched shed in good time, and the combined exertions of the assembled villagers and others, to the number of 800, within half an hour after the alarm of fire was given, in conjunction with the Staines and Egham fire-engines. The estimated loss was about £1000, all insured. The flakes of flame and fire and the occasional bursts from the smouldering ricks had nearly communicated to one of Mr. Gyll's farms, in the occupancy of Mr. Thomas Buckland, but by the praiseworthy exertions of the latter, and the effective working of the machines for the subduing of the fiery element, that calamity was avoided, and the loss chiefly fell on the insurance companies.

This part of Wraysbury belonged to Mr. Powell, fine, 12 George I. 1725. Thomas Ringer, Esq., who married Mary, daughter of —, died in 1722. The widow remarried with Simon Harcourt, Esq., who deceased in 1724, and she died in 1745, leaving a son, the Rev. Thomas Ringer; and the fine with Sir Philip Harcourt, Knt. and Roger Phillips relates to the moiety of some (probably this) estate in Wraysbury. There is another fine levied, Easter 1746, by which Thomas Powell, Esq. and Harcourt Powell, Esq. sell lands in Langley, Iver, and Colnbrook, to Charles Owen, Gent., and in 1786 Harcourt Powell, Esq. is admitted a copyholder on the surrender of Thomas Tower, Esq. This Mr. Harcourt Powell died in 1782, and his son John Harcourt Powell takes up his copy, and in 1803 he has power to fell timber.

There is a recovery deed, Michaelmas 1812, in which John Harcourt Powell, Esq. was vouchee. The specifications are 4 messuages, 2 tofts, 1 water corn-mill, 2 dovecots, 6 gardens, 100 acres arable, 100 meadow, 100 pasture, 20 wood, 20 furze and briar, and free fishery in Langley Marsh, Iver and Wraysbury; and in 1813, 26th March, there is a power of attorney from John Harcourt Powell, Senior, and John Harcourt Powell, Junior, to Joseph White, late Cornet in 10th Light Dragoons. Hence a recovery is suffered and a surrender made to Sir William Parker and Joshua Grigby, who surrender to John Blagrove, Esq., of Ankerwycke, the same year.

In Easter term 1829 another recovery is entered, to which John Harcourt Powell is vouchee, by which 8 acres of meadow land, 8 acres pasture, in Wraysbury, are sold. This is the last portion of property held by the Powells, and it reverted again to the Harcourt family; the surrender is made to Randolph Horne, of Staines. There was a relationship between William Holcombe, of Yeoveny, and Mr. Powell, who died in 1782. He was son of Admiral Essex Holcombe, of Pembrokeshire.

## PEDIGREE OF POWELL AND RINGER.

Arms of POWELL:

Arms of RINGER: G. a bell O. between 3 fleurs de lis A.

SIR PHILIP HARCOURT.=ELIZABETH, d. of John Lee, of Ankerwycke.

THOMAS RINGER, ob. circa 1722, citizen of London.=MARY, d. of —, buried 26 Jany. 1745; will pr. 1 Feb. 1745.=SIMON HARCOURT, of Pendley, Herts. bd. 30 May, 1724, sp.

ANNE.=THOMAS POWELL, of the 6 Clerks Office, will dated 30 July, 1751, and proved 7 July 1761, cited in Court Rolls in 1743, and his death in 1761.

—, dau. or cousin, related to — Holcombe.

THOMAS RINGER, Vicar of Offley, Herts, ob. 8 Jany. 1755, æt. 52, will pr. same year.=SARAH, only child of Rev. John Bower, Settl. 14 May 1729, ob. 29 April, 1743, æt. 42.

MARY, of London, d. 2 May, 1757, will proved 17th following.

HARCOURT POWELL, will d. 17 March, 1776, and prov. 1782, admitted copyholder, 1765.=BEATA, d. of Hyde Parker, 3rd son of Sir Henry Parker, Bart.

THOMAS RINGER, d. y.

HARCOURT RINGER, d. y.

SARAH, died unm. 27 August, 1754, æt. 20.

JOHN HARCOURT POWELL, b. 23 May, 1762.=— d. of Joshua Grigby of Drinkeston, Suffolk.

WILLIAM POWELL, b. 27 May, 1769.

JOHN HARCOURT POWELL, b. 1791, ob. 15 Feb. 1855, æt. 63.

MARY AGNES POWELL, m. 24 Sept. 1856, W. W. Drake.

EMMA, m. 12 March, 1855, Rev. Henry William Haygarth, son of William Haygarth, of Lond.

## HYTHE END MILL AND FERRY.

The dwelling houses are few in this section of the parish, which, with farm and beerhouses, do not exceed twenty, comprising the paper mill on the Colne stream, to approach which we enter a narrow lane, rather muddy in winter; we cross a small bridge and pass some cottages on the right till we reach a mill, now the property in fee of Messrs. Ibotson and Ladell, and lately belonging for some time to Messrs. Ashby; the land around it, of some 8 acres, is the freehold of Messrs. Ibotson, bought of Messrs. Ashby.

There is a small island planted with willows and osiers, on the banks of the quickly gliding current which moves to empty itself into the Thames.

The paper warehouses and machinery are correspondent with the Wraysbury mills, but are smaller, yet the same art, industry, and good management are apparent, and with the same sterling results. The number of men employed on an average is 35, and of women 46, while the wages vary for boys 3s. 6d. to men five or six times that amount per week; the women earn 1s. a day, and some men obtain 30s. weekly. The manufacture here is coarse boards made from rope, and on the waste is found a drying ground, aided by exposure to sun and wind. The two mills are about two miles apart by the Colne, and here, as at Wraysbury, the award map allows eight yards on the Colne banks for passage.

It is not unlikely that this mill is on the site of one of the two mills mentioned in Domesday Book, for a mill once founded is rarely abandoned. In 1755, at the Court, a presentment was made that the watercourse on Coltnet river at the mill was pent up so high by Ralph Carter that the common had been flooded and the ford dangerous, and in 1756 the same complaint was repeated that the stream at Coltnet mill was dammed up by Richard Streatley the tenant.

These mills were demised by deed, 12th September, 1740, by Philip and John Harcourt to Ralph Carter for 99 years; subsequently Mr. John Harcourt said the party demising had no right to lease for more than 21 years by Lady Harcourt's will in 1713. In 1801, — Ashby was served with a notice to surrender his holding, made under Mrs. Mary Gyll, whose husband, William Gyll, had bought them, and which were once held by John Winch, fisherman, for 20s. a year.

Counterparts of a lease, 30th March 1756, between Ralph Carter and Richard, son of Richard Streatley of Wraysbury, to hold the corn mills for 83½ years at £32 per annum. On the 27th May 1762 an assignment between Stephen Edwards, &c., and the mills were granted to William Gyll, Esq., for the remainder of the term of 99 years; a suit ensued which Thomas Ashby gained and continued in the mills. The Ashbys are of Staines, brewers, &c., a distinguished and opulent Quaker family, of much influence and property in that town. Thomas Ashby first appears on the Court Roll in 1787, and in 1801 Robert and William Ashby buy lands of Nathaniel Wilmot, and in the same year Thomas Ashby buys the eyots on the Thames of William Chandler; and, 1815, an admission of Thomas Ashby, under the will of his father Thomas, of 32 acres in Queen's mead; and the death of William Ashby is noticed in 1832, and John Ashby is admitted as devisee of the will of William Ashby, his father, and Charlotte Morris admitted also—fine for moiety £50.

In the same year there was a presentment about the height of the water at Hythe End by George Simon Harcourt, Esq., and an enrolment of the award in action brought by Mr. Harcourt v. Robert Ashby and others—water to rise only to two inches above the floor of the arch near Hythe End Green, and Mr. Harcourt may set a stone to indicate the extreme height relative to the water; the stone is distinguished by letters F. T. and by figures 1832. This was the award made by Frederick Thesiger, Esq., 1st July, 1832. The upright stone, some 4½ feet high, based on another large stone of 2 yards length, is in a field near Hythe End Bridge, on the left side going from Wraysbury to Staines, and on the Staines side of the bridge. The words on the stone are: "Two inches above the bottom or floor, and 24 inches below the inside crown of the adjacent archway, under the adjoining road, is the height beyond which according to law the water of the river Colne and the mill head cannot be penned up; as ascertained in 1832 by the award of Fred. Thesiger, Esq., Barrister at Law, to whom it was referred in an action of Harcourt v. Ashby, to ascertain how far the occupiers of the adjoining mill had a right to pen up the water.

"This pedestal was erected by G. S. Harcourt, Esq., pursuant to the aforesaid award, in order to perpetuate the rights of all parties interested, and in the hope it may prevent disputes in time to come. August 1832."

The lower part of the stone is rather obliterated.

Mr. Gyll owns a farm of some value in Hythe End which belonged to his ancestors, and came to him through a younger brother, Bellenden Charles Gyll, (who died, 1822,) as heir-at-law. There was formerly a manor at Hythe End, but whether in the right of Mr. Gyll or Mr. Harcourt there are no Court Rolls to determine. It may be that Lewin's farm was the old Manor House.

We continue our route to the father of waters, the Thames, to cross which there must have been a ferry in continual ply, a traject to that portion of Wraysbury across the stream, commonly called Roake's ferry, from one of that appellation who here resided and kept with the ferry a public house; the residence is in the occupancy of Messrs. James and Charles Aldane, army-clothiers from London, whose taste is displayed in the embellishment of the house and the grounds which surround it. The freehold is in Mr. Skidmore Ashby, whose ancestor let it to Henry Bell, and he resided in it 52 years; then his son Henry Bell had it, Mr. Ashby also had the eyots down the river. And for the accommodation of foot-passengers there is now a commodious path of gravel laid down to the edge of the water, to which there is access by some steps; and a long wire crosses the fluid suspended from lofty poles of 40 feet high, to which a bell is attached, notifying the arrival of wayfarers. The traffic is inconsiderable, not averaging more than two persons a day, and this does not pay the salary of the boy who directs the boat or punt. Small craft and punts are let by the hour or day by Mr. Samuel Dickenson of the Angler's Rest, an inn with land belonging to Mr. Thomas Harris Brewer of Staines—about 1½ acres. And many are the attractions which induce Londoners to resort hither for piscatory pastime. The Thames is here subject to considerable overflowings, either from excess of water by rain or melting of snow, or by closing the dams up stream;—in fact it is much apprehended that the locks will soon fall into serious dilapidation, owing to the traffic being removed from the water and transferred to railways, though barges full of freight yet navigate the fluid—not however more than two, being a reduction from eight a day.

The depth of water here averages from six to seven feet in the deepest part, except at the weir where it is said to be about 20 feet, or three times that profundity; the current is about three miles an hour, and the gravelled bottom is at low water sometimes clearly exposed a little below the Angler's Rest.

There is a fall of water at the weir, where fishermen most do congregate, while the noise of the reverberation heard afar is not unpleasant to the auditory nerves—*The Wraysbury Niagara*—and shadow of that cataract whose sounds are heard 40 miles distant, and whose descent is 164 feet at the Horse-Shoe Fall: and such is the violence of its rush of waters into the boiling abyss, that it disintegrates the bottom, and it is thought in the lapse of ages that it will be lost in the Lake Erie by annual retrogradation.

Locks and canals are not of ancient invention or use here—the earliest known in England dates only from 1563; the aggregate length of canals is some 2200 miles, and as railways increase their use will be less required.

The family of Kederminster, old proprietors in Wraysbury, had some portion of land here; but their chief residence was at Langley, which parish and park were united in general grants with Wraysbury, as well as being spiritually associated.

It may not be inopportune to add, that the village of Cippenham was thrown into these grants. A famous archæologist and son of letters resided here, Jacob Bryant, and died in 1804, ætat. 89. He was considered one of the most erudite of the 18th century, as his analysis of the Ancient Mythology evinces. He left his valuable library to King's College, Cambridge; and what was superior to his erudition, he bequeathed £2000 for propagating the Gospel, besides other appropriate legacies, all which embalm his name in the memory of the wise and good.

The first notice I have of the Kederminsters relative to our parish is a deed of recovery, 1554, in which* George Freville, Esq. of Shelford, Cambridgeshire, and others, seek against John Kyderminster, Gent., lands in Wraysbury, with diverse other adjacent places. A deed of 1547 states, that John Kiderminster bought lands in Langley of Reginald Cripps and Elizabeth his wife: one Richard Cripps had lands in our parish in 1560.

In 1609 Robert Style purchased some lands of John Kederminster in Slough and elsewhere; and in 1616 Sir John Kederminster repurchased these lands of Robert Style. This gentleman, who had a grant of the manor of Langley, 8th December 1626, founded a divinity library, which had been pent up for a century or more, and was discovered behind the wainscot of the manor-pew at Langley about 30 years ago, and is now placed over the south porch of the old church, part of which is

---

* George Freville (the descendant of Baldwin de Freville, temp. Henry III., and Lucy daughter of Richard de Scalers, of Wydial, Herts) was Baron of the Exchequer 1558, and died 1578, sp. He sold his property at Little Shelford, Cambridge, to John Banks, Esq., and he to Sir Toby Pallavicini, Kt., which was bought, 1625, by John, son of Sir George Gyll, Kt. (page 64).

Norman, with the chancel, and its chapel has a square-headed decorated door and east windows with tracery. On the pew are engraved the arms of Kederminster, one of whom built the tower in 1649, and founded the picturesque alms-houses contiguous to the church.

## PEDIGREE OF KEDERMINSTER.

Arms: Az. 2 chevronels O. between 3 bezants.

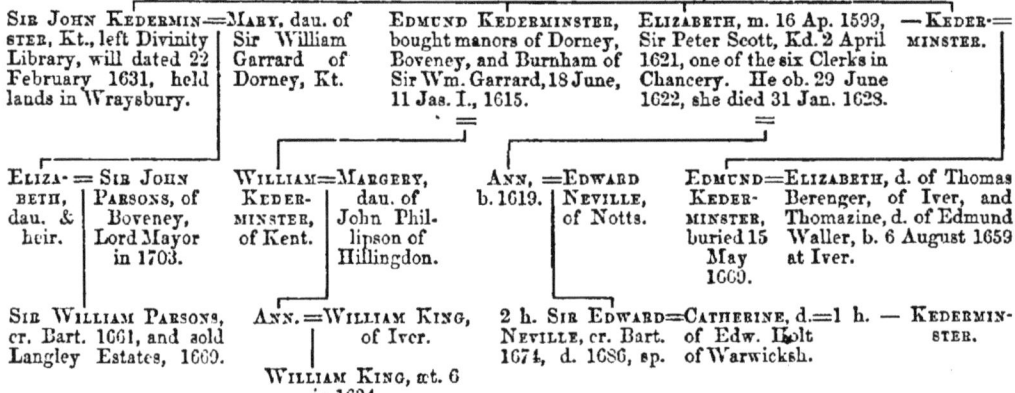

## STAINES BOUNDARY OF THE PARISH AND TINSEY MEAD.

The parish is bounded here by the county-ditch, which extends in a zigzag course directly to the Thames, near to the London mark-stone erected in 1781; and opposite this stone on the Egham side stands a post, on which are the arms of the City of London in iron; and formerly on a moulding round the upper part of the stone was, "God preserve the City of London 1280" (page 67). These bearings were granted by King Richard II., in commemoration of the then Lord Mayor, in 1374, Sir William Walworth, who felled Wat Tyler, and afterwards despatched him with a dagger. This is the city line of demarcation. There is a Court of Conservancy eight times a year in Middlesex, Surrey, Kent, and Essex. Opposite to the Lammas Land where the London-stone is placed is the Colne ditch, which bounds Middlesex and Bucks; directly across the water to the Surrey side is a bed of osiers, about half an acre, which is in our parish belonging to Mr. Ashby. These trees abut on the property of the Staines and Egham Gas Company, where large gasometers built in 1833 tower above the surrounding buildings. The last erected is about 25 feet high and 40 feet in diameter. The towing path here is in Surrey, and continues to the *raised* horse-bridge, which forms the boundary of our parish, and extends to some 100 yards beyond the lock adjacent to the Thames.

The tide is not felt here, and the common belief is, that its influence reaches no higher than Teddington, and hence styled Tide-end-town; but the true etymology is Totyngton, as old deeds prove, and is the same as Tooting, Tottenham, &c. It is some twelve miles from London, and was formerly an appurtenance of Staines, which is the limit of the jurisdiction of the Lord Mayor. To establish this right a stone was set, hence the name Stane.

The bridge here is of celebrity, and formerly the passage was over that built by Thomas de Oxenford, temp. Henry III., for which end three oaks out of Windsor Forest were accorded for repairs in 1262, and grants of frontage levied (page 51).

Dr. Stukeley the antiquarian supposes a Roman road, *via trinobantica*, to have passed through Staines, which was enveloped in a dense forest, part of which was Hounslow Heath: but it was diswarrened and disforested in 1227. That the limits of the forest of Windsor, where it bordered on Surrey, should be as far as Staines Bridge, along the Thames to Loders Hatch, where the three counties of Surrey, Berks, and Bucks meet, dated 26th December 1272.

Windsor Forest did not extend to the Surrey side on the accession of Henry II., as is shewn by a report of a jury of knights on a perambulation made about seventy years afterwards, whose presentment is still on record.

The attempt of the king to afforest land became a general grievance, and petitions were sent to the king that lands should be disafforested. Hence the Charta de Foresta, signed with that of Magna Charta, 1215. This forest, once 120 miles in circumference, is now about 56 miles.

The manor of Staines belonged to Westminster, temp. Edward the Confessor, 1066. It bounds Wraysbury on the Moorside, and has been in the Taylor family some years since. The manor of Yeoveny belongs to Westminster, and the lessees have been in the Gyll family more than a century; the extant Court Rolls of which date 19th May, 6 Edward VI., 1552. The common or moor extends to Moor Bridge or Nott's Green, also Towte's Green, and the stream belongs to the manor, as recognised temp. Elizabeth, and confirmed at a Court Baron held 3rd September 1641. The Dolben family were Lords of the manor in the 17th century. History mentions as Lord here Sir Nicholas Brembre, four times Lord Mayor of London, in 1377, 1383, 1384, and 1385; and on being attainted was executed in 1388, during the perilous reign of King Richard II., when a cadet branch of the royal family, as lately in France, superseded the elder line. The new Staines bridge, costing some £40,000, was opened in 1832. The produce of the tolls in 1803 was £1200; but since the introduction of railways they have everywhere declined.

We now pass across the Thames, and as there are about 12 acres of land appertaining to Old Windsor adjacent to Ankerwycke, so there are little less here belonging to Wraysbury on the Surrey side. The Thames stream is sometimes deep and sometimes shallow, as it was in 1716, when it was so exhausted of water as to allow an almost dry-shod passage above and below London Bridge.

The fact of 10 or 12 acres being across the water at Old Windsor and Egham would induce a suggestive mind to infer that the course of the Thames had been changed, which must be the case since parochial boundaries were fixed in King Alfred's days—who died A.D. 901 (page 68).

The lock-house has been kept by Henry Fennimore since 1843. The lock was bought of —— by the Marlow Company, and belongs to the Thames Commissioners, while the Angler's Rest is the freehold of Thomas Harris the brewer, of about 1½ acres; and the meadow of some 8 acres behind it, called Tinsey Mead, is in the Gyll family. There is a towing path to the horse-bridge, raised about 12 feet from the water and some 30 yards long, with a small strip of land which coincides with the county ditch on the opposite side, all comprised within the precincts of Wraysbury.

Osiers are thickly planted here, and in a moist ground they delight. Some belong to Mr. Grantham of the Strand, London: the soil is gravel and light clay. The meadow of Runnimede, on the opposite side of the road, some 160 acres in extent, is fertile land, and not the worse for its annual submersion from the Thames, snow and rain, that rich food from heaven called water, but it is oxygen and hydrogen.

Tinsey Mead has a gulley running through it, which is supposed to be an old division between Egham and Wraysbury, part of which traverses the yard of Mr. Parris, who has a house here, for the Windsor soap, sale and make, I believe. This manufactory was heretofore, in 1816, in Windsor town. Some willow beds interpose between his premises and Tinsey Mead, which once belonged to Lord Ashbrook, of Beaumont Lodge, Old Windsor (page 68), who owned land in Wraysbury.

It is a mile from Staines Bridge to the locks at the ferry here, and from thence to Datchet Bridge it is computed at 5¼ miles. These locks were erected in 1815. It is a quarter of a mile from the lock to the raised horse-bridge, and the boundary of Wraysbury is by a sort of brook at the back of the lock, extending to a barn or shed about 50 yards up the stream towards Ankerwycke point, at the bend, known in maps as Milson's point.

Mr. Parris' house with grounds, through which Wraysbury parish runs, abuts on the Egham road, and outside on an elm tree is written on a board, "The only manufacture for the *original Windsor soap*—Warehouse, 139, Strand."

## PEDIGREE OF ASHBROOK.

Arms: A. on a chevron voided, S. 3 ravens, each holding in the beak an erm. spot as many pellets.

WILLIAM FLOWER, raised to the peerage of Ireland as Baron, 27 Oct. 1733, ob. 29 April 1746. =EDITH, dau. of Hon. Toby Caulfield, of Clone, Kilkenny.

HENRY, 2nd Baron, created Viscount Ashbrook, 30 Sept. 1751, ob. 27 June 1752. =ELIZABETH, dau. of Lieut.-Gen. Wm. Tatton.

WILLIAM, 2nd Viscount. ob. 1808.=ELIZABETH, dau. of — Ridge.

SUSANNA DEBORAH, dau. and heir of Rev. Maximilian Friend, m. 1802, ob. 1810. =HENRY JEFFERY, 4th Viscount, of Old Windsor, ob. 185 . =EMILY THEOPHILA, dau. of Sir Thos. Metcalf, Bart.

CHARLOTTE AUGUSTA.

HENRY, 5th Viscount.=FRANCES, dau. of Sir J. Robinson, Bart. m. 1823. SUSANNA SOPHIA, m. Wm. Robinson, Clerk. CAROLINE, ob. 17 Ap. 1840.=HENRY, son and h. of Sir H. Every Bart. ob. 1856.

## WRAYSBURY HOUSE.

This house, originally the Rectory House, may have received no spiritual tenant since 1349, when it was appropriated, and the living made a Vicarage. How long the Vicarage House has existed is not known, but probably it was used as such immediately after the appropriation, in which case the last clergyman who lived in the Rectory was John de Melton, presented by King Edward III. and confirmed Rector 6th July 1347. He did not reside long in the parish, for we find his successor in William de Ashley, when the Vicarage was instituted, who was presented by the Custos and College of Windsor as their first presentation, 1st Feb. 1349, and from this period it is presumed that the house has been leased by laymen, as there is no distinct record of a spiritual tenant. We are certain that from 1639 no Vicar resided here, although during the Reformation times, it is not clear if laymen always dwelt in it, but the presumption is that they did, if it was leased with the rest of the College lands.

The Grimshaw family finding the *Vicarage* residence damp and agueish, obtained a dispensation from Archbishop Laud, 1st April 1639, to remove to Langley, spiritually incorporated with Wraysbury.

This house, the vicarage, is now in the occupancy of Mr. Henry Tailor, parish clerk, at a rent of

£54, which comprises the use of 18 acres of land. This Vicarage is the remnant of a larger house, and is very antique, with massive oak beams, &c. and badly distributed rooms. It stands on an acre of land, and adjacent to it lies a field of some 4 acres of loam soil; and if a spiritual residence were exacted, this site might be made appropriate, as nearer to the church than the old rectory house, both of which require pulling down and modern buildings substituted, in these utilitarian times, when comfort means real existence, and existence comfort. Before the alteration of the road this house, which is now more remote, was adjacent to the public way, but by the footpath it is nearer to the church than the rectory house. The high ground contiguous to the church would be an eligible spot for a parsonage, and exchanges might be made to secure this *desideratum*.

The Rectory House stands on the glebe a short distance from the Colne on the right bank, from which it is divided by a brook and meadow, and is held by the present lessee as parcel of the Rectory, he having on lease for the usual terms the great tithes, comprising also the house.

When this residence was erected no data are found, unless the Chapter Records supply them, and as they are private records for the use of the corporation, the Chapter Clerks think they can afford no accommodation for an insight to guide the inquirer in this piece of reasonable curiosity. The usual covenants are that the house should be kept tenantable, &c. and that in it a suitable reception should be afforded for man and beast, should the Dean and his reverend company visit the parish for spiritual purposes.

It is strongly built, as far as walls go, but *tempus edax rerum* has visited it with corroding influences. The date may be of the time of Henry VIII. or later, but its outward and visible signs indicate no architectural triumphs. The rooms are small, low, and most inconveniently distributed, and little else than superseding it by a better could raise the residence to the level of modern comfort.

The garden at the side of the house is of a conventual character, enclosed within four walls, but on the western part outside the wall is one agreeable promenade in summer, at the *terminus* of which was a very noble and expansive chestnut tree, now in decay, still it rears its high top and makes a noise when "it is fretted with the gusts of heaven." It may be coeval with Henry VIII. or Elizabeth. Its bulk and circumference is 18 feet at 5 feet from the ground, and in its day of glory, proud in its altitude and foliage it towered aloft a noble object in the villages, as well as from the surrounding heights. This retreat commands a view of the church, of Ankerwycke, and Cooper's Hill; the soil very fair, and in the garden is a fruit-bearing mulberry tree, now white and bald with dry antiquity, and probably planted when these trees were first introduced, temp. James I. into our isle; the fruit comes very late, but it is good, large and sweet, and like good wine, is mellowed by time.

Contiguous to the Rectory House stands a farm-house tenanted by Mr. Wm. Thomas Buckland, successor of his father, who lived there in 1784, but its nearness is not so pleasant to the moderns as to our ancestors, when bad roads precluded frequent travelling, even for provisions—what time a quagmire was to be avoided, and limbs and vehicles equally suffered by the temerarious experiment of an expedition for pleasure or necessity. In a family dwelling-house we now covet the balmy air laden with fragrance from flowers of every hue, rather than the *aroma* of a farm however savoury to agriculturists.

It was a custom heretofore to have bowling-greens where we now find lawns, and this peculiarity marks the ground opposite the façade to this house. The old doorway to the entrance contiguous to the farm has been changed, for the spot where three roads converge, and an ivy mantled wall of considerable age, as appears by its caducity, bounds a very ancient orchard, part of which is the freehold of Mr. Gyll, with half of the united barns which lie beyond the walls. A chestnut tree, lately planted, is opposite to the carriage entrance, which one day in its leafy expansion it may adorn and protect.

## LESSEES OF THE RECTORY AND COLLEGE LANDS.

We have shewn that the impropriation took place in 1349, and there is little doubt but that the Rectory House and the great tithes went together. Dr. Lipscomb asserts that a lease had been prior to this date in the hands of Richard Fitzwalter, under the Abbey of Gloucester, if so, he may have been kin to Robert Fitzwalter, one of the rebellious barons against King John, styled Marshal of the army of God and Holy Church. He was son of Robert, and grandson of Richard FitzGilbert, whose son Gilbert FitzRichard, of Clare, had a daughter Margaret, wife of William Gernon, who took the surname of *Mountfitchet,* and held lands in Wraysbury, 1125. His son Sir Gilbert founded Ankerwycke Priory (page 27). But at the time of the appropriation (of which more under ecclesiastical matters) the lessee was Ralph Goodyear—a very old name in England—the principal family lived at Poynton, Cheshire, and Sir Richard Goodyear married Ann, daughter of Thomas Clare, son of — Earl of Gloucester, descendant of the above Gilbert FitzRichard Clare.

It may be true that both these persons were lessees here, and, if so, it is singular that in the time of King Henry VIII. the very same names should occur as lessees—for Richard Fitzwater, Gent. appears in a deed of indenture and recovery, 4th February, 29 Hen.VIII. 1537, and buys of Thomas Archer and Ann his wife, lands in Wraysbury—11 acres—and it is recorded in the Exchequer Rolls that Richard was to pay £26. for the same in sundry instalments, and to enter possession one month following the date of the writing.

As all the names of intermediate lessees are lost, I shall presume that Ralph Goodyear was the next in order, and that he held *Shaw* Manor in Old Windsor in 1548, which he sold to William Harvey, who was Norroy King of Arms in 1549, and died in 1566. This manor was also in the Aldworth family (page 83). There is a deed in 1562 whereby Robert Bedyll buys property of Jocomina Goodyear, in Langley Marsh and Iver; and a Michael, son of Michael Goodyeare, is buried in Horton Church in 1593, and several entries of this name follow. This Michael was interred 1603.

It is probable that this Ralph was father of Thomas Goodyeare, of Old Windsor, who had a grant of arms 19th October 1575, and his children, viz., Jane was married at Windsor 1564 to Reginald Pilgrim, and Elizabeth in 1665 to Thomas Goade, of Horton. Another, Ann Goodyear, married 1595 to Thomas W. Norwode. The family of this patronymic and of Herefordshire were created baronets 1707, the last of which house, Sir John Dinely Goodyere, was a Poor Knight of Windsor, and was buried on the south side of St. George's Chapel in 1809, æt. 80. He was a man of great singularity, and of him some portraits and sketches are given, which appear from their grotesqueness to be caricatures—the pencil may be as graphic as the pen, if we look at the famous caricatures for which England is celebrated—an art which took its rise in the days of Sir Robert Walpole. The present representative of a branch of this family is George Dinely Goodyear, of Barton House, Gloucester, son of the Rev. George Dinely Goodyear, and his wife Harriet, only child of Thomas Chudleigh Sanders, and Susan, daughter of William Gyll, Esq. of Wraysbury House.

The next lessee was Walter Prunes in 1654, and how long he remained I cannot say, but he retired to Langford, Berks, where he was interred. His will was proved in London, 1st March 1594, by his widow, Mary daughter of — Pleydell, of the same county, to whom he left his fortune for life, then to his niece Alice Baker. His arms are given (which he mentions in his will) as of *Wraysbury,* and in Harl. MSS. 1391, fol. 139. Visitation Bucks, 1566.

O. lion ramp. Az. on a chief of the last an ostrich feather of the first, between two others A.

## BIOGRAPHICAL NOTICE OF SIR DUDLEY CARLETON.

We now come to a gentleman of note in his day, who was lessee in 1621, of the college lands and of Wraysbury House. The name of Carleton is of antiquity in Lincolnshire, temp. Edward I. The predecessor of the London branch was Thomas Carleton, citizen, merchant tailor and broderer of London, who was a benefactor to that Company, and whose will bears date 20th Dec. 1382.

Sir Dudley Carleton was created Viscount Dorchester in 1628, and died 1631 without issue male, when his house became extinct. Born in 1573, he became an eminent statesman, his life and energies being concentrated on diplomacy and administrative occupations. He went to France as secretary to our Ambassador there in 1600; while in Parliament he was considered at once an efficient member and an able orator. He was said to have been implicated in the Gunpowder Plot, but on investigation his innocence was established. In 1610 the Sovereign knighted him, and he was accredited to the Embassy at Venice, and this office he so well discharged that he was similarly appointed to the States General of Holland, sitting in the Council of State for the United Provinces. These and many recognized services induced Charles I. to call him to the Upper House as Baron Carleton in 1626, after which he was again accredited to France on an extraordinary mission. Here he gave such satisfaction that he was again promoted a step in the peerage, the highest honour he was destined to attain, and was styled in his patent of 1628, Viscount Dorchester. The Sovereign now entrusted him with the seals of Secretary of State, and he superseded Lord Conway, (of whom page 60). This worthy peer was considered a most able foreign minister, and better acquainted with external affairs than most of his contemporaries.

The stirring and woful times of King Charles I. came on, owing to an over-weening assumption and a false conception of constitutional prerogatives in the sovereign. Anxiety and public solicitude about the future arose in the mind of Carleton, like to him of whom Milton speaks (Sir James Ley, a man of eminence in the law, who was raised to the coif, and eventually created Earl of Marlborough, 1625, and died 1628. In 1679 the Earldom became extinct.)

> "That good Earl, once President
> Of England's Council and her Treasury,
> Who lived in both unstained with gold or fee;
> And left them both, more in himself content
> Till sad the breaking of that Parliament
> Broke him."

No doubt existing convulsions of State, and the forecast of his active mind anticipating worse—"present fears were less than horrible imaginings"—aggravated a natural infirmity, the stone, styled *morbus studentium*, (and like consumption or atrophy, *opprobrium medicorum*), until Baron Heurteloup recently introduced the science of lithotrophy, which assuages its pangs or cures it. This was the proximate cause of his death, which took place 15th February 1631, in his 58th year. His body was honoured with interment in Westminster Abbey's holy precincts, "with ashes which make it holier."

Both Anthony Wood and Horace Walpole have given a summary of his works, comprising Letters, &c. published in 1757 by the Earl of Hardwicke, who has done justice to his character. We here append a pedigree of Carleton in union with others connected with Wraysbury.

# HISTORY OF WRAYSBURY.

## PEDIGREE OF CARLETON.

Arms, A on a bend S, 3 mascles of the field.

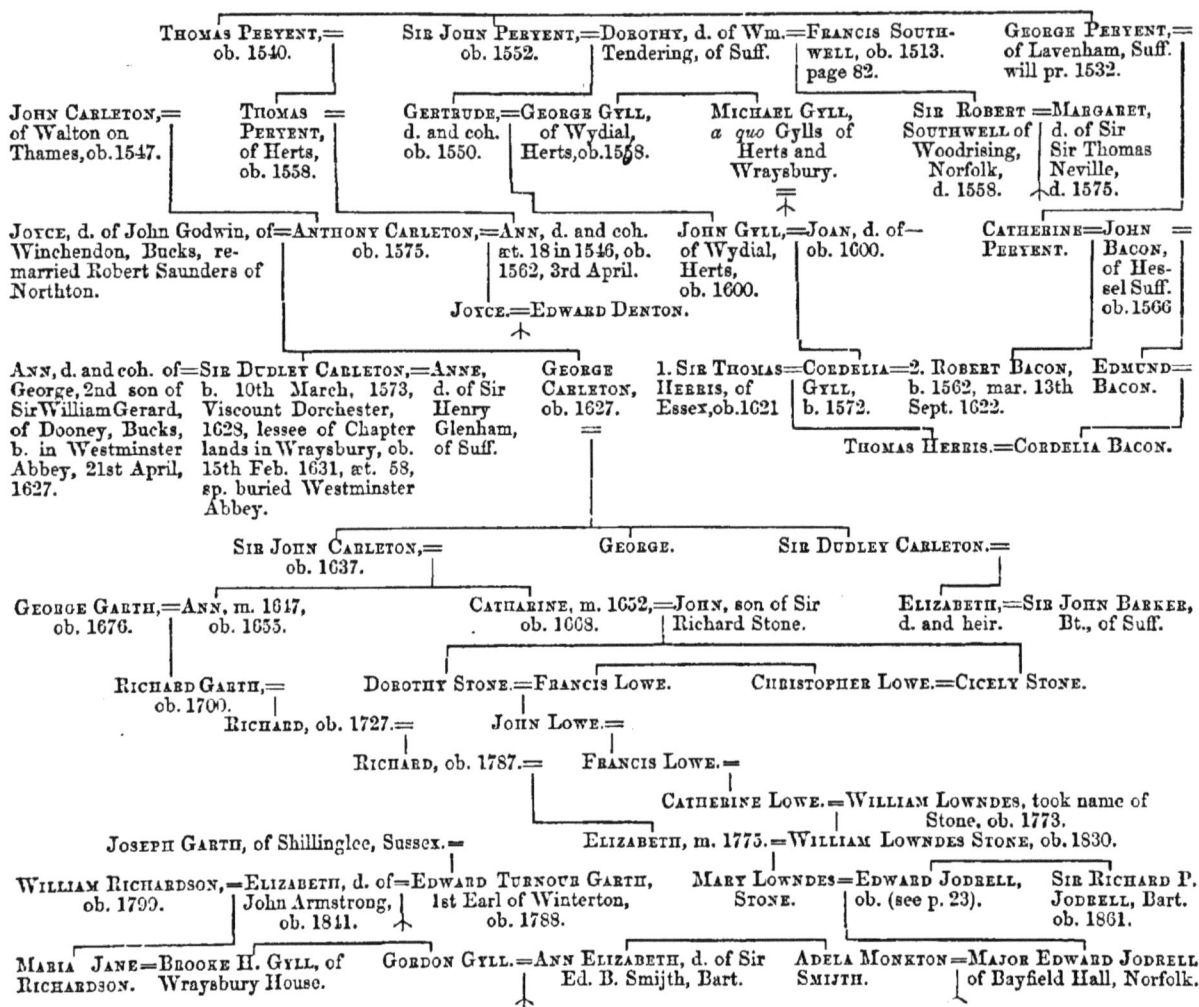

## CONTINUATION OF LESSEES.

The lesseeship of the College lands came now into the hands of John Sharowe, who was Lord of the Manor in 1627 to whom I have adverted, page 18. He died in 1631, and his widow Mary, who remarried Sir Andrew King, had a lease for 21 years, dating to December 1635. The lesseeship had been renewed in 1629, in the name of John Whistler, of the family of Goddington, Oxon. He afterwards lived at Windsor, and his will was proved by his son, John Whistler, of Gray's Inn, London, 21st March, 1644, leaving a son Thomas, and a daughter married to Nathaniel Hagthorne, of Cookham, Berks.

Henry Beckingham follows next, whose lease with the Chapter dates 20th April, 1663, for 21 years, and during his tenure of it a lawsuit arose, dated Monday, 17th November, 1673, between Sir Andrew King of Ankerwycke, and Henry Smith, exhibiting a complaint, and stating that the Dean and Canons were seised of the Rectory and Parsonage, and glebe, &c. with tithes and all manner of profits, commodities, and that by deed of indenture these were granted to Henry Beckingham, Esq. for 21 years, and that his yearly rents were reserved in trust, and that one William Pinchon should have the use and rents, and that H. Beckingham, by indenture, 16th July, 1672, assigned to Sir Andrew King, Kt., all the said tithes for the remainder of his term, the tithes being worth £20. per annum, and that the defendant Smith evaded paying these tithes to Sir Andrew: that the Chapter had demised the tithes and Rectory House to Mary, widow of John Sharrow, gentleman (who died 1634), by indenture, 10th December, 1635, for 21 years at £19. per annum; and that afterwards Sir Andrew intermarried with Mary Sharowe, and that then he and his wife by indenture, 5th December, 1658, assigned the site of the rectory and glebe lands to Henry Smith, in trust for William Pinchon, gentleman, under whom the defendant now claims, in consideration of £260. (Page 20.)

The glebe lands were to be enjoyed tithe free, plaintiff buying the reversion of the premises also in the name of John Bland, of some persons authorised in the late times, and affirming that the glebe lands were to be tithe free, did for £1360 paid to William Pinchon, gentleman, convey the site and lands to William Pinchon, his heirs and assigns, and they were so enjoyed. That Sir Andrew King and William Pinchon, addressing themselves to the Chapter, required separate leases, but it was refused, the College granting only to one party at a time. The deed mentions land to the amount of 15 acres, a meadow, 20 acres arable, and 20 pasture. The tithes of them were worth £4. a year. William Pinchon also addresses the Chapter to have the whole lands and tithes, he in the meantime paying *pro tanto*.

This difference caused another suit in the Exchequer Court, in which articles, of date 15th May, 1661, were cited, and it was agreed that plaintiff should bring his debt against the defendant Smith, in the Court of Pleas, according to the statute of King Edward VI. for not setting forth his tithes in kind, value £4. The case to be heard at the next assizes. (See Martin's Index, Deed Repository). There are deeds of fine, 1653, between Nicholas Pinchon, gentleman, and Andrew King, Esq., and also between the former and John Bland, Esq., of Wraysbury, (page 20). Having found no further prosecution of the suit, perhaps the litigants settled it between themselves.

John Topham next resided at Wraysbury Rectory House, and he leased the tithes in 1679 to 1707 inclusive. In 1689 this gentleman buys land of John Pinchon, Sen., Esq., and others in our parish; and this is followed by another deed of the same date between Richard Fryar and John Pinchon, gentleman, in Wraysbury.

This Mr. Topham I take to be he who married at Windsor in 1655, Joan, daughter of — Stoughton, Esq. He dwelt at and had property in Windsor, but I have not found his will. One Richard Topham gave £100 to the Free School at Windsor, a branch of the same who dwelt at Clewer.

The next lessee is a widow lady, as in the case of Mary Sharowe, and if we write our annals true, as reported to me by the late Mr. William de St. Croix, Chapter Clerk, to whom I am beholden for his general and useful courtesy, Elizabeth, widow of Benjamin Hassel, deceased, leased these lands and the house, 20th June, 1707, and here she dwelt till her death in 1714, when the remainder of the lease devolved on her only son John Hassell, Esq., who did not long survive his mother and predecessor here, dying in 1718. But as this property could be held on a combined lease, the name of John Rowland was inserted after the expiry of the first Hassel lease in 1721, and so continued till 1742. There was a relationship between the Hassels and Rowlands, and the former then inhabited Wraysbury House, as the rate book and the parish registers demonstrate.

Mr. Rowland was originally of Newbury, Berks, but dwelt in London, and his sister married John Hutton and had a son John, and a daughter Elizabeth, who was wife of Robert Prowse Hassel, as is shewn in the Pedigree of Hassel (page 77). There was a connection with John Boulter, Esq. whose will was proved in 1736. Mr. Rowland died after the close of his lease, 27th January, 1744, and his will was proved, 1745, by his nephew, John Hutton; by the will he gives to the poor of the parish of Wraysbury £5.

From this the leases of the Rectory House were renewed in the name of Robert Prowse Hassel, Esq., who dwelt here, although he had a very handsome mansion at Croydon, of which mention is made in his will and other documents; and he had a picture drawn in Indian ink of the Rectory in 1724, still extant, the architectural points of the building, the trees, and garden being identical with those at the present writing. "*Rectory House of Raisbury*, near Windsor and Staines, belonging to Mr. Hassel, taken 1724, Charles Pearce fecit, 1724."

This gentleman was admitted, on the death of his father John, in 1718, to the Copy Rolls of Yeoveny, for the estate he held, though he seems to have had right there in 1712, and homage was paid in 1730, and he is rated in 1734 in Wraysbury. From this period to his death he continued to make the Rectory his head-quarters, and on the renewal of the lease in 1752, the name of his son-in-law, William Gyll, Esq. was associated with his, since which period all the leases have been granted to members of this latter family. Mr. Hassel, by will dated 27th October 1759, directs all his freehold and copyhold messuages, lands, &c. in or near Wraysbury to be sold, and to be equally divided between his four daughters and co-heirs. The eldest of whom Elizabeth, married William Gyll, Esq., and she succeeding to her purparty or 4th share of the estate, her husband purchased the interests of the remaining co-heirs, and took up his permanent residence in the parish; and he enters his admission on the Court Rolls in 1760; was trustee of the Bridge Church lands in 1761. He augmented his possessions in this locality, but having another residence near London he then let Wraysbury House to John Harcourt, Esq. from 1764 to 1773. He returned to it, and again let it in 1781 to Richard Stackpole, Esq. who was made by Louis XVIII. Baron Stackpole in France, and his son, Richard Fitz-George, who died 1848, was created a Marquis, and then Duke of Stackpole. He married Elizabeth, eldest daughter of Major Francis Tulloch, of Tanachie, Scotland, who left surviving male issue, Colonel Thomas Tulloch, 42nd Highlanders.

In the year 1788 Mr. Gyll was chosen to the highest civic honours of the City of London, and he attended in 1789 his Majesty King George III. on his visit to St. Paul's Church to return thanks for his restoration to health, and a patent was prepared and announced in all the public papers, 18th and 19th April 1789, to create him a Baronet, which is usual when the King honours the City on any great occasion, but the proffered advancement was not accepted for family reasons.* Nor was the claim revived until his son William Gyll, Captain 2nd Life Guards, who had in 1803 at his own expense raised two troops of cavalry on the threat of invasion, solicited the favour which his father had injudiciously declined, when he too unfortunately died prematurely, and the expected honour has not since been conferred.

William Gyll, Esq. was a London merchant, and was Treasurer of Christ's Hospital, to which

* His wife Mary induced him to forego the honour, because there was then a son by his first wife, who only survived a few years and died unmarried. Women may be very affectionate, but not always discreet. They have a fibre more in their hearts and a cell less in their brains than men.

institution he liberally contributed, having nearly rebuilt the Grammar School at the College of Hertford in 1793.

He endowed the town of Maidstone, his name being on the list of benefactors inscribed in the church. He was also a benefactor to Wraysbury during his life, and at his death. He had been associated in business in London with his great uncle James Brooke, Esq., who was Sheriff of Kent, 1731. Having passed a life of activity, industry and honour, and being in his 75th year, he died 26th March 1798, honoured and lamented by all who knew him, and justly venerated by his own family whom he had zealously instructed in virtue and religion. He was buried in the family vault in Wraysbury chancel, and while a handsome monument consecrates his memory, his character may be transmitted as amongst the best heir-looms of his posterity.

Mr. Gyll left an only son, William Gyll, Captain in the 2nd Life Guards, who died in 1806, aged 31, and his mother, Mary Gyll, eldest daughter and co-heir of John Brome, Esq. of Ludlow, held the leased estates till her death in 1820, in her 89th year. Since which time they have been in the tenure of the present lessee, Brooke Hamilton Gyll, Esq. of the Rectory House, and of Yeoveny Hall, Middlesex.

There is a village in Bucks styled Gyllesbury, and a family of this name, William Gylle, appears amongst the gentry of Bucks, returned by the Commissioners, 12 Henry VI. 1433, and William Gylle, of Berks, whose will is proved in London 1493. John Gylle was in the Battle of Agincourt 1414, in the retinue of Sir Richard Hastings, and his name is 354 on the roll of those who were in that engagement. Also Richard Gyll, Serjeant of the Palace to Henry VII. and VIII. He was of Berkshire, and died 7th August 1511, (a very handsome effigy of him in armour, with a monumental inscription in brass, exists still in Shotesbrooke Church, Berks), leaving Joanna an only child.

Thomas Gyll of Upton, was buried there in 1591, and John Gyll of Windsor was buried there in 1637, having married Barbara Aldridge, 14th November 1630, at Windsor. See fine 1618, with Ambrose Aldridge of Wraysbury.

But the house whence spring the lessees of the College lands was of Wydial, Herts, a cadet branch of a numerous progeny settled in Kent, temp. Elizabeth, from whence they came to London; and as the pedigree with the diverging branches is given *in extenso* in Lipscomb's Bucks, and in Burke's Landed Gentry, and the Collectanea Topog., the main line will be only inserted here, limited space not permitting collaterals. We premise, however, the early history of the house. The family of Ghyl, Gyll, Gylle, Gille, Gill, for it is recorded in all these ways, is derived from that one which resided in the North, temp. Edward the Confessor, 1041, at Gille's Land, in Cumberland. This estate was wrested from the proprietor by William the Conqueror and bestowed on one of his followers named Hubert, who slew the owner Bueth Gille, and with the possessions took also the *name*, for the signification of *Gille* is valley, hence Hubert styled himself Hubert de Vaux or Vallis. In Denton's MS. of the History of Cumberland, is recorded minutely the history of Lanercost Abbey, which was founded by Hubert de Vallibus, to appease the wrath of Heaven towards his ancestor for the inhuman murder of Bueth Gille. Sir Henry Ellis' Domesday Book says that Ghyl, of Yorkshire, held lands there, temp. Edward the Confessor. *See* Gale's Houoris de Richmond, Camden's Britannia, Vol. iv. and Dugdale's Monasticon, Vol. ii. about Gille of Gille's land.

A branch of this family descended from Yorkshire to the adjacent shire of Lincoln, where we find Richard, son of Michael Gylle, paying 66 marks (about £44) to King John in 1200. This is about £528 of our money. Henry Gille of Lincoln, pays to King John in 1203, 6s, and Godfrey, son of Robert Gylle, was living in Lincolnshire 1278, and descended into Cambridgeshire, where we find the *same family* in the Rolls of the Hundreds published by Royal Commission, 1812-18.

From this time the family is traced to John Gylle, of Buckland, Herts, who died 1499, and in his will he leaves money for prayers to be said for his parents in Cambridgeshire. Richard Gyll was a householder in Shelford Parva, Cambridgeshire 1278, as were Walter and Bateman Gyll, at Foxton, in the same shire, and at the same period. This village is near Buckland, Herts, where deeds and wills and monuments* shew what property the Gyll family had there and at Wydial, the contiguous village, where they were Lords of the Manor, with the advowson of the Church.

\* On the monuments and the pedigree, for uniformity, the *y* instead of *i* has been adopted, which was formerly used interchangeably in the orthography, and that there have been diverging branches of this family in Hunts, Northamptonshire, and Kent—with arms identical, Harl. MS. 6065. Kent. In 1278 Walter le Gille served as a juryman at Tonbridge, and in 1400 — Gille's daughter and heir married John Sybell, of Sutton-at-Hone. In Fuller's Church of England Abroad, he mentions Michael Gyll, then in Germany 1575, who may be the one who was of Deptford, and whose will was proved 1580, Prerogative Office, and brother of George Gyll, whose will he witnessed in 1568, traditionary ancestor of the Kent line.

## PEDIGREE OF GYLL.

Arms: S. two Chevrons A. each charged with 3 mullets of the field, on a dexter Canton O. a lion pass. guard. G. Also, Lozenges O. and Vert. a lion ramp. guard. G.

JOHN GYLLE, of Buckland, Herts. b. circ. 1430, deed of fine, 1485,=JOANNA, dau. and coh. of Sir William Littlebury ats Horne, ob. 23 Jan. 1499, will prov. 8 Feb. 1499, Pr. Off. M.I. | of Buckland, buried in Buckland Church. M.I.

| ANDREW GYLLE, of Linton, Camb. 1526. | WILLIAM GYLLE, of do. proved his father's will in 1500. | — dau. of Leonard Hyde, of Throcking, Herts. | RICHARD, of do. ad-min. 5 July, 1535. Pr. Off. | ELIZABETH, dau. of —, living 1535, adm. |

| 1 h. JOHN GYLLE, of Buckland, Herts, and Wydial Hall, of the Petty Bag Office, ob. 15 March 1546, will prov. 25 Jan. 1547, bd. Wydial Church, M.I. | MARGARET, dau. and h. of George Canon, of Wydial Hall, m. 1509. | 2 h. JOHN WRENG-HAM, m. 1548, ob. 1579, will proved Pr. Office. | LEONARD GYLL, Priest of Jesus Coll. Camb. will proved 14 July, 1547, at Camb. | RICHARD GYLL, of Easton, Hunts, dead in 1547, *a quo* Gylls of Northton. Visn. |

# HISTORY OF WRAYSBURY.

A family pedigree/genealogical tree of the Gyll family:

**Generation 1:**
- **George Gyll**, of do., b. 1510, married twice and had 14 children, ob. 29 Oct. 1568, æt. 58, will pr. 2 Dec. foll. and witnessed by Michael Gyll, M.I. = **Gertrude**, d. and coh. of Sir John Peryent, Knt. of Herts. m. 1535, ob. 1551. p. 95.
- **Rich. Gyll** = **Agnes**, d. of Swaffham, Camb. ob. 2 April 1579. | of —, bd. 17 April, 1575.
- **Margaret**, dau. and h. m. Michael Pigot, of Beds.
- **Dorothy**.
- **Francis Gyll**, of Heydon, Essex, buried 20 May, 1595. = **Marcia**, dau. of Robt. Aspland, of Heydon, Essex, m. 30 Oct. 1560, ob. 1600.
- 4th son, **Michael Gyll**, of Deptford, Kent, will pr. 5 Oct. 1590. Harl. MSS. 6065 for arms of Gyll of Kent.

**Generation 2:**
- **John Gyll**, of do. High Sheriff of Herts. 1575, ob. 22 Oct. 1600, æt. 62, will pr. 1601, M.I. = **Joan**, d. of —, ob. 1600.
- **Edward Gyll**, of Anstey, Herts. ob. 1616. = **Margaret**, dau. of Thomas Campion, m. 10 Feb. 1574, d. 1605.
- Other children.
- **John Gyll**, of Sutton at Hone, near Dartford, Kent, bd. 6 Apr. 1624. = **Ann**, d. of —, bd. 12 April, 1626.

**Generation 3:**
- **Sir George Gyll**, b. 1563, Officer at siege of Cadiz, 1597, Knighted 23 July, 1603, ob. 17 Nov. 1619, adm. 30 Nov. following. = **Alice**, d. of Thomas, son and h. of Sir Thomas Essex of Berks. by Margaret, d. of Lord Sands of the Vine, m. 1595, ob. 1627. p. 45.
- **Sir John Gyll**, Knighted 26 Nov. 1613, M.P. for Minehead, will pr. 20 May, 1651, ob. sp. Pr. Off. = **Jane**, d. of Hugh Trevilian, of Yarnescombe, Devon.
- **Catherine**, m. 1, Wm. Hyde, 2, Sir R. Lovelace, cr. Lord Lovelace, p. 82.
- Daughters.
- **John Gyll**, of do. and of Dartford, bd. 6 April, 1646. = **Ursula**, dau. of Thomas Langridge, m. at Sutton at Hone, 14 June, 1611.

**Generation 4:**
- **John Gyll**, of do. b. 2 Sept. 1597, sold Wydial, 1627, and of Shelford pa. Camb. will pr. 27 April 1661, Pr. Off. = **Mary**, dau. of —, m. 1625, buried 23 April, 1644. = **Martha**, d. of — Spilman of Norfolk, m. 1645.
- 1w. **Ann** = —, adm. 1633, Pr. Office. = **George Gyll**, of Littlecourt Layston, Herts. living 1659. = 2w. **Helena**, d. of —, m. 29 June, 1652, bd. 25 June, 1659, at Layston.
- **Thomas Gyll**, of Dartford and Boxley, Kent, buried 18 Sept. 1667, admin. 1 Oct. 1667 by son George. = **Alice**, d. of — Jennings, m. 1645, adm. by son George Gyll, 18 Jan. 1672, at Rochester.
- **Martha**, b. 1646.

**Generation 5:**
- **Charles Gyll**, of Shelford Par. which he sold 1662, b. 17 Aug. 1630. p. 64.
- **Henry**, 1632.
- **Francis**, 1634.
- **Joseph**, living 1661.
- **George**, born 1637.
- **George Gyll**, bpt. 16 June, 1653.
- **George Gyll**, born 1648, of Boxley, Kent, bd. 25 Jan. 1726, æt. 77, will prov. 2 Feb. following. = **Susanna**, d. of Thomas Cox, m. 25 Feb. 1676, buried 7 July, 1721, æt. 70.
- **Thomas Gyll**, bd. 4 Oct. 1664, sp.

**Generation 6:**
- **Thomas Gyll**, buried 1693, æt. 15.
- **George**, d. y. **George**, d. y.
- **Elizabeth**, bpt. 17 March, 1680, m. 24 Sept. 1700, Thomas Newman.
- **Ann**, m. Thomas Walter, of Fawkham, Kent.
- **Susanna**, bd. 4 Dec. 1703.
- **William Gyll**, of Boxley, bpt. 30 Sept. 1686, ob. 10 Aug. 1654, æt. 68, = **Elizabeth**, d. and h. of John Lawrence of Deptford, b. 1690, m. 8 Sept. 1713, bd. 28 April, 1750.

**Generation 7:**
- **Brooke Gyll**, b. 1714, buried 13 March, 1744, sp.
- **Thomas**, ob. 1744.
- **Elizabeth**, m. 20 June, 1751, Thos. Baytop, of Rochester, m. 2ndly 13 May, 1784, James Kincaid. She ob. 13 Oct. 1800, æt. 82.
- **Ann**, m. 18 Nov. 1746, Thomas Wright of Dulwich, ob. 4 May 1809, æt. 82.
- **Elizabeth**, dau. and coh. of Robert Prowse Hassell, of Wraysbury House, m. 4 Oct. 1751, ob. 29 June, 1769, æt. 39. = **William Gyll**, of Wraysbury House, b. 1723, ob. 26 March, 1798, will prov. 26 April following. = **Mary**, eldest dau. and coh. of John Brome, of Ludlow, Salop. m. 20 Dec. 1773, ob. 11 Mar. 1820, æt. 88, descended from Sir W. de Brome, Standard Bearer to Ed. III. Visn. Salop.

**Generation 8:**
- **Robert Hutton Gyll**, b. 4 Dec. 1758, ob. 29 Oct. 1792, sp.
- **Elizabeth**, b. 1752, ob. 1776.
- **Margaret**, b. 1753, m. 7 Ap. 1772, John Deschamps. She ob. 1799.
- **Susanna**, b. 1756, m. 1st, 11 Feb. 1779, Thomas Chudleigh Sanders; m. 2nd, 10 June, 1819, Wm. Bailey of Tonbridge Castle, Kent. She ob. 7 Dec. 1833.
- **Frances**, ob. 1785.
- **Harriet**, m. 17 Feb. 1784, Arch. Paxton, of Watford, Herts. She ob. 1794.
- **Grace**, b. 1763, ob. 1847.
- **William Gyll**, b. 13 Sept. 1774, Capt. 2nd Life Guards, Equerry to D. of Sussex, ob. 10 Feb. 1806, will pr. 3 Feb. 1808. = **Lady Harriet Flemyng**, d. and h. of Hon. Hamilton Flemyng, 9th and last Earl of Wigtoun, m. 13 Oct. 1794, at Wraysbury, ob. 1813, æt. 37.

**Generation 9:**
- **Louisa Jane Gyll**, m. 12 May, 1819, Sir Jasper Atkinson, Kt. Provost of the Moneyers of the Royal Mint. He died 1856.
- **Brooke Hamilton Gyll**, of Wraysbury House and Yeoveny Hall, Middlx. b. 16 July, 1795. = **Maria Jane**, d. of Wm. Richardson & Eliz. d. of John Armstrong, & wid. of Edw. 1st E. of Winterton, m. 3 May, 1821, ob. 21 July following.
- **William Thomas Mariamne**, d. y.
- **Bellenden Charles Gyll**, of Hythe End, b. 1799, ob. 1822, sp.
- **Gordon Willoughby James Gyll**, b. 1 Aug. 1803, of Wraysbury. = **Ann Elizabeth**, d. of Sir Edw. Bowyer Smijth, Bt. m. 20 Aug. 1839.
- **Hamilton Gyll**, of Shenley, Herts. ob. 1844. = **Frances Caroline**, d. and coh. of Sir John Murray, Bt. m. 30 Sept. 1835, 5th in descent from Sir D. Murray and Lady Lilias Flemyng. See page 102.
- **Sir Robert Gyll**, Kt. 1831, b. 1805. = **Jane Price**, dau. of Sir John Pinhorn, Kt. of Ningwood, Isle of Wight, m. 21 Ap. 1847.

**Generation 10:**
- **Flemyng George Gyll**, born 1841, Lieutenant Royal Artillery.
- **Edward Gordon**, b. 1845.
- **Brooke Flemyng**, b. 1847.
- **Letitia Elizabeth**, m. 4 Oct. 1859, Charles Campbell Prinsep.
- **Cordelia Adela**.
- **Lilias Flemyng**.
- **Hamilton Flemyng Campbell**, b. 1836.
- **Bellenden Charles John**, b. 1838.

## PEDIGREE OF FLEMYNG EARL OF WIGTOUN.

BALDWIN FLEMYNG, settled in Scotland under K. David I. at Biggar. = Had various manors. See Douglas Peerage.  
Arms: G. A. chevron within a double tressure flory, counterflory A.

SIR MALCOLM FLEMYNG, witnessed a donation of Walter, High Steward of Scotland temp. Alexander III. Sheriff of Dumbarton. = ROBERT BRUCE, King of Scotland.

ROBERT FLEMYNG, 4th in succession from Baldwin, was a Peer of Scotland, 1289, ob. 1314 =

SIR MALCOLM FLEMYNG. | SIR PATRICK FLEMYNG, of Biggar. = —, d. and coh. of Sir Simon Frazer, who was executed 1306. | WALTER, the Steward. = MARGERY, d. & heir.

SIR MALCOLM FLEMYNG, created Earl of Wigtoun, 9 Nov. 1341. = MARJORIE, foster sister of K. David II. | SIR MALCOLM FLEMYNG, 1346. = CHRISTIAN | K. ROBERT II. ob. 1390.

JOHN, ob. circa 1361. | SIR DAVID FLEMYNG, murdered in 1405, by James Earl of Douglas. = | PATRICK a quo Fleming of Boord. | ROBERT Duke of Albany, ob. 1419. | K. ROBERT III. ob. 1406.

THOMAS, 2nd Earl of Wigtoun, sold the Earldom to Archibald Douglas, 8 Feb. 1371, d. sp. | SIR MALCOLM FLEMYNG, beheaded 24 Nov. 1440. = LADY ELIZABETH STEWART.

ROBERT, 1st Lord Flemyng, 1450, ob. 1495. = LADY JANET DOUGLAS, d. of James 7th Earl of Douglas.

SIR MALCOLM FLEMYNG, ob. v. p. = EUPHEME, d. of James Lord Livingstone. = WILLIAM FLEMYNG of Boord.

JOHN, 2nd Lord Flemyng, d. 1524, by assassination. = EUPHEME, d. of David Lord Drummond, poisoned 1504.

MALCOLM, 3rd Lord, d. 1547, at Pinkiefield. = LADY JANET STEWART, nat. d. of K. James IV. of Scotland.

JAMES, 4th Lord, d. 1558, æt. 24. = LADY BARBARA HAMILTON, d. of James Duke of Chatelheraut. | JOHN, 5th Lord, d. 1572, of a gunshot wound. = ELIZABETH, d. and h. of Robert, son of Ninian, 3rd Lord Ross.

JOHN, 6th Lord Flemyng and 1st Earl of Wigtoun, 1606, d. 1615. = LADY LILIAS GRAHAM, d. of John, 3rd Earl of Montrose.

JOHN, 2nd Earl of Wigtoun, d. 1650. | JAMES FLEMYNG, d. 1625. = | MALCOLM FLEMYNG, d. 1650. = | ALEXANDER FLEMYNG, was dead in 1654. = See bond, Wm. Flemyng to Jas. Flemyng, son of Alex. Flemyng, son of John, 1st Earl of Wigtoun. Reg. House, Edinburgh. | LADY LILIAS, m. 1627. = SIR DAVID MURRAY, Kt. of Stanhope, co. Peebles.

JOHN, 3rd Earl of Wigtoun, d. 1665. = | JOHN FLEMYNG, d. 1667. sp. | JOHN FLEMYNG, Col. d. sp. 1684. | DR. JAMES FLEMYNG, Rector of Raymochy, in Ireland, d. 1684. = JANET, d. of Rev. Dr. Alexander Forsyth, contract 11 Sept. 1660. Regist. House, Edin. | SIR WILLIAM MURRAY, cr. Bart. 1664. = JANET, dau. of James 1st Earl of Hartfield, and Lady Margaret, dau. of William 1st Earl of Queensbury.

JOHN, 4th Earl of Wigtoun, d. 1668. sp. m. = | WILLIAM, 5th Earl of Wigtoun, d. 1681. = | DR. JAMES FLEMYNG, Clk. will d. 11 Sept. 1729. = MAGDALENE, d. of Dr. Thos. Way, m. 1700. | SIR DAVID MURRAY.

JOHN, 6th Earl of Wigtoun and 11th Lord Flemyng, d. 1744. = | CHARLES, 7th Earl of Wigtoun, d. 1747, with him expired the heir male in the direct line. | CHARLES ROSS FLEMYNG, b. 1711, on decease of Charles, 7th E. of Wigtoun, assumed the honours, as 13th Lord Flemyng and 8th Earl of Wigtoun, d. 18 Oct. 1769. = ANNE, sister of Wm. Hamilton of Dublin, m. 26 Dec. 1743. | SIR JOHN MURRAY, ob. 1777.

LADY CLEMENTINA FLEMYNG, d. and h. m. 1735, Charles, 10th Lord Elphinstone.

HAMILTON FLEMYNG, b. 1745, 14th Lord Flemyng and 9th and last Earl of Wigtoun, d. 13 June, 1809, MI. Wraysbury Chancel. = MARY CHARLOTTE, d. and h. of Wm. Child of Birthwaite Hall, Darton, York, and Saranmaria, d. and coh. of Wm. Rooke, of Barnesley, York, m. 14 Dec. 1769, d. 31 Jan. 1797. | SIR ROBERT MURRAY, ob. 1794.

LADY HARRIET JANE FLEMYNG, only child, married at Wraysbury, 13 Oct. 1794, d. 1813, MI. = WILLIAM GYLL, Captain 2nd Life Guards, died 10 Feb. 1806, æt. 31. | SIR JOHN MURRAY, ob. 1848.

BROOKE HAMILTON GYLL, of Wraysbury House, served heir of line, p. 100. | GORDON WILLOUGHBY JAMES GYLL. | HAMILTON GYLL. = FRANCES CAROLINE, p. 100.

FLEMYNG GEORGE GYLL.

## HISTORY OF WRAYSBURY.

### PEDIGREE OF HOWARD, WYNDHAM, AND SMIJTH, OF HILL HALL, ESSEX.

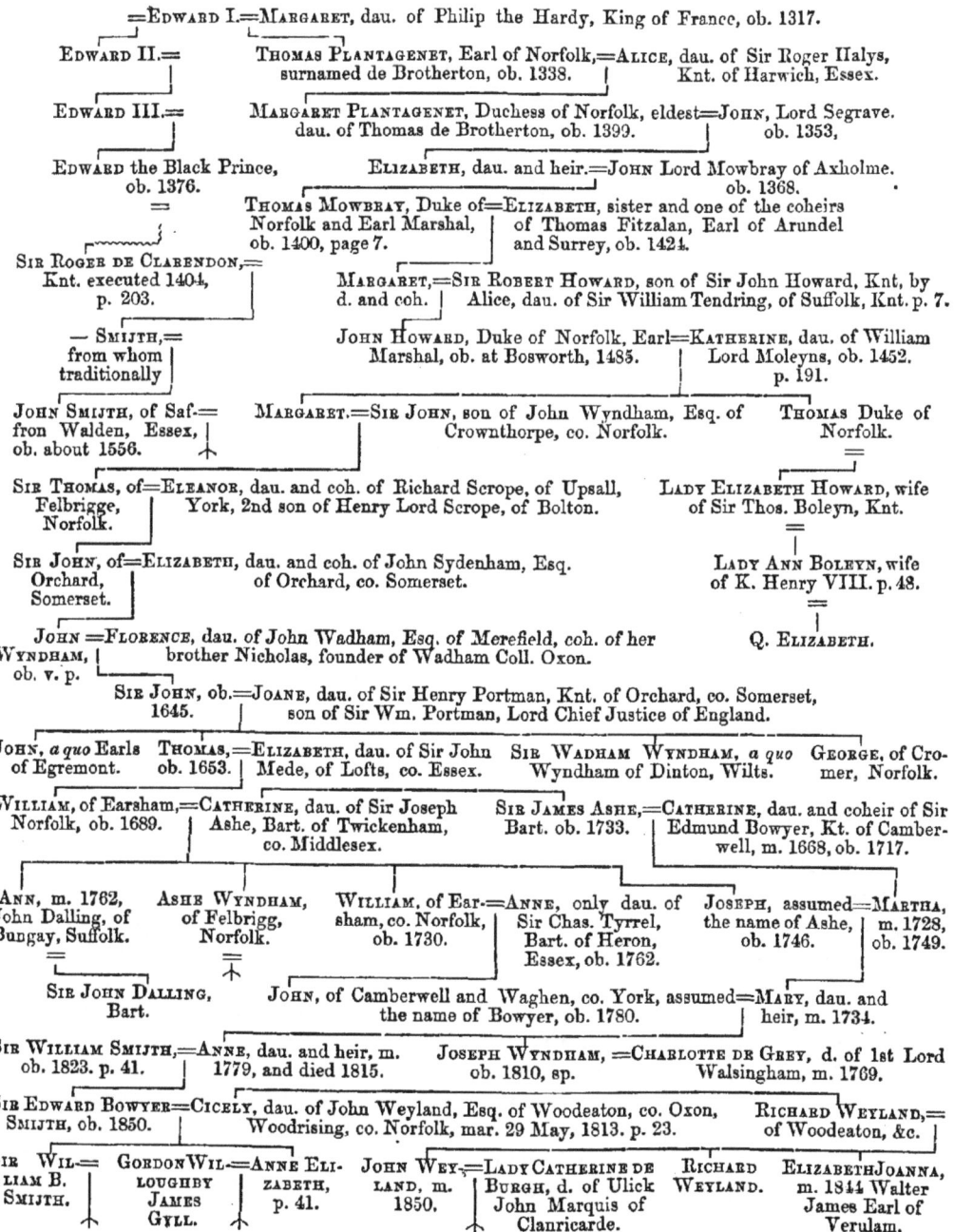

## ECCLESIASTICAL HISTORY AND STATISTICS.

How long prior to the Conquest Wraysbury had a church is not known; but at this period a church existed, and it was also the mother-church to Langley, which was included in the survey, and was appendant, as far as relates to the spiritualities, until the last incumbent died, Rev. Charles Champnes, in 1855, when Langley was separated. It is now under the care of the Rev. William D. Scoones, who preached his first sermon there on Good Friday, 1856. The separation took place after a union of nearly nine centuries, and the Rev. Seymour Neville was appointed, by the Dean and Chapter of Windsor, Vicar of Wraysbury, and was inducted July 1855. It seems that one of the Montfitchets who held Wraysbury in fee gave the church to St. Peter's of Gloucester.

Langley is a scattered village of some 2½ miles from Colnbrook, and part of it is in that parish: it is about 3820 acres, nearly double that of Wraysbury, and yet the larger was comprised within the smaller parish. Its population was some 1797, and in 1861 . It is in Stoke Hundred. The great tithes of Langley, subject to the payment of £20 to the Vicar, were formerly in the hands of the Upton family.

A parish was identical with a diocese, the Bishop being sole incumbent; but in the sixth and seventh centuries, as the nation grew more populous and opulent, the Thanes and Lords founded churches for their own tenants, and if additional churches were built they became parochial.

The Lord was allowed to appoint to the church called the *advocation* or advowson, and these were sometimes devolved on the clergy in perpetuity. Although they were appropriated, and went under two heads, plenary, and in this case rectories were turned into vicarages, and the Vicar got the small tithes and oblations. After the appropriation was made the bodies so endowed were called impropriators, and the distinction arose between great tithes of corn, hay, wood, and small tithes predial, and those called mixed and personal. No tithes belong to the Vicar of common right, but by endowment and prescription only. Some benefices at the Reformation were granted to laymen, hence lay impropriators (page 34).

The appropriation of Wraysbury belonged to the abbey of St. Peter in Gloucester; and Richard de Gernon, in 1112, gave to St. Peter's of Gloucester several donations, and Wraysbury may have been in the list (page 4); when it was a rectory, the earliest name mentioned is Robert de Burnell, Archdeacon of Bucks, who resigned it in 1219 (page 10); and from this time it continued a rectory until it was appropriated in 1349, since which it has been a vicarage.

It was exchanged with King Edward III., by whom it was given to the foundation of his Chapel of St. George at Windsor, and it is said to have been in the hands of the Fitzwalter family (page 6).

The practice of appropriating livings came in with the Normans, and within 300 years the monks were proprietors of one-third of all the *benefices* of the realm, which, by Act 27 & 31 Henry VIII., would have been disappropriated, had not a clause been inserted to give them to the King in as ample a manner as the Abbots held them—hence one-third became the King's (page 34).

There are 3845 appropriators in England, who receive great tithes, estimated at £1,639,730, leaving only the vicarial tithes or other minor endowments for the maintenance of incumbents. Henry VIII. allowed the union of churches when only a mile apart, and under the value of £6, about £70 a year. Plurality has since been partially abolished, for there were many unions, nearly 3000, and abuses were multifarious by dispensations, &c., a clergyman being once able to hold as many benefices without cure as he could hold under £8 a year in value; but in 1603 the holdings were restricted to the distance of 30 miles asunder. In some parts of England, especially the north, the parishes are very large indeed.

In the Church of England the Canon of 1603 contains the code of legislation and discipline. Ten parishes form a deanery, and several archdeaconries as territorial divisions have been created. The total number in 1854 was 71. The archbishoprick or province of Canterbury comprehends 20 dioceses, with a population of some 13 millions. The archbishoprick of York comprises 7 dioceses, with a 6 million population. There are 11,728 benefices in England and Wales. The Cathedral Chapters and other dignitaries have about 993 livings, and in private or lay-hands there are about 6092. The total revenue payable to the Church yearly is about £4,292,885—comprising all sources.

The Tithe Commission general average for 18 years is £99. 7s 8½d. In 1837 the rent charge or tithe-commutation act begun. It has risen to £105. 12s 2d in 1843; and in 8 years the average was over £100. In 12 years about £12,000 in value, £720 per annum, or £60 a year, has been restored to the church under the tithe redemption trust. The annual value of tithes in the lands of laymen is £765,429; clerical corporations and their lessees, £678,335; schools, colleges, hospitals, and their lessees, £195,946: total, £1,639,730.

There are 297 benefices in England and Wales under £50 per annum, 1629 over £50 and under £100, 1602 over £100 and under £150, and 1354 over £150 and under £200.

Since 1821 more than 2000 new churches have been built, equal to about £600,000 income; and the pew accommodation is enough for 5 millions of persons.

The average of all livings is £300 per annum. The livings in Bucks are poorly endowed. In the diocese of Oxford there are 72 livings under £100 a year, 85 under £150, and 66 under £200.

The first mention of tithes in England dates A.D. 786, in a decree of a Synod: but tithes were first specifically granted to the clergy by Ethelwolfe, King of the West Saxons, A.D. 844, at Wilton, at the feast of Easter.

The parochial beneficed clergy number some 12,000, and about 5000 curates. Deaneries and chapters have about 800 livings, private persons about 5000, while the revenues of the chapters are about £154,000 a year. The revenue of all benefices are set at some £3,000,000 sterling, that of curates £400,000, giving an average of £300 for each incumbent, and £80 for curates.

Wraysbury is in the gift of the Dean and Canons of Windsor. This corporate body has an income of £19,972. 4s 7d per annum, according to the return of cathedral revenues and expenditure made by the Commissioners for 1852, and published in 1855. The total being £313,005. 2s.

The Chapter of Christ Church declined to give any return, on the ground that their property is strictly collegiate; and the Cathedral of Bangor has no corporate property. There are two collegiate churches—Westminster and Windsor: the income of the former is £30,657.

The endowments wherewith King Edward III. invested this College of Windsor by his letters patent of foundation, were first the advowson of the Church of Wraysbury, Bucks; of South Taunton in the diocese of Exeter; and Uttoxeter in that of Coventry and Lichfield. These he gave to the custos, canons, alms, knights, and ministers of the college, to hold in fee pure and perpetual alms thoroughly and perpetually free from all exactions, with licence to appropriate the same to the college, notwithstanding the statute of mortmain.

Pat. de anno 22 Edw. III. 1347, and in 24 Edw. III. 28 January 1346, the royal founder gave unto the custos and college, by the name of Custos and Chaplains of his free Chapel of Windsor, 1 messuage, 17 acres of land, 1 acre of pasture, 3s rent, with appurtenances in Wraysbury, which had been conveyed to him by Richard de Gloucester, one of the heirs of Isabel de Dutton (page 29).

Hugh de Spenser, son of the Earl of Winchester, and, according to Camden, Earl of Gloster, *jure uxoris,* Lord Chamberlain and chief favourite, after Gaveston, of King Edward II., was accused of seducing the King and of oppressing the State; and by the order of the Queen was drawn on a hurdle through the streets of Hereford on St. Andrew's Eve, 29 November 1326, and was beheaded on a gallows of 50 feet high, and his head was fixed on London Bridge. He left three sons— Hugh, Edward, and Gilbert, from the eldest of whom descended Thomas created Earl of Gloucester: he was beheaded at Bristol (page 29).

On the 23rd May 1349 (the year of the appropriation of Wraysbury Rectory, whereby it became a vicarage), the King granted to Windsor the advowson of the church of Datchet, to appropriate it to them and their successors.

At the same time the King gave the advowson of the Church of Iver to the Collegiate Church of St. George, Windsor: but it reverted by exchange to the crown, while the Manors of Langley and Cippenham, attached to Wraysbury, paid yearly salaries for thirteen chaplains and four clerks, to maintain the Royal Chapel in the park of Windsor, temp. Edward II., which establishment, being after removed into the castle, formed the foundation of the more splendid chapel of St. George's in the next reign.

The value of the living of Wraysbury in the King's Books, or *Liber Regis*, is £14. 10s 5d yearly; tenth, £1. 9s 0½d; Archdeaconry, 10s 7¾d; Dean and Canonry of Windsor, £65. 19s 6d certified value; and before the separation from Langley its value was about £445 per annum. The vicarage is commuted at £166; afternoon duty, £26; average surplice fees, £10; land and house about £50, from which there is a deduction of some £10. The entire living now, 1861, may be worth some £350 a year. There is a vicarage-house let to Mr. Henry Tailor the parish clerk, with lands, the rent of which goes to the vicar (page 91). The church-rate averages 2s 6d in the pound.

The parish was inclosed in 1799, and in the act of Parliament there is no mention made of allotment of tithes. There is an allotment for the Deans and Canons as proprietors having manorial rights, but not for tithes; the clause enacting that the new allotments were to be for the same uses, &c., and for cottage rights to the lord of the manor for right of soil, and willow plantations for the copyholders to be held in severalty by copy of Court Roll. A parcel of the waste was allotted for holding a fair every Friday in Whitsun week, pursuant to ancient custom (page 83). Fairs were formerly kept in the churchyards, and the citizens of London had the privilege of frequenting fairs by statute, temp. Henry VII.

The church lands consist of 5 acres, 2 roods, 8 poles—part arable, part meadow in this parish, realising from £10 to £12 a year. In 1736 the church lands were rented by John Winch for £1. 16s 7d yearly. They were let to George Leno for seven years from 14th October 1829, at the rent of £1. 17s per annum, amounting to £10. 3s 6d yearly. The rent is carried to the account of the church-rate after payment of a quitrent, the exact amount of which does not appear; but in 1828 a payment of £1. 3s 11d is entered in the books for quitrent to Michaelmas 1827, without saying for how many years.

It is uncertain to whom the church is indebted for these acres (page 14), whether to Sir Thomas Smyth of Ankerwycke, or to his predecessor Lord Windsor; and it is a reflection on somebody, whether the parish or the church, that the benefactor's name is not recorded, at once to recognise endowments or to encourage them.

There is a gift of £20 per annum given by John Lee, Esq., of which mention will be made under donations and benefactions to the church with other charities; but it is not necessary that either the vicar or the curate of the parish be selected, the appointment may be given to any clergyman obtaining two certificates from his own body, and these endorsed by the bishop of the diocese.

Under the Wraysbury tithe apportionment and value of rent-charge we find that the average great tithe is 7s in the pound, and the vicar's tithe 1s 6d. The vicar clears about £166, and the lay-rector about £390, out of a net return of £413. 19s 2d. See more under tithe apportionment.

There are about 15 acres of vicarial glebe, and the curates get about £70 per annum; and there are also about 52 acres of land belonging to the Church, held by the lay rector with the Rectory House, for which he pays a septennial fine, on renewal of lease, of about £700, or £100 a-year, and £56. 15s to the Chapter annually; £15 for vicarial tithes, and 14s every two years to the diocese of Lincoln, now I presume payable to Oxford. These leases are not to continue after 1884, when the Church property will revert entirely to that body, and perhaps be made more under the control and direction of the Ecclesiastical Commissioners.

The Church of England is pre-eminent for its doctrine, discipline, and morality. She need fear no dissenters, who generally on becoming wealthy join the Church, where they find dignity and faith. The Romanists instead of increasing with the population do not advance, and abroad Protestantism is beginning to be appreciated, as is seen by the Pope's allocutions, which are a series of *groanings* over everything Protestant and progressive, caring for little beyond the supremacy of Ecclesiastical polity—one prominent idea forms the key-note of all their arguments and positions. Grant but *toleration* abroad, and let our Divines, like Jewel and Taylor, &c. be *translated*, and the continent will become Protestant, which it is now, save in its *unproved* doctrines.

True Christianity in all its details squares with every political and social relation, meets every moral necessity, and applies itself equally to the conscience of the most unlettered peasant and the councils of the most powerful princes. It is uniform everywhere, and as its origin is divine, so its utility is human; and lately the Church of England has worked in her vocation admirably; she has taken in hand the poor, and has directed her labours to the moral recovery of the lowest, by calling into existence homes, refuges, and penitentaries. She has sent out Bishops and Clergy to our Colonies, and has planted in foreign soils the seed which has borne so good fruit among ourselves.

## RECTORS AND VICARS.

### Rectors.

1219. Robert de Burnel, Archdeacon of Buckingham, resigned 1219, and on his cession Martin de Patteshall was presented by the Abbot and Convent of Gloucester.

In the same year was presented William de Hereford.

1230. Silvester de Anagn, *see* Deed 15 Henry III. among fines.

1234. Robert Holbeche by the same convent, Robert or Richard de Montfitchet renouncing his claim.

1260. Hugh, probably brother of William de Windsor. *See* fines, Horton, 1261.

1299. Robert de Gloucester, resigned.

1300. 30th Nov. Robert le Wyse, Subdeacon, presented.

1312. Ingeland de Warle.

1323. 3rd Dec. John de Staunton.

John de Shareshall exchanged for the Preceptorship of Exeter with

1334. 1st Sept. Adam Murimoth.

1347. 6th July, John de Melton presented by the King, and confirmed Rector.

### Vicars.

The Rectory was appropriated and made a Vicarage, 1349.

### Vicars.

1349. 1st Feb. William de Ashley, presented by the Custos and College of Windsor.

Here there is an *hiatus* of 85 years as to dates, probably Hugh, Vicar of Wraysbury, cited in Deed 1361, comes in here.

1424. John Smart, resigned.

Ditto, 12th Dec. Robert Steppingley.

1432. Robert Holbeche, probably related to Robert Holbeche, Rector in 1230.

Ric. or Rob. Chapell, resigned.

1441. 28th Jan. William English.

Walter Beseley, resigned.

1457. 28th Feb. John Veysey.

Richard Weston, resigned.

1462. 4th Nov. John Norton, died.

1464. 23rd June, Richard Leving, resigned.

1466. 30th June, John Cokson.

1476. 12th Oct. Thomas Dixon.

1479. 29th Oct. John Burton, resigned.

1483. 23rd June, Nicholas Rewys, resigned.

1485. 16th Feb. Peter Boyle.

1490. Robert Long, resigned.

15th May, William Harryson.

1497. Hugh Livesay, resigned.

17th Feb. Wm. Duston, by Southwark Convent.

## Vicars.

1520. 16th March, William Hand.
1529. 21st Nov. Henry Woodward,
1548. 4th July, Richard Palmer, but neglecting to pay his tenths.
1552. 17th June, Thomas Blackwood.
1561. 14th Nov. Thomas Clement.
1564. Peter Walthowe.
1580. 21st June, John Whitnall.
1582. George Eyles. *See* Par. Registers.
1626. Ellis Beverley, Rector of Quainton, Bucks, and there buried 26th March 1657.
1630. James Scrimshaw.(¹)
1640. Adam Dominique, resigned.
1642. 2nd June, John Dutton.
1645. 31st Aug. Richard Bachelour. *See* Par. Reg.
1647. 19th Nov. Robert Temple.
1656. William Reeve.
1661. 4th June, William Black.

## Vicars.

1667. 4th Oct. James Dallian,—was deprived on account of not taking the oath—a non-juror occurs as Vicar in 1669. *See* Par. Registers.
1690. 8th Nov. John Conradus Werndly, by the Bishop on lapse.(²)
1724. 16th Dec. John Amy.
1757. 21st May, Richard Blacon.
1758. 28th Jan. Richard Wilmot.
1763. 29th July, Fretwell Vandernan, ob. 24th Jan. 1803, æt. 86. Buried at Wraysbury.
1803. 20th April, William Clarke, ob. 1821.
1821. 19th Feb. Thomas Weldon Champnes, resigned.(³)
1829. 13th April, Richard Webb, ob. 13th April 1829.(⁴)
Charles Champnes, ob. 1st June 1855, æt. 72.
1855. July, Seymour Neville, Minor Canon of Windsor.

There are 16 resignations from 1219 to our time.

(¹) James Scrimshaw had a dispensation from Archbishop Laud, April 1639, stating he had lived for nine years in the *Vicarage* House situated near the Thames, in an unhealthy soil, to the loss of his health, he begged to remove to Langley, more peopled, and three miles from Wraysbury.

(²) Easter Term, 6th May 1702, there was a lawsuit in the Exchequer between Mr. Werndley and Sir Edward Seymour, Bart. and John Ball, defendant. The plaintiff in Michaelmas Term 1700, exhibited his bill in Court, and set forth that he was for three years next before the exhibiting Vicar of Wraysbury with the Chapel of Langley, which Vicarage before the year 1258 had been a Vicarage endowed, and that the Vicarage and said Church and Chapel were and for the time aforesaid had been instituted to the whole alterage, and particularly to the tithe within Langley, as by the endowment appears. That the plaintiff in 1689 was inducted, and that the Dean and Canons of Windsor had demised to Sir Edward Seymour the tithes of the place, and that he let the same to John Ball as under tenant. That the Dean and Canons, by deed of January 1697, let it to Seymour for 21 years, who leased it to Ball by virtue of a prior agreement with Sir Henry Seymour, father of Sir Edward Seymour. Reference was made to an old terrier purporting to be a valuation of the Vicarage in 1258, and of the profits taken in the cause. The dispute lay about the tithe of hay, &c. and the result was that it was ordered and adjudged that the Plaintiff's said bill be dismissed the Court with costs.

(³) In the presentation document of Thomas W. Champnes, Langley precedes Wraysbury.

(⁴) George Adolphus Hopkins, licensed Curate, during part of the incumbency of Mr. Champnes, was appointed in May 1835 to be under-master of Stroud School, Egham, and the Rev. James Phillips was Lecturer here (died 4th June 1825) of Lee's Charity, 30th March 1824.

Mr. Hopkins came to Wraysbury in 1828, and left in 1855, and died 13th February 1856, æt. 54. He founded the day-school in 1828, and the clothing-club on the 19th December 1849; the village gentry, &c. gave him a dinner at which he was presented with a silver salver, one dozen table forks, one dozen spoons, two gravy spoons, and four silver sauce ladles, purchased by the subscriptions of 720 parishioners and friends, as a testimony of his faithful services for 22 years. On the 9th August 1855, a farewell dinner was given to him on retiring from a curate's duty and a church which he had so faithfully served for 27 years; at which time 106 of the parishioners presented him a silver milk-jug, tea-pot, and sugar basin, tongs and butter-knife.

In March 1858 there was a subscription raised in Wraysbury for Elizabeth, daughter of David Hobbs, of Windsor, and widow of Rev. G. Hopkins. He was an excellent specimen of a clergyman in morals and religion.

>He preached the joys of Heaven and pains of Hell,
>And warned the sinner with becoming zeal,
>But on Eternal mercy loved to dwell.—*Dryden's Good Parson.*

The names of the Curates since are Rev. Thomas Grainger, 1855; Rev. John Garrett, 1856; John Holcomb, 1857; George Taylor, 1859, Master of the Stroud School, Egham, who received a flattering testimonial on his retirement, of a pocket communion service and a silver ink-stand. Presented by the parishioners of Wraysbury to the Rev. George Taylor, in testimony of their respect and friendship, February 1861. In the same year Mr. West, of Datchet, became curate here.

## CHURCHYARD AND MONUMENTAL INSCRIPTIONS.

Before we reach the Church we are stopped at the precincts by the Churchyard, called by the Germans *God's acre.* To enter our cemetery we pass through an old porch, known in architecture as a Lich-gate, from the Saxon *lic,* a body or corpse. Underneath these porches bodies were laid before the priest could attend to the sanctimonious ceremony of burial, and sometimes part of the service was recited here, and the body, generally exposed, was placed out of sun and rain.

There are many fine specimens of Lich-gates, especially in Devonshire, which impress a character of antiquity as well as afford a reverential entrance to the last resting place, where the rich and the rude forefathers of the hamlet sleep.

Time was when our antecessors were buried in fields and obscure places, to prevent bodies being desecrated or mangled by wild animals, hence it was found expedient to close in spaces as churchyards for their reception; but from the earliest periods some sanctuary seems to have been devoted to the honoured remains of all destined to the inevitable grave. The ashes of burnt bodies were collected and laid in cinerary urns styled *Columbaria*—dovecots. Modern monuments in graveyards do not occur earlier than the 17th century, (mounds of earth being their precursors,) and were mostly erected in the eastern division of the churchyard.

There were often yew-trees planted here, mournful accompaniments, like the cypress, and a fit emblem of the departed. They were also used for making bows, (of which page 49). We have an old yew-tree of some centuries growth, on the south-west side, and one on the opposite side, lately planted by the author of this history. Prior to Protestant days churchyards were charged with crucifixes, while the churches also were over-laden with these badges of Christianity; but Reformers used the ornament sparingly, lest brute matter, becoming objects of love as in some countries, idolatry might supersede the worship "in spirit and truth."

There are about ten handsome altar tombs in the cemetery, including the Harcourt monuments, inclosed within high iron-rails, and nearly 90 monuments besides, but no date anterior to the last century. Nor is there one of extraordinary longevity, although the village is exceedingly healthy. The present cemetery is more than an acre in area, and is nearly circular, with trees at the edges on the north side. I append memorials to give satisfaction or consolation to any who may here seek the last resting depository of friends or relatives, when time shall have swept away every vestige.

## MONUMENTAL INSCRIPTIONS IN WRAYSBURY CHURCHYARD.

**North Side—**

In Memory of John Lovegrove, who died 23rd July 1786, aged 38 years.

In Memory of Mary Lovegrove, widow of John Lovegrove, who died 22nd January 1787, aged 49 years.

*Altar tomb*—Here lyeth the body of John Goodman, who died February 1776, aged 70. Also Mary and Sarah Goodman, wife of the above John Goodman, who departed this life 10th February 1788, aged 86.

Henry Goodman, died — February —, aged —

In Memory of Mrs. Ann Goodman, who died February 12th 1803, aged 76 years.

In Memory of Mr. John Goodman, junior, who departed this life December 1785, aged 49 years.

**East Side, enclosed in rails—**

In Memory of Mrs. Ann Buckland, relict of the late Thomas Buckland, who departed this life 21st April 1828, aged 74. Also of Mary Ann, daughter of Charles and Martha Hewlitt, and grandchild of the above, who died in infancy.

Mr. John Virgo Buckland, son of the above, died 24th November 1833, aged 41 years.

In Memory of Mr. Thomas Buckland, of this parish, who departed this life 14th January 1812, aged 65 years. Also to the Memory of Martha, the beloved wife of Charles Hewlitt, of Herefordshire, and daughter of the above, who departed this life 16th April 1830, aged 54 years.

In Memory of Mr. Francis Virgo Buckland, son of Virgo and Ann Buckland, who departed this life 22nd April, 1824, aged 11 years. Also of William Virgo Buckland, brother of the above, who died 14th November 1827, aged 17. Also of Charles Thomas Buckland, brother of the above, who died 19th November 1845, aged 25 years.

In Memory of Mr. Virgo Buckland, late of this parish, who departed this life 12th September 1825, aged 39.

Sacred to the Memory of Alfred, son of John and Maria Dyson, late of Botolph Lane, London, died 6th Sept. 1845, aged 26.

Here lyeth the body of David Wingrove, of this parish, who departed this life 28th March 1785, aged 76 years.

Here lyeth the body of Mrs. Mary Wingrove, wife of Mr. David Wingrove, of this parish, she departed this life 10th February 1781, aged 66.

Here lie the remains of Martha West, wife of Thomas West, who departed this life 5th July 1814, aged 42 years.

Here lieth the body of Mr. William Moore, who departed this life, 19th April, 1771, aged 66. Here also lieth the body of Elizabeth Moore, wife of the above, who departed this life 30th September 1771, aged 61 years. Likewise near this place is the body of Mrs. Mary Pocock. She departed this life 19th April 1773, aged 91.

In Memory of Mary Morgan, who died 22nd April 1828, aged 61 years.

*Altar tomb*—In Memory of Mr. Arthur Palmer, of this parish, who departed this life 20th September 1780, aged 54. Also Arthur and Martha Palmer, who departed this life 15th July 1782, aged 10 months. To the Memory of Arthur Palmer, who departed this life 1st April 1799, in the — year of his age.

In Memory of William Downham, Parish Clerk, who died 27th January 1834, aged 77.

In Memory of Mrs. Martha Herbert, of the parish of Isleworth, Middlesex, who died 18th January 1822, aged 64. Also Elizabeth Hester, daughter of James and Mary Ann Herbert, who died 12th February 1828, aged 15 months. Also Mr. Thomas Herbert, father of the above, who departed this life 29th August 1832, aged 63 years.

In Memory of William Sills, who departed this life 11th March 1824, aged 24. Also Daniel Sills, father of the above, who died 1st April 1831, aged 53 years.

In Memory of Mrs. Ann Sills, of this parish, who died 27th November 1823, aged 74 years. Also Mr. Daniel Sills, husband of the above, who departed this life 3rd January 1832, aged 76 years.

In Memory of Mr. John Barrow, of this parish, and formerly of Waverham in Cheshire, who departed this life 15th December 1820, in his 54th year. Also of Elizabeth Barrow, wife of the above, who died 27th January 1854, aged 86, respected and lamented by all who knew him.

110                    HISTORY OF WRAYSBURY.

SOUTH SIDE—

Here lyeth the body of Ellis Style, who departed this life — 1775. Here lyeth the body of Mr. Robert Style, who departed this life November 1770, aged — and 10 months.

Sacred to the Memory of Mrs. Ann Style, widow of Robert Style, who died 28th September 1807, aged 30 years.

In Memory of Mr. Robert Style, who died 27th April 1828, aged 73. Also three children, Peter, died 9th April 1810; Mary Ann, died 23rd July 1824; Charlotte, died March 30th 1827. Also of Martha Style, daughter of the above, died 23rd February 1831, aged 14. Also Elizabeth, daughter of the above, and wife of William Clarke, of Datchet, who died 7th January 1846, in the 54th year of her age.

Here lyeth the body of Mrs. Mary Winch, relict of Mr. John Winch, of this parish, who died 2nd Dec. 1755, aged 89.

Here lyeth the body of Mr. John Winch, late of this parish, who died 21st January 1745, aged 72 years.

In Memory of Mrs. Ann Martin, relict of Mr. Samuel Martin, of this parish, who departed this life 14th January 1769, aged 62 years.

Here lyeth the body of Mr. Samuel Martin, who died 15th May 1765, aged 70 years.

Here lyeth the body of James Fleming, son of David and Jane Fleming, of the parish of ——, in Midlothian, who departed this life 1814, aged —

In Memory of Daniel Taylor, son of Wm. and Eliz. Taylor, of this parish, who died 8th February 1806, aged 23.

Hester, wife of Richard Taylor, who died 28th September 1806, aged 51.

Robert Taylor, died 19th May 1795, aged 75.

Sacred to the Memory of Mr. William Taylor, died 11th January 1827, aged 88. Also Mrs. Elizabeth Taylor, wife of the above, died 5th July, 1830, aged 36. Also Robert, son of the above, died 19th May, 1795, aged 25 years. Also Richard, son of the above, died 27th June, 1827, aged 55 years. Also George, son of the above, died November 1837, aged 50 years.

William Wilmot, died 15th April 1803, aged 89 years.

In Memory of Mrs. Elizabeth Style, wife of H. Style, of New Windsor, died 10th April 1790, aged 33. Also Martha, their daughter, died 23rd September 1794, aged 3 months and 20 days. Mr. H. Style departed this life 10th May 1802, aged 39.

Here lies the body of Mary Jordan, who died 14th December 1760, aged 21 years.

Beneath this stone lyeth interred the remains of Samuel Taylor, who died 20th April 1790, aged 27.

In Memory of Samuel Plastow, who died 1st March 1828, aged 56.

In Memory of Mr. Edward Stevens, who departed this life 27th February 1810, aged 76.

Sacred to the Memory of Mr. William Milbourne, of —— London, who died 24th June, 1780, aged 41. Also Mrs. Martha Milbourne, wife of the above, who died 17th January 1827, in her 72nd year.

In Memory of Mr. Joseph Keates, late of the parish of Egham, who died 15th October, 1810, aged 53 years. Also of Charlotte Keates, wife of the above, who died 19th November 1835, aged 74.

In Memory of Mr. Robert Butler, of this parish, who died 14th December 1836, aged 45. Also Mrs. Joanna Butler, relict of the above, died 26th October 1847, aged 61.

Sacred to the Memory of Mr. James Sims, an old inhabitant of this parish, who departed this life 19th April 1824, aged 87.

Sacred to the Memory of Mrs. Ann Sims, daughter of James and Mary Sims, of this parish, who departed this life 14th July 1800, aged 23 years.

In Memory of Mrs. Mary Sims, wife of Mr. James Sims of this parish, who died 1st April 1809, aged 64.

Here lieth the body of Mr. Richard Very, late of this parish, who departed this life May 1745, aged 57.

On a tomb is inscribed E. B. 1754.

Here lieth the body of Joan Lewin, wife of Richard Lewin, of this parish, who died 27th Dec. 17—.

In Memory of Mr. William Cooper, son of Daniel and Mary Cooper, who died 14th September 1759, aged 64.

In Memory of Elizabeth, daughter of Richard and Elizabeth Withers, died Jan. 1828. Also Emily Jane, died Jan. 1839.

In Memory of Mrs. Jane Hodgson, who died 31st December 1815, aged 35.

Here lyeth interred the remains of Thomas Robinson, who died 2nd August 1820, aged 50. Also his sister, Jane Robinson, who departed this life 11th Feb. 1824, aged 48.

In Memory of Elizabeth, wife of George Trash, who departed this life 16 Jan. 1815, aged 27.

WEST SIDE—

In Memory of Mrs. Sarah Haines, wife of Thomas Haines, of this parish, who departed this life 28th Dec. 1809, aged 63 years. Also Mr. Thomas Haines, husband of the above, died 28th September 1814, aged —.

Sacred to the Memory of Mr. William Groom, who departed this life 10th day of June 1811, aged 72.

In Memory of Mr. Thos. Groom, son of William and Mary Groom, of this parish, who departed this life 31st October 1805, aged 45.

In Memory of Mrs. Mary Groom, wife of Mr. William Groom, who died 10th March 1816, aged 65 years.

In Memory of John Harris, who died 14th June 1752, aged 56 years.

In Memory of Mr. John Hodgson, who died 20th June 1821, aged 63.

In Memory of Mr. John Sanders, of this parish, who died 6th November 1766, aged 72.

In Memory of Mr. Simon Sanders, son of Mr. John and Mary Sanders, died 28th April 1798, aged 76.

In Memory of Mary, relict of Mr. John Sanders, she departed this life 5th April 1781, aged 81. Also near this place lie 10 of their children, 7 sons and 3 daughters.

In Memory of Mrs. Jane Thomas, wife of Mr. William Thomas, who departed this life 17th Feb. 1810, aged 39.

In Memory of Mr. William Thomas, of this parish, died 24th December, 1822, aged 72.

In Memory of Miss Mary Thomas, daughter of William and Catherine Thomas, departed this life 23rd June 1794, aged 19.

In Memory of Catherine, wife of William Thomas, died 13th Feb. 1793, aged 44.

In Memory of Richard Grove, who departed this life 7th Feb. 1726, aged 76.

Here lyeth the body of Martha, wife of Mr. Richard Grove, who died 30th July 1756, aged 64 years. Also Martha, daughter of Richard and Martha Grove, died 16th April 1757, aged 38.

*Altar tomb*—Here lieth the body of Elizabeth, wife of John Russel, who died 9th April 1759, aged 48 years. Here lyeth the body of John Russel, departed this life 6th November 1706.

*Altar tomb*—Here lieth the body of Ambrose Adkins, of the parish of Stanwell, Middlesex, yeoman, who died 2nd September 1706, aged 66.

Here also lyeth interred Mary, wife of the said Ambrose Adkins, who departed this world 27th April 1735, aged 87.

WEST SIDE—

Sacred to the Memory of Michael Willis, son of Michael and Mary Willis, who departed this life 2nd July 1788, aged 15. Also Mary Willis, she died 16th August 1804, aged 51. Also Mr. Michael Willis, died 8th Oct. 1814, aged 68.

SOUTH SIDE—

Sacred to the Memory of John Painter, who died 10th November 1831, aged 67.

In Memory of Elizabeth Hood, daughter of William and Ellis Hood, and niece of John Painter, who died 20th September 1834, aged 22.

Sacred to the Memory of Sarah Taplin, died 13th March 1850, in her 62nd year.

In Memory of Christian Mathews, of this parish, died 10th August 1781, aged 70.

Sacred to the Memory of William Darling, who was 58 years employed in Mr. Godwin's family of Datchet, died 18th April 1848, aged 84. Also Elizabeth, wife of William Darling, departed this life 3rd Feb. 1836, aged 67 years.

Mrs. Mary Wilmot, wife of Nathaniel Wilmot, of this parish, who departed this life 28th Feb. 1807, aged 47.

In Memory of Mr. Shadrach Child, late of this parish, who died 22nd October 1780, aged 69. Also near this place lie the bodies of Shadrach Child, his father, who died 26th November, 1745, aged 71; Elizabeth Child, his mother, died 12th March 1749, aged 75; Thomas Child, his brother, died 21st October 1767, aged 66. His five sisters also died, Elizabeth, 5th June 1746, aged 44; Margaret, 14th October 1751, aged 35; Anne, 18th August 1775, aged 66; Jane, 2nd October 1776, aged 62; Martha, 25th November 1780, aged 66.

In Memory of John Crowder, who died 15th October 1759, aged 73.

Here lieth the body of Elizabeth Smith, in expectation of that great day—what sort of person she was that great day will best discover—she died 28th March 1749, aged 32.

Here lieth the body of Mrs. Sarah Trotman, who died 24th June 1735, aged 31.

In Memory of Mr. Joshua Bonnett, who died 29th Feb. 1856, aged 57, after a long and painful illness.—*South side.*

Sacred to the Memory of Bathsheba Gurney, who died 4th April 1856, aged 73. Cruciform headstone.—*West side.*

Sacred to the Memory of Mrs. Sarah Tappin, who died 3rd March 1850, in her 62nd year, after a long and painful illness, which she bore with Christian fortitude and patient resignation.—*East side.*

Sophia Louisa Ibotson, died 1st June 1854. Richard Ibotson, Esq. father of the above, died 24th March 1858, aged 59 years. Also Grace, wife of the above, died 30th December, 1858, aged 52.—*West side.*

To the Memory of Matthew Combe Westaway, 3rd son of Mark Alpheus and Elizabeth Westaway, of Hythe End Farm, Ankerwycke, who departed this life 28th July 1858, in the 29th year of his age.

On the South-eastern side of the Churchyard—

Agnes Mary Neville, born 1st March 1821, died 13th October 1860. "She is not dead but sleepeth." The stone is horizontal, on which is a recumbent cross.

Upon a high altar tomb of black marble environed with iron rails, on the South-side of the Church to the right of the entrance porch, are inscribed these words on the tomb, and also on the side of the tomb—

Here lyeth the body of Mary Lee, relict of John Lee, Esq. late of Ankerwycke within this parish, she departed this life 13th day of April 1725, in the 69th year of her age.

At the West-end of the Church and against the belfry wall, is a mural tablet to the Harcourt family, bearing the following inscription—

Ann Harcourt, wife of John Harcourt, Esq. of this Manor of Wraysbury, who died in the year of Our Lord 1770. "The just shall be had in everlasting remembrance."

Also several altar tombs over the vault of the Harcourt family, shewing the following records—

Sacred to the Memory of Philip Harcourt, Esq. of Wigsell, in the parish of Salehurst, county Sussex, where he was buried 18th July 1708. He was eldest son of Sir Philip Harcourt, Kt., of Stanton Harcourt in the county of Oxford, by Elizabeth his 2nd wife, daughter of John Lee, Esq. of London and Ankerwycke House, in this parish, and younger brother of Simon, Viscount and Baron Harcourt, some time Lord High Chancellor of Great Britain.

John Harcourt, Esq. of Ankerwycke, Lord of this Manor, 3rd but eldest surviving son and heir of Philip Harcourt, Esq. of Wigsell, who was buried here 5th October 1789, aged 77.

Sacred to the Memory of Lee Harcourt, 2nd son of Philip Harcourt, Esq. of Wigsell, who died at Bombay, in the East Indies, A.D. 1726, unmarried.

And of Elizabeth, eldest daughter of Philip Harcourt, Esq. and Sarah his wife, who was here buried 5th May 1735.

Sacred to the Memory of Elizabeth, wife of Philip Harcourt, Esq. of Wigsell, daughter and heir of Timothy Woodroffe, M.D., who died 16th December 1728, aged 57.

And of Philip Harcourt, Esq., some time of the Middle Temple, and Lord of this Manor, eldest son of Philip Harcourt, Esq. of Wigsell, and Elizabeth his wife, who died without surviving issue 16th March 1759, aged 61.

Also of Anne, first wife of John Harcourt, Esq. of Ankerwycke, who was Lord of this Manor. She died without issue, and was here buried 20th December 1770.

Sacred to the Memory of George W. Richard, 3rd and youngest son of John Harcourt, Esq. of Ankerwycke, and Mary Irene his 2nd wife; a Major-General and Colonel of the 12th Regiment of Foot, and Governor of the Island of St. Croix, where he died unmarried 19th December 1812, aged 37.

Sacred to the Memory of John Simon Harcourt, Esq. of Ankerwycke, Lord of this Manor, sometime M.P. for Westbury, co. Wilts, eldest son and heir of John Harcourt, Esq. and Margaret Irene his wife. He died 21st Feb. 1810, aged 37 years.

And of Margaret Irene, 2nd wife of John Harcourt, Esq. and daughter of John Sarney Esq. of Somerset House, afterwards married to Admiral Molyneux,* Lord Shuldham, and lastly to John, Earl of Clanwilliam. She died at Silberg, on her estates near Clagenfurth, in Carinthia, 22nd Feb. 1811.

Also of Elizabeth Dale, wife of John Simon Harcourt, Esq. of Ankerwycke, daughter of Major Henniker, Esq., and niece to John, Lord Henniker, who died 10th May 1811, aged 27.

---

* Second son of Rev. Samuel Shuldham, of the Diocese of Ossory, Ireland, co. Baron, 24th June 1776, ob. 1798, sp. (p. 24). Some children of the Harcourts who died infants have been omitted.

Sacred to the Memory of Jessy, 2nd daughter of John Rolls, Esq. of the Hendre, county Monmouth, the beloved wife of George Simon Harcourt, Esq. Lord of this Manor, A.D. 1834, High Sheriff, and sometime one of the representatives in Parliament for this County, She was born 25th June 1809, married 24th June 1833, and died universally beloved, respected and lamented, suddenly at Paris, 29th July 1842.

## THE CHURCH AND MONUMENTS.

The Church, seated on an eminence, the highest ground in the parish, is in the centre of the cemetery, and is dedicated to St. Andrew, brother of St. Peter. St. Andrew's Cross, or Saltire, is represented like an X, and in that shape are some churches which were dedicated to the Saint.

It is impossible to say at what period this sacred edifice was built, and if it be not coeval with Horton Church, which is Saxon, or may be as old as the Edwards. Nor do tradition or history hint at what period the south aisle was taken away, whose absence disfigures the building, and which we trust will soon be restored, as funds are in course of collection for this devoutly to be wished consummation, with plans drawn for improvements of the south and west sides of the sacred edifice.

The Church is a moderate edifice, with its mullioned and transom windows; there are figures representing human faces sculptured on it, mouths which serve for sewers, in architecture termed gargylles or spouts. The stone though good is of course corroded by time, which puts to flight all antiseptic expedients to arrest decay. Such substances are said to be found in a new material called *zopissa*,* which has been applied to the induration of stone, cement, bricks, and other mineral products; and a Committee is now sitting to inquire into the best mode of preserving the stone of the New Parliament Houses, as well as timber, against oceanic action and the ravages of marine insects. The Church is well calculated for a small parish, and could contain sittings for about 200 persons. The population at the commencement of this century may not have exceeded 400, and now it is under 800; but being the mother church to Langley, it ought to have been kept in its integrity; for the latter has not been suffered to decline as our church has. The material of which it is constructed is brick, covered with a sort of cement; the principal entrance is under a huge porch on the south side; the windows are irregular and have stone mullions and tracery variously disposed. The steeple is not very lofty, and is made of wood, being surmounted with a weather vane.

The body of the building consists of a nave and a north aisle, at the east end of which there is a small Lady Chapel, oratory or chantry. The chancel is small, and if the south aisle extended to the end of the church and ran parallel with the chancel, it is likely there was a chantry here correspondent with that in the north aisle. There is now a deep outside gutter to carry off moisture, and prevent the mouldering of the materials of the fabric.

At the west end of the building is the lately erected vestry-room, 12 feet by 14, rather small, but adapted for parochial uses. Heretofore the vestries were held in the body of the church, or at the George Inn, until 1821, when Mr. Brooke Gyll caused a vestry-room to be set up at the corner of the north aisle; but this so completely obstructed the light of a handsome window adorned with mullions and tracery work, that it was deemed expedient after many years to remove it to the western side, which was done by virtue of a faculty in 1851, and at the charge of a member of the Gyll family. It would be better to remove this too, if the Lady Chapel could be assigned for vestry purposes, and an entrance to it would be from the chancel, as well as one from the aisle.

The length of the Church from the eastern extremity to the entrance of the vestry is 60 feet. The length of the chancel is 20 feet by 14, and the width at the transept from the northern to the

* Ζωος πισσα, *live pitch*, a composition of pitch and wax for arresting decay, used by the Greeks, but of doubtful virtue.

southern door is about 38 feet, but which would be enlarged by 13 feet 6 inches if the south wing or aisle were restored. The north aisle is 50 feet long.

Between the chancel and the vestry at the west is a high pointed Gothic arch (the circular is older than the pointed or Saxon arch) which was till lately thickly incrusted with chalk and whitewash, and was recovered from its coating at the same time that all the huge beams in the Church were restored to their pristine state, and were varnished and the church repaved at the expense of a member of the Gyll family, so that now the beauty of the grain, oak or chesnut, is completely developed, giving a cheerful appearance to the vast masses of wood, indicative of the primitive condition of the building.

There is a gallery under the pointed arch westwards, where formerly there was an organ, given in 1839 by Mr. G. S. Harcourt, on the day of a confirmation held here by the Bishop of Lincoln, and the organ loft was enlarged to accommodate a choir at the pious instance of Jessy, wife of Mr. G. Harcourt. This organ has been removed, either from decay or from its being inadequate to the necessities of time and place. The gallery is opened, and has lights behind, and an *harmonium* contributes to the choral wants of the church. It will afford room on either side for ten male and ten female choristers. In 1856, Mr. Neville, the vicar, introduced choral classes into the service of the church, for the realisation of which a subscription of some £25 was raised. A fine organ of moderate size would be a great boon, the means of elevating the soul to religious rapture, a spiritual expedient of great antiquity in the church.

High above the organ loft is the wooden tower, wherein are five bells, four of which are situated towards the east, with the *tenor* at the west side, which is of considerable weight. It is 2 feet 8 in. high, and its diameter 3 feet 2 inches, and at the top 20 inches in diameter; it has on it X. s. q. 1. + sit nomen × Domini—Henesell.

Bell No. 1 is the smallest, for they decrease gradually, 2 feet 2 inches high, and it is *cracked*; its diameter is 2 feet 2 inches below, the top diameter is 14 inches, and it has on it, T.H. R.L. H.W. 1657. Bell No. 2 has on it Bryanus Eldridge me fecit 1657. Bell No. 3 has on it William Eldridge made me, 1664.

The bells are not deficient in an emission of melody and power. These services to the church are of great antiquity, from about the 7th century, and in Romanist days bells were *baptized* and *anointed* with holy oil, and had fantastic verses on them; prior to the invention of bells at Nola in Italy, congregations were called to church by wooden rattles, *sacra lignea*. The largest bell known is one in Russia, said to weigh 432,000 lbs., and stands near 20 feet high, 21 yards round and 23 inches thick. The ringing of bells in change is said to be peculiar to Great Britain, which has ringing colleges, while chiming is practised on the Continent by means of a particular apparatus added to a clock.

The font has a very antique character with a high wooden covering, large, circular, plain and columnar, standing on a square plinth under the gallery, between the nave and the aisle, where arches are supported by massive square piles; it is said there are more than 70 circular fonts in Bucks, all very ancient; and adjacent to the font is a stove which was generously given in 1852 by Felix Pryor, Esq., then tenant of Ankerwycke, at the cost of £60. It passes through a tube to the northern entrance, and the external brickwork runs up considerably, so that the smoke may rise above the building level. To many who have dwelt at Ankerwycke, as well as to the present tenant, Mr. C. Scholefield, this parish is beholden for charity and gifts, and it may not be irrelevant here to notice that the principal families resident in this secluded village seem to have very laudably vied with each other in contributing to the service and decoration of the church, affording to every admirer of these interesting repositories of the sacred remains of our departed ancestors and friends, an example worthy general imitation. There is an account of the gift of John Lee, Esq. on a stone panel set in oak, affixed to the south side wall.

An extract from the Codicil annexed to the last will and testament of John Lee, Esq. of London, dated 21st February, 1697, and the codicil, 11th July, 1704:—

"I do hereby give, devise, and bequeath unto the Governors of the Charity for the Relief of Poor Children of Clergymen, and their successors for ever, all that annual sum of £52. 16s, now reduced to a moiety, payable out of the hereditary revenue of Excise, and which were granted by Gilbert Whitehall by a certain deed poll or writing under his hand and seal, bearing date 29th April, 1678, unto my late father, John Lee of London, Esq., since dead, whose estate and interest therein is now come to and vested in me and my heirs; and also all that other annual sum of £18, now reduced to a moiety, payable also out of the said hereditary revenue of excise, and which was granted by the said Gilbert Whitehall by another deed poll or writing under his hand and seal, dated 29th April, 1678, unto the said John Lee the testator, and my heirs and assigns for ever; and all my estate, right, title, interest, claim and demand whatsoever, of, in and to the said several sums, to have, hold and enjoy the said several annual sums unto the said Governors of the Charity for the Relief of Poor Widows and Children of Clergymen, and their successors for ever, upon trust, and to the intent and purpose that the said Governors and their successors shall from time to time, and at all times from and after my decease for ever, employ and dispose of all such sums of money as shall be by them, their bayliffs or agents, from time to time received by virtue of these presents or the devises hereby made, or permit or suffer the same to be from time to time for ever, and upon my decease employed and dispersed by the Court of Assistants of the said Corporation, for the paying unto such orthodox minister of the Church of England, as by law established, as shall be in that behalf elected, nominated and appointed by the said Court of Assistants, the sum of £20 every year for ever, to read divine service and preach a sermon in the parish church of Wyrardisbury, on every Sunday in every year in the afternoon for ever: and also for the paying unto such person as shall officiate then and there as clerk for the time being, £1 of the like money yearly for ever; and also for the providing 12 pennyworth of bread to be distributed every Sunday to and among such poor persons of the parish of Wyrardisbury aforesaid, who shall be most necessitous and most deserving, and who shall be present at the said divine service and sermon; and also upon trust to dispose of all the rest and surplusage of the premises remaining after all charges by reason of the trust aforesaid, shall be defrayed yearly for ever, in and for the relief of poor widows and children of clergymen, in such manner as by the said Court of Assistants of the said Corporation shall be ordered or directed. A.D. 1807. Rev. Wm. Clarke, Vicar. John Barrow, Joseph Adkins, Churchwardens."

On a panel of stone bordered with yellow, in the south aisle, is this Benefaction left by the will of William Gyll, Esq., who died in 1798:—

"I give and bequeath to the Minister and Churchwardens of the parish of Wyrardisbury for the time being, and their successors, the sum of £300, 3 per cent. consols, upon trust to pay the dividends thereof yearly on every Christmas day for ever, unto and equally among 24 such poor housekeepers of the same parish who do not receive alms, as they the said minister and churchwardens for the time being, or the major part of them, deem most proper objects of charity."

Likewise the following:—

"I give to the Minister and Churchwardens for the time being of the parish of Wyrardisbury the sum of £100, 4 per cent. Bank Annuities, upon trust to lay out the dividends and yearly products thereof in the purchase of bread, to be distributed at their discretion among the poor of the parish every Christmas day, or within one week after. Fretwell Vanderman, Vicar. William Groom, William Thomas, Churchwardens. A.D. 1798."

Upon the same pillar there is an exceeding handsome monument of white marble, with a shield of the arms of Harcourt and Rolls encircled with cypress boughs, and surmounted with a graceful peacock on a ducal coronet, the crest of Harcourt; on the sides are two seraphs holding a shroud, and underneath is written—" Sacred to the memory of Jessy Harcourt, the beloved wife of George Simon Harcourt, Esq. of Ankerwycke House in this parish, late one of the representatives of this county in Parliament. She was the second daughter of John Rolls, Esq., of the Hendre, in the county of Monmouth, and died suddenly at Paris, 29th July, 1842, aged 33 years, nine days after the birth of a daughter, still-born. Her remains with those of her infant are deposited in the family vault here, awaiting the blessed resurrection."*

Not far from this monument is a grey stone, inlaid with brass figures of a gentleman and a lady; above the head of the latter is a shield with a chevron between three eagles displayed. The arms over the gentleman are hidden by the floor of a pew, together with the inscription and the whole of the effigy of the lady. It may be the family of Gould, of Wraysbury (see page 75).

This part of the shire is not at all famous for its antiquities, nor have there been any stone coffins found, into which bodies were laid when in the church, as they were too heavy to move with the tenant within; but there is a description of *relics* here, temp. Richard II., ascribed to Sir John Shorne (it was customary to knight the clergy), but that conjecture requires proof; it is not however impossible but some tomb or rood, or superstitious relics were here as elsewhere, " when all our fathers worshipped stocks and stones." Richard II. was a benefactor to Ankerwycke, page 29.

Sir John Shorne was Rector of North Marston in Bucks, 1290, and a native of Kent. His will is dated 9th May, 1308, in which he left his *little* to the poor, "his blessed part to heaven, and slept in peace."

The superstition of his days ascribed superhuman potency to this son of sanctity, and it relates how he blessed a well whose medicinal virtues were a specific for all cutaneous disorders, derivable from the prayers of Shorne, whose flesh and muscles had become *horny* from certain postures of devotion, "and who oftener upon his *knees* than on his *feet*, died every day he lived." Some lives narrate how he conjured the devil into a *boot*, and this miracle is as well attested as the impudent impostures in our day of *winking madonnas*, Hohenlöhe's marvels, &c.—to hoodwink the credulous two-footed animals.

> Sir John Shorne, gentleman born,
> Conjured the devil into a *Boot*.

Ceremonies were performed at Shorne's well, and this may be referred to the superstitions of *well*-worship practised by the Britons, Saxons and Germans; formerly a species of *Saturnalia*, which were fortunately converted into rustic diversions, and terminated in the decoration of wells with garlands and boughs of trees—hence probably the *Dedication* feasts of Churches.

Several sepulchral slabs have been despoiled of their brasses: there are some in the floor of the nave, but so battered by ancient contusion and the brush of time as to be scarce recognizable.

Richard Bennet died 1st May, 1733, aged .

Here lyeth the body of Mary, wife of Henry Gibbons, of this parish, died 8th May, 1687, in the 35th year of her age.

* Want of space obliges us to omit the latter part of the inscription, detailing the shining and acknowledged virtues of the lady, which is to be found *in extenso* in Dr. Lipscomb's History of Bucks.

Here also lyeth the body of Henry, son of Henry Gibbons of this parish. Hee was husband to the deceased Mary Gibbons. Hee died 3rd July, 1687, aged 50 years.

In the north aisle.—Underneath this stone is interred the body of Mr. Robert Style, late of this parish, who departed this life 28th June, 1786, aged 68 years.

Also Mrs. Martha Style, wife of the above, who died 10th December, 1815, aged 89 years.

At the west end of the north aisle.—Here lieth interred y$^e$ body of Ellis Trippick, who died 20th February, 1710, aged 49 years.

Here lieth the body of Martha, widow of James Sayer of Staines; she was also wife to the above mentioned Ellis Trippick of this parish. She died 6th May, 1727, aged 61.

Here lieth the body of Mr. Ellis Trippick, late of this parish, yeoman, who died y$^e$ 10th August, 1752, aged 57.

On a mural tablet in the north aisle.—This monument is erected by a disconsolate widow to the memory of Isaac Holmes, of Ely Place, London, who died 27th January, 1793, aged 39, and is buried in a vault near this spot.

In the same place lie the bodies of four of his children. William Style Holmes, died 23rd October, 1786. Mary Ann Holmes, died 17th November, 1790. Harriot, 1798. Carolus Holmes, 1792: all infants.

Sacred to the memory of Henry Davies, who died 3rd May, 1852, aged 68. *In cœlo quies.*

On a black marble in the pavement of the east end of the north aisle.

> In certain hope that day to see,
> Wherein the dead shall raised be.

Catharine, the wife of Mr. Francis Bowry, of this parish of Wyrardisbury, departed this life 20th day of January, A.D. 1692-3, in the 49th year of her age.

Some verses.

In like manner the above named Mr. Francis Bowry departed this life 5th September, 1726, in the 77th year of his age, and is here also interred.

Some verses.

Here lyeth —— the daughter of —— of this parish, and citizen of —— died 1720. A pew conceals the rest of the inscription.

This section of the church was once a chapel or chantry for priests, probably dedicated to the Virgin, as there are cavities in the wall for holy water, and a deep recess for the Virgin or some image; the last remaining ones of which were to come away in 1547 by Act of Parliament.

Round the four corners are cantons for armorial ensigns, and which are now filled with those of Harcourt and Gyll, Smijth and Williams, painted according to the emblazonment of each.

There is a door here which conducts to the chancel; it seems of a later construction than the partition wall. The large window is here in which some stained glass has been repaired, and there is now no obstruction to the light,

> "Right against the Eastern gate,
> Where the great sun begins his state."

It was against this mullioned window that the old vestry stood, since transported to the west of the church. The windows in the north aisle are improved by the addition of stained glass.

The pulpit and reading-desk are together, and of old oak highly varnished; the former has a sounding board of oak also, they stand nearly in the centre of the church; and opposite to them is the beautifully ornamented oak-pew belonging to Ankerwycke House. It has moulded panels, with the upper compartments very richly carved with perforated work, the foliage and execution in the style of Grindling Gibbons,* of wood-carving memory, an art since brought to incredible perfection.

Steele, in his account of this church, mentions a beautiful pew of right wainscot on the south side appropriated to the sole use of Mr. Leigh (Lee), over which was a large hatchment of arms. G. a fesse counter-compony O. and Az. between 10 billets of the 2d—4, 3, 2, 1 quartering Az., a cinque foil within a bordure engrailed erm.

Crest, on a torse A. and G. a squirrel ppr. browsing on a branch of hazel, vert. fructed O. on the north side of the nave on a tablet of marble.

In memory of John Simon Harcourt, Esq., who departed this life 21st February 1810, aged 37 years, eldest son of John Harcourt, Esq. Also Elizabeth Dale Harcourt, wife of the above, who departed this life 10th May 1811, aged 27 years: daughter of Major Henniker, Esq., and Mary his wife. They left two infant children, viz. George Simon, born 25th February 1807; and Elizabeth, born 22nd May 1808. On a mural monument—Elizabeth relict of Philip Harcourt, Esq., daughter of Timothy Woodroffe, M.D., died XVI December MDCCXXVIII, aged XXVII. This monument was erected by her son Philip Harcourt, Esq., late Lord of the Manor, who died XVI day of March MDCCLIX, aged LXI, and lies also interred near this place.

Above fixed to a pyramid of marble are arms on a gilt shield in relievo, 9 quarterings of Harcourt:—†

1. Two bars in chief a crescent. 2. Three lions passant gard. 3. Fretté a canton erm. 4. A cross moline. 5. The sun in splendour. 6. Lion ramp. within a tressure flory. 7. Three eagles displayed. 8. A fesse chequé between 10 billets. 9. A bend erm. within a bordure charged with a rose or cinquefoil.

Crest on a ducal coronet a peacock ppr. close. Motto: Le bon temps viendra.

There are several hatchments of Harcourt and one of Lord Shuldham (page 112) on a mural tablet of white marble.—Sacred to the memory of George Simon, infant son of George Simon and Jesse Harcourt, of Ankerwycke House in this parish, born 24th May, and died 10 June 1834.

## THE CHANCEL.

This division of the church measures about 21 feet from the eastern window to the pointed or Saxon arch, which separates it from the body of the holy edifice; and there are about 14 feet across the chancel. This section is rather small, but it is lofty and neatly kept, and contains 13 monuments to the Gyll and Hassel family, under which is the family vault. There are also two horizontal slabs containing brasses; and probably there were others which have disappeared. The inscription of one to the memory of the Gould family has been preserved, but the slab of brass is gone.

Here lyeth the body of Edward Gould, Esq., Sarvant of King Charles II., son of Alexander Gould, Esq. of Wyrardisbury. Died 25th December 1680, aged 69.

He may have been buried in the vault below. After the system of cremation or burning corpses was abolished, some 180 A.D., in consequence of the progress of Christianity, cemeteries became

---

* It is not known where this wood-carver was born, but he was of English parents residing in Holland. Charles II. gave him a place in the Board of Works, and he was employed at Windsor in his vocation. He carved the much-admired foliage in St. George's Chapel; and at Burleigh, Chatsworth, and Petworth are his carvings found, a noble profusion of which decorates these British palaces. He died in London, 3rd August 1721.

† We omit the general detail of the arms on hatchments from circumscription of space. Some account of this church was taken in 1718 by E. Steele, a house-painter at Bromley: the MSS. are in the possession of J. B. Nichols, Esq., F.S.A.

general; and by degrees superstition raised its head, and thought that the nearer a corpse was interred to the church the safer the spirit was: and this idea further degenerated, so that bodies were buried in the church itself, and at last they were deposited under the Communion Table. In 1855 all intramural burials were prohibited, although it has not been universally carried out in thinly populated parishes, where ancient vaults exist.

The smallest brass is the oldest extant here, and is in good preservation, and was formerly under the feet of the servants in the pew belonging to the lay rector; but Mr. Gyll procured its removal to the south side of the chancel, to prevent *abrasion* from pressure, and it is now opposite to the brass slab to the memory of Dame Elizabeth Hoby, sister of Mr. John Stonor. A brass plate is affixed to the sepulchral slab. It exhibits an Eton Scholar's dress, attired in a cap or hood drawn over the head, a long gown girded and faced with fur, having tight sleeves, and fastened at the right side, with these words in old English.

"Here lyeth John Stonor the Sone of Walter Stonor Squyer, that departed this worlde ye xxix day of August in the yere of our Lorde mbxii."

On the north side of the chancel are three escutcheons of arms, viz.:—

Quarterly: 1 and 4, a fesse between 6 martlets; 2 and 3, chevron between 3 roses, 2 party per fesse and pale of 9 coats. 1. Quarterly: 1 and 4, a fesse between 6 martlets; 2 and 3, a chevron between 3 roses. 2. Two bars indented: in chief. 3. Three roses. 4. On a bend 3 mullets pierced. 5. Six lioncels ramp. on a canton a mullet. 6. A fesse charged with an annulet between 3 leopards faces. 7. A chevron between 3 lions ganbs erased. 8. A fesse checqué. 9. Two bars gemelles, impaling a saltire vaire between 4 mullets.—The last described coat impaling a saltire vaire between 4 mullets. N.B. Same arms are on the windows of Place Farm (page 64.)

Below is the following inscription in old English letters on the horizontal monument:—

"Here lyeth buried Dame Elizabeth Hobby, doughter and heire to Sr. Walter Stonor of Stonor in ye county of Oxon., Knight, sometime wyfe to Walter Walsh of Elmeley in the Countie of Worcester, Esquier, sarbant to King Henry ye VIII of his Pribey Chamber, which Dame Elizabeth dyed the xyd day of August Ao Dni mdlx: Also here lyeth buryed Walter Walsh late of this parishe of Wyrardsbury in ye countie of Bucks, Esquier, sone and heire to the said Walter Walsh and Dame Elizabeth, whiche Walter the sone dyed xxb day of February in the yere of oure Lorde God Mccccclxi."

Brasses in churches are not much older than the time of King Edward I. 1271, or in the 12th century; and in the days of Cromwell, it is said, that monuments were despoiled for the metal, but the example is much anterior to the epoch of the Commonwealth. They were very numerous in England, about as many are lost as are preserved, viz. 4000. Out of 190 churches in Bucks some 90 retain brasses, and the number preserved is about 240. The oldest brass dates 1349, and it is at Ivinghoe to the memory of Ralph Fullywolle and his wife Lucy, to whom there is also a brass of 1368 date. The next oldest is in Taplow Church, 1350, to Nichole de Aunnberdene, (Ambrosden), Oxon. Thomas Cheyne, at Drayton Beauchamp, has a brass to his memory, who was shield-bearer to King Edward III., 1368; and one to William Cheyne, 1375. There are several of early date subsequent.

In the 12th century figures are represented on coffins in effigy, while crosses are as early as the 9th century.

The art of enamelling came from Venice, so did that of staining glass, about the 10th century. The earliest recorded brass is 1208, and there are very few abroad. Some brasses were taken up, the engraving effaced, and new engraving superimposed — like manuscripts, whose writing was obliterated or partially expunged and new writing inserted, hence they took the same name, *palimpsest*. The plates were called cullen plate from Cöln. In modern times the art of rubbing brasses has been discovered: it is done with heel ball or pouch ball, like lithographic ink, brought to great perfection; and can be transferred to stone or zinc. The principal brasses of England have been published in folio volumes.

Some brasses were of colossal size, one at Durham being 16 feet by 9 feet, on the floor; and some so diminutive as to be only 6 or 7 inches long, inserted into walls.

On the north side of the chancel is a large mural monument, consisting of a sarcophagus of alabaster, with an urn beautifully carved in relievo, leaves, tendrils, &c.

Arms above and below. Erm. 2 chevronels, one S. the other Az. between 3 mullets in pale of the last, Paxton impaling Gyll.

Sacred to the memory of Harriet Paxton, wife of Archibald Paxton, Esq., of Watford Place, Herts, and daughter of William Gyll, Esq. of this parish, who, during the period of a few years, having fulfilled the duties of a long life, and having held out an eminent example to others, as a daughter, as a sister, as a wife, and as a parent, left her sorrowing relations and her disconsolate husband to deplore her irreparable loss. She died x day of Nov. MDCCXCIV, in the XXXIII year of her age. A. Paxton, Esq. died 11th August MDCCCXVII, aged LXXX years, leaving an only child, William Gyll Paxton, Esq., who died III May MDCCCL, aged LXII.

On another mural monument of white statuary marble—

In memory of William, son of George Gyll, Esq., who died 10th August 1754, aged 68. Also his son William Gyll, Esq., of Wyrardisbury House in this parish, died 26th March 1798, aged 74, of the family of Gyll, of Wydial, Herts, and of Boxley, Kent. Also Mary, wife of William Gyll, Esq., eldest daughter and coheir of John Brome, Esq., of Ludlow, Salop; died 11th March 1820, aged 88. Mr. Brome married Mary, daughter and heir of Samuel Bowdler, Esq., of Ludlow, Salop.

Arms:—S. 2 chev. A. each charged with three mullets of the 1st, in base a cinquefoil A. on a canton O. a lion passant guard. G. impaling. 4thly. 1 and 4. Vert. 3 snakes in pale A. 2 and 3. S. on a chevron O. 3 green leaves slipped.

Crest:—A demi eagle, with wings displayed Az. fretté O. beaked of the last. Gyll in the centre impaling Hassel and Brome.

On a very handsome monument of white marble, on which is a figure of Faith bending over a column, is this inscription, the proper names being in red colour,—

Sacred to the memory of the Right Hon. Hamilton Flemyng, ninth and last Earl of Wigtoun and Baron Cumbernauld in Scotland, who departed this life 13th June 1809, aged 64. Also of the Right Hon. Mary Countess of Wigtoun his wife, daughter and heir of William Child, of Birthwaite Hall, Darton, co. York; and Saranmaria, daughter and coheir of William Rooke, Esq., of Barnsley, co. York, who died 31st January 1797, aged 57 years. Also of Lady Harriet Jane Flemyng, only child of the above, and wife of William Gyll, Esq., of Wyrardisbury House in this parish, and Yeoveny Hall, Middlesex, who died 6th November, 1813, aged 37 years. Also Bellenden Charles Gyll, Esq. of Hythe End, Wyrardisbury, son of the above, whose decease took place 24th September 1822, aged 23 years.

This monument is erected by their descendants as a token of their unfeigned affection.

Arms:—1 and 4. A. a chevron within a double tressure, flory and counterflory, E. Flemyng. 3. Az. 3 cinquefoils A. Frazer. Crest:—A goat's head erased A. armed O. Supporters 2 stags ppr. attired and unguled O, each gorged with a collar Az. charged with 3 cinquefoils A. Motto: Let deed shaw.

On another mural monument, with a very elegant marble figure in relievo of Hope resting on an anchor, and holding a shield, containing arms of Gyll impaling Flemyng.

Sacred to the memory of William Gyll, Captain of 2nd Regiment of Life Guards, and first Equerry to H.R.H. the Duke of Sussex, who departed this life in the thirty-second year of his age, 16th February 1806, after a long and painful illness which he bore with exemplary piety and resignation. He was only son of Wm. Gyll, Esq. of this parish. This monument is erected by his widow, as a small token of the respect and affection she bore him through life, and of her regret for his death.

Underneath a neat mural slab (scroll pattern with cypress boughs), the south side of the chancel, are the arms of Gyll impaling Richardson, erm. on a chief Az. 3 lions' heads erased A. cinqued G.

Sacred to the memory of Maria Jane, the much-beloved and affectionate wife of Brooke Hamilton Gyll, Esq. of this parish, daughter of the late William Richardson, Esq., Accountant-General of the Hon. East India Company, and the Right Hon. Elizabeth, Dowager Countess of Winterton, his second wife, born xii May 1794, married 3rd May 1821, and alas! prematurely died 21st July following, aged 27 years. (Some extracts from Job.)

On a very handsome mural monument, south of the communion table, surmounted with a sarcophagus enveloped with flowers, with an inscription, "Sacred to conjugal and maternal affection," underneath a shield of Pytches impaling Hassel and Prowse.

This marble is inscribed in memory of a tenderly beloved child, Sophia Pytches, third daughter of Sir Abraham Pytches, Kt. of Streatham, co. Surrey, and Dame Jane his wife, granddaughter of Robert Prowse Hassel, Esq., and Elizabeth his wife, who, with other relatives, are interred in a vault under the communion table: born 3rd September 1761, died July 1779. Also in memory of a dear and ever beloved child, Penelope, wife of the Rev. Robert Sheffield, fourth daughter of the above-named Abraham and Jane Pytches: born 12th January 1764, died 22nd January 1787.

In the same vault are deposited the remains of the Right Hon. Emily Elizabeth Coventry, daughter of the Right Honourable Lord Viscount Deerhurst and the Right Hon. Peggy, his wife, daughter of the above Sir Abraham and Jane Pytches: died 17th March, 1789, aged 18 months. To these great and several losses has his afflicted wife to add with deepest regret that of her beloved husband, Sir Abraham Pytches, Kt., a sincere friend, a kind father, and affectionate husband. He closed a life of strict rectitude, 10th April 1792, aged 72. Dame Jane Pytches died 30th March 1796, aged 62. Four surviving daughters lament the loss of so excellent a parent, and from filial affection and gratitude inscribe this small tribute of their duty to her beloved memory.

On another large mural monument, white and grey, having an urn from which issues a flame above, and underneath the arms of Gyll impaling Hassel and Prowse.—(South side of the chancel.)

In memory of Elizabeth Gyll, eldest daughter of Robert Prowse Hassel, Esq., wife of William Gyll, Esq., of this parish: died 9th June 1769, aged 39; and left issue, one son and six daughters. (Here follow six lines in verse.) Elizabeth Gyll, ob. 28th November 1776, ætat. 24. Frances Gyll, ob. 28th January 1785, ætat. 24. Robert Hutton Gyll, ob. 28th October 1792, ætat. 34. Margaret, wife of John Deschamps, Esq., ob. 9th December 1799, ætat. 46. Susanna, married first Thomas Chudleigh Sanders, Esq.; secondly, William Bailey, Esq., of Tonbridge Castle, Kent, ob. 7th December 1833, ætat. 77. Grace Gyll, ob. 1st June 1847, ætat. 84.

On the north side of the chancel a very white mural monument on a black marble slab, surmounted with an urn enveloped in a shroud; and at the base between the feet are the arms of Gyll impaling Murray and Frazer. A hunting horn S. stringed and garnished G. on a chief Az. 3 stars of the first. In the epitaph black and red letters are interchanged.

In the vault beneath repose the remains of Hamilton Gyll, Esq., of Shenley Lodge, and Salisbury Hall, co. Herts, who died 21st February 1844, aged 39. Also Captain William and Lady Harriet Gyll of Wyrardisbury House: he has left to deplore his loss two sons and his widow Frances Caroline, who, during a protracted illness, attended him with exemplary affection, daughter and coheir of Sir John Murray, eleventh Baronet, descended lineally from Sir David Murray, Kt. of Stanhope, co. Peebles, Scotland, and the Lady Lilias Flemyng, daughter of John sixth Lord Flemyng and first Earl of Wigtoun.

On another square mural tablet, with a shield set in cypress boughs, are the cognizances of Wright and Gyll in pale. O. a chevron Az. charged with cross crosslets fitché A. between 3 greyhounds courant S. Sacred to the memory of Thomas Wright, Esq., Alderman of the City of London, who died ix April MDCCLXXXIV, aged LXXVI: he was son of Edward Wright, Esq. of Aldington, Kent; and he married Ann, daughter of William Gyll, Esq.

On another slab of marble.—In memory of Ann Wright, widow of the late Thomas Wright, Esq., who died 4th May, 1809, aged 82 years. Also Mrs. Elizabeth Kincaid, who died 21st October, 1800, aged 82; daughters of William Gyll, Esq. of Maidstone, Kent. Extract from the Bible. Arms in lozenge, Wright impaling Gyll.

Underneath there is another slab containing the words:—In memory of Ann Willes, widow of John Willes, Esq. of Dulwich, Surrey, daughter of Thomas Wright, Esq. of the same place, and Ann, daughter of William Gyll, Esq. of Boxley, Kent. William Gyll married Elizabeth, daughter and heir of John Lawrence, Esq., and Elizabeth, daughter of Richard Brooke, Esq. of Kent, and sister of James Brooke, Esq. of Lewisham, Kent, High Sheriff of Kent, 1731.

A small marble monument, surmounted by an urn, is thus inscribed:—William Wentworth Deschamps, Esq., who died 27th December, 1830, æt. 56. Also Lieutenant Henry Price Deschamps, R.N., third son of the above, who died at the Island of Ascension, 8th February, 1838, æt. 35. Also Frances Ann, wife of W. W. Deschamps, ob. 16th October, 1840, æt. 68, grandson of William Gyll, Esq.

A large square monument ornamented, south side of the chancel.—To the memory of Robert Prowse Hassel, Esq. died 2nd April, 1760, aged 64. John Hutton, Esq. died 14th February, 1764, aged 70 years. Elizabeth Hassel died 9th June, 1773, aged 80. This mark of esteem and affection is testified by William Gyll, Esq. 1785.

For many years the picture (6 feet high by 9 long, an oil painting on leather, highly varnished, in the centre of which is the monogram I.H.S., with angels at the four corners), now placed behind the communion table, which is railed in with cushioned forms for communicants to kneel on, and which was painted by a Mr. Hassel, an amateur in this graceful and scientific art, was formerly fixed against the eastern window, and obstructed incoming light. When the new windows were set, in 1845, this picture was removed to the great advantage of the chancel and church. The eastern window is a good specimen of its period, which is that of decorated gothic architecture. It has a triplet and three quatrefoils in the head, with four other small openings, all of which have been filled with beautiful stained glass, and executed by Ward and Nixon, who supplied similar windows in St. George's Chapel, Windsor.

Of the three quatrefoils above, the uppermost has in it a cross of ancient ruby glass, formerly in a window here, and of great antiquity. Another quatrefoil has the crown of thorns, and the third has the sacramental cup, all surrounded with scrollages and borders.

The three large lights are filled with very elegant mosaic and scrollage patterns, and are the same as once adorned a church at Cologne on the Rhine.

In the centre are inserted the armorial ensigns of Gyll, quartering Flemyng and impaling those of Bowyer Smijth. The two side lights bearing the crests of Gyll and Flemyng.

It is not unusual to insert on presentation or memorial windows the name of the donor, or the party on whose account the window or glass was given, but here arms are introduced. In all such windows places assigned to heraldry would be better filled with sacred and more congenial subjects.

The south window in the chancel, of stained glass, is of smaller dimensions, and it has well replaced a window which excluded light and had no recommendation to compensate. The present window has its mullions and architectural adornments carved in stone like its eastern neighbour.

At the summit are two small openings of painted glass, and in the centre is a quatrefoil with a handsome pattern of the same, in which the letters G.W.J.G. are convoluted; while below, the window consists of two lights of scrollage pattern, but not quite so rich in execution as the adjoining lights in the eastern window. On the dexter side are the arms of Gyll with six quarterings, and on the sinister side those of Flemyng with as many. The play of colours on the monuments when the sun is brilliant, affords a pleasing variegation.

The Saracenic or gothic stone arch supported on pillars of massy proof, which separates the chancel from the nave, was once encumbered with an immense board containing the Decalogue, Lord's prayer and Creed (and a scrap of Greek, &c.) which have been transferred to the oak wainscot over the Communion Table, and are inserted in golden letters, at once adorning the wall and relieving its obscurity, which the intervention of the board under the point of the arch caused. Its removal has restored the architectural symmetry to the arch, and now the large eastern window may be clearly seen from the western extremity of the church.

In lieu of the darkness at the eastern parts caused by the picture against the window, the painted glass "richly dight casts a dim religious light," such as befits a receptacle consecrated to devotion.*

We here take leave of the church and the cemetery, and repassing the Lich-gate we find ourselves in a file of young chestnut trees, which were planted a few years since by the author of this history, while the old bushes and shrubs which obstructed the access to the church have totally disappeared. In time, this contemplated improvement, which gives an open space, will also secure an umbrageous passage to the church, with the beauty of verdure and fragrance superadded.

The house known as Church Farm is an object of deserved admiration, and is tenanted by Mr. James Pullin, whose taste has completed improvements commenced by his predecessor and father-

---

\* In the "Windsor and Eton Express," 31st May, 1845.

"The small but neat parish church of this place has lately received an accession to its internal embellishment by the addition of a very handsome stained glass window in the chancel, the gift of Gordon W. J. Gyll, Esq. brother of Brooke Hamilton Gyll, Esq. lay rector of the parish, to which family, long residents in the place, the church and parish have been indebted for various acts of munificence.

"Its equal in Bucks is only to be found in the elaborate stained glass window presented to the new church in the town of Buckingham by his Grace the Duke of Buckingham, which with this window comprise the only two specimens of this kind of fenestral church ornaments extant in the shire.

"The window is a facsimile of one originally in a church, now destroyed, at Cologne on the Rhine, and the public will appreciate the beauty of the execution by Messrs. Ward and Nixon, of Frith Street, Soho, who have been engaged in similar artistic operations in St. George's Chapel, Windsor.

"The exquisitely chiselled marble figures of monumental art which grace and enrich our village church, with this beautiful stained glass window and the suspension bridge in the parish, &c., constitute features in Bucks worthy the period and the shire, and will reflect credit on those whose laudable ambition incites them to imitate and rival each other in embellishments suitable to the locality."

R

in-law, Mr. Henry Stevens, sometime of Horton. Mr. Pullin rents nearly all the land owned in this parish by Colonel Williams, and it is no more than justice to add that the property has improved under the lesseeship of one who concentrates his energies on the amelioration of the soil committed to his superintendance.

We now descend the inclined plane where the avenue conducts to the village, and we wish that it had crossed the opposite field, belonging to Mr. Francis Buckland; so passing a slated barn of a commodious size, which is a good substitute for the former one consumed a few years ago by a fierce fire of 12 hours duration, at the loss of some £500,—that the thoroughfare had joined the old road leading to Place Farm. By this adoption the way now used, and which in winter is, from its low level, often full of water, could be avoided. This would be of admitted utility to the farmers, and let us suggest that if another access to Wraysbury, through a field belonging to Colonel Williams, and conducting to the wharf on the bank of the Thames were effected, and a solid bridge thrown across at a point below Ankerwycke, which in the map of 1770 is styled Pay-gate, whereby a new entrance to the village would be made, unequivocal advantages would accrue to the parish, already made better by good avenues into it, good roads through it, and a railway which has been most serviceable to a once sequestered hamlet. The bridge would terminate nearly opposite to the Bells of Ouseley, and so afford a quicker passage into Old and New Windsor, Staines and Datchet.

The present access to the Wharf House, already a defined road, would facilitate the completion of a better one, and a bridge to traverse the stream would be ornamental and a *desideratum* to the parish and the entire vicinity. It might be costly at first, yet it would give a return in increased commerce, and we must remember that good is seldom conferred but at the price of money and labour, and these combined appliances rarely fail to yield adequate reward.

## DAY AND SUNDAY SCHOOLS.

In this parish are two schools supported by voluntary subscriptions. That attached to the Established Church is a day and Sunday school, and it consists of a school room 28 feet by 15, for boys as well as girls, with a master and mistress. That supported by Dissenters is only a Sunday school, and may be said just to have a local habitation and a name; the children are beholden to Mrs. William Thomas Buckland for tuition. The only dissenters here are Baptists, not *Anabaptists;* there is some stress laid on these distinctions. By *particular* Baptists (of which at Horton, Egham, and Wraysbury there are many) are intended those who have been *solemnly immersed* in water upon personal confession of faith—which is, that there are three Divine persons in the Godhead, eternal and personal election, original sin, particular redemption, efficacious grace in regeneration and sanctification, free justification by the imputed righteousness of Christ, and the final perseverance of the *saints*. These are styled Calvinistic Baptists. One of the greatest authorities in their faith is Dr. John Gill, D.D. a shining light in theology, morals, and erudition. His father Edward taught a Baptist congregation at Kettering in Northamptonshire, and died in 1723, having been induced to become Baptist by some very zealous Presbyterians and Baptists, and in this persuasion he educated his son, Dr. John, one of the most learned Hebraists and commentators on the Scriptures. His style resembled himself, manly, nervous, plain—conscious of the unutterable dignity, value, and importance of the freight it conveyed. His learning and labours were only exceeded by the invariable sanctity of his life and conversation. He died, aged 74, in 1771. He bore the armorial ensigns of Gyll of Herts, which are on all his pictures taken in manhood and age. He is supposed to descend from a junior branch of that of Wydial, Herts, settled in Northamptonshire, to illustrate which I add a few descents and an engraving of the arms:—

GYLL OF WYDIAL HALL

RICHARD GYLL, of Easton, Hunts, brother of John Gyll, of Wydial, Herts, who died 1547.

Arms: S. 2 chevrons A. each charged with 3 mullets of the field, in a base a cinquefoil of the 2nd, on a canton O. lion pass. guard. G.

JOHN GYLL, cited in the will of Leonard Gyll, proved 14 July, 1547, at Cambridge. Visn. London, 1634, p. 99.

JOHN GYLL, of Sudbro', Northamptonshire, will proved 2 Oct. 1616.=SARAH, d. of — Ward, extrix. 1616.

2. JOHN GYLL.= 1. PHILIP GYLL, of Edmonton,=ELIZABETH, d. of Tho. Bateman, m. 19 Feb. 1632. M.D. ob. 1652, will pr. 1653.

JOHN, of Kettering, ob. 1718, presumed to be his son.=THOMAS GYLL, M.D. b. 1642, ob. 1714.=MARTHA, d. of — ob. 1702. will pr. Commissary Court, Lond.

EDWARD, of do. b. 1 July, 1672, will proved 20 April, 1723.=

DR. JOHN GILL, the Baptist Divine, b. 1697,= Dr. in 1748. Will pr. 1771.   EDWARD GILL.=   THOMAS GYLL, ob. 1719. sp.

JOHN, ob. sp. 1804, æt. 78.   MARY, m. George Keith.   JOHN GILL, Baptist Divine, will prov. 24 March, 1809, sp. æt. 79.

There was a Dr. Joseph Stennet, poet and Baptist, of some consideration in his day, who died in 1713, and was buried in Hitchendon, Bucks. He married the daughter of one George Gill, a merchant.

Much praise is to be given to the officiating minister of the Baptists in Wraysbury, Mr. William Thomas Buckland, who exercises his vocation at the chapel here to a well disposed and confiding auditory, while to his wife and family are entrusted the religious education of the Baptist flock. Mr. Buckland has now laboured without fee or reward for 35 years; his sole object being to promote piety, to diffuse the heavenly word, and reinforce it by precept and example; the pleasure he has had in doing it pays itself, for there is not in the scale of nature a more inseparable connection of cause and effect than in the case of happiness and virtue.

To revert to the school of the Established Church, it seems not to have assumed a specific character before the year 1828, when a Sunday and day school was opened at the instance of the

Curate, the Rev. George A. Hopkins, co-operating with the Rev. James Phillips, who was lecturer of Mr. Lee's Charity in 1824. After his death, the following year, Mr. Hopkins joined Mr. Virgo Buckland and Mr. Butler of this parish, to found an establishment which has since become defined and matured, yielding abundant fruit.

The number of boys on the Register is about 60, and girls about 50—the average weekly attendance some 80. Lists have been published since 1843, and the sum collected is about £50 yearly. Mr. Elias Ellis was appointed schoolmaster, and his wife schoolmistress, in 1851, at a joint salary of £20 per annum, with house free and some additional emolument according to the fluctuation of the children, ranging from £6 to £10 a year. Mr. Ellis left the parish in 1861.

The present school rooms, of from 28 feet by 15, are in the original poorhouse of the parish, and it is rented of the trustees at £10 per annum with rates about £1.

Previously to the school being transferred here the place of attendance was in a cottage opposite the George Inn, belonging to Mr. Harcourt, and let by him for £7. 10s a year only.

The school is managed by a committee of some seven persons, and the Vicar, Rev. Seymour Neville, is secretary, while Mr. James Pullin is treasurer, and they issue the yearly report, and a diocesan inspector visits the school. The children pay a slight quota every Monday morning, as the payment of a small sum for education preserves the principle of independence. The number of subscribers is between 50 and 60, and the cash results are from £40 to £50 a year. The two chief points of funds and attendance evince sustained interest in the cause on the part of the promoters of the Establishment, and there is a growing appreciation of and demand for Christian education on the part of the poorer portion of the community. The charity of our times consists in keeping people from the union by diligence, from alcohol palaces by teaching temperance and sobriety, and from worthless publications by diffusing virtuous knowledge and planting efficient schools. Statistics shew that in 1856 the proportion of criminals to the population was 1 in 923; in 1859 it stood at 1 in 1117; and that in 1860 it stood at 1 in 1217, while the proportion of offences committed by *children* has diminished still more sensibly. Education is like health, the most venerable of the powers of heaven; in its presence blooms the spring of pleasure, and without it no one is happy.

*The following notice was issued previous to the re-opening of the School in* 1851.

"This School as a Day and Sunday School, will be re-opened for the reception of the Children of those residing in Wyrardisbury, on Monday, September 29th, 1851.

It consists of a Day and Sunday School. There will be a resident Master and Mistress, fully competent to manage and instruct the Children.

The principles of the Master and Mistress are those of the Established Church, but the Children of Dissenters will be allowed—at the request of their parents—to attend Chapel, provided such be open in the parish, and they produce, if required, a certificate to that effect; it being indispensably necessary that the children instructed at this School should attend regularly some place of Public Worship.

The Children will be required to meet every Sunday morning at the school, at half-past nine o'clock, and parishioners will be requested, if necessary, to assist in the instruction on that morning.

There will be one whole holiday every week; two vacations, viz. one fortnight at Christmas, and one month during harvest.

Children paying one penny per week will be instructed to spell and read correctly.

Those paying twopence per week, to read, write, and cipher as far as practice.

Practical instruction in plain needlework will be afforded to the girls, and for this purpose work will be taken in at the school.

The books in general use will be the Old and New Testament, secular reading books, an approved Spelling Book, and Crossman's Introduction to the Knowledge of the Christian Religion; these, with slates, will be supplied by the Committee; all beyond these will be supplied at the school by the master, and must be paid for by the parents.

In order to meet the great extra expenses of this school, voluntary contributions will be thankfully received by the Committee of Management: B. H. Gyll, Esq., G. W. Gyll, Esq., R. Ibotson, Esq., Mr. Pullin, Mr. Roumieu, Mr. Jordan. Rev. G. A. Hopkins, Hon. Secretary. Wyrardisbury, September, 1851.

### Report of the Committee of Management.

The subscribers to the Wyrardisbury Day and Sunday School met July 30th, 1851, at the Vestry Room, for the purpose of adopting and carrying out the best possible method of conducting and managing the affairs of the same, and as every subscriber is considered a member of the general Committee, it was agreed that a Committee of management should be elected for the purpose of superintending all things belonging to the said School—the undermentioned willingly undertook the office, viz:—B. H. Gyll, Esq., G. W. Gyll, Esq., R. Ibotson, Esq., Mr. Pullin, Mr. Roumieu, Mr. Jordan, and Rev. Geo. Adol. Hopkins, M.A.

It was unanimously resolved that the Rev. G. A. Hopkins should continue Honorary Secretary, and that he also take the office of Treasurer.

The Committee having agreed with Mr. F. Buckland—trustee to the Church property—to rent of him half of the old workhouse for the sum of £5 per annum, and that they might have immediate possession of the premises, agreed to pay the rent from Midsummer day last, and to recompence the then tenant, by paying him 10s at Michaelmas next for any inconvenience he might be put to in removing upon so short a notice; and he is also allowed to take his crops off the ground when the proper period arrives.

The Committee of management, anxious that no time should be lost, forthwith sent for Mr. Clark to prepare an estimate for the thorough repairing and painting the premises, as well as the fitting up of the two lower rooms for the schools; his estimate having been laid before the Committee, and having had their serious attention, it was agreed between the parties that the sum of £13 should be paid for the same, and Mr. Clark undertook to fulfil his agreement by the 13th of September, provided two new grates were found by the Committee, which has been done.

The Committee then took into consideration the appointment of a Master and Mistress; it was resolved that the Secretary should advertise and obtain the most eligible parties he possibly could, and their joint emolument should be £20 per annum from the Treasurer—the children's pence (according to the rules laid down by the Committee)—apartments over the school-rooms—and any profit that may accrue from their providing the scholars with copy and ciphering books, pencils, or any article that may not be found by the subscribers.

The Committee of management then called upon the inhabitants of the parish, soliciting their kind aid to support that which must be acknowledged so desirable an object, and it is with grateful thanks they have to report that their exertions were met in the most liberal manner; yet they would wish to impress most respectfully upon all not to relax in any way from obtaining donations and subscriptions.

The Committee have elected, through the Secretary, Mr. and Mrs. Ellis, as School-master and School-mistress, and sincerely do they trust, under Divine Providence, that there will be Christian charity amongst all, and that their endeavours to carry out the wishes of the subscribers may prove beneficial to the families of the labouring classes of the parish of Wyrardisbury.

The Committee announce that all subscriptions are due on the 29th of September, and will be collected on that day or within one week afterwards.

By order of the Committee,  Geo. Adol. Hopkins, Hon. Secretary and Treasurer.
September, 1851.

## CHARITIES.

The county of Bucks, is celebrated for its public charities, and the returns give to it the sum of £7479 annually, out of nearly a million of money collected from the counties of England and Wales, independent of Scotland and Ireland.

It is stated in the Parliamentary returns of 1786, that Philip Harcourt, Esq., in 1758, left land for the purpose of giving bread to the poor of the parish, then vested in John Harcourt Powell, Esq., to produce £2. 12s yearly, which Mr. George Simon Harcourt used to cause to be distributed in eight penny loaves every Sunday; but on 6th February, 1831, he ceased to do so, alleging that *no claim* existed, but that he would distribute an *equivalent* in voluntary donations. It appears from a minute in the vestry books, 4th May, 1831, that the churchwardens then stated that they had made an enquiry as to the cause of the bread not being sent as heretofore to the church on the 6th February last past, which in their remembrance had been paid from Hythe End Farm, formerly belonging to Harcourt Powell, Esq., and since from the estate, and that on their applying to Mr. Harcourt they received the same answer as above.

Philip Harcourt, the donor in 1758.=     *Ann.=Thomas Powell, ob. 1761.
John Harcourt.=                           Harcourt Powell, ob. 1782.=
John.=                                    John Harcourt Powell.

George Simon Harcourt, discontinued the donation in 1831.

According to the records of the parish many charities have been given and the names of the benefactors have been *unrighteously* forgotten—as in the case of the Bridge lands, supposed to have been the gift of Andrew Lord Windsor in 1543. Also the glebe lands, the gift of which is uncertain, probably from Sir Thomas Smyth, on his coming to Ankerwycke in 1550. In 1704, John Lee, Esq., gave a donation, to which we again advert. (p. 115.)

## THE PARISH REGISTERS.

The evidence afforded by Parochial Registers is of the first class, and there is scarcely a claim of peerage or case of heirship on record which has not been proved in part by them.

At the dissolution of the Monasteries in 1535, the dispersion of the monks who were to that period the principal registrars, gave rise to the mandate issued in 1538, for keeping registers of baptisms, marriages and burials, in each parish. And again in 1558, on the accession of Queen Elizabeth, it was ordered that every Minister at his institution should subscribe to this protestation —"I shall keepe the Register Booke according to the Queene's Majesties injunction." Again, on 25th October 1597, it was ordained that parchment Register Books should be purchased at the expense of the parish, and that all the registers then kept and written on paper should be transcribed on parchment, and that all subsequent baptisms, marriages, and burials be duly entered, and certified at the end of the page by the clergyman and churchwardens; and copies be sent to the Register of the diocese to be faithfully preserved in the episcopal archives, which regulations were confirmed by the 70th Ecclesiastical Canon of 1603. Some interruption occurred during the Commonwealth, from 1644 to the restoration of monarchy in 1660. Since which time the registers have been generally pretty well kept. It seems incredible how our ancestors did without some certificates of marriages or baptisms, at least, seeing the important interests which are jeopardised in case of subsequent litigation, by the difficulty of proving the legality of a marriage and the legitimacy of the offspring of any union.

In many cases these national muniments are lost, stolen, mislaid, or burnt, and to prevent the evils arising from these contingencies, the injunction of Elizabeth went to enforce their being forwarded to the episcopal archives for *certain* preservation, and it was imperative on the clergy, in whose custody these indispensable documents were, to send them there, but as there was *no fee* for so doing, and the duties entailed were *unprofitable*, they were unrighteously neglected, and at the present time the duplicate registers are not perfect in any diocese in the kingdom.

Unluckily for our parish the registers have been destroyed by fire, and even the last book seen

* In page 85 it is stated that this lady married about 1760; that date relates to her son's marriage.

or known, dated 1629, is not now in existence. The earliest extant bears date 29th September 1733, but no entry is made before 1734. Prior to the reign of King George I. all unmarried ladies were entered as mistress. In 1813, the New Registration Act came into operation, in which the ages of persons were entered at their death. In 1665, the affidavit that persons were buried in woollen began, by reason of the plague, and the order was repealed in 1814.

### IN THE OLD REGISTRY.

*Baptisms.*

1633. 4th Oct. Ursula, daughter of Sir William Salter, Kt. He then rented Ankerwycke House of the Smijth family.
1634. 17th Nov. William, son of Sir William Salter, Kt.
1646. 5th Sept. Mary, daughter of Richard and Mary Batchelaur.
1669. 20th Oct. Elizabeth, daughter of James Dallian, Vicar.

*Marriages.*

1647, 9th June, John Harris and Amie Batchelaur, at Ashsmanworth, Hants.
N.B.—Ancient registers sometimes recorded marriages which did not take place in the parish.

*Burials.*

1640. 25th May, Katherine, wife of Mr. Andrew Warde.
21st Aug. Sarah Eyles, widow.
1641. 17th Aug. James Parke, gent.
7th Sept. Rachel, daughter of Mrs. Mary Sharowe, widow of John Sharowe, Lord of the Manor here in 1627; he died in 1634.
1643. 24th Dec. Andrew Warde.
1645. 30th Jan. Mary, daughter of Richard and Mary Batchelaur.
1662. 7th Nov. William Pinchon (*see* page 21).

The present Register Book begins 1734, from which the following selections are made—

### IN THE LATER REGISTRY.

*Baptisms.*

1734. 8th April, Gibbons, Sarah, daughter of William and Sarah.
20th April, Prowse Hassel, Jane, daughter of Robert, Esq., and Elizabeth, his wife.
18th Oct. Crowder, William, son of Samuel and Elizabeth.
27th Dec. Child, Martha, daughter of Thomas and Rebecca.
1735. 1st Aug. Harcourt, Philippa, daughter of Philip, Esq. and Sarah.
1736. 7th April, Gibbons, Elizabeth, daughter of Richard and Elizabeth.
1737. 3rd July, Lewington, William, son of Henry and Sarah.
16th Feb. Hassel, Sarah, daughter of Robert Prowse Hassel, Esq.
1738. 25th Feb. Pembrook, Ann, daughter of John and Ann.
1739. 17th June, Dosett, Mary, daughter of John and Elizabeth.
29th July, Smith, Diana, daughter of Simon.
18th Sept. Gibbons, Thomas, son of William and Sarah.
26th Sept. Stephens, Mary, daughter of Solomon and Mary.

*Baptisms.*

1740. 7th April, Atkins, Joseph, son of Joseph and Sarah.
22nd April, Child, Shadrach, son of Thomas and Rebecca.
1742. 29th May, Godman, Elizabeth, daughter of John and Sarah.
13th Feb. West, Elizabeth, daughter of William and Mary.
1743. Partington, Thomas, son of Richard and Elizabeth.
1744. Gourney, William, son of Daniel and Susanna.
Bennett, Thomas, son of Richard and Ann.
1745. Stevens, Milicent, daughter of Solomon and Mary.
1746. Lewin, James, son of Robert and Sarah.
1748. Byde, Samuel, son of William and Elizabeth.
1751. Boddington, Timothy, son of Timothy and Ann.
1753. Bullock, Mary, daughter of Thomas and Sarah.
1755. Bullock, Ann, daughter of Thomas and Sarah.
Bunce, John, son of John and Martha.
Style, Martha, daughter of Robert and Martha.
1756. Anderson, Mary Martin, daughter of Mary.
Burt, Eleanor, daughter of William and Mary.
Wilmot, Mary, daughter of Richard and Mary.
Style, Robert, son of Robert and Martha.
1757. Style, Mary, daughter of Robert and Martha.

*Baptisms.*

1759. Style, Elizabeth, daughter of Robt. and Martha.
Sturges, William, son of William and Mary.
1761. Style, Charlotte, daughter of Robt. and Martha
Buckland, William, son of William and Elizabeth.
1762. Mossington, James, son of John and Martha.
1763. Style, Henry, son of Robert and Martha.
Gould, Elizabeth, daughter of James and Elizabeth.
Graves, Elizabeth, daughter of William and Elizabeth.
1764. Style, Peter, son of Robert and Martha.
1765. Gould, Ann, daughter of James and Elizabeth.
Style, Ellis, son of Robert and Martha.
1767. Style, Bathsheba, daughter of Rob. and Martha.
Taylor, George, son of Samuel and Mary.
Hammerton, Alice, daughter of Thomas and Rachel.
1769. Taylor, Robert, son of William and Elizabeth.
1774. Biddle, Diana, daughter of William and Mary.
15th Sept. Gyll, William, son of William and Mary Gyll, Esq.
1778. Gould, Thomas, son of James and Elizabeth.
1779. Lovegrove, Mary, daughter of John and Mary.
1780. Sills, Sarah, daughter of Daniel and Ann.
1778. Haines, Mary, daughter of John and Mary.
1780. Downham, Elizabeth, daughter of William and Elizabeth.
1781. Sills, Richard, son of Daniel and Ann.
1783. Buckland, Elizabeth, daughter of William and Jane.
Buckland, Mary, daughter of — Sarah.
1784. 8th Feb. Willis, John, son of Rev. John Willis, Curate, and Sarah.
Willis, Francis, son of William and Ann.
1785. Willis, Richard, son of Rev. John Willis, Curate.
1786. Buckland, William, son of William and Jane.
Buckland, Virgo, son of Thomas and Ann.
17th Sept. Bouverie, George Augustus, son of Hon. Edward and Arabella, at Ankerwycke House.
1787. Sills, Priscilla, daughter of Daniel and Ann.
Willis, Louisa, daughter of Rev. John Willis and Sarah.
25th Dec. Buckland, Francis, son of Thomas and Ann.
1789. Buckland, John, son of William and Jane.
Batt, Elizabeth, daughter of John and Hannah.
1790. Buckland, Mary Ann, daughter of Thomas and Ann.
Sills, William, son of Daniel and Ann.
Style, Robert, son of Robert and Ann.
1791. Buckland, Thomas, son of William and Jane.

*Baptisms.*

1792. Style, Henry, son of Robert and Ann.
Buckland, John Virgo, son of Thomas and Ann.
1793. Buckland, James, son of William and Jane.
1794. Style, William, son of Robert and Ann.
Buckland, Martha, daughter of Thomas and Ann.
Style, Martha, daughter of Robert and Ann.
1795. Buckland, Henry, son of William and Jane.
1796. Gould, John, son of John and Ann.
27th Aug. Gyll, William Wright, son of Capt. William.
1797. Buckland, William Thomas, son of William and Ann.
1798. Buckland, Jane, daughter of William and Jane.
Hopkins, Rowland, son of Thomas and Mary.
1799. Style, Isaac, son of Robert and Ann.
Buckland, Robert, son of William and Jane.
1801. Giles, Henry Western, son of John and Martha.
Buckland, Joseph, son of William and Jane.
Style, Edmund, son of Robert and Ann.
1805. Buckland, Martha, daughter of William and Jane.
1808. Leno, George, son of George and Mary.
1809. Sills, Mary Ann, daughter of Daniel and Mary.
1810. Style, Peter, son of Robert and Elizabeth.
1811. Buckland, William Virgo, son of Virgo and Ann.
Style, Elizabeth Ann, daughter of Robert and Elizabeth.
1813. Buckland, Francis Virgo, son of Virgo and Ann.
1827. Stile, Sidney, son of Robert and Elizabeth.
1836. 11th Oct. Harcourt, John Simon Chandos, son of George and Jessy Harcourt, Esq.
1838. 28th July, Hopkins, Elizabeth, daughter of George Adolphus Hopkins, Curate.
1840. 24th June, Harcourt, Mary, daughter of Simon and Jessy, Esq.
1841. 28th May, Hopkins, Georgina, daughter of Geo. Adolphus, Curate.
1843. Pullin, John Hutton, son of James and Mary.
1844. Pullin, Elizabeth, daughter of James and Mary.
1846. Pullin, James Stephens, son of James and Mary.
1847. Tillyer, James, son of James and Jane.
28th Oct. Harcourt, Gertrude Minette, daughter of George and Gertrude Charlotte, Esq.
1849. 25th Jan. Harcourt, Otto Simon Henry, son of George and Gertrude Charlotte, Esq.
Tillyer, Helen, daughter of James and Jane.
1850. 19th Jan. Harcourt, Grace Isabella Rolle, daughter of George and Gertrude Charlotte, Esq.
Slocock, Benjamin, son of Benjamin and Sarah Chapman.

*Baptisms.*

1850. Roumieu, George Frederick, son of Charles and Eliza Jane.
1855. Scholefield, Cottrill, son of Cottrill Scholefield, Esq., of Ankerwycke.

*Marriages.*

1746. 5th Nov. John Jervis White, of St. James's, Westminster, and Elizabeth Fletewode, of Amersham, Bucks. p. 42.
1747. 21th Jan. Thomas Jervis, of Harmsworth, and Ann Crowder, of Wraysbury.
1748. 25th May, William Byde and Elizabeth Povey.
1748. 19th July, Sir Watkin Williams Wynn, Bt. of Wynstay, co. Denbigh, and Frances Shakerley, daughter of George Shakerley, of Gwersilt, co. Denbigh.
1750. 2nd Dec. John Russell and Elizabeth Lewin.
11th July, Richard Lazell, of Egham, and Jane Harfield.
1752. 11th June, Henry Lewington and Rose Chitty.
1762. 10th Jan. William Grove, Wraysbury, and Eliza Gill, of Yeatley, Hants.
1763. 6th Oct. Robert Child, Esq., of Heston, Middlesex, and Sarah Jodrell, of this parish—Signed Gilbert Jodrell.
1766. William Taylor and Elizabeth Wise.
1767. Thomas Stockley, of Old Windsor, and Elizabeth More.
1769. Richard Streatly and Ann Tyrel, of Reading, Berks.
1770. William Whitmarsh and Ann Evans.
1771. 17th Aug. John Harcourt, Esq. and Margaret Irene Sarney, of St. Mary, Strand, spinster.
John Lovegrove and Mary Godman.
1775. William King and Elizabeth Wilmot.
William Milbourne and Mary Style.
1778. Thomas Haines and Sarah Smith, of Old Windsor.
1779. Isaac Holmes, of St. Sepulchre, London, and Mary Style.
James Fletcher and Kezia Fettiplace Aaron Blake.
1782. 6th May, William Buckland and Jane Burt.
1782. 8th Sept. George Rous, Esq. and Charlotte Thomas.
1783. William Buckland and Ann Virgo.
1785. William Harris and Elizabeth Webb, of Stoke Pogis.
Edmund Winder, of Burnham, and Elizabeth Style.
1788. Samuel Johnson and Ann Gurney.
1789. William Brambly and Mary Collier.
1789. Robert Style and Ann Whitmarsh.

*Marriages.*

1790. 1st March, William Codrington, of Stanton Drew, Somerset, and Mary Rudhall, of Wraysbury.
1791. John Gould and Ann Stone.
1792. Shadrach Trotman and Martha Prior.
1793. William Sturges and Sarah Morecock.
1794. Evan Hopkins, of New Windsor, and Ann Thomas.
John Davies and Martha Gould.
13th Sept. Capt. William Gyll, of this parish, and the Right Hon. Lady Harriet Jane Flemyng, of Richmond Hill, Surrey, spinster and minor. Signed Wigtoun.
William Eastern and Ann Chandler.
1795. John Willis and Mary Hunt.
1796. Isaac Cane and Rebecca Rosier.
John Caley and Sarah Parker.
1799. William Evelin and Ann Pullin.
Thomas Randell and Mary Groom.
Thomas Groves and Mary Skuller.
1803. John Buckland and Sarah Simons.
1807. 19th Dec. Frederick Wm. Coore, of Great Winchester Street, London, and Isabella Blagrove.
1808. Edward Godden and Ann Adkins.
1809. Virgo Buckland and Ann Wood of Langley, Bucks.
1812. Henry Mole and Ann Hampton.
1816. 25th Nov. Hugh Parkin, Esq. and Mary Charlotte Blagrove.
1817. George Groom and Sarah Slaughter.
1821. James Buckland, and Elizabeth Farnell.
1826. Robert Style and Mary Thomas, widow.
1830. Henry Style and Mary Thomas.
William Lipscombe and Maria White.
1834. Henry Eldborough and Rebecca Buckland.
1836. Charles Hastings and Charlotte Pullin.
Mathew Stevens and Eliza Glascott.

*Burials.*

1734. 24th June, Elizabeth Lewington.
14th Nov. William Crowder.
1735. 5th May, Elizabeth, daughter of Philip Harcourt, Esq.
1737. 14th March, Philippina Harcourt.
1738. Mary Atkins, widow of Horton.
8th Oct. Sarah, daughter of Mr. Hassel.
19th Jan. Simon Morse, Esq. of Thorpe, Surrey.
Jane Gibbons.
1739. Elizabeth, daughter of Linward Street.
27th June, Rev. Mr. Charles, Holloway.
Jane Bowden.

*Burials.*

1739. Mary Stephens.
1740. Richard Gibbons.
Elizabeth Moles, widow.
John Cane.
1741. Elizabeth Cane.
Edward Child, by Thomas Beighton, Lecturer, of Wraysbury.
William Morse, Esq. æt. 30. Ped. of Lee, p. 23.
1742. William Grove.
John Grove.
William Gibbons.
John Bowry, from London.
John Gibbons.
Richard Gibbons.
Dinah Bowry.
1744. Sarah Percival, widow.
1745. Thomas Bowry.
Robert Lewin.
1749. Mary Stephens, widow.
1750. Edmund Bowry.
Dorothy Bowry.
Eliza Atterbury.
1752. Ellis Trippick.
1753. Elizabeth, widow of Edm. Phipps.
John Pembroke.
1754. Sarah, widow of Joseph Adkins.
1755. Mary Winch, widow.
Solomon Stevens.
1756. Sarah Woodford, widow.
Edmund Bowry, from London.
Martha, widow of Richard Grove.
Martha Grove.
1757. Mary Lewin, widow.
Marlborough, son of William and Ann Vaughan.
1758. Edward Phipps.
1759. Edmund Bowry.
23rd March, Philip Harcourt, Esq.
1760. William Holloway.
Mary, wife of John Spicer.
Elizabeth, daughter of John Spicer.
4th April, Mr. Robert Prowse Hassel.
1761. Thomas Dean, from Weybridge.
1763. Richard Grove.
1764. 23rd Feb. Mr. John Hutton.
1765. Henry Lewington.
Joseph Maxfield.
7th Oct. William, Robert, and Arabella Barbaroux.
1766. Mary Barbaroux. Ped. of Hassell, 77.
1767. Mary Wiltshire.
Eliza, daughter of William Grove.
Ann, wife of Francis Bowry.

*Burials.*

1769. 5th July, Mrs. Elizabeth, wife of William Gyll, Esq.
1770. Alice Wilmot.
20th Dec. Mrs. Ann Harcourt.
1772. Mary Crowder, widow.
1773. Elizabeth Pretty, widow.
16th June, Mrs. Elizabeth Hassel.
1774. Philip Francis, son of John Harcourt, Esq.
1776. 3rd Dec. Miss Elizabeth, daughter of William Gyll, Esq.
1781. Mary Wingrove.
Richard, son of Daniel and Ann Sills.
1783. Elizabeth, wife of Francis Gibbons.
1785. 31st. Jan. Miss Frances, daughter of William Gyll, Esq.
David Wingrove, a farmer.
5th Oct. John Harcourt, Esq.
John Godman, a farmer.
1786. Robert Style.
John Lovegrove.
William Style Holmes.
Charlotte Sills.
1787. 30th June, Mrs. Penelope Sheffield. p. 77.
1788. Henry Steevens.
Michael Willis.
1789. 23rd May, Hon. Emily Elizabeth Coventry. p.77.
1792. 20th April, Sir Abraham Pytches, Kt. p. 77.
William Buckland.
3rd Dec. Robert Hutton Gyll, Esq.
1793. Joseph Adkins.
1796. 27th Aug. William Wright, son of William Gyll, Esq.
1797. Samuel Adkins.
10th April, Dame Jane Pytches.
George, son of Col. King.
1798. 4th April, William Gyll, Esq.
17th April, Thomas Wright, Esq.
Elizabeth Buckland.
1799. 29th Sept. Right Hon. Lord Shuldham.
Robert Buckland.
1802. 18th Feb. Thomas Wright Gyll.
Henry Style.
1806. 23rd      , William Gyll, Esq. aged 31.
Ann Style.
1808. 22nd Nov. Penelope Sheffield. p. 77.
1809. 12th May, Ann, widow of Thos. Wright, Esq.
1811. 17th May, Mrs. Elizabeth Dale Harcourt, aged 28 years.
1812. Thomas Buckland.
1814. James Fleming.
1815. Martha Style
1817. Sarah Buckland.

## Burials.

1817. Jane Buckland.
Nov. Mrs. Ann Willes.
1820. 20th March, Mary, widow of William Gyll, Esq.
1821. 31st July, Maria Jane Gyll, wife of Brooke Hamilton Gyll, Esq.
1824. Francis Buckland.
1825. Virgo Buckland.
1828. Ann Buckland.
Robert Style.
1830. 4th Jan. Wm. Henry Deschamps, Esq. p. 100.
1833. Robert Style.
John Virgo Buckland.
1837. Philip Simon Harcourt.

## Burials.

1840. 23rd Oct. Frances, widow of William H. Deschamps, Esq.
1841. William Buckland.
1842. 13th Aug. Jessy, wife of George Simon Harcourt, Esq.
1844. 28th Feb. Hamilton Gyll, Esq. aged 39 years.
1846. Elizabeth Buckland.
1847. 7th June, Grace Gyll, aged 84.
Charles Thomas Buckland.
1848. 21st Nov. Mary Harcourt.
1849. James Buckland.
1854. Sophia Louisa Ibotson.
1856. Mary Sills.

## GYLL AND WRIGHT CHARITY.

In 1798, the sum of £300 consols was left by William Gyll, Esq. of Wraysbury House, in trust to the minister and churchwardens of the parish and their successors, to pay on Christmas day a dividend to 24 poor housekeepers of the said parish 8s 4d each; there is also some bread distributed every Sunday.

In 1798, Thomas Wright, Esq. (who married Ann, sister of said William Gyll, Esq.) of Dulwich, Surrey, gave to the minister and churchwardens for the time being in trust to lay out the dividends of £100, 4 per cent Bank Annuities, in the purchase of bread every Christmas day. The stock now stands at £446. 18s 6d, in the names of Rev. Richard Webb (who died vicar here in 1829), Virgo Buckland, Francis Buckland, and Robert Butler. Dividends are £13. 8s.

Since 18— the names of William Thomas Buckland, Francis Buckland, and Edward Pasmore were substituted; the latter subsequently emigrated to Canada.

By resolution in vestry, 19th December, 1827, it was agreed to give in future £10 of this dividend in money, and the remainder £3. 8s in bread. But the same persons do not receive money and bread; and the names of all participating the charity are entered in the account book.

In 1820, Mary, widow of William Gyll, Esq. of Wraysbury House, gave by will £50 to the poor of this parish.

## CHARITIES AND GIFTS TO THE CHURCH.

In 1855 the subscriptions raised in Wraysbury, that is in four months ending March 1855, were £45. 1s, Schools; £13. 12s 4d, Clothing Club; £24. 15s 2d, Patriotic Club; £5, Bread from Mrs. Pryor; 10s ditto, Mrs. Davies; £17. 11s 6d, Coals; £5, Bread, G. S. Harcourt, Esq. Total, £111. 10s.

Gifts to the Church at various times :—

1710. John Hassel, Esq. of Wraysbury House, gave a large oil painting of angels, &c. now placed behind the communion table, formerly against the eastern window in the chancel of the church. p. 122.
1822. Brooke Hamilton Gyll, Esq. of Wraysbury House, gave a vestry room, and a large Bible for the use of the clergyman.

1830. Rev. Charles Champnes, the vicar, gave a violoncello, bow and case.
1839. George Simon Harcourt, Esq., and Jessy his wife, gave an organ to the church.
1842. George Simon Harcourt, Esq. gave the large iron Suspension Bridge at the cost of £500, and he raised the road from Hythe End Bridge to Lammas Gate at his own charge, when the new road in the parish was made.
1845. Gordon Gyll, Esq. of Wraysbury, gave the eastern painted glass window in the church.
1848. Ditto, the stained glass window in the south of the chancel, with two communion table books and two oak chairs for the communion table, hassocks and carpet for ditto; also red cloth cover for the pulpit and reading desk, and a pair of commandment tables above the communion table, in lieu of the old ones, which were fixed over the pointed arch which divides the chancel from the nave, and whose size and position intercepted the light; he also gave the stained glass windows in the north aisle.
1851. Ditto, gave a new vestry, now on the western side of the church, in lieu of the old one given by B. H. Gyll, Esq. in 1822, and which was removed, as obstructing the light of the eastern window of the north aisle, by a faculty.
1852. Felix Pryor, Esq. then tenanting Ankerwycke House, gave a most useful stove to the church.
1853. Gordon Gyll, Esq. relaid the whole of the pavement of the church, new painted and varnished the pews, and recovered all the beams of oak and chestnut wood from an incrustation of chalk and whitewash.
1856. There was a liberal collection made at the church for the Coal and Clothing Club, uniting the Choral Club expenses.
1857. A concert was held at the paper mill by the permission of Mr. Richard Ibotson, and the proceeds were applied to purchase a new organ, as the old one, given by Mr. Harcourt in 1839, was considered unserviceable.
1858. Captain William Shelton gave some dead lights for the back of the organ loft.

## ALMS HOUSES.

There are six cottages on that part of the parish which is near the George Inn. They are almshouses, and are or ought to be assigned rent free to certain aged poor persons, placed there by the parish officers. There is no document relative to these tenements, but they are kept in repair by the parish, and the occupants generally receive parochial relief.

There are also four cottages which were received from the then Lord of the Manor, Mr. Blagrove, in exchange for four other cottages, which are supposed to have been built by the trustees with money that had accumulated in their hands; they are let to different holders at £4. a year each.

These rents are applied to pay quit rents and church expenses, and interest, and part of the principal money, viz. £200, due to Mr. Ambrose Cane, borrowed 18th June, 1828, and the surplus, if any, after repairs, is given to the parish surveyor towards the repairs of the bridges.

The Bridge Lands consist of 10 a. 3 r. 23 p. part tilth and part meadow, forming with the church land one field at the Staines end of the parish, and were formerly let to George Leno for 37s an acre, and for a lease, rental £20. 2s 3d.

An annual quit rent of 8s 4d is paid to the Lord of the Manor in respect of these lands. Mr. Cane's loan was partly borrowed for sustentation of bridges, &c. and Mr. W. Thomas Buckland was to be treasurer, and to produce an account, 25th March yearly, till it was liquidated, which it is.

On 5th July, 1790, John Rockley, of Hounslow, Middlesex, lent the parish £100, all since repaid.

The Bridge land history as to the donor is in the same predicament as the donor of the Church lands, all parties' names have been ungratefully allowed to drop into hopeless oblivion, as if to *encourage* others in acts of charity.

The old workhouse, built 1798, (for in Vestry, 12th March of that year, they agreed to build one) is the same where the Parish School is now kept. Outside the workhouse is inscribed on a stone, Erected Anno Domini 1798. William Groom, William Thomas, Churchwardens. Joseph Adkins, Michael Willis, Overseers. Nathaniel Wilmot, Builder.

On 26th July, 1861, Mr. Elias Ellis left the parish, having been there as master to the parish school for almost ten years. At the time of his quitting the appointment the parish gave him and his wife a donation in the shape of a purse of money of some £10, and a testimonial of good conduct for himself and wife.

## CLOTHING CLUB.

This Club forms a part of the charitable donations in which this parish abounds.

It appears that the idea, whose principle has worked so well throughout Great Britain, has been adopted in our small parish, and the results are most satisfactory. The working of the Club resolves itself into sums received and depositors.

It began in 1844, in which year only £10. 5s was received. In 1849, £66. was received. In 1850, £79. 18s 6d; and there were 117 depositors realising £67. 8s 6d. The intermediate years are about the same until 1854, when the realised sum for all was £71. 7s; the depositors being 70 in number, and the sum returned was £48. 10s 8d.

The Club partially ceased, but in 1859 it revived, under the auspices of the Rev. Mr. Seymour Neville, the vicar.

## CHURCHWARDENS OF WRAYSBURY PARISH SINCE 1734.

Rates and Minutes of Vestries begin 1734. The Book was bought 15th April, 1734.

1734. Philip Harcourt, Esq. and Wm. Pearson.
1735. Ditto and Henry Pinnock.
1736. H. Pinnock and John Grove.
1737. John Harris and John Crowder, and so remained till 1744.
1744. Samuel Martin and Richard Verry.
1745. John Harris and Samuel Martin.
1746. William Cooper and Ralph Carter.
1747. Ditto.
1748. Ditto and John Crowder, Sen.
1749. Ditto.
1750. Ditto to 1753.
1753. Samuel Martin and John Godman to 1755.
1755. David Wingrove and Samuel Martin.
1756. Ditto.
1757. Robert Style and Samuel Martin.
1758. Ditto and Thomas Rolfe.
1759. Ditto and John Crowder, Jun.
1760. Ditto ditto to 1763.
1764. Richard Jones and John Crowder.
1765. Ditto and John Povey.
1766. Ditto and Richard Walker.
1767. Ditto and John Povey.
1769. Rich. Jones and Shadrach Child, so to 1771.
1771. John Povey and Richard Streatley.
1772. William Whitmarsh and David Wingrove, so till 1777.
1778. Arthur Palmer and David Wingrove, so till 1780.
1781. Arthur Palmer and Robert Styles, so till 1784.
1785. Daniel Rosier and William Wilmot.
1786. Ditto and Michael Willis.
1787. Ditto, ditto.
1788. James Sims and M. Willis.
Here the books are lost till 1797.
1797. William Groom and William Thomas.
1798. Ditto.

1799. Ambrose Cane and William Thomas.
1800. Nathaniel Wilmot.
1801. Daniel Rosier and Daniel Sills.
1802. Ditto and Nathaniel Wilmot.
1803. Daniel Sills and Charles Palmer.
1804. Robert Style and ditto.
1805. Ditto and James Sims.
1806. Thomas Buckland and ditto.
1807. John Barrow and Joseph Adkins.
1808. William Grove and ditto.
1809. Ditto and Robert Style.
1810. Evan Evans and ditto.
1811. Ditto and Daniel Sills.
1812. Evan Evans and Ambrose Cane.
1813. Ditto and ditto.
1814. Ditto and Daniel Sills.
1815. Ditto and Thomas Buckland.
1816. Virgo Buckland and Robert Styles.
1817. Daniel Sills and ditto.
1818. Ditto and John Blagrove, Esq.
1819. Virgo Buckland and ditto.
1820. Ditto and Robert Styles.
1821. Daniel Sills and ditto.
1822. Virgo Buckland and ditto.
1823. Ditto and Henry Mole.
1824. George Leno and ditto.
1825. Ditto and Thomas Buckland.
1826. Joseph Davis and Edward Pasmore.
1827. Ditto and ditto.
1828. Francis Buckland and ditto.
1829. Robert Style and Solomon Willis.
1830. Ditto and Francis Buckland.
1831. Ditto and ditto.
1832. George Simon Harcourt, Esq. and ditto.
1833. Francis Buckland and William Taylor, and so continued for ten years.
1844. James Pullin and William Taylor.
1845. Ditto and Samuel Jordan, and so continued till 1848.
1849. James Pullin and Benjamin Slocock.
1850. Ditto and John Taylor.
1851. Ditto and Francis Buckland.
1852. Ditto and Richard Ibotson, and so to 1856.
1857. Cottrill Scholefield, Esq. and Richard Ibotson; in March 1858 Richard Ibotson died, and Mr. Scholefield was appointed the vicar's churchwarden.
1858. Cottrill Scholefield, Esq. and Capt. William Shelton.
1859. William Ladell, gentleman, and John Taylor.
1860. Ditto.
1861. William Clifford and John Henry Skinner, Overseers.

## PROPRIETORS OF LAND IN WRAYSBURY.—FREEHOLDERS IN 1860.

ACREAGE, ABOUT.

| A. | R. | P. | |
|---|---|---|---|
| 730 | 0 | 0 | George Simon Harcourt, Esq., of Ankerwycke House. |
| 340 | 0 | 0 | Brooke Hamilton Gyll, Esq. |
| 300 | 0 | 0 | Thomas Peers Williams, Esq. |
| 7 | 0 | 0 | Rev. Mr. Seymour Neville. |
| 8 | 0 | 0 | Messrs. Ibotson and Ladell. Mr. Skidmore Ashby, holds the Eyots at Hythe End. |
| 4 | 0 | 0 | Mr. Francis Buckland. |
| 6 | 0 | 0 | Mr. John Taylor. |
| 9 | 2 | 3 | Mr. John Palmer. |
| 12 | 1 | 4 | Bridge Trust Lands. |
| 0 | 2 | 0 | Baptist Chapel Lands. |
| 52 | 2 | 23 | Dean and Canons of Windsor. |

ACREAGE.

| A. | R. | P. | |
|---|---|---|---|
| 5 | 3 | 21 | Church Land in trust. |
| 2 | 2 | 37 | Thames Commissioners. Parish Lands. |
| 70 | 0 | 0 | Gordon Willoughby Jas. Gyll, Esq. |
| 5 | 1 | 36 | Neville Reid, Esq., sold to Capt. Shelton. |
| 1 | 2 | 21 | Crown Lands, Farm of P. Augusta and K. George, 3 qrs. Lord Braybroke was lessee. |
| 58 | 0 | 0 | River Thames. |
| 19 | 2 | 28 | Roads. |
| 18 | 2 | 36 | Church Glebe, vicarial. |
| 0 | 0 | 10 | Chapel Trust. |
| 3 | 0 | 0 | Mr. Thomas Harris. |

## NAMES OF THOSE WHO HELD LANDS IN WRAYSBURY,

### According to the Award Map of 1798 and 1803.

| ACREAGE | | | | ACREAGE | | | |
|---|---|---|---|---|---|---|---|
| A. | R. | P. | | A. | R. | P. | |
| 4 | 3 | 30 | Adkins, Joseph. | 2 | 1 | 4 | Monnery, William and Josiah. |
| 1 | 1 | 2 | } Ashby, Thomas and Wm. Chandler. | 3 | 2 | 5 | Matthews, Nathaniel. |
| 42 | 0 | 22 | | 2 | 0 | 37 | Novell, John. |
| 31 | 0 | 7 | Thomas Buckland. | 1 | 2 | 26 | Newman, Elizabeth. |
| 11 | 1 | 34 | Duchess of Bucclough. | 113 | 9 | 14 | Powell, John Harcourt, Esq. |
| 1 | 1 | 4 | Boult, Mary. | 0 | 0 | 29 | Porter, Thomas. |
| 1 | 0 | 35 | Chandler, William. | 0 | 3 | 16 | Packer, John, and William Thurbin. |
| 283 | 2 | 2 | Downshire, Marquis of. | 9 | 1 | 19 | Stanton, Thomas, holds Gill's Close. |
| 28 | 0 | 11 | Williams, Thomas, Esq. | 136 | 1 | 26 | Style, Robert. |
| 4 | 2 | 12 | | 3 | 3 | 4 | Trotman, Shadrach. |
| 24 | 2 | 20 | William Gyll, Esq., Dean and Canons | 16 | 1 | 38 | Taylor, William. |
| 63 | 3 | 24 | of Windsor, and allotment for ma- | 1 | 3 | 0 | Taylor, John. |
| 170 | 3 | 7 | norial rights. | 0 | 2 | 6 | Thurbin, William. |
| 49 | 3 | 35 | | 1 | 0 | 25 | Tanner, Elizabeth. |
| 28 | 2 | 23 | | 5 | 3 | 12 | Trustees of Church Lands. |
| 4 | 2 | 12 | | 11 | 1 | 3 | Ditto of Bridge Lands. |
| 0 | 3 | 23 | Herbert, James. | 18 | 2 | 36 | Wraysbury, Vicar of. |
| 412 | 1 | 36 | Harcourt, John, Esq. | 28 | 0 | 11 | Williams, Thomas, Esq. |
| 1 | 2 | 25 | King George III. held by Lord Bray- | 2 | 0 | 21 | Whitmarsh, William. |
| | | | broke as lessee. | 2 | 0 | 0 | Parish Gravel Pits. |
| 16 | 2 | 20 | King, Mary. | 21 | 1 | 4 | Wilmot, Nathaniel. |
| 0 | 3 | 25 | Mills, Samuel Hugh. | 1 | 3 | 6 | Walker, George. |
| 2 | 2 | 2 | Widow of Robert Mackason, Esq. | 4 | 1 | 3 | Whitfield, Robert. |

## THE WRAYSBURY PARISH OVERSEERS' ACCOUNTS.

### Rates and Minutes of Vestry begin 1744. First Book ends 1789.

At a vestry held 30th May 1741, the poor-rate relief was 6d in the pound. Philip Harcourt's house, 5s; ditto for Ankerwycke, 10s. William Cooper for —— Trumball, Esq. £4. 12s 3d. William Pearson and John Crowder for Mr. Bullock, the mills, £1. 16s. Mr. Swain for Mr. Hassel, 13s 6d. Do. Samuel Martin for ditto, £3. 12s. David Wingrove for Mr. Trippick, 5s. Thomas Child for Welly, 5s 9d. John Willis for Mr. Hassel—several entries for Mr. Hassel. The names appended are John Harris and Richard Verry.

Henry Pinnock, William Cooper, Samuel Verry: sum collected, £39. 9s 9d; another rate, 10th October 1744: total, £52. 11s 8d. Various entries of losses by Great Ankerwycke; new house built there. In overseers' hands £2. 0s 3d. Signed Philip Harcourt and Christopher Tower, 17th April 1745.

On the 18th August 1745 another rate collected, £5. 8s 9d; ditto, 2nd March, 1745-6, £45. 8s Seen and allowed by two of His Majesty's Justices of Peace for Bucks, 7th March, 1745, £39. 9s 6d.

```
£91 19  6
  1 15  4
─────────
 93 14 10
 83  1 11   disbursed.
─────────
£10 12  1
```

Signed 2nd April, 1746—Philip Harcourt, George Tash.

2nd April 1746: David Wingrove, John Sanders, John Crowder, Ralph Crowder, John Harris, Samuel Martin—Churchwardens. William Cooper, Edward Godman—Overseers. William Lewin, Henry Pinnock, Shadrach Child, John Crowder, Edward Hughes, Jeffrey Tucker, John Godman.

Poor rate, 14th May 1746, 6d in the pound. Shadrach Child for Welly, 5s 9d—Signatures of Philip Harcourt and Thomas Parr, 23rd January 1746.

```
£39  9  6   rate.
 10  4 11   overseers' hands.
  0 16  6   ditto.
─────────
£50 10 11
 42  2  8   disbursed.
─────────
 £8  8  3   surplus.
```

Total disbursements of rates in 1747, £42. 3s 2d.

It appears that about this year Mr. Hassel let Wraysbury House, as various names are entered for him and his property. 26th December 1747, at 6d in the pound, rate £39. 2s; disbursements, £69. 8s 10d. Rate in 1748, £86. 17 3d. Total received, £41. 14s 2d; disbursed, £32. 13s; surplus, £9. 2s 2d.

In the rate made in 1749, Mr. Hassel returns home, and there is a rate of 13s 6d—£37. 12s 6d. The names for Mr. Hassel are Martin, Godman, Pain, Willis, Lewington. Signatures: Thomas Parr, Christopher Tower.

In 1750, rate at 6d in the pound. John Crowder for Henry Bullock; Widow White for Welly House; William Styles for his Grace the Duke of Montagu, 2s 6d. Rate, £37. 18s 1d; subsequently, £44. 11s 8d. Rate made in October 1750, £37. 18s 1d. Gilbert Jodrell, Esq., for Philip Harcourt, Esq., £1. 2s 6d; Mr. Hassel, 5s; David Wingrove for Mr. Hassel; William Style for the Duchess of Montagu; Widow Pritty for Mr. Bullock. In 1751, 23rd June: rate 6d in the pound, £37. 19s 7d. Gilbert Jodrell, Esq.; William Cooper for William Trumball, Esq.; William Style for the late Duchess of Montagu; Richard Barnett for Thomas Tower, Esq.; the widow of Wm. Pritty for Mr. Bullock.

```
1752  .  £38  1  2
          16  8  4
         ─────────
         £54  9  7
          49 13  0   disbursed.
         ─────────
          £4 16  7
```

On the 9th August 1752, rate 6d: £37. 16s 10d. Burt for Welly House; William Style for Lady Cardigan, 15th March 1753, rate 12d: £74. 13s 9d. Jeffrey Tucker for Judge Carter; Richard Grove for Mr. Bowry; Richard Bonnett for Thomas Tower, Esq.; Richard Bonnett for William Allat, Esq.; William Style for Lady Cardigan; Thomas Bullock. 14th November 1753, rate 12d: £76. 5s 3d. John Montagu for Lady Cardigan.

In 1754, Judge Carter appealed against his rate of £40; and in 1755, at Wraysbury, the Bench took off £8. He held a mill in Wraysbury. Simon Padnore for Philip Hare, Esq., 16s 5d. Rate in 1754 came to £101. 17s 11d. Accounts swore before Philip Harcourt—George Tash, Thomas Parr.

31st March 1755, a 6d rate: £38. 4s 2d; Gilbert Jodrell, Esq. for Great Ankerwycke House and meadow; Mr. Hassel for his orchard and gardens; Judge Carter; John Budin for Samuel Verry; John Godman for Mr. Hassel; John Godman for Cold Harbour; Samuel Martin for Mr. Hassel; Samuel Martin for late Bowry's barn now Jennings'; Jeffrey Tucker for late Judge Carter; William Lewin for Mr. Dorlthen ats Dalton; John Buat, late Bowry, now Jennings; Thomas Downham for Catherine Cummins; Francis Bowry Denham for Cummins; John Montagu for late Duke of Montagu.

1759. Cornelius Townshend, Esq. rented Great Ankerwycke, and John Powey, Esq. was in Little Ankerwycke; John Harcourt Powell, Esq., Mrs. Mewes for late Sanders, for Nichols; David Wingrove for Mr. Gyll, £9. 10s.

1760. John Goodman for late Mr. Hassel, £4. 16s; David Wingrove for Mr. Gyll, £9. 10s; William Whitmarsh for Mr. Bowry.

1761. Harcourt Powell; Gilbert Jodrell; Widow Crowder for Mr. Bullock; John Godman for Mr. Gyll; David Wingrove for Mr. Gyll; Richard Jones for late Squire William Trumball.

1762. John Godman for Mr. Gyll; David Wingrove for Mr. Gyll; Mr. Jordan for Mr. Gyll; Henry Lewington for Mr. Gyll.

1763. Robert Styles for Hythe End Farm; Joseph Mocock for Mr. Gyll; Joseph Mocock for Mr. Gyll's house and Orchard, £1. 7s; Richard Streatly for Mr. Gyll; H. Lewington for Mr. Gyll.

1765. John Harcourt for Mr. Gyll; Geo. Barne, Esq. for Harcourt Powell, Esq.; John Crowder for Rev. Mr. Vandernan; Richard Bennett for — Jennings, Esq.; Widow Pritty for Mr. Henry Bullock.

1766. John Harcourt, Esq. for M. Gyll's house (rented Wraysbury House); Richard Jones for Colonel Sandys.

1767. George Barne, Esq. for Harcourt Powell, Esq.; John Harcourt, Esq. for Mr. Gyll; John Crowder for Duchess of Montagu.

1769. Harcourt Powell, Esq. for Hythe End Farm.

1770. Richard Jones for late Lady Sandys; received of Mrs. Buckland for Rose Lewington, 7s 6d.

1771. Mr. Barne leaves and Harcourt Powel comes in, and still holds Hythe End farm; Mr. Jodrell paid £1. 16s in rates, and in 1772 ditto.

1772. Jukes Colson for the iron mill, £1. 16s.

1773. Mr. Gyll returns to live in Wraysbury House, and Mr. John Harcourt retires from it as lessee; Richard Jones for — Sandys, Esq.; Thomas Ashby; William Taylor; Roger Carter, for Harcourt Powell, Esq.

1774. Sir Edwin Wynn, Bart. resides at Little Ankerwycke; and in July, Mrs. Jodrell, widow of Gilbert Jodrell, quits Great Ankerwycke, and is succeeded by Thomas Rous, Esq.; and Mrs. Hewett comes into Little Ankerwycke.

1775. Jukes Colson, Esq. for the iron mill.

1776. Thomas Bates Rous, Esq.

1777. The Gnoll Company took the copper mills and the river on the Common.

1778. Duchess of Buccleugh rated; and Daniel Sills for William Gyll, Esq.

## RATES.

| Year | £ s. d. | Year | £ s. d. | Year | £ s. d. |
|---|---|---|---|---|---|
| 1744 | £52 11 8 | | 42 17 7 | | 138 3 1 |
| 1745 | 45 8 0 | | 42 17 7 | 1805 | 138 3 1 |
| 1746 | 50 10 11 | 1775 | 43 2 1 | | 138 3 1 |
| 1747 | 39 12 0 | | 43 2 7 | | 138 3 1 |
| 1748 | 36 17 3 | | 43 2 7 | 1806 | 138 3 1 |
| 1749 | 37 12 6 | | 42 13 7 | | 138 3 1 |
| 1750 | 37 18 2 | | 42 12 11 | | 138 3 1 |
| 1751 | 37 19 2 | 1776 | 45 6 11 | 1807 | 132 19 7 |
| 1752 | 38 1 2 | | 45 17 7 | | 133 17 0 |
| 1753 | 74 13 9 | | 45 17 4 | | 133 17 0 |
| 1754 | 101 17 11 | | 45 12 2 | 1808 | 130 19 0 |
| 1755 | 77 2 3 | 1777 | 45 12 2 | | 261 18 0 |
| 1756 | 76 18 6 | | 45 12 2 | | 131 15 0 |
| 1757 | 76 14 9 | | 45 12 2 | | 131 16 0 |
| 1758 | 76 1 9 | 1778 | 92 3 1 | 1809 | 131 16 1 |
| | 42 18 4 | | 46 6 2 | | 131 16 1 |
| 1759 | 77 11 6 | | 46 6 2 | | 131 16 1 |
| | 78 15 6 | 1779 | 92 11 5 | | 131 16 1 |
| 1760 | 78 15 6 | | 92 11 5 | 1810 | 131 16 1 |
| 1761 | 39 7 9 | | 92 11 5 | | 197 14 1 |
| | 79 12 3 | 1780 | 92 13 11 | | 198 14 7 |
| 1762 | 39 14 7 | | 46 6 11 | | 132 14 2 |
| | 79 16 9 | | 97 0 5 | 1811 | 132 14 2 |
| 1763 | 80 12 3 | 1781 | 48 11 2 | Not cast up or entered. | |
| 1764 | 40 2 1 | | 96 17 11 | | 132 14 2 |
| | 40 2 1 | 1782 | 97 6 11 | | 132 14 2 |
| 1765 | 42 0 5 | | 96 4 5 | | 132 14 2 |
| 1766 | 40 2 4 | | 96 3 11 | 1812 | 132 14 2 |
| 1767 | 40 5 4 | 1783 | 96 3 11 | | 132 14 2 |
| | 81 0 9 | Torn out. | | | 132 14 2 |
| 1768 | 41 0 4 | 1801 | 137 14 4 | The Books are wanting. | |
| 1769 | 40 14 10 | | 137 14 4 | 1821 | 133 10 0 |
| | 41 17 10 | | 137 14 4 | | 143 16 3 |
| 1770 | 41 14 0 | 1802 | 137 14 4 | 1822 | 135 12 6 |
| | 41 12 11 | | 137 14 4 | | 134 10 10 |
| 1771 | 41 14 5 | | 137 14 4 | 1823 | 144 17 0 |
| | 91 12 1 | | 137 14 4 | | 145 4 11 |
| | 41 16 8 | | 137 14 4 | | 145 4 11 |
| | 41 18 2 | 1803 | 137 11 2 | 1824 | 145 4 11 |
| At the George Inn. | | | 276 6 2 | | 147 7 1 |
| 1772 | 42 0 2 | | 138 3 1 | | 146 6 4 |
| 1773 | 41 11 10 | | 138 3 1 | 1825 | 145 18 0 |
| | 41 18 10 | | 138 3 1 | | 143 18 2 |
| | 41 8 7 | 1804 | 138 3 1 | | 145 15 11 |
| | 41 13 7 | | 138 3 1 | | 146 8 11 |
| 1774 | 41 13 7 | | 138 3 1 | | 144 2 11 |

## RATES—continued.

| Year | £ | s | d | Year | £ | s | d | Year | £ | s | d | |
|---|---|---|---|---|---|---|---|---|---|---|---|---|
| 1826 | 152 | 19 | 11 | | 145 | 4 | 8 | 1830 | 34 | 9 | 6 | |
| | 151 | 0 | 3 | | 145 | 4 | 8 | 1831 | 25 | 6 | 3 | |
| | 145 | 17 | 7 | | 145 | 4 | 8 | 1832 | 23 | 5 | 9 | |
| | 144 | 8 | 4 | | 145 | 6 | 2 | | 70 | 17 | 1 | |
| 1827 | 146 | 5 | 1 | 1833 | 145 | 4 | 8 | 1833 | 77 | 7 | 2 | |
| | 146 | 11 | 7 | | 145 | 9 | 1 | 1834 | 76 | 2 | 5 | |
| | 146 | 8 | 1 | | 145 | 9 | 1 | | 71 | 3 | 6 | |
| | 146 | 13 | 1 | | 145 | 9 | 1 | 1835 | 85 | 5 | 1 | |
| 1828 | 146 | 13 | 4 | | 145 | 6 | 1 | 1836 | 121 | 1 | 10 | |
| | 146 | 10 | 1 | 1834 | 145 | 0 | 1 | 1837 | 44 | 14 | 2 | |
| | 145 | 9 | 7 | | 145 | 0 | 1 | | 28 | 13 | 3 | |
| 1829 | 145 | 9 | 7 | | 145 | 0 | 1 | 1838 | 84 | 3 | 7 | |
| | 146 | 5 | 0 | | 145 | 7 | 4 | 1839 | 18 | 18 | 2 | |
| | 145 | 16 | 10 | 1835 | 145 | 7 | 4 | | 45 | 10 | 7 | |
| 1830 | 146 | 13 | 3 | In 1827 £70 18 3 {collected as Church Rate. | | | | 1840 | 38 | 10 | 5 | |
| | 146 | 19 | 7 | | | | | 1841 | 17 | 13 | 3 | |
| | 145 | 14 | 10 | | | | | | 45 | 12 | 7 | on 121 people |
| | 145 | 14 | 10 | 26 10 7 { Church land. | | | | 1842 | 33 | 0 | 10 | on 84 ,, |
| 1831 | Not cast-up. | | | | | | | 1843 | 6 | 5 | 7 | on 28 ,, |
| | 145 | 14 | 10 | £97 | 8 | 10 | | | 43 | 9 | 3 | on 134 ,, |
| | 145 | 8 | 8 | | | | | 1844 | 61 | 15 | 1 | on 119 ,, |
| 1832 | 145 | 7 | 8 | 1828 £36 | 5 | 1 | | | 41 | 16 | 2 | on 136 ,, |
| | | | | 1829 35 | 5 | 1 | | | | | | |

The average rate of rates is 3d in the pound, so it has not been thought expedient to continue the series till the present year.

In 1801, 1734 persons and houses, collected on about 70, &c. at which time the valuation of the parish was £2743. 8s.

In 1844, the rated value of the parish on 136 people was £3774. 11s.

In 1858, the gross rate was £4677 2s 6d. Net or rateable value, £4251. 4s, and in 1859, the result was the same.

In 1860, the rates about 2s 6d in the pound, but the average rate is 20d, raising £650, average some £500.

On one occasion the gross rate was £4722. 12s 6d. Net or rateable levy was £4290. 19s.

## CHURCHWARDENS' ACCOUNT.

### RATES AND MINUTES OF VESTRIES BEGINS FROM 1734.

Philip Harcourt, Esq. and William Pearson, paper-maker, Churchwardens, 1734.

6s 8d accustomed fee for interment of a parishioner within the Church, payable to Churchwardens for the use of the Church.

Received of Mr. John Winch £1. 16s 7d for Church land, due Lady-day, a year's rent, 15th April 1734.

Names of some parishioners at Vestry, April 1735, Charles Holoway, John Harris, Simon Smith, Robert Lewin, John Crowder, John Grove, John Cox, the mark of John Winch, H. Pinnock, William Lewin, mark of John Russel, Richard Denny, Richard Frogley.

An 8d rate on 74 persons or houses, 12th Jan. 1734-5. Philip Harcourt for his house 13s 4d; Simon Smith for Mr. Harcourt, £6. 2s 8d; John Grove for Mr. Trumbal, £6. 16s 4d; Mr. Pearson and Crowder for the mills, £2. 13s 4d; Mr. Robert Hassel for his house, 16s; Mr. Martin for Mr. Hassel's Spur's land, 8s 4d; Shadrach Child, £2. 8s 8d; Mr. Trippick for Francis Bowry, £2. 10s; Edmund Bowry, 5s; ditto for Francis Bowry, his cousin, 6s; Sir Henry Ashurst, 2s; J. Winch for Mr. Harcourt, £1.; Henry Pinnock for Philip Harcourt, £4. 3s; Edward Godman for Mr. Verwins, 16s; John Godman for Mr. Hassel, £1. 4s; R. Verry for Mr. Harcourt, £1. 4s; Thomas Haynes for Francis Bowry, 6s; ditto for Poltock, 4s; Richard Barnet for Mr. Hales, 8s; John Gill for Th. Russel, 7s; James Bond for John Russel, 9s; Francis Perkins for his own land, 1s; William Shears for Widow Leaders, 1s; William Terry, Thomas Wildman for Mr. Hassel, 2s; Mrs. Adkins for Mr. Binfield, 2d; Mrs. Styles, 3s; John Rolfe for Mr. Harcourt, 4s; R. Parrington for Trippick's, 1s; Richard Frogley for Mr. Harcourt, 5s; H. Lewington for Mr. Hassel, 2s; Edward Phipps for Mr. Harcourt, 2s; Widow Rolfe for Mr. Hassel.

12th Jan. 1735. Rate for Church repair of pews, &c. £47. 7s 10d. Signatures—Robert Prowse Hassel, Philip Harcourt, and 12 others.

7th April 1735. Three Churchwardens appointed—Mr. H. Pinnock, by Mr. John Amy, Vicar; Mr. Philip Harcourt, and William Pearson—11 names appended.

Disbursements for the parish, 1733-4, £47. 10s 1d. In Churchwardens' hands, £15. 12s 11d. Paid Mr. Stanny for painting the Church, £1. 5s 6d. Ditto, painting steeple, £11. 11s 6d. Oct. 1735, due 3rd May 1736, due to Churchwardens, £3. 8s 11d. 20th Dec. 1735, John Willis paid £1. 10s for Sarah, daughter of his wife, late Ann Perkins, till she attains 15 years.

26th April 1736. Henry Pinnock and John Grove, Churchwardens elect—10 signatures. Remaining in Churchwardens' hands, £12. 3s 5d in June 1735. Rate, 12th May 1739, at 4d in the pound. Philip Harcourt for his new house, 3s 4d; William Mitchell, Esq. for Mr. Harcourt, 10s 8d; John Grove for Mr. Trumball, £3. 1s 6d; Messrs. Pearson and Crowder, of the mills, for Mr. Bullock, £1. 4s; Mr. Pearson for Mr. Allen, 9s; ditto for Mr. Hassel for his mansion-house, 7s 2d; Mr. Martin for Mr. Hassel, Spur's land, 4s 2d; Shadrach Child for Thomas Tower, Esq. £1. 1s 10d; Ellis Trippick for Mr. Adkins, £1. 10s 6d; Edmund Bowry 2s 6d, for his kinsman, Francis Bowry, 3s; ditto for Lady Ashurst, 1s; Thomas Haynes for Francis Bowry, 2s 2d; Richard Barrett for Thomas Tower, Esq. 4d; Samuel Kerett for Welly House, 3s 10d; Richard Gibbons, John Russel, William Rolfe, John Willis for George Child, John Walford, Mrs. Styles for Mrs. Davenport, Widow Rolfe for Mr. Hassel, Thomas Stevens for Mr. Atkins. Total £23. 17s 6d. There are five names attached to the rate disbursements. Dr. Lee for his bill, 7s 6d. Mr. Sykes for painting Church gates, 10s 6d. Four days' ringing of bells, 12s. Overcharged Mr. Hassel in the rate, 3s 8d. Total, £46. 15s 4d. 30th March 1741, Churchwardens John Harris and John Crowder, seven names are appended. Disbursements are £28. 4s 7d.

6th March 1743. In vestry a rate of 6d in the pound. Philip Harcourt for his house, 5s; for Day Mead, 3s; Mrs. Savan for Mr. Hassel, 13s 6d; John Godman for ditto, 12s 3d; ditto for late Wildman, 1s 6d; Thomas Child for Welly House, 5s 9d; John Willis for Mr. Hassel, 1s 6d; Henry Lewington for ditto, 1s 6d, &c. Total, £36. 6s. Seven names attached.

26th March 1744. Churchwardens, Samuel Martin and Richard Verry—10 names attached. In 1745, six names attached—J. Landen, H. Pinnock, R. Lewin, Jeffrey Tucker, David Wingrove, Edward Godman.

Old Ankerwycke, rate 10s. Squire Harcourt's new house, 1s 8d; Mr. Crowder for Mr. Bullock, 12s; Shadrach Child for Squire Tower, 10s 11d. Several entries for Mr. Hassel. Thomas Child for Welly House. Total, £12. 2s 11d. Disbursements. Copy of Squire Lee's will, 9s 6d. Lost by Ankerwycke great house, 8s. Churchwardens for 31st March 1748, W. Cooper and Ralph Carter, with 11 names appended to the book.

1749, John Crowder and William Cooper, Churchwardens. 8th April 1751, John Crowder, sen. and W. Cooper, Churchwardens; Richard Dipple, Curate. 30th March 1752, £6. 1s 2d, for Overseers. Ditto, eight persons pricked down to serve as Churchwardens. 1753, R. Dipple, Curate, appointed Churchwarden, 10 names affixed. Disbursements, £5. 7s 5d. 26th May 1757, Richard Blacon inducted Minister. 1760, John Crowder and Robert Styles, Churchwardens; Styles to have the right of building a seat or pew for himself and family. 1764, Fretwell Vanderman, Vicar. In 1744, a dispute between John Harris and Richard Verry, Churchwardens, and Robert Lewin, the parson's tenant, for the vicarage farm at Wraysbury, it was decided by Counsellor Bell at the Visitation, that as the parson leased out his farm, it must pay to the church and poor-rate.

## MISCELLANEOUS NAMES OF GENTLEMEN WHO HAVE HELD PROPERTY IN WYRARDISBURY.

1041. Wraysbury was held by a *Thane* of K. Edward Confessor — of which there were Regis, mediocres, minores, or lowest class of freeholders.
1066. Robert de Gernon, by gift of William I.
1125. William de Gernon, took name of Montfitchet.
1157. Sir Gilbert de Montfitchet founded Ankerwycke Priory, and dying, his property here went to Richard de Montfitchet, and in 1258 it devolved to females.
1219. Robert de Burnell, and he was followed by Robert de Burnell.
1230. Alexander de Wyredesbir, Ralph de Wyrardesbyr.
Robert Burnel, Bishop of Bath and Wells, and died 1292.
1275. William de Huntercombe.
1280. Christiana de Mauriscis.
1283. Elias de Coventrie.
1289. John de Remenham.
1299. William le Ken, and his son Ralph le Ken.
1312. Sir Roger de Norwode.
1320. Sir Humphrey de Walden.
Walter de la Grave.
1323. Richard Ikene.
1325. Richard de Wynferthing.
1327. John de Shobenangre, also of High Wycombe.
1326. Sir Hugh le Despenser, Earl of Winchester, beheaded 1326.
1330. Alicia de la Gardinière.
1334. John de Lancaster, Peer of Parliament, died 1334.
1340. Ralph de Plaiz, Baron.
1350. Isabel de Duton.
Richard de Gloster, of the De Clare family.
1360. Richard de Plaiz, died Peer of Parliament, 1360.
1369. John Jourdelay, of Place Farm, with Thomas de Remenham.
1376. Robert le Smyth held the manor of the Crown.
1377. Henry atte Water, do.
1384. William de Windsor, Lord Windsor, Peer, ob. 1384.
1420. Richard Frowyn, of Colnbrook.
1436. Sir John de Fray, Baron of Exchequer, died 1460.
1460. Sir David Brecknock, and John Brecknock, Esq.
1461. Sir Richard Wylly, of Welly House.
William Paulet, Esq.
John Pollard, Gent. and John Ball, Gent. jointly at Place Farm until 1537.
In this century the family of De Vere held lands through the De Plaiz, whose male line became extinct in 1360.
1480. Sir Walter Stonor, of Place Farm. Held also the manor. Constable of the Tower of London.
Thomas Archer, Esq.
George Windsor, Esq.
1520. Richard Fitzwater, Esq.
1522. John Oxenbridge, Canon of Windsor, d. 1522.
1523. Sir Henry Norris, of Oxon. beheaded 1537.
Dr. Thomas Aldridge, Provost of Eton, d. 1556.

1537. Sir William Windsor, of Bradenham, Knt. of the Shire.
Thomas Archer, Esq.
John Norris, Esq. d. 1563, of Ankerwycke.
1539. John Polard, Gent. and Ralph Hamersley, Esq.
1542. Andrew Lord Windsor, of Ankerwycke, d. 1543.
Reginald Digby, Esq. of Horton, d. 1549.
1548. Sir Philip Hoby, died 1558. Secretary of State.
1549. Ralph Goodyeare leased College lands.
1550 Sir Thomas Smyth, Knt. of Ankerwycke, d. 1577. Principal Secretary of State and thrice Ambassador to France.
1554. John Kyderminster, Esq. of Langley.
George Frevylle, Esq. Baron of Exchequer, 1558, d. 1578.
1560. Walter Walshe, of Place Farm, d. 1561.
1564. Walter Prunes held College lands.
1577. George, brother and heir of Sir Thomas Smyth of Ankerwycke, d. 1584.
1583. Edmund Kederminster, father of Sir John Kederminster, d. 1607.
1584. Sir William Smijth, Knt. of Ankerwycke, d. 1626.
Sir Robert Oxenbridge, relative of Rev. John Oxenbridge, Canon of Windsor, who died 1574.
1591. John Pennar, Esq.
William Peters, Gent. d. 1611.
1600. Henry Bulstrode, Lord of the manor, died 1632.
1620. Sir Dudley Carleton, Lord Dorchester, College lands, d. 1631.
Felix Wilson, Gent. of Place Farm.
1622. Sir William Walshe, d. 1622.
1627. John Sharowe, Esq. Lord of the manor, died 1627.
1625. William Sandford, Esq. and Edward Sandford, Esq.
1629. John Whistler, Esq. College lands.
1631. Sir William Salter rented Ankerwycke of the Smijths, d. 1643.
William Trumball, Esq. d. 1635.
1636. Edward Bulstrode, Esq. and Edward Woodward, Gent.
1641. William Sharowe, Esq.
James Parkes, Esq. died 1641.
1642. Andrew King, Lord of the Manor, d. 1659.

1643. Andrew Warde, Gent.
1647. Robert Hall, Gent.
1652. John Lee, Esq. bought Ankerwycke Purnish, and in 1678 Ankerwycke Priory, d. 1682.
Isaac Pennington, Esq.
Richard Hale, Esq. Place Farm, d. 1678.
Nicholas Pyncheon, Gent.
1654. William Pyncheon, held College lands, died 1662.
George Brome, Esq. d. 1652.
Edward Bulstrode, Alexander Croke, Esq. &c.
Alexander Gould, Esq., father of Edward Gould, who d. 1680.
1660. Henry Beckingham, Esq. College lands.
1672. Richard Hale, M.D., Place Farm, d. 1728.
John Topham, Esq., College lands in 1707.
1679. Sir Andrew King, Lord of the Manor in 1659, d. 1679.
1687. John Pyncheon, Esq.
Sir William Trumball, Knt. d. 1716.
Francis Bowry, d. 1726.
1696. Elizabeth, widow of Benjamin Hassel, Esq., College lands, d. 1714.
John Hassel, Esq. of do.
1704. John Lee, of Ankerwycke, d. 1704.
John Rowland, Esq. College lands, d. 1744.
1714. John Hassel, Esq. of Wraysbury House. d. 1718.
1724. George Northey, Esq., Thomas Ringer, Esq.
1727. Robert Prowse Hassel, Esq. of do. d. 1760.
Thomas Tower, Esq. of Place Farm, d. 1778.
Mary, widow of John Lee, Esq., d. 1725.
Philip, grandson of Sir Philip Harcourt, Kt. d. 1759.
1735. Edward Borrett, Gent.
1745. William Camden, Gent. and Charles Saltmarsh, Gent.
1748. John, 2nd Duke of Montagu, d. 1749.
1750. William Gyll, Esq. of Wraysbury House, and Yeoveny Hall, Middlesex, d. 1798.
1752. Countess of Cardigan, wife of George, 4th Earl of Cardigan, d. 1790.
1759. John Harcourt, Esq. d. 1785.
1760. Christopher Tower, Esq. d. 1771.
K. George III. d. 1820.
Col. Martin Sandys, d. 1768.

1766. George, 4th Earl of Cardigan, created Duke of Montagu, d. 1790.
1767. Francis Hargrave, Gent., Christopher Hargrave.
1775. — Partington, Esq. and Edward Bodle, Esq. John Vernon, Esq.
1780. Pascoe Grenfell, Esq. of Taplow, d. 1838. Arthur Marquis of Downshire, d. 1801.
1785. John Simon Harcourt, Esq. d. 1810.
1788. John Barrington, son of Sir Fitzwilliam Barrington, Bart.
1790. Duke of Buccleugh, d. 1812.
1798. Captain William Gyll, of Wraysbury House, d. 1806.
1799. Harcourt Powell, Esq. Mary, widow of William Gyll, Esq. of Wraysbury House, d. 1820.
1800. Lord Boston, d. 1856.
1800. Robert Mackason, Gent. Lord Braybroke, d. 1858.
1803. John Blagrove, Esq. of Ankerwycke, died 1824.
1819. Walter Francis Duke of Buccleugh.
1820. Princess Augusta, d. 1840. Brooke Hamilton Gyll, Esq. Wraysbury House, and Yeoveny Hall, Middlesex. Bellenden Charles Gyll, Esq. of Hythe End, d. 1822.
1828. Hugh Parkin, Esq. of Ankerwycke.
1829. George Simon Harcourt, Esq. Lord of the Manor, M.P. for the County.
1839. Neville Reid, Esq. Gordon Willoughby James Gyll, Esq.
1855. Rev. Seymour Neville, Vicar of Wraysbury. Thomas Harris, of Staines.
1860. Captain William Shelton.

## PROPRIETARY ACCORDING TO THE AWARD MAPS OF 1798 AND 1803.

Adkins, Joseph.
Ashby, Thomas.
Buckland, Thomas.
Chandler, William.
Downshire, Marquis of.
Gyll, William, Esq.
Herbert, James.
Harcourt, John, Esq.
King George III.
King, Mary.
Mackason, widow of Robert, Esq.
Monnery, William.

Monnery, Josiah.
Mills, Samuel Hugh.
Mathew, Nathaniel.
Newman, Elizabeth.
Nowell, John.
Powell, John Harcourt, Esq.
Packer, Josiah.
Porter, Thomas.
Stanton, Thomas.
Style, Robert.
Tanner, Elizabeth.
Taylor, William.

Taylor, John.
Thurbin, William.
Trotman, Shadrach.
Trustees of Church lands.
Do. of Bridge lands.
Parish Gravel pits.
Walker, George.
Whitfield, Robert.
Whitmarsh, William.
Williams, Thomas, Esq.
Wilmot, Nathaniel.

## NAMES OF LITERARY AND DISTINGUISHED CHARACTERS OF WRAYSBURY.

1292. Robert Burnell, Bishop of Bath and Wells.
1326. Sir Hugh le Despenser, Peer of Parliament.
1436. Sir John Fray, Baron of Exchequer.
1480. Sir Walter Stonor, Knt. Constable of the Tower.
1522. John Oxenbridge, Canon of Windsor.
1548. Sir Philip Hoby, Secretary of State.
1554. George Frevylle, Baron of Exchequer, 1558.
1577. Sir Thomas Smyth, Knt. Secretary of State.
1620. Sir Dudley Carleton and Lord Dorchester.
1622. Sir William Walshe, Knt. Sir William Smijth, Knt. Col. in the Army, M.P. for Aylesbury.
1661. Sir Thomas Smijth, created Bart. 1661. William Trumball, Esq. M.P. for Bucks. 1631.
1662. William Pynchoon, "The meritorious Prince of our redemption."
1679. Isaac Pennington, Esq., various religious works.
1707. William Walshe, the famous critic, grandson of Sir William Walshe.
1716. Sir William Trumball, Knt. statesman and publicist.
1728. Dr. Richard Hale, M.D. medical tracts.

1749. John 2nd Duke of Montagu.
1760. King George III.
1766. George 4th Earl of Cardigan and Duke of Montagu.
William Gyll, Esq. Lord Mayor of London, 1788.
1790. Thomas Williams, Esq. M.P. for Marlow, Vice President of the Literary Fund, &c.
Col. Martin Sandys, son of Samuel Lord Sandys.
1796. Owen Williams, Esq. M.P. for Marlow.
1800. Arthur Hill, 2nd Marquis of Downshire.
1806. William Gyll, Captain Life Guards, Equerry to the Duke of Sussex.
1807. Pascoe Grenfell, Esq. M.P. for Marlow.
1812. Henry, 3rd Duke of Buccleugh.
1820. Thomas Peers Williams, Esq., M.P. for Marlow.
1837. George Simon Harcourt, Esq., M.P. for Bucks.
Henry James Lord Montagu.
Walter Francis Duke of Buccleugh.
1860. Gordon Willoughby James Gyll, Esq.: Tractate on Language; History of Wraysbury, Horton, and Colnbrook; Translation from the Spanish of Don Guzman de Alfarache; History of the House of Flemyng Earl of Wigtoun; Fugitive Pieces.

## HOUSES AND THEIR PROPRIETORS.

| | |
|---|---|
| Ankerwycke House, | George Simon Harcourt, Esq. |
| Wraysbury House, | Brooke Hamilton Gyll, Esq. |
| —— House, | Rev. Seymour Neville, Vicar. |
| —— House, | Captain William Shelton. |
| Vicarage House, | Tenanted by Mr. Henry Taylor. |
| Wraysbury Mills, | Messrs. Ibotson and Ladell. |
| Whitehall, | Colonel Thomas Williams. |
| —— House, | Mr. Francis Buckland. |
| Ivy Cottage, | Buckland property. |
| Hythe End Mills, | Messrs. Ibotson and Ladell. |
| Farm house, near Wraysbury House, | Mr. William Thomas Buckland. |
| Private house, | Mr. Thomas Buckland. |
| Farm house, | Mr. Benjamin Slocock. |
| Do. Church Farm, | Mr. James Pullin. |
| Place Farm, | Mr. Samuel Jordan. |
| Hythe End Farm, | Mr. Mark Westaway. |
| Do. Ferry, | Messrs. Charles and James Aldane. |

## GENTRY WHO HAVE RENTED HOUSES IN THE PARISH.

1734. Sir Henry Ashurst.
Mr. Verwins.
1747. —— White, to 1752.
1749. Cornelius Townshend, Esq.
1750. Francis Bowry Denham.
1754. Philip Hare, Esq.
1755. Dalton or Dotton.
Richard Carter, d. 1755, a Welsh Judge.
1759. Mrs. Mewes or Meux.
1765. George Barne, Esq.
1772. Gilbert Jodrell, Esq.
Thomas Bates Rous, Esq., M.P. for Worcester, d. 1800.
Lord Shuldham.
1774. Mr. Beauchamp.
1774. Sir Edwin Wynn, Bart.
1778. Mr. Aylet.
1780. James Bonnel, of Pelham Place, Old Windsor, Esq. tenanted Wraysbury House.
Richard Stackpole, Esq., Count Stackpole in France; father of Richard, Duke of Stackpole.
1810. Charles Peto, Esq.
Lamont Norman, Esq.
—— Aberdeen, Esq.
John Kirkland, Esq.
John Cricket, Esq. d. 1811.
Lord Kingsborough.
William Mackreath, Esq.
William Hopkins, father of Rev. George A. Hopkins, —— Laurel Cottage.
Francis Goodrich, Esq. Laurel Cottage.

## TENANTS OF ANKERWYCKE HOUSE.

1537. John Norris, Esq.
1542. Andrew Lord Windsor.
1550. Sir Thomas Smyth, Kt.
1584. George Smijth, Esq.
1630. Sir William Salter, Kt.
1641. Andrew King.
1659. Sir Andrew King.

1680. John Lee, Esq.
1725. Harcourt family.
1772. Gilbert Jodrell, Esq.
Mr. Bouverie.
1798. Lord Shuldham.
1805. John Blagrove, Esq.
1811. John Crickett, Esq.

1811. Sir Edwin Wynn, Bart.
Hugh Parkin, Esq.
Lord Charles Beauclerk.
Capt. William Brooke.
Countess of Norbury.
1850. Felix Pryor, Esq.
1854. Cottril Scholefield, Esq.

## NAMES OF SOME OLD INHABITANTS OF THE PARISH.

1299. Hamond, John.
1533. Andrew, John.
1600. Atkins, William.
Ambrose, William.
1535. Henry Balnett.
1600. Bowry, Henry.
1672. Bernard, Ann.
1629. Child, William.
1699. Cobham, Richard.
1600. Domley, William.
1603. Edwardes, Thomas.
Filse, Henry.
1614. Green, William.

1514. Hamond, John.
1630. Harris, John.
Hellen, John.
1683. Hellen, William.
Hearne, William.
Helperley, Ralph.
Halfacre.
1583. Kederminster, Edward.
1608. Ledgold, Richard.
——— William.
1583. Moore, Thomas.
1617. Moore, Richard.
1606. Moore, Thomas.

1610. Peters, William.
——— John.
1646. Pilgrim, William.
1570. Rudstone, Robert.
1610. Reeve, Richard.
Snape, Thomas.
Smith, Ann.
Style, Anthony.
Virgo, William.
Weston, Ann.
1570. Wexham, Thomas.
1620. Wilson, Felix.

## NAMES OF PERSONS RATED IN 1734.

Harcourt, Philip, Esq.
Smith, Simon, for Mr. Harcourt.
Grove, Mr. John, for William Trumball, Esq.
Pearson and Crowder, for the Wraysbury Mills.
Hassel, Robert Prowse, Esq.
Martin, Mrs. for Mr. Hassel's Spur-land.
Cockman, ——
Child, Shadrach, for Mrs. Hall.
Tupp, Mr. for Francis Bowry.
Easom, ——
Aylet, Mr.
Bowry, Edmund.
Ashurst, Sir Henry, Bart.
Winch, John.
Urwin, ——
Brown's lands.
Pinnock, Henry.

Goodman, Edward.
——— John.
Verry, Richard.
——— Samuel.
Limings, James.
Lewing, William.
——— Robert.
Trippick, Ellis.
Haynes, Thomas, for F. Bowry.
Poltock.
Barnett, Richard, for Mrs. Halls.
Street, John.
Keen, Samuel.
Barsett, John.
Long, Francis.
Bond, James.
Russel, John.
New, John.
Blake, William.
Gill, John.

Cock, John.
Perkins, Francis.
——— James.
Stevens, William, for widow Leaders.
Terry, William.
Wildman, Thomas, for Mr. Hassel.
Livard, Thomas.
Thomas, John.
Phillips, Edward.
Pretty, William.
Rolfe, William.
——— John.
Shrub, Thomas.
Martin, Mrs.
Woolford, John.
Adkins, Mrs.
Binfield.
Styles, Mrs., for Davenport.

Saunders, Joseph.
——— John.
Ride, John.
Holway, Charles.
Mills, John.
Strike, Leonard.
Parrington, Richard.
Pain, John.
Duck, Edward.
Frogley, Richard.
Wade, Richard.

Love.
Lewington, Henry.

NAMES APPENDED TO
THIS RATE.

Holway, Charles.
Harcourt, Philip.
Pearson, William.
Child, Shadrach.
Harris, John.

Verry, William.
——— Richard.
Bond, James.
Trippick, Ellis.
Crowder, John.
Pinnock, Henry.
Smith, Simon.
Grove, John.
Frogley, Richard.
Hassel, Robert Prowse, with his autograph.

## NAMES OF ELECTORS, 1861.

Ashby, Skidmore.
——— William.
Bell, Charles.
Buckland, William Thomas.
——— Francis.
Cornish, George.
Clifford, William.
Davies, Joseph.
Gyll, Brooke Hamilton.

Gyll, Gordon Willoughby James.
Gordon, James.
Harcourt, George Simon.
Harris, South.
Poulter, Thomas.
Ibotson, William.
Jordan, Samuel.
Ladell, William.
Neville, Rev. Seymour.

Palmer, John.
Pullin, James.
Slocock, Benjamin.
Scholefield, Cottrill.
Shelton, William.
Taylor, John Painter.
——— James.
——— Henry.
Westaway, Mark Adolphus.

There were 5761 registered electors in Bucks, in 1837, and the county returns 11 members to Parliament.

    2233. George Simon Harcourt . Tory.
     982. George Henry Dashwood . Liberal.

1837, July and August,—

    2993. Marquis of Chandos ⎫
    2704. George Simon Harcourt ⎬ Tories.
    2633. Sir William Young ⎭
    2071. George R. Smith           Liberal.

The proportion of the population to the £10 holders, and again that of the £10 holders to the householders of every class, is very considerable. There is a marked difference in the proportion between the population and the enfranchised class. The electors of Great Britain are some 945,000.

## AGRICULTURAL AFFAIRS.

### WRAYSBURY AND HORTON PLOUGHING ASSOCIATION.

This Association comprises some 90 to 100 members for the encouragement of industrious labourers and servants. Among other benefits conferred on the parish and carried out by Mr. Harcourt, was the annual Ploughing Match, which generally takes place in September, when the united farmers of Wraysbury and Horton vie with each other in the exposition of their roots for competition. The ploughboys meet early in the field to try their skill and capacity in the primitive and now almost perfected art of turning the soil, and however well the plough may do it (for these stupendous machines have almost superseded the hands of ploughmen), it may be a question if the work is better executed, although it can be accomplished more easily, in a shorter time, and at lesser charge.

These meetings are of the most social kind, and the number of agriculturists of both parishes who assemble at the principal inns give courage and impart happiness to each other. Good cheer and good fellowship are promoted, and interchanges of opinions predominate, so that these small parishes have prospered, and even rival the great agricultural societies which annually meet in the field, especially the South Bucks, which holds its yearly sessions at Salt Hill, for the furtherance of a science once neglected, but to which all must cede—for sustentation of body precedes all cultivation of science.

The Wraysbury and Horton ploughing matches commenced in 1845, under the presidency of Mr. Harcourt, of Ankerwycke, and the average annual sums collected since that period have reached £45.

The presidential chair is taken by a resident or proprietor in the village, and the holdings alternate between one and the other. The vice-president is generally president the ensuing year. The names of those who have officiated *seriatim* are G. S. Harcourt, Gordon Gyll of Wraysbury, Edward Tyrrell of Berkyn Manor House, William Ashton of Horton House, Cotterill Scholefield of Ankerwycke, and this 1861 William Antony Greatorex of Horton.

The display of fruits, flowers and vegetables is always creditable, while prizes are awarded to every class of labourer, with rewards to the boys and girls of the schools for writing, needle work, &c. A special fund is subscribed to purchase two silver cups for mangold, &c.

There is an annual report published with the names of subscribers, among which we are proud to see that of H. R. H. the Prince Consort, who takes a lively interest in the villages.

Time was when game abounded in the parish of Wraysbury, under Mr. Blagrove and Mr. Harcourt, but since 1855 the shooting has been let to Mr. Francis Goodrich who lives at Laurel Cottage, a tenant on the Ankerwycke Estates, while Sir William Yardley rents what shooting there is belonging to Colonel Williams. As there is no cover for game it is too much exposed for anything like preservation, and all have been allowed to sport promiscuously, so that there is little left to hunt or shoot; however, the Prince Consort occasionally visits the locality with his harriers, and sometimes greyhounds are seen, but there must be little hope of sport where game is not duly secured.

## AGRICULTURAL STATISTICS.

The counties of the north of England are larger than those of the south, the largest being Yorkshire and the smallest Rutland, while the shire of Bucks is a *medium* size, its acreage being 513,400; its length is 45 miles, and its breadth 18 miles; its narrowest breadth is 10 miles.

It is a corn-growing country: the division for arable purposes being 352,000, for pasture 170,000. The circumference is 138 miles. The county of York contains 3,669,410 acres, while Rutland is only 95,360 acres. Buckinghamshire is one of the seven counties lying together, without a city among them or a cathedral. The largest parish in it is Chesham, with its eight appendages in Burnham Hundred, containing 11,880 acres. The entire acreage of Great Britain is 32,160,000, producing in round numbers some £37,412,000; 27 millions at £1. 7s 2d an acre is £36,675,000; two millions at 5s is £500,000, while 3,160,000 of moor and mountain produce £237,000, which tallies nearly with the rental as determined by assessment under the property and income tax acts in 1842, exclusive of Middlesex, the circumstances being exceptional, which is £387,861. Total, £37,408,014.

Some parishes are equal to 7000 or 8000 acres in area, while Stony Stratford is only 70 acres.

The exact area of Wraysbury parish is 1656 acres 1 rood, comprising water, and Stoke, which is the smallest hundred, contains 28,140 acres.

Of Wraysbury two-thirds are arable and one-third grass. The soil is generally a sort of black and blue loam and gravel, and it is a cereal village in a generally cereal shire; yet the roots grown here are peculiarly fine, especially mangold and turnip. The parish is chiefly cultivated by about ten yeomen farmers, not one being a large owner.

Geology, of which we treat little here, embraces the study of the globe in general, while mineralogy is the alphabet to geology.

The soil is generally fertile, and has an admixture of London clay, a plastic material which forms the substratum of the metropolis. There are varieties of clay of divers colours, alternating with pebbles mixed with marine shells, extending from the south of Essex to Hungerford in Berks, and known as Uxbridge clay.

Caird remarks that the south-eastern part of Bucks is chalky soil. The stiff blue clay round and beneath London is a marine deposit containing sea animals, and this lies under the fine bed of gravel on which the metropolis is erected. The strata overlaying the clay contain bones of all animals, domestic and wild: even of the hippopotamus, tapir, and animals peculiar to America. On Wraysbury Green echini or hedgehogs have been found, a prickly shell fish. The Thames drains the village.

Speed fancifully describes the shape of Bucks in 1611:—"In form it somewhat resembles a lion rampant, whose head or north points touch the counties of Northampton and Beds, whose back or east part is backed by Bedford and Herts. His loins or south borders rest upon Berks, and his breast, the west side, is butted upon wholly by Oxfordshire."

The length thereof from Wraysbury in the south to Cold Brayfield in the north is 39 miles, the breadth at the broadest from Ashridge in the east to Bernwood Forest in the west is 18 miles. The whole circumference being 138 miles.

In 1814 the annual value of real property here was £3774. 11s. In 1831 it fell to £3305, and in 1860 it rose to about £4000 per annum.

The average rate of wages was 8s 6d weekly: it has now reached 12s, and this suffices, for there are very few paupers here, and fewer go to the treadmill.

The poor rate is 2s 6d in the pound, including county rate, but there is a heavy land-tax. The condition of the poor is very creditable to the parish, and equally so to the rich; the former looking to the latter to redress the balance of their lot, and they are not deceived.

The Union is at Slough, in which refuge there are generally about two to three hundred souls. The magisterial benches are at Slough or Eton.

The land-tax in this shire is 1s 5d in the pound, one-third of which only is redeemed. This tax is of very ancient date, records assigning it to Ethelred, and was called Danegelt; but the continuous land-tax bears date only from the Revolution in 1688.

The first tax on personal property was instituted by King Henry II. at 2d in the pound on net effects, and this was raised to 1s 10d. It was a payment in lieu of military service.

There are no turnpikes here or in Horton, but anciently levies were made for waggon passages, of some 5d in the pound; the modern or macadam system of road making was introduced in 1818, which answers very well on high roads, but not so well in very populous cities like London, where there is a partial return to the old stone paving.

In 1850 the average of wages of all northern counties was 11s weekly, while in southern counties it was only 8s 5d, the general average being 9s 6d. Between the northern and southern counties the disparity of wages is more than a third; the difference between 15s and 6s a week in South Wilts, arranging the counties under two divisions, of the corn counties of the East and South Coast, and the mixed corn and grass of the Midland and Western Counties.

The higher wages of the north are due to the proximity of manufacturing and mining enterprise, which adds 37 per cent. to the wages of the agricultural labourer of the north as compared to those of the south. Since 1770 in all agricultural shires wages have increased 66 per cent., and in the south 14 per cent., while in some counties no increase is visible. The counties which stand high in the scale of poor rates, stand low in the scale of wages.

Free trade has done most for those who feared it most, the producers themselves. Some of the lamentable causes of the American differences is that the South are free traders and the North are not. In fact, free trade in politics is what toleration is in religion, but there are nationalities as well as individuals who will not be aided.

Real property is not to be confounded with landed interest. The annual value of all property in England is 514 millions sterling says Alison, and the value of manufacturing property is about 150 millions sterling.

Wages are at a very fair rate in Wraysbury and Horton villages, seldom less than 12s a week to the labourer, which forms a contrast to the times of King Edward III., when in 1352 haymaker's wages was 1d a day, and reapers of corn 2d a day in August, increasing till the end of the harvest. This depends much on the price of wheat and other grain, of which there is now annually consumed 12 million quarters of wheat and 36 millions of other grain. The climate is improved from cultivation and draining, and felling wood, &c. It is remarkable that in the 12th century excellent wine was grown in England; the climate since has become more moist and humid; some 32 inches of rain fall annually, while the thermometer has sunk to 5° zero, and it has rose to 90° in the shade.

The trade in corn has been unexceptionable under free trade, prior to which circumstance prices fluctuated from 36 to 73 per cent., and in 1822 corn fell to 42s a quarter. The fluctuations of grain in 1689 was 252 per cent.; in 1791 it was 280 per cent., and in 1814 it was 203 per cent. In 1815 again fluctuation was 196 per cent., and in 1828, the year of the introduction of the sliding scale, the fluctuation was 119 per cent., "labitur et labetur in omne volubilis ævum." The people consumed six millions of quarters of corn less than after the corn laws were abrogated.

The common incidences of landed property, the characteristics of a landed estate, are that it should fluctuate. In agriculture we are annually inventing and perfecting labour: machinery and steam engines add incalculable horse power to the business of farming.

The flail, the sickle and plough are departing from the hands of the labourer, who no longer sows his seed; only a portion of the hoeing and harvesting falls to his share, and yet his wages are higher and his services more in demand than ever.

The reaping machine was a novelty of questionable promise in 1851: it is now an established implement of agriculture. Traction engines moved by steam can with ease draw 60 and 70 tons on ordinary turnpike roads, at the rate of four miles an hour, while thousands of acres are ploughed by steam, and the happy result will no doubt be a continual increase of produce and fertility, the sources of national happiness and national greatness.

To these advantages is added guano, largely used now in Great Britain, as a new and superior fertiliser of soil; much is already imported, and much is on its way from Peru, where the *penguin* deposit is chiefly found: a source of national income to that part of South America, of such importance to its fiscal welfare, that on it *their debt* is secured, while England is the principal market for its sale and consumption. It warms the soil and prevents seed dying, it quickens moist land, for wet kills the seeds, hence the utility of draining.

Freedom is a fruitful mother, and industry is one of her first-born sons. With these appliances never did England stand so high and look with such confidence to the future, now that all legislative protection is withdrawn. Its prosperity depends on the unaided resources of science, skill, capital and perseverance.

Perhaps under this section of the village history it may not be irrelevant to advert cursorily to the poor laws, a distinctive feature in English polity.

By the 13th Car. II. 1661, certain townships and villages maintained their own poor, hence they became so many parishes. There are some 200 extra parochial localities, many of which are as large as parishes, and they are exempt from poor rate.

The 43rd Elizabeth, 1600, created poor rates on all visible and productive property, exempting only stock in trade; and this has shown us that a decent provision for the poor is the true test of civilisation, while the condition of the lower orders is the best mark of national discrimination and feeling. There were some statutes about poor laws in 1495 which consigned to the parish best known all who were unable to work. In 1531 even a license to beg was granted in certain districts, and in 1536 a voluntary provision was made for all poor dwelling three years in the parish, and again in 1563 and 1572 sums were levied for supporting the poor, the precursor of our poor laws. In 1830 the poor law provision reached £6,553,442.

Formerly the poor, having no property, paid in manual labour for their houses, and specific services were entered in the Court Roll. Some of these were ploughing the lord's lands, making his hay, and helping in the harvest, for which the lord found implements, but not sustenance.

The lord would not let his *villain* be emancipated or remove from the locality lest he should lose his services, nor could he marry without permission, or even sell goods, so stringent were the usages of *villenage*; and this, like all tyranny, caused rebellions, such as that of Wat Tyler in 1382. Attempts were made to repeal the feudal laws, and a Bill was introduced into the House of Lords for the manumission of serfs. It was read three times in one day, and yet it was ejected at last. Stowe relates that Sir Symon Burley went to Gravesend to claim a bondman, and demanded 300 lbs. of silver for his liberation, which being refused, he caused the man to be imprisoned in Rochester Castle.

Anciently Book-land was that for which rent was paid with suit and service. Folk-land was that which was not guaranteed by writing, but liable to be resumed at pleasure by the lord, and was held in villenage.

## MISCELLANEOUS MATTER, WITH THE CIVIL GOVERNMENT OF THE PARISH.

The Police-station is in a central part of the village, and was at the house of one Mrs. Sexton, widow of James Sexton, an old resident here, who still lives in the house of her father, Thomas Porter. This parish employs but one policeman at 16s a week, without a house. This appointment is the power which appoints policemen for the county in general.

Most parish officers consist of two Churchwardens, two Overseers, two Surveyors, and two Headboroughs, who are appointed by the Magistrates; the Surveyors are chosen yearly by the Ratepayers to inspect and assess. The Waywardens are the acting Magistrates, and should act as a Board. There are few subjects of social economy which it more imports to attempt to improve than the means of internal communication, especially as there is a change in the relative importance of highways by the adoption of railways—good roads improve agriculture.

The length of the parish from Lammas Gate, Staines, to the junction with the parish of Horton at the extremity near the mill, is about 3¼ miles; it is, however, circuitous. Its breadth from Lammas Gate to the Thames is about 3 miles in a straight line, and the circumference is about

17 miles, about 3½ miles of water and 3½ of land. In a straight line the length of the parish is about 2¼ miles.

The distance from Staines Bridge to Fleet Ditch, beyond Welly House, is nearly 5 miles, taking in the sinuosities of the Thames; and from Welly to Egham Hythe it is about 4 miles. From Staines Bridge to Datchet Bridge the distance is some 7 miles.

The ancient estimate of the parish was that it contained 1610 acres, but a new admeasurement makes it 1656 acres. It contained formerly, in 1831, 135 inhabited houses and 135 families, with no building in progress. Some 62 families were employed in agriculture, and 68 families were engaged in handicraft or the mills. In parts of this county straw and plait and lace-making occupy the peasants, and were exercised for trades as at Hanslape; bone or thread lace is wrought near Olney. Neither in Wraysbury nor Horton is any handicraft exercised, more living by land than by hand.

The males in Wraysbury were 331, and the females 351; total 682 in population, but the census of this year 1861 makes only 735, with 150 houses. The census of the kingdom in 1861 is 29,031,164, increase of 12 per cent., and the decrease in Ireland is 12 per cent. The difference in population over the last census in 1851, is 1,519,306.

Railways have much improved the locality and the condition of the people also, and it is a powerful solvent to diminish provincial rusticity, local and self-importance; class prejudice and all the elements of isolation melt away in its presence. The railway through our parish has been of great use to it; has enhanced the value of property, as is the case wherever such a project has been executed, despite the fears of those who repressed the enterprise. Railway reports comprise the essence of agricultural statistics; receipts dwindle if trade is bad, and it will be bad if the corn crop is deficient—hence they indicate the general prosperity of the nation with greater accuracy than the funds. Elevation and depression of funds denote the same results in both. As yet we have witnessed no scene of collision, or indeed disaster of any magnitude; a boy and a man wilfully threw themselves under the train in its passage, and were crushed to death, some 10 years ago; but deaths either accidental or by malice prepense are very rare. Occasionally those dreary land-marks in the vast desert of human misery, called Coroner's inquests, arise in Wraysbury.

Our line does us great credit, and is of infinite accommodation, not less so now the station is removed (page 79). We have also a telegraph apparatus on it. Perhaps the civilised world is much indebted to Mr. Reuter, a gentleman of German extraction, for the perfection of this invention, a process effected by an organised system of agencies, so that intelligence may be flashed round "this punctual spot," for the advantage and comfort of diplomacy and commerce.

Englishmen owe to Professor Wheatstone a debt of gratitude for his share in this discovery in 1838, and we live in reasonable expectation that as ocean telegraphy is becoming more necessary, it may eventually be effectuated, and so be realised in us the boast of Puck in the Midsummer Night's Dream to "Put a girdle round the earth in 40 minutes;" thus shall we accelerate intelligence, and make both time and space *pant*.

Some apprehensions are entertained about a future continuation of this mode of proceeding, by reason of the enormous consumption of coal, a mineral of the first utility to a commercial nation; and though it may have been used by the ancients and the Anglo-Saxons, it was not before 1259 that King Henry III. granted a charter to the freemen of Newcastle for liberty to dig coal. The produce of our mines, which cover a space of 2779 square miles, is 70 millions of tons annually; and to comfort the inhabitants of a cold region, the geologists think the mines may yet last 5000 years.

## FINES AND DEEDS.

A fine is *finalis concordia*, or last agreement between two parties to buy, sell, or exchange. That party who seeks against the other is termed *querent* or plaintiff, and is he who purchases; that which keeps the party out is termed *deforciant*, as keeping the owner out of his rightful possession. The *querent* stands first in the deed, and then the *deforciant*; a fine is levied on a supposed breach of covenant. These actions come under the term *ouster* in law, or *putting out*.

The use of recoveries did not openly take place until 12 Edward IV. 1472, from which period the records of them are preserved, and the information to be obtained from fines and recoveries is the name of the freeholder levying the fine—if married generally that of his wife, and occasionally that of his eldest son and heir. There are fines preserved as early as the days of King John, but with more certainty from Richard I. to our own times. Pursuant to a statute 3 and 4 William IV. 1834, was passed an act for the abolition of fines and recoveries, and for the substitution of a simpler mode of assurance, and an officer under the Registrar has been appointed.

Mich. 7 Richard I. 1195. Walter de Ramgrove *v.* Salomon Piscator, lands in Datchet.

Mich. 7 Richard I. 1197. Cecelia de ———— *v.* Ostibus de la Gaue, lands and tents in Langley.

Trin. 15 Henry III. 1230. Silvester de Anagn, parson of Wraysbury Parish *v.* Alexander de Wyredesbir and wife in Wraysbury, p. 106.

Trin. 15 Henry III. Roll. 93. An acre of land. One Dionysius, of Wraysbury, and Cecilia his wife, and Matilda sister to Cecilia, sold to Silvester lands, &c. containing 1 messuage, 5 acres, with appurtenants. There is a recital of 2 acres sold with a messuage adjacent, all under tillage, called Waytebrech; some conditions are annexed after the deaths of Cecilia and Matilda.

44 Henry III. 1259, Roll 46. Between Thomas, son of Oder de Ponte and Geoffrey de Gervan, deforciant, of 30 acres of land and 6*s* 8*d* rent, all held in fee of Ric. de Montfitchet. Rents in Wraysbury.

Easter, 2 Edward I. 1273. Christopher de Pover *v.* Henry de Weincham, messuage, lands, rents, island of fishery in the Thames, in Wyrardisbury, Langley, Datchet, and Staines.

Mich. 4. Edward I. 1275. ———— and William de Huntercumbe and wife, lands in Wraysbury and Langley.

Hil. 12 Edward I. 1283. John le Boller of London *v.* Elias de Coventric and wife, messuage and lands in Wyrhardesbyr'.

Trin. 18 Edward I. 1289. John de Remenham and wife *v.* Walter Cappe and wife, lands and mill in Wraysbury, p. 56.

East. 24 Edward I. 1295. John de la More *v.* Ralph de Wyrardesbyr and wife, messuage and lands in Wraysbury.

Trin. 20 Edward I. 1291. John de Remenham and wife *v.* John de la Halle, — Wexford and wife, lands and rents in Horton.

Hil. 24 Edward I. 1295. Geffrey de Mariscis and Giles de la Stonystrete of Stoke, and wife, messuage and lands in Datchet.

Mich. 25 Edward I. 1296. John de Walden and wife *v.* Aunger de Horton and wife, lands in Langley and Montfitchet, p. 9.

Mich. 29 Edward I. 1300. Hugh le Despenser *v.* John de Merton and wife, rents in Datchet. N.B.—There are two deeds of similar dates and names, and Thomas de Brotherton, Earl of Norfolk, had a grant of the manor of Datchet as part of the possessions of Hugh le Despenser, 1 Edward III. 1327, p. 29.

Mich. 29 Edward I. 1301. Mabilia de Membyry and the Countess of Champaye *v.* Christiana de Mariscis, lands in Datchet. I find John de Champesey was Lord of the Manor of Iver in 1316, the name may be Champeney.

Hil. 3 Edward II. 1309. John de Remenham and wife *v.* Hugh de Remenham, lands in Horton.

Trin. 6 Edward II. 1312. William de Clifford, Chaplain, *v.* Ralph le Ken of Langley, and wife, messuage, lands, rents in Langley.

Trin. 12 Edward II. 1318. John de Langley, Chaplain, *v.* Ralph le Ken and wife, messuage and lands in Langley.

Trin. 19 Edward II. 1325. Walter de la Grave of Langley *v.* William atte Stoke and wife, messuage, land, mill, rents in Wraysbury and Horton.

Mich. 4 Edward III. 1330. Alicia la Gardinière of Langley *v.* John Wardock, of Evre (Iver), and wife, messuage and lands in Langley and Wraysbury.

Mich. 17 Edward III. 1343. Walter Rabbe *v.* John de Remenham, jun. messuage, rents, mill in Wraysbury and Horton.

A charity endowed at Hillingdon was styled Rabbe's Charity, lands and a chaplain to pray for the soul of this Walter Rabbe. Escheat 46 Edward III. 1372.

Mich. 42 Edward III. 1368. John Wyott of Wyrardsbury *v.* William Langford and wife, messuage and lands in Horton.

Mich. 45 Edward III. 1372. Richard Pope and wife *v.* Thomas Wyott and wife, lands in Langley.

Mich. 45 Edward III. 1372. William Forde, Clerk, *v.* Thomas Wyott and wife, messuage and lands in Langley and Horton.

A Thomas Wyott was Rector of Eton 1421.

Alice, daughter of Richard Kniffe, was joint-heir of John Wyott, she married Richard Bulstrode. *See* pedigree of Bulstrode.

Mich. 8 Henry V. 1420. Thomas Melreth of Horton *v.* Richard Frowyn of Colbrok, and wife, messuage, lands, and rents in Wraysbury and Langley.

N.B.—Here occurs a gap in the records of fines, and the references made to Wraysbury, nearly 20, relative to leases, &c. temp. Henry VIII. Edward VI. and Mary, called abstracts of leases, are lost or misplaced.

Mich. 8 Henry VIII. 1518. Robert Honeywood, Esq. *v.* Richard Fitzwater and others, rents in Langley Marsh, Wexham, Upton, Datchet, Fulmer, &c.

Trin. 8 Henry VIII. 1521. George Windsor, Esq. *v.* Robert Palmer and others, tents in Langley and Wraysbury.

Trin. 8 Henry VIII. 1539. John Polard, Gent. *v.* Sir Walter Stonor, Kt. manor of Remingham and Cokke, with tents in Wraysbury, Langley Marsh, Horton, Stoke, and Datchet.

Trin. 8 Henry VIII. 1539. Ralph Hamersley, Esq. *v.* Thomas Archer, Esq. tents in Colbrok, Wraysbury, Thorney Parish, and Langley Marsh.

Trin. 8 Henry VIII. 1539. Richard Fitzwater *v.* Thomas Archer, Esq. meadow in Wraysbury.

Trin. 8 Henry VIII. 1539. Thomas Aldridge, property in Eton. A branch of this family settled in Wraysbury, originally of Burnham, one Dr. Robert Aldrich, whose history is recorded in Fuller's Worthies of Bucks, corresponded with Erasmus, and Dr. Aldrich was Provost of Eton and

Bishop of Carlisle 1537, and died March 1556, and was succeeded by Sir Thomas Smyth as Provost in 1547. He was a Canon of Windsor and had been Proctor in Cambridge 1525, and was of King's College.

Trin. 8 Henry VIII. 1539. William Sparry and others v. Reginald Digby, Esq. the manor of Horton and the advowson in Colnbrooke, Langley Marsh, Iver, Wyrardsbury, &c.

Trin. 1537. Henry Caldwell and William Sadler, and Margaret, wife, v. Henry Walger and Ursula his wife, property in Old Windsor.

Mich. 1 Edward VI. 1547. John Kederminster and Reginald Cripps, and Elizabeth, wife, lands in Langley.

Hil. 6 and 7 Edward VI. 1553. George Freville, Esq. and others v. John Kyderminster, Gent. lands in Wexham, Stoke Poges, Fulner, Langley, Upton, Ditton, Wraysbury, p. 88.

Mich. 1 Mary, 1553. Thomas Windsor, Esq. v. George Bulstrode, Esq. manor of Maperlings in Iver, with free passage in Colnbrook stream, with messuage and lands in Colnbrook and Langley.

Hil. 3 and 4 Philip and Mary 1556, John Calthorpe, Esq. and Frances, Countess of Hunts, manor of Stoke Poges, and advowson of the Church.

1560, 2 Elizabeth. Richard Mascall v. Richard Cripps, John Living and Ann his wife, daughter of Richard and Elizabeth Mascall, a messuage, 3 acres of land in Wexton, Fulner, and Wraysbury.

1560, 2 Elizabeth. George Edwards v. Henry Balnett, property in Langley, Horton, and Wraysbury.

1560, 2 Elizabeth. Thomas Wyche and Agnes his wife, property in Langley, Horton, and Wraysbury.

1560, 2 Elizabeth. John Jeffrey v. Anthony Heydon, tents in Wraysbury.

Hil. 5 Elizabeth, 1562. Robert Bedyll or Bevill v. Jacomina Goodyer, lands in Langley and Iver.

Hil. 8 Elizabeth, 1565. Reginald Marshall v. Richard Marshall, property in Wexham, Wraysbury, and Datchet.

Mich. 1572. George Edwards and Andrew Burton, tents in Wraysbury.

Hil. 29 Elizabeth, 1586. John Hill, Gent. and others v. George Woodward, Gent. property in Langley and Montfitchet.

Hil. 35 Elizabeth, 1591. The manor of Cornwallis in Iver, sold by James Heblethwayte.

1593. Roger Gyll v. William Tuching, tent in Buckingham.

1594. William Marsham and John Pinnar, Esq. v. William Peters, 4 messuages, 4 gardens, 100 acres land, 400 acres land, and 4 pasture, 100 waste, 12d rent in Horton, Wraysbury, Iver, and Stoke Poges.

1594. William Peters and Sir Michael Blunt, tent in Horton.

1596. Samuel Enderbie v. John Bowser, Gent. in Langley.

1601. Thomas Nelson, Gent. v. Thomas Hale, recapitulation of lands in Datchet.

1602. William Baker v. Ambrose Aldridge, 7 acres of pasture, &c. in Wraysbury. William Walshe, Esq. vouchee.

1603. Michael Goodyear v. Henry Bulstrode, Esq. Langley Marsh.

1604. Thomas Hanbury, Esq. v. Richard Hanbury, tent in Langley Marsh.

1607. Robert Style v. William Gregge, Gent. and John Fabian, Gent. (the lawyer), the manor of Wexham, Fulmer, Stoke Poges.

1608. George Salter buys the manor of Denham of Sir Henry Maynard, Kt. and William Bowyer, Esq.

1612. Robert Style v. Mary Verney, widow, tent in Langley Marsh.

1609. Robert Style *v.* John Kederminster, Esq. Langley, &c.
1612. Henry Gould of Iver *v.* Thomas Russel of Iver, property there.
1612. Robert Bankworth *v.* Edmund Salter, property in Langley Marsh.
1612. Edward Woodward *v.* Edmund Arthur, Gent. manor of Wexham.
1616. Sir John Kederminster *v.* Robert Style, property in Wexham.
1617. Bartholomew Beale, Gent. and William Robson, Gent. *v.* Charles Docket, Gent. and William Denny, Esq. manor of Weferling and Cornwallis, with lands and tents in Iver, Langley, Wraysbury, Colnbrook, Horton, &c. Vouchee, Edmund Walter, Esq.
1618. Felix Wilson, Esq. *v.* Henry Bulstrode, Esq. manor of Horton and advowson, Langley, Datchet, Wraysbury, Upton, Iver. Sir Robert Digby, vouchee.
1620. Margaret Lovelace, widow, *v.* John Croke, Esq. manor of Chilton, Bucks.
1620. Felix Wilson, Gent. *v.* Ambrose Aldridge, Place Farm, Wraysbury.
1620. Thomas Pytt *v.* Henry Bulstrode, Langley Marsh.
1622. Felix Wilson, Gent. and Richard Bedd, Gent. *v.* Daniel Salter, Gent., property in Iver and Langley.
1624. Sir John Kederminster and Messrs, Palmer (Roger and Thomas), sell to Geoffrey Tupper, Gent. and Walter Morgan, Gent. sells about this neighbourhood diverse property with the advowson of Dorney Church. The vouchees are four of the Garrard family and Sir Francis Cottington, Bart. join to sell. In 1631 he was raised to the title of Lord Cottington, of Hanworth, Middlesex, died 1653.
1624. Felix Wilson, Gent. and Joseph Lane, Gent. (the lawyers) *v.* Henry Bulstrode, Esq., one messuage, one garden, 30 of acres land, &c. in Horton and Langley Marsh. George Cowardclow, vouchee.
1624. The same parties, one messuage, one garden, five acres of pasture, one acre of wood, with common of pasture in Horton, Wraysbury, Langley, &c. George Edwards, vouchee.
1625. Francis Bowry *v.* Thomas Bulstrode, Esq. property in Wraysbury.
1625. William Sandford, Esq. *v.* Edward Sandford, Esq. property in Wraysbury.
1627. George Style *v.* Lazarus Currington, property in Langley Marsh.
1629. Sir Edmund Verney *v.* James Palmer, Esq. in Langley Marsh.
1630. Felix Wilson, Gent. *v.* Richard Hurley, Gent. and George Warren, Gent. property in Iver.
1633. Laurence Washington, Esq. and Laurence Isaac *v.* Richard Edwards and Richard Dorrington, the manor of Wersbury or Werbbury. This may not be Wraysbury.
1636. Thomas Harris and William Burle *v.* Francis Ridley, Gent. two messuages, two *agnats*, 70 acres land, 18 acres land, with 20 acres pasture in Langley and Colnbrook.
1636. Edmund Bulstrode, Esq. and Richard Edwards *v.* Edward Woodward, 18 messuages, one garden, *agnat*, 200 acres land, 40 pasture, 60 ditto in Horton, Colnbrook, Wresbury. Vouchee, Thomas Bulstrode, Esq.
1638. Edward Seares and John Hall, in Datchet.
1647. George Brome, Gent. and Robert Hall, Gent. *v.* William Sandford, Esq. and Robert Brome, Gent. three messuages, two mills, six gardens, 20 acres arable, and sundry acres of pasture and waste in Wraysbury. Edmund Bulstrode, Esq. vouchee.
1651. Richard Hale, Gent. *v.* Thomas Smyth (of Horham Hall, Essex), manor of Remenham and Cow, Wraysbury.
1653. Nicholas Pinchon, Gent. *v.* Andrew Kinge, Esq. Wraysbury.

1653. John Sibley *v.* Andrew Kinge, Esq. Wraysbury.

1657. Richard West *v.* Edward Bulstrode, Esq. Wraysbury. William West appears in a deed with Charles Feldoe, Harris Prettie, in Langley Marsh.

1658. John Poundey, Gent. *v.* John Sandford, Gent. in Langley.

1662. John Pinchon, Gent. *v.* Edward Bulstrode, Esq. Wraysbury.

1667. John West and William Fry Hampton, Wraysbury.

1669. Mary Goodyear and John Harcourt, Esq. Langley Marsh.

1671. Richard Hale, Gent., senior, *v.* George Penyman, Wraysbury.

1677. Robert Bampton *v.* John Slocombe, five messuages, 10 gardens, five acres arable, 18 meadow, eight pasture, in Horton and Wraysbury. Vouchee, Charles Peters, Gent.

1686. John Topham, Esq. *v.* John Pinchon, senior and others, in Wraysbury.

1686. Richard Fryar *v.* John Pinchon, Gent. in Wraysbury.

1689. Henry Guy *v.* Sir — Leigh, Kt. four messuages, three gardens, 50 acres arable, 20 acres meadow, 30 acres pasture, in Horton, Iver, and Wraysbury.

1693. Ambrose Adkins *v.* Elisha Gill, Wraysbury.

1694. Edward Belitha, Frances Fryar, widow, and — Peake, in Wraysbury.

1694. Thomas Robbins, junior *v.* Edward Belitha, Langley Marsh.

1696. John Hassel, Esq., Frances Fryer, widow, — Peake, and Edward Belitha, in Wraysbury.

1696. Josias Darby *v.* John Hassel, Gent. two messuages, four gardens, 26 acres arable, seven acres meadow, 12 acres pasture, in Wraysbury and Horton. William Peake, vouchee, with Susan his wife, and Frances Fryer, widow.

1697. Thomas Rowe, Gent. *v.* Joseph Yate, Gent. the manor of Langley Marsh. Henry Seymour, Esq. vouchee.

1699. George Harrison, Esq. *v.* Arthur Keck, the manor of Stoke Poges, and in a similar recovery of the same date, John Levy *v.* John Goodwin, the manor of Cippenham.

1701. William Turton *v.* Henry Stevens, Esq. five messuages, 10 gardens, 180 arable, 25 meadow, 30 pasture, one wood, in Horton and Wraysbury.

1704. Ambrose Adkins and John Slocombe, Wraysbury.

1722. Willam Gill and Robert Collins, and Elizabeth his wife, property in Olney, Bucks, £200.

1724. George Northey, Gent. and Frances Style, wife of James Style, Wraysbury.

1725. Thomas Ringer, Esq. and Mary Harcourt, widow, Thomas Powell, Gent., and Roger Phillips, Esq., a moiety of some Wraysbury property.

1726. Henry Browne, Gent. *v.* George North, Gent., 12 acres meadow, &c. in Wraysbury. Vouchees, Thomas Style, and Bridget his wife, James Style.

1728. Joseph Wanynough, Gent. *v.* Giles Horseman, Gent., two messuages, three gardens, 15 acres meadow, seven pasture, in Wraysbury and Horton. Vouchee, Francis Bowry.

1733. John Allett *v.* Edmund Bowry, Gent. and wife, Wraysbury.

1735. Edward Leigh and Hatton Tash, Esq., manor of Delaford, Iver.

1735. Samuel Holderness *v.* Edward Borrett, Gent., four gardens, 40 acres land, seven meadow, three pasture, and common of pasture in Horton and Wraysbury. Vouchee, Stephen West.

1745. William Camden, Gent. *v.* Charles Saltmarsh, one messuage, one toft, two gardens, 16 acres land, 16 meadow, 10 pasture, in Horton and Wraysbury. Vouchee, Mary Binfield, widow.

1759. Francis Ayscough, D.D. *v.* Robert Palmer, Gent. manor of Delaford, Iver. Vouchee, George Tash, Esq.

1760. William Folkes, Esq. *v.* Maurice Robinson, manor of Ditton, with appurtenants in Langley, Stoke, and Datchet. Vouchee, George Earl of Cardigan, and Mary his wife, who call Hon. John Montagu.

1767. Francis Hargrave, Gent. *v.* Christopher Hargrave, Gent. two messuages, two gardens, 200 acres land, 100 meadow, 20 pasture, and common in pasture, Wraysbury. Vouchee, Martin Sands, Esq., Mary his wife, daughter of William Trumball, Esq.

1776. Edward Bodle, Gent. *v.* Thomas Walley, — Partington, Esq., manor of Parlant, and lands in Langley, Iver, and Wraysbury, to which Frederick Lord Boston is vouchee.

1778. John Elderton, Gent. *v.* John Vernon, Gent. the manor of Remingham and Cow, and Cornwallis, 20 messuages, 15 gardens, 900 acres land, 350 meadow, 350 pasture, five acres ozier, and common of pasture, with two fisheries with appurtenants, in Wraysbury, Langley, Datchet, Old Windsor, Iver, &c. Vouchee, Christopher Tower, Esq.

1794. Cornthwaite Ommaney, Esq. *v.* William Johnson, the manor of Wraysbury, &c. 10 messuages, four dove-cots, 20 gardens, 300 acres land, 100 meadow, 100 pasture, 50 wood, 200 furze and heath, common of pasture, free fishery, liberty of frankpledge, courts leet and baron, view of frankpledge in Wraysbury and Horton. Vouchee, John Simon Harcourt, Esq.

1803. Henry Hoyle Oddie *v.* John Forster, one messuage, two gardens, 12 acres land, eight acres meadow, eight pasture, in Wraysbury and Horton. Vouchee, Charles William Montagu, Earl of Dalkeith.

1809. John Throsby *v.* Ralph Dunn, manor of Sudeley, in Datchet, Wraysbury, &c. Vouchees, Edward Earl of Harwood and Edward Lascelles.

1812. Percival White, Gent. *v.* Ralph Dun, Gent. four messuages, two tofts, one water corn mill, two dove-cots, six gardens, 100 acres land, 100 meadow, 100 pasture, 20 wood, 20 furze, free fishing, &c. in Langley, Iver, Wraysbury. Vouchee, John Harcourt Powell, Esq.

1814. Charles William, Duke of Buccleugh, is vouchee to the sale of the manor of Datchet.

1819. Francis White *v.* Joseph Morris, 20 acres land, 20 meadow, 20 pasture, and common of pasture in Wraysbury. Vouchees, Thomas Palmer, and John Palmer, and Mary his wife.

1825. Christopher Tower, Esq. is vouchee in the sale of the manor of Remenham, and Cow and Cornwallis, 50 messuages, 50 gardens, 1000 acres land, 500 acres meadow, 200 pasture, 50 acres oziers, 30 acres land with water, two separate fisheries in Iver, Thorney, and Langley Marsh.

1825. The manor of Taplow was sold. Vouchee, John Hamilton Fitzmaurice, Viscount Kirkwall.

1828. John Lake, Gent. *v.* John Wilkinson, 12 acres meadow and common of pasture in Wraysbury. Vouchee, George Simon Harcourt, Esq.

1829. John Lake *v.* John Winter, eight acres land, eight pasture, eight meadow, in Wraysbury. Vouchee, John Harcourt Powell, Esq.

There is great difficulty in ascertaining the parties associated in fines and recoveries from 1759, as neither the christian names nor the places are given in the abstracts or calendars, which omissions were allowed merely to save the clerks the trouble of inserting them, and which tends to nullify the intention of preserving the records. In periods prior to 1759, 33 George II. the christian names, and places and abstracts of the fines were transcribed, which is a great convenience to the searcher, for this *precis* stands in lieu of the identical deeds, if no *more* is required. The fines and recoveries cease in 1833.

REFERENCE TO THE MAP OF THE PARISH OF WRAYSBURY, IN THE COUNTY OF BUCKS,
Surveyed by Wm. Thos. Buckland, 1845.

|  | Description. | Quantity. | | | Cultivation. | Owner. | Occupier. |
|---|---|---|---|---|---|---|---|
|  |  | A. | R. | P. |  |  |  |
| 1 | Osier grounds | 2 | 0 | 0 | Osiers |  | Wm. Osman |
| 2 |  | 0 | 0 | 28 | Do. |  | Do. |
| 3 | Queen Mead | 11 | 1 | 15 | Arable and meadow | Bridge Trustees | Francis Buckland |
| 4 | Osier ground | 0 | 2 | 16 | Osiers | Do. | Wm. Wears |
| 5 | Queen Mead | 0 | 0 | 32 | Meadow | Miss Mackason | Francis Buckland |
| 6 | Do. | 5 | 2 | 19 | Arable and meadow | Church Trust | Do. |
| 6a | Old road | 0 | 1 | 0 | *Gravel pit* | *Parish* | Parish |
| 7 | Gravel pit | 0 | 2 | 0 | Meadow | B. H. Gyll, Esq. | Mary Ann Sills |
| 8 | Queen Mead | 17 | 3 | 28 | Arable and meadow | Do. | Do. |
| 9 | Osier ground | 0 | 3 | 6 | Osiers | Do. | Wm. Osman |
| 10 | Meadow | 0 | 3 | 12 | Meadow | Miss Mackason | Thos. Paris |
| 11 | Osier ground | 0 | 3 | 36 | Osiers | Do. | Joseph Osman |
| 12 | Do. | 1 | 2 | 21 | Do. | G. S. Harcourt, Esq. | — Grantham |
| 13 | Do. | 0 | 1 | 18 | Do. | Do. | Do. |
| 14 | Tuisey Mead | 6 | 3 | 18 | Meadow | Do. | Job Winckworth |
| 15 | Osier ground | 0 | 1 | 39 | Osiers | — Grantham | — Grantham |
| 16 | House, orchard and Garden | 1 | 0 | 29 | House, &c. | Do. | Do. |
| 17 | Lock-house and eyott | 0 | 1 | 23 | Lock-house, &c. | Thames Commissioners. | Thames Commissioners |
| 18 | Pasture | 2 | 1 | 0 | Pasture | Do. | Thomas Roake |
| 19 | Osier bed | 0 | 0 | 14 | Osiers | Do. | Do. |
| 20 | Do. | 4 | 0 | 34 | Do. | Mrs. Morris | Wm. Osman |
| 21 | Driftway | 0 | 2 | 29 | Pasture | Do. | Thomas Roake |
| 22 | Ferry-house garden | 1 | 0 | 32 | House and garden | Do. | Do. |
| 23 | Orchard | 0 | 1 | 20 | Orchard | — Thompson | Wm. Smart |
| 24 | Cottage & garden | 0 | 0 | 16 | Lot and garden | Do. | Do. |
| 25 | Drift (part off) | 0 | 0 | 35 | Pasture | Do. | Do. |
| 26 | Queen Mead | 33 | 1 | 36 | Arable | Messrs. Ashby | Messrs. Ashby |
| 27 | Further Queen Mead | 17 | 3 | 22 | Meadow | T. P. Williams | Henry Stevens |
| 28 | First ditto | 16 | 3 | 31 | Do. | Do. | Do. |
| 29 | Queen Mead | 14 | 0 | 11 | Do. | Rev. C. Champnes | Wm. Taylor |
| 30 | Great Hamlet Close | 4 | 1 | 16 | Arable | B. H. Gyll, Esq. | Mary Ann Sills |
| 31 | Drift to mill | 0 | 0 | 37 | Pasture | Messrs. Ashby | Messrs. Ibotson |
| 32 | Eyott | 0 | 2 | 33 | Osiers | Do. | Do. |
| 33 | Do. | 1 | 1 | 4 | Do. | Do. | Do. |
| 34 | Do. | 0 | 1 | 38 | Do. | Do. | Do. |
| 35 | Cottages and gardens | 0 | 2 | 3 | Cottages and gardens | Mrs. Tubb | Henry Stevens and others |
| 36 | Eyott | 0 | 1 | 25 | Osiers | Messrs. Ashby | Messrs. Ibotson |
| 37 |  | 0 | 2 | 28 | Do. | Do. | Do. |
| 38 | Paper-mills and premises | 0 | 1 | 2 | Mill, &c. | Do. | Do. |
| 39 | Eyott & garden | 0 | 1 | 22 | Osiers and garden | Do. | Do. |
| 40 | Driftway | 0 | 3 | 15 | Pasture | Do. | Do. |
| 41 | The nine acres | 8 | 3 | 0 | Arable | B. H. Gyll, Esq. | Mary Ann Sills |
| 42 | The six acres | 6 | 0 | 8 | Do. | Do. | Do. |
| 43 | The five acres | 4 | 2 | 15 | Do. | Do. | Do. |
| 44 | Cherry orchard | 2 | 0 | 27 | Meadow | Do. | Do. |

## HISTORY OF WRAYSBURY.

| | Description. | Quantity. A. R. P. | Cultivation. | Owner. | Occupier. |
|---|---|---|---|---|---|
| 45 | Cottage, barn, and premises | 0 1 28 | Cottage and barn | B. H. Gyll, Esq. | Mary Ann Sills |
| 46 | Pasture | 1 1 39 | Pasture | Do. | Do. |
| 46a | Old road ditto | 0 3 5 | Do. | Do. | Do. |
| 47 | Do. | 2 0 27 | Do. | G. S. Harcourt | James Pullin |
| 48 | Cottages & gardens | 0 1 30 | Cottage and gardens | Do. | Martin and Penton |
| 49 | The orchard | 1 3 10 | Orchard | G. S. Harcourt, Esq. | James Pullin |
| 50 | Homstead | 2 0 36 | Homestead | Do. | Do. |
| 51 | The six and eight acres | 13 2 29 | Arable | Do. | Do. |
| 52 | Eyott | 3 2 11 | Osiers | Do. | George Grantham |
| 53 | Fisher's Eyott | 5 0 16 | Do. | Do. | Do. |
| 54 | Scoules' Eyott | 2 2 19 | Wood | Do. | G. S. Harcourt, Esq. |
| 55 | Scoules & 12 acres | 16 2 23 | Arable | Do. | James Pullin |
| 56 | 12 acres | 10 3 9 | Do. | Do. | Do. |
| 57 | The four acres | 3 3 27 | Do. | Do. | Do. |
| 58 | Cottages & gardens | 0 3 7 | Cottages and gardens | Charles Bell | C. Bell and W. Wise |
| 59 | Pettidge | 3 1 6 | Meadow | B. H. Gyll, Esq. | Mary Ann Sills |
| 60 | The 7 & 11 acres | 13 1 23 | Arable | Do. | |
| 61 | Pasture | 0 1 15 | Pasture | | |
| | Old road | 0 0 10 | | Parish gravel-pit | Parish |
| 62 | Orchard | 0 2 8 | Orchard | G. S. Harcourt, Esq. | James Collins |
| 63 | Cottages & gardens | 0 1 16 | Cottages and gardens | Do. | Collins and Garlick |
| 64 | Homestead | 0 2 13 | Homestead | B. H. Gyll, Esq. | Mary Ann Sills |
| 65 | Pasture | 0 2 10 | Pasture | Do. | Do. |
| 66 | Orchard | 0 2 36 | Orchard | Do. | Do. |
| 67 | Wilkinson's Close | 3 0 6 | Arable | Do. | Do. |
| 68 | Part of Cambers | 10 0 37 | Do. | G. S. Harcourt, Esq. | James Pullin |
| 68a | Do. | 7 3 5 | Do. | Do. | Do. |
| 69 | Osiers | 1 0 22 | Osiers | Do. | Do. |
| 70 | Cun Mead | 9 3 34 | Meadow | Do. | Do. |
| 71 | Meadow | 4 3 23 | Do. | Do. | Do. |
| 72 | Moorfield | 15 3 29 | Do. | Do. | Do. |
| 72a | Plantation | 0 0 9 | Plantation | Do. | Do. |
| 73 | Watt's Hill | 6 3 3 | Arable | Do. | Do. |
| 74 | College garden, shed, part of meadow. | 0 1 12 | Cottage, garden and meadow | Do. | Do. |
| 75 | Meadow next Moor Meadow | 1 3 10 | Meadow | Do. | Do. |
| 75a | Do. | 0 1 12 | Do. | Do. | Do. |
| 76 | Little Hamlet Close | 1 3 6 | Do. | Do. | Do. |
| 77 | The 18 acres | 18 1 3 | Do. | Do. | Do. |
| 78 | First Common | 11 2 5 | Do. | Do. | Do. |
| 79 | Middle do. | 11 0 6 | Do. | Do. | Do. |
| 80 | Further do. | 12 1 4 | Do. | Do. | Do. |
| 81 | Black Ground | 32 0 19 | Arable and meadow | Mr. Gyll | Wm. Thos. Buckland |
| 82 | The Common | 26 3 1 | Meadow | Mr. Harcourt | — Cornish |
| 83 | Lower Rye side | 9 2 7 | Arable | Do. | James Pullin |
| 84 | Further do. | 14 3 15 | Do. | Do. | Do. |
| 85 | High Worplefield | 8 2 16 | Do. | Do. | Do. |
| 86 | Lower Warbridge | 14 0 0 | Do. | Do. | Samuel Jordan |
| 86a | Driftway | 0 1 25 | Driftway | Do. | James Pullin |
| 87 | Craw Bush | 7 3 38 | Arable | Mr. Harcourt | James Pullin |
| 88 | Upper Warbridge | 7 0 33 | Do. | Do. | Samuel Jordan |
| 89 | The 16 acres | 13 2 10 | Do. | Do. | Robert Cornish |
| 90 | Frontage | 0 1 27 | Do. | Do. | Do. |
| 91 | Homestead | 1 0 15 | Homestead | Do. | Do. |
| 91a | Portion of old road | 0 1 0 | Old road | Do. | Do. |

| | Description. | Quantity. | | | Cultivation. | Owner. | Occupier. |
|---|---|---|---|---|---|---|---|
| | | A. | R. | P. | | | |
| 92 | Cottage & garden | 0 | 1 | 10 | Cottage and garden | Mrs. Painter | Mrs. Painter |
| 93 | Orchard | 0 | 2 | 17 | Orchard | Do. | Do. |
| | Old road | 0 | 0 | 12 | | | |
| 94 | Garden | 0 | 1 | 15 | Garden | G. S. Harcourt, Esq. | John Tailor |
| 95 | Cottages & gardens | 0 | 0 | 22 | Cottages and gardens | Do. | Thos. Paine |
| 96 | Do. | 0 | 0 | 31 | Do. | Do. | Manders and others |
| 97 | Part of Upper Warbridge | 0 | 0 | 24 | Plantation | Do. | G. S. Harcourt, Esq. |
| 98 | Do. | 0 | 2 | 30 | Gardens | Do. | Manders and others |
| 99 | Plantation | 0 | 2 | 36 | Plantation | Do. | G. S. Harcourt, Esq. |
| 100 | Pasture | 0 | 2 | 13 | Do. | Do. | Samuel Jordan |
| | Old road | 0 | 2 | 0 | Do. | Do. | G. S. Harcourt, Esq. |
| 101 | Do. | 0 | 0 | 11 | Do. | Do. | Do. |
| 102 | Do. | 0 | 2 | 8 | Do. | Do. | Legrande |
| 103 | Plantation | 0 | 0 | 22 | Do. | Do. | G. S. Harcourt, Esq. |
| 103a | Do. | 0 | 0 | 10 | Do. | Do. | Do. |
| 104 | Orchard | 1 | 0 | 2 | Orchard | Do. | Legrande |
| 105 | House & premises | 0 | 2 | 9 | House, &c. | Do. | Do. |
| 106 | Meadow | 1 | 3 | 23 | Meadow | Do. | Do. |
| | Old road | 0 | 3 | 22 | | Do. | |
| 107 | Cottages & gardens | 0 | 2 | 27 | Cottages and gardens | Do. | Jackson and others |
| 108 | Cock Allens | 14 | 0 | 26 | Arable | Do. | Samuel Jordan |
| 109 | Plantation | 0 | 0 | 22 | Plantation | Do. | G. S. Harcourt, Esq. |
| 110 | Scoles | 3 | 1 | 31 | Mead | Do. | Samuel Jordan |
| | Part of old road | 0 | 2 | 0 | Old road | Do. | |
| 111 | Part of park | 16 | 3 | 25 | Do. | Do. | |
| 111a | Do. | 12 | 0 | 6 | Do. | Do. | |
| 112 | Ankerwycke Eyott | 2 | 3 | 1 | Wood | Do. | Lord Ch. Beauclerk |
| 113 | Wood, part of Ankerwycke Mead | 2 | 1 | 1 | Do. | Do. | Do. |
| 114 | Meadow | 3 | 1 | 35 | Meadow | Do. | Do. |
| 115 | Pleasure grounds | 4 | 1 | 12 | Pleasure ground | Do. | Do. |
| 115a | Garden | 0 | 1 | 0 | Garden | Do. | Samuel Jordan |
| 116 | Part of Ankerwycke Mead | 2 | 3 | 25 | Meadow | Do. | Do. |
| 116a | Do. | 5 | 3 | 24 | Do. | Do. | Do. |
| 117 | Littleday Mead | 2 | 2 | 7 | Do. | Do. | Lord Ch. Beauclerk |
| 118 | The Canal | 1 | 2 | 9 | Water | Do. | Do. |
| 119 | The Grove | 3 | 2 | 2 | Meadow | Do. | Do. |
| 120 | Mansion & gardens | 7 | 1 | 23 | Mansion and grounds | Do. | Do. |
| 121 | Kitchen garden | 1 | 0 | 0 | Garden | Do. | Do. |
| 122 | House and orchard | 4 | 0 | 6 | Orchard | Mr. Harcourt | Samuel Jordan |
| 123 | Homestead | 1 | 1 | 37 | Homestead | Do. | Do. |
| 124 | The Dairy and premises | 0 | 2 | 14 | Dairy, &c. | Do. | Do. |
| 125 | Dairy orchard | 10 | 0 | 26 | Meadow | G. S. Harcourt, Esq. | Do. |
| 126 | Vicarage Close | 3 | 0 | 8 | Arable | Rev. C. Champnes | Wm. Taylor |
| 127 | House & premises | 0 | 1 | 30 | Homestead | Do. | Do. |
| | Old road | 0 | 0 | 12 | | | |
| 128 | Pasture | 0 | 2 | 17 | Pasture | Do. | Do. |
| 129 | Orchard | 0 | 1 | 23 | Orchard | G. S. Harcourt | Robert Cornish |
| 130 | Willow ground | 0 | 0 | 25 | Willows | Do. | Samuel Jordan |
| 131 | Cottages & gardens | 0 | 2 | 10 | Cottages and gardens | G. S. Harcourt | W. Randall & others |
| 132 | Woodhall | 8 | 0 | 6 | Arable | Do. | Samuel Jordan |
| 133 | Part Garsons' Mead and Plantation | 12 | 1 | 36 | Grass | Do. | Do. |
| 133a | Do. | 1 | 1 | 6 | Do. | Do. | Do. |
| 134a | Part Upper Warrenfield | 2 | 2 | 15 | Do. | Do. | Do. |
| 134 | Lower Warrenfield | 31 | 0 | 15 | Do. | Do. | Do. |

|  | Description. | Quantity. | | | Cultivation. | Owner. | Occupier. |
|---|---|---|---|---|---|---|---|
|  |  | A. | R. | P. |  |  |  |
| 135 | Plantation | 0 | 1 | 8 | Wood | G. S. Harcourt | G. S. Harcourt, Esq. |
| 136 | Osier ground | 0 | 1 | 5 | Osiers | Do. | Lord Beauclerk |
| 137 | Fir plantation | 0 | 1 | 6 | Plantation | Do. | Mr. Harcourt |
| 138 | Runnymeade piece | 1 | 2 | 10 | Meadow | Do. | James Deane |
| 139 | Magna Charta Isle | 3 | 0 | 36 | Do. | Do. | Lord Ch. Beauclerk |
| 139a | The Pool | 1 | 1 | 29 | Water | Do. | Do. |
| 140 | Upper Warrenfield | 15 | 0 | 9 | Arable | Do. | Samuel Jordan |
| 141 | Plantation in do. | 0 | 1 | 22 | Wood | Do. | G. S. Harcourt, Esq. |
| 142 | Duck Puddle | 5 | 2 | 32 | Arable | Do. | Samuel Jordan |
| 143 | The Marsh | 13 | 1 | 7 | Do. | Do. | Do. |
| 144 | Bushy Close | 8 | 0 | 14 | Meadow | T. P. Williams, Esq. | Henry Stevens |
| 145 | Patcroft | 7 | 0 | 37 | Arable | Mr. Harcourt | Samuel Jordan |
| 145a | Osiers in do. | 0 | 3 | 2 | Osiers | Do. | George Grantham |
| 146 | Osiers | 0 | 2 | 2 | Do. | Do. | Do. |
| 147 | Fir plantation | 0 | 3 | 5 | Wood | Do. | G. S. Harcourt, Esq. |
| 148 | Eyott | 3 | 0 | 5 | Osiers | G. S. Harcourt, Esq. | George Grantham |
| 149 | Slope | 0 | 2 | 18 | Arable | T. P. Williams, Esq. | Henry Stevens |
| 150 | Thomas' Field | 36 | 0 | 35 | Do. | Do. | Do. |
| 151 | The Wharf | 0 | 1 | 32 | Wharf | Do. | Ibotson |
| 151a | Road to do. | 1 | 2 | 6 | Road | Do. | Do. |
| 152 | Eyott | 0 | 0 | 21 | Osiers | Mr. Harcourt | George Grantham |
| 153 | The 12 acres | 11 | 3 | 18 | Meadow | T. P. Williams, Esq. | Henry Stevens |
| 154 | Further Close | 9 | 2 | 17 | Arable | Do. | Do. |
| 155 | Part of Royles | 4 | 2 | 13 | Do. | B. H. Gyll, Esq. | Ann Buckland |
| 156 | Do. | 13 | 2 | 26 | Meadow | Do. | Do. |
| 157 | Part of eyott | 0 | 3 | 28 | Osiers | Do. | William Haines |
| 158 | Orchard | 0 | 1 | 22 | Orchard | Do. | Do. |
| 159 | Ferry-house and garden | 0 | 0 | 28 | House, &c. | Do. | Do. |
| 160 | Orchard | 3 | 1 | 0 | Orchard | Do. | Ann Buckland |
| 161 | The kitchen 5 acres | 3 | 2 | 36 | Meadow | Do. | Do. |
| 162 | Eyott | 1 | 1 | 2 | Osiers | Do. | William Haines |
| 163 | Do. | 0 | 3 | 1 | Do. | Do. | Do. |
| 164 | Osiers | 1 | 3 | 30 | Do. | Do. | Do. |
| 165 | Upper Leys | 3 | 3 | 11 | Meadow | Do. | Do. |
| 166 | Townford or Shagbags | 19 | 2 | 2 | Arable | Do. | Ann Buckland |
| 167 | The Leys | 17 | 2 | 2 | Meadow | Do. | Do. |
| 168 | The long 8 acres | 7 | 3 | 39 | Do. | Do. | Do. |
| 169 | Homestead | 1 | 5 | 15 | Homestead | Do. | Do. |
| 170 | Garden | 0 | 1 | 33 | Garden | Do. | Do. |
| 171 | Barley Close | 5 | 3 | 29 | Arable | Do. | Do. |
| 172 | The nine acres | 9 | 3 | 16 | Do. | T. P. Williams, Esq. | Henry Stevens |
| 173 | Great Lease | 46 | 1 | 30 | Do. | Do. | Do. |
| 174 | The Marsh | 13 | 0 | 12 | Do. | Do. | Do. |
| 175 | Churchfield or Court Close | 8 | 2 | 32 | Meadow | Do. | Do. |
| 176 | Great Parsonage Close | 8 | 3 | 38 | Arable | Mr. Gyll | W. Thos. Buckland |
| 177 | Garsons' Mead | 6 | 0 | 10 | Meadow | Do. | Ann Buckland |
| 177a | Drift do. | 0 | 2 | 32 | Drift | Do. | Do. |
| 178 | Meadow | 2 | 2 | 14 | Meadow | Mr. Harcourt | Robert Cornish |
| 179 | Cottage & garden | 0 | 1 | 21 | Cottage and garden | B. H. Gyll, Esq. | Joseph Newell |
| 180 | Waras Close | 3 | 0 | 6 | Arable | Do. | W. T. Buckland |
| 181 | Orchard | 0 | 3 | 26 | Orchard | Do. | Joseph Newell |
| 182 | Do. | 1 | 2 | 2 | Do. | Joseph Davis | Joseph Davis |
| 183 | House & premises | 0 | 1 | 23 | House, &c. | Do. | Do. |
| 184 | Orchard | 1 | 0 | 37 | Orchard | Do. | Do. |
|  | Old road | 0 | 1 | 0 |  |  |  |
| 185 | House and garden | 0 | 0 | 27 | House | James Sexton | James Sexton |

## HISTORY OF WRAYSBURY.

| | Description. | Quantity. A. R. P. | Cultivation. | Owner. | Occupier. |
|---|---|---|---|---|---|
| 186 | Orchard & garden | 0 2 30 | Orchard | Ann Buckland | Thomas Jugby |
| | Old road | 0 0 20 | | | |
| 187 | Cottage & garden | 0 1 28 | Cottage and garden | Do. | Do. |
| 188 | House, garden, &c. | 0 3 3 | House and Garden | Francis Buckland | Francis Buckland |
| 189 | Barton Hall | 5 0 6 | Arable | Mr. Harcourt | Robert Cornish |
| 189a | Long Close | 2 0 21 | Do. | Do. | Do. |
| 190 | The Butts | 1 1 17 | Meadow | Do. | Do. |
| 190a | Orchard | 0 1 0 | Do. | Do. | Do. |
| 191 | Do. | 0 2 22 | Do. | Do. | Do. |
| 192 | Burnt Mead | 6 2 35 | Do. | T. P. Williams, Esq. | Henry Stevens |
| 193 | Church and yard | 0 2 20 | Church and yard | Parish | Parish |
| 194 | Stack-yard | 0 3 25 | Stack-yard | T. P. Williams, Esq. | Henry Stevens |
| 195 | Homestead | 0 2 38 | Homestead | Do. | Do. |
| 196 | Orchard | 0 1 29 | Orchard | Mr. Harcourt | Edward Downham |
| 197 | School houses and garden | 0 2 32 | Houses | Do. | Jugby and others |
| 198 | Garden | 0 0 9 | Garden | T. P. Williams, Esq. | Henry Stevens |
| 199 | Cock's Close | 2 2 33 | Meadow | Mr. Harcourt | Robert Cornish |
| 200 | Do. and part of river | 3 0 27 | Do. | Do. | Do. |
| 201 | Meadow and part of river | 1 0 37 | Do. | Benjamin Clark | Benjamin Clark |
| | Old road | 0 1 27 | | Do. | Do. |
| 202 | Orchard | 0 3 10 | Orchard | Do. | Do. |
| 203 | Houses & gardens | 0 2 36 | Houses, &c. | Do. | Braisher and others |
| 204 | House, garden and orchard | 0 2 10 | Do. | John Atkins | Mary Style |
| | Old road | 0 0 25 | | Do. | |
| 205 | Key garden | 36 2 13 | Arable | Mr. Harcourt | Benjamin Slocock |
| 206 | Craw Bush | 37 3 20 | Do. | Do. | Do. |
| 207 | Old field, or Rye side | 41 1 28 | Do. | Mr. Gyll | W. T. Buckland |
| 208 | Barley close | 4 1 28 | Do. | Do. | Do. |
| 209 | House, garden and premises | 1 3 0 | House, &c. | Do. | Mr. Gyll |
| 210 | Farm stead | 0 3 35 | Homestead | Do. | W. T. Buckland |
| 211 | Part of orchard | 1 2 10 | Orchard | B. H. Gyll, Esq. | B. H. Gyll, Esq. |
| 212 | Meadow | 2 3 5 | Meadow | Do. | Do. |
| 213 | Lone meadow | 2 3 38 | Do. | Do. | Do. |
| 214 | Livingston's do. | 3 0 28 | Do. | Do. | W. T. Buckland |
| 215 | The Common | 20 2 13 | Pasture | Do. | Do. |
| 216 | Wyrardisbury Moor | 20 3 6 | Do. | T. P. Williams, Esq. | Benjamin Slocock |
| 217 | Rushy close | 3 3 28 | Meadow | Mr. Gyll | W. T. Buckland |
| 218 | The 4 acres | 4 2 14 | Do. | Do. | Do. |
| 219 | Ford's field | 2 1 21 | Arable and meadow | Do. | Do. |
| 220 | Cottage & garden | 1 0 5 | Cottage and garden | Do., bought in 1850 by Gordon Willoughby Jas. Gyll | Jas. Hammond |
| 221 | Little Cockmans | 3 1 3 | Meadow | Do. | W. T. Buckland |
| 222 | Upper do. | 1 1 6 | Do. | Do. | Do. |
| 223 | Wyrardisbury Moor | 4 2 12 | Pasture | T. P. Williams, Esq. | Benjamin Slocock |
| 224 | Do. | 1 0 0 | Do. | Parish | Do. |
| 225 | Do. | 20 2 21 | Do. | Mr. Williams | Do. |
| 225a | Do. | 4 1 24 | Do. | Mr. Gyll | W. T. Buckland |
| 226 | Mills, cottages and gardens | 2 0 21 | Mills | Mr. Williams | Messrs. Ibotson |
| 227 | Pasture | 0 3 26 | Pasture | Do. | Do. |
| 228 | Cottage & gardens | 0 1 17 | Cottage and gardens | Do. | Do. |

## HISTORY OF WRAYSBURY.

|  | Description. | Quantity. A. R. P. | Cultivation. | Owner. | Occupation. |
|---|---|---|---|---|---|
| 229 | Mill, house and garden | 2 0 23 | House and gardens | Mr. Williams | Messrs. Ibotson |
| 230 | Close house | 1 0 13 | Meadow | Mr. Gyll | Do. |
| 231 | House, barn, &c. | 0 0 39 | House, &c. | Do. | Do. |
| 232 | Part of meadow | 0 0 20 | Meadow | T. P. Williams, Esq. | Do. |
| 233 | Whitehall and garden | 2 1 36 | House | Do. | Do. |
| 234 | Meadow | 1 3 1 | Meadow | Do. | Do. |
| 235 | Part of Mill field | 8 3 37 | Arable | Do. | Joseph Reffell |
| 236 | Do. | 0 0 39 | Do. | Do. | Do. |
| 237 | Little Flatcombs | 0 2 34 | Do. | Do. | Do. |
| 238 | Styles | 10 0 27 | Do. | Do. | Do. |
| 239 | Meadow | 2 0 12 | Meadow | Francis Buckland | Edw. Downham |
| 240 | Do. | 1 2 34 | Do. | Mr. Williams | Ibotson |
| 241 | Cottage & garden | 0 1 8 | Cottage and garden | Mr. Gyll | Timothy Cuthbert |
| 242 | Part of orchard | 1 2 10 | Orchard | Do. | Mr. Gyll |
| 243 | Stable yard and garden | 0 0 35 | Yard and garden | Do. | Do. |
| 244 | Orchard and rick-yard | 0 3 11 | Orchard, &c. | Do. | W. T. Buckland |
| 245 | Cottages & gardens | 0 1 3 | Cottage and garden | Do. | Higgs and Jackson |
| 246 | Houses & gardens | 0 1 7 | Do. | Francis Buckland | Downham & Weston |
| 247 | The Green | 0 3 24 | Pasture | Mr. Harcourt | Benjamin Slocock |
| 248 | Do. | 0 2 27 | Do. | Do. | Do. |
| 249 | Homestead | 1 2 20 | Homestead | Do. | Do. |
| 250 | Orchard | 0 3 20 | Orchard | Do. | Do. |
| 251 | Beer shop and garden | 0 0 23 | Beershop | Thomas Harris | Wm. Goddard |
| 252 | Orchard | 0 1 30 | Orchard | Do. | Do. |
| 253 | Meadow & garden | 0 3 10 | Meadow | Do. | Do. |
| 254 | Randall's Green | 1 1 10 | Do. | Mr. Harcourt | Benjamin Slocock |
| 255 | Floury field | 2 3 10 | Do. | Do. | Do. |
| 256 | Garden | 0 0 24 | Garden | Do. | Do. |
| 257 | Bowry's barn and yard | 0 1 12 | Barn, &c. | Do. | Do. |
| 258 | Bowry's barn and part of field. | 0 1 0 | Arable | Do. | Do. |
| 259 |  | 0 0 36 | Do. | Do. | Do. |
| 260 |  | 2 2 4 | Do. | Do. | Do. |
| 261 | Piece of gravel pit | 0 0 39 | Pit | Mr. Cox | John Millest |
|  | Old road | 0 1 26 |  |  |  |
| 262 | Polly's meadow | 1 1 22 | Meadow | Do. | Do. |
| 263 | Cottages & gardens | 0 3 33 | Cottages and gardens | Do. | Bradley |
|  |  | 0 0 24 | Do. | John Taylor | Goody |
| 264 | Old road | 0 0 22 |  |  |  |
| 265 | Beer shop and premises | 0 0 30 | Beershop | Mr. Barnes | Rachael Baker |
|  | Old road | 0 0 24 |  |  |  |
| 266 | Chapel and yard | 0 0 6 | Chapel and yard | Chapel Trust | Chapel Trust |
|  | Old road | 0 0 4 |  |  |  |
| 267 | Houses & gardens | 0 2 5 | Houses, &c. | Mary Leno | Funnel, Leno & other |
|  | Old road | 0 1 0 |  |  |  |
| 268 |  | 0 0 29 |  |  |  |
|  | Old road | 0 0 8 | Do. | Joanna Butler | Butler, Sims, &c. |
| 269 | Houses & gardens | 0 1 18 | Houses and gardens | Martha Hewlett | Dyson, Ware, Spong |
|  | Old road | 0 0 12 |  |  |  |
| 270 | Meadow and part of river | 0 3 29 | Meadow | Barnes | Rachael Baker |
| 271 | Do. | 0 3 14 | Do. | Francis Buckland | Francis Buckland |
| 272 | Do. | 2 0 17 | Do. | Mr. Harcourt | John Millest |

| | Description. | Quantity. | | | Cultivation. | Owner. | Occupation. |
|---|---|---|---|---|---|---|---|
| | | A. | R. | P. | | | |
| 273 | Meadow and part of river | 1 | 2 | 22 | Meadow | Mary Leno | John Taylor |
| 274 | Orchard | 1 | 0 | 24 | Orchard | Samuel Atkins | John Millest |
| 275 | Cottages & gardens | 0 | 0 | 23 | Cottages and gardens | Joanna Butler | Monger and others |
| 276 | Do. | 0 | 0 | 17 | Do. | Do. | Robert Roe |
| 277 | Do. | 0 | 1 | 2 | Do. | Church Trustees | Tappin, Prew, &c. |
| 278 | George Inn and premises | 0 | 2 | 34 | Inn, &c. | Neville Reid & Co. | Wm. Clarke |
| 279 | Cottages & gardens | 1 | 1 | 8 | Cottages and gardens | Mr. Harcourt | Shanks and others |
| 280 | Cottage & garden, barn & orchard | 0 | 1 | 27 | Barn | Francis Buckland | Francis Buckland |
| 281 | Arable | 3 | 0 | 4 | Arable | Do. | Do. |
| 282 | High barn and yard | 0 | 1 | 22 | Barn and yard | Mr. Williams | Henry Stevens |
| 283 | Arable field | 2 | 1 | 28 | Arable | Neville Reid | Wm. Clarke |
| 284 | Meadow | 2 | 1 | 14 | Meadow | Do. | Do. |
| 285 | Cottage & garden | 0 | 1 | 13 | Cottage and garden | Bridge Trust | Jackson, Watts, &c. |
| 286 | Do. | 0 | 0 | 31 | Do. | Francis Buckland | Clark and Day |
| 287 | Homestead | 0 | 1 | 18 | Homestead | Mr. Harcourt | John Millest |
| 288 | Little meadow close | 0 | 3 | 2 | Meadow | Do. | Do. |
| 289 | Arable field | 6 | 3 | 15 | Arable | Do. | Do. |
| 290 | Cottage & garden | 0 | 1 | 24 | Cottage and garden | Mrs. Tanner | Mrs. Tanner |
| 291 | Do. | 0 | 1 | 17 | Do. | Joseph Davis | Chas. Caley & others |
| 292 | Goater's close | 3 | 1 | 9 | Meadow | Do. | Joseph Davis |
| 293 | Part of ditto | 0 | 2 | 16 | Do. | Ann Buckland | Do. |
| 294 | Meadow | 2 | 3 | 31 | Do. | Mr. Harcourt | John Millest |
| 295 | Douglas | 23 | 3 | 12 | Arable | Do. | Benjamin Slocock |
| 295a | Part of do. | 3 | 0 | 0 | Do. | Do. | John Millest |
| 296 | New close | 10 | 1 | 0 | Do. | Do. | Benjamin Slocock |
| 297 | Great meadow | 9 | 1 | 26 | Meadow | Do. | Do. |
| 298 | Gyll's close | 9 | 2 | 34 | Arable | Mary Palmer | Wm. Taylor |
| 299 | The 10 acres | 10 | 1 | 21 | Do. | Mr. Harcourt | John Millest |
| 300 | Long Ham | 12 | 2 | 18 | Meadow | Do. | Benjamin Slocock |
| 301 | Do. | 19 | 3 | 39 | Arable | Do. | Do. |
| 302 | Wandsor Hill | 10 | 2 | 5 | Do. | T. P. Williams, Esq. | Henry Stevens |
| 303 | The 7 acres | 8 | 0 | 2 | Meadow | Do. | Do. |
| 304 | Barnfield | 40 | 1 | 31 | Arable | Do. | Do. |
| 305 | Princess Augusta | 1 | 2 | 21 | Do. | Princess Augusta | Francis Buckland |
| 306 | Gravel pit | 0 | 1 | 36 | Gravel pit | Parish | Parish |
| 307 | Sand hill | 13 | 2 | 21 | Arable | Mr. Harcourt | John Millest |
| 308 | Do. | 23 | 0 | 18 | Do. | Mr. Gyll | Ann Buckland |
| 309 | Welly House piece | 10 | 0 | 6 | Do. | Do. | Do. |
| 310 | Do. | 4 | 0 | 1 | Meadow | Do. | Do. |
| 311 | Do. | 1 | 1 | 27 | Do. | Do. | Do. |
| 312 | Arable field | 4 | 1 | 26 | Arable | Do. | Thomas Holderness |
| 313 | Millstream, &c. to Colnbrook Bridge | 1 | 3 | 0 | Water | | Ibotson |
| 314 | Do. from Thames to Upper Mill Bridge | 14 | 2 | 23 | Do. | | Do. |
| | River Thames | 58 | 0 | 0 | | | |
| | Roads, &c. | 19 | 2 | 28 | | | |
| | Total acres in Wyrardisbury Parish | 1656 | 1 | 18 | | | |

## ABSTRACT OF THE COMMISSIONERS' AWARD,

Relative to the Enclosure of the Parish of Wyrardisbury, County Bucks.

The Commissioners were James Taylor of Islington, gentleman; Richard Davis of Lewknor, Oxon, gentleman; and Thomas Wyatt of Fordhouse, county Wilts, gentleman, appointed by Act of Parliament passed 39 George III. entitled an Act for dividing, allotting and inclosing the open and common fields, common meadows, commons and waste grounds within the parish and manor of Wyrardisbury. John Simon Harcourt, Esq., late of Ankerwycke Place, in the parish of Egham, Surrey, but now of Trimley, county Surrey; Archibald Paxton, Esq., and Richard Dalton, Esq., (trustees named and appointed in and by the last will and testament of Wm. Gyll, Esq. for and on behalf of his widow Mary Gyll, now of Wraysbury House), John Peccock, of St. Saviour, Southwark, wharfinger, and John Cowderoy, of Deptford, county Kent, butcher (trustees for Mary, daughter of William Perkins, deceased, wife of John King, wharfinger), Robert Style of Wyrardisbury, yeoman, and Nathaniel Wilmot of Wyrardisbury, carpenter, all which are parties to certain exchanges hereinafter particularly mentioned, severally send greeting, &c. &c.

A true and perfect survey and admeasurement of the common fields, meadows, commons and waste grounds was made by Thomas Bainbridge, Esq. of Gray's Inn, which has been reduced to writing, with a map or plan taken with the number of acres, roods and perches, &c. in statute measure belonging to each proprietor, which was verified on oath before the said Commissioners, consisting of the following, &c.:—Public roads, Staines and Colnbrook ditto, Datchet ditto, Lower Ankerwycke ditto, Upper Ankerwycke ditto, Road over Wraysbury Green, Repairs of ditto, Herbage of ditto to be enjoyed by proprietors of lands adjoining. No trees to be planted in the hedges adjoining the road nearer to each other than 50 yards. Roads not to be stocked within ten years. Private roads:—private road leading to Thomas Stanton and Mr. King's; private carriage road over Hythe End Green; gates; herbage of private roads. Footpaths:—to Horton, Datchet, from Ankerwycke to the Church; ditto to Old Windsor ferry; to Staines; footpath over old field, to be also used as public carriage roads in floodtime; gates and styles. Public drains:—Horton drain; drain on the Green; Queen's Mead drain; repairs of the drains. Allotment of the space of 8 yards on each side of the river Colne; allotment for gravel pits; ditto on the common. Fences:—Allotment on Queen's mead; fences, in town field; fences in Mrs. King's close; fences and herbage of allotments for gravel pits, &c. Allotments to the Lords of the several manors, in lieu of their right of soil:—to John Simon Harcourt, Esq.; to the Dean and Canons of Windsor. Fences:—Allotments for glebe to the Dean and Canons of Windsor and their Lessee; allotments to the Vicar; allotment of the residue: allotment subject to the wake; allotment to Joseph Adkin, subject to the right of the inhabitants of the parish to hold a wake or fair thereon annually; allotments to Thomas Ashby; ditto to Thomas Ashby and William Chandler; ditto to Thomas Buckland, with fences, &c.; ditto to the Duchess of Buccleugh; ditto to Mary Boult; ditto to William Chandler; ditto to the Marquis of Downshire, sold to Thomas Williams, Esq.; ditto to the Trustees of William Gyll, Esq.; ditto to William Gyll, Esq., Captain Horse-Guards; ditto to John Goodwin; ditto to James Herbert, subject to the wake; ditto to John Simon Harcourt, Esq.; tithe free ditto. Exchanges the pightle from Nathaniel Wilmot; Cocks Close from Gyll's Trustees; Garson's Close from ditto; allotment to the King and to Lord Braybrooke as lessee; allotment to Mrs. King's trustees. Exchange for the allotment for the gravel pit; ditto to Mrs. Mackason; ditto to Samuel Hugh Mills; ditto to Messrs. William and Josiah Monnery; ditto to Nathaniel Matthews;

ditto to John Novell; ditto to Elizabeth Newman; ditto to Thomas Porter; ditto to John Harcourt Powell, Esq.; ditto to Joseph Packer and William Thurbin; ditto to Thomas Stanton; ditto to Robert Style; Exchange Helmet Close from the Trustees of the late William Gyll, Esq.; allotment to Shadrach Trotman; ditto to William Taylor; ditto to John Taylor; ditto to Elizabeth Tanner; ditto to Thomas Williams, Esq.; ditto to Nathaniel Wilmot; Exchange Grove Close from Robert Style; allotment to William Whitmarsh; ditto to George Walker; ditto to Robert Whitfield; ditto to the Trustees of Wyrardisbury Church land; ditto to the Trustees of Wyrardisbury Bridge land. General orders for fencing.

Signed, 1803, by the Commissioners, viz.—James Taylor, R. Davis, Thomas Wyatt, A. Paxton, Richard Dalton, John Simon Harcourt, John Peecock, Mary King, Robert Style, Nathaniel Wilmot.

Inrolled in His Majesty's Court of Common Pleas at Westminster, of the term of the Holy Trinity in the 44th year of the reign of King George III. Keane Fitzgerald. Roll 2.

And whereas after the engrossment, but previous to the execution of the foregoing part of this award, application was made for further allotments, &c., the Commissioners the same as before. 1803. Enrolled 44th George III. Roll 23.

## WYRARDISBURY TITHE APPORTIONMENT,

### VALUE OF RENT CHARGES FOR 1843.

Average Great Tithes 7s in the £.   Vicar's Tithes, 1s 6d.

| Landowners. | Occupiers. | Vicar. £ s. d. | Rector. £ s. d. | Value of Rector's Payment. £ s. d. |
|---|---|---|---|---|
| Ashby, Thomas | Himself | 2 0 3 | 13 8 3 | 14 13 10 |
| Atkins, John | Mary Styles | 0 5 0 | | |
| Atkins, Joseph | John Millest | 0 12 6 | | |
| Augusta, Princess | Francis Buckland | 1 10 0 | 0 11 2 | 0 11 9¼ |
| Bell, Charles | Himself | 1 6 6 | | |
| Ditto | William Wise | 0 11 0 | | |
| Buckland, Ann | Thomas Tugbey | 0 16 0 | | |
| | Joseph Davies | 0 4 0 | | |
| Buckland, Francis | Himself | 1 1 0 | | |
| | | 0 3 9 | 1 6 3 | 1 7 8½ |
| Ditto | John Brazier | 0 2 0 | 0 11 6 | 0 12 1¼ |
| Bridge Land, Trustees of | William Osborn | 0 1 6 | | |
| | George Leno | 0 7 6 ⎫ 0 5 0 ⎭ | 3 19 6 | 4 3 11 |
| Clark, Benjamin | Himself | 0 1 0 ⎫ 0 17 6 ⎭ | 0 7 6 | 0 7 10¾ |
| Cox, Daniel | William Taylor | 0 1 6 ⎫ 0 8 6 0 12 6 ⎭ | 5 2 0 | 5 7 8 |
| Church Land, Trustees of | George Leno | 0 5 0 ⎫ 0 1 9 ⎭ | 2 1 3 | 2 3 6¼ |
| Daniel, Joseph | Himself | 2 4 6 ⎫ 0 3 0 ⎭ | 1 2 0 | 1 3 2 |
| Dyson, John | Joseph Davy | 0 2 0 | 0 15 0 | 0 15 10 |
| Gyll, B. Hamilton, Esq. | Mary Sills | 1 12 0 ⎫ 3 0 8 ⎭ | 23 6 10 | 24 13 0 |
| Ditto | Thomas Wm. Buckland | 2 0 0 ⎫ 4 3 0 1 3 6 ⎭ | 29 13 6 | 31 6 9½ |

| Landowners. | Occupiers. | Vicar. | Rector. | Value of Rector's Payment. |
|---|---|---|---|---|
| | | £ s. d. | £ s. d. | £ s. d. |
| B. H. Gyll, Esq. | Thomas W. Buckland | 0 8 0 | | |
| Ditto | Ann Buckland | 2 6 6 ⎫ | | |
| | | 3 15 0 ⎬ | 29 15 6 | 31 8 10¼ |
| | | 2 11 0 ⎭ | | |
| Ditto | William Haynes | 3 6 0 | | |
| Ditto | — Pickersgill | 0 2 3 ⎱ | 0 6 6 | 0 6 10¼ |
| | | 0 1 3 ⎰ | | |
| Ditto | Timothy Cuthbert | 0 4 6 | | |
| Ditto | Himself | 1 2 6 | | |
| George Simon Harcourt, Esq. | Charles Bell | 3 17 0 ⎱ | 1 19 0 | 2 1 2 |
| Ditto | George Milner | 0 7 0 ⎰ | | |
| Ditto | James Collins | 1 1 6 | | |
| Ditto | — Martin and another | 0 4 6 | | |
| Ditto | Edward Passmore | 2 8 9 ⎫ | | |
| | | 5 12 6 ⎬ | 41 18 9 | 44 5 9¼ |
| | | 0 16 6 ⎭ | | |
| | | 11 18 6 | | |
| Ditto | Himself | 12 2 6 ⎫ | | |
| Jordan, Pullen, Harcourt | 25 | 4 12 0 ⎬ | 37 1 0 | 39 2 6¼ |
| | 4 | 1 13 0 ⎭ | | |
| | 8 odd | | | |
| George Simon Harcourt, Esq. | Edward Downham | 0 15 9 ⎫ | | |
| | Robert Cornish | 1 4 6 ⎬ | 12 3 9 | 12 17 5 |
| | Henry Taylor | 0 10 0 ⎭ | | |
| | | 7 0 6 | | |
| Ditto | — Tildersley | 1 0 0 | 0 8 9 | 0 9 2¼ |
| | | 0 1 9 | | |
| Ditto | Thomas Jackson | 0 7 6 | | |
| Ditto | Francis Buckland | 1 8 7 | | |
| Benjamin Slocock and Henry Taylor hold about 17 acres | | 9 1 0 ⎱ | 67 0 3 | 70 15 5¼ |
| | | 1 7 8 ⎰ | | |
| Mr. Harcourt | Thomas Bramford | 0 5 0 | | |
| Ditto | James Dean | 0 6 0 | | |
| Ditto | Benj. Walker and others | 0 7 6 | | |
| Ditto | Robert Edmead | 0 5 6 | | |
| Ditto | Empty | 0 3 0 | | |
| Ditto | John Dixon | 0 3 6 | 1 2 6 | 1 3 8¼ |
| Ditto | John Millest and John Dyson | 0 8 6 | 3 6 6 | 3 10 2½ |
| Thomas and John Harris | Sarah Lucas | 0 13 6 | | |
| Ann Herbert | Rachel Baker | 0 2 0 | | |
| Ditto | George Leno | 0 7 0 | | |
| Martha Hewlett | John Dyson | 0 3 0 | | |
| Ashby Skidmore | Mary Ann Sills | | | |
| Ditto | Richard & Percy Ibotson | 3 1 6 | | |
| Thomas Jackson | Passingham and others | 0 18 6 | | |
| George Leno | Himself | 0 4 6 ⎱ | 0 12 0 | 0 12 8 |
| | | 0 1 6 ⎰ | | |
| John Morris | William Osborn | 1 11 0 | | |
| Ditto | Thomas Roakes | 0 18 10 ⎫ | | |
| | | 2 18 8 ⎬ | | 1 1 1¼ |
| | | 0 3 0 ⎭ | | |
| Sarah Mackason | George Leno | 0 1 6 | | |
| Ditto | Thomas Parris | 0 5 0 | | |
| Ditto | William Osborn | 0 13 6 | | |
| Parish of Wyrardisbury | Mary Ann Sills | 0 3 6 | | |
| Ditto | Francis Buckland | 0 6 0 | | |
| Ditto | Surveyors of the Highway | 0 1 6 | | |

| Landowners. | Occupiers. | Vicar. | Rector. | Value of Rector's Payment. |
|---|---|---|---|---|
| | | £ s. d. | £ s. d. | £ s. d. |
| Mary Palmer . . . | William Taylor . . | 0 7 0 | 3 15 0 | |
| | | 0 4 0 | 0 1 6 | 3 19 2¼ |
| Reid and Co. . . . | John Millest . . | 0 7 6 | 0 0 4 | |
| | | 0 2 6 | 1 16 6 | 1 18 6¼ |
| | | 0 2 6 | | |
| Robert Thompson . . | John Smart . . | 0 1 2 | | |
| | | 0 5 8 | | |
| | | 0 2 2 | | |
| Sarah Tubb . . | Winchcombe and others | 0 7 0 | | |
| John Taylor . . | Himself . . | 0 13 0 | | |
| Thomas Tanner . . | Himself . . | 0 6 0 | | |
| Thomas Peers Williams, Esq. | Henry Stevens . . | 0 18 0 | | |
| | | 10 0 0 | 81 8 6 | 85 19 10¼ |
| | | 4 0 0 | | |
| Ditto . . . | — Pickersgill . . | 1 18 6 | | |
| | | 0 6 0 | | |
| Ditto . . . | George Glascott . | 1 1 3 | | |
| | | 0 3 6 | 1 0 3 | 1 1 4¼ |
| Ditto . . . | Francis Buckland . | 8 14 0 | | |
| Ditto . . . | Joseph Reffell, Horton | 1 5 0 | 7 16 0 | 8 4 9 |
| Robert Whitfield . . | James Holderness . | 0 5 6 | 1 14 6 | 1 16 4¾ |
| Ditto . . . | William Wears . | 0 3 6 | | |
| | | 153 0 0 | 377 0 0 | |
| Vicarial Glebe . . | | | | |
| Rev. Charles Champnes . | William Taylor . . | 2 0 0 | 5 0 0 | 5 5 7¼ |
| Rectorial Glebe . . | B. H. Gyll, Esq. | | | |
| Dean and Canons of Windsor | | | | |
| B. H. Gyll, Esq., their lessee . | Thomas Wm. Buckland | | 10 0 0 | 10 11 2½ |
| | | | £392 0 0 | £413 19 2½ |
| Rectorial Glebe . . | Thomas Wm. Buckland | | | |
| | Total . . . | 10 0 0 | 10 0 0 | 10 11 2½ |
| Ditto . . . . | Thomas Wm. Buckland | 1 0 0 | | |
| Manorial allotment not in the Schedule in Tithe agreement | Amount payable to the | 153 0 0 | 377 0 0 | |
| | Vicar . . | 154 0 0 | 377 0 0 | |
| | Amount payable for the Rectorial Glebe . | 10 0 0 | 10 0 0 | 10 11 2½ |
| | Amount for Vicarial Glebe . . | 2 0 0 | 5 0 0 | 5 7 7¼ |
| | Totals . | £166 0 0 | £392 0 0 | |

---

Lincoln's Inn, 22nd August, 1838.

Dear Sir,

We have the pleasure to inform you that we have arranged a Meeting in the Parish of Wraysbury to effect a Commutation of Tithes, which meets the convenience of the principal parties concerned. The day appointed is the 6th September, when one of us will attend on your behalf, accompanied by Captain Deschamps.

We send you on the other side a statement of the data upon which, with reference to the late Act of Parliament, we think the Commutation will take place. The first average, £339. 2*s* 2*d*, is 1-7th of your gross receipts in respect of Great Tithes, during the last seven years (exclusive of the Tithe of the Glebes

# HISTORY OF WRAYSBURY. 171

and of Ann Buckland's Farm). The sum of £32. 11s 5d is the proportion of Tithe to be attributed to Ann Buckland's Farm. With reference to the rest of the Tithe in the parish, and the two sums of £6. 0s 6d and £5. 7s 11d, are 1-7th of the average receipts for seven years in respect of the Glebe.

The reason why the Tithe on Ann Buckland's Farm is calculated separately, is because for some years past the Tithe has been sunk in her rent, so that we have not been able, as in the other cases, to arrive at any average from her payment of Tithe.

The reason why the Tithe on the Glebe is distinguished is, that Glebe when in the *actual* holding of the Rector or Vicar, is not subject to Tithe, consequently it is necessary to take a separate account of this. At present both the Rector's and Vicar's Glebe is let out, and therefore pays Tithe. The Act of Parliament requires the Glebe to be kept distinct.

We believe it is the Vicar's intention to propose a Commutation of the Small Tithe upon an average of his last seven years' receipts.

We have communicated with the Dean and Canons of Windsor, and the several landowners in the parish. We hope we have made ourselves intelligible.

We remain, Dear Sir,
Your faithful and obliged Servants,
COLLEY SMITH, HUNTER & GWATKIN.

B. H. Gyll, Esq., Wraysbury House.

## DATA FOR THE WRAYSBURY TITHE COMMUTATION.

|  | A. | R. | P. |
|---|---|---|---|
| Total Quantity of Land in the Parish, exclusive of water | 1522 | 1 | 38 |
| Arable . . . . . . 873 0 35 |  |  |  |
| Meadow or Pasture, including Ozier Homestead, Orchards and Gardens . 649 1 3 | 1522 | 1 | 38 |
| Titheable . . . . . 1049 0 13 R. T. |  |  |  |
|  278 2 26 V. T. | 1327 | 3 | 1 |
| Rectorial Glebe . . . . . | 49 | 3 | 35 |
| Vicar's ditto . . . . . . | 18 | 2 | 36 |
| Exempt from Tithe as formerly belonging to Ankerwycke Priory . | 126 | 0 | 6 |
|  | 1522 | 1 | 38 |

### RECTORIAL TITHES RECEIVED, &c.

| 1829 | £351 | 9 | 4 |
| 1830 | 351 | 14 | 4 |
| 1831 | 354 | 6 | 1 |
| 1832 | 354 | 2 | 4 |
| 1833 | 320 | 14 | 3 |
| 1834 | 321 | 17 | 3 |
| 1835 | 319 | 11 | 3 |
|  | 2373 | 14 | 10 |

1-7th is £339  2  2
Value of the Tithes of Ann Buckland's Farm, 92a. 0r. 18p. . . £32 11 5

| Tithe of Rectorial Glebe in William Buckland's hands | £6 3 2<br>6 3 2<br>6 3 2<br>6 3 2<br>5 17 0<br>5 17 0<br>5 17 0 | Tithe of Vicarial Glebe in W. Taylor's hands, and paid by him | £5 12 0<br>5 12 0<br>5 12 0<br>5 12 0<br>5 2 6<br>5 2 6<br>5 2 6 |
|---|---|---|---|
|  | 42 3 8  1-7th is 6 0 6 |  | 37 15 6  1-7th is £5 7 11 |

## WRAYSBURY COURT ROLLS.

It appears from an inspection of the Court Rolls of Wraysbury, county Bucks, that all the Rolls which are said to be extant are contained in four books, the earliest date being 14th October, 1725.

Feudal law, or the tenure of land by suit and service to the owner of it, was introduced into England by the Saxons about 600 A.D., and the slavery of it was increased under William I. in 1066. Hence the kingdom was divided into baronies, which were entrusted to nobles, who furnished the king with money and soldiers. Money made soldiers, and soldiers made money.

The name of Vavasors, who ranked next to barons, merged into *liberi homines* or freemen. The persons called afferatores or affeerers levied fines styled amerciaments.

Commons of soil or water, pasture or turbary, turf estovers, wood for fuel, &c., while piscaries were right of fishing in rivers not navigable.

The Lords formerly obliged their tenants to grind their corn at their mills. The word grist is the past tense of the Saxon gerisan, to crush. Hand mills were called querne; and the common oven or *furnagium* belonged to the Lord, who forced his tenants to bake there also.

All *botes* came under the term *estoveria*, as fire-bote, wood-bote, &c. p. 17, note.

Villani were entered on Court Rolls for protection and services according to the custom of the manor. Leet is a lawday court, superior to the Wapentake (weapon take) or hundred. The homage is a jury and an act of submission of a tenant to his Lord as an acknowledgment for lands. The statute of 12 Carolus II. 1661, discharged all tenures from the incident of homage, because it was incident to Knight's service, which that statute abolished.

The first Jury on the Wraysbury Rolls, 1725, consists of 19 persons, viz. Francis Bowry, John Winch, Richard Cobham, James Liming, John Perry, Shadrach Child, Henry Pinnock, Richard Perry, Thomas Wildman, Henry Vincent, William Lewin, John Godman, John Saunders, Robert Lewen, Charles Liming, jun., Weedon Grove, John Gyles, John Russel, Ellis Trippick.

Admission of Thomas Tower, Esq. on the surrender of Thomas Potter, 19th November, 1724, citizen and hippiatrus (farrier) who came before Mary Lee, Lady of the Manor, messuage, 30 acres land, 40 meadow, 40 pasture, &c., osiers, &c.

Admission of William Chandler of Staines, on the surrender of James Meeres, paper-maker.

Admission of Thomas Wapshot of Thorpe, Surrey, farmer, son of B. Wapshot, of Wraysbury, yeoman, deceased. This is the oldest name in these parts; Wapshote Farm being granted temp. Alfred, to Reginald de Wapshote. John Leader of Wraysbury, cited, paper maker. Gilbert Urwin, gentleman, and Mary ux. 1732.

Death of Francis Bowry; and his son is Francis Bowry. Edmund Bowry admitted by the will of his grandfather, Francis Bowry. Edmund Bowry, nephew. Will of Francis Bowry, dated 27th June, 1726, cites property bought of Mr. Robert Porter, of New Windsor; and my brother, Thomas Bowry, my second son Edmund Bowry, and his son Edmund Bowry, and his sister Mary Bowry, and Dinah. Grandson Thomas Bowry, son of Edmund Bowry, and Samuel Bowry his brother.

1732. William Harris, (distiller, son and heir of John Harris).

Surrender of Henry Pinnock and Mary ux. daughter of Ellis Trippick, dead.

On the death of John Bowry, Francis his son, an infant, was admitted; æt. 9. Francis Bowry, his uncle and guardian. Martha Sawyer, late ux. James Sawyer, and widow and relict of Ellis Trippick, dead; and Ellis Trippick is his son and heir. Francis Long of Wraysbury, tailor, was admitted on the surrender of Richard Legg of Langley. Thomas Hinton, son and heir of Thomas Hinton, dead, 1727.

Weedon Grove of Wraysbury, brazier, &c. 1726, surrender to the use of James Tillier of Harmondsworth, yeoman; Gilbert Urwin, gentleman, and Mary ux.

Esther Duck, widow of — Duck; Thomas Duck, son and heir. John Russell cuts down certain elms. Surrender conditional of Francis Long to the use of James Liming, sen. Ann was widow of said James Liming, 21st October, 1737. Francis Perkins makes a surrender.

Jury sworn, 1729, in which year Ellis Trippick was admitted on the surrender of William Harris.

Jury sworn, 1729, Joyce, lately wife of John Richardson, of St. Giles's, Cripplegate, bricklayer, granddaughter and coheiress of Susanna Wood, formerly of Wraysbury. Runwell Richardson is son and heir. Henry admitted, and again surrendered to John Thomas of Wraysbury. There are surrenders of John Russell and Richard Verry.

In 1730 there is an admission of Thomas Russell on the surrender of Thomas Haynes. Admission of Thomas Duck on the death of his mother, Esther Duck, widow.

1731. Admission of Samuel Mills on Richard Verry's surrender.

1732. Francis Bowry dies, and his brother, Edmund Bowry, is heir, and sought admission. Death of Elizabeth Pretty, and Thomas Pretty is her eldest son and heir. Thomas Duck dies and his brother Edward Duck is his heir. Christopher Clarke of New Windsor is admitted on the surrender of James Tillyar, Weedon Grove. William Winson of Hinton Marsh, yeoman, nephew and heir of William Leversedge of Wraysbury, property called Gaston's, to the use of John Russell. William Winson surrenders to the use of James Perkins of Southwark, Surrey, mealman, and John Perkins, son of James Perkins. Admission of Thomas Pretty, and the surrender of James Liming. Surrender of John Leader. Judith ux. John Leader. John Meale, son of John Meale, Seneschall. Samuel Mills admitted 1731. In 1731 the jurors appoint 25th October for *staking* day, and the meeting to be at 9 in the morning at the George Inn, Wraysbury, on pain of 1s forfeit for non-attendance. Judith Leader, widow of John Leader, admitted. His will dated 13th March last past. Death of Samuel Bowry and his wife Elizabeth, and their son, Francis Bowry, admitted. Surrender of Samuel Bowry to Robert Style of Iver, gentleman (since deceased).

It appears that Gilbert Urwin and Mary ux. were at a Court held for this manor, 7th December, 1674, and were admitted tenants; bought lands of Thomas Matthews and Martha ux., which had been bought of James Parkes, 38 acres of land are herriotable, and that 2 herriots are due to the Lord of the Manor, viz. the best living or dead goods. Relief on the death of Thomas Child, of Richmond, Surrey.

1734. Death of Christopher Clarke, and his brother's admission, viz. Samuel Clarke. Thomas Pretty surrendered by the *rod* into the hands of the Lord, by the hands of Christopher Clarke and Samuel Verry.

1735. Samuel Clarke surrenders to Martha Lisney of New Windsor. Satisfaction on surrender of Samuel Bowry to Robert Style of £157. 10s, 10th October, 1733. Elizabeth Stanney, Anna Peeling, and Hannah Styles, executors of will and residuary legatees of Robert Style. Elizabeth Bowry and Francis Bowry admitted on the surrender and will of Samuel Bowry deceased.

1737. Death of James Liming. Death of William Chandler. Edward Duck surrendered to Mary Pinnock, spinster; and Joseph Russell admitted on the surrender of Francis Long.

1738. Death of Mary Adkins, widow of Samuel (son of Ambrose Adkins) whose only son is William Adkins, now æt. 16, was admitted by John Burcombe, his guardian. Ann Chandler admitted under the will of William Chandler, her late husband; will dated 9th October, 1728.

z

1739. Dinah Bowry admitted on will of her father, Edmund Bowry. Edmund Bowry, jun. came to Court, cites deed poll, 8th November, 1739, of Thomas Virgo and Mary ux. daughter of Edmund Bowry, sen., son of Francis Bowry.

1740. Additional surrender of Thomas Pretty to James Belson, of Wood Street, London, for £55. 10s.

1741. James Perkins of St. Mary Magdalen, Bermondsey, mealman, admitted on the surrender of Francis, son of John Bowry. Admission of Mary Ann and Sarah Leader, daughters and co-heirs of Judith Leader.

1742. John Harris, maltster, admitted on surrender of Francis Thomas, son of John Thomas. Francis Bowry, son of Samuel Bowry, admitted on the surrender of Elizabeth and Francis Bowry. Elizabeth, widow of Samuel Bowry, and Francis Bowry, brother of Samuel. Francis Bowry surrenders to the use of Mary Mackay of Staines, widow, for £250. John Russell and Ann ux. late Ann Bond.

1743. Thomas Tower, Esq. surrenders property of 45 acres in the occupation of William Weyland, and some land belonging to Lady Salter and Gilbert Unwin, gentleman. Also some land surrendered by Thomas Potter, citizen and farrier of London. Surrendered to the use of Sir Philip Hall of Upton, Kt., and Thomas Powell, of the Six Clerks Office, gentleman. Indenture tripartite of 17th October 1728, between Philip Harcourt, Esq., and Henry Hall, Esq., and Sarah Hall, daughter of said Henry Hall, and John Wiseman, Esq. and Thomas Tower. John Harris surrenders to John Russell and Shadrach Child, senior, to the use of his will, 8th March 1742. Deaths of Dinah Bowry and Ann Liming.

1744. Edmund Bowry admitted in trust, 12th October 1743, by will of Dinah Bowry, daughter of Edmund Bowry, her sister Catherine Bowry, brother Thomas Bowry. Surrender of Shadrach Child to John Wyeth. Elizabeth Pretty, widow, and James Belson to Henry Bullock of Poyle, gentleman. William Adkins, gentleman, surrenders to will. Lands bought by Ambrose Adkins, grandfather of William Adkins, of John Gibbons. Surrendered to the use of Walter Holt of Holborn, gentleman, £1050. Acknowledgment of satisfaction by Mary Mackay to Francis Bowry, son of Samuel Bowry, and Elizabeth ux., followed by a recovery between Francis Bowry and Henry Bullock, and the surrender of Francis Bowry to William Pearson. William Gibbons cited in the deed. William Pearson of Horton, admitted, paper-maker.

1745. It is presented by the homage that Thomas Bowry, grandson of Francis Bowry, a customary tenant, surrenders to Silvester Andrews, of Colnbrook, gentleman. Edward Bowry surrenders to John Harris, 21st Oct. 1747. Satisfaction. William Adkins surrenders to Walter Holt of Holborn, London, £366. 0s 10d. Death of George Urwin, gentleman; sister, Elizabeth Urwin ux. William Nicholls; will 27th July, 1740, of George Urwin. Admitted. To go to the heirs and assignees of William Nicholls. Mary Herbert admitted, ux. James Herbert, granddaughter of James Liming, whose will dated 18th March, 1732. Death of Thomas Bowry.

1746. John Wyeth, of Hartley Waspell, Southton, yeoman, and William Wyeth. Satisfaction from Shadrach Child. John Winch died, and Ann Winch, spinster, daughter is admitted, who surrendered to the use of her will. Francis Bowry, of Denham, admitted as eldest brother and heir of Thomas Bowry. Shadrach Child and Elizabeth Verry die; daughter of — Child. Elizabeth Child, spinster, daughter of Shadrach Child, produced her father's will, dated 19th Dec. 1744, and is admitted; and surrenders to the use of John Russell. Satisfaction admitted. William Nicholls surrenders to the use of his will.

1747. Walter Holt, by deed poll, acknowledges satisfaction of William Adkins, 1744, and

William Adkins is admitted and surrenders to Ellis Trippick, and he surrenders to Peter Style, gentleman of Chippenham, Burnham. Henry Bullock is admitted, and Samuel Mills surrenders to his will. William Adkins surrenders to Ralph Carter, miller, of Wraysbury, and to Joseph Adkins. Edmund Bowry, junior, surrenders to John Harris. License to demise the Bridge lands (trustees Thomas Tower, Esq., Ellis Trippick, and Henry Pinnock) to John Russell for 21 years.

1748. Thomas Russell surrenders to John Maxwell, gentleman of Colnbrook. Sarah Keterich, widow, of Hampsted, Middlesex, administrix of goods of Silvester Andrews of Colnbrook, receives satisfaction of Francis Bowry, of Denham, Bucks. Francis Benny surrenders to Mathew Palmer, of Ditton Stoke, yeoman, £51. 5s. Ann Fisher, late ux. — Fisher, and widow of William Chandler, whose will dated 9th Oct. 1728. William Chandler admitted and surrenders. Samuel Verry and Ann Russell die; widow of John Russell. Thomas Read of London, gentleman, admitted. Shadrach Child admitted on death of Elizabeth Child, spinster. Thomas Child, brother of Shadrach.

1749. John Harris, maltster, receives satisfaction on conditional surrender made by Edmund Bowry, jun. John New, husbandman; daughter, Mary New, ux. John New; daughter of Henry Russell, widow of John Russell.

1750. Thomas Reed, gentleman, surrendered to John Russell.

1751. Mary Stanney admitted, and Martha Pinnock, daughter of Henry Pinnock, admitted. Will of Ellis Trippick, 2nd May, 1752. John Maxwell receives satisfaction from Thomas Russell, £40.

1753. William, son and heir of Samuel Adkins, after admission surrenders to John Norton of New Windsor. Deed citing a marriage to take place between Martha Pinnock and Robert Style of New Windsor, gentleman, and they were subsequently admitted as tenants. Death of James Perkins, whose will dated 26th October, 1752; nephew, Stephen Brown, property in Wraysbury; daughter, Sarah Perkins; grandson, Francis, son of Francis Perkins, and Sarah ux.; grandaughter, Mary Perkins, daughter of Francis Perkins. Stephen Brown admitted. Will of Dinah Bowry, 26th February, 1742, daughter of Edmund Bowry. Catharine Bowry admitted. Francis Bowry, conditional surrender to Elizabeth Style for £50.

1754. Thomas Russell, dead, and Mary Pinnock, dead.

1755. Complaint by presentment that the water-course in Colnett river at the mill is penned up so high by Ralph Carter, that Wraysbury Common has been flooded, and so the ford is dangerous.

1756. Mary Pinnock, dead, devised by her will her property to Martha, ux. Robert Style, gentleman; her daughter, said Mary, was sister of Ellis Trippick.

23rd October, 1758. Presentment that Francis Bowry, of Horton, held Brome's Corner, and there felled and carried off 80 trees *sans licence* of the Lord; and satisfaction was made.

1756. Surrender of Anne Winch to Samuel Martin, her future husband; and they were admitted and surrendered to Richard Styles. Death of Roger Jenyns, 1753, will dated 4th August, 1753. Son, John Harvey Jenyns, who is admitted, paying £400. George Child, dead, and Shadrach Child is his cousin. Ralph Carter, dead. Elizabeth Brunson, late Elizabeth Perkins. Elizabeth, ux. William Nicholls, dead. Presented that the water at Colnett Mill is dammed up by Richard Streatley the tenant.

1759. Elizabeth Brunson, dead, and Nanny is her daughter and heir; and is admitted. Samuel Pope admitted on death of Ralph Carter.

1760. Death of Robert Prowse Hassel, Esq. Surrender to William Gyll, Esq. and John

Stracey, and their heirs, who were admitted. William Trumball, Esq. dead, leaving one child, Mary ux. Hon. Colonel Sandys.

1761. Will of Martha Lisney, 24th April, 1758, devises property in Wraysbury to Hannah Avery, now ux. James Burt, admitted and surrenders to Joseph Burt, apothecary, and John Peyton, in trust, latter a stationer in London. John Norton admitted, and surrenders to John Harvey Jenyns, Esq. Catherine Bowry surrenders to Joseph Adkins, cordwainer. Trustees of Bridge Trust Lands: William Gyll, Esq., Shadrach Child, Richard Style, and Thomas Crowder. William Gyll, Esq. and John Stracey surrender to Thomas Constable, of Abchurch Lane, gentleman, who again surrenders to William Gyll. Henry Bullock, dead, and John Bullock is his son and heir of full age. Death of Thomas Powell, Esq., seized of the moiety of Hythe End Farm, and that Harcourt Powell, Esq. is his son and heir, and of full age.

1764. Surrender of Francis Bowry, of Horton, gentleman. Surrender to Nathan Mathews and Christian ux. William Nicholls surrenders to William Whitmore, of Shepperton, Esq.

1765. Thomas Pearson is son of William Pearson; will dated 18th March, 1763, makes William Gyll his trustee for his Wraysbury estates. Daughter Susanna, and sons Thomas and James Pearson. William Gyll admitted on trust.

1768. Thomas Beauchamp admitted by virtue of the will of Thomas Russell. James Trout admitted. Sampson Stephens and Hannah ux. late Russell. Admission of James Harrison, of London, stable-keeper, on surrender of William Nicholls, of Sunbury, Middlesex, gentleman, who was admitted at Court 9th October, 1745. James Harrison paid a fine of £50 to the Lord, and on his surrender William Gyll, Esq. was admitted. On the surrender of James Harrison, William Dingley and John Chandler are admitted. Admission of Thomas Rolfe, of Staines, maltster, on surrender of John Harvey Jenyngs, gentleman. Francis Bowry on death of his father Francis Bowry. Admission of Harcourt Powell, Esq. on death of his father Thomas Powell, Esq. Harcourt Powell, Esq. admitted on surrender of Thomas Tower, Esq.

1769. Ann Martin surrenders to uses. Mary Sanders and Elizabeth Goldsmith admitted, under will of Ann Martin, widow of Samuel Martin; her sisters-in-law. John Harvey Jenyns, Esq. of Eye, Suffolk, son of Roger Jenyns, surrendered to the use of Thomas Rolfe of Staines, Middlesex. William Gyll, Esq. surrenders to will. Death of Mary Sandys, widow of Colonel Sandys; and William Trumball Sandys is son and heir, and is admitted.

1772. Elizabeth Goldsmith surrenders to Mary Sanders, and Francis Bowry surrenders to John Nowell. Death of Mary New wife of John New, who were admitted in 1749, and John New is son and heir. Thomas Rolfe surrenders to William Whitmarsh.

1773. Samuel Pope surrenders and suffers a recovery. Samuel Pope and Stephen Edmonds surrenders to Simon Sanders.

1775. William Adkins surrenders to William Whitmarsh, and John Bullock of Poyle, Esq. to Jeffrey Tucker, of Wraysbury. John Dalton and Mary ux. late Stanney, surrenders to William Wilmot. Thomas Rolfe, conditional surrender to Richard Howell, who was admitted; and he surrenders to Richard Smith of Stonwell. Nanny Brunson surrenders for suffering recovery; daughter and heir of Elizabeth Brunson, daughter of Francis Perkins, to the use of Thomas Jarvis of Longford, Middlesex, auctioneer. A surrender also by said Nanny Brunson to Joseph Adkins.

1777. Admission of Elizabeth Tanner under will of Jeffrey Tucker, his will dated 1775, bequeaths to Elizabeth, his daughter, ux. William Tanner, of Wraysbury, labourer. John New surrenders to Nathanial Mathews. Death of Thomas Rolfe, and of Mary Dalton wife of John Dalton, formerly Mary Stonney, widow, niece of Ellis Trippick.

1779. Admission of Mary Keene under the will of James Perkins, her grandfather. Robert Style and Martha ux. late Martha Pinnock, surrenders to William Gyll, Esq. Here are mutual surrenders between William Gyll and Martha Style.

1781. Admission of Mary Boult (heir of Mary Stonney, afterwards Mary Dalton) wife of Stephen Boult. Mary Singer admitted under the will of Thomas Rolfe. Shadrach Child and Catherine Mills, dead.

1782. Deaths of Joseph Burt and John Peyton.

1783. Death of Mary Saunders, widow. Surrender of Simon Saunders. Surrender of Thomas Beauchamp, of Hatton Church, Bedford, and Mary ux. to William Taylor, who surrenders to William Thomas, copper-roller.

1787. Death of William Trumball Sandys, Esq., and that Mary ux. of Arthur Hill, Lord Fairford, sister and heir of William Trumball Sandys. Death of Harcourt Powell, Esq. and that John Harcourt Powell is his eldest son and heir. Admission of Mary Reeves and Sarah Lyons. Death of Samuel Verry, grandson of John Verry; daughters of Samuel Verry. Nathaniel Mathews surrenders to William Combes. Joseph Bradley of Horton, labourer, and Mary ux. and John Meredew, of Datchet, and Sarah ux. surrenders to Thomas Ashby. Thomas Harris admitted on the death of William Dingley, and surrenders to Thomas Marshall. Deaths of Mary Sanders and Elizabeth Goldsmith, and admission of Simon Sanders and Mary Novell. Surrender of Martha Style to Robert Style, her son. Thomas Harris surrenders to Thomas Ashby, who was admitted to lands near the Thames, eyots, &c. Death of William Sandys, Esq. and the admission of Lady Fairford. Death of William Perkins; daughter Mary ux. John King. John Peacock and John Cowderoy admitted under will of William Perkins.

1788. John Barrington, Esq. son of Fitzwilliam Barrington, admitted as trustee for the will of Harcourt Powell, Esq. whose will is dated 20th March, 1776. Joseph Snow and Simon Saunders admitted under will of Shadrach Child. John Herbert, son of Mary Herbert, widow, admitted intail under will of James Liming. Mary Reeves and Sarah Lyons surrender to John Taylor, of Peter Street, Golden Square. William Combes, brewer, surrenders to John Chippendale of Harmondsworth, brewer. Mary Lady Fairford surrenders to uses. Lord Fairfax, represented by Robert Mackason, his attorney, prays admission.

1791. William Gyll, Esq. surrenders to William Augustus Towsey, of Thames Street, gentleman, son and heir of Susannah Towsey, ux. Charles Towsey of Wantage, Berks, gentleman, daughter and devisee of William Pearson of Horton, Bucks, paper-maker; a recovery was suffered by Towsey, and he surrenders to John Godwin, of Datchet, butcher.

1794. Hannah Burt surrenders to Josiah Monnery, senior, and Josiah Monnery, junior, who were admitted. Joseph Parker admitted on surrender of John Chippendale. William Whitmarsh, of Wraysbury, blacksmith, surrenders to Edward Winder, of Burnham, yeoman. Admission of Joseph Adkins under will of his father Joseph Adkins. Thomas Porter on the surrender of Shadrach Trotman; and Robert Singer and Mary ux. daughter of Thomas Rolfe, surrender to Thomas Buckland, yeoman.

1795. Nathaniel, son of Nathaniel Mathews admitted; and Thomas Buckland on surrender of James Trout. Admission of Mary Haines on death of her father. Rolfe, William and Mary Haines surrender to Thomas Buckland. Robert Style surrenders to Nathaniel Wilmot. Death of Shadrach Child, and Shadrach Trotman admitted on his death and under his will, and Elizabeth Trotman admitted. George Urwin presented on death of his mother Mary Urwin, and her husband Gilbert Urwin. This is followed by a recovery between George Urwin, gentleman, and Edward Gilbourne. Property bought of Thomas Mathews and Martha ux. now in tenure of John Winch and Joseph Sanders. Henry Pinnock named in the deed, and is admitted, and Edward Gilbourne demanded against him.

1799. Thomas Porter's admission on surrender of Shadrach Trotman. Mary Boult's surrender to Richard Dalton, gentleman. Death of Josiah Monnery, and his son Josiah Monnery admitted, and William Monnery admitted on the death of his father Josiah Monnery, leather-seller of London.

1800. Nathaniel Wilmot on the surrender of William Wilmot; and Mary Wilmot's admission on the death and under the will of Simon Saunders. Mary Gyll, widow of William Gyll, Esq. admission for her life. Mary Boult surrenders to Richard Dalton, who was admitted. Joseph Packer surrenders to William Thurbin, brewer, of Harmondsworth. Samuel Hugh Mills on the death of Catherine Mills. Nathaniel Wilmot surrenders to Richard Shirley for securing £200 and interest. License to John Peacock and John Cowderoy, trustees for Mr. King, to demise their copyholds for 21 years. Nathaniel Mathews surrenders to his will.

1801. William Perkins, dead, by a Court Baron held 6th December, 1787; will dated 2nd March, 1784; daughter, Mary King ux. John King. She died without issue, and the property was bought by Thomas Williams, Esq. who was admitted. He had Goddard's lands. Admission of the Marchioness of Downshire for life, on death of the Marquis of Downshire, her husband; lands were surrendered with homage presented, 3rd June, 1784. Martha Shirley, acknowledgment of satisfaction on surrender of Nathaniel Wilmot, wheelwright, to her late husband, Richard Shirley, of Horton, Bucks. Nathaniel Wilmot surrenders to Richard and William Ashby as tenants in common. Arthur Harding surrenders to William Chandler, eyots at Hythe End, &c. and he surrenders to Thomas Ashby; and again, William Chandler surrenders to Charles Bell of Maiden Lane, Covent Garden. The Homage presents the death of Thomas Williams, Esq. Nathaniel Wilmot surrenders to Thomas Buckland for securing £1200. Shadrach Trotman surrenders to Thomas Buckland for securing £200. William Taylor, deed of surcharge to William Thomas for securing sum of £250.

1804. Nathaniel Mathews surrenders to William Virgoe, and he is admitted, was of Langly Marsh, gentleman.

1807. Nathaniel Wilmot surrenders to Thomas Buckland, and his admission, and he surrendered to John Blagrove, Esq. Richard Style surrenders to Thomas Buckland piece of copyhold of 16 acres, No. 206 on the award map, by the Colnet or Colne stream, or Mill river. Fine £27, on which a further surrender is made to John Blagrove, Esq. Shadrach Trotman surrenders to Thomas Buckland. Richard and William Ashby presented for penning up the water of Colne too high. N.B.—The first General Court Baron and Court of Survey of John Blagrove, Esq., Lord of the Manor of Wraysbury, Tuesday, 17th February, 47 George III. 1807.

1808. Robert Style of Wraysbury, eldest son of Richard Style, and Martha ux. daughter of — Pinnock, surrenders to John Blagrove, Esq. Owen Williams admitted under will of his father, Thomas Williams, Esq. William Wright surrenders to William Grace, and Thomas Buckland to John Longman, of New Windsor, baker. William Taylor surrenders to Richard Taylor, of Colnbrook, tailor. John Harcourt Powell, Esq., license to fell timber. William Virgoe surrenders to Francis Buckland his nephew.

1812. Robert Style, conditional surrender to Richard Pope, admission on death of William Whitmarsh and Ann ux.; and a subsequent surrender of Robert Style to George Leno, who surrenders to William Virgoe, for securing £200 and interest; and Virgo Buckland is presented as heir at law of Thomas Buckland.

1813. Power of attorney from John Henry Powell, jun. to Joseph White, 26th March, 1813, late Cornet in 10th Light Dragoons. They suffer a recovery, and a surrender is made to Sir William Parker and Joshua Grigby. Charles Bell, a copyhold at Hythe End, surrendered to Daniel Sills. Sir William Parker and Joshua Grigby surrender to John Blagrove, Esq. John Taylor surrenders to John Blagrove, Esq. (John Taylor admitted tenant, 13th June, 1788, on surrender of Mary Reeves and Sarah Lyons). Edmund Winder admitted on surrender of William Whitmarsh, and he with Richard Style surrenders to John Blagrove, Esq. Death of Thomas Buckland. Elizabeth Tanner, presentment of sale to Thomas Buckland.

1814. Ann, ux. Thomas Buckland, by virtue of his will dated 6th May, 1812, gives all his Wraysbury freeholds which he bought of Shadrach Trotman, and Edward Newman, and William Haynes and ux. Mary, admitted 1799.

1815. Admission of Thomas Ashby, under will of Thomas Ashby, his father, 32 acres in Queen's Mead, No. 238. Robert Style surrenders to William Virgoe, and he to John Blagrove, Esq.; and admission of William Virgoe, William Hagar, and William Thomson as trustees to Thomas Buckland, as part of his estate.

1816. Admission of William Ashby under will of Thomas Ashby. Admission of Robert Ashby, Robert and William Ashby surrender to John Blagrove, Esq. Philip Bridger admitted as trustee under will of John Novell.

1819. Death of Josiah Monnery, and admission of William Monnery, his brother. William Thomson surrenders to Henry Emlyn. Death of William Virgoe. Admission of Charles Hewlett by surrender of William Thomas and Ann Buckland. Admission of Joseph Davis. John Longman surrenders to John Glynn. Admission of Frederick Thurbin on the death of William Thurbin. Fine arbitrary £25. 4s. Surrender to Thomas Billings of Dover Street, Piccadilly. Deaths of Joseph Adkins, John Godwin, Elizabeth Tanner. Surrender of George Leno to Frances Rolfe. Philip Bridger surrenders to James Passingham. Death of William Virgo.

1822. Surrender of Frederick Thurbin and Thomas Billings to William Harris of Staines, brewer, admitted, fine arbitrary £18. 18s. Admission of John Godwin under will of his uncle, John Godwin. Death of Richard Dalton presented; and admission of Thomas, son of Elizabeth Tanner, who surrenders absolutely to Virgo Buckland. Death of Mary Gyll, holding under will of William Gyll, Esq. Brooke Hamilton Gyll, Esq. admitted. Charles Hewlett surrenders to Richard Stanton of Islington.

1823. Admission of Joseph Adkins and Susan Adkins. Admission of Susan Richards. Joseph Adkins surrenders to Robert Butler, and John Glynn surrenders to Robert Butler. Admission of Ann Buckland, Mary Roberts, Ann Birks, Catherine Bowry Minchin on the death of William Virgo, who surrenders to William Thomson. Proclamation for the heirs of William Gyll, Esq.

6th June, 1828. A General Court Baron of James Bradshaw, Hugh Parkins, and Augustus Hill Bradshaw, Lords of the Manor of Wraysbury. Surrender of Susan Adkins to Robert Morgan. Surrender of Mr. William and Mrs. Susan Richards to Thomas Jackson. Will and death of Mary King, and admission of Mr. and Mrs. Cox under will of Mary King. Surrender of Hannah and Mary Porter to James Sexton. Death of Robert Style, and his place filled up in Bridge trust, fine £24. Deaths of Ann Buckland, William Taylor, and Richard Taylor. Third proclamation for the heirs of William Gyll, Esq. but no one comes. Conditional surrender from James Passingham to Thomas Jackson, to secure £200. Ditto from William Taylor to Dr. Robert Pope of Staines, M.D. to secure £600.

12th Sept. 1828. Brooke Hamilton Gyll, Esq. produced the will of William Gyll, Esq., dated

Dec. 1795. Homage find that Mary and William Gyll the younger, are both dead, and that Brooke Hamilton Gyll is heir-at-law, and he is admitted, and surrenders to John Henry Howard preparatory to a recovery, and Ralph Colley Smith, gentleman, comes and complains against John Henry Howard of a plea of land, &c. and the land is surrendered by Brooke Hamilton Gyll; he Gyll paying £4. 10s 8d fine certain. Presentment of the will of Virgo Buckland, dated August 1825, gives his copyhold Broxhunter to William Thomas Buckland, of Hammersmith Terrace, baker, and Francis Tanner. Admission of William Taylor as trustee in his father's will, William Taylor.

1829. John Harcourt Powell, senior, and John Harcourt Powell, junior, are admitted, and they surrendered to Randolph Horne of Staines. Suffer a recovery. Admission of Sir Fitzwilliam Barrington, Bart. as heir-at-law of his father, Sir John Barrington. Admission of Robert Style, junior, on the death of his father, Robert Style, senior.

2 Nov. 1829. At a Special Customary Court of George Simon Harcourt, Esq. Lord of the Manor, Charles Thomas Buckland, infant, and eldest son of Virgo Buckland, deceased, eldest son of Ann Buckland, widow, deceased, sister of William Virgo, and Eleanor, daughter of Hugh Jones of Trifin, Anglesea, admitted with other of his relations by marriage. Surrender of William Thomson, Francis Buckland, John Virgo Buckland, William Thomas Buckland, Joseph Davis, and Mary Ann ux. and Charles Hewlett, for whom the said Thomson is trustee, and sell their property to G. S. Harcourt for £8340. There was also a payment of £452.

1829. Conditional surrender from Charles Hewlett to the Messrs. Buckland for £290.

1831. Mary, Marchioness of Downshire, Baroness Sandys, and Arthur Blundell Sandys Trumball, Marquis of Downshire, indenture for rent, 29th November, 1800; and Thomas Williams, Esq. and Pascoe Grenfell, Esq. for £450. House of Ambrose Adkins, fine £40. Absolute surrender of Charles Thomas Buckland, an infant, to G. S. Harcourt, Esq. Ditto of William Ashby to Charles Bell, eyot in the Thames; and he to his nephew Charles Bell.

1832. Death of William Ashby. Presentment about height of the water by George Simon Harcourt, Esq., and inrolment of the award, in an action brought by Mr. Harcourt against Richard Ashby and others; water to rise only to *two* inches above the floor of the arch near Hythe End Green, and plaintiff Harcourt may set up a stone to indicate extreme height to which water may be pent. Stone distinguished by letters F.T, and by figures 1832. This was the award of Frederick Thessiger, 1st July, 1832. John Ashby admitted as devisee of the will of William Ashby his father, and Charlotte Morris admitted as devisee of William Ashby her father; fine for moiety, £50. Death of Daniel Sills presented, and his devisees Francis Buckland and Joseph Sills admitted; on the surrender of Charles Bell in 1813 he became a tenant; will dated 31st May, 1827, and 11th November, 1831. Francis Buckland and Joseph Sills surrender to Sarah Tubb, widow. William Monnery surrenders to Benjamin Clark, and William Taylor to Robert Pope.

1834. Richard Dalton, Esq. admitted in 1801 on surrender of Mary Boult: now Thos. Dalton his brother is admitted, who surrenders to B. Hamilton Gyll, Esq. James Herbert admitted intail under the will of James Liming. Death of Owen Williams, Esq.; admitted in 1808 under will of his father Thomas Williams. Death of Virgo Buckland presented, and William Harris.

1835. Thomas Peers Williams, Esq. admitted; fine £40. Sophia Harris, Robert Harris, and Henry Mills admitted as devisees of William Harris; fines £63.

1839. Samuel Hugh Mills admitted to allotment who surrenders to Francis Buckland; and Thomas Ashby surrenders to Thomas Ashby, junior. Henry Gundry admitted, and Samuel Tubb surrenders to Henry Tunnell. George Leno surrenders to Frances Rolfe, and also to Charles Gordon. Thomas Jackson to Thomas Dyson, gentleman, of Wraysbury, and John Dyson admitted.

1842. Thomas Jackson to John Hewens. Death of John Jackson. Surrender to Henry Field Wilkins. Ditto, George Leno to William Leach. Admission of William Philip Harris: will dated 8th August, 1852. Surrender to devisees. Admission of South Harris. Thomas West surrenders to Henry Lake; and John Godwin of Datchet, gentleman, surrenders to Hon. Major Henniker, in trust, for £1990, paid to G. S. Harcourt, Esq. Death of Hon. Major Henniker and Lord Henniker presented. License to South Harris to demise.

1844. By will of William Perkins, Mary King admitted, on which Daniel and Ann Cox are admitted for their lives. Daniel Perkins Cox admitted. Death of George Leno, and Mary Leno admitted.

1848. Sarah Tubb surrenders to Henry Farnell. Lord Henniker surrenders to Henry Lake, gentleman, by direction of G. S. Harcourt, Esq. Death of Thomas Tanner. Will of Charles Bell, and his widow married to George Grantham. Admission of Elizabeth Grantham. Surrender to Henry Farnell. Death of Richard Butler and Benjamin Clark, and Mary Leno. Henry Andrews admitted. Sarah Tubb surrenders to William Jennings.

1856. Lord Henniker surrenders to Seymour Neville, clerk. James Bedingfield presented. Raymond Reffell and Ann ux., late Butler, surrender to George Cornish. Henry Lake, gentleman, absolute surrender to Gordon W. James Gyll, Esq. for £525; 22nd April admitted. William and Jane Leno admitted under will of William Leno. John Francis Buckland, only surviving brother and heir of Charles Thomas Buckland, eldest son and heir of Virgo Buckland. James Sexton's death presented. Thomas Ashby, jun., presentment and enfranchisement. Conditional surrender of Sarah Tubb to Mr. Joseph Tucker for £100, for land at Hythe End. James Sexton and Mary Ann Sexton admitted. Charlotte Morris admitted, fine £50; and John Morris admitted, who surrenders to Skidmore Ashby; moderate fine, £42. Charles Hewlett to William Thomas Buckland; and William Chapman surrenders to George Cornish. Enrolment of disentailing deed of G. S. Harcourt, 20th February, 1858. Re-settlement on John Simon Chandos Harcourt, Esq. Admission of John Tucker, tanner, and his absolute surrender to Henry Bunnin of Wraysbury. Francis Buckland to Thomas Johnson, £150. 27th July, 1860, Francis Buckland of Wraysbury received £180 from B. H. Gyll, Esq. for land, about 2 acres—1 acre, 2 roods.

## THE COURT ROLLS OF THE MANOR OF YEOVENEY, MIDDLESEX,
### Date from 5 Edward VI. 1552.

In the possession of the Cathedral of St. Peter's, Westminster, 19th May, 6 Edward VI.; formerly written Zeveny, Yeveny. David Eyre, Andrew Durdant, William Baldwyn, Richard Wood, Leonard Rutter.

John Fylce died seized of a grove and wood called Cockmans. Johanna Baldnet held a barn, meadow, &c. by the death of Eleanor Hardwicke. Johanna Prince, a tent. and 6 acres land and meadow by the death of Isabella Spencer. Juliana Towte, a messuage and parcel of land in Yeveny by the death of Juliana her mother.

1554. Thomas Fylce, administrator and guardian, parcel of land, Cockmans, by death of John Fylce. Alice Towte, widow, admitted to the premises. John Towte. Leonard Rutter admitted to a croft—Penny Croft—by death of John Rutter.

1 Queen Mary. Thomas Holmes, admitted to land in Yeveny. Juliana Fewaters; Richard Fewaters admitted by death of Juliana, late wife of William Fewaters, daughter and heiress of Alice Towte. Thomas Hayward, by death of Joane Prince. Andrew Durdant, lands in Steyne Hill, Yeveny. Thomas Holmes. Robert Goode, gentleman, admitted, messuage and 8 acres, 2

meadow, and in Newlands by surrender of Jo. Hatton, gentleman, and Joan his wife, late wife of Andrew Baldnet. Robert Good had license to demise the same lands for 60 years. David Eyre, a customary tenant, lands called Greneshyll, lying in Rivol, lands in lordship of Stanwey, parcel of Yeveny manor.

3 and 4 Philip and Mary. William Gyles of Stanes died seized of a tent. and 3 acres in Yeoveny. Robert Goode died, and Peter Goode was his son and heir.

1 Elizabeth, 1558. William Gyles, son and heir of William Gyles. Margaret, ux. William Gyles, admitted on death of William Gyles. Joan Woode died seized of lands called Harchells. Robert Woode, son and heir. George Bulstrode, son of Edward Bulstrode (and Mary, daughter of Sir Richard Empson), admitted, died seized 5 acres in Yeoveny called Harechyll, and Thomas Bulstrode is son and heir. Joan Hayward and Alicia Hayward admitted on death of Robert Hayward. Thomas Bourde admitted to Towmede, Yeveny, on surrender of Edward Stockwood. Andrew Durdant. Andrew Durdant and Joan his wife admitted on surrender of Richard Fewaters. Ditto admitted to lands in Westfield, near Richard Wood's lands, lately Hayward's by surrender of William Baldwyn. Leonard Rutter admitted.

3 Elizabeth. John Stockman admitted, 1 messuage and 8 acres of land, &c. called Roundacre, lying in Bridgecroft and the moiety of a *gurges* lying in More Lane. Barne abutting on Swan Mede, north to Stanes Moor, lying in lands of Lodowicke Rede, near Bridge Croft and Stanes Moor. Andrew Durdant and William Baldwyn. John Bonyon on surrender of Alice Hayward, sister and heiress of Thomas Hayward, deceased. Homage on death of Thomas Bulstrode, Edward Bulstrode is son and heir. Robert Woode. Andrew Durdant, a surrender from David Eyre to Andrew Durdant, and extract of certain Court Rolls belonging to Yeoveny manor, the original rolls are not extant.

8 Elizabeth. Robert Woode admitted on death of Joan Symonds, widow, his mother.

14 Elizabeth. Stephen Durdant on death of Andrew Durdant. Andrew Durdant, son of Andrew Durdant.

24 Elizabeth. Ralph Durdant again renders homage, formerly William Baldwyn, to the use of Elizabeth Durdant, lately Alice Haywards. Remembrance of diverse things to be presented and recorded at the Court holden at Yeoveny, 8th October, 1585. A piece of land called Languages, of 15 acres, to which Jo. Notte laid claim, but did not substantiate it. The farmer of it was Richard Holte, who brought an action against William Symondes, Lady Gresham's tenant, about land in Swan Mede, but Symondes lost the case. The Common or Moor extends to Nott's Green, also Towtes' Green, and the stream belongs to the manor.

7 James I. Andrew Durdant admitted to Pennycroft on surrender of Alexander Barney and Judith his wife.

2nd Sept. 1626. Andrew Durdant, senior and junior, admitted on surrender of Edmund Burde.

30th August, 1634. Homage, Henry Bulstrode, armiger, Walter Holte, gentleman, and Andrew Durdant, gentleman. Henry Bulstrode took it on decease of Edward Bulstrode. Homage on death of Ralph Crewe of Southmede, near the Bush in Stanes, seven acres.

Dean and Canons of Westminster held a Court 3rd September, 1638. Andrew Durdant, William Ludgold, John Miller, gentleman, Thomas Fylce, Henry Napton, John Horne. William Offley, gentleman, son and heir of Margery Offley, deceased, daughter and heiress of Ralph Crewe, dead; and William Offley surrendered the same to the use of John Cooke for £60. It was afterwards surrendered to Henry White for £56.

Court Baron held 3rd September 1641. It was declared that Towte's Green was parcel of the manor. Henry Fielde, who held lands on the west of Stanes Church, aliened them to William Ludgolde. A true account of the acreage of Yeveny manor—total 44 acres. Harehill nine acres, and I think copyhold.

1661. John Wix admitted to lands near London Stone in the Chantry Mede on death of Thomas Wix his father. John Pettiward, Esq., and Sarah his wife (daughter and heir of Henry White of Putney) admitted.

1664. Charles Durdant, fine £22. 10s. Thomas Holte, gentleman, admitted on death of Thomas Holte, his father, to a mansion and 25 acres at Towte's. Ann Baker, widow, admitted to a cottage in Towte's Green.

1665. Joseph Sheldon admitted to all tents. of Charles Durdant (John Dolben married Catherine, daughter of Ralph Sheldon and niece of Gilbert Sheldon, Archbishop of Canterbury.)

1667. John Newland, on the surrender of Thomas Holte, gentleman. Surrender to the use of Henry Jackson by Charles Durdant, gentleman.

7th November, 1669. Names of tenants that owe suit and service: Samuel Berry, gentleman, John Pettiward, gentleman, Richard Fryer, gentleman, John Wix, gentleman, William Baker.

1664. These paid suit and service: William Steers, Henry Smith, Jacob Cornwall, John Billinghurst, Thomas Webster, Walter Moore, Richard Hipkin, John Fulmer, Obadiah Wicks.

1668. William Ludgolde, John Miller, Thomas Filce, Henry Napton, John Horne. Here is entered an account of some lands recovered to the manor by Mr. Croame.

1671. A surrender from John Newland taken before Mr. Dolben, Lord of the manor, to the use of Samuel Berry, junior, for life, and then to his heirs, and to his father Samuel Berry.

1676. John Pettyward, admitted by Mary or Sarah Pettyward his mother. Fine £25.

1680. Samuel Berry, junior, to the use of Elizabeth Newland, widow and relict of John Newland.

1687. Conditional surrender from Samuel Berry, junior, to the use of Elizabeth Newland, £978. 10s. In 1689 the surrender was found by the Homage Jury.

1681. A surrender by Sir Joseph Sheldon to Sir Thomas Meeres, Knt. and Dame Sheldon, taken by William Dolben, Lord of the Manor.

1682. The will of Anne Baker, wherein she devises her copyhold cottage, &c. to William Baker, her youngest son.

1685. John Pinchon, of New England (and of Wraysbury), his letter of attorney to William Whiteing, surrenders his lands called Cockmans in Yeovency, and William Whiteing, by virtue of the said letter of attorney did surrender the said lands called Cockmans to the use of Richard Fryer.

1703. Elizabeth Hassel, widow of Benjamin Hassel, admitted to Cockmans land, she being assignee in the Commission of Bankruptcy awarded against Peter Fryer, son of Richard Fryer, who was a tenant here in 1669.

1691, August. Walter Holte admitted, £20; Edward Birde and John Burde, £10; Henry Bulstrode, £2. 3s 4d. Total £32. 3s 4d.

May, 1664. Charles Durdant admitted on death of Andrew Durdant, £22; Ditto, Mr. Houlte on death of — Houlte, his father, £33. Total, £55.

1703. Charles Singleton, son and heir of John Singleton, admitted on death of said John Singleton; £33 fine. Mr. Steeres for lands late Wix's.

9th October, 1712. Court Baron, Sir Gilbert Dolben, Knt. and Baron, John Pettiward and

## STAINES.

As an appendix to the History of Wraysbury, the Court Rolls of Yeoveny have been added, and a few extracts from the Parish Registers of Staines have been permitted to be taken by the Rev. Mr. Stokes, the Vicar, to whom the author is much beholden for his courtesy.

The Registers begin 1688, and are even imperfect afterwards.

### Baptisms.

Susanna Maria, daughter of John Shorter, Gent. and Elizabeth, 11th Sept. 1705.
Thomas, son of Thomas Aldridge and Mary, 1707.
Elizabeth, daughter of Richard Wyat, Gent. 1709.
John, son of John Mackason, of Staines, 1713.
Andrew, son of John Mackason 1714, and Mary, daughter of ditto
James, son of John Mackason, 1717.
Elizabeth, daughter of Moses and Mary Peters, 1731.

### Marriages.

John Hudley, of Wraysbury, and Jane Bishop, 1689.
Charles Windsor and Mary Palmer, 1692.
Richard Wapshot and Mary Janaway, 1694.
Henry Pinnock, of Wraysbury, and Mary Trippick, 29th May, 1716.
Thomas Skinner, Esq., of Dorset, and Barbara Opie, of Stoke Newington, 2nd Aug. 1733.
Richard Taylor of Staines, and Ann Street of Wraysbury, 18th May, 1755.

### Burials.

Mary, wife of John Weyland, 1704.
Thomas Hearne, Gent. 1705.
Humphrey Westen of Raisbury, 1712.
Mr. Windham, 31st Jan. 1719.
Mary Windham, 1721.
Joseph Morecock, 1722.
—— his widow, 1727.
Madame Shorter, 1729.
Mr. Walden, from London, 1732.
Henry Styles, 1733.
John Ludgold, 1733.

### Burials.

Mr. Peter Estwick, 1735.
John Wolkot of Wraysbury, 1741.
Mrs. Trippot of do. 1746.
William Morecock, 1746.
Lady Bradford, wife of Theophilus Bradford, 11th Oct. 1748.
William Style, 1749.
William Wingrove, 1749.
Ann, wife of Mr. Eusebius Williams, 1750.
Theophilus Bradford, 7th Aug. 1752.
Richard Bradford, 1753.
Rev. Eusebius Williams, 1754.
Joseph Peters, 1758.
Joseph Morecock, 1761.
Henry Styles, 1763.
Elizabeth Nevill, 1763.
Thomas Hubbard, 1763.
John Goring, 1763.
Mr. James Witherstone, Vicar, 1766.
James Styles, 1766.
Mary Paxton, 1768.
Six people drowned at New Years' Bridge, Staines, in the Exeter Coach, Monday, 5th Dec. 1768.
John Styles, 1771.
Moses Peters, 1781.
Mrs. Willoughby Stevens, 1786.
Mr. George Carter, 1788.
Mr. William Palmer, 1788.
Mr. Stephen Boult, 1796.
Francis Henry Duke of Harcourt, buried 24th July, 1802.
John Edmead, 1802.
John Goring, 1806.

# APPENDIX.

### WRAYSBURY VOLUNTEERS, 1860.

| | | |
|---|---|---|
| J. P. Taylor. | William Pendry. | William Taylor (2). |
| G. Cornish. | John Holloway. | John Crook. |
| J. Green. | Robert Holloway. | George Ridgway. |
| James Horton. | John Watson. | Wm. W. Ladell, Gent. |
| John Tolley. | William Taylor (1). | |

Perhaps it would not be just to our village to omit the names of those who have enlisted as Volunteers, a body now become indispensable to the State, whereby some 150,000 men are at the service of the nation, and are most useful auxiliaries to the army.

The War Office has just issued a circular which will materially promote the efficiency of this body; the expense and machinery of its organization has been left to the Volunteers themselves for the two and a half years of their embodiment. The Government gave Enfield rifles to them, and appointed paid Adjutants to each corps. The circular will not only relieve the different corps from a large item of cost, but will provide means of instruction in the shape of drill instructors taken from the line, from pensioners, or from the disembodied militia staff, in the proportion of one to every two companies of volunteers. This body has been in need of proper and efficient instructors; the rank and file knowing more about the duty of soldiers than the officers who command them. By this system the Government does not subsidise the Volunteers, but contributes to realise useful and practical ends, the two cardinal virtues of a military force, discipline and tactics. The drill instructors are to receive liberal remuneration, and in addition to their pensions will receive 2s 4d a day, and if they have no pension, then 2s 7d. They will be subject to military law, and act under the immediate direction of the Adjutant. This domestic force is not to be under the absolute control of the Horse Guards. Thanks are due to the Secretary of State for War, for this discriminative bounty, and thanks are due by the country to Lords Elcho and Ranelagh for the ardour they have evinced in perfecting as much as was within their reach the forming and disciplining of the Volunteers, to make them fit for anything for which a soldier is fit, and ripen into a veteran. Thus with our wooden walls and hearts of oak, England never shall lie at the proud foot of a conqueror, if we are put on a par with a nation of warriors, and we give to the bravest people on earth the full use of its bravery.

### PETITION OF JONE TANNER RELATIVE TO SIR WALTER STONOR, KNIGHT.

It has been deemed useful to insert the whole of this document (page 57) as a specimen of the character of a petition in the days of King Henry VII. with the orthography and diction :—

PLEADINGS AND SURVEYS, &c. TEMP. HEN. VII. VOL. 2.

T. 2.

To the Kyng our soūcon lord.

In the most . . . . . wise scheweth unto yor highnes Jone Tanner wiffe of Thoms Tanner of ye lordschip of Wyrardesbur in the countie of [Buckingham] . . . . oñ Walter Stonor of the same countie gentilmā hath of long tyme hadde to ferme . . . . . . . land of ye seid lordschip of

Wyrardesbyr to yᵉ grett hurte . . . grace and yoʳ tennt of the same town so that wᵗhin xxvᵗⁱ yeres there beth decayid wᵗhin ye seid lordship xx . . . . . labor of late was made be the seid Thomͣs Tanner my husbond and other of yoʳ tennt to my lorde of Garlyn of Seynt Dauid and Robᵗ Southwell wᵗ other of yoʳ Surveyours of the seid lordschip to haue the same yoʳ demene lond seūed among yoʳ tennt to the Mayntennce of yoʳ tenntrys and grette awantage to yoʳ grace In fynes and other wysse to the valure of cc mc wiche yoʳ said hoñabill councell rith well p̃ceyvth and entendith the same said lond to be deuidid among yoʳ tennt wherfor the seid Walter Stonner p̃cevyng color thus may be the scid Thomͣs Tanner and other of yoʳ tennt for yoʳ emprouemet hath of his cruell mynde made laboʳ to indite theym in foreyn counteis and wᵗ threting and diūse other . . . . . grevosly trowbillyd them to put them in . . . that schuld make no ferther laboʳ for the emprouement of yoʳ seid lond wheruppon the seid Walter Stonner of late hath causid and forcid diūse p̃sons of his . . . tennt to surmyse treason on the said Thomͣs Tanner my husbond that he schuld speke obprobrious word ageynst yoʳ heynes be the space of a quarᵗ of a yer passid the wiche thing as god knoweth he never dide nor thochte and yᵗ I take god to my gogge (gage) And if he hadd so done the seid Walter Stoner nor his tennt awthe nott to have conselid treson be so long tyme frome yoʳ grace. Wheruppon he has now sedicõsli causid my seid husbond to be comittid into yoʳ prison of yᵉ Marshalse. Wherfor hit may plese yoʳ grace as well for the declarcõn of my said husbond as for the conceylemet of the said Walter Stoner and his tennt to comaund yoʳ Chaunseler of yoʳ Duchie and the scid Sʳ Robt. Southewell wᵗ other of yoʳ counsell lernyd at London be cause thei be ner yoʳ Marshalsee to haue the Examinacõn of the pmiss for the forther trewth therin to be knowen And yoʳ seid Orator shall eūmor pray for the p̃sruacē (preservation) of yoʳ grace long to induere.

Indorsed: Committitur cᵃ mrõ Hemson et
mrõ Southewell

JOHN EDNAM.

## SOME MONUMENTAL INSCRIPTIONS TO THE FAMILY OF GYLL, (pp. 5, 99.)

### EPITAPHS IN BUCKLAND CHURCH, HERTS.

"Orate pro anima Johannis Gyll qui obiit xxiii die Jan. Anno Domini Mccccxxxxix. Cujus anime propitietur Deus."

This is placed under the effigies of a man, six sons, and five daughters, in brass.

"Orate pro anima Johanne Gyll que obiit Anno Domini Milessimo . . . . . Cujus anime propitietur Deus."

With the figure of a woman in brass.

### IN THE CHAPEL NORTH OF THE CHANCEL IN WYDDIAL, HERTS.

"Hic jacet Georgius Canon gen'. nuper unus Dominorum istius ville, qui istam insulam propriis sumptibus construxit, Anno Mdxxxii. et obiit ib die Septembris, Anno xxbi. Illustrissimi Regis Henrici Octabi. Cujus anime propitietur Deus."

The arms of Canon have been torn off. The inscription is in brass, (pp. 5, 31.)

### IN THE CHANCEL OF WYDDIAL CHURCH, HERTS.

"Of poure charitye praye for the soule of John Gille, Esq. late Lorde of this towne, and Patron of the same, who departed this worlde, xb daye of Marche, in the xxxbii yere of the raigne of oure Soberaigne Lorde the Ring Henry VIII. of whose soule Jesu habe mercie."

Under him the arms of Gyll impaling Canon, and the figures of a man and woman in brass, with five sons, and eight daughters.

"Under this stone was buried George Gyll, Esquier, bringe Lorde of this towne, whiche had two wyves, be whome he had rib chyldren, and dyed the xxix daye of October, the fifty-eight yere of his age, in the yere of oure Lord God MDlxviii.

Under him arms of Gyll impaling Peryent, in brass.

"Præterita pariter atq. futura mandentur oblivioni.

"Sub isto marmore posita sunt corpora Johannis Gille Armigeri, et Johanne charissime Conjugis ejus, qui cum per spacium 37 annorum perquam amice pariter vixerunt—Ambo mense Octobris 1600 in eternam vitam per J͠sum Christum obdormierunt in pace. Relinquentes duos filios et tres filias." In brass.

IN THE CHANCEL OF BISHOP STORTFORD CHURCH, HERTS.

Arms quarterly 1st and 4th St. two chevronels A, each charged with three mullets of the 1st on a canton O, a lion passant G. 2nd and 3rd lozengy O and V, a lion ramp. guard. G. for Gyll impaling A, two bars S in chief, three buckles az. for Luther, crest on a wreath, a hawk's head eraz. az. between two wings frettée vert. for Gyll MS. The bodies of John Gill, Gent. and Dorothy his wife, lie here interred. He died June y$^e$ 4th, 1711, aged 56 years. She Jan. 23rd, 1700, aged 40. Filius natu maximus P. H. M. (p. 125.) In the same chancel of Bishop Stortford are monuments to the memories of Denny, son of John Sandford, Gent. and Ann, his wife (see page 22), and to John Denny, son of John and Cordelia Brome, William Brome and Cordelia Brome, &c.

EPITAPHS AT MAIDSTONE, KENT.

On the north side of a four-sided monument surrounded by rails in the Cemetery :—

"In memory of William Gyll, Esq. who died 10th August 1754, aged 68 years. Son of George Gyll, Esq. of Dartford and Boxley, who died 25th January 1726, and Susanna, his wife, who died 7th July 1721; of the family of Gyll, of Wyddial, Herts."

*South Side.*—" Also Elizabeth, wife of William Gyll, Esq. who died 21st April 1750, aged 60 years."

*East Side.*—" Brooke, son of William and Elizabeth Gyll, died 15th March 1744, aged 30 years."

*West Side.*—" Also four children of William and Elizabeth Gyll, who died infants."

On the top of the same monument :—

"To the memory of Elizabeth Lawrence,* widow, who died 9th October 1758, aged 91.

"Example fair of virtue truly wise
Who did the short-lived joys of sense despise,
Did humbly hope, and patiently await,
The change that doth ensue this mortal state;
Just and benevolent, thee joys attend
With bliss celestial, O thou more than friend,
May undisturbed thy ashes here remain,
Till time shall prove thou hast not lived in vain."

*Verses under the inscription on the monument of Elizabeth, wife of William Gyll, Esq. at Wyrardisbury, Bucks.*

" Long in affliction's thorny paths she trod,
Supported by just confidence in God.
Here life in every act of duty spent;
Virtuous, sincere, faithful, benevolent.
To sure reward the last great day shall raise
Her sleeping dust, and join the saints in praise."

* Elizabeth Lawrence was mother of Elizabeth, wife of William Gyll, Esq.

## GENERALIS RETORNATUS BROOKE HAMILTON GYLL, TRITAVO 1843.

The Service of B. H. Gyll, Esq. of Wyrardisbury House, Bucks, as nearest and lawful heir of line, and of the body of the Hon. Alexander Flemyng, son of John sixth Lord Flemyng, and first Earl of Wigtoun.

Hæc Inquisitio facta fuit in Curiâ Vicecomitis Vicecomitatûs de Edingburgo decimo quarto die mensis Maij anno Domini millessimo octingentesimo, quadrigessimo quarto coram Honorabili viro Georgio Tait Armigero, Advocato Vicecomite substituto dicti Vicecomitatûs per hos probos et fideles Dominos patriæ, videlicet, Christopherum Douglas Armigerum Scribam Signeto regio Cancellarium, Hamilton Gray Gardiner, Joannem Bruce et Joannem Browne Armigeros, Scribas Signeto regio, Jacobum Weir de Tollcross Medicinæ Doctorem, Capitaneum Edwardum Marjoribanks, nuper in Honorabilis Orientalis Indiæ Societatis Ministerio, Georgium Gordon Capitaneum in Honorabilis Orientalis Indiæ Societatis Ministerio, Andream Smith, Georgium Home, Andream Strachan, Davidem M<sup>c</sup>Neillie, Gulielmum Wright, Jacobum Pringle Halley, Gulielmum Currie et Davidem Telford, omnes Scribas in Edingburgo. Qui Jurati dicunt magno Sacramento interveniente, Quod Alexander Flemying, filius legitimus Joannis quondam Sexti Domini Flemyng et Primi Comitis de Wigtoun Tritavus de Brooke Hamilton Gyll Armigeri de Wyrardisbury House in Comitatu de Bucks, et Yeoveny Hall in Comitatu de Middlesex obiit ad fidem et pacem regiam, Quod dictus Brooke Hamilton Gyll lator præsentium est filius legitimus natu maximus Dominæ Harriot Janæ Flemying quæ nupsit Gulielmo Gyll Armigero de Wyrardisbury House prædicti Capitaneo in Secundo Regimento regiorum Satellitum de Life Guards ejus patri, Quæ Domina Harriot Jane Flemyng unica legitima proles fuit Hamilton Flemyng qui ad titulum Domini Flemyng durante vitâ patris ejus succedebat et super mortem ejus ad titulum noni Comitis de Wigtoun. Quis Hamilton Comes de Wigtoun filius et hæres fuit Caroli Ross Flemyng Medicinæ Doctoris Dublinensis, qui ad titulum octavi Comitis de Wigtoun succedebat anno Domini millessimo septengentesimo quadrigessimo septimo super mortem Caroli septimi Comitis tanquam propinquioris et legitiomi hæredis masculi dicti Joannis primi Comitis de Wigtoun. Quis Carolus Ross Flemyng eo postea Comes de Wigtoun filius legitimus natu secundus fuit Jacobi Flemyng Rectoris de Castlane, Kilderry, Mothell, &c. in Regno Hiberniæ, Thoma filio natu maximo dicti Jacobi præmortuo, dictus pater ejus sine legitimâ prole relinquendo. Quis Jacobus Flemyng Rector de Castlane &c. filius legitimus natu maximus fuit Jacobi Flemyng Rectoris de Ramochy vel Ray in Comitatu de Donegal in Regno Hiberniæ. Quis Jacobus Flemyng Rector de Ramochy vel Ray unicus legitimus filius fuit dicti Alexandri Flemyng. Et quod dictus Brooke Hamilton Gyll lator præsentium est propinquior et legitimus hæres lineæ et de corpore dicti Alexandri Flemyng filii dicti Joannis primiti Comitis de Wigtoun, Tritavi sui. Et quod est legitimæ ætatis. In cujus rei testimonium Sigill a quorundam eorum qui dictæ Inquisitioni intererant cum Brevi S. M. Reginæ direct. intus clausa una cum subscriptione Joannis Archibaldi Campbell Clerici dicti Vicecomitatûs de Edingburgo sunt appensa apud Edinburgum die mensis et anno Domini primo suprascript.

(Sic Subscribitur)      J. A. Campbell, Sheriff Clerk.

Hæc est vera Copia principalis Retornatûs super præmissis in Cancellariâ S. M. Reginæ remanente. Extract. Copiat. et Collat. per me Archibaldum M<sup>c</sup>Neill ejusdem Cancellariæ Directorem sub hoc meâ subscriptione.

Arch<sup>d</sup>. M<sup>c</sup>Neill, C. D.

WILLIAM GYLL, Esq. of Wraysbury House, Bucks, Captain 2nd Life Guards, married the Lady Harriet Jane Flemyng, only daughter and heir of Hamilton Flemyng, 9th and last Earl of Wigtoun, in Scotland, which entitles the issue of that alliance to bear the arms and quarterings of the noble and regally descended house of Flemyng. The College of Arms in Scotland, have also accorded to the family of Gyll, representatives of the Cadet branch of Flemyng, (whence they deduce their origin,) to bear and use the crest and motto of Flemyng, in addition to their own paternal crest; and Mr. Gyll, as eldest son of the family, had a service made to him which was duly returned to Chancery, in Edinburgh, serving him ".as nearest and lawful heir of line and of the body of Alexander Flemyng, son of John, 6th Lord Flemyng, and 1st Earl of Wigtoun." The pedigree of Flemyng has been considered, approved, and registered in the Lyon Office, with the evidence deducing their lineage, from the youngest son of the 1st Earl of Wigtoun, from which some extracts are made. The principal proof in sustentation of this descent, is an original Scotch bond still extant, dated 31st July, 1654, and afterwards registered in Scotland, in which James Fflemyng is styled " sone lawful to umquhle Alexander Fflemyng, brother-german to ane noble Earl, John, Earl of Wigtoun." This James was subsequently ordained, and became Rector of Raymochy, in the county of Donegal, Ireland, as appears by the bishop's registry and by his original marriage settlements, deposited with all the other deeds at the Register House or the Lyon Office (p. 101), 1843, Edinburgh, dated 11th Sept. 1660, in which he is styled " only son of Alexander Fflemyng, of the kingdom of Scotland, and grandson of the deceased Earl of Wigtoun." He died in 1684, and was succeeded by his son James, Rector of Castlane, Kilderry, &c. in Ireland, and Chaplain to all the Lords Lieutenants of his time there, and was buried under the communion table at Dunmore, Kilkenny, in 1729. His son Charles Ross Flemyng, on the demise, in 1747, of Charles, 7th Earl of Wigtoun, *s.p.* claimed the honours as 8th Earl of Wigtoun, and exercised all the prerogatives of his title, and at his decease, in 1769, his only son and heir, Hamilton Flemyng, followed as 9th and last Earl of that name. He died in 1809, leaving an only child, married to William Gyll, Esq. by virtue of which union, their issue are entitled to quarter the armorial ensigns of that noble house, although the honours are extinct, the Barony of Flemyng being a male fee.

Arms of Flemyng. G. a chevron within a double tressure flory, counterflory A. Gyll Quarterly. First and fourth, sa. two chevrons arg. each charged with three mullets of the field, in base, a cinquefoil of the second, on a canton or, a lion passant guardant gu. Second and third lozengy, or, and vert, a lion rampant guardant gu.

Robert, Duke of Albany, and Regent of Scotland (brother of King Robert III. son of King Robert II., grandson of King Robert Bruce), had a daughter, the Lady Elizabeth Stewart, married to Sir Malcolm Flemyng, whose son Robert was created Lord Flemyng, about 1450. His ancestor Robert Flemyng was a Peer of Scotland in 1289. His great-grandson, Malcolm, 3rd Lord Flemyng, married 26th Feb. 1524, Lady Janet Stewart, natural daughter of King James IV. of Scotland, by Agnes, Countess of Bothwell, daughter of James, Earl of Buchan, and their issue thus descend from John of Gaunt, Duke of Lancaster, who derives from King William the Conqueror.

*An omission in page 14, line 8, is here inserted.*

We find that the King granted this Manor of Wraysbury about the period of 1447-8 to Sir John Fray, Knight (p. 16), and he was succeeded here by the College of Eton in 1457, and the manor was granted to Sir Richard Wylly in 1460 (p. 14), in 1461 William Paulet had it. Pedigree of Paulet (p. 15).

I presume the grant of Wraysbury Manor to Sir William Moleyns was a few years before his death at the siege of Orleans in 1429. The words are—By the subsequent charter, 25 Henry VI. 1447, the King granted the Manor of Langley Marys, with the Manor of Wraysbury, parcel of the said manor with all the Lordships, lands, tents., &c. lately belonging to Sir Robert Hungerford, Knight, Lord Moleyns, in the town and fields of Eton, and also in the towns of Old and New Windsor, held by Robert in right of his wife Alianor, daughter and heir of Sir William Moleyns, late deceased.

The family of Hungerford was of great celebrity in Wilts at Farley, from which place they could ride to Salisbury without going off their own estates; for extensive holdings see page 69 of this history.

As the parties seem to have had a long tenure here, a detailed notice may not be irrelevant, their property being also in Stoke Poges, the adjacent parish, whose proprietary were much connected with Wraysbury.

About 1291 Robert Poges, of a patrician family, married Amicia de Stokes, hence the two names were blended. Stoke means *place*. Stoke Farm, Place Farm (p. 55.) His daughter Margaret married Sir John Molines, say some genealogists. This family was of French extraction, and one took the appellation of *Leumesin*, or Water-house, and the arms cross Moline refer to mills, denoting mill-wind, William de Molines, or of the Mills. Sir John Molines left a widow Egidia, ob. 41 Edward III. 1367, cousin and heir of John Manduit and Margaret Poges his wife. He held 12 manors in Bucks, one of which Stoke was girdled by his possessions, Datchet on one side, Fulmer, with lands in Burnham, Ditton (p. 69), and Cippenham, which was often incorporated with Wraysbury (p. 10). This Magnate seemed wedded to calamity, for in 1340 all his lands were seized and himself thrown into *durance*. Stow surmises that it was for mismanagement of the Exchequer. In 1346 he was released, and again re-cast into prison where he expired, and his son William succeeded to all but Stoke, which did not devolve to him before the death of his mother Egidia, 1367. He died in 1381, and his son in 1385, and his grandson in 1425, leaving the subject of our inquiry, the lessee of Wraysbury, Sir William de Molines, who fell at the famous siege of Orleans whilst defending a bridge against a *sortie* from the French garrison in 1429. His body was transported to England, and he sleeps in Stoke with his ancestors. His line was reduced to a daughter, Alianore, who had only attained the age of 13 when her parent was slain. Early marriages were in vogue then, as in Eastern climes where they exercise this advantage to the full, and as she was now an heiress, an orphan, and under age, some one had the custody of her marriage (p.12). Hence she is reported to have been united to Robert, Lord Hungerford, at the age of 15 years, probably betrothed only ; the Hungerfords got the estates. As the father of Alianore died by casualty in the battle-field, destiny so arranged it that her husband should experience the vicissitudes of life in war and peace. He was made prisoner in France for seven years, after his capture, consequent on the fight at Chastillon in 1453, and again on his return to his native country, he was victimised in the wars of the Roses, and at Newcastle his head paid the forfeit of his venture. His wife Alianore obtained restoration of some of his forfeited estates, and then Sir Oliver Manningham "took his stand on the widow's jointure land," with whom she lived until she calm reclined in death. Her body was consigned " to the vault of the Capulets "—where all her buried ancestors were packed—and now her time-worn grave-stone with an epitaph may yet be seen under the *piscina* by the communion table.

At this point of the chancel are to be seen four graves within the elevation around the communion table, two without and two within the rails. The grave-stone on the north side is over the burial place of Sir William and Lady Margaret Molines, he who fell at Orleans, 1429.

Two well preserved effigies remain on this grave-stone, that of Sir William Molines of Wraysbury, who is represented in his knightly armour, but with mailed hands clasped in prayer, as if to intimate the connection between the spirit of chivalry and the devotion of the Christian.

The other exhibits the effigy of Lady Margaret Molines. Catherine, daughter of William, Lord Moleyns, married John Howard, Duke of Norfolk (p. 7).

On the south side rests Lady Eleanor, daughter of Sir William Molines, and wife of the unfortunate Lord Hungerford, who by right of his wife, was lessee of Wraysbury Manor.

One of the graves has been sadly mutilated and despoiled of part of its brass, nothing can deter the sacrilegious hand of man, neither stone, wood, nor corruption itself. The inscription is in Latin, thus rendered—"Here, beneath this stone, is buried the body of the venerable Lady Alianor Molins, Baroness, who in first espousals had to her husband Lord Robert Hungerford, Knight and Baron. She afterwards married the honourable Lord Oliver Manningham, Knight, on whose souls the Lord have mercy."

Within the rails are two graves containing the remains of four of the Hampdyn family of Bucks ; and the centre grave that of Dr. Philip Gyll, doctor in physicke, tithe-holder, and parish overseer. He was buried in 1653, son of John Gyll of Northampton county, whose pedigree is printed, page 125.

Here lyeth the body of Phillip Gill, Doctor in Physicke, late of this parish of Stoke Poges, who departed this life 10th day of September in the yeare of our Lord God 1653, aged 52 yeares.

## ADDITIONAL NOTES.

Page 3. At the compilation of the Liber Censualis there were 57 Proprietors of land in Bucks and Robert Gernon is 21st on the list. [*Bochinghsire. Terra Roberti Gernon. In Stoches Hd'* ⓂROBERTUS GERNON *ten'* WIRECESBERIE *p'XX. hid' se defd'. Trā ē xxv. cār. In dnīo V hidæ 7. ibi sunt IIæ. cār' 7. XXXII. uilli cū XVIII. bord' hn̄t XV. cār 7. adhuc VIII*[o] *cār pōss. fieri. Ibi VII. serui II. molini de XL. p'annū ptu V. cār 7 fenū ad animalia curiæ. Silua q'ngent' porc' 7 IIII. piscār in Tamesia de XXVII. sot' IIII. den min'. In totis ualent' uat' 7 ualuit XX. lib' TRE XXII. lib'. Hoc.* Ⓜ *tenuit Edmund' teign' RE. Lib. Censual. Tom. I. f.* 149.

Page 4. 10 Edw. 1. 12 R. comīsit Cristiane de Mariscis Maner' R. de Langele & Wyrardebir' cum ptin' tenend de R. ad firmam quamdiu R. placuerit redd' inde R. p annum centum et decem libras, &c. Rot. 2. Abbr. p. 40.

Testa de Nevill, p. 261. D'. Galfro de Marisco ij m̄r' d uno feodo in Linford Buk.' of the honour of Wallingford.

Page 5. Idem esc' de exit' Maner de Langele & Wyrardbury, (Wyrardebury, Wyrardesbury, Wyrardisbury), cum pertin' que fuerunt Edmundi frīs R. & Aveline uxoris sue defuncti de heredibus ipsius Aveline cum omnibus inde precept' medio temporē, &c. Rot. 3. Abbreviatio Rotulorum Originalium 1 Edward I. son of Henry III. p. 22, Vol. I. 3 Hen. III.

Page 8. Orig. VI. Edward II. p. 194. R. comīsit Rogō de Norwode Manerium de Baketon, Norfolk, &c. Manerium de Cypenham cum hameletto de Eton & Manerium de Langeleye cum Wyrardisburi cum pertin. in Com Buck' custodiend' quamdiu R. placuerit. Rot. 6.

Page 9. Extract' grossor' finium. Edward II. 12 Edward II. p. 252. R. constituit Humfrm̄ de Waleden senescallum R. castrorum, &c. vidett' Man'ii de Brustwyck, &c. Man'iorum de Chippenham & Langelo Mareys cum hameletto de Wyrardebury cum pert' in com Buk' parci de Wyndesore cum pert' in com Berk', &c.

Page 9. Edward II. Extract e finium Cancell' de S'c'da parte de anno, &c. 17, p. 276. R. constituit Humfridum de Waleden et Ricm̄ de Ikene senescallos R. castrorum, &c. vidett Man'ii de Brustwyk cum ptin' Castrī, &c.

Man'ii de Chippenham cum ptin' Man'ii de Langeleye Mareys & Wyrardesbury cum ptin' Man'ii de Fulmere cum ptin' Man'ii de Bolecroft (Bulstrode) cum pert in com Buk', &c.

Testa de Nevill temp. Edw. II. p. 245. Dn̄s Ric̄s de Mūfichet tenet Langele cū Waredesbur' in capite de Dn̄o Rege ptinentes ad baroniam suam de Stanstede in com' Essex' nec inde facit Militare Sviciū.

P. 260. Heres. Ric̄i de Munfichet tenet Langeley.

Page 10. In Origin' de anno R. E. fil' *R. E.* XVIII. p. 281. R. &c. Saltm Sciatis qd constituimus Ricm̄ de Wynferthyng & Ricm̄ de Ikene senescallos n̄ros castrorum, &c. vidett, Man'ii de Brustwyk cum pt', &c. Man'ii de Chippenham cum ptin Man'ii de Langeley Mareys in Wyrardesbury cum ptin' Man'ii de Fulmere, cum ptin Man'ii de Bolecroft cum ptin in com Buk'.

Page 10. Extract o Rot. C'rar' Sub sigillo tam Regine et Ducis, &c. anno r. R. f. R. E. XX[o] applicuerunt, &c. Roll 15, page 305. Edward II. R. commisit Johñ de Shobonangre Custodiam Man'iorum R. de Cippenham, Langeley Marays et Wyrardesbury tiend quamdiu, &c. Johēs de Shobenhangre de Custodia Man'ii de Wycomb. cum pert £62 per ann.

Page 10. In Orig. de anno RR. Edwardi t'cii XLIX. Rot. I. p. 335. R. commisit Robto. le Smyth, custodiam Man'ii de Wyrardesbury cum ptin. in com Buk tiend ad finem decem annorum reddo iñde R. p ann' quadragiñta et quatuor libras, &c.

Page 10. Edw. III. In orig' de anno r. r. Edw. t'cii 50. R. p bono servicio quod Henry atte Water hostiar' Aule R. fecit, impendit, &c. Commisit ei custodiam Man'ii de Wyrardesbury com ptn̄ in Com. Buk' tiend usque ad finem decem annorum reddo inde R. p[r] ann' quadraginta, & quatuor libras, &c.

Page 14. In Orig' de anno. r. r. Edwardi I. t'cii post conquestum xxiiij (1350). Rot. 32. p. 212. Vol. II. Ricūs de Glouc' heres Isabelle de Duton dedit et concessit dño Edwardo Regi Angl' et Franc' et heredbz & assignatis suis unū messagiū, decem et septem acras t're et unam acram pti et tres solidos redditus in villa de Wyrardesbury in com. Buck'. Et predictus Ricūs warrantizabit, &c.

Page 56. De redisseisinis Edward III. 43 (1369), Roll 17, p. 310, Vol. II. Abbr. Rot. Le roi ad g' ante et a ferme lesse a Johan Jourdelay et Thomas Remenham de Wyrardesbury, les maisons de son Manoir de Wyrardesbury en le comitee de Buk, cesassovoir une veille salle et une boverie coṽtz de streyin, et une graunge coṽte de tegle, ove les gardyns adjoingnantz; et ove deux centz et trent et sept acres et une rode de trē arable, et seize acres trois rodes et set pches de pasture severable, prticulierement gisantz in Radelakeneyt quatorze acres, &c. đi en Warneslade đi acre et set pches, et en Gosmere une acre et trois rodes ensemblement, ove une piece de feble et seckepree appelée le Westmede, contenant quindize acres et đi, a avoir et tenir au fin de trent ans rendant oet livres dest' linges et sustendront touz les maisons, &c.

Et ils au'ont resonables housbote, &c. deinz le Park de Langele Mareys p vewe.

Page 194. *Bockinghsire—Domesday Book, Vol. I. F. 151. Terra Walterij Filij Other in Stoches. Hund'—. Hortune—(the 30th on the list of Owners). Walterius filius Otheri ten STOCHES. p X. hiđ se defđ. Trā ē IX. cār. In dn̄io II. hide 7. ibi sunt II. cār. 7. XV. uilli cū V. bord. hn̄t VI. cār 7. VII.ma pot' fieri. Ibi IIII. Serui 7. I. molin' de XX. Sot. patū III. car'. In totis ualent nat. VI. liƀ. q̄ndo recēp L. sot TRE. VI. liƀ. Hoc. Ⓜ Eldred hō Stig' archiepi 7. uend' pot'.*

Witts de Windeshore tenet medietate ville de HORTON in capite de dño Rege & ptinz ad medietatē baronie sue de Wyndeshore quā defendit p. Ward scitz. p xl. dies p—Castri de Wyndeshore XVI.ˢ VIII.ᵈ.

Pret'ea infra illam medietatē ville de Horton Adam de Horton tenet de dc̄o Witto q̄rta prte uni' feodi.

Aliam vero medietatē ville de HORTON pñoiātus Witts tenet de Hug' de Hodengf' & Thom' de Lacell' reddendo eis annuati unū par calcarioz deauratoz.

Witts de Wyndlesor' debet VI. milit' & di'. Duncann' de Lascell' & Rad' Hoddeng—deb VII. milit & di'.

Abbrev. Placit. p. 306. Henr' Chelsey p cartam suā dat dño Henr' Spigurnell mit & heredbz suis XXI. Sot. v den. redđ. Simul cum omnibz. aliis redditibz & serviciis de omnibz tenentibz suis in Hortone & Stanewell—temp. Edw. II.

Abb. Pl. p. 89. Walter' de Upenour dicit in placitando q̄d cōia pasture in Horton partita fuit gratis int' tenentes. Witti de Windlesore in eadē villā ita q̄d quelibet hida habuit secundū q̄d habere debuit.

Do. p. 319. Rela' Roƀti fit & her' Rogi de Suthcote facta Henrico Spigurnell mit de toto jure suo in omnibz terris & ten' in Chalfhunte Sc̄i Petri Chalfhunte Sc̄i Egidii Isnamsted Cheyney que quondā fuer' Thome de Aignenz.

In the Rolls of the Hundreds, temp. Henry III. and Edward I. Vered'cm de Langl.—Dic'q̄d Ric. de Munfichet tenet Langl' de dño Rege ptin ente ad baron' Suā & dic q̄d đns Ric' habet visū franpleg' set nessim' q° waranto. Villata solvit-pannū đni Rege p hidagio XXXVIII. s. & dat se sect V.s.

Vered'cm de Horton—Dic q̄d đns Ric de Oxeye tenet Villā de Horton de Witto de Winđs. & Walt'o de Willesdē de dño Rege in capite ptinente ad baron' Suā & villata solvit p. annū de hidagio XX. S. & dat de secta XVI. S. de visu franpt j marc'.

Vered'cm de Stok'—Dic q̄d đns Hunƀtus le Pugeis habet Stok' in custodia & est de honore de Dudeley' & ħt visū franptg. & villata subtraxit se de hidagio p XX. annos elapsos scilⁱᵒ q° libet anno de XXX. S. eo q̄d est de honore de Duddeleya Nessim q° waranto & ño facit sectā.

In defalta—Langl. Dn̄s Ric. de Munfichet—Thom' de Ponte.

  Horton—Ric. de Oxehey. Prior de Hurnle. ađ Mansel panet' đni Reg'.

  Stok—Dn̄us Humƀtus le Pugeis—Galfr' Cusan.

  Hupton—Prior de M'ton—Galfr' Cumbaud.

  Eure (Iyer)—Mag' Witts Coc' in s'vico đn. Edw. fit. Reg'—Jot̄nes Captt̄us.

# HISTORY OF HORTON.

## INTRODUCTION.

**Horton.** This name is written Hortune in Domesday Book, and its derivation is from *Ort* or *Wort*, meaning herbs or vegetables; and *tun* an inclosure or garden. Ortgears, Hortgeard, Hortus. *Tun* means hedge in Gaëlic, hence *dun* a fort or town.

This name is a patronymic in some families, and the same word is used for ten other parishes in England. There is another Horton in this county, which is partly in Ivinghoe, and is a hamlet of Edlesborough in the Hundred of Cotlesloe, about 33 miles from London. It is also a manor, which was for some centuries in the hands of the Brocas family, one of whom was ancestor of Henry Beckingham of Pudlicot, Oxon, p. 96, whose daughter Agnes married William Brocas, from whose ancestors the Brocas at Eton was called, p. 2. One John Brocas was appointed to conduct the works at Windsor Castle, 25 Edward III. 1351.

William Brocas was subsequently of Horton, and dying in 1484, his son Sir John succeeded. The manor was alienated in 1461 by Bernard Brocas to John Malter of London, merchant; it came in 1613 to John Theed, Esq., and finally to the Hall family, and then to Mr. Charles Augustus Hoare, in whose family it is.

The Horton of which we treat is a parish and a manor also, about 17 miles from the capital of the kingdom. It is the smallest, save Wexham, of all our 13 parishes, in the Hundred of Stoke, which is also the smallest of the 9 hundreds into which this shire is subdivided.

To the north of it runs the town of Colnbrook, which bounds it by the road. The county of Middlesex occupies the eastern side, and at its south lies Wraysbury, while on the west is a part of Stoke Poges looking towards Datchet and Windsor.

It is in the deanery of Burnham, and now in the diocese of Oxford. The shape of it has something of a triangular form, having one and its more definite point abutting on Wraysbury.

The length of the parish from its junction with Wraysbury to Colnbrook is about three miles, and its breadth where it enters from Datchet parish and continues to Stanwell, about two miles.

It is bounded by the Colne Bridge, and the stream running to the extremity of the parish and joining Langley Marsh, is more than a mile.

Its received admeasurement in acreage is 1610, and the major part of the families are employed in agriculture or at the mills in the village, which, like many other mills in this vicinity, have been used for divers purposes, as corn, paper, silk, shawls, &c., engaging many hands, and subserving the wants of the place.

In acreage it differs little from its neighbour Wraysbury, and in statistical particulars both resemble each other, as both are in the same hundred, which contains 28,140 acres of land, with a population in 1841 of 15,647.

In 1798 the general land tax in this division was £3730. 8s 4d, and the annual value of property in 1843 was £83,520. 0s 2d.

The census which has yielded so much useful and indispensable information to the nation, in

1801 made the population in Horton to be 647 souls; in 1811 it rose to 723; in 1821 to 776; and in 1831 it touched 1804, so to 1841 to 873.

A Colnbrook return for 1861 gives the population:—

|  |  |  |  |  |
|---|---|---|---|---|
| Horton | . | 179 . 187 . | 366 |
| Langley | . | 231 . 268 . | 498 |
|  | Total | . 410 . 455 . | 865 |
| Houses . | Horton . | Inhabited 77 . Uninhabited | 2 |
| ,, . | Langley . | ,, 105 . ,, | 4 |
|  | Total | . 182 . . | 6 |

The houses and annual value of property, rateable value of messuages, lands, &c. pursuant to the order of the Poor Law Commissioners in 1838, was £4198. The estimated rental was £4575. 16s.

There are about 50 cottages besides Horton Manor House, Berkyn Manor, the Cedars, Horton Lodge, &c. besides a few farm houses.

The parish is described in Domesday Book as then held of the Windsors of Stanwell, and its specific proprietor was Walter-fitz-Other, whose father held the same, temp. Edward the Confessor in 1041. This once powerful house possessed three lordships in Surrey, two in Hants, and three in Bucks, with four more in Middlesex, and of the demesnes Stanwell was the centre and metropolis. The words are these:—Walter, son of Other, held Horton in Stoke Poges, and answered for ten hides, and there is land enough to employ nine ploughs. Two hides are in the demesnes, and there are two ploughs and 15 villains, with five bordars who have six ploughs, and even a seventh may be made. There are four bondmen and a mill of 20s, and meadow for three ploughs. Its whole value is £6, when received 50s. In the King's time (Edward the Confessor) there were six ploughs. Eldred, vassal of Stigand, Archbishop of Canterbury, held this manor, and might sell it. Stigand was one possessed of great authority and ample revenues. He was made Archbishop of Canterbury 1052, and had been Chaplain to King Harold. He was said to be very covetous and very ignorant, and under William the Conqueror he suffered imprisonment, and died 1070.

The parish of Horton has several resident families. It is of much salubrity, and now divested of woods, in which it once abounded. It is in the Chilterns, as Mathew Paris writes, "per totam Ciltriam nemora spatiosa densa et copiosa," in which were wild beasts, besides robbers, exiles and fugitives, *usque Londinum fere*. "How meny bestys of venery there were, that monastic Mistress Juliana Barnes, temp. Henry VI. testifies, in treating of the Companyes of bestys and foules, and route of wulves."

## THE SOIL.

The object of this work is more historic than delineative, hence what relates to the soil may not have its full share of description.

I will avail myself of some of Mr. Masson's remarks, and add that the soil is a rich teeming verdurous flat, charming by its appearance of plenty, and the goodly show of wood along the fields and pasture in the nooks where the houses nestle—that all is grateful to the eye in all directions to the sky-bound verge of the landscape.

There is no lack of trees, and the beech which attains perfection in the Chilterns, though rare, yet is found here.

Bucks is esteemed for the beech, ash and willow, that *sad* tree, whereof, says an old penman, "such who have lost their love make their mourning garlands, and the Jews hung up their harps on these *doleful* supporters." This tree grows very fast, and it has been remarked that the owner of willows will buy a *horse* before that by other trees will pay for his *saddle*. An acre of willows will turn to more profit than an acre of land.

One great dissight there is which blemishes the locality, the ugly pollards on the banks of streams and on the hedge borders, which trees are cut and maimed, and truncated so as to resemble stunted giants. Some pleasing compensation however exists in the noble elms, the alders which delight in a very moist soil, poplars and lofty cedars, with no lack of shrubbery or hedge, and in the vernal equinox the apple and pear bloom with a white and pink blossom, a various sylvan scene, where now and in past times,

> Poplars and alders ever quivering played,
> And nodding cypress formed a fragrant shade.

In the rectory ground here there is a very fine *white elm*, an unusual specimen. Neither are the gardens deficient in fatness of soil, for I learn that asparagus will grow any where, almost in gravel.

In a region intersected with rivers no wonder the distribution of water is considerable, and fish abound such as fresh water produces, and trout are common, a fish reported to have the propension of eels, which travel by night, for we hear of trout on a gravel walk. There are rivulets brimming through the meadows, among rushes and water plants, where streamlets or runnels connect with the Colne, a river which continues for miles, and separates Bucks from Middlesex on its erratic journey to the father of waters, the silver Thames, which like all waters follows a sinuous course, owing to the mobility of the element and the obstacles it encounters, a useful provision in extending the means of irrigation and intercommunication, which prevents the current from acquiring a too great velocity whereby facile navigation would be interrupted. Many rivers flow at a very moderate level, like the vast Amazon in South America, which has only a fall of twelve feet in the course of 700 miles.

The streams turn many mills in the vicinity. The locality is grassy and the soil cereal. It is probable during Milton's *sejour* here that Horton abounded in meadow land. Mills were not yet in use for manufactures, rural occupations being chiefly agricultural, and small sections were devoted to pasture husbandry.

## THE PARISH.

In the centre of the village adjacent to the sign post which marks two miles to Datchet, three and a-half to Windsor, and three to Stanwell, stands in full-blown dignity a large and umbrageous elm tree, where three roads converge.

It is traditionary that this very tree was planted in 1726 to commemorate a mournful circumstance, the death of a child of Mr. John Ashton, innholder here, who was accidentally killed by the fall of a Maypole at this identical spot.

One of the diverging branches goes to Colnbrook, which is one mile distant; that to Datchet is nearly two miles off; passing the lane where the old Horton and Wraysbury roads met, and which was closed in 1800; the path to Wraysbury is about a mile and a-half. On its approach to Wraysbury the road passed by the Colne Bridge mill, now in the tenure of Messrs. Ibotson and Ladell, leaving Horton at a house then the property of Mr. Booker Darby, and which now belongs to the daughters of the late Mr. Cobbett Darby. It is known as Horton Grove, a red-bricked mansion, square and sufficiently commodious, usually let to substantial tenants.

Opposite to this is a white house, the property of Mr. George Tupp, with a garden and some land adjoining in a large and fruitful orchard. It is called the *Cedars*, from some fine specimens of that stately tree being near the house. There are many of this tree in the neighbourhood, although it is an Eastern production; and in our time an American tree of great amplitude and beauty also, the *Araucaria*, is being largely and widely planted in our gardens and groves.

The cedar of Lebanon is said never to be found indigenous in any other locality than the Syrian mountains, a wood whose bitterness prevents its being attacked by insects, and whose vitality and age are such as to recede to biblical times. A singularity in the tree is its inclining branches, being one of the noblest productions of the vegetable kingdom: and it is said that, on an approaching storm of snow, it will turn up its branches to meet the additional weight to be superimposed.

> "The broad round spreading branches, when they felt
> The snow, rose upward in a point to heaven."

There are some houses in the parish known as the Albion houses, formerly the workhouse, and in 1842 they were metamorphosed into a school for boys: these belong to the Tupp family.

Opposite another substantial residence, heretofore a farm house, the property of Colonel Williams, are some ornamental trees clad with ivy, and in the tenure of William Anthony Greatorex, Esq. of London, a lawyer; the house is at the point of juncture of three roads, viz. to Datchet, Colnbrook, and through the village to Moor Farm, conducting to Stanwell.

Nearly in face of the church is a small neat house, whose owner is Mr. William Stevens, nephew of the late Mr. Henry Stevens, formerly proprietor of some 20 acres of land here in fee, which were disposed of at his death. He rented lands in Wraysbury, and resided until he died at the Church Farm (page 124) now tenanted by Mr. James Pullin, his son-in-law.

Another section of the village contains a house which formerly belonged to Mr. James Holderness, called *Ash Farm*, and is not far from the church. Since Mr. Holderness' death it has been in the occupancy of Mr. George Trumper, and it was sold to Mr. Tyrell in 1853. James was brother of John Holderness, High Constable for the Hundred of Stoke, who died 1851, another brother was Alexander Holderness, who died the following year, a most respectable tradesman in Colnbrook, whose son still conducts the business as builder, &c.

Beyond the Rectory on the Colnbrook road stands a house, formerly tenanted by Captain Richard Stovin Maw, R.N., now of Ashford. Its present owner is Edward Temple Watson, Esq., and it is styled Horton Cottage; it belonged to Mrs. John Taylor, widow of Mr. Watson, and is now in the right of her daughters.

A Mr. Emlyn of Wales, owns a small house nearly opposite.

Not far from the mill, to which I shall again advert, in a recess is a small house where Mr. Robert Long Groom dwells, who has performed the office of churchwarden, and to him I am indebted for his kind consideration in cheerfully allowing me to inspect the parish rate-books.

At the back of the mill there are sundry houses, one known as Mill House, where the *quondam* owners of this establishment dwelt, and once the residence of Mr. Tippet. All these houses went with the mill when it came it came into the hands of Mr. Tyrrell in 1859. In this part of the village a tan-house and yard formerly existed, which abounded hereabouts.

Mr. Raymond Reffels has a farm-house at the back of the high road, which he rents of Colonel Williams, with about 400 acres of land.

Proceeding onwards towards Stanwell we find a farm-house in which the above-mentioned Mr. Henry Stevens dwelt for years, known as Hoglane Farm, now more appropriately termed Moor Farm. It is tenanted by Mr. Henry Pullin, and it has been much improved under his tenancy. To this is attached that considerable farm heretofore Moor Farm, which consists of two capacious barns, sheds, and a dwelling-house, and the property abuts on Wraysbury, comprising many acres of excellent soil, which it ought to be if let for a rent of 40s an acre. The tenant holds some 300 acres, half pasture, half arable, of Colonel Williams.

We may add without hyperbole that this parish, as if dedicated to good genius and good fortune, is well stocked with picturesque farms, all denoting the care and taste of the tenants, but to describe them as topographical equity would expect interferes too much with the limited character of the history of this improving and interesting locality, honoured as the residence of Milton, and as the burial place of his revered mother.

It was also the cure of Rev. Dr. John Blair, the laborious and erudite author of the Chronology, of whom more under Church affairs.

On the road tending towards Colnbrook, there is a farm known as Butt's Green Farm, in the occupancy of Mr. Henry Lamb, who now rents under his landlord, Mr. Tyrrell, who bought it some few years ago.

Passing Millbridge Farm, to which access is attained by a bridge, we attain another called Mildridge Farm, of some 600 acres in extent, recognised in the older records, a house square and of solid stamp, with barns of considerable extent and durability, such as attach a real credit to the county, and awaken pride in those who possess them.

The spot is noted for a curious box hedge planted by Mr. Pullin, who was tenant here for many years, at whose decease it passed into the tenure of his son Stephen Pullin, a yeoman, thoroughly versed in the mysteries of agriculture. Mr. Pullin has been Churchwarden several years, and in his custody were lodged the parochial books, the conduct of the parish business; the locality is noted for the attention given to tillage and farming operations.

Sir John Gibbons, Bart. Lord of the Manor of Stanwell, holds a small property also in Horton. Perhaps the next objects worthy notice are the inns and beer-houses. There is ample room for two inns as well for the use of parishioners as wayfarers, and the dinners consequent on the ploughing match here are held biennially at the Bells, by the church, near a clump of trees where fairs were wont to be held; and at the Crown Inn, opposite the large isolated elm tree, as we observed before, at the junction of the high roads.

There are several beer-shops, indispensable to the needs of the parish and its population, for in no time could parishes forego these much frequented houses of resort, which to the poor are places of refuge after the day's toil, and serve as clubs to learn news and indulge in potations of beer, as good as wine for the body's sake if not abused. No nation or time has gone on without such places of some sort, and an old law of King Ina of Wessex, in Saxon days, recognizes them, although licences to vend spirituous fluids were not introduced before 1551.

Before the antique entrance to the old *Place House*, when rented by the Brierwoods and possessed by the Scawens, are two brick posterns now united by a wall; in one of these is an aperture made for the convenience of receiving letters, that crowning *addendum* to civilization, page 80. This depository acts as a receiving house, having been transferred hither in 1860. A Post Office had existed here since 1855, and now is felt the improvement known as the prepayment plan of 1d for half-an-ounce, which uniform rate of postage came into operation in 1840. There are two deliveries daily from Colnbrook at 8 a.m. and 3 p.m.

The Brewers' Company, a very ancient body, incorporated in 1427, hold about 30 acres of land and one cottage in the parish, rented by — Williams, a farmer and shopkeeper here. This land was purchased with some funded property which was left by a Mr. Baker for the support of almshouses at Mile End, London.

There is also a cottage adjacent owned by Rev. Arthur Hubbard, and rented also by Williams.

By the side of the bridle and foot road called Horton Lane, which is just one mile from Colnbrook, there are four cottages, one a beer house belonging to Mr. Harman of Uxbridge. This road is very convenient for Colnbrook, and was originally the principal transit to the town, but it is not used for carts or vehicles. In winter parts of it are subject to deep inundations, but in summer it is very agreeable as it intersects some spacious and well-cultivated fields, which receive free access of wind and sun, and are unincumbered by timber.

Here I introduce, alphabetically, the names of the landed proprietary of Horton in 1800, as taken from the award map—

| | | | |
|---|---|---|---|
| Buccleugh, Duchess of | Cole, T. R. | Harrison, Robert | Sheppard, John |
| Buckland, Thomas | Clarkson, Abner | Haynes, Francis | Shirley, R. |
| Bennett, R. | Crew, M. | Holderness, — | Thurbin, William |
| Bullock, Henry | Darby, Booker | Jones, Rev. R. | Tupp, John |
| Baker, William | Evans, W. M. | Morrell, A. G. | Whitaker, John |
| Biddle, Dr. William | Formel, Thomas | Philpot, John | Williams, Thomas, Esq. |
| Bishop, Elizabeth | Gay, M. A. | Rayner, Thomas | Williamson, Harriet |
| Beauly, Robert | Gray, Margaret Ann | Reeves, William | Williams, Frances |
| Cox, R. | Hetherington, Joel | Snowden, — | Wingfield, R. |

### PROPRIETORS IN 1861.

| | | |
|---|---|---|
| Thomas Peers Williams, Esq. Lord of the Manor and Patron of the Church. | The Rector of the Parish Edward Tyrrell, Esq. Cobbett Darby, Esq. George Tupp, Esq. | Miss Eliza Cane Edward Temple Watson, Esq. |

### YEOMEN AND GENTRY.

| | | | |
|---|---|---|---|
| William Anthony Greatorex, Esq. Mr. Stephen Pullin | Mr. Henry Pullin Mr. George Trumper | Mr. Long Groom Mr. Henry Lamb | Mr. Raymond Reffells Mr. Stephens. |

### THE MILLS.

This locality from its superfluity of water is peculiarly suited for mills turned by this element. As wind-mills were not in use until about 1155, it is not improbable that the water-mill of 20s value mentioned in Domesday Book, is that which is still so conveniently placed on the Coln stream, and which has subserved so many useful purposes from its original one of merely grinding grain, to the making of fine paper, boards, iron works, silk and shawl printing, which was the last use to which it was applied.

This mill seems not to have been gainful to the proprietors, Messrs. Tippet and Co. who employed nearly 60 persons of both sexes in various departments at wages ranging from £2. to 8s a week, earned by girls and lads.

In the year 1859 a decline in business caused a total suspension of it, and after an auction of two days, all the goods, and subsequently the mill-house and the residence of the proprietor, were jointly brought to the hammer.

The earliest name as mill owner here is Richard West, paper-maker, in 1649. The mill is mentioned as in full operation at the period that *Place House* was tenanted by the Brierwoods, who obtained from the proprietor or lessee of it leave to make openings to feed the canals from the main river at the expense of £300, which was discharged by Mr. Brierwood.

It was in the tenure of William Pearson in 1758, the same who held the Wraysbury Mills in 1760. The mill-house formerly rented by Mr. — Keane of London, and used as a residence, is a brick building coated with a white cement; commodious and almost surrounded with water.

In front of it the Colne forms an island, or else a moat has been artificially made, the waters of which used to be applied to the factory, but now it is not so. It is of a horse-shoe form, rather deep, and formerly it had neat gravel walks around it, on which are various trees of age and youth. The Colne also forms islets beyond the bridge leading through the parish by reason of its circuitous route, for the stream enters at the Colne bridge and divides the parish and the counties of Bucks and Middlesex.

It bounds it on the eastern side for more than half a mile, and re-entering passes on until it reaches these mills, and crosses the road under two bridges close together, one with iron rails and the other of wood, and so continues its course to the termination of the parish at its junction with the Wraysbury Nail Mill, comprising a circuit of some two miles in its meanderings.

The greatest depth of the stream at the mill head may be 8 or 10 feet at the lock. In winter the course is rapid, while the fluid submerges the fields and roads adjacent to Wraysbury.

There is a long and spacious garden behind the mill house parallel with the factory houses, occupied by the operatives, which are eight in number, and the garden adorned with deep box borders, is not deficient in fruit yielding trees, standards, espaliers, &c.

The foreman of the works lived in the central house of three, tenanted by the workmen, now that of the lessee.

The pile of building is very extensive for there were several factories, having the houses slated, and there is one very tall chimney for central purposes.

A communication across a branch of water is made by a cast-iron bridge. There are also drying lofts and cutting apartments. That part of the factory used for boards only belongs to Colonel Williams, and this he retains in possession because it secures a right of water. The rest of the mill belongs to Mr. Tyrrell, who bought it after the public sale of goods and chattels.

On the 26th Sept. 1860, these mill contents were exposed for auction by Mr. W. T. Buckland, with all the implements and machinery, fixtures, etc. Steam coppers, vats, steam-pipes, and brass taps, with 4000 printing blocks, slate top tables, &c.

And on the following day, the 27th, were disposed of all the surplus household furniture of the mill-house residences, brewing utensils, garden tools, board quarterings, panelling, door-frames, and sundries belonging to the print works.

In 1860 it was announced in the public papers that for sometime past a new place of worship had been in course of preparation, and that a portion of the Horton print works had been appropriated to the purpose.

The room in the lower factory is capable of holding some 100 persons, and this is to be or has been permanently enlarged by the removal of an intervening partition wall, so as to accommodate 250 persons in comfort.

An instrument (harmonium) is placed within its walls to assist in the psalmody, and the service is to be conducted as nearly as possible after the form of the Established Church.

The minister is a gentleman from New College, London, Mr. Hasson, and in January the augmented accommodation was completed for the benefit of the worshippers, who are chiefly of the village. The room has not yet been licensed for prayer purposes.

The cause of the secession arose about a misunderstanding between the Rev. Richard Gorges

Foot, Rector of Horton, and the Churchwardens, relative to the distribution of bread to the poor under the will of the late Rector Browne, and about the Rector's right to appoint Churchwardens. It is alleged that by the ancient minute book of the Horton Vestries it is not a right or a custom in this parish for the Rector to appoint any Churchwarden; and to obtain opinions, a meeting was held at the Five Bells Inn on the 4th July, 1860, when the Chairman, Edward Tyrrell, Esq. read a report from Mr. Stephen Pullin and Mr. Robert Long Groom, Churchwardens.

In the sequel, unhappily some assaults were affirmed to have been committed, arrests followed, and an action was brought by the Churchwardens against the Churchwarden nominated by the Rector, and the case was tried at Gloucester.

As these are temporary disturbances which often dash the tranquillity of a parish and seriously ruffle the parishioners, it may be within the scope of the historian just to mention them *en passant*, but on their merits he should not enter as he could give satisfaction to neither party, and to take part in a parish fray he would find it easier to keep off than to win a battle.

It belongs to him only to regret that any differences should arise to neutralise the harmony which should religiously subsist between the pastor and his flock.

It is to be hoped the schism will be of very brief duration, and that this well-conducted village will be restored to the spiritual equilibrium of years, and that the memory of disunion will be utterly obliterated, and with a renewed amity promoting virtuous communion which strengthens the ligaments of friendship and obedience,

"That love between them like the palm will flourish,
And peace shall still her wheaten garland wear."

The writer of this history begs here to acknowledge his obligations to Mr. Foot for his hospitality, as well as his general courtesy, in affording him the means of ascertaining what otherwise had not been within his reach. He likewise thanks all parishioners who have considerately contributed to supply any local information, for without such aid parish histories would be incomplete, and he solicits his informants also to remember—how a grateful mind,

"By owing owes not, but still pays, at once
Indebted and discharged."

## DESCENT OF THE MANOR.

It were vain to ascertain precisely through how many or whose hands this manor has passed; from the earliest times it seems generally to have been in the tenure of the Windsor family until the time of King Henry VIII., yet occasional alienations are found through the fines and recoveries, which may have been family arrangements or settlements, for this manor was not wholly wrenched off the large Wyndsor property until the forcible abstraction of it by the second monarch of the Tudor Dynasty, as will be shown in chronological order.

This village being small in area and numbers, and inconsiderable in wealth, was held in conjunction with larger demesnes, hence few records are preserved of it apart from the usual transfers of property, and it is not unlikely that its neighbour Wraysbury had been even more neglected had it not been annexed to Crown royalties, besides having the advantage of a celebrated Benedictine Nunnery, of which annals are preserved.

William, son of Walter Fitz Other, being Castellan or Warder of the Castle of Windsor, was the first to assume the patronymic of Windsor, and his son William procured from King Henry II. a confirmation of all the lands which had belonged to his grandfather. He is reported to have deceased in 1194, leaving two sons, Walter and William, who divided the Barony of Windsor, the Stanwell moiety falling to William, who died seized of it about 1275.

The proprietor had paid into the Exchequer £100 for livery of some part of his estates, which subsequently devolved to his nieces, Christian, wife of Duncan de Lascelles, and Gunnora, wife of Ralph de Hodleseng, children of his brother Walter.

A fine was levied, 1287, Easter term, about the Beaconsfield advowson and other lands. Horton was held as of the manor of Stanwell, and Hugh de Windsor was presented in 1218 to the Rectory of Horton by William de Windsor, and it is to be noted that this is the only presentation to this living of any member of the Windsor family.

The public records tell us of some who not sole proprietors here, had yet latent claims on the manor and territory, for by a deed preserved among the Charter Rolls, 5 John, 1203, p. 116, that monarch by letters patent granted to Robert, son of Roger, certain property which Constantin de Cramavill had made over to him; which in the deed the daughter of this lady and Robert de Cramavill, viz. Waleron, had put in trust for her with this very town and lordship of Horton, until she should come of age or be married, which first should happen, and there is an especial proviso that the trustees should not damnify the estates.

In 5 John, 1203, Roll 93, a fine is levied between William the Prior of Merton, and William de Windleshore, relative to an acre of land and a croft called Rudding in Horseley Parish. This William Windsor gave to the Convent of St. Mary Merton and the Canoness the land which Geffrey son of William Okey hath in Horton, with all the waste belonging thereto; also two acres belonging to the demesnes, styled Buttes, with the closes "*et tota sequela sua*," besides other property and *appurts*.

Another fine, 6 John, 1204, shews how Richard de Hakeburne buys lands in Horton of William de Windleshore.

In another deed in the same Charter Roll, p. 181; 10 John, 1208, the letters patent that we the King cede to Robert Ruffo of Kenebanton, in Papewick, and Robert de Braybroc and his heirs, by gift of Matilda Countess of Clare, daughter of James St. Hilary, various properties *inter alia* from the gift of William de Windleshore, 4 acres of meadow in Horton, p. 29.

Fine, 14 John, 1212, Roll 147, between Hamond, son of Henry Rex, and William de Wyndleshore, a tenement and a virgate of land in Horton, and a mill with three acres of land.

Also in 15 John, 1213, Walter de Upenon says in a plea that a common pasture was allowed *gratis* among the tenants of William de Wyndesore in the town of Horton, so that each tenant had a hide of land for pasturing according to his wants, Rot. 4.

Another deed, 15 John, 1213, states that — son of Henry de Wendleshore, obtains lands and tenements in Horton.

Another instrument bearing date, 8 Henry III. 1223, shews that William de Wendleshore buys lands of Geoffrey de Mauriscis of Wraysbury. He was governor of Ireland, 1215 and 1230 (page 29), and in the time of this king, Richard de Oxeye, who had married Joan, daughter of William de Wyndesore, who died 1275, held the manor of Horton, of whom William de Wyndesore and Walter de Willesden held of the king in capite, paying 20s for hidage, and 16s for suit and service, with two marks for frankpledge. The deed suggests some defaults, and also about the Prior of Harley, and ends "*ad mansel panet Domini Regis.*"

A deed Hil. 25, Henry III. 1240, states that John, son of the King (this is John of Eltham, created Earl of Cornwall, who died *sp.* 1334) bought lands of Andrew, son of John of Horton.

A deed 45 Henry III. 1260, Roll 64, fine between Eustace Prior of Merton, and Henry Maunsel and Joan his wife, of 13s 6d rents and *appurts.* in Horton and Wexham, Bucks.

In 46 Henry III. 1261, Roll 46, between John, son of Walter de Horton, and Richard de Oxeheye, whom Hugh, Vicar of Wraysbury, calls to warrant, and for whom he is bail, for two messuages, two virgates, four acres of land, and two acres in Horton. We do not find any Hugh at this time on the list of Wraysbury incumbents—he may have been curate only; but as there is a long period between 1234 and 1299, the dates of the two rectors at this period, the name of Hugh in 1261 may have been lost in the Registry, p. 106.

In Trinity term, 51 Henry III. 1266, Aunger de Chauncumbe and Joan his wife seek against Ada de Maunsel, probably widow of the above Henry de Maunsel, deforciant of lands, &c. in Horton and Langley.

These transfers of property shew that at this early period the entire parish of Horton, whose area is only 1610 acres, was not wholly in the feudal tenure of the Wyndsors, yet there is no positive alienation of the manor.

In a deed, Trin. 2 Edward I. 1273, Rot. 21 and 71, Ass. and Jur., Alberic de Whytlebyr recovers seizin of 20 acres of pasture in Raveneston, belonging to his tenements in Horton, and of William de Barantyne and Joan his wife in another moiety.

I here refer the reader to the abstract of Horton fines for the intermediate periods, and I pass to the first notice we have of the manor devolving into other hands, after I transcribe the purport of the deed, 2 Edward II. in 1308, to be found in the Common Plea records, whereby Henry Chelsea by deed gives to Sir Henry Spigurnell and his heirs 21s and 5s rent, with all his other rents and services, and all other holdings in Horton and Stanwell, Rot. 1.

It appears that Sir Richard de Wyndsor died 1326, and that his wife Joan soon followed him to the last bourn in 1328, which gives cause why a new name should be assigned in a fine as proprietor here in fee, for by Mich. 2 Edward II. 1308, John, son of Richard de Cadamo, and William de Thobiner de Wyselech are said to have bought the manor and the advowson of Horton. Some marriages or conveyances took place probably before, because in 1306 the same Richard de Cadamo presents to the living of Horton one Stephen de Cheshunt, who continued Rector for nine years, when his place was supplied in 1315 by William de Harpesfield, who was not presented by a Windsor, but by John son of Geffrey de Whethamsted, who the Register says was dispensed with for two years to perform the obsequies of Ralph de Windsor.

From this time it does not appear that any Windsor presented to the incumbency, so I presume they invariably sold the right of presentation which had been attached to the manor, until the day when William Lord Windsor was so unceremoniously heaved out of his ancestral demesnes by Henry VIII. as will be seen in the sequel.

In the Nomina Villarum one Nicholas Came, and John son of Geoffrey were Lords here in 1316, and for the village of Horton the name of Hugh le Despenser is assigned. This is *pro temp.* I suppose. The next in succession to these hereditary estates was Richard de Windsor, whose inquisition took place in 1367. He married for his third wife Claricia, daughter of John Drokensfield, widow of John Yorke, while a former William de Wyndsor had espoused Margaret daughter and heir of John Drokensfield, whose daughter Margaret took the veil and became a nun at Ankerwycke (p. 35).

In 1357, Mich. 31 Edward III., evidences denote that the said manor passed into the tenure of Sir Roger le Louthe, High Sheriff of Essex 1358, and Robert Tame and his wife, which implies some union of the families or trusteeship, for it returns into the Wyndsor tenure. Hence it appears that the next occupant for life was Sir James Wyndsor, whose escheat is recorded 1370; then followed his son Sir Miles, who dropped in 1387, all holders of Stanwell and Horton, the former as of the manor of Horton.

I could have wished to give more detailed accounts of the distinguished members of this house, but lest the personal biographies should augment the narrative too much, I rather refer to the genealogy, in which the descents may be traced. I now pass to the brother of the last owner, viz. Sir William de Wyndsor, a man honoured in his day and exalted to trust and profit. He was constituted Lord Lieutenant or Governor of Ireland in 1369 and 1373, and was succeeded there by James Earl of Ormond in 1377. These chief governors were instituted 1173, and Richard de Clare Earl of Pembroke, surnamed Strongbow, was Lord Warden in 1173, and they have been continued to our days, although propositions have been made to abolish the office of Lord Lieutenant, and to govern Ireland like Scotland.

This Sir William de Wyndsor it was who remarried with the beautiful Alice Perrers, a lady of much worth, but who was also much persecuted in her time, perhaps less from her own demerits than from jealousy; albeit she won golden opinions, purchased as much by her practical virtues as her feminine smiles and blandishments. She was in such credit with the King, Edward III., by reason of her handsome physiognomy, ever a sweet spectacle, and the enchantment of her address, that she sat at the King's bedside when all the Council and the Privy Chamber stood waiting without doors, and she moved suits to her royal lover when they *dared* not, in which he concurred *sympathetically*, for the loveliest harmony is the sound of the voice we love. Her fault was too great amiability, and a credible historian alleges that she was friendly to many, but all were not friendly to her, through that envy which is innate in vulgar souls.

This Dame Alice Perrers, although she had been the *chere amie* of King Edward III., was not ignobly born, and was either daughter or granddaughter of Richard Perrers of Essex, Sheriff of Essex and Herts for four years from 1329, and had been Sheriff 1313. His arms were quarterly A and S. She died *sp.* by her second husband Wyndsor, to whom she was really married. This is confirmed by her *Inq. p. m.* taken before Sir Nicholas Brembre, Lord Mayor of London in the years 1377, 1383-4-5, and who possessed Yeoveny manor (page 90).

This lady was the Helen of her time, and she had been previously wedded, as her will denotes, made in 1400, in which she cites her son John, but not his surname, and her daughter Joane, wife of Robert Skerne of Kingston on Thames, to whom there is a monumental brass there, dated 1437.

Edmund, son and heir of Henry Skerne, heir to Robert Skerne, sells property in Bagshot, Close Rolls, 6 Edward IV. 1467.

Before we quit the subject of this interlude, Alice Perrers, one of the Ladies of the Bedchamber to Queen Philippa, wife of Edward III., who died 1359, we may remark she was above the common intelligence of her sex, and if her beauty was flattered and she succumbed, she had redeeming qualities, for persons occasionally lost to rectitude are not altogether lost to a sense of it.

Entertainments were made for her at much cost, and the people took it ill that their taxes, grievous to be borne, were lavished on this favourite—above all a tournament held in Smithfield gave great umbrage, where Alice Perrers, to whom the King gave the name of "*the Lady of the Sun,*" appeared by his side in a triumphant chariot, and attended by many ladies of quality, each leading a knight by his horse's bridle. A petition was got up soliciting the King to remove from his person the Duke of Lancaster, his son (John of Gaunt, time-honoured Lancaster), Alice Perrers, Latimer Lord Chamberlain, and others most in favour—all done at the suggestion of the *Black Prince*, who died *untimely*, 1376, leaving one son, King Richard II. and a natural son, Sir Roger de Clarendon, the reputed ancestor of the Smijths of Hill Hall, Essex (p. 41). Sir Roger was executed in 1402, with eight grey friars, for high treason. He married Margaret, (who died 21st September, 1382, under age, as her *Inq. p. m.* shews, 28th October, 1382) daughter of Mariotte, daughter of William de la Roche of Cornwall, son of Thomas de la Roche or De la Rupe, as detailed in the Inquisition.

Sir William Wyndsor expired 15th September, 8 Richard II. 1384, leaving three sisters his coheirs. He made a nuncupative will, and dying without issue male the barony fell into abeyance, while the estates continued in the Wyndsor house, and one John Wyndsor held a *quota* of them, against whom the said Dame Alice stoutly protests in this her *emphatic* phrase, "On pain of my soul he hath no right there nor *ever* had," while she bequeaths to her two daughters her manors which John Wyndsor and others had usurped. She died seized of the extensive manor of Bradwell, Essex, which had been granted to her by King Edward III. To her was given the manor of Philiberds Court, Berks, on whose attainder it came to John Holland Earl of Huntingdon, 12 Richard II. 1388. He was also attainted and executed, 1400, at Plessy in Essex, on the very spot where the Duke of Gloucester had suffered, in whose death he had been mainly instrumental. In 1400 this estate came to John Wyndsor by marriage with one of the Beckingham family, p. 96. Pat. Roll, 1 Henry IV.

There was a gentleman here of some local importance who bought and sold lands at this epoch of our story, *ycleped* Wyot, and the earliest record of him is found in a fine, Hil. 3 Henry IV. 1401, when he buys of Dionysia wife of Richard Overton certain messuage, lands, rents, &c. in Horton; and the next purchase of magnitude is Hil. 6 Henry VI. 1427, when Richard Wyot and his wife buy or have a transfer made of the manor of Horton and the advowson. In the Close Rolls 5 Henry VI. 1426, Robert Dru, brother of Richard or Thomas Dru, children of Laurence Dru by his late wife Lucy, grants to Richard Wyot part of the manor of Horton with the advowson of Horton Church. Richard Wyot was M.P. for the Shire 1414, 1421, and 1426.

In 1404 John Wyot was collated to Horton Rectory, and no doubt this is the same family who held lands in Wraysbury about a century later (page 155).

According to the chronological currency of events, we may insert here that in 1427 this manor as of the Manor of Huntercomb was held by Sir Richard Wyndsore, who deceased the following year, and if we advance to another escheat, 30 Henry VI. 1452, it is shewn that his son, Sir Myles Wyndsore held three parts of Horton as of the Manor of Stanwell. He also held Poyle of this manor, and all were held of the Castle of Windsor.

The Poyle property where the mills belonging to Messrs. Ibotson now stand, and where mills have been for many centuries, formed the estate of William de la Poyle in 1267, and of William de Langele of Horton, who conveyed the Manor of Poyle to John de la Poyle and Isabel his wife.

This John deceased in 1318, having demised the manor to his wife for life; then to Richard de Waleden or Walden relative of Humphrey de Walden, who died 1331, and was a crown tenant of the Wraysbury estates and manor, &c. (page 9).

In 1256, Alice de Middleton bought of Alexander, son of Richard de Langele, certain lands in Horton, and it is not improbable that either connection by marriage or consanguinity existed.

The reversion of Poyle was in Elizabeth, sole heir of John de la Poyle, and she was 24 years old at her father's decease. Escheat, 2 Edward III. 1337. Sir Thomas de la Poyle died seized of this estate in 1424, and in 1452 the same manor was possessed by John Gainsford of Crowhurst, Surrey, who held it under the Windsors by the service of half a knight's fee, and so it continued, and was part of the estates included in the forced exchange between Lord Windsor and King Henry VIII.

In the Patent Rolls, 29 November, 1488, there is a license to John Gainsford to alienate the manor of Poyle to the use of Alice his wife, with remainder to John Gaynsford and the issue of his former wife, daughter of Otwell Worseley, Esq. Again there is another deed, 6 Henry VII. 1490, by which license is given to Richard Batenor, clerk, to alienate the same manor to Thomas Oxenbridge, brother of John, (page 64), to the use of Alice, wife of John Gaynsford, and the issue of his former wife, Ann Worseley. Sir Thomas Oxenbridge married Catherine, daughter of Sir John Gaynsford, and he was magistrate for Bucks in 1496. Ralph Leigh of Stockwell married Joyce, another daughter of this Sir John, who died 1510, and the manor continued in the Leigh family, and was eventually purchased by Sir John Gibbons, Bart. with other estates in Stanwell in 1754, and in 1781 the Poyle mills were conveyed by his son, Sir William Gibbons, Bart. to John and Henry Bullock. John Bullock died 1762, leaving a daughter Mary, who was married to Sir James Hodges, of London, Kt. Mr. Bullock held the Wraysbury conjointly with the Poyle mills, and both now belong to or are rented by the Ibotsons. Sir John Gibbons is the present Lord of the Manor of Stanwell, and holds property in Colnbrook and Horton.

As in the alliances made by the Gaynsfords, there are names connected with the villages under consideration in this history, I subjoin a pedigree of that family with that of Whethill.

### PEDIGREE OF GAYNSFORD AND WHETHILL.

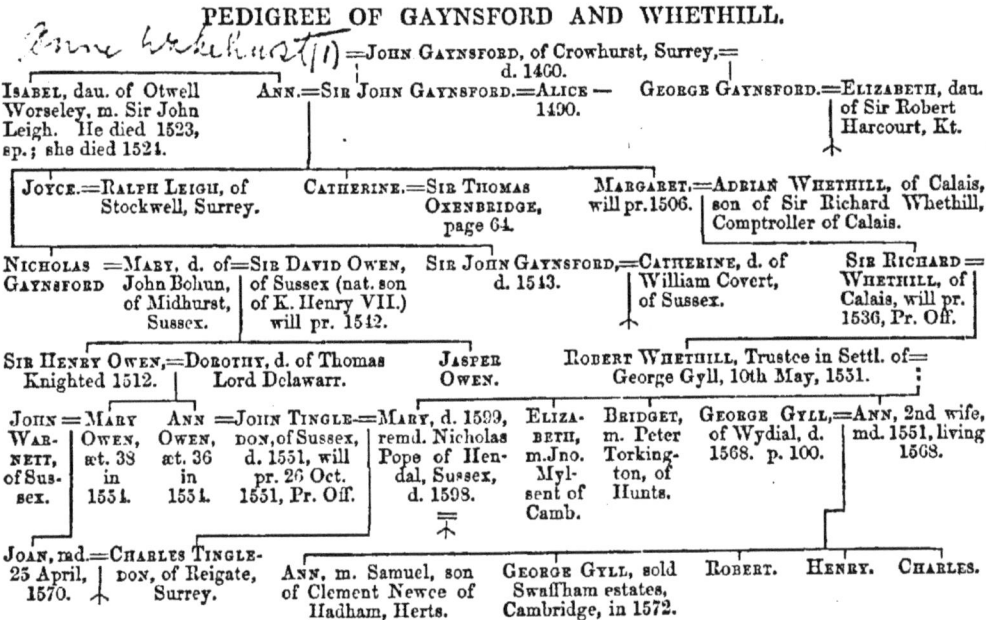

From this digression about Poyle, which is not in the parish of Horton or in the township of Colnbrook, let us advert to another family destined to play a part in the county, and the history of the kingdom,—Bulstrode,—of whom mention has already been made.

They took their name from the manor of Temple Bulstrode, and it was in the possession, as the Placita Rolls shew, of the Prior of Butlesham Montagu, 1351.

By a deed Trin. 12 Edward II. 1338, Robert Pogeys and Peter his son buy lands of John de Bulstrode, and his wife Margery lands in Datchet called *Mora*, (fenny part). Richard Bulstrode is the ninth name of a list of 36 names among the Knights and Squires of Bucks in 1501. He was son of William and grandson of John Shobingdon, who assumed the name of Bulstrode, because he married Agnes the sole heir of Robert Bulstrode. This lady remarried with William Brudenell, father of Edward, who by escheat 9 Edward IV. 1469, held lands in Langley and Horton; from this union descend the Earls of Cardigan, created 1661. George Brudenell assumed the patronymic of Montagu from his union with Mary, one of the daughters and coheirs of John, Duke of Montagu, and Mary, daughter and coheir of John Churchill, the famous Duke of Marlborough, page 69.

Edmund Brudenell, Lord of Raans, had an only daughter, Aliason, married to Richard Waller of Kent, the same who took the Duke of Orleans prisoner at Agincourt, 1415. Dying in 1475 he was the direct ancestor of Edmund Waller the poet. This match brought the Wallers into the shire of Bucks.

There is a pedigree of Brudenell of Stoke Mandeville, so I shall insert one here to illustrate this portion of the work.

### PEDIGREE OF BRUDENELL, OF STOKE MANDEVILLE.

RICHARD BRUDENELL, of Aynho, Northamptonshire.=

WILLIAM BRUDENELL, of ditto.=AGNES, d. of Thomas de la Grove, and ALICE, d. and h. of Walter de Raan, of Raans in Agmondesham, Bucks.

WILLIAM BRUDENELL, buried at Hedgerley.=AGNES, d. and h. of Robert Bulstrode.|JOHN DE SHOBBINGDON.|EDMUND BRUDENELL, temp. Edward III. will dated 1425, sp.|HENRY, from whom the Brudenells of Shardeloe, Bucks.

ALICE, d. of Thomas Dipden.=EDMUND BRUDENELL, Lord of Raans,=PHILIPPA, d. of Philip Englefield, M.P. for Bucks, 1406. of the Green,

ALICE, d. and h. of her mother, md. Richard Waller, son of Richard Waller, who took the Duke of Orleans prisoner at Agincourt. | DRU BRUDENELL,= H. Sheriff of Bucks 1474, d. 1479. | SIR ROBERT BRUDENELL,=MARY, d. and coh. of Chief Justice of the Com. Thomas Entwisle. Pleas, d. 1531.

EDMUND BRUDENELL, of= Chalfont St. Peters. | SIR THOMAS BRUDENELL,=ELIZABETH, d. of Sir William d. 1548. Fitzwilliam.

ELIZABETH, md. Sir Robert Drury, of Hedgerly, Bucks. | SIR THOMAS BRUDENELL, d. 1586.=

ROBERT BRUDENELL.=

SIR THOMAS BRUDENELL, cr. Baronet 1611, cr. Baron 1627, and= Earl of Cardigan 1661, d. 1663.

ROBERT, 2nd Earl.=

FRANCIS, d. 1678.=

GEORGE, 3rd Earl of Cardigan.=LADY ELIZABETH BRUCE, d. of Thomas Earl of Aylesbury.

GEORGE, 4th Earl of Cardigan, Duke of Montagu, see p. 69. | JAMES, 5th Earl of Cardigan. | ROBERT, d. 1770.=

ROBERT, 6th Earl of Cardigan, d. 1826.==

1st wife, ELIZABETH JANE HENRIETTA,=JAMES THOMAS, 7th Earl of=2nd wife, ADELINA LOUISA MARIA, d. of
d. of Admiral J. R. Tollemache, d. 1850. Cardigan, K.C.B. Spencer de Horsey, and LADY LOUISA MARIA JUDITH, d. of Earl of Stradbroke, md. September 1858.

With the lands in Stanwell, conveyed in 1476 by Sir Peter Ardern and others, probably came some of the Horton property, which the Bulstrodes held. It appears at this time that the once famous name of Bulstrode is found now at Horton, for Richard Bulstrode presented John Daniel to the rectory here in 1478, and this is the only presentation made by them, although they were occasionally lords of the manor with the Digby family, with the advowson, until Henry Bulstrode of Wraysbury presented in 1631. Although the property of the Windsors diminished here, yet the family continued in opulence and honour, and what may be termed the second race after the estates fell into abeyance on the demise of Sir William Wyndsore in 1394, so I shall pass to a Sir Myles Windsor who is *said* to have been brother of William the last Baron.

In certain genealogies some affiliate Thomas Windsor, who died 1486, with this Myles Windsor. He it was who espoused Elizabeth, daughter and heir of John Andrews of Norfolk, and from this alliance came Andrews, created Lord Windsor, 1529, apparently in favour with Henry VIII. who gave him various offices, and in July, 1505, made him Keeper of the Wardrobe, (in room of Sir Robert Lytton, Knight, of Knebworth, Herts), and subsequently, in 1540, Ankerwycke Priory and its demesnes. He was the last of a long and continuous line, to have and to hold the Stanwell possessions with those of Horton, which his antecessors had owned since the era of Edward the Confessor; a valiant family, which had enjoyed every post of military and civil honour. Henry de Windsor received £100 a year for his services in Brittany, by grants 6 Henry VII. 1490, Pat. Rolls.

Prior to the death of Andrews, Lord Windsor, in 1543, this arbitrary King Henry VIII., what especial cause moving is unknown, thought fit to effect a certain exchange of land, and for this purpose he sent a message to Lord Windsor that he would *dine* with him at Stanwell, when doubtless a feast worthy a monarch and a peer was prepared.

The repast finished, the *facetious* monarch, "flushed with imperiousness and wine," and with a foregone conclusion, averred that " he liked so well of that place as that he resolved to have it,"— but not without a *consideration*.

The Lord of Stanwell reasonably alarmed at the *modest hint*, stammered out a hope that his Majesty (for in this reign the flattering title of Majesty was first used, which has given so much umbrage to Quakers) was only in a jocose and playful humour, and that he willed not *really* to deprive him of his beloved seat, where lay the hopes of his issue and the relics of his ancestors. But Henry, who like Louis XIV. of France, said, *" La loi, c'est Moi,"* was not to be appeased, diverted, or deprecated by entreaties, commanded my Lord on pain of his *allegiance* to apply to his Attorney-General and settle the exchange with him *sans* delay or murmur, viz. Bordelay Abbey, in Worcestershire. The obsequious functionary, Sir Richard Rich (subsequently Lord Chancellor Rich in 1547), handed him a conveyance ready made, and dated 14th March, 1541, and thus arbitrarily these lands so long dear to himself and ancestors, who were the eyes of Stanwell, were wrested from the House of Windsor.

In this deed the Parsonage of Stanwell is stated to be parcel of the possessions of the Priory of Ankerwycke, and the Manor of Stanwell is described as extending into the shires of Bucks, Berks, Surrey and Hants, each parish being enumerated in the deed in the Augmentation Office.

The *unkind cut* of the monarch to the peer, "shore his old thread in twain," for he departed the next year from a world of woe, where one chagrin and mutation treads on the vestige of another.

Subsequently, Sir Thomas Hoby got his estate, house, and manor for a season, and having passed into the tenure of Lord Knyvett, for services rendered to the Crown, and especially for his suppression of the Gunpowder Plot; it owned various proprietors, and it is now the fee of the Gibbons family with the Lordship of the Manor.

To conclude the detail of the Windsor family, the honours continued in the line of the first Baron, until the title fell into abeyance, when the Committee of Privileges in the House of Lords determined in favour of Thomas Hickman, Esq. who was eventually raised to the Earldom of Plymouth in 1682, representing a house for antiquity, lustre, and good fortune, little inferior to any of those in Great Britain, which by pursuing virtue and incited by useful industry, have reached the path of brilliant fame.

## PEDIGREE OF WINDSOR.

WALTER FITZOTHER, 1041.=     Arms: A, a Saltire G.

- WILLIAM assumed the patronymic of Windsor, 1066.=    RICHARD.=
- WILLIAM confirmed in estates by King Henry II. d. 1194.=    WILLIAM.=    HENRY.=
  - WALTER took a moiety of the Barony.=
  - WILLIAM of Stanwell, see fines Horton, 1203-4.=
  - HUGH of Horsley, Surrey, temp. H.I.
  - DELICIA, m. Robert de Hastings, Lord of Eastern Sussex.=
  - Son — see fines, 1213.
- CHRISTIAN, m. Duncan de Lascelles.
- GUNNORA, m. Ralph de Hodenge.
- WILLIAM of Stanwell, d. 1275.=
- RALPH or HENRY de CORNHILL, page 12.=
- DELICIA=GODFREY de LOUVAINE.
- MATHEW of Eton, Bucks, d. 1261.
- WILLIAM, d. 1279. Inq. p.m.=MARGARET, dau. of John de Drokensfield.
- JOAN.=SIR RICHARD OXEY. See fine 1261.
- HUGH, probably Rector of Wraysbury. See fine 1261, page 106.
- RICHARD, d. 1326.=JOAN —    WALTER.    MARGARET, Nun at Ankerwycke, page 35.
- RICHARD, d. 1367, æt. 30, in 1326.=CLARICIA, dau. of John Drokensfield.=JOHN YORKE.    WILLIAM, Rector of Stanwell.
- SIR JAMES WINDSOR, d. 1370.=
- SIR WILLIAM de WYNDSOR, Lieut. of Ireland, d. 1383.=ALICE, dau. of Richard Perrers= 1st h— m. 1378, d. 1400.
- Three sisters co-heirs.
- SIR MILES WINDSOR, d. 1387.=    JANE, m. Robert Skerne of Kington-on-Thames.    JOHN.
- BRYAN WINDSOR, d. 1399.=
- RICHARD, d. 1428.=
- MILES, d. 1452.= *Joan da of Walter Green*
- THOMAS WINDSOR, d. 1486, M.I. Stanwell Chancel.=ELIZABETH, dau. of John Andrews of Suffolk.
- ANDREWS LORD WINDSOR of Ankerwycke Priory, by deed 4th August, 1540, d. 1543.=ELIZABETH, dau. of John Blunt, son of Walter, Lord Mountjoy.
  - WILLIAM LORD WINDSOR of Ankerwycke Priory, d. 1558.=
  - SIR EDWARD WINDSOR of Stoke, entailed in Ankerwycke.
  - THOMAS WINDSOR of Bentley.=MARY, dau. of Thos Beckingham, from whom Henry Beckingham of Wraysbury, p. 96.=
  - EDWARD, 3rd Lord, d. 1575.    HENRY, d. 1605.=
- THOMAS, 5th Lord, d. 1642, left estates to Thomas Hickman.
- ANDREW, d. sp.
- ELIZABETH=DIXIE HICKMAN of Oxon.
- PETER of Fenditton, Camb.
- THOMAS, 7th Baron Windsor, cr. Earl of Plymouth, 1682.
- EDWARD, son of Sir John Harcourt, who d. 1566.=ANN=JOHN PUREFOY of Bucks.
- THOMAS, æt 55, in 1623.=
- ANDREW, æt. 11, in 1632.    WILLIAM, æt. 7, in 1623.

In deeds subsequent to the alienation of Stanwell from the Windsors we still find them holding property in the locality, and the family of Digby about this period enter and sustain influence for many annual revolutions. A recovery fine, Trin. 24 Henry VIII. 1532, shews how William Sparry and William Wheeler (probably of Datchet) seek against Reginald Digby, Esq., and his wife Ann, certain property in Colnbrook, Langley Marsh, Iver and Wraysbury, and to these are added not only the advowson of Horton, subject to perpetual alienation and recovery, but also the Manor of Horton, and this with the consent of the Wyndsor proprietor.

This transaction is followed and confirmed by a fine, Hil. 29 Henry VIII. 1539, with the same parties, and from this juncture the Digby family appears prominently in Horton, as the next recorded evidence shews, Easter 34 Henry VIII. 1544, Sir Andrew Windsor buying of Reginald Digby, Esq. various pieces of property in Horton.

An intermarriage of the Brome family also introduces them into this parish. This is a distinct house from that of Brome who held lands in Wraysbury in the 17th century (page 22).

By fine, Trin. 6 Ed. VI. 1553, Ralph Brome, Esq. and others, are querents against Ann Digby, widow, who is deforcient of the Manor of Horton with appurtenants in Colnbrook and Langley Marsh, with the advowson of the church.

Ralph, son of Sir Nicholas Brome of Baddisley, county Warwick, had married Alice, daughter of Reginald Digby, so it was very likely to be some marriage arrangement which suggested his appearing as plaintiff in the cited deed of conveyance, which instrument is followed by one, Easter 1569, when Edward Windsor, son of Andrew Lord Windsor, seeks against Ambrose Digby, senior, in which reference is made to certain rents and *annates* with George Digby in Horton, Colnbrook, Langley, &c.

The same proprietors continue here for some 80 years longer, when their possessions passed by purchase to the Bulstrodes, although there were some intermediary changes between the Digbys, as the fine, Trin. 4 Jac. I. 1606, evinces, when Abigail Digby, widow, obtains property here of Robert Digby, and in 1611 the same lady sells to Sir John Jackson her interests in some Colnbrook tenements.

The remainder of the Digby possessions seem to end by the Michaelmas deed 1617, when Henry Bulstrode acquires by purchase the manor of Sir Richard Digby, which terminates their territorial alliance with the parish, and the chief proprietorship devolved on the Bulstrodes, whose connection with Horton had been unbroken since the exciting æra of King Edward IV. and the relentless wars of the Roses, which made all England to tremble and wail.

Before I insert a succinct pedigree of Digby to illustrate this section of the Horton history, I will advert to a case in Chancery, dated 6th October, 1596, between William Higgins and Thomas Glisson and others, relative to a claim by lease of a farm or grange in Horton, with divers lands in the parish demised to the plaintiff by deed of indenture, 26th May, 1579, for 21 years at £50. yearly by Sir George Digby, Knight, deceased (second son of Sir Everard Digby of Drystoke,) and the Lady Abigail, his wife; and afterwards to Robert, son and heir of the same.

There was an answer put in to this suit, 13th November, 1596, by Thomas Glisson, who alleged that the lease of the farm was *distended* to Robert Digby for £40, for a term yet unexpired, and he complains of the non-fulfilment of the conditions.

## PEDIGREE OF DIGBY.

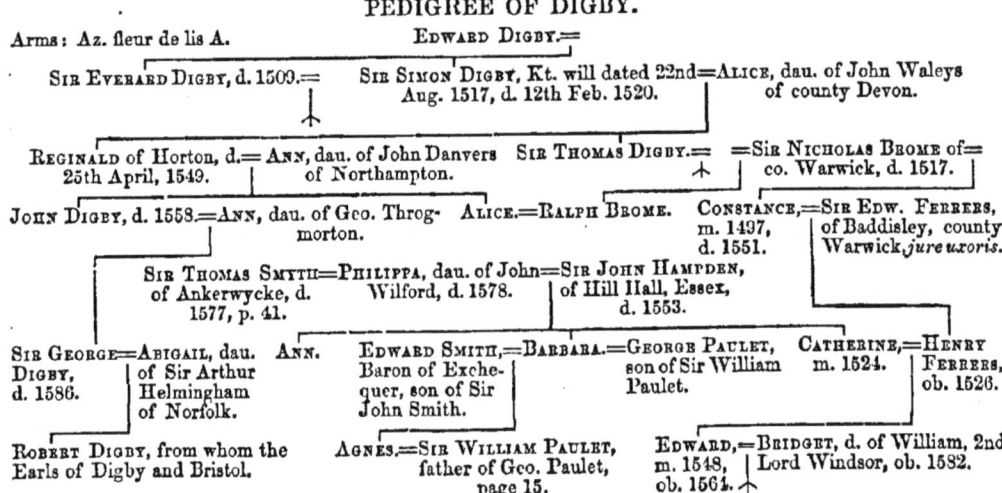

Before I treat of the next substantial owner of this manor, I will mention *en passant* that the Crown had interests here, and by deed, 20th April, 36 Elizabeth, 1593, one William Gerevend occupied under lease of the Crown for 21 years, at 5s rent per annum, the church house, probably some houses or tenements adjacent to the holy edifice.

The next proceeding of consequence bears date 2nd July, 1595, whereby we find the family of Tredway first introduced into Horton—a name conspicuous in the parish registers. Richard Tredway, Esq. of Beaconsfield (who presented to the Church of Stoke Poges in 1592, and his son Walter in 1601, from whom Henry Tredway in 1658) had dealings with John Chamberlayne, jun. gentleman, and Elizabeth his wife, daughter of Richard Tredway, were seized by virtue of the said Elizabeth in the church and advowson of Stoke Poges, and of two messuages and 7½ acres of land in Colnbrook, with divers lands in Iver and Horton, &c. which they did, 29 Elizabeth, 1586, convey to Robert and William Chamberlayne, and after the death of Elizabeth his wife, daughter of Thomas Bowser, son of Thomas Bowser, old inhabitants. It seems that William Higgins and Jane his wife bought the same of John and Elizabeth Chamberlayne, which lands were then in the tenure of Thomas Reader and John Andrews, and that the said Richard Tredway had compounded with — Gille, Esq. of London,* (probably Thomas or Ralph Gille of the Tower of London—see Topographer, Vol. VIII. p. 208) for £200, and this was the origin of the lawsuit. The parties were proprietors of the George Inn, Colnbrook, as is shewn in the answer of William Tredway, 10th July, 1595. Chancery proceedings:—In law phraseology the case and object of the suit was for relief against recognisances affecting the plaintiff's purchase, comprising the manor and parsonage of Stoke Poges, sold and conveyed to the plaintiff by John Chamberlayne, who disposed of it to Higgins, and entered into recognisance for performance of covenants, by which the defendants seek to restrain land, all which or part of them were parcel of the manor of Langley Marsh, and were held by defendant of the Crown. The deed of fine assuring to Richard Tredway the manor of Stoke Poges, &c. which he bought of John Chamberlayne, is 31 Elizabeth, 1588.

About this date we find the name of Peters, destined to hold influence in Horton, appears, of whom mention is made in Wraysbury (page 61). In Hil. 1594, William Marsham and John Pennar, Esq. buy of William Peters, gentleman, 4 messuages, 4 gardens, 100 acres land, 100 meadow, 4 pasture, 4 wood, 10 briar and waste, and 12d rent in Horton, Wraysbury, Iver and Stoke, and a very considerable purchase was effected in Horton and the adjacent parishes by Sir William Bulstrode and Nicholas Georgey, gentleman, from John Gyles, gentleman, and John Woodward, gentleman, comprising more than 1000 acres, besides tenements and gardens, &c. Also Sir Michael Greene in 1605 buys of Henry Rysley, gentleman, the manor of Mansfield, in which deed there is a recapitulation of divers pieces of property in Horton, Langley, &c.

The name of Edwards was of some significance in the time of Elizabeth, 1560, and in this year there is a fine between George Edwards and Henry Balnett of Horton, who either went to reside in Wraysbury, as a yeoman farmer, or who held lands in that parish.

* This branch of the family of Gyll distended were "Keepers of the Queen's Lyons," and it may not be uninteresting to state that in 1235, Frederick, Emperor of Germany, sent to King Henry III. of England, three leopards, &c. which were removed to Woodstock Park, and afterwards to the Tower as a royal appendage to the state. King Edward II. ordered the Sheriffs of London to pay the Lion Keeper sixpence a day for the beasts, and three halfpence a day for the keeper out of the fee-farm of the city. By degrees it became a *patent place*, and was filled by the following individuals:—John Boure, 1343; Robert Mansfield, 1438 and 1459; Thomas Rooke, 1460; Richard Hastings, 1464; Humphrey, Duke of Buckingham, 1483; Aubrey de Vere, Earl of Oxford, 1485; Sir James Worseley, 1512, relative of Otwell Worsely, p. 205; Ralph Worsely, 1531, who appointed Thomas Gyll, 1573-1586; Ralph Gyll, 1605; and in 1613 Michael and Thomas Heneage held it conjointly with Gyll; Robert Gyll, 1620; William Gyll, 1673, who is buried in St. Peter's Church, Tower of London, as Captain Gill Lyon Keeper, 10th September, 1686. His two daughters and coheirs sold the appointment which the Gyll family had held for 113 years. The Zoological Gardens, Regent's Park, received the wild animals, which were sold some years since.

The respectable name of Croke, of whom mention is made, and a pedigree given (page 61) as united in several unions with the house of Bulstrode, is found in a deed of fine, 39 Elizabeth, while William Peters, gentleman, and George Higgins, gentleman (may be son of William Higgins before cited), are found in deeds of date 1604.

Before the manor was given by King James I. to Sir Thomas Knyvett, I will briefly recapitulate the names of John Brockett, Esq. and Edmund Salter, gentleman, a branch of the Iver House. Sir Thomas Cheney and Henry Cheney, who interchanged properties at Horton in 1613, and John Cheney, buried at Horton 1600, and the family of Shorter, one of whom was a landowner here, all among the dominant proprietary in Horton, of whom more under Colnbrook.

This stage now conducts us to the notable grant by King James I. to the family of Knyvett.

Sir Thomas Knyvett was in high favour with this king, hence these lands with the manor of Stanwell, which was ceded to him by grant, 5th August, 1603, and which had lately been in the possession of Geoffrey Child, gentleman, with the manor of Poyle, and subsequently the manor of Horton, were granted 23rd March, 1613, to Sir T. Knyvett, Kt., on payment of £1459, and a fee farm rent to the Crown from lands late in the possession of Ann Peters, William Peters, and John Peters, senior. This Knight did good service to the Crown, and was raised to the honour and dignity of a Baron in 1607. He paid for lands in Horton annually £3. 8s 10d, holding a cottage, two closes, and a tenement, and other lands of a yearly value of 9s 6d: to hold to Lord Knyvett and his heirs as of the manor of Hampton Court by Knight's service, Parliamentary Rolls, 11 Jac. I. Test. 22, March 1613. By deed dated 23rd December, 1613, Lord Knyvett was made Lord of the manor of Staines for £80, and there is cited a previous deed, 29th May, 42 Elizabeth, 1600, in which mention is made of one Edward Ferrers, of London, mercer, and Francis Phelips, of London, gentleman, who held property in the vicinity.

Sir Thomas Knyvett was one of those influential aristocrats who had been appointed Gentlemen of the Privy Chamber to James I., who in 1605, upon the *mysterious* information conveyed by letter to Lord Mounteagle, was sent, being Justice of Peace also in Westminster, to make search with others in the vaults and cellars under the House of Lords, where Guy Fawkes was discovered, and so the gunpowder treason was detected and averted, which annual search continued till lately under Sir Seymour Sadler, Kt. sometime exon of the Royal body guards.

This Baron seemed to have given proof of his loyalty, and satisfaction to his royal master during his life, which was closed in 1622. He died issueless, hence his newly acquired honours became extinct, and singular too that either grief or some other stroke of fate caused his wife to end her pilgrimage in the very same year with her husband, to whom she had been united many decades.

They both lie buried under a gorgeous monument in Stanwell Church, a pair to that noble monument erected there to the memory of Thomas, father of Lord Windsor, who was despoiled of his estate. It is of veined marble, supported by columns of the Corinthian order, their effigies large as life, and the postures kneeling, indicative of supplication for grace. The Baron left instructions in his will for the building of a free school in Stanwell, and a house for the master to instruct poor children in that parish, for the sustentation of which a farm was bought in this county, which let at £40 a year, although the prescription and injunction in the will was that it should realise £20 per annum at least.

This gentleman, of a noble stock, was also fashioned to much honour, so I annex a short pedigree; but the curious I refer to Blomfild's Norfolk, which draws his lineage from very remote ancestry, nobles in that shire of credit and renown. It does not appear that the manor of Horton was long in the tenure of Lord Knyvett, although he continued to dwell at Stanwell, and made it his chief quarters, where he expired.

## HISTORY OF HORTON.

### PEDIGREE OF KNYVETT.

Arg. a bend S. within a bordure engrailed of the same.

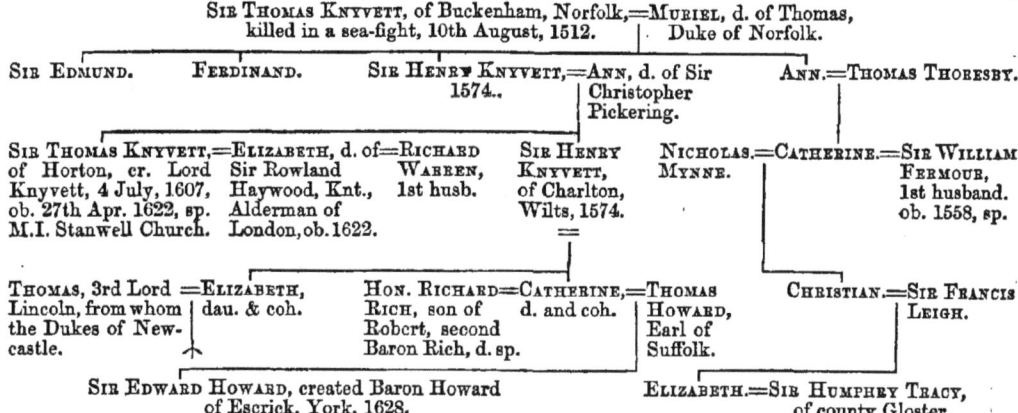

In Jones' Records, Vol. II., 13 James I., 1615, there are letters patent about the concession of the court leet and view of frankpledge relative to the manor of Horton, and this was a prelude to its next alienation, for by fine Mich. 15 James I., 1617, the manor or claims on it seem to have been still in the right of Sir Richard Digby, who is styled *deforciant* when it was bought by Henry Bulstrode, Esq. He was then tenant of the Mills at Wraysbury, and by patent 24th April, 1616, had a right of free warren in Wraysbury and Horton, while various fines of the period shew that large increments were made to his possessions in this section of the shire.

The manor and rectory now came into the hands of Felix Wilson, gentleman, who buys them of Henry Bulstrode, Esq. by recovery deed Trin. 16 James I. 1618. This comprised also the advowson, 14 acres waste, 4 cottages, 10 gardens, 300 acres land, 50 meadow, 400 briar, &c., with certain specific money rents in Horton, Wraysbury, and adjacent localities. The name appended to the deed as vouchee is that of Sir Robert Digby, Knt. This was a mere conveyance effected through the lawyer, Mr. Wilson, whose name is conspicuous in many analogous transactions in the neighbourhood. He also bought Place Farm, Wraysbury (page 58), and was a man of some distinction and utility here and at Colnbrook, where he resided, for we find he had two children buried in the Horton Cemetery in 1613, and in 1639 the wife of Felix Wilson the younger is here interred.

The Bulstrodes were now lords in Horton, and they possessed the advowson, which they seem not to have done since their connection with the parish in 1478; and so to fortify their hands the fines and recoveries indicate various sales and purchases in Wraysbury, here, and in the vicinity.

In 1618 a transaction is recorded between Henry Rawson and Henry Bulstrode, relative to *tents.* in Horton and Iver, and in 1624 Mr. Bulstrode obtains some of the Edwards' property in Horton. He added still more in 1633, bought from John Reeve and Samuel Enderby. In 1624 Felix Wilson and Joseph Lane, the two lawyers, buy of Henry Bulstrode some tenements and about 50 acres of land, to which deed the name of Thomas Cowardelow is annexed. In 1633 Philip Smith appears as querent against Henry Bulstrode for some additional 50 acres in Horton and Wraysbury. The same Mr. Bulstrode is found in a transaction with George Goade in Colnbrook, and from this time he ceases to be a purchaser. The son of this Henry, of the same name, was buried 29th October, 1604, and in 1629 his sister Dorothy is also recorded as buried in Horton. Parish registers.

Mr. Bulstrode married very young about 1598, for he had a daughter baptized in 1600, and a son Edward (of Wraysbury) baptized in 1608. Several children followed at Horton.

He himself was baptized 5th January 1578, at Upton, being son and heir of Edward Bulstrode, who died 1596, and was interred at Upton. Mr. Henry Bulstrode departed this world in 1632, aged only 54, and his first wife Mary, daughter and heir of Thomas Read of Abingdon, predeceased him in 1614. Henry Bulstrode, who appears as purchaser of some property in Horton, succeeded as son and heir, and died also in 1643 unmarried.

To continue the chain of evidence I shall cite the next deed, which is Hil. 12 Charles I. 1636, in which Edward Bulstrode and Richard Edwards seek against Edward Woodward, a relative of the Bulstrodes, 18 messuages, 1 garden, 200 acres land, 40 pasture, 60 ditto, with *appurts.* in Horton, Colnbrook and Wraysbury, and the name appended as vouchee is Thomas Bulstrode. In another deed of 1641, between Thomas Knight, brother-in-law of Henry and Thomas Bulstrode, *v.* Robert Hall and Thomas Tredway, there is a conveyance of some magnitude, in which the Bulstrodes again appear.

The second brother, Thomas, was now in entire possession of Horton manor, with the advowson which he inherited by the decease of his elder brother Henry Bulstrode unmarried. But as his will is not in London, and indeed there are very few of the Bulstrode wills there, it is not certain if he obtained his property by descent or bequest. He was not so enamoured of Horton as not to alienate very soon after his succession, for in 1646 Elizabeth Draper, widow, buys land of him, and in 1647 we find his brother-in-law, Thomas Knight, again releasing him of his acres. This is followed by another portion of soil of the once concentrated holdings here, disposed of to William Fletcher in 1648, to be a precursor of further alienations.

This family were considerable holders in Hedgerly, Upton and Horton. Thomas Bulstrode, now in entire possession of Horton manor and advowson, probably deemed it advisable to concentrate himself in Hedgerly; a deed of 1650 with Ann Durdant, widow, is to this effect, as well as three deeds enrolled in sequence, Close Rolls, 1649. Indenture between Thomas Bulstrode, Esq. and his wife Susanna, and Edward Goodall, gentleman, of Horton (son of Edward Goodall, Rector here). The latter gives £600 to the former for certain lands in the parish, viz., Flad Campe, 23 acres, in the occupation of John Haines, yeoman; Duke's Close, adjoining the dwelling house of Mr. John Peters, 7 acres; a cottage and meadow in Wyrardisbury mead, in the tenure of Thomas Ashby of Horton, with *tents.* garden, eyots, &c. formerly held by Richard Cripps, deceased, and now held by Richard Norris, maltster.

Another indenture, 20th November, 1649, between the very same parties, when Mr. Goodall receives of Mr. Bulstrode £130 for a close, pasture, &c. in Barrowfield, and six acres in Deeplake Common, in the occupation of John Helperly, near a freehold belonging to — Lydgold, widow, late purchased by Edward Goodall and Sarah his wife.

The third indenture of the same date, Thomas Bulstrode, Esq. and Susanna his wife sell to Richard West, papermaker, for £140, a messuage and *tent.* in Horton, where John Helperly dwells, some land, garden and orchard, with a piece of meadow in Wyrardisbury Mead, and an eyot; property in Colebrooke field, near Newbridge Green, and 17 acres in High Cross, Horton; and a part of Fisher's Farm, near Ditton Hatch, held by Tobias Osgood.

In order that the succession of property may be traced (although these conveyances may be uninteresting to the general reader it may not so be with those topographers who minutely scrutinize the passes from one hand to another) I shall detail another fine, Easter 1650, between Daniel Cox, gentleman, of Windsor and Sir John Pettus, Knt. *v.* Thomas Bulstrode, Esq. and Susanna his wife, deforciants of the manor of Horton, viz., 3 messuages, 3 cottages, 4 barns, 2 dovecots, 6 gardens, 6 orchards, 160 acres of land, 24 meadow, 34 pasture, 6 ditto water, and 40s rent, view of frankpledge, &c. in Horton and Wraysbury.

Also the advowson of Horton Church. This sale was effected after the second proclamation made consequent on a fine 27th May, 1650.

The manor was now completely out of the hands of the Bulstrode family, and to its purchase, 17 Charles I. 1640, of Robert Hall, gentleman, the lawyer, by Thomas Bulstrode, I advert, as well as to the deed of indenture, 26th November, 1627, between John Sharowe, gentleman, citizen and merchant tailor, relative to the sale of Wraysbury manor, which was acquired by Henry, father of Thomas Bulstrode, (page 18).

There seem to be sundry windings and doublings about this manor, for in a deed, 1641, Robert Hall buys the manor again.

Of Daniel Cox, as joint Lord here with Sir John Pettus, I have no information, but the knight was of some transient notoriety in his day. He was son of Sir Thomas Pettus, Bart., of Rackheath, Norfolk, and married in 1637 Elizabeth, daughter of Sir Richard Gurney, Lord Mayor of London in 1641. His wife's sister Ann was wife of Thomas Richardson, second Lord Cramond, grandson of Chief Justice Richardson who issued an order against *wakes*, and directed it to be read in churches. This alarmed the Bishops, and a certificate was signed by 70 clergymen to prove the antiquity and *inoffensiveness* of wakes and fairs, which being sent, a Bishop reported it at the Council table, where the Chief Justice was so severely reprimanded that he came out of Court facetiously complaining that he had been nearly *choked* by a pair of *lawn sleeves*. The Judge died in 1634. One Sir John Pettus had been M.P. for Dunwich, Suffolk, but he died ultimately in the Fleet Prison in 1690. He wrote a treatise, in 1683, on mines, and a work called *Fleta Minor*, or the art of assaying metals.

Before we come to the last conveyance of Horton manor to the family of Scawen, I must advert to the fact that there is hardly one purchase on the part of the Bulstrodes to balance his frequent dispossessions.

In 1663 Timothy West relieves Thomas Bulstrode of his solid property here, and there are conveyances in 1669, 1670 and 1671, indicative of a downward tendency. The year 1671 records a conveyance to William Sandford, Esq. (page 21), and in the same year Thomas Bowry became proprietor in fee by purchase of more of the Bulstrode estates, and so until 1676, when Thomas Bulstrode died. The last of the name hereabouts is Henry Bulstrode, his son, who appears in the Court Rolls of Yeoveny manor in 1691, where an ancestor, George Bulstrode, who died in 1558, held lands, and Thomas was his heir.

The family of Bulstrode had towered above the common mark, and were much above mediocrity for talents, position, opulence and descent. A short *precis* may not be uninteresting to qualify the aridity of land conveyances, which are the staple in topographical researches.

The manor of Temple Bulstrode is in Hedgerly, and in 1537 it was bestowed on Bisham Abbey, which was endowed as a mitred abbey for Benedictine monks, as Ankerwycke had been.

In the family records of the Bulstrodes it is alleged that William the Conqueror granted the estate of the Shobbingtons, whose capital seat, now called Bulstrode, was situated in the centre of a fine park at Gerard's Cross, Beaconsfield, to a Norman lord; but that the Shobbingtons would not render possession to one who wished to wrench it by force, hence they collected friends, ammunition and cattle, to repulse the Norman invader, and this they did so effectually that they retained their hold. Shobbington was cited into the presence of the Conqueror, William I. and he, with his seven sons, came before Majesty riding on a BULL, and being asked why he resisted when the *whole* island had yielded, he replied that his antecessors had there dwelt time out of mind whereof the memory of man ran not to the contrary; but he promised if he were allowed to enjoy the inheritance he would become a faithful vassal to the successful sovereign. A distich runs:

"When William conquered English ground,—Bulstrode had *per ann.* 300 pound."

On this the King passed his royal word, and so—uniting equity and liberality in a knot—the estates confirmed to the petitioner were transmitted in the right line, until the inheritance dwindled into a *female*, the fate of most estates and titles.

This is probably one of the many dubious and vain oral transmissions which abound in most counties and kingdoms and private families, especially in Scotland, where tradition is as rife and is held as tenaciously as in Rome; and it brings to mind Dr. Johnson's remark, in his Tour to the Hebrides, "that a Scotchman loves Scotland better than truth; he will always love it better than inquiry, and if *falsehood* flatters his vanity he will not be very diligent to detect it." This may be predicated of most family *traditions*. The legend of the bull-striding occasioned the name *Bul-strode*, and the crest of the family, a bull's head and neck between two wings expanded, indicate the furious *momentum* of the naturally tardy beast. It is not unlikely the word may mean only a *pasture* for bulls.

Bulstrode Park was once the seat of the Duke of Somerset, and it also was the residence of the infamous Lord Chancellor Jeffries—the only Chancellor known for bloodthirstiness—who in 1685 held the *bloody assize*, which King James II., who sanctioned his tendency, jocosely called *Jeffries' campaign*, when neither age, sex, nor character escaped vengeance; and as he was the worst judge (morally) that ever soiled the ermine (some have been convicted of bribery, as Bacon and Earl Macclesfield), so his deeds are recorded in the annals of his country in letters of *blood*, and he lived to reap in grief what he had sowed in shame. This *model* Chancellor under the *tolerant* reign of King James II. had a daughter Mary, who married Charles Dyve of Lincoln's Inn, and he sold Bulstrode to the Duke of Portland. It is known that Jeffries built the house in 1686, but it was subsequently improved, and it stands in a park of 800 acres, displaying all the charms that can be produced by diversified surface, commanding situation, and sylvan grandeur.

To remount genealogically to the early history, let us revert to Robert Bulstrode in 1339, who, by marrying into the Sampson family, got the Hedgerly estates, where they dwelt, concurrently with Upton and Horton—for Thomas Bulstrode, in his will of 1560, adverts to these mansions, leaving them to his wife Ann for life, with this injunction, that she is to support them and keep them in repair, and not to *let* them.

The earliest records enrolled of this name is John, in 1311. His line died out in his great-granddaughter Agnes, daughter and sole heir of Robert Bulstrode. She married for her first husband John Shobingdon, who assumed the patronymic of Bulstrode. Nicholas de Shobingdon, one of the same family, was Prior of Burchester, Oxon, in 1349, and William, son of this John, died in 1472, leaving Richard, the eldest of nine sons, who deceased 1496. He made a marriage which secured to him the Chalvey estate, and through the Wyots of Wraysbury and Iver he obtained Horton property, and presented to the living of the latter in 1478. He was in the commission of the peace for Bucks to the end of his life, as were Edward and William Bulstrode in 1502; the latter was appointed to the Cocket Seal, and was collector of the customs on wool, hides, &c. in the ports of London, 10th July, 1509. Richard's son Edward carried on the line; whose brother or kin, William Bulstrode, was Minor Canon of Windsor.

"Pray for the soule of William Bulstrod, late Pety Canon of Windsore, whiche deceased the first day of May, the yeare of Our Lord mbxrii. on whose soule Jhu habe mercy."

Let us turn to the Thomas Bulstrode, mentioned before, whose will was proved in the Prerogative Office, 24th November, 1560, and in it he cites his second son Francis, to whom he leaves his Berkyn estate, but Francis died the next year, and it devolved on Edward, his elder brother. His mother, Joan Pigot, died the same year, and was interred at Horton. The Mr. Bulstrode (brother of

Thomas) had a son John of Horton, who died 1579, and the Woodwards are cited as relatives. George Woodward was Clerk of the Constable of Windsor Castle, and succeeded John Gaudon, 20th October, 1509. They had a grant of arms in 1527, and appear in the early Visitations of Bucks.

Henry Bulstrode, son of Edward, who died 1596, was Lord of this Manor, and he died in 1632, while his son of the same name became a partisan in the civil wars. He it was who is mentioned in a decree of Parliament, 20th October, 1642, as publicly signalised. Taking notice of the good affections of Heny Bulstrode, he was authorised and appointed to raise all the forces of foot of the trained bands and volunteers within the three Hundreds of the Chilterns, viz., Burnham, Desborough, and Stoke, and to lead and conduct them against the threatening invaders, and to command them as their Colonel. They were assembled at Aylesbury, of which town he was made Governor, and Colonel of the Regiment late Fleetwood's. London Journals, Vol. vii. I insert here a letter of John Hampden, the patriot, addressed,—

"To my noble friends Colonell Bulstrod, Captaine Grenfield, Captaine Tyrrell, Captaine West, or any of them.

"Gentlemen,—The army is now at North Hampton, moving every day nearer to you, if you disband not wee may be a mutuall succour each to other, but if you disperse you make yourselves and y$^{rs}$ a *pray*. You shall hear daily fro' y$^{or}$ servant, J. HAMPDEN. North$^a$. 1 Nov. 1642."

There was another celebrity in this family, Edward, son of Edward Bulstrode of Hedgerly, who died 1596, and was a lawyer known for his Reports of Cases, temp. James and Charles I.; one of the Justices of North Wales in 1649, by the interest of his nephew, the celebrated Bulstrode Whitelock, he died 1659. A no less celebrated man was Sir Richard Bulstrode, whose unbending loyalty urged him to follow the fortunes of King James II. when he retired to France at the age of 80 years, and ended his days at St. Germains en Laye, 3rd October, 1711, aged 101 *years*, leaving 17 children alive, the eldest being 72, and the youngest only 13 years of age. Here was activity to the last; an ancient author compared old age to *straw*, which once filled with grain, became empty and ready to be reduced to dust; the emblem was adopted because it paints by a single stroke the transition from flourishing youth to barren decrepitude. Who would know more* of this eminent family and of the Bulstrode estate, would be pleased to read the Vicissitudes of Great Families by Sir Bernard Burke, Knight, who was made Ulster King at Arms in 1854, on the death of Sir William Betham. The father of Sir Bernard Burke and himself have done more for diffusing heraldry and genealogy, and popularising them, than any of their predecessors in these attractive pursuits, which almost come within the periphery of science.

From this episode let us now revert to the descent of the Manor, which, until its alienation to Cox and Pettus, had never been out of the hands of parties connected by birth and property with the parish from the days of the Confessor.

By indenture, 16th June, 1658, Close Rolls, Daniel Cox of New Windsor, gentleman, and Sir John Pettus, Knight, and Robert Scawen of Isleworth, Middlesex, and Russel Alsop of London, merchant, for and in consideration of a competent sum sell to Robert Scawen the Manor or Lordship, site, capital messuage, or Mansion House of Horton, with a close of pasture called Leaze, of six acres, late in the occupation of Alice Gilman. Ford's Close, part of Barrowfield, five acres; Osgood's Farm, or the Ashe Farm, late occupied by Thomas Hilliard. Also Colley Mead, Shollen, Colbrookefield, and other parts in the possession of Robert Biddle and Joseph Flatt of Horton, yeomen, and

---

* Bulstrode Wills, Prerogative Office. William Bulstrode, 1479. Sir William Bulstrode, 1525. Dame Matilda, 1532. Thomas, 1559. Margaret, 1541. Ann, 1561. Joane, 1617. John, 1625. Richard Bulstrode was Recorder of Reading, 1656. Henry Bulstrode gave £30. for the rebuilding of the new school of Eton College, which was begun in 1689 and finished at the cost of £2286. 9s 1d. This is one of the four endowed schools in Bucks, with Amersham, Aylesbury, and Buckingham.

of Richard Norris, lands with a malt-house and barns; Bulstrode Close, Barrowfields, Ray Hill and Deeplake Pond Close, in the occupation of Edward Haynes and Edward Herne; Ambrose Barnes, Robert Sharpe, with the eyots and osier plots by Richard Reeves.

It cites an indenture, 28th April 1650, between Thomas Bulstrode of the Inner Temple, and Daniel Cox and Sir John Pettus, Knight; also recites a fine of conveyance and details an account of the Rectory, advowson, donation, right of patronage, presentation, and free disposition of Horton Church, &c. all estates of freehold and inheritance, &c.

After so long a continuance in this especial parish and vicinity, in a few years not *one* of the many ramifications of this house is to be found. We have observed that Richard Bulstrode, who died 1496, was the eldest of nine sons, and nearly all married and had issue, but there is not a soul at this day that is known.* Sir Richard Bulstrode attained the patriarchal age of 101, and died in 1711, leaving 17 children; and Thomas Bulstrode who sold Horton, left also four sons, of whom nothing is recorded. Some straggling cadet branch may yet exist, but not in the shire of Bucks or the adjacent counties; shewing the instability of families who rarely continue more than a century in one locality, but are swiftly followed by others to be again displaced—like Time

"Truditur dies die,
Novæque pergunt interire Lunæ."

## PEDIGREE OF BULSTRODE AND CROKE.

Arms, S. a stag's head embossed A. In the mouth an arrow of the last; on the scalp between the attires, a cross formée fitchée O.

JOHN DE BULSTRODE, 5 Edward II. 1311.=

JOHN, fine 1338.=MARGERY, d. of Hugh Montford, of Chalfont, Bucks.

ROBERT, b. 1339.=—— d. of — Sampson, of Hedgerly, Bucks.

2nd hus. JOHN CHOPINDEN or=AGNES, d. and coheir.=1st hus. WILLIAM BRUDENELL, | ALICE, *ux.* Richard Widwick, of
SHOBBINGDON, took name of | See Pedigree of Brudenell. p. 206. | Rickmansworth, Herts.
Bulstrode.

WILLIAM BULSTRODE, Lord of Hedgerly by=AGNES, d. of William Norris, of | EDMUND BRUDENELL,=PHILIPPA, d. of Philip
right of his mother, devisee in remainder of | Bray, page 17. | will dated 7 Oct. 1457. | Englefield, of the Green.
lands in Chalfont, Iver, &c. in default of John
and Henry Brudenell, d. 1472.

RICHARD BULSTRODE,=ALICE, d. of Richard | ISABEL, *ux.* William | GEORGE, of London, | SIR ROBERT, of=MARGARET,
M.P. 1473, High She- | Knyffe, of Chalvey, | Langley, of Coln- | merchant. | Hawridge, 1478. d. of ——
riff, Bucks; 1473, pre- | heir of John Wyot, | brook.
sented to Horton Rec- | page 155, fine 1368,
tory, 1478, Inq. p. m. | m. 20th April, 1457.
1496.

| JOHN.=— d. of ——=WILLIAM PENNAR, WALTER, EDWARD, THOMAS. ROGER. HENRY=ELIZABETH,
| Germands· of Langley; fine Draper in a Fish- BUL- | d. of Thos.
SIR RICHARD= | worth. 1594. London. monger. STRODE. | Mow, of
EMPSON, p. 21. | Rochester.

JOHN PYNCHEON, of=JANE. | MARY, relict of=EDWARD BULSTRODE, High=2nd wife, ELLEN. | WILLIAM BULSTRODE, Minor
Writtle, Essex, d. | John Ashfield. | Sheriff of Bucks, 1503, died=3rd w. MARGARET. | Canon of Windsor, d. 1 May,
1578, p. 21. | 2nd August, 1517. | 1522, M.I. Eton.

FRANCIS PIGOT, of Stratton, Beds, | JOAN, buried at Horton,=GEORGE BULSTRODE of ditto, and Yeoveny,
d. 1553. | cited in the will of | Middlesex, d. 1558. p. 182.
| Thomas, her son.

A                 B

* Had this patronymic been Smith we had not been so sure of its extinction. The Patronymica Britannica remarks that out of 50 of the most common surnames of England and Wales in the entries of baptisms and burials for 1853, the name of Smith is found 33,557 times, while every 73rd person is of *that* name.

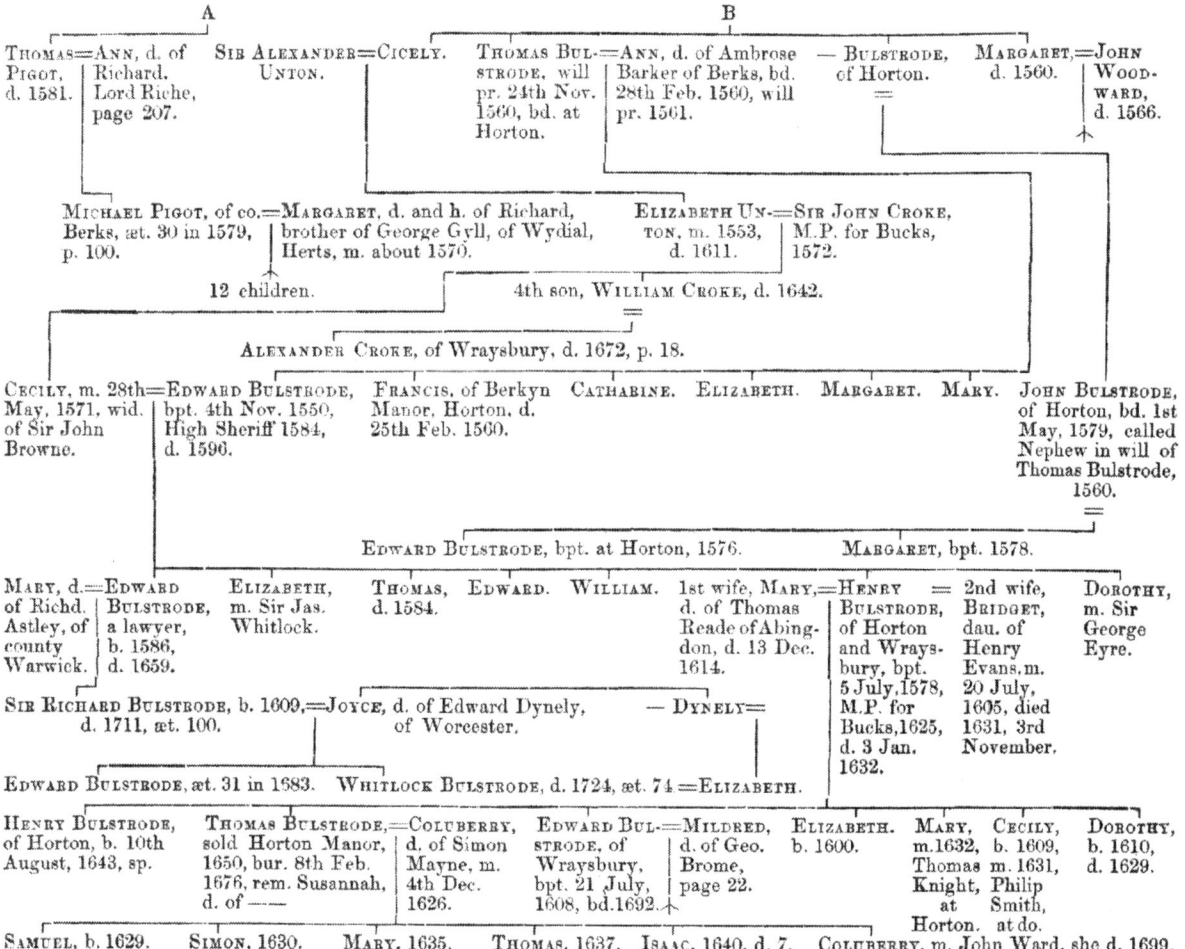

What tempted Robert Scawen to fix his capital residence in Horton lands must be left to conjecture, but being a citizen and a merchant, he was probably intimate with Sir John Pettus, Knight, of London, who vouched for it as a good investment. I have not found that either Cox or Pettus dwelt in Place House, or the mansion; they probably let it. When Scawen came he doubtless had a view to reside here as a country squire, and he put the mansion into repair for the reception of himself and family.

At this time, in 1657, there is an indenture between Philip Earl of Chesterfield, and this Robert Scawen, Esq. and Christopher Dodsworth; and another of the same date, with Robert Scawen and Sir Henry Spiller, Knight, of Laleham, Middlesex. This latter gentleman, who died 1649, had the site of the Manor of Laleham leased to him with the tithes in 1606 for 40 years, and his daughter Catherine brought them in marriage to Sir Thomas Reynell, Knight, who died 1655. Towards the end of the 17th century these tithes became the property of John Phillips, whose grandson, Phillips Gibbon, Esq. had a daughter Elizabeth, married to Philip Jodrell, Esq. who died 1763, younger brother of Gilbert Jodrell of Ankerwycke (page 23). Hence small investments in the vicinity may have been the prelude to the purchase of Horton Manor by Robert Scawen, whose family continued here till 1782. It may not be considered inappropriate to give a succinct detail of this family, originally from Cornwall.

The name is pronounced *Skoin*, and is found in Boscawen and Lanscawen. In fact the name is merely an abridgment of Lanscawen as the pedigree will show. To this name the figure *apocope* has only been applied, but many surnames lose all identity by *compression*, as Ollerenshaw is contracted into *Wrench*, a respected member of which family has been mentioned, p. 68. Besides the authority of Lysons, there are in the College of Arms 10 very ancient deeds in sustentation of the descent from Roger de Lanscawen, temp. Edward I. and the pedigree is entered in *Visitation*, 1620. The younger branch of this house left Cornwall, and those who remain, if any, are in obscurity.

The inquisition of Robert Scawen of Mollenich, was taken in 1630, and this Robert of Horton was his son and heir. He it was who entered business, although he inherited the manor of Anthony Mollenich in Cornwall from his ancestors; yet he and his brothers and sisters seem to have done well in their earthly pilgrimages as their wills denote. Robert was immediate ancestor of two knights, and some descendants who had credit for being among the wealthiest of commoners, and he came to dwell at Place House soon after his purchase in 1658, for in that year he baptizes his son, Humphrey at Horton, and he himself was the first of his family to be buried in the family vault in 1669, within the precincts of the church.

Whether he was popular, or what was his character no records shew. His will is dated 5th Jan. 1667, and proved 21st March, 1699, and by it his widow became Lady of the Manor for her life. She was Catherine, daughter of Cavendish Alsop, sister of Russel Alsop, joint-purchaser with Mr. Scawen, in 1658, hence she might through her brother have a collateral interest in the property. She outlived her husband 15 years, and was consigned to the same resting-place 12th August, 1684. Mr. Scawen left the manor in trust with others to his brother Francis Scawen, who died issueless in 1669. His will cites only his cousins Jane, Alice, Mary Scawen. The manor passed to Edward Scawen, Robert's brother, who was buried in Horton Church, 29th Sept. 1691, and in the entry he is styled Lord of the Manor. Occasion will be given to speak of Rev. John Scawen, Rector here, and a younger brother, who was buried in 1695, under the Ecclesiastical history of this village.

After the death of Catherine Scawen in 1684, by deed of fine, Trin. 1686, Thomas Hinton, Gent. buys of Thomas Child, Gent. the manor of Horton with appurtenants, six messuages, one mill, 12 gardens, 160 acres land arable, 24 meadow, 34 pasture, six acres of water course, and 40s rent, with frankpledge (pledge or surety for the good behaviour of freemen) in Horton, Wraysbury, Colnbrook, and adjacent places, with the advowson of Horton Church, and to this deed the name of Edward Swatkin is attached as vouchee.

This was only some family arrangement, as we find Edward Scawen, Esq. died Lord here in 1691, for the estate now passed in all its plenitude to Robert's eldest son, Sir Thomas Scawen, Knight, and Alderman of London, whose wealth enabled him to buy largely in Surrey, and so he settled himself at Reigate. His birth took place about 1644, and his will suggests that his marriage was in 1691, as the settlements are dated 3rd September of that year. He chose Martha, daughter of Abraham Wessell, a very rich Dutch merchant, with whose dowry he swelled his own large possessions. His will is dated 4th July, 1730, by which he shews that he was associated in business with Richard Stockdale, whose son John married at Horton 9th February, 1661, Catherine, sister of Sir Thomas Scawen, while another sister, Ann, was here united in matrimony to John Hussey, 27th March 1676.

Sir Thomas died shortly after the date of his will, and on the 1st October 1730, his mortal remains were deposited in Horton, and had the same earth to cover him and his parents. By his will, proved 10th October following his decease, he makes large provision for his children. The eldest, Thomas, got the Horton estates in addition to a large succession from his uncle Sir William Scawen, Knight, who had departed this world 17th October 1722, without any family. Amongst his charities is that of £100. for repair of Eton College Chapel in 1699 and 1700. He was 7th son of his father, and had been Governor of the Bank of England, 1695, and M.P. for Surrey, 4, 6, 7 Ann. He exercised some influence here after the decease of his uncle Edward, and presented to the Rectory his relative William Nanney. His very extensive property at Carshalton descended to his nephew, while his widow Mary, daughter of Sir William Maynard of Essex, who died in 1700, had an ample jointure. His brother's widow Martha, who did not die till 1766, presented to the same living in 1750 Edward Dicey.

The next successor was Thomas Scawen, son and heir of his father of both names, M.P. for Surrey 1727, and is styled of Maidwell, Northampton. He did not reside here, and in fact the mansion was let. His brothers, three in number, were interred in Horton; Robert and Colonel Francis in 1708, and the new successor was Sir Thomas in 1725. The Rector, Robert Nanney, their relative, is shewn by his monument in the chancel to have become a lifeless tenant in the same vault in 1734.

We now come to another family arrangement, whereby the manor was again ostensibly alienated from the house of Scawen, for by fine, Trin. 1772, Samuel Swenfen and William Cornish, Gent. buy for the fictitious sum of £1000, of Sir Thomas Scawen, Knight, and Martha his wife, the manor of Horton, six messuages, two dove-cots, 130 acres land, 50 meadow, 30 pasture, &c. with the advowson of the church. Robert Nanney, their relative, was presented to the living in 1721, and dying, as remarked before, in 1734, the presentation was in Dame Martha Scawen, Sir Thomas' widow, so it is manifest that the Scawen interest was loath to leave. In 1750 this lady again appointed to the incumbency, nor was it until 1782 that the perpetual advowson of the Rectory was transferred from Scawen to John Brown, Esq. of Tottenham, Middlesex, who in July of that year presented the Rev. Thomas Roberts *vice* John Blair, the celebrated compiler of the Chronological Tables, of whom under the Ecclesiastical history.

A new adjustment caused the Horton estates to pass apparently into other hands, and to be bought by deed, Easter 13 George I. 1725. Catherine, daughter of Sir Thomas Scawen, had married 21st May 1717, Sir John Shelley, Bart. of Sussex, and she died unluckily by a fall from her horse in 1726. Of this family was Percy Bysshe Shelley the poet, drowned off Leghorn, and buried in Rome, 1822.

A relative of this house, Robert Shelley, continued in the parish and was Churchwarden in 1789, and Mary, sister of Sir John Shelley, married Sir John Lawson, Bart. and singular that there is a monument to Miss Emilia Lawson, only daughter of Sir Gilfred Lawson, Bart. in the middle of the nave, but they are two distinct families.

The deed of fine goes to the alienation of the entire property, in which Sir John Shelley disposes of it to William Gaskarth, Gent. the lawyer, and the specification in the instrument is the manor of Horton, six messuages, 130 acres of land, 50 meadow, 30 pasture, courts leet and baron and frankpledge, with the advowson of Horton Church; vouchees, Sir Thomas Walker and Thomas Walker. This seems a copy of the transfer made in 1722.

In 1745, died Thomas Scawen, Esq. of Horton, who in 1725 had been Esquire of Lord Delawarr's Company, and was said to be the *richest* commoner in England. He married 8th June 1725, Tryphena, daughter and sole heir of Lord James Russell, 6th son of the 1st Duke of Bedford. His son and heir James Scawen, was M.P. for Surrey in 1774, and died issueless in 1800. He it was who sold the Horton estates in 1782, as an indenture goes to certify. His sister Tryphena married 14th June 1759, to Henry, 2nd Earl of Bathurst, son of the famous Earl, patron of Pope and a friend of literature in all its branches, and eventually the estates and accumulations of the industry, good fortune, and frugality of the Scawens became centred in the house of Bathurst, whose junior branches yet bear the cherished and *euphonious* baptismal name of Tryphena. A member of this family, Frances, sister of Tryphena, daughter of Henry Bathurst, son of Dr. Henry Bathurst, Bishop of Norwich, was married in 1830 to John Graver, Esq. who assumed the name of Browne, and acquired the estate of Morley Hall in the county of Norfolk; he died 1861, and his only son and heir, John Bathurst Graver Browne, is the worthy representative of his house.

Lewis Scawen, the second son of Sir Thomas, who is styled of Horton House, deceased in 1740, and before the death of his wife all their children departed without leaving issue. I shall turn therefore to another brother connected with Horton, viz. William Scawen, an unfortunate member of a very prosperous house, who, it was said, was poisoned in 1775, by one Mrs. Butterfield.

The reader may pardon a digression here, which relates to the trial consequent on the alleged poison case. The apothecary, Mr. Cochran, deposed that William Scawen was greatly emaciated, and that his arm was in a gangrenous condition. Mr. Panxy said he saw him on the 4th May, and that on the 14th of June the patient complained of a *brassy* taste in his mouth, and that he was in a state of salivation, and that on being removed to Panxy's house he made a fresh will and soon after died. Miss Butterfield procured her defence to be read, and she therein alleged that at 14 years of age she was abducted from her parents by one of her own sex, and brought to Mr. Scawen, and that the circumstance broke her father's heart. That she loved Mr. Scawen, who in addition to great personal kindness had been very liberal towards her education, and that she by her conduct for many years had convinced him of her unfeigned affection and gratitude; and that during a protracted illness she had watched over him and dispensed his food and medicines; that she was treated by the neighbours as his *wife*, and that she repudiated with horror the imputation of murder with which she was charged; she warmly invoked *equity* of decision in her favour, which is not only justice, but a rectification and amendment of it.

She called many most reputable witnesses to sustain her character, so that after only *a quarter* of an hour's deliberation the jury returned a verdict of *not guilty*.

The trial lasted from seven in the morning till the afternoon. Mr. Scawen's will was disputed, but it was ultimately established in 1760; the bulk of the property, some part being in Horton, was bequeathed to Mrs. Butterfield, who, according to the opinion of the Judge, had not *tampered* with Mr. Scawen, and so the accused lady was exonerated from all suspicion.

A brief allusion to the remaining brother, Robert Scawen, will close this account of a house whose territorial influence subsisted from 1658 to the end of the 18th century in Horton; and as the transfer of property generally characterises these details, an occasional anecdote or incident may not be considered *de trop* to assist a creeping narrative.

The Reigate property was very extensive, and this Robert seems to have selected by preference the shire of Surrey for his general residence; and dying in 1778, he left by his wife Winifred, daughter of John Borret of Sussex, an only son John. Thomas Borret, her brother, had married, 16th Sept. 1735, Susanna, sister of this Robert Scawen, and in 1782 there was an administration granted to Louis Scawen, executor of her father's will and goods unadministered; and her only brother John, had a commission in the army as officer in the Guards. A duel took place between him and a Mr. Fitzgerald, 1st September 1773, at Lisle in the Austrian dominions, and the incident redounds to his credit, for having received his adversary's fire, he discharged his own pistol in the air, and on making an apology for the cause of the hostile meeting, the parties were reconciled. He died in India in 1800, leaving no issue by his wife, a daughter of the Earl of Albemarle. His surviving sister Winifred, married William Blunt of Springfield House, Sussex, a branch of the Blunts of Horton, collaterals of that of Lord Mountjoy.

Samuel Blunt, brother of this William, had a son Henry, who married Mary, sister of Henry William Atkinson, Esq. Provost of the Moneyers of the Royal Mint, whose son, Sir Jasper Atkinson, also Provost of the Mint, espoused Louisa, only daughter of Captain William Gyll of Wraysbury House (see Pedigree of Gyll, p. 100).

Mr. Robert Scawen was buried in a crypt of the church of Horton in 1778; Mary Nanney in 1787; and the last interment of any member of this opulent family was Martha, daughter of Louis Scawen, at the age of 67, in 1798.

Previous to the final disposal of the Horton estates in 1782, there was a deed of conveyance of this manor, Mich. 1778, when Samuel Duplick, Gent. buys of Thomas Winckley the manor of Horton with appurtenants, and the advowson of the Church. This again was a family arrangement.

It is to be remarked that during a period of nearly a century and a half how few purchases were effected by the Scawen family. In 1692 Thomas Rowe, Esq. buys property at Horton of John Scawen, Clerk, and in 1759 Thomas Scawen, Esq. and James Scawen, his son, are vouchees to some property bought in Boveney and Cippenham. These are all the deeds which public records disclose. Their wills evince they were not unmindful of parochial claims, and the memory of a time-honoured house is embalmed in a locality where Blair compiled the Chronicles of time and where Milton's hymns inspired piety, and his poems a thirst for glory.

It may be remarked also that of the once widely divergent branches of this family, there is not *one* person in England now bearing the appellation of Scawen—of almost corresponding antiquity with the Bulstrodes—both houses are declined to dust; and a memorable family of whom I shall write under the Manor House, of antiquity of birth and acknowledged intelligence, who resided here on lease for a protracted period, the Brierwoods, not one of that patronymic remains, or else vegetate in obscurity; families like individuals come up and are cut down like flowers, fade and rarely continue in one stay—it is the pride of families to boast *antiquity* of residence, and lay foundations for long-lasting, yet uniform is the dirge of generations over hopes blossoming but to perish.

The public records do not indicate precisely into whose hands the manor fell after 1782, while the rate-book of Horton gives the name of Mrs. Hugford as holding the house in 1787. She was probably widow of James Hugford, who was Churchwarden in 1777. The date of the earliest rate-book is 26th May 1787, and she is rated for Spillings and the manor £6. 7s 6d, and so continued until 1791, when the house was in the tenure of a widow named Hickman, whose husband's father had been master of an assembly room in Brewer Street, Golden Square. She is reported to have purchased the manor of a Mr. Cooke or Croke of Beaconsfield; a John Croke there died in 1764, one of the ancient house of Studley (page 19).

Subsequently the manor came into the hands of William Hancox, Gent. of Slough, and Mary, his wife (rated in the parish books), and Henry Sexton, Gent. The former was probably son or related to Nicholas Hancox of Stoke, who died 21st April 1790, æt. 62, leaving a son William, who died in 1795, æt. 29.

The next possessor was Thomas Williams, Esq. who had previously bought lands in Wraysbury, and was of Llanidan in Anglesea. He purchased the Temple Mills and erected Temple House on the banks of the Thames at Bisham, Berks, in 1788. He was M.P. for Marlow from 1790 to 1802, and by deed, 15th June 1795, he bought of the parties above recited, viz., Hancox and Sexton, the manor of Horton with the advowson of Horton Church—of which more under the Manor House. Having traced the descent of this manor in almost unbroken succession from 1044 to 1861, a pedigree of Williams will close the next chapter, as this is closed with one of Scawen.

# HISTORY OF HORTON.

## PEDIGREE OF SCAWEN, BLUNT, AND ATKINSON.

Arms granted 19th Feb. 1601: A. a chevron G. between three griffins' heads, erased S.

ROGER DE LANSCAWEN of Cornwall.=
    |
RICHARD.=
    |
WILLIAM SCAWEN of Mollenick, temp. Edw. I. from whom — in succession.=
    |
EDWARD SCAWEN, ob. 13th May, 40 Eliz. 1598.=

WILLIAM SCAWEN,=ALICE, dau. of Nicholas Saule. æt. 20, in 1620.

ROBERT SCAWEN of Mollenich, Inq.=ISABEL, dau. of Humphry Nicholls of Cornwall. p. m. 5 Car. I. 1630, æt. 30, in 1598.

ROBERT of Horton Place, æt.18, in 1620, bought Horton 1658. Buried there 15th March 1669, will dated 5th Jan. 1669, and pr. 21 Mar. 1669. = CATHERINE, dau. of Cavendish Alsop, m. about 1642, buried 1684.

EDWARD SCAWEN, Lord of Horton Manor, will dated 21st Sept. 1619, and pr. 9 June 1693.

JOHN, Rector of Horton, ob. 1695.

HENRY, ob. 1679.

MAUDE ELIZABETH.

FRANCIS SCAWEN of Camb. ob. 11th March 1669, will dated 13th March, and pr. 8th April 1670. = MARY, will pr. 1684.

SIR THOMAS SCAWEN, Kt. of Horton Place, Alderman of London, ob. 22nd Sept. 1730. Buried at Horton, will dated 4th July 1730, and pr. 10th Oct. foll. = MARTHA, dau. of Lennard Wessel, by Ann Crawford, m. 3rd Sept. 1691, ob. 29th June, 1766, presented to the living 1750.

SIR WILLIAM SCAWEN of Surrey, knighted 29th Oct. 1692, of Carshalton, 1696 and 1712. Governor of the Bank of England 1695. M.P. for Surrey 4, 6, 7 Q. Ann, ob. 17th Oct. 1722, æt. 75, sp. = MARY, dau. of Sir Wm. Maynard of Essex, ob. 30, Oct. 1700, æt. 33.

MARY, ob. 1731.=GEOFFREY NANNEY, ob. 1695.

WILLIAM NANNEY, ob. 1695.

ROBERT NANNEY, Rector of Horton 1721, ob. 1734, æt. 42.

HUMPHREY, bpt. at Horton, 12th Feb. 1658.

CATHERINE, m. at Horton, 9th Feb.1661, John Stockdale.

ANN, m. 27th March 1676, at Horton, John Hussey.

1. THOMAS SCAWEN of Horton, M.P. for Surrey 1727, and of Maidwell, Northampton, ob. 11th Feb. 1745. Squire to Lord Delawarr, 1725. = TRYPHENA, dau. and h. of Lord James Russell, 6th son of Wm. 1st Duke of Bedford, m. 8th June 1725.

1st wife =2. LEWIS= 2nd wife MARY, dau. and coh. of Abraham Foster of High Laver, Essex. Buried at Horton 1741.
MARY, SCAWEN, ob. 1730. ob. Aug. 1840.

MARY, wife of Wm. Watkinson, m. about 1707.

4. WILLIAM SCAWEN, ob. June 1775. Bd. at Horton, supposed to be poisoned.

CATHERINE, m. 21st May 1717, Sir Jo. Shelley, Bart. He ob. 1771. She ob. 1726.

MARTHA, m. Sir Nathanl. Mead of Essex.

ANN, m. — Trenchard, of co. Dorset.

JAMES SCAWEN, born 1734, M.P. for Surrey 1774, ob. 7 Jan. 1800, sp. Sold Horton in 1782, will dated 27 June 1797, pr. 12 Feb. 1800.

LETITIA, ob. 1819.

TRYPHENA, m.=HENRY, 2 Earl of Bathurst, Lord Chancellor, 1771, d. 1794. 14 June 1759, ob. 2 Dec. 1807.

MARTHA, m. — Dicas.

ROBERT, ob. 1710.

COL. FRANCIS SCAWEN, ob. 1710.

THOMAS, will pr. 12th Feb. 1755.

ABRAHAM, ob. 1746.

MARTHA, ob. 1798.

HENRY LORD APSLEY, b.1762, 3rd Earl of Bathurst.=

MARY, ob. 5th Aug. 1725.

3. ROBERT SCAWEN of Reigate, Surrey, ob. 8th Nov. 1778, will da. 25th Oct. and pr. 12th Nov. 1778. Executors, Louisa Scawen and S. Blunt. = WINIFRED, dau. of John Borret of Shoreham, Sussex.

THOMAS BORRET.= SUSANNA SCAWEN, m. 16th Sept. 1735.

JOHN SCAWEN, officer in the Guards, died in India, Jan. 1800, sp. = — dau. of Earl of Albemarle.

MATILDA, ob. 1752.

CHARLOTTE, ob. 1752.

LOUISA.

WINIFRED.=WILLIAM BLUNT, of Springfield House, Essex.

SAMUEL BLUNT.=

HENRY WILLIAM ATKINSON, Provost of the Moneyers of the Royal Mint, ob. 13th Sept. 1834, æt. 82.=

MARY, m. 30 July, 1792.=HENRY BLUNT, of Chelsea.

LOUISA JANE GRACE, only d. of Captain Wm. Gyll of Wraysbury House, m.1819. = SIR JASPER ATKINSON, Kt. Provost of the Royal Moneyers, of North Frith, Kent, d. 6 Oct. 1856, æt. 66.

REV. HENRY BLUNT, ob. 1843, æt. 49.

SAMUEL JASPER BLUNT.=

JANE LAURA, only child, m. 30 Oct. 1850=WILLIAM, son and h. of Wm. Green Gowing.

## MANOR HOUSE, FORMERLY PLACE HOUSE, NOW HORTON HOUSE.

It is the opinion of some that the old house, known as Place House, was built about the beginning of the reign of Elizabeth, 1558, and was adjacent to the south side of the tower of the Church. We have a picture of this edifice preserved in the Gentleman's Magazine for 1791, from a drawing made by Francis Brerewood, Esq. who dwelt in it; on which engraving are the words F. Brerewood pinxit, 1773, and Cook sculpsit, presenting a detailed view of the then mansion, which abutted on the south side of the ivy porch of the tower of the Church, situated behind a wall of some 15 inches thick by 7 inches, made from the clay extracted from the spot inclosing the gardens and park.

This seat had a most rural and ornate appearance, not unworthy the talents of the famous Lancelot Brown, known by his *sobriquet* of Capability Brown, who had been head gardener to King George II. in 1759, and who, after having embellished by virtue of his ingenuity nearly all the fancy gardens of England, died in 1783, and to whom this country is indebted, for he exploded the stiff Dutch style introduced by King William III., and discovered a more cultivated taste, which commanded the admiration of native and foreign horticulturists.

In the front façade was a portico, over which was a vast window divided into four compartments; a huge chimney, not unworthy the altitude of a tall Lancashire one, arose on the left wing, and on the opposite side on the corresponding wing there towered also three more chimneys in a stack. It is not unlikely that this was the very same spot which was inhabited by the tenants and lords of the manor in the early part of the 16th century,—the mansion either modified or rebuilt,—but it remained moated round. In the gardens, as altered by the Brerewoods, were canals. With the earth from these excavations a mount about 18 feet high was formed near the boundary of the garden, and at its basis was placed a leaden canister containing coins, together with the names of persons present at the ceremony of laying the foundation. An arch was thrown over the principal canal, on which was erected a pavilion, elegantly furnished, and containing that essential in a country residence, a well selected library.

The canals, covering about an acre, lay below the bed of the Colne, from which they were separated by a bank, and a right was purchased from the proprietors of the adjoining mill for an opening to feed them from the main stream at the expense of £300.

It was here that Robert Scawen lived soon after his investment, for we find his son Humphrey baptized at Horton Church, 12th February, 1658-9, and the same was buried 5th January, 1676; where his other children were baptized I know not, nor was there another baptism here till that of William, son of Edward Scawen, in 1693. Three marriages in 1661, 1676, 1735, shew that the Scawens dwelt on the spot, and it may not have been till after the death of Mr. Robert Scawen in 1710 that Place House was let to the Brerewoods.

From this period we may date the advent of the family in Thomas Brerewood, whose son Charles, dying prematurely, was interred 26th December, 1718. This is the only entry of Brerewood in the parish register, and it will permit me to introduce a succinct notice of a family which rose from small beginnings, and attained very great opulence and literary renown—comprising within its folds a mathematician of celebrity, a lawyer of celebrity, and a poet above mediocrity; and it is painful to think that all the accumulations of wealth and the splendour of genius could not retard or parry a reverse, which reduced them to comparative penury. The hand of the diligent made rich, but neglect or prodigality, like a small perforation in a vast vessel, was the inroad to ruin. All the aggregate of wealth had been secured, as far as prudence and sobriety, which is the strength of the soul, could interpose, yet the younger branches of this once opulent house dwindled into poverty, and the money destined to support the descendants of its careful predecessors, was dissipated, the last male heir of the family dying in 1781, taught by stern necessity, *augustam pauperiem pati*.

As this family resided at Horton Place, or was associated with the parish for some half a century, the reader may forgive a digression which will qualify a history whose general characteristic is a record of interchange of property; and as the proper study of mankind is man, biography may be a medium of entertainment and instruction not out of place in a topographical dissertation.

The name of Brierwood is uncommon, and perhaps there is not now any person of this patronymic left. The only one I have seen is of the Vicar of Colyton in Devon in 1529, whose armorial cognisance was a *bundle of briars bound*. This resembled that of the same name in Chester, of whom we treat, and who rented Place House, and spent large sums with magnificence on the place and grounds, to justify which outlays the liberality of the Scawens must have shone in their leases to the Brierwoods.

It may be that the marriage of Sir Robert Brerewood, Kt. with Catherine, daughter of Sir Richard Lee of Cheshire, brought them into Bucks: for history records that a distended branch of Lee settled at Quarendon, and a Sir Robert Lee, who died 22nd December, 1608, was fourth son of Sir Anthony Lee, some accounts of which family is noticed in Dr. Lipscomb's history of the County, and in the Harl. MS. 1535 and 2163. In the Pat. Rolls there is a grant, 7th December, 1499, to Richard Lee and Joan his wife, of the manor of Quarendon for 50 years.

Robert Brierwood, the patriarch of his house, was of Chester town, a man eminent in his day from his having been chosen three times mayor of that antique city, and he was buried in St. Werburgh's Abbey there, under a very splendid monument, standing in a fine chapel, at the upper end of which and surmounting it, are the coat, crest and streamer advanced over him, with the significant words, Labore, Patientiâ, Equitate. This alderman, like Whittington of London, was thrice mayor of Chester, and was what in trade is styled a *wet-glover*. The dates of his mayoralties are 1583, 1587, 1600, and he died leaving his money and talents to his sons, one of whom, Edward, evinced superior abilities; born in 1565 he early betrayed great promise, and was removed to Brazen-nose College, Oxford, in 1581, and was styled by general recognition the *learned* mathematician and antiquary. In 1596 he was elected the *first* professor of Astronomy in Gresham College, London, and he also composed many treatises on divinity, so that his name and renown are embalmed in Fuller's Worthies. The erudite Wood says that he saw his Commentaries on Aristotle written in the *smallest* and *neatest* hand he ever beheld. He lived not to publish anything, having been called to his great account, 9th November, 1613, at the age of 48. Among his miscellaneous writings was an Inquiry on Language, a subject dear to the author of the "Tractate on Language,"—who with deference also presents to the public this piece of topography.

The will of Edward Brierwood is dated 3rd November, 1613, when he was *in articulo mortis*, and proved almost immediately after his decease, as the wont was then, by his nephew Sir Robert Brierwood, to whom he leaves his *manuscripts*, not to lose his chance of usefulness with posterity, and the bulk of his apparently moderate property,—some legacies to Alexander Rose his kinsman, and to his cousin John Brierwood and Mrs. Jane Ratcliff, &c. Sir Robert inherited his worldly means and the virtues of his uncle, and during his pilgrimage on earth he laboured diligently, and added to the fortune bequeathed by his frugal father.

Sir Robert was son of John Brierwood, of whom Wood in his Athenæ, Vol. I. makes honourable mention—a man of mark and likelihood, and who was pricked for Sheriff; but as his name is not found on the roll, he may not have served or paid forfeit. This gentleman deceased about 1630, having taken such care of the education of his talented son Robert, that he sent him to Brazen-nose College in 1605. His destiny was for the law, and to it he applied, finding little difficult to diligence and skill. In 1637, being then 50 years old, he was constituted Justice for several counties, and in 1639 he was appointed Recorder of his native city Chester. A career of sobriety and equity induced the Sovereign to confer on him the title of Knight, 5th December, 1643, for he was a zealous adherent of the royal cause, and supported King Charles I. by his influence and wealth, esteeming such good actions the most acceptable sacrifices.

This gentleman is noticed in various works, as we find in Daniel King's Vale Royal of England, or County Palatine of Chester, fol. 1656, part II. p. 43. Where a eulogy of his accomplishments and merits is written by a competent hand. His fame and wealth enabled him to contract suitable alliances, and by both his wives he had issue; one the only daughter of Sir Randall Mainwaring of Peover, Cheshire, whose sister Elizabeth married Adam Leicester. The latter, in his memoirs, adverts to Sir Robert and to his widow Catherine Lee, who lived 37 years in doleful widowhood, dying 1691. This lady finds honourable notice in the memoirs of Dr. Edmund Mainwaring, Topog. I. p. 74, who remarks that Sir Robert was constituted one of the Judges of the King's Bench. Having fulfilled all his sublunary duties, Sir Robert yielded to the stroke of fate, at the age of 67, in 1654, and was interred in his native town of Chester, where his will is probably also proved, as it is not in London.

Thomas Brierwood, his son and heir, it was who first rented Horton Place, and who inherited a very large fortune from his father and grandfather, the savings of industry, frugality and talent judiciously applied. A good layer up is a good layer out of capital, hence their son Thomas had to give and had to save, and he found also that *thrift* is the fuel of magnificence, happiness and ease, in a retired as well as in the noisy walk of artificial society.

Despite the pains which pride of place, deep knowledge of the law, practice, will and means to bind in succession, the inheritance he thought to leave in indissoluble entail—but envy, which is the production of hatred, and that common arbitrator time, counterworked his projects, and in the brief space of less than a century the wealth of centuries was dissipated, and though the family did not so far decline as to merit a niche in Burke's Vicissitudes of Families, yet enough was spent to reinforce the aphorism, that what frugal parents collect, prodigal descendants squander.

Sir Robert Brerewood is reputed to have died worth full £8000 a year, a vast sum in 1654, which he put into security with his pecuniary accessions from his ancestors, and effected entails on the issues of both his marriages, and this providential forethought availed till 1748. At the death of his son, Thomas Brerewood, the entail was in its integrity, when a sister took possession of the property, to whom Francis Brerewood was unknown or unnoticed; and hence followed alienation by her, regardless of the remonstrance of her friends, and she also repudiated the injunctions unmistakingly expressed in the wishes of her progenitors in their respective testaments and settlements.

Francis, the second son of Thomas Brerewood, was now involved in lawsuits in quest of his rights, and that he had right on his side, and the *magic* of being in the right, is evinced by the statements made in courts of law, and the answers received from the best legal judgments:—but equity failed him, and by destiny he was wedded to calamity, like others who had been in fortune's lap high fed.

> Nor Blackstone any pleasure brings,
> His right of persons or of things,
> Would make us beggars were we kings.

This same Francis Brerewood, who had lived at and loved Horton Place, to whom we are indebted

## HISTORY OF HORTON.

for the steel plate representation of the mansion to which I have referred, and whose bent it was unthriftily to lavish money on the embellishment of another's property; he it was who was forced from home and all its pleasures, to lodge for 15 years obscurely in the Strand, and was beset by carking care and biting penury, so that at his death all his fond relics were sold by auction, and among his goods was a large chest containing many writings and collections of his own doings and life, its antecedents and consequents, and those of his relatives for centuries, who had benefited their kind by their genius or exalted it by their example, which had been sedulously preserved from loss or encroaching decay. Unconscious of the literary value of the box it was purchased by a broker, of whom however it was *redeemed*, and its recovery disclosed to those who retrieved it the mysteries of the Brierwood House. Some of the treasures were verses written to Lord Baltimore in Gunpowder Forest, Maryland, U.S., and sundry choice poetical effusions by Thomas Brierwood the poet, son and heir of Sir Robert, who inherited the combined talents of his gifted antecessors.

I cannot find the will of this Thomas, who deceased issueless in 1748; but that of his brother, the last remnant of the stock, is dated 7th July, 1781. He is styled of St. George the Martyr, London, and his will assigns to his widow Mary all his disposable property, and she administers within three days of his death to all his effects. Thus ends the eventful history of Brierwood of Horton Place, now extinct in the male line.

I will annex a Pedigree, although they were merely tenants, and at no time proprietors of any land in the locality, not a single deed being extant to indicate any possessions in fee.

### PEDIGREE OF BRIERWOOD.

Arms:—Erm. 2 pales Vaire, O. and A: on a chevron Az. a bezant between 2 garbs O. crest on a wreath, two swords in saltire G. pommels and hilts, O piercing a ducal coronet ppr.

ROBERT BRIERWOOD, of Chester.=

| — d. of — Oulton, m. about 1563. | =ROBERT BRIERWOOD, Mayor of Chester, 1583, 1587, 1600, in which year he died. | =— d. of Thomas Parry, of Cheshire. | =— Powell, of Horsley. | — BRIERWOOD.= |
|---|---|---|---|---|
| EDWARD BRIERWOOD, of London, Professor of Astronomy, &c. ob. 4th Nov. 1613, æt. 48 sp. will dated 3rd Nov. and prov. 13th following. | | JOHN BRIERWOOD, of Chester, a man of some eminence. | =MARY, d. of John Parry. | JOHN BRIERWOOD, cited as cousin in 1613. |

| CHRISTIANA, d. of Richard Grosvenor. | =SIR FRANCIS GAMUL, of Chester, ob. 1654, Mayor of Chester, 1634. | =ELIZABETH. | JANE, d. of SirRandall Mainwaring of Over Peover, Cheshire, Mayor of Chester, 1618, 1625, she ob.1630. | =SIR ROBERT BRIER b. 1583, High Sheriff of Chester, Recorder of ditto, 1639, knighted 1643, and Justice of Common Pleas, ob. 1654, æt. 67, M.I. St. Mary's, Chester. | =CATHARINE, d. of Sir Richard Lee of Chester, ob. 1691. | JOHN BRIERWOOD. | =SARAH, d. of Robert Wall, of Chester. | JOAN, m. John Ratcliffe, Alderman of Chester. |
|---|---|---|---|---|---|---|---|---|

SYDNEY GAMUL, m. about 1692.=THOMAS BRIERWOOD, of Horton, ob. about 1730.

| THOMAS BRIERWOOD, the Poet, b. about 1694, ob. 1748, sp. | CHARLES, buried at Horton, 26th Dec. 1718, sp. | FRANCIS BRIERWOOD, of Horton, and St. George the Martyr, London, will dated 7th July, and pr. 10th July, 1781, ob. sp. | =MARY, d. of —— Executrix. | A daughter, of whom little is known: but who got the property. |
|---|---|---|---|---|

After the departure or the secession of the Brierwoods, the park and mansion seem to have declined into unmerited abandonment, until the gardens alone were rented for the mere profit derivable from the soil.

One Mayhew, a gardener, who for 40 years long was grieved with the sight of approaching decay and desolation, hired the garden and ornamental parts, which may have been considerable.

The house which now neglect was precipitating into decay, was partially taken down in 1785, and subsequently the lease or rent was in one Cox, at the rate of £22. 10s yearly. There were still remnants of brickwork, whose disintegration was not entirely removed till 1832, at the suggestion of George Thomas Ellison, Esq. (brother of Mr. Ellison, Vicar of New Windsor), the legal adviser of Colonel Williams, hence the park is disencumbered of the unsightly fragments of a once substantial manor house.

A new mansion, which now adorns the park, was designed and executed. It is pleasantly situated near a piece of running water, an offshoot from the Colne, being surrounded with trees which give a lively appearance, and cast a gratefully umbrageous shade in the heats of summer.

The edifice is modern in architecture, constructed of brick coated with stucco, raised on arches to defend it from floods, while the chief door is entered by a flight of some dozen stone steps. The hall is commodious, so are the principal apartments on the ground floor, containing a library, drawing room and dining room *en suite*, all looking on the south aspect of the park, and to this a verandah is added, uniting ornament and utility.

Let me here append a Pedigree of Williams, Lord of the Manor and impropriator of the advowson of Horton since 1795, who also holds largely in Wraysbury, as well as owns extensive properties in Berkshire and in South Wales. The Temple Mills at Bisham belonged originally to the Knights Templars. Various kinds of manufactures have been wrought here, as of brass kettles, &c. up to 1759. They were bought by Mr. Thomas Williams in 1788 of George Pengree, whose uncle had succeeded Mr. William Ockenden, M.P. for Marlow.

## PEDIGREE OF WILLIAMS.

Arms: A chevron S. between 3 Cornish choughs, in the beak of each an ermine spot ppr.

THOMAS WILLIAMS of Llanidan, in Anglesea, purchased Temple Mills, Bisham, Berks, in 1788, and erected Temple House. M.P. for Marlow from 1790 to 1802. Bought Horton manor and advowson in 1795. Vice-President of the Literary Fund Society. Died at Bath, 29th Nov. 1802, æt. —=CATHERINE, dau. of — Lloyd.

| OWEN WILLIAMS of do., b. 1764, M.P. for Marlow in 10 Parliaments from 1796, died 23 Feb. 1832. =MARGARET, eldest d. of Rev. Edward Hughes of Kenmell Park, co. Denbigh, and sister to the 1st Lord Dinorben, m. July 1792, ob. 1821. | JOHN WILLIAMS.=ELIZABETH, d. of Dr. — Currie of Boughlin Hall, Cheshire. | MARY, ob. unm. 1830. | JANE, m. 20 Jan. 1796, Major-Gen. Wheatley. |

| THOMAS PEERS WILLIAMS, of do., M.P. for Marlow, Dep. Lieut. of Berks and Bucks, Col. of the Royal Anglesea Militia. Born March, 1795. =EMILY, d. of Anthony Bacon of Aberavon, m. 27 Aug. 1833. | OWEN EDWARD WILLIAMS, b. Jan. 1798. | 1st h. LIEUT.-COL. THOMAS KNOX, nephew of Viscount Northland. =EMMA, m. 1st 31 Oct. 1795, m. 2ndly | 2d h. LIEUT.-GEN. SIR HENRY FREDERICK CAMPBELL, K.C.B. |

OWEN LEWYS COPE WILLIAMS, b. 13 July, 1836.   ANTHONY COPE WILLIAMS.

There is a walled garden and shrubberies, imparting grace, charm and use to this spot in a park consisting of some 25 acres of grass land, which the present distinguished occupant holds in his hands for agricultural purposes, with about as much more of mixed land. Sir William Yardley, knighted 1847, was Chief Justice in Bombay, 1852-7, and he married in 1847 Amelia, daughter of T. Wilken, Esq. To him a tribute of respect may be paid in consideration of his judicial labours in

India, and for his magisterial and his social services in a vicinity which knows how to appreciate both mind and moral worth.

The soil here is very good, the country flat and intersected with streams from the prolific source of the Colne, which river traverses the village and disembogues in Wraysbury parish. The park is walled in part and fenced with oak paling, while an appropriate brick lodge indicates the *entrée* under well-grown trees extending to its extremities.

There is a small tenement by the gardens in the park, adjacent to the Manor House, where tradition, that deathless chronicler in every parish, alleges that one Cantrell lived, who was a friend of the *historic minion of the moon*, Richard Turpin, and who like unto him having "spent his time in riot most uncouth," ended his unquiet days on a gibbet at Hounslow Heath, and the chequered biography of one of the *par nobile fratrum* is inscribed in Newgate Calendar. Fable likes to invent, and tradition loves to promulgate myths, which time sanctifies; so here they show a mound under which it is said that Cantrell secured and fed his horse in a deep cavity below, and that this *underfed* quadruped conveyed him to the heath to exercise his *vocation* as a *conveyancer* after his own heart.

Many years before the inclosure, both Horton and Wraysbury Green displayed a large flat and wild superficies as far as Hythe End, "ample verge and room enough the characters of *theft* to trace," what time the law could do little more than afford a negative repression to rapine and wrong. Now all is order and security, so that civilisation, like wisdom, is justified of her laws, and the tenants of Horton House enjoy without molestation their *otium* amidst the elms and ashes, plane trees and tall cedars, and other such children of the earth as dignify a moderate-sized park, lacking neither wood nor water. The mildness of the climate here enables all trees to flourish as if in a tropical clime, for it is remarked that all fruit trees ripen and throw out a very attractive deep colour as they grow mellow. Horton is also rich in botany.

I will subjoin here the names of several who have tenanted the Manor House during this century, and whom the villagers love to remember, for the present proprietors have never inhabited Horton House:—General Capel, — Boehm,* Marchioness of Downshire, Mrs. Catherine, widow of Rev. Isaac Gosset, whose son Isaac was Curate of Colnbrook in 1841. Colonel James Ballard Gardiner, brother-in-law of Mr. Gosset, Colonel Colderton Wood, Captain George Bulkeley, William Ashton, and in 1859 Sir William Yardley, present tenant.

There was another family of some antiquity in the county, the Aubreys of Boarstall, and one of the members, Sir John Aubrey, Bart. sold his possessions in Horton to the family of Williams. The last heir male of this house was Sir Thomas Digby Aubrey, High Sheriff in 1815. There was an intermarriage with the Carters, one of whom tenanted Ankerwycke House, p. 139, so I shall give the united genealogy for a few descents.

### PEDIGREE OF AUBREY AND CARTER.

Sir John Aubrey, Bart. of Boarstall, Bucks, *jure uxoris*=Mary, d. and h. of William Lewis, d. 1700.

Sir John Aubrey, d. 1743.=    Richard Carter, of Ankerwycke, a Welsh Judge,=Martha, d. of — Cornish. d. 6th January, 1755, æt. 83.

Sir Thomas Aubrey,=Martha, d. 5th Dec. 1788, æt. 76.    George Richard Carter, High Sheriff of=Julia, d. and h. of Bucks, 1766, d. 1771, æt. 51.   James Spillman.
d. 1786.

Richard Aubrey,=   Mary, d. of Sir James=Sir John Aubrey, 6th Bart.=Martha Catherine, d. and h.
d. 1808.   Colebroke, Bt. d. 1781.   sold Horton lands, d. 1826, sp.   m. 26th May, 1783, d. 3rd Sept. 1815, sp.

Sir Thomas Digby Aubrey, Bart. High Sheriff of Bucks, 1815, d. 1860, sp.

* A Mr. Anthony William Boehm, clerk, who died 1722, æt. 50, established a German school in England; was reader at St. James's Chapel, and Chaplain to Prince George of Denmark.

As the family of Gosset were residents in Horton House, and Mr. Isaac Gosset was Curate of Colnbrook and Rector of Datchet, I give a Pedigree.

## PEDIGREE OF GOSSET.

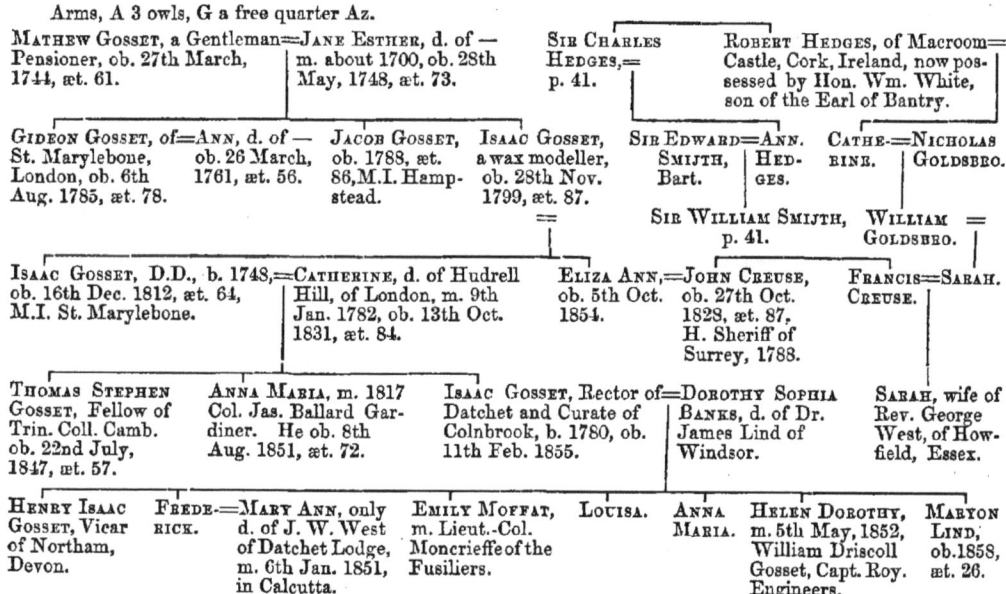

Arms, A 3 owls, G a free quarter Az.

MATHEW GOSSET, a Gentleman=JANE ESTHER, d. of — Pensioner, ob. 27th March, m. about 1700, ob. 28th 1744, æt. 61. May, 1748, æt. 73.

SIR CHARLES HEDGES,= p. 41.

ROBERT HEDGES, of Macroom= Castle, Cork, Ireland, now possessed by Hon. Wm. White, son of the Earl of Bantry.

GIDEON GOSSET, of=ANN, d. of — St. Marylebone, ob. 26 March, London, ob. 6th 1761, æt. 56. Aug. 1785, æt. 78.

JACOB GOSSET, ob. 1788, æt. 86, M.I. Hampstead.

ISAAC GOSSET, a wax modeller, ob. 28th Nov. 1799, æt. 87.

SIR EDWARD=ANN SMIJTH, HEDBart. GES.

CATHE-=NICHOLAS RINE. GOLDSBRO.

SIR WILLIAM SMIJTH, WILLIAM = p. 41. GOLDSBRO.

ISAAC GOSSET, D.D., b. 1748,=CATHERINE, d. of Hudrell ob. 16th Dec. 1812, æt. 64, Hill, of London, m. 9th M.I. St. Marylebone. Jan. 1782, ob. 13th Oct. 1831, æt. 84.

ELIZA ANN,=JOHN CREUSE, ob. 5th Oct. ob. 27th Oct. 1854. 1828, æt. 87, H. Sheriff of Surrey, 1788.

FRANCIS=SARAH. CREUSE.

THOMAS STEPHEN GOSSET, Fellow of Trin. Coll. Camb. ob. 22nd July, 1847, æt. 57.

ANNA MARIA, m. 1817 Col. Jas. Ballard Gardiner. He ob. 8th Aug. 1851, æt. 72.

ISAAC GOSSET, Rector of=DOROTHY SOPHIA Datchet and Curate of BANKS, d. of Dr. Colnbrook, b. 1780, ob. James Lind of 11th Feb. 1855. Windsor.

SARAH, wife of Rev. George West, of Howfield, Essex.

HENRY ISAAC GOSSET, Vicar of Northam, Devon.

FREDE-=MARY ANN, only RICK. d. of J. W. West of Datchet Lodge, m. 6th Jan. 1851, in Calcutta.

EMILY MOFFAT, m. Lieut.-Col. Moncrieffe of the Fusiliers.

LOUISA.

ANNA MARIA.

HELEN DOROTHY, m. 5th May, 1852, William Driscoll Gosset, Capt. Roy. Engineers.

MARYON LIND, ob. 1858, æt. 26.

## NOTICE OF LESSER PROPRIETORS OF LANDS IN HORTON.

The writer has not deemed it inexpedient to advert briefly to some who bear names in history as well as in these localities, but the limit of such a work must of necessity circumscribe a desire, although persons of note may be cited incidentally; and to the end that all who are interested in such investigations may know who were the proprietary in times past the author had sedulously made inquisition into the public muniments of the realm to supply a desideratum and adduce topographical facts. Hence he has diligently extracted from or copied every fine, recovery, and deed within reach, that he might at once give satisfaction, awaken curiosity, or furnish aid to any future historical inquirer as to what relates to this section of Bucks or the county generally.

The author is not acquainted with any topographical history where *every* deed of fine and recovery is partially transcribed for a given locality, and he with deference takes credit to himself for suggesting this idea and reinforcing it by example.

The parish of Horton is of small area, yet have its acres been conveyed and reconveyed incessantly since it reclamation from the savage life which once prevailed, and that nation evinces a system of advanced civilisation which can furnish unbroken records of transference of soil and tenements so interesting to future ages—and may the genealogist or historiographer who requires it be able to avail himself of these local annals.

Domesday Book informs us who held lordship here at the era of William the Norman, and in times anterior, while well authenticated documents declare in days as remote as King John, who they were that had interests in Horton and Wraysbury.

To these I must refer the curious, where will be seen in chronological series the conveyances that time has spared, which, with the parish registers, although defective for the first 20 years, introduce us to the early as well as to the fixed and fugitive proprietary.

After the records of the Wyndsors in Domesday Book, who maintained territorial ascendancy here until dislodged by King Henry VIII. in 1543, p. 207, the first record of exchange of lands occurs in a fine 6 John 1204, between Richard de Hakeburne and William Wyndleshore. This relates to a sale in Horton, and few are the parishes of small extent which can boast of fines recorded of so early a date. There is a fine of the same time, 1203, between William Prior of Merton and William de Wyndleshore relative to an acre of land, and a croft styled Rudding, in Horseley parish.

The next conveyance is in 1212, between William Hamond, and John son of Henry *Rex* (the King), and William de Wyndleshore, a tenement and a virgate of land in Horton, with a mill and three acres of land. This is succeeded by another fine in 1213, where the family of Windsor again shew pre-eminence here.

Ten years later, in 1223, the same William de Wyndleshore buys lands and tenements of Geoffrey de Mauriscis, a house of notoriety settled in Wraysbury (page 11), and in 1231 the name of Walter de Horton occurs. In 1240 John the son of the King buys of Andrew, son of another John of Horton. As Henry III. was reigning I do not find any of the baptismal name of John amongst his children who lived to majority.

The name of Hall is common; a family of that patronymic was of some importance, temp. Elizabeth and the sequent reigns, in this parish, and may be the progenitor is to be found in Walter de la Halle, who appears in a fine of sale at Horton in 1254.

The name of Langley is a patronymic, and of territorial importance in Horton; the Richard de Langley whose son Alexander sold lands to Alice de Middleton in 1256 may be the common ancestor of the many Langleys of this and the neighbouring places.

In 1261, John son of Walter de Horton buys lands of Richard de Oxeheye, whom Hugh, Vicar of Wraysbury, calls to warrant, and to whom he is bail for sundry parcels of lands, tenements, &c. (page 106.)

A family by name Middleton were early proprietors here, as well as Maunsell, in the 13th century.

Under the descent of the manor I have alluded to its alienation from the Windsors, and how it came into the hands of the Cadamo family in 1328, one of whom had presented in 1306. Another house of manorial influence is found in the Remenhams, which gave name to the manor in Wraysbury, held by them of the Crown. John de Remenham and his wife buy lands in Horton of John de Halle in 1291, from which period until their extinction they held sway in all the circumjacent parishes, p. 56.

To pretermit other holders I again advert to the subsequently influential family of Bulstrode, whose cradle seems to be in Bulstrode and Datchet, where we find them holders in 1338.

There is another family, ycleped Eyre, whose descendants retained possession here in later days, and it is not unlikely that the William le Eyre of Langley, who acquired Horton lands of John de Taunton of London, 10 Edward III., may be a progenitor of the house.

Let us not, in the enumeration of small holders, pass by the family of Aunger at this period; nor that of Wyot, one of whom is recognized in Richard Wyot, who purchased lands of Dionysia, widow of Richard Overton. His relative is found in John Wyot, collated to the Horton Rectory in 1404. This family settled eventually in Wraysbury, and were of distinction there. Richard Wyot was High Sheriff for the shire in 1410, 1416, and 1424, and M.P. for it in 1407 and 1426.

The year 1409 brings us to a classic person, for in him we discover the cherished name of Thomas Chaucer, who with Robert Chichele, citizen and grocer of London, dealt in lands in Horton.

Let me advert that Sir Robert Chicheley was Lord Mayor of London in 1411 and 1422, and that he deceased in 1440, having been brother of Henry Chichele, Archbishop of Canterbury, who died in 1443, sons of Thos. Chichele of Higham Ferrers, county Northampton, a *tailor* there, who departed this world about the commencement of the 15th century. This latter was eminent in his time, and had married Agnes, daughter of William Pynchon, ancestor of those of Essex (p. 21), the first of whom was an opulent *butcher*, and from him descended a line of important personages, whose issue gave off Baronets and Squires of high degree. They were lessees of Wraysbury House, (p. 96.)

A party to the deed to which reference has been made is Thomas, son of Sir Thomas Chaucer of Eweline, Oxon; he died in 1434, being only son of the famous Geoffrey Chaucer,* the poet, who died in 1400. Sir Thomas Chaucer made a high alliance in Maude, daughter and heir of Sir John Burghersh, and at her death in 1436 her only child Alice was selected to be wife of Thomas Montagu Earl of Shrewsbury. She married, secondly, William de la Pole, Duke of Suffolk, whose son John espoused Elizabeth, daughter of Richard Plantagenet, Duke of York, and sister to King Edward IV. This Sir John de la Pole had a natural daughter, Joan, who became the spouse of Thomas Stonor, and his son again was father of Sir Walter Stonor of Place Farm, in Wraysbury (p. 57). Thomas Chaucer was Sheriff of Berks in 1399, and he gave a manor in Edlesborough, Bucks, to his daughter Alice, and she bestowed it on her husband William de la Pole, and his son John left it to the Dean and Canons of Windsor in 1480.

Advert that there is a mysterious *hiatus* in the fines between the times of Henry VI. and those of Henry VIII., at which latter period the family of Digby predominated here, as has been already shewn.

A gentleman by name John Wyllyams in 1535 buys of Simon Mynyfield certain property, and the family of Edwards, destined to hold sway in Horton, in conjunction with that of Peters, now appear.

John Edwards of Horton, gentleman, had a son, and also a daughter Elizabeth, who was united as third wife to Thomas Eyre of Burnham, to whose ancestor of the same names a grant of arms was conceded, 16 Edward IV. 1476. Thomas Eyre married Alice, daughter of William Plastrell of Langley, Bucks, and Mr. Eyre's fourth wife was Beatrix, daughter of Richard Husband of Cowley, Middlesex, by whom he had a daughter Elizabeth, married about 1570 to George Edwards of Horton; and about a century later, 25th May, 1676, Francis Bowry of Wraysbury married Catherine, daughter of — Edwards of Stoke Poges, who was interred in Wraysbury Church in 1692. Some notices of this family are found in Alice Edwards, buried 1572. George Edwards, buried 1601, buys lands here in 1560 of Thomas Wyche, and of Henry Balnett of Horton and Wraysbury of the same date. James Edwards buried in 1612, and Thomas Edwards in 1624.

Coeval with this family was that of Peters, from whom the close in Wraysbury took its name (page 61), which was sold by John Slocomb of Colnbrook, and Elizabeth his wife, daughter of John Peters, in 1683, to Richard Hale of Place Farm.

I add here skeleton pedigrees of Peters, Salter, Nichols, Urwin and Slocomb. David Salter was the first Bailiff of Colnbrook town, and Daniel Salter in 1626 gave the Cripple House there. Samuel Salter, gentleman, buys property of William Staunton in Horton in 1614, and Christopher Salter buys of John Peters in 1645. Charles Salter appears in a sale at Colnbrook in 1679, and Elliot Salter, of Stoke Poges, married 27th August, 1861, Edith, only child of Henry St. George Priaulx of Guernsey.

* In 1390 King Richard II. appoints Geoffrey Chaucer, father of English poetry, to superintend repairs at St. George's Chapel, and on the 12th July, 1370, *inter alia*, he was nominated Superintendent of the King's Falcons at Charing Cross Mews, page 55. His salary as Clerk of the Works was 2s a day, and £36.10s *per annum*, or some £657 of our denomination of money.

## PEDIGREES OF SALTER, PETERS, NICHOLLS, AND SLOCOMB.

[Pedigree chart:]

WILLIAM SALTER of Iver, p. 43.

- DAVID SALTER = CATHERINE, d. of —, buried 11 Nov. 1649.
- SIR EDWARD SALTER, b. 13 Jan. 1645. = URSULA, d. of Edward Brocket of Herts, b. 11 April, 1649.
- WILLIAM PETERS, of co. Dorset, Visn. 1575, Bucks. Held lands here in 1590, d. 1611. = ANN, d. of John Hilpe of Thamebery, Gloucestershire, d. 1628.

Children:
- JOHN, bpt. 9 March 1610.
- SIR WILLIAM SMITH of Ankerwycke, d. 1631. p. 41. = ANN, d. of Edw. Croft, d. 1675.
- SIR WILLIAM SALTER, of Iver, m. 1632, d. 1643.
- MARY SALTER, m. 18 May, 1623.
- JOHN PETERS, of Iver. = ALICE, daughter of Sir Edmund Wheeler, of Datchet, H. Sheriff of Bucks, 1616, d. 1648, m. dau. and coh. of Richard Hanbury of Datchet.
- AGNES, b. 1592.
- MARY, d. 1590.
- THOMAS PETERS.

- DANIEL SALTER, of Colnbrook.
- JOHN PETERS, æt. 18 in 1634.
- ANN, a twin.
- WILLIAM, b. 1621.
- CLEMENT, b. 1620, see deed 1661.
- URSULA, m. 23 June, 1636. Edward Hatche.
- MARY, m. 2 Sept. 1635, Thomas Newberye.
- GRACE, b. 1623.
- ELIZABETH, b. 1627.
- ALICE, ux. George Cooke, of Gloucestershire.
- ELIZABETH, b. 1623.
- SUSANNA, b. 1627.

MARGARET, m. 3 Nov. 1666, — Stradling, Vicar of Iver.

JOHN SLOCOMB, d. 1607.

- EDWARD NICHOLLS, of Wraysbury, p. 83. = MARY. = JOHN PETERS, 1649.
- WILLIAM, d. 1672.
- URSULA, b. 1611.
- ELIZABETH, b. 1642.
- EDMUND SLOCOMB, bpt. 14 Sept. 1600, fine, 1659, d. 1658. = —, d. of —, d. 1635.

- WILLIAM NICHOLLS, sold Wraysbury property to Jas. Harrison in 1767, and he to William Gyll, Esq. = ELIZABETH URWIN.
- JAMES URWIN, of Wraysbury, will d. 27 July, 1741, and pr. 2 Nov. 1741.
- CHARLES PETERS, d. 1679.
- ELIZABETH, d. 1714. = JOHN SLOCOMBE, of Colnbrook, Mercer, who sold Peter's Close, living 1682.

JOHN SLOCOMB, 1695.

In 1686 Henry Peters married — Guenint; afterwards this family disappears from the Registers. Agnes Peters, from Windsor, buried in Horton Cemetery, 1847.

In 1649, John Peters junior appears in a deed as vouchee for Edmund Slocombe, and in 1666 William Peters sells property in Horton to John Durdant and George Cooke, who married John Peters' daughter Alice. In 1677 he is vouchee in a deed of fine relating to Horton and Wraysbury for John Slocombe.

Another family which rose from small beginnings dwelt here for years, and were benefactors to the poor, so I append a skeleton pedigree.

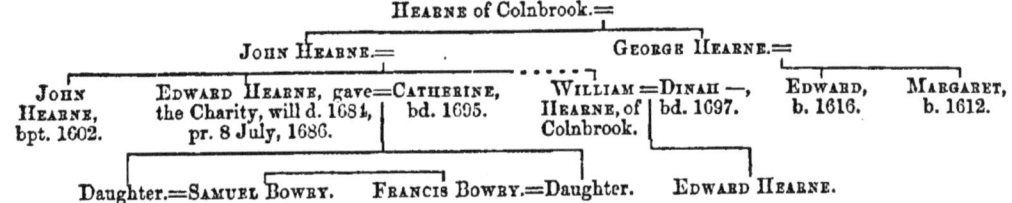

[Pedigree chart:]

HEARNE of Colnbrook.

- JOHN HEARNE.
- GEORGE HEARNE.

- JOHN HEARNE, bpt. 1602.
- EDWARD HEARNE, gave the Charity, will d. 1684, pr. 8 July, 1686. = CATHERINE, bd. 1695.
- WILLIAM HEARNE, of Colnbrook. = DINAH —, bd. 1697.
- EDWARD, b. 1616.
- MARGARET, b. 1612.

- Daughter. = SAMUEL BOWRY.
- FRANCIS BOWRY. = Daughter.
- EDWARD HEARNE.

The name of Tredway, p. 210, is found here and in Stoke Poges, as purchasers in 1588; also those of Higgins and Bowser.

On a brass beneath the figure of a man in Langley Church, in a furred and embroidered gown, with a long beard, wearing a quilted ruff, is inscribed in old English:—

"𝔥ere lyeth the bodie of John Bowser, Gent. and sonn of Thomas Bows' of Coole-Broke, who in ye 61th yeare of his age dyed in the faith of our Lord Jesus Christ, and in ye 50th yeare of the peace of the Gospel in England (dating from the accession of Queen Elizabeth), leaving behind issue one sonne and one daughter, Ao. Dni. 1608, March ye 23rd."

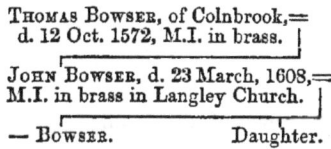

In 1641, the names of Robert Hall and Thomas Tredway are attached to a considerable conveyance of lands in Horton, &c., in which Thomas Bulstrode, Esq., is vouchee. In 1648 a similar deed with John Hall, gentleman, and 1649 one with Robert Hall. In 1664 Richard Hall sells property to James Seymour, senior, one of the Langley family, descended from Edward Duke of Somerset, the Protector.

A branch of the time-honoured house of Blount holds lands in Horton and Colnbrook, descended from Walter Blount, who bore for arms Barry nebulee of 6, O. and S.

### PEDIGREE OF BLOUNT.

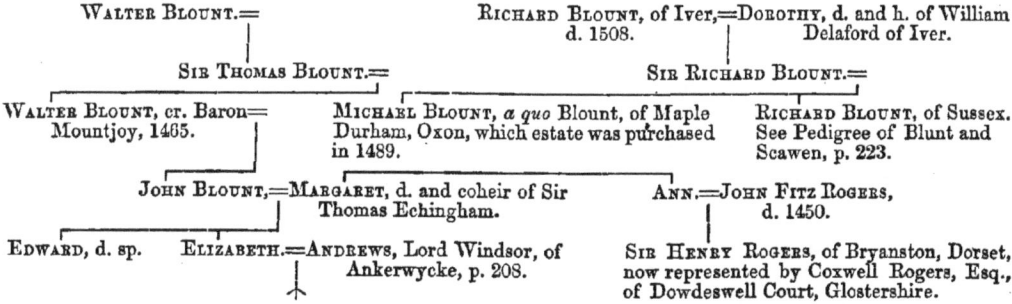

For a more extended acquaintance with the old proprietors who figured in sales and exchanges, we must commend the curious to the list of fines and recoveries; for those who lived and died in the parish, we refer to the parish registers.

We here recapitulate some well-known Horton names, to whom references have been made in the course of the history, viz., Bowscr, Higgins, Tredway, Peters, Pytt, Blunt, Burcomb, Edwards, Bowry, Holderness, Stevens, Virgo, Bullock, Pullin, &c.

An early name in the parochial registers is that of Darby, members of which house still continue proprietors. In a deed of fine, Hilary 1696, Josias Darby buys property here of John Hassel, gentleman, of Wraysbury, of whom mention has been made, page 77.

### BERKYN MANOR HOUSE.

The boundaries of a parish (παροικία), so called from its proximity to the Bishop's House, were ascertained by those of a manor, which seldom extended over more than one parish, and these parishes agree with our present divisions.

From investigations of old local deeds it appears that there were small manors in Horton parish, as in most others of larger dimensions (imperia in imperio), and which were ancient alienations from the demesne lands belonging to the manor.

These demesne lands, *terræ dominicales*, were such lands as the lords kept in their own hands *out* of the manor, while the residue of unlet lands were termed *waste*, on which all sorts of cattle were depastured.

I find mention made of one John Berkyn, who deceased 36 Hen. VI. 1458, in a deed in which the Rev. Dr. William Westbury, Provost of Eton College, who died 1477, is cited 10th April, 37 Henry VI. He was the fourth Provost of Eton College, which was dedicated "to the blessed Marie of Etone beside Wyndesore." This Provost was of celebrity in his day, and his merit was strenuously and successfully to oppose the union of Eton College with Windsor College, proposed by King Edward IV. Harl. MS. 5564.

John Berkyn held and had the fishery in the Thames with a *Weir*, called *Horne de Were* in Edeston, being the house, lands and fishery belonging to the Provost of Eton. The deed is in the public Record Depository, and the reference is to be found in Martin's Index to deeds of grant. In another grant of 1494, this same weir and fishery was granted to Eton—a deed 1 Henry VII. (which the Bailiffs of Cookham and Bray, previously granted to Charles Rippon), is cited.

It may not be remote from verisimilitude, for we have no express testimony, that this manor was either so called from John Berkyn himself, or that he was of Horton, and took for patronymic the place of his nativity, suffice to add, that this is indubitably the site of a manor, and it was given by the will of Thomas Bulstrode, proved 24th November, 1560, to his second son, Thomas, from whom it came to his elder brother, Edward, as appears in its proper place.—See Pedigree of Bulstrode, p. 217. The name has been revived by the present owner of a handsome edifice, built on the identical area where our great epic Poet lived and sung.

Traditions exist, which are referred to our own times, although curiosity has not been until lately so ardent about the spot, and point to the ground where Berkyn House now stands as the *veritable endroit*, where until recently flourished an apple tree, and where yet exists in all its solidity of architecture a red-bricked pigeon house, recognised and respected as the *identical* one extant in the Bard's time, a *columbarium* adequate for the family, and such as were appendant to country residences. The modern residence, approached from the road through very handsome iron gates, to which a lodge is attached of a corresponding character, is of deep red brick, Elizabethan style, with stone insertions, comprising all the *indispensables* of modern comfort, and constructed with a becoming and judicious taste by Edward Tyrrell, Esq. the City Remembrancer, an office of trust and honour, also held by his late father, Timothy Tyrrell, Esq.

This ground, and the house then upon it, were acquired from the trustees of Mr. John Cooke in 1848, and the improvements effected since the purchase justifies the village in its praise on account of the exchange. The park, though small, is reduced to order; the streams humectate without o'erflowing the land, and the picturesque stamp of the spot enlivens the spirit and charms the eye. The gardens have produced all requisites in a very brief space, like the fabulous ones of old, "which one day bloomed and fruitful were the next."

This *locale* is then traditionally the hallowed spot, and the old house now demolished is adjudged to have been the same which the Poet's father rented of the Earl of Bridgewater, Sir John Egerton, who with his elder brother, Sir Thomas Egerton, "par nobile fratrum," served under the Earl of Essex at the siege of Cadiz in 1597, and were *both* knighted for their valour. Sir John was advanced to the dignity of Earl of Bridgewater in 1617, and died in 1649, being ancestor of an illustrious race, since exalted to the rank of Duke of Bridgewater. Sir John was son of the celebrated Sir Thomas Egerton, Lord Keeper of the Seals and Baron Ellesmere in 1602, who died in 1616; a person, says Dugdale, of quick apprehension, profound judgment, and of a most venerable gravity, having been seldom seen to *smile,* unlike the gay Lord Keeper Hatton, who led the brawls when "seals and maces danced before him." Sir Christopher Hatton had a property at Padbury, near Colnbrook, with the estate of Perry Oaks in 1587. How this Horton property came to Sir John Egerton I do not find, as there are neither fines nor recoveries to indicate where he obtained it, whether by purchase, gift, or inheritance. Estates were occasionally conveyed not by bargain and sale, but by deeds of feoffment, which it was not necessary to enrol.

After the plague in London, when whole families withdrew to the provinces, this was the selected spot for nearly six years of the useful life of the English Homer—a place immortalised by his *sejour* here; yet is it to be lamented that he does not specifically mention Horton in his correspondence, unless by his *suburban* retreat this locality be implied.

A few touching remarks had still more embalmed the house, grounds and village, and have shrouded it in an undecaying renown, imparting a ray of glory to a site beloved of all who honour Milton's memory this side idolatry. As Mr. Tyrrell* is the fortunate possessor of the venerated spot, I shall annex a short pedigree of his family, which came from the county of Berks. The name is one also well known in this shire as an offshoot from the great house of Tyrel of Essex.

## PEDIGREE OF TYRRELL.

WALTER TYRRELL=

AVERY TYRRELL, of Stamford, Berks,=

GEORGE HATCH, of Windsor.=MARY, d. and co-heir.

ANN HATCH.=DR. ILTYD NICHOL, D.D., d. 1787.

TIMOTHY TYRRELL, b. 1754,=ELIZABETH, only daughter of John Dollond, of St. Paul's, London, md. 29th May, 1789.
City Remembrancer, 1793, d. 9th July, 1832.

Arms. A 2 chevrons A z —a Bordure engrailed G.

1. JOHN TYRRELL, Barrister-at-law, d. sp. 1840. = DIANA, d. of — Wylde, 1861.

WILLIAM MARTIN ATKYNS, 1861. = 2. GEORGE TYRRELL, of Foordhook, co. Middlesex, Capt. R.N. = JULIANA, d. of — Porteus.

GEORGE. ELIZABETH.

3. EDWARD T., City Remembrancer, 1861, of Berkyn Manor House, Horton, co. Bucks. = FANNY, only child of William Lingham, of Ewel Surrey, md. 2nd Oct. 1823.

AVERY TYRRELL, b. 1840.

4. FREDERICK TYRRELL, Surgeon of St. Thomas's Hospital, died May, 1843. = FRANCES SUSANNA, d. of Rev. Samuel Lovick Cooper, Rector of Ingoldsthorpe, co. Norfolk, married June, 1823. Seven children.

SIR CHARLES GEO. YOUNG, Kt. Garter King at Arms, D.C.L., F.S.A., md. 2nd August, 1854.

5. CHARLES TYRRELL, Architect, died sp. = JEMIMA CHEMINANT, ob.

ANNE, d. 1861.

ELIZABETH DOLLOND, md. 27th June, 1839, Francis J. Blandy, Clk. sp.

6. TIMOTHY TYRRELL, of Guildhall, Lond.

7. RICHARD TYRRELL.=ELIZABETH, d. of — Dowdeswell, d. 1861.
GERALDINE, 1861, only child.

8. WILLIAM TYRRELL, younger son, Rector of Beaulieu, now Bishop of Newcastle, N. S. Wales.

It would be interesting to record the names of the several proprietors of the Miltonian residence. Prior to the family of Cooke, one Mr. Thomas Woodward dwelt here, and he died in 1840, almost a nonagenarian, and was father of the wife of the present Mr. William Thomas Buckland, of Wraysbury, and of the wife of Mr. Richardson, of Colnbrook. Mr. John Cooke left a son, John Parsons Cooke, the same who was poisoned by William Palmer, in 1855; and Mr. Tyrrell bought the property of the trustees of Cooke and Stevens: Mr. Cooke's mother had married a Mr. Stevens, of London.

* The author regrets to say that he must apologise here for *scanty materials,* in consequence of his not receiving the promised information from Mr. Tyrrell as to his family, the dates of his Horton purchases, and the names of the previous proprietors of Berkyn Manor House. Authors of topographical history are *especially* dependant on the judicious *courtesy* of landed proprietors, without which much of this now so popular kind of history would be either *incognitum aut vagum.*

As the circumstance of the Palmer poisonings gave rise to much excitement in the kingdom, it may not be *mal-àpropos* to advert to the law proceedings, as the victim was a Horton man.

Mr. John Parsons Cook, styled of Lutterworth, aged 28 in 1855, was a racing and a betting worthy, and either owner or had a share in certain race-horses; and his acquaintance was one William Palmer, a surgeon at Rugeley, Staffordshire. It came to pass that Cook's horse Polestar won a large stake at Shrewsbury races, and on this event an *ominous illness* surprised him, and to do him *good* Mr. William Palmer prescribed morphine pills, which he took, but much against his will, as he had some *prophetic* alarm that his *friend* Palmer purposed " drugging his posset." The prescription threw him into strong convulsions, and spasms followed by *tetanus* ensued, so that he died; and on the *autopsy* there was found antimony in his intestines. The case was heard before counsel and judge, and the verdict of the jury declared that the man had died of poison administered by his associate, William Palmer, on the 15th November, 1855. It was proved that a chemist's apprentice had sold strychnine to Palmer.

It appears that Cook had received £700, which was not found at his death, and the opinion obtained that Cook not only knew, but was participant in the schemes of his subtle friend, by which immense gains were effected through a systematic traffic in murder, and that he could not resist his influence, because resistance might lead to worse consequences. The investigation disclosed that Palmer insured certain lives, and that in a brief period after effecting the policies death followed. Palmer's wife was among the *choice insurances* for £13,000, and the coroner's inquest alleged in its verdict that Palmer had murdered her. To this was added a charge of murdering his own brother, Walter, and in this suggestion the jury concurred, for he had also insured his life for £23,450, to cover a debt of £400. So many similar murders done by Palmer, some *sixteen*, were consequent on transactions with him; but his memory needs no new accusations to render him an object of general execration, and having been executed in December, 1855, he as much as most sons of earth and wrath, left a name at which the world grew pale.

## BIOGRAPHICAL NOTICE OF MILTON.

Many enthusiastic biographers of Milton have made rambles to Colnbrook and Horton, and by reiterated explorations in tradition and documents, something more has been unfolded. But not the least of judicious inquirers is that gentleman, whose elegant and comprehensive life of Milton now ranks among the best of that useful species of writing, biography, for which England is celebrated.

He who would know all that is disclosed about the rival of the Greek and Roman epic bards would do well to consult Mr. Masson, and to him I have turned for information, some of which is interwoven in this *precis* of a life also written by the Colossus of literature, Dr. Johnson, but which is rather critical than social, and which, despite the *acumen* therein displayed, has been as much criticised and has given as little satisfaction as any piece of biography from the pen of him who compiled the Lives of the Poets. His best lives are of those he liked best, whilst Milton and others encountered his unmitigable aversion. Johnson says of Milton, accusing him of malignity, that hell looked *darker* at his frown; and at *thine*, added *meek* Cowper, the poet.

This is but a succinct account of the poet—a sojourner for many years at Horton. On leaving Cambridge, Milton returned to his father's roof, not then in the metropolis, but in a *suburban* retreat, by which Horton is meant, whither his father had retired to pass some years in the sweet quiet village where he dwelt, as being of that complexion " which seemed made for one who his mortality had felt."

With his aged parent Milton lived, whom he only quitted occasionally to repair to London, with the philosophic purpose of acquiring new *pabulum*, that no craving void should be left aching in his breast for want of books.

Many causes suggested to him a longing to visit the Continent, and especially that section of it, Italy, which ever had the fatal gift of beauty, and this with his parent's concurrence.

Dates assign his sojourn at Horton from the beginning of June, 1632, until the April of 1638. Here he became familiar with the ancient and opulent house of Bulstrode, which family came to reside permanently at the Manor House, after the death of Edward Bulstrode, in 1595, and when Milton joined the village the Bulstrodes were in the height and blossom of renown.

This incited the representative of Bulstrode to become solicitous about his ancestry, whose names he would not willingly let die—for we seem to live in the persons of our forefathers; and it is the labour and reward of vanity to extend the term of this ideal longevity, remarks the historian of the Decline and Fall of Rome.

To this end he referred his pedigree to the College of Arms (the only competent authority then for analysing and giving an *ultimatum* on such points), in a letter dated from Horton, 14th July, 1634, inclosing a genealogy and armorial ensigns, but which was not approved by the College, because it was alleged that the *scocheon* had more quarterings than at a previous visitation, so it was returned for further proof, or for what was of *equal* consequence, "the Herald's fees."

This rejection was disregarded by Henry Bulstrode, hence a citation was issued ordering him to appear before the Earl Marshal, then the Earl of Arundel (this office is hereditary in the family of Howard, Dukes of Norfolk), to answer for contempt, under penalty of £10 and consequences.

This very heraldic inquiry urged Milton to set out his pedigree, and either to obtain a grant of arms, or to have confirmed legally the coat which his father used. A similar case occurred with Shakspeare in 1599—O on a bend S, a spear of the first—of whom it was said:—

> He seemed to shake a lance
> As brandished at the eyes of ignorance.

The Manor House of Horton was now bedizened with armorial cognizances of Bulstrode, some of which were traceable in 1812, when the last fragment was removed from that portion of the building which was in the rear of the church. Add MSS. 9439. British Museum.

To this *retreat* it was in the salubrious village, for age that lessens the enjoyment still increases the desire of living, that the venerable paternity of Milton retired at the limit of man's age, 70 years, to obtain fresh accessions of health and to enjoy the company of his son John, and his daughter Anne, wife of Edward Phillips, in the autumnal felicity of his life.

The second son, Christopher Milton, visited the *retreat* also, as appears by the burial of his infant son here in 1639. He was a lawyer, being admitted of the Inner Temple, 22nd September, 1632, and in 1638 he married at St. Andrew's, Holborn, Thomazine, daughter of William Webber of that parish. Their daughter Sarah, so called from her grandmother, was here baptized in 1640.

The county of Bucks has been famed for its bards, and so breathes of poetry (page 50). Spenser resided at Whaddon when under Secretary to Lord Grey, who died 1593, which place was honoured by a visit from Queen Elizabeth in her progress through Bucks in 1568.

Milton, Denham, Waller, Gray, Cowper, found homes here, and doubtless the seclusion of Horton and the repeated strains of the sweet bird of eve, for nightingales abound in the village, awakened an inspiration, together with the scenery and the society, in the thoughtful mind of the young philosopher and child of song. A welcome reception at the Manor House endeared him to his companions, and as the Sabbath revolved, he found himself in the centre of a congregation animated with warm devotion and gratitude, whose expansion is a virtue and a pleasure.

Report affirms that here in the sequestered hamlets he exercised his early muse, and that Comus, from a hand more electrifying than a wizard's wand, was composed in 1634, to be followed by his plaintive Lycidas in 1637, with that enchanting sonnet to *Philomela,*\* commencing:—

> Oh, nightingale, that from yon bloomy spray,
> Warblest at eve, when all the woods are still,
> Thou with fresh hope the lover's heart doth fill.

Who does not love Horton and all about it? For ever sacred be the place that has part in Penseroso and Allegro—for ever classic be its silent streams, for ever hallowed by the memory of the past, its sheltering groves!

It is to be regretted that Milton does not insinuate that Horton contributed to his gathering the sweetly pastoral imagery of his poems, and that beneath the pear-tree, bending under its overburdening store of fruit, he heard

> The lark begin its flight,
> And singing, startle the dull night.

Though he could not predicate of this flat country,

> Mountains on whose barren breast
> The labouring clouds do often rest.

The poet had evidently a predilection for this county, and his imagination, fed by the rural sights and sounds, burst into its most beauteous bloom, for he lived also at Chalfont St. Giles, in a small house at the extremity of the village belonging to the Fleetwood family, and their arms graven over the door of the façade betoken antiquity, a woodcut of which is given in Vol. III. of Dr. Lipscomb's Bucks. It is to be remarked here that a connection with the county was kept up by his nephew Thomas, son of Sir Christopher Milton, Kt. who took to wife Martha, daughter of Charles Fleetwood, son of Sir George Fleetwood, of the Vache, Bucks, p. 42.

At Harefield Court, the residence of Alice, daughter of Sir John Spencer, who died 1637, and then Countess of Derby, widow of Ferdinand 5th Earl of Derby, who report said was poisoned in 1594, was the *Arcades* performed in 1634 by the grand-children of this peeress, who remarried with Thomas Egerton, Lord Keeper of the Seals, and to her is addressed the compliment in the Allegro, "the cynosure of neighbouring eyes," p. 235.

At this stately mansion, the repertory of wit, beauty and learning, masques then in vogue were exhibited, as private theatricals, one of which Queen Elizabeth attended from 31st July to 3rd August, 1602.

Milton was certainly in Horton in 1634, for on the 4th day of December in that year he indited a letter to Dr. Alexander Gille, the younger, and he dates it from his *suburban* retreat; but from this period there exists no further trace of Milton's correspondence. With the just mentioned family he was familiar; his preceptor Alexander Gille, the elder, died 17th November, 1635, æt. 71, and his son, the correspondent, was appointed to succeed his father at St. Paul's School, London, where Milton had been educated. He was Head Master of this school for 35 years, and died in 1642. The family was from Lincolnshire, and took out a grant of arms in 1607, p. 98. In 1636 he was admitted D.D. at Oxford, and history records some literary scuffles between this grave Doctor and Ben Jonson, who with age grew irritable and querulous, and in consequence of pre-

---

\* Nightingales abounded in this parish. This bird, with singing birds in general, in Holland are protected from molestation, and even bird-nesting and every other injury to the melodists of the wood, are there punished by local laws. Destruction of birds is impolitic, as they are of great importance to agriculture, and devour insects which would desolate woods, fruit and grain.

vious provocations, Dr. Gille in 1632 circulated a philippic to the discredit and discomfort of *Rare Ben*. The insulted poet retaliated in a sharp rejoinder, and exercised his spleen and venom to the full, as he had previously done with Inigo Jones the architect, when the turbulent temper of Jonson took care to be in the wrong, being generally unconscious of the magic of the right.

The father of our John Milton, *decus Angliæ*, was a scrivener for 40 years long, and conducted a thriving business with two partners. He quitted London in 1632, and continued to reside in Horton until the decease of his wife, who was buried in the chancel of the church in 1637. She was a most approved mother, and widely known for her works of charity, and her discernment taught her to perceive how nature had displayed in her son her mysterious energies. The monumental inscription is given under the Church history.

The poet's parents, well stricken in years, repaired to the metropolis, and listened again to the swinging of the sign, the Spread Eagle, the arms of Milton, for every wind did make it ejaculate a sound.

The mode of indicating the contents of a shop by outward sign is very ancient, and is supposed to have been instrumental in the culture and encouragement of painting, for many artists of celebrity have begun their career in towns as mere sign-painters, a usage as old as our Edwards, as well as those painters of nature who, surrounded by pleasing images, experience the divine glow of inspiration.

After the death of his mother our bard sighed for *bella Italia*, to which he betook himself, a country for which he had a predilection; and his aptitude in her language, which like herself has the gift of beauty, is evinced in the production of some graceful sonnets written in *most choice* Italian.

This broke the tie which linked him to Horton. His excursion was interrupted by civil wars at home, for he had purposed to visit Athens, the eye of Greece, so famous for arts and eloquence.

He returned home after an absence of nearly two years, in 1639, as he himself observes, "free and untouched by any kind of profligacy or vice," full of merit and shining virtues as times went.

Politics ran high, and being of a stern, unbending spirit, he espoused, through *conviction*, the side of the republican and puritan party; yet was he no *democrat*, or for authority vested absolutely in the people, thinking then, with swarms of aristocratic and intelligent cotemporaries, that although monarchy may be a good institution, it is by no means *better* or more *sacred* than any other political institution; for government is but a national association, acting on the principles of society, and each nation may freely adopt its own form of government, there being no divine prescription for a monarchy more than a republic.

Soon his abilities were recognised, and he became Latin Secretary to the Protector, and so having offered the nation the homage of his talents, he was in daily communion with those impulsive spirits who opposed *traditionary* usages, until the advent of the Long Parliament, in which Dr. Warburton asserted there was an assemblage of the greatest geniuses for government that ever met, which employed Blake on the seas, Cromwell in the army, and Milton in the cabinet.

Milton was Latin Secretary to the Council of State in 1649, at a salary of £290 a year, which in 1655 was reduced to £150 during his life. There are 46 Latin letters extant of classic elegance, besides his polemical writings, in which he wielded the weapons of irony on subjects of ecclesiastical solemnity, and all his acts and publications were the result of *honest conviction*, not nature's rebellion done in the blaze of youth. He had a strong will, "quod vult valde vult," yet always sustaining himself by a good conscience and a lofty purpose—witness the reply he gave to one who asked him on *what* he was thinking, he replied, on *Immortality*.

He prosecuted his literary and political toils until 1651, when he lost an eye from paralysis of the optic nerve; and in 1654 the calamity was followed by total privation of sight. Yet blindness did not affect the appearance of his eyes; the same dark grey orb bent on nature without the power of expressive flashes, indicative of superior intellect.

"When sorrow comes, it comes not in single spies, but whole battalions,"—so his wife died, and thus being deprived of sight and with three young children, he might feelingly complain of being in darkness, and in danger compassed round, and solitude—

"He that is stricken blind, never forgets
The precious treasure of his eye-sight lost."

And even this bereavement he was wont to say would be tolerable were it not for the gout.

Subsequently to the change of political opinion, when, from the voluntary abandonment of the supremacy by Oliver's son, who only coveted *tranquillity*, the nation accidentally returned to kingly predominance, which has since been matured into a constitutional government, now the model of all polities, Milton narrowly escaped with his life, for he was hunted like a partridge on the mountains, and repaired, after the scourge of the plague in London in 1660, to Chalfont in Bucks, and there he completed and published his Paradise Lost.

Becoming acquainted with Thomas Elwood the Quaker, who died 1713, and who had been Milton's reader in his blindness, and the original editor of George Fox's Journal (probably related to John Elwood, who married at Iver in 1639, Mary, daughter of David Salter, p. 43), through Isaac Pennington, p. 18; at the suggestion of the follower of George Fox, he added his Paradise Regained, which, great and attractive as it is, some regret that he had not extended, and caused the poem to terminate with the Crucifixion, the most stupendous event since the creation.

He now felt happier in himself, although perplexed by domestic differences with his own children, who, like Lear's daughters, were not kind to their parent, yet he tolerated all and forgave them.

Having attained his 66th year, his old foe the gout, the *eighth* plague, prevailed over the enfeebled powers of nature, and on the 10th November, 1674, he paid a debt due to time and mortal custom, while in his garden house in London, and his mortal part was interred near his father's grave.

A sculptured monument is raised to the memory of this great heir of fame in Westminster Abbey, at Poet's Corner, "in whose holy precincts lie ashes that make it holier."

At his decease he was full of renown though not of years, yet did he live long enough for the attainment of ever-during fame, that last infirmity of noble minds.

A reviewer of his works remarks, that at its appointed time the aspiring spirit ascended before the Infinite, when perhaps one of the most richly stored intellects which ever spent itself in acquiring knowledge, appeared in the presence of the Omniscient.

They who knew him say he was wont to sit in a small chamber hung with rusty green, in an elbow chair, dressed neatly in black, pale but not cadaverous.

He sometimes wore a grey coarse coat at the door of his house in sunny weather, when he received his visitors; and he used to recline and dictate with his legs over the arm of a chair; but when he walked his uprightness gave him an air of courage and undauntedness, for his spirit shone through him. His physical and social ills had a little dashed his spirit, and blighted that hope which will always tinge with a dark shade the evening of life.

His was a soul, which like a star, dwelt apart, for his virtue never trembled before temptation, an impersonation of moral greatness. His memory is still cherished by the inhabitants of Horton,

And it is their pride,
An honest pride, and let it be their praise,
To offer to the passing stranger's gaze,

the site of a residence, Berkyn Manor, where Milton loved to dwell.

## PEDIGREE OF MILTON.

Arms of Milton—A. eagle displayed with two heads, G. beaked and with legged Az.

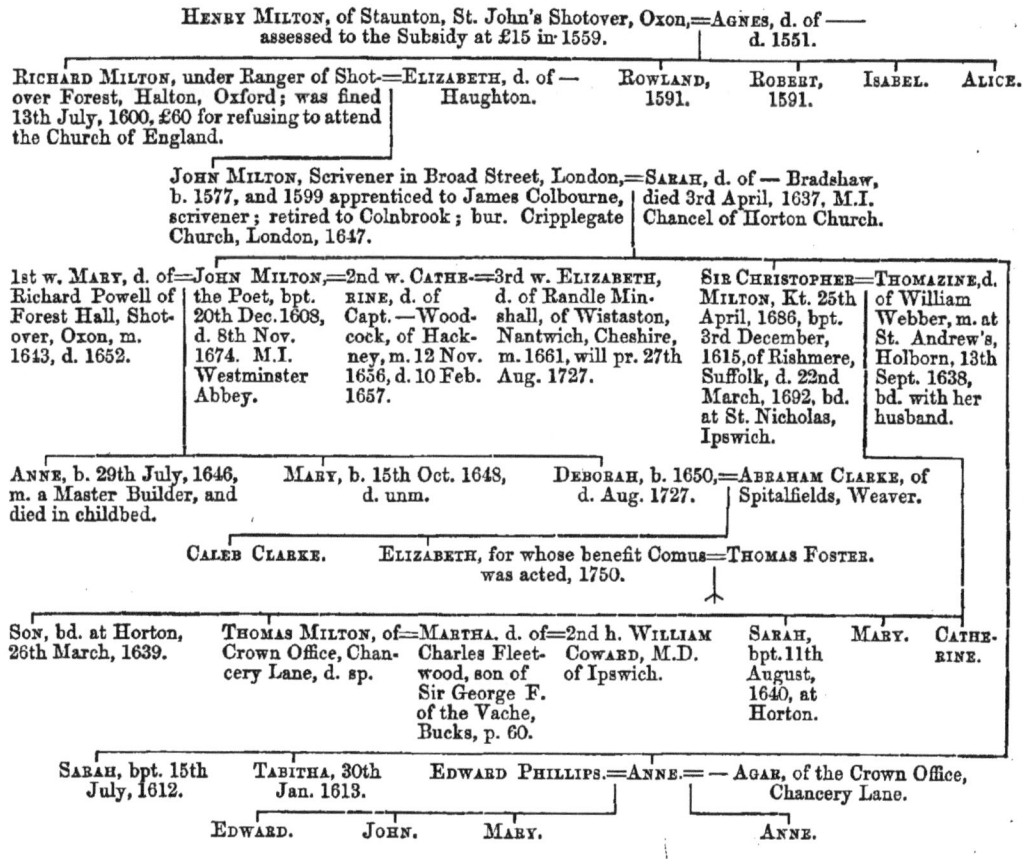

## THE CHURCH.

This church, dedicated to St. Michael the Archangel, is the mother church of Eton, and is in the diocese of Lincoln. Anciently there was supposed to be a dignity attached to the Rectorial office, now in abeyance, but of which mention is made in an antique black-letter book still extant at Lincoln; and that two scholarships, or the right of sending to Eton College foundation, is inherent by reason of this original connection between Horton and Eton.

The Church has been justly admired for its picturesque character, and it is surmised that it was raised in the twelfth century, if not earlier, judging from the semi-circular arch on the front floor, which is well preserved with its waved mouldings, recognized as Norman architecture. This style was disused after the reign of King Henry III., or about 1250, when the Saracenic, or pointed arch, known also as Gothic, prevailed.

This antique edifice stands in a cemetery of about an acre in extent, on the south side of the high road through the village. Its length is about 70 feet, very irregular, being chequered and pieced with flints and brickwork. The tower is square and ample, lofty (between 70 and 80 feet in altitude), and very picturesque from its deep-green ivy mantle, which has not been injurious to the structure. On the north face of the tower is a large clock, some 10 feet in diameter, and above it are large mullioned windows. Within the north porch is a fine old Norman arch, with a double row of zigzag, like the vertebræ of a fish; and between the nave and aisle, within short circular columns, supporting pointed arches have been modernised. The fretwork is so called from *frettan*, signifying fishes' teeth. A reel plain Saxon arch, then zigzag with single nail-head ornament externally blended, is supported on a plain ancient capital. The outer arch is a reel pattern to the ground. Third division four-fold zigzag.

The Church consists of a nave with two aisles, a chancel, and at the west end a square embattled tower, having a small turret projecting from its north-east angle; but one aisle is only a recess.

There are two porches with deep sloping gable roofs on each side of the nave, and a short cross aisle projecting on the north side, between the nave and the chancel.

On the south side, at the eastern end of the aisle, is a small vestry room of modern erection, and has been used for a Sunday school.

In the western face of the tower is a door, under a plain square moulding, above which is a mullion window of three lights, cinquefoil-headed, having trefoils in the point of its arch.

In the upper story of the tower, which contains five bells and a clock, are four windows, and in the roof above the south aisle are three irregular lights. Others of smaller size have been made in the wall below them.

On the east and west sides of the cross aisle are two modern sashes under pointed arches. The east window has stone mullions and trefoils, with some fragments of painted glass, but of what age is uncertain. History does not clearly define when painted glass was introduced for the transmission of light and other optical purposes. Bede quotes it in the seventh century, and it is known that artists came from Venice to introduce them into our architecture.

The roof is ceiled, but the beams project rudely through the stucco. On a corbel in the north-east pier of the nave is a shield with three chevronels, and at the termination of the moulding of the west door are several small blank escutcheons.

The font, which is probably coeval with the building, has been removed from its former situation, and is placed at the west end of the nave. It is very large, plain, and cylindrical, and stands on a circular basement, having its basin lined with lead, p. 114.

At the west end of the nave is a gallery, erected by voluntary contributions in 1789, when Robert Sayer and Richard Shelley were churchwardens. There is an harmonium used for aiding psalmody, the joint gift of the Rev. Tracey Coxwell and Edward Tyrrell, Esq. of Berkyn Manor.

The communion table of oak is supported by a carved and painted frame, and on a panel above is inscribed "Do this in remembrance of me."

On the sides of the eastern window were painted the Decalogue, Creed, and Lord's Prayer; but these have been removed. There are two foot-stools of needlework, the gift of Mr. Edward Tyrrell, of Berkyn Manor House; and two arm-chairs of oak of an antique form, on one is written, "God is love," and on the other, "Watch and pray." The monogram IHS is carved in the centre of each chair. The same gentleman gave also a memorial stained-glass window in 1857. The centre represents our Saviour with a cross and a flag between four Roman soldiers. In the centre light are the four Evangelists, surmounted by IHS. Above in a round light is a white dove, and the twelve Apostles disposed on either side, with their names underwritten.

The window is about 8 feet by 6 feet broad. The writing is fading, as it is only painted on and not burnt into the glass. There are two Archangels in the two lights right and left of our Saviour.

By the communion table there are two windows, north and south, with curtains.

There is really only one aisle, the recess on the north side is the manorial pew, which is separated from the large black Scawen monument. Within the interior of the walls of the church, when it was repaired in 1827, numerous figures were found of saints and the Virgin Mary; an entire figure of the latter is still pent up in the sides, with crucifixes and other emblems of bygone superstitions. Painting the walls in churches is not traceable higher than the eleventh century, and from this probably arose the illuminating of missals, exquisitely achieved, and, like painted glass, beyond the reach of modern art, owing to certain peculiar chemical combinations, unknown to modern science.

By the side of the pulpit are stone steps, seven in number, very steep, the lowest about two feet from the floor, which lead to the rood-loft, and this crossed the chancel. Perhaps some evidence of superstition. Ashmole says that the College of Windsor lost 100 marks yearly in the profit made by St. Anthony's pigs, and not less than £500 a year by the offerings of Sir John Schorne's shrine, page 116.

The chancel contains some mural slabs.

To the memory of Mary Brown, wife of the Rev. William Brown, Rector of this parish, who departed this life 26th September, 1848, at an advanced age. Here follows a citation from Scripture.

Also, the above Rev. William Brown, born March, 1771, died 26th September, 1850, having been Rector of this parish 55 years.

The monument is of white statuary marble; above the crest of Brown, a pigeon.

In this chancel, on a plain slab, laid crosswise on the floor, near the communion rails on the north side—

Under this stone are deposited the remains of Jane, wife of John Tupp, of this parish, who died 28th February, 1796, aged 59 years.

On another, in the middle of the floor:—

Beneath this stone are deposited the remains of John Tupp, Esq. of this parish, who died 8th March, 1813, aged 68 years.

On a blue stone horizontal within the chancel, opposite the door of the Rector's pew:—

Here lyeth the body of Sara Milton, the wife of John Milton, who died the 3rd of April, 1637.

An ancient slab retains clear marks of two principal figures, and the other smaller plates of brass below them, with a shield of arms at the west end of the stone, and Robert Nanney, 1734, more recently cut at the other extremity.

Also on a mural slab on the south side are Arms O, a Lion ramp. Az. crest on a wreath the same as in the arms; it is rather highly infixed on the wall, and the inscription dull from the brush of time.

        Hoc subter marmore
        Humati requiescunt cineres
        Roberti Nanney AM cujus Ecclesiæ
        per tredecim plus minus annos Rectoris.
        Galfridi Fil Nanniæ stirpe pervetustâ,
        Nanneiorum de Nanney in agro Merviniensi.
        Hujus etiam Ecclesiæ non ita pridem Rectoris,
        Et
        Mariæ filiæ Francisci Scawen Armigeri
        Tali majorum nobilis splendore Armiger
        Propriâ tamen dignitate clarior exstitit

## HISTORY OF HORTON.

> Nullâ non instructus Virtute quâ veram
> deceret libertatem
> Aut gravius exigeret Sacerdotii munus
> Morum suavitate pariter Spectabilis de Sanctimoniâ
> Relictis sibi superstitibus
> Nata altera novenni Catherina
> Atteraq. posthuma Maria Martha
> Mortales hasce posuit exuvias
> Die 29 Maij Anno { Dom. 1734
> æt. 42.

At the entrance to the manorial pew is a horizontal slab dedicated to Samuel Tipper, of Horton Mills, in this parish. Died 12th February, 1832, in the 56th year of his age.

The Scawen monument is very large and in the north portion of this recess in the church which is divided from the manorial pew. On this mysterious marble mass is not one word for whom it was erected; not even the sculptor's name. It consists of a basement divided into three compartments of veined marble, on which stands a large sarcophagus with a pyramid of black and gold, surmounted by a white fluted urn, whence issue flames of gold. This costly design was erected to the Scawen family, whose vault is under the pew which occupies the front of the aisle, but from some cause unexplained, neither inscription nor arms have been inscribed on it. As there are no single monuments to the members of this family in the church, it may have been intended to engrave thereon the principal names, as there were more than twenty members of this house buried here, including Mr. Robert Scawen, who purchased the manor in 1658, and died in 1669; with his son, Sir Thomas Scawen, in 1730; and Dame Martha Scawen, in 1766. Martha, daughter of Louis Scawen, closed the vault in 1798.

Monuments either perish or are unknown, and as in this case, they are only proofs of the artist's skill, and may be the vanity of those by whom they were erected; they are alone but transient records of men and deeds, and often inadequate to incite posterity to emulation.

NORTH WALL. White marble on black.

Sacred to the memory of Mrs. Sarah Wagstaff, wife of Mr. John W. and daughter of Edmond and Ann Haynes, of this parish, who departed this life 21st March, 1826, in the 70th year of her age. Who left for the poor of the parish for ever at the discretion of the Minister and Churchwardens, £100 new 4 per Cent. Stock, to be given on Christmas Day and Good Friday.

On a white marble slab, in the middle of the nave:—

In memory of Miss Emilia Lawson, only daughter of Sir Gilfred Lawson, Bart. of Brayton Hall, in the county of Cheshire, and sister to the present Sir Wilfred Lawson, Bart., who departed this life 23rd September, 1796, in the 33rd year of her age.

On a plain stone:—

Here rest the remains of Mrs. Mary Martha Evans, of this parish, relict of John Evans, Esq., late of Kingston, Jamaica, who died 12th December, 1812, aged 80.

On sepulchral stones in the pavement of the belfry are the initials and dates E T. 1730, and W T. 1733.

Here lieth buried the body of Edward Hazal, senr., Citizen and Button Seller of London. He died 18th December, A°. Dñ. 1669.

Here lieth the body of Thomas Haynes, husband of Martha Haynes, of this parish, tanner. He died 26th January, 1674, aged 43.

SOUTH AISLE. On a black marble:—

Here lieth the body of Elizabeth Griffin, wife of Edwin Griffin, of the Lordship of Batherton, in Cheshire, gentleman, and daughter of Thomas Pitt, of Colnbrook, mercer. Ob. 5 die Mart. An. Dom. 1670.

On another stone: Arms: fesse chequé, between 3 annulets; Crest on a wreath a Stork:—

Hereunder lyeth buried y$^e$ body of Agnes, y$^e$ wife of Thomas Pitt, of Colnbroke, in this parish, mercer, who died y$^e$ first of January, 1659, aged 62. Alsoe y$^e$ body of Thomas Pitt, husband of the said Agnes, who died y$^e$ 29th June, 1667, aged 83. They had 9 children, viz. Thomas, William, John, Edward, Anne, Elizabeth, Mikanell, Katharine, and Martha.

Here also lyeth buried in this isle the bodies of Katharine, John, and Mickanell Pitt; and also Edwin Blunt, son of Robert Blunt, gentleman, by Ann his wife, who died 14th August, 1664, aged 23. And also William Duglis, Martha and Elizabeth, children of William Clifton, junior, by Martha his wife, all lye buried here.

And also here lyeth y$^e$ body of Anne, the wife of Robert Blunt, gentleman, and Anne, daughter of Thomas Pitt, who died 17th March, aged 70 years.

WEST SIDE:—

Here lies the body of Sarah Willingham, mother to Mary wife of Joseph Holderness, of this parish, who died 31st December, 1823, aged 64.

The slab is horizontal, and has on it five lines in verse.

SOUTH SIDE. On a white marble set on black, simple and supported on claws:—

In memory of Elizabeth, wife of Cobbett Derby, of the Inner Temple, Esq. who departed this life 14th July, 1832.

Also, of Frances Elizabeth Harriet, wife of Cobbett Derby, junior, who died 3rd July, 1826; and their daughter Helen Maria Harriet, who died 25th July, 1826. Also, of Elizabeth Caroline, only daughter of Cobbett Derby, senior, Esq. and Elizabeth his wife, who died 23rd February, 1844.

Booker Derby, father of Cobbett Derby, Esq. died 1860, aged 91.

Near this is a pew assigned to the teaching of the children, kindly superintended by Mrs. Tupp; and in a desk there are books which are used for a lending library to the children.

In the church was found, some years since, a large coffin of 6 feet long, in an upright position; unfortunately it was broken to pieces, and the metal appropriated.

There is also a spacious iron stove in the Church, which is heated on Saturday and Sunday.

This Church underwent a thorough repair in 1827, at the cost of £1000, including the clock. John Cook and Stephen Pullin, Churchwardens. There is a list of the benefactors at the west end of the Church painted on a board, in six compartments, the centre making a seventh compartment, on which is the statement of repairs.

Benefactions to the Church:—

1. The public-house known by the sign of the Five Bells, with garden and meadow on the south side of the road opposite Horton Lane, 3r. 35p. situated in this parish.
2. Four cottages and gardens, near a piece of meadow ground on Horton Moor, 3a. 2r. 10p. bounded by the roadside to Stanwell on the north, the county ditch at the east, lands belonging to Peers Williams, Esq. on the south, and the parish gravel-pit on the west. The rest of the above property is for the repairs of the church of this parish.
4. Whereas for many years a rent-charge of 30s. per annum has been paid by the Lord of the Manor of Horton, and given away in bread by the Churchwardens to the poor of this parish.
5. Sarah Wagstaff, late of N. Windsor, who died 21st March, 1826, by her last will and testament left £100.
6. Also Mrs. Gosset, late of this parish, left £20, the interest arising to be distributed in bread to the poor of the parish.

7. The several sums of £100 and £20 are now invested in 3 per Cent. Consols, in the name of the Rector and Churchwardens, and the interest is distributed in bread, agreeable to the wills of the said Mrs. Wagstaff and Mrs. Gosset.

Under this gallery there is a passage to the Tower, which is reached by some much worn spiral steps to a cock loft. The clock is locked up, but it is wound every Monday by a man from Egham, at a fixed salary. The second flight of steps conducts to the belfry. On the right, looking north, is the large tenor bell, which strikes for the *clock* by means of a wire attached to it. The four remaining bells are arranged in a line towards the south, and are uniform in size. The belfry is constructed of solid oak, with ashen spars for the bells, one of which was founded, according to a minute in the Churchwardens' account, 1753-4, viz.: Casting the bell, £10. 10s; paid part casting the bell, £3. 8s 8d. Oil for ditto, 1757-8. The ringers receive a pound sterling annually, and ring on specific as well as on ordinary occasions; besides emulative contests with neighbours.

The tenor bell bearing to the north has on it—Praise the Lord * 636. Diameter, —; it is 129 inches round, and 38 inches high.

On the first of the other four bells is, Richard Phelps made me, 1727. Second bell, Feare God, 1647. Third bell, Edmund Bowry, William Wells, Ch. W. R. P. fecit, 1719, Honour God. Fourth bell, pointing north-west, has on it, Francis Bowry, Robert Singer, Churchwardens, Thomas Swain made me, 1753.

## CHURCHYARD.

The Churchyard is about an acre in area, and cleanly kept. In it northwards are two very picturesque and antique yews, coevals, male and female, probably 6 or 700 years old. Under the male tree, which bears fruit, there is a large commodious bench. These trees are common to most churchyards. At Bedfont, on the London Road, there are two cut in *topiary*,* or clipped work, exhibiting figures of 1704, while the tops of the trees are formed into the shape of peacocks.

This cemetery is not very full of monuments, and it is alleged that head-stones have been removed in large quantities. Part of the cemetery towards the north, abutting on the road, is unconsecrated ground. A large dense brick wall surrounds it on three sides, which divides it from Horton Park. It is of great thickness, bricks 12 inches long and 3 broad, overtopped with ivy, and strengthened with several large round buttresses, whose use is not clearly defined. A door leads into the Park near the site of the old mansion.

The exterior of the church walls, in which are no monuments, have some inscriptions on them. On a white stone, affixed to the outside of the north wall of the aisle—

Near this place lies yᵉ bodie of William Goade, yᵉ father, and William his son, both late of Colebroke, Physitians. Also Joseph and Sarah Fellowes, son and daughter of George Fellowes, Surgeon, and Priscilla his wife, and kinsman of the late William Goade.

*On a small stone :*—Elizabeth Thompson died 10th October, 1777.

*On another slab :*—Here lyeth the body of Lazarus Holderness, who departed this life the 2nd day of June, 1756, in the 75th year of his age. Some citations follow.

Also the body of Mr. Henry Holderness, son of the above, who departed this life 1st June, 1800, aged 82 years. Some verses.

On an altar tomb in the churchyard, near the east end of the chancel—

William Child, Citizen and Haberdasher of London, died 16th December, 1715, aged 50 years.

* This form of cutting hedges and *clipping beards* is noticed in a distich among the fragmentary pieces by the author of Hudibras.

No topiary hedge of quickset
Was e'er so neatly cut or thickset.

Also, Henry Child, twin with the abovementioned, died 31st August, 1718.

Also, Elizabeth Child, daughter of the above William Child, died 22nd July, 1727, aged 37 years.

Also, Judith Child, wife of the above William Child, died 21st June, 1730, aged 65 years.

Also, Mr. Joseph Child, Gent. of Richmond, Surrey, son of the above William Child. He died 16th May, 1749, aged 61 years.

*On a grave-stone near:*—John Virgo, of Brompton, in the parish of Kensington, died 25th March, 1810, aged 49.

On the north side:—

Sacred to the memory of Mr. Francis Virgo, Citizen of London, who departed this life 30th March, 1810, aged 58 years.

*On another altar tomb:*—Sacred to the memory of William Virgo, Esq. of Wraysbury, Bucks, son of Thomas Virgo, late of Mildridge, in this parish, who departed this life 14th May, 1819, in the 70th year of his age.

On the north-west side of the Churchyard is a stone to—

John Dowse, died 26th September, 1850, aged 73. Mrs. Lucy Dowse died 27th December, 1857, aged 82. Also, John Curtis, died 10th February, 1851, aged 75. Also, Richard John Frear died 8th November, 1845, aged 61. John Broughton, died 4th September, 1841, aged 80.

*On an altar tomb:*—Mary Webster, widow, daughter of Henry Holderness, died 8th June, 1853, aged 88.

John Plumridge, 33 years Clerk of this Church, died 1st June, 1843, aged 70. Mrs. Martha Plumridge, widow, died 4th September, 1855, aged 78. Mr. Thomas Plumridge, died 27th April, 1846, aged 33.

Mr. Richard Fonnereau, died 7th February, 1814, aged 28.

*On an altar tomb:*—Mr. William Howard, Citizen and Grocer of London, died 11th October, 1723, aged 63. Ann his wife, died 7th April, 1721, aged 63.

*Altar tomb:*—Mr. Thomas Biddle, late of Colebroke. Figures erased. Mrs. Elizabeth Biddle his wife. Also, Susanna Smith, widow, daughter of Thomas and Elizabeth Biddle, died October, aged 49. Mr. Robert Biddle, died December, 1743, aged 60.

*An altar tomb*—To the memory of Thomas Wynch.

There are two stones united, north side, to—

John Burcombe, late of Colebroke, Mercer, died 6th December, 1714, aged 56. Ann, wife of ditto, died 11th September, 1708, aged 49.

*A stone*—To Edward Perkins, and one to Mary Godden, died 8th January, 1860, aged 70. Edward Godden, husband of ditto, died 23rd April, 1837, aged 52. James, their son, died 21st February, 1842, aged 15. William Atkins, brother of Mary Godden, died 12th March, 1859, aged 76.

*A slab close to the wall:*—Elizabeth Yeates, daughter of Wilson Yeates, Esq. died 2nd November, 1834, aged 4. Frances Mary Yeates, sister, aged 15 years.

Several altar tombs in the Churchyard, whose inscriptions are quite illegible. One to the family of Lisle.

Susan, daughter of James House, died 10th December, 1722, aged 32.

Susanna, wife of Henry Bullock, of Poyle, 1840. Ditto, Mr. James Holderness, died 23rd April, 1853, aged 70.

Rebecca Burcombe, died 22nd April, 1765, aged 40. William Burcombe, husband of the above, died 25th March, 1779, aged 54. William Burcombe, son of the above, died 9th July, 1799, aged 34. Ditto, Rebecca Burcombe, late of Kingston, Surrey, died 5th January, 1830, aged 67.

*Altar tomb:*—William Derby, Esq. died 23rd November, 1837, aged 74. John Derby, Esq. late of the Bank of England, died 5th January, 1843, aged 82. Also, Mrs. Frances Holderness, widow of James Holderness, died 10th October, 1848, aged 80.

A large Monument to the memory of Alexander Wicherly, Esq. died 8th February, 1766, aged 80, servant of the removing Wardrobe to King George I. II. and III. with a good character.

*Upright stone:*—Mr. Leamer, died 1801. *Flat stone:*—Mr. Henry Forth, 1819. One to a family of Jennings. Large handsome iron railing containing a monument—

To the memory of Adelaide Gardiner Laing, died young.

Ditto of Lydia Whiteford Laing, born 3rd January, 1808, died 26th April, 1836.

Several upright stones to the memory of the Haynes' family.

*Large stone*—To the memory of Thomas, son of Edward and Mary Biddle, died 3rd August, 1717, aged 29. Ditto of Edward Biddle, of Richmond, Gent. and Mary his wife, died 13th March, 1743, aged 73. She died 12th December, 1747, aged 69.

John Ashton, of Woolwich, died 20th May, 1792, aged 56. Frances his wife, died 3rd August, 1791, aged 50. Also, John Ashton, died 4th July, 1804, aged 74.

Fanny, wife of John Fulkes, of Colnbroke, daughter of the above, died 24th November, 1813, aged 43.

There are six stones to the family of Maish, of Colnbroke; also to Stevenson, Hibbard and Thurley, Oak, Stretton.

A stone horizontal slab, in the shape of a coffin, on the north-west side, near the church door—

The Rev. T. Tracey Coxwell, Rector of Horton, died 8th December, 1852, aged 76.

William Rogers, poulterer and citizen of London, son of William and Ann Rogers, of Stratfieldsay, Hants, died 11th December, 1816, aged 42.

A very handsome stone column, surmounted with a sarcophagus—

Sacred to the memory of Mary, wife of Mr. William Stevens, died 15th January, 1852, aged 69. William Stevens died in 1852, aged 72.

On an elevated piece of ground at the back of the female yew tree, within a tall iron rail, is another tomb, on the top of which—

Sacred to the memory of Mary, the beloved wife of Henry Stevens, died 2nd February, 1848, aged 60. Sacred to the memory of Henry, husband of the said Mary Stevens, died 21st October, 1851, aged 60.

On the north side of the same tomb—

Ann, wife of Edward Hall, Esq., who died 28th July 1829, æt. 45. Also Ann, wife of John Littlewood, Esq., died 22nd August, 1833, æt. 36.

On the south side—

William Littlewood Stevens, son of Henry Stevens of this parish and Mary his wife, died 24th September, 1835, æt. 9.

Mary Ann Fowles of Stanwell, daughter of the above Henry and Mary Stevens of Wyrardisbury, died 16th June, 1847, æt. 30.

Also John Hutton Stevens, son of the above, died 24th September, 1850, æt. 32.

*Tombstone:*—Jane Louisa, wife of Thomas Stevens, of Dock Street, Whitechapel, London, died 19th October, 1851, æt. 67.

Ditto. Mr. Thomas Stevens of ditto, died 16th March, 1853, æt. 68.

Elizabeth Jane, daughter of Thomas Stevens, died 28th July, 1847, æt. 25.

Mr. James Stevens, son of Thomas and Jane Stevens, died 11th October, 1831, æt. 21. Do. Thomas, son of Thomas and Jane Stevens, died 10th April, 1836, æt. 23.

Frances, daughter of William and Mary Stevens, died 1821, æt. 6; and Harriet Ann, daughter of ditto, died 1832, æt. 21.

Mr. James Stevens, died 20th February, 1828, æt. 60. Do. Elizabeth, wife of Mr. Joseph Stevens, died 7th September, 1821, æt. 68.

Jane, wife of Thomas Northcroft, died 31st March, 1808, æt. 21. Ann, daughter of — Stevens. Some children of James and Elizabeth Stevens, 1784.

Mrs. Elizabeth Brook, of Tottenham Court Road, died 7th February, 1847, æt. 89.

250 HISTORY OF HORTON.

Mr. Thomas Bennett, died 2nd February, 1815, æt. 56. Other records of Bennett.

Sundry monuments to the families of May, Stretton, Shurley, Hibbard, &c.

Spencer Percival Enoe, son of Spencer and Ann Enoe, died 1816, æt. 21. Some verses.

Mrs Agnes Peters, wife of Henry Peters of New Windsor, died 30th September, 1847, aged 25 years.

Mr. Joseph Reffell of the Manor Farm, in this parish, died 13th September, 1848, aged 59.

Alfred, son of Joseph and Elizabeth Reffell, died 20th January, 1844, aged 22.

On a horizontal slab, surrounded with iron rails, north-west side of the cemetery—

In this vault lieth the remains of Mrs. Ann Pullin, wife of Mr. Stephen Pullin, of Mildridge Farm in this parish, died 4th July, 1818, aged 38. Jane, daughter of the above, died 20th December, 1811.

Also, Mrs. Elizabeth, 2nd wife of Mr. Stephen Pullin, died 19th April, 1833, aged 62. Also, Mr. Stephen Pullin of Mildridge, died 19th March, 1853, aged 80. A son, Nelson Edward Pullin, died 1854.

## PLAGUE BURIAL STATISTICS.

These statistics of burials for 12 years preceding and including 1636, each year commencing 25th March (see Masson's Life of Milton, Vol. I.), relate to Colnbrook burials.

1625, 11 burials; 1626, 34 ditto, of the plague; 1627, 7 ditto; 1628, 17 ditto; 1629, 11 ditto; 1630, 13 ditto; 1631, 8 ditto; 1632, 8 ditto; 1633, 3 ditto; 1634, 13 ditto; 1635, 13 ditto; 1636, 11 ditto.

Hence it is to be noted that the mortality rises here to triple in the plague, 1626, but singular that in the year of the second visitation of the plague, 1630, it seems to be unscathed, and on its third appearance no change in mortality for the worse occurs. In 1637 the Horton Registers record 31, that is only three fewer than in the Great Plague year, 1626. In London, 35,000 persons died of the plague in the autumn of 1626.

1636.
March. Wife of Thomas Porter.
April. Susan, daughter of Morris and Martha Fisher.
" 6. Sara, uxor Johñis Milton, generosi, obiit 30.
" 9. Infant son of John and Susan Hawkins.
" 24. John, son of ditto.
" 28. Catherine, wife of John Ballinour, of Colebroke.
May 15. Richard Vicar, Gent. and Innkeeper, out of the Talbot, of the plague.
" " Frances, dau. of Richard Vicar, Gent.
" " John, son of John Paine, tapster, out of the Talbot, of the plague.
June 13. John, son of John Cooke, Gent., out of the Talbot, of the plague.
" 26. John Withers, sadler, of Colebroke, of the plague.
" " Mary, dau. of Henry Heydon, glover, of Colebrook.
" " Alice, wife of Gilbert Brandon, vintner of London, out of the Talbot, of the plague.

June 27. Susanna, wife of Robert Taylor, cobler, of Colebrook, of the plague.
July 7. Jonathan, son of ditto, of ditto.
" 10. Henry Heydon, glover, died of consumption, ditto.
" 30. Thomas Head, Mayor of Colnbrook, surfeited by drinking.
Aug. 20. Brigida, wife of Thomas Harris, died of a *staid* pestilence.
" 29. William Snowdon, servant of John Haines, husbandman, of the plague.
Sept. 29. William Stanton, carpenter.
" " Martha, wife of Maurice Fisher.
Nov. 13. Alice, wife of Thomas Field.
Dec. 23. Peter, son of Peter Jannings.
Jan. 4. John, son of John and Margaret Browne, of Colebroke.
" 9. Richard Farmer, Gent. aged 92.
" 28. Elizabeth, daughter of Judge Grayhew, of Colebroke, of a consumption.
Feb. 4. Margaret, wife of William Mitchell, of Colebroke.
Mar. 13. Margaret, wife of John Browne, of Colebroke.

By these entries it seems that of the 31 deaths of the year, 14, or almost half, were from plague, and mostly from that side of Colnbrook town which is geographically in Horton parish.

Bills of mortality took rise in 1592, in which year began a great pestilence, which continued till the 18th December, 1595, and afterwards discontinued and returned in 1603.

By care and skill and experience we now baffle or keep at bay cholera and disease. There are more centenarians amongst us now, even in proportion to our vastly increased population, than in any former times. The average duration of human life has been perceptibly increased, and this is symptomatic of a still more important advance in the general condition of public health. Statistics do not give us quite so favourable a list of infant life, its mortality being beyond the proper ratio, swelling the death rate of the country. Infanticide is not practised as a system, but want, misery and shame all tell fearfully in the balance against the ties of parental affection; and from infant mortality it is presumed that two-fifths of our whole population is cut off—within five years of their first entry upon life.

## ECCLESIASTICAL MATTERS.

The Rectory was impropriate, but on enclosing the parish in 1800 the lands given in lieu were directed by the Act of Parliament to be awarded to the then Rector and his successors, Rectors of Horton, thus letting the incumbent into the direct ownership of the Rectory, which is in the Archdeaconry of Buckingham, and now in the diocese of Oxford. Horton St. Michael's value in the King's Books is £22. 9s 4½d, Archdeacon 10s 7¾d, Bishop 4s 5½d; and now the clear value is about £385 per annum, but in 1650 the living was valued at £100 per annum. The tithes, great and small, were originally common, with a few acres on the Rectory ground and one field excepted, and were commuted for land, some of which was enclosed. They consist of glebe, tithes, and corn rent, the latter is about £6. 10s, and surplice fees £10, *communibus annis*. In 1791 there was an allotment for gravel to the Lord of the Manor, and to the Rector for glebe and tithes, while a corn rent was to be substituted for old inclosures when the land is an insufficient allotment for the common right of cottagers. The gravel pit, which was on the left side of the new road of Horton Lane, leading from Wraysbury, has been changed to the opposite corner, leading towards Hog Lane—this land is full of water in winter—and the former pit is now converted into meadow, and is possessed by the Lord of the Manor.

30th June, 1760. Glebe land terrier—Colly mead, High field, Hare field, Low field, Home close, Parsonage house, with garden, orchard and yard, 9 acres and 1 rood. The perpetual advowson or right of presentation of the Rectory of Horton St. Michael's, Bucks, was transferred from the family of Scawen, in 1782, to John Brown, Esq. of Tottenham, Middlesex, who in July of that year presented Rev. Thomas Roberts, *vice* Rev. John Blair, and in May, 1796, Mr. Roberts resigned it to Rev. William Brown, son of John Brown, who was inducted 10th June, 1796. He was also patron of the living then, and he sold this right to Thomas Williams, Esq., who in 1799 purchased the advowson. There are about 250 acres of land on the north-west side of the parish, belonging to the incumbent. The old common consisted of some 300 acres.

The earliest date transmitted to us of an appointment to the living was 1218, when William de Windlesore presented a relative in Hugo de Windlesore, since which time the personal right of presentation has varied with almost every appointment, nor do we find it again positively in the hands of the Windsor family, or even the name of Windsor connected with the Rectors, save where William de Harpesfield, presented in 1315, and had a dispensation for two years to perform the obsequies of Ralph de Windsor. In fact, the right of presentation became wholly marketable, a custom introduced into England with the Conqueror. Saxon tything was the origin of our manor, the judicature of which is still termed *tything* courts. The division into shires before Alfred's time is mentioned in the laws of Ina, at the close of the 7th century. Tything, township and vill were synonymous, and the words city and borough are equivalent.

In the taxation of Pope Nicholas, the Church of Eton was at £10. 13s 4d; Datchet, with the Chapel of Fulmer, £13. 6s 8d; Upton the same; Stoke, £12; Dorney, £6. 13s 4d; Wraysbury and Langley, £33. 6s 8d; Burnham, £30, and the Vicarage £10. This taxation is of great importance, because all taxes, as well to Kings as to Popes, were regulated by it until the Survey, 26 Henry VIII. 1534.

## RECTORY HOUSE.

The present Rectory, though very old, does not seem to be the identical one cited in ancient deeds of conveyance, being a comparatively modern house, dating from 1700 perhaps. It is a large brick building, pleasantly situated in a recess environed with trees, and improved under the present Rector's taste; the front abuts on the high road to Colnbrook, commanding a clear prospect of Windsor Castle, and it stands on some two acres of ground with an appropriate garden, stables and offices, with some large cedars, &c. and a beautiful specimen of a white elm, of which some seedlings are in growth.

On the 20th May, 1788, a terrier makes the site of the Rectory to consist of about two acres, with a brick dwelling, &c., an acre of meadow land and one of arable, with one acre, one rood and 13 poles in Lowfield, with sundry *addenda*. All tithes were then paid to the Rector in kind, and not subject to any modus or custom. "The churchyard belongs to the Rector, and the chancel is repaired by the Lord of the Rectory, and the walls of the Church by the Lady of the Manor." There are some houses let to parishioners for repairs of the Church, about £8; viz., one let to John Seames, another bit of land abutting on Sir John Aubrey's land, p. 229 (this land was subsequently purchased partly by the Williams' family, and some 20 acres of it was in the possession of Mr. Henry Steevens, which was sold to Miss Elizabeth Cane and others, after his death in 1851), and there were five cottages, yielding about £7 yearly. There is a terrier of Horton in 1749, which contains no allusion to Church lands, and a terrier of glebe, 1770, of five items, £9. 1s. There is also a very old black letter terrier, in which are found the names of Henry and Thomas Bulstrode, with that of Edward Goodall, who succeeds in 1631 *Francis* Boswell, and not William Boswell, as is found in the Rectorial list, which the parish registers affirm—assistant to the celebrated Puritan minister, Thomas Gataker,* of Rotherhithe. Goodall did the duties here for £100 per annum, from 1631 to 1652, and dwelt at the Rectory with his wife, Sarah Goodall, p. 213.

There is another terrier, *sans date*, belonging to the Parsonage of Horton in the time of Sir Thomas Scawen, who in his will left £30 for the poor of the parish, at which time no lands were exempt from payment of tithes, nor subject to any particular modus. This terrier states there are five bells in the church, one clock, one Bible, two Common Prayer books, one pulpit cloth and cushion, one communion table cloth, two pewter flagons, two pewter dishes, two plates, one silver chalice and cover weighing eight ounces nine pennyweights, and no lands or money in store for the repairs of the church or utensils. Robert Nanney, Rector of Horton.

The Sunday School has about 50 children, and from 20 to 30 in the Infant Day School: the elder children attend the Horton and Colnbrook Day School, at Colnbrook, which was erected by joint subscription. The Sunday School is free; the charge in the Infant School is 1d weekly for each child.

---

* Instituted to Rotherhithe in 1612, and was Rector 42 years; wrote a treatise on the purity of the language of the Greek Testament, and was called by Anthony Wood the learned Presbyterian; known for his controversy with Lilly the astronomer. He died 1654.

For this and other information relative to the parish, for permission to search the Parish Registers, &c., I am much beholden to the Rev. Mr. Foote, whose courtesy was not wanting in either personal or epistolary communications, besides hospitality.

## RECTORS.

1208. Hugh de Windlesore, by William de Windlesore.

1306. John London died Rector.

„ 4th November. Stephen de Cheshunt was presented by Richard de Cadamo, whose son John bought the manor and advowson, 1328.

1315, 4th July. William de Harpesfield, presented by John, son of Jeffrey de Whethamsted. Had a dispensation for two years for the obsequies of Ralph de Windsor. He died 1349.

1349, 4th August. Roger de Kimbell, by Nicholas Langtoft de Lethingburg.

1361, 11th October. John de Gestlinthorp, by Sir Roger de Louth, who in 1357 had bought the manor of Horton.

1394. John Chamber died Rector.

„ 3rd August. John Forest was collated by the Bishop on lapse.

1404, 9th August. John Wyat was collated by Bishop on lapse. He exchanged for Wymondham, Norfolk.

1405, 18th December. Walter Piers, by Adam at Wood, patron.

1408. Nicholas Calton resigned.

1414, 15th October. Richard Petworth, by Edmund Duke of York. Exchanged with Simon Marchford.

1415, 5th March. Simon Marchford for Stowe in Lindsay, Prebend Lincoln Cathedral. He was Canon of Windsor, and died 1444, and was buried at Hammersmith, Middlesex, having exchanged for Burwescote Rectory, Yorkshire.

1434, 17th November. William Palmer.

1468. Thomas Bengewyn died Recter.

„ 3rd November. Bartholomew Geryng, by J. Pury, Esq., resigned.

1477, 22nd October. Ambrose Repyngton, by J. Pury, resigned.

1478, 17th October. John Daniel, by Richard Bulstrode, Esq.

1485, 12th October. William Stanley.

James Blith, presentation unknown.

1546, 20th October. Roger Griffith, by Reginald Digby, Esq., in right of his wife Ann, (daughter of John Danvers, Esq.)

1560. William Barker, who resigned.

1570, 16th February. Elizeus Rothwell, by William Bromfyld, Esq.

1584, 26th March. Roger Meyrick, resigned 1592.

1590, 25th November. Edward Wickham, by Q. Elizabeth; afterwards Archdeacon of Dorset.

1592, 2nd March. Richard Langley, by Q. Elizabeth during the minority of Robert Digby, he being the Queen's ward.

1612, 9th March. Anthony Maxie, Canon of Windsor, by Thomas Langley, executor of Thomas Langley deceased, the patron.

1618. Francis Boswell, by Lord Digby. He was buried in St. Lawrence Jewry Church, London. p. 252.

1631. Edward Goodall, by Henry Bulstrode, Esq., and occurs Rector in 1650, when the living was valued at £100 a year. His son of the same name was born here—of King's Coll. Camb. 1661,—became a Romanist and resigned his living of Prescott, co. Lancashire, on the abdication of James II.

1652. James Worthington, and was ejected from this living and mastership of Jesus Coll. Cambridge.

1661. Robert Peade.

1691, 10th December. Thomas Roe, S.T.P., by King William and Mary.

1692, 28th January. John Scawen, by William Scawen, merchant of London, the Crown title being set aside.

1695, 9th December. William Nanney, by Sir William Scawen, Kt.

2 K

1721, 31st January. Robert Nanney, son of Geffrey Nanney, who married Mary (ob. 1731) daughter of Francis Scawen, brother of Robert Scawen, who bought the manor of Horton in 1658.

1734, 29th August. John Edwards, by Dame Martha, widow of Sir Thomas Scawen, Kt. who died 1730. She died 1766.

1750, 12th July. Edward Dicey, by Dame Martha Scawen. He exchanged for Marsh Gibbon, Bucks.

1772. Mathew Schutz, D.D.

John Blair, LL.D. and F.R.S. In 1776 inducted to the Rectory of St. John Evangelist, Westminster, which he held with Horton by dispensation. He recast his famous Chronological Tables at the Rectory House. He was related to Dr. Hugh Blair, and died 24th June, 1782. He had a brother, Capt. Blair, killed at the sea-fight, 12th April, 1782, which shock accelerated his death. He was an able officer, and bravely distinguished himself under Sir George Rodney—falling in the bed of honour, he became one of the three heroes to whom their country, by its representatives, voted a public monument.

1782, 15th July. Thomas Robarts, on the presentation of John Brown, Esq., of Tottenham. He resigned to his son Thomas.

1795, 11th April. Thomas Robarts, by William Brown, Esq. of Magdalen Coll. Oxon, and on his cession,

1796, 1st June. William Browne, son of the above, was inducted and admitted as patron in full right on his own presentation.

1851. Tracey Coxwell, on the presentation of Thomas Peers Williams, Esq., whose grandfather, Thomas Williams, Esq., bought the advowson, in 1799, of Rev. William Brown. Mr. Coxwell was son of Charles Coxwell, of Ablington, Gloucestershire, a family whose head is Richard Rogers Coxwell, who assumed the name of Rogers as representative of the ancient house of Rogers of Dowdeswell Court, near Cheltenham, co. Gloucester, and of Bryanston, co. Dorset. p. 234.

1855, August. Richard Gorges Foot, on the presentation of Thomas Peers Williams, Esq.

## CHARITIES.

The Report of the Commissioners for inquiries concerning Charities, 10th July, 1832, on the parish of Horton lands. There is a public house called the Five Bells, let to George Taylor as yearly tenant, at the rent of £29; also five cottages, let to several poor persons, producing £9 per annum; and four acres of land let to Henry Stevens as yearly tenant at £8. The whole of these rents, some £40, are carried to the Churchwardens' accounts.

Hearne's Charity. This is a sum of £1. 10s annually, by the Minister and Churchwardens, from Thomas Williams, Esq. We find that nothing was known distinctly in the parish as to the nature and origin of this charity, but guided by a statement in the Parliamentary returns in 1786, we obtained at Doctors' Commons an extract of the will of Edmund Hearne, dated 14th December, 1684, and proved 8th July, 1686. He devised all his messuages, lands and tents., with appurts. in Horton or elsewhere (which he had lately purchased of Mr. Charles Peters in 1675) to his wife for life, and after her death to Edward Hearne, son of his brother William Hearne, and the heirs of their two bodies, and for default, to his sons-in-law Francis and Samuel Bowry, and Thomas Bowry and his daughter-in-law, Anne Cook, their heirs and assigns for ever. Upon special trust, and that certain sums be paid yearly for ever after his decease, on the feast of St. Thomas the Apostle, to his executors or survivors, and that the yearly sum of 30s by them disposed and given amongst such poor of the parish who receive no collection of the said parish yearly, to issue from such land for ever.

An old receipt for rent, dated 26th April, 1728, was produced to us at Colnbrook, which had been for some time in the family of a late Churchwarden of Horton, on which there is an endorsement in the handwriting of the Churchwarden, "Mr. Bowry and Mr. Hern had equal share in Spillings when let to John Webb." The receipt is signed by Francis Bowry, and on the left hand corner the whole money received, £9. 5s, is divided into two parts, and £4. 17s is expressed to be the money, £2. 8s land and poor, and in the right hand corner the same sum of £2. 8s is again divided into two parts, £1. 10s of which is termed poor's money, and the remaining 18s land tax: Some land called Spillings, near the Manor House of Horton, now belongs to Mr. Williams, in respect of which this payment of £1. 10s is made, and it is laid out by the Minister and Churchwardens in the purchase of bread, which is given to the poor at Christmas.

Wagstaffe's Charity. On a tablet in the church it is stated that Mrs. Sarah Wagstaff, who died 21st March, 1826, left for the poor of the parish for ever, at the discretion of the Minister and Churchwardens, the interest of £100 new 4 per cent. Annuities, to be given in bread on Christmas day and Good Friday. The funds of this Charity now consist of £94. 7s 5d, 3¼ per Cent. standing in the names of Stephen Pullin, Rev. William Brown, and John Cook. The dividends are applied as is stated in the account of the next charity.

Parishes of Horton and Langley Marsh Chapelry, and Colnbrook:—

Gosset's Charity. Mrs. Catherine Gosset (widow of Rev. Isaac Gosset, died 1812, and daughter of Hudrell Hill of London), who died 1831, within 12 months of the date of this inquiry, by her will gave £20 to the poor of the parish of Horton, to be laid out at the discretion of the Minister and Churchwardens. With this sum £22. 4s new 3¼ per Cents. was purchased, standing in the same names as the stock of Wagstaff's Charity, the interest of the combined sums amounting to £4. 1s 10d yearly, to be laid out where the latter is received in the purchase of bread (as the interest of the former has hitherto been) to be distributed on Good Friday, on the Sunday next before or after Christmas, to the poor of the parish.

Chapel and Land. This relates to 2¼ acres, yielding £6 per annum, applicable to repairs of Colnbrook Church. The land is in Langley Marsh, and there is no mention of Horton.

Goade's Charity. 2 acres, 3 roods, and 4 poles, yielding £6. 10s, applicable to the Minister and poor of Colnbrook.

Town Houses.—By indenture, 3rd April, 1657, Thomas Pitt of Colnbrook, mercer, conveyed to Francis Ridley, Esq. and others, and their heirs, all those three cottages or tenements situated in Colnbrook, in the parish of Horton, therein particularly described, with all the lands, buildings and appurtenants to the only proper use and behoof of the poor inhabitants of the town of Colnbrook, within the two several parishes of Horton and Langley Marsh, after the buildings and reparations shall be satisfied, equally to be divided between the two hamlets, one as much as the other for ever; with a covenant that whereof if only half of the feoffees should survive, the said surviving six should convey the premises unto twenty at the least other honest and substantial inhabitants of the town of Colnbrook, and of the parishes of Langley and Horton, and their heirs, for the purposes in the said indenture, &c.; also that the said feoffees, or the greater number of them, should yearly on the Friday in Easter week meet in some convenient place within the town of Colnbrook.

Rector William Brown's Charity.—By will dated 28th April, 1849, he gave the interest of £500 3 per cent. annuities, to be distributed in the purchase of half-quartern loaves of household bread, by the Rector and Churchwardens of the parish of Horton, monthly, and on the first Sunday of every month for ever after divine service, to such poor of the parish as shall be at the morning service of the said Church, except sickness prevent. Also that a board be set up at the south-west end of the Church in plain and legible characters declaring his intention. He appoints two persons executors to his will, proved 2nd December, 1850.

Church Land's Charity.—The scheme for the management and administration of the estates and revenues of this trust was approved by the Court of Chancery on the 14th day of May last, and a printed copy of the scheme has been forwarded to each of the trustees. The certificate of the Charity Commissioners for England and Wales recommend the establishment of a scheme for this charity, bearing date 23rd March, 1858. It appears therefore that considerable time has been taken up in the prosecution and perfecting of the scheme, if we take the date of the Charity Commissioners' Certificate. In the beginning of May of this year the scheme came before the Master of the Rolls at Chambers, there being present the solicitors of the Attorney General of the Trustees, and of the Rector and his Churchwarden respectively, when it was ordered, That the land and any term or estate therein belonging to the Charity be vested in the official Trustee of Charity lands for all the estate and interest therein holden in trust.

That the Rector for the time being of the said parish of Horton and the Lord for the time being of the manor of Horton, be appointed trustees in conjunction with the existing or continuing Trustees.

The scheme as to the Parish Church.—The Trustees shall out of the annual income of the Charity administer after certain provisions. The Churchwardens shall annually lay before the Trustees a statement and estimate, for visitations, sacramental wine, clerk's salary, for the ordinary repair of the parish Church, including the vestry, clock and bells (there are five), but excluding the chancel. And the Trustees shall in every year pay to the said Churchwardens the amount of the estimate under the first head, if equal or less than £25; if more than that sum, then the sum of £25 at the least. Should any surplus remain to be invested, and go into the names of Trustees to form a fund for the periodical renovation of the fabric of the church.

Church estate disbursed £112. 16s 7¼d to defray church expenses in 1823. In 1828 a new clock. There was a faculty in 1789 to erect a gallery in the church; five bells and the repairing, of which a lease was granted to Messrs. Jennings. Repair of the tower, 1818. Weather-cock, 1838.

## CHURCHWARDENS.

The earliest extant book of Churchwardens dates from 1737, for which Edmund Bowry paid 13s 6d; but there are some few names recoverable as Churchwardens prior to 1736, which I have inserted.

1615. Thomas Pitt.
1616. Ditto and Maurice Fisher.
1637. John Hawkins and Thomas Bowden.
1638. John Hieron and John Spencer.
1639. Nicholas Michel.
1736 to 1738. Edmund Bowry and Thomas Virgo.
1739 to 1741. Moses Brads and ditto.
1741. Henry Crowder was nominated by the Rector, Mr. Edwards, in room of Moses Brads, but he was rejected by the Parish; notwithstanding Crowder was sworn at the visitation, the Rector having a right to choose one, but the Court ordered that Brads should have his costs paid him. Henry Crowder and William Warden nominated for Overseers.
1742. Missing leaf.
1743. Thomas Virgo and Francis Haynes.
1744 to 1745. Ditto and Thomas Bowry.
1746 to 1747. Thomas Webb and William Shortland.
1748 to 1749. William Pearson and Rich. Hibbard.
1750. Ditto and Moses Brads.
1751. Robert Singer and ditto.

1752 to 1753. Robert Singer and Francis Bowry.
1754 to 1755. Edm. Haynes and Francis Bowler.
1756. Peter Levery and ditto.
1757. Ditto and Richard Mayo.
1758. Thomas Fennel and ditto.
1759. Ditto and Charles Prince.
1760. William Cobbet and ditto.
1761. Ditto and Francis Haynes.
1762. James or William Pearson and John Holland.
1763. Francis Haynes and ditto.
1764. Ditto and William Trout.
1765. Ditto, James Pearson, and William Trout.
1766. Ditto and William Trout.
1767 to 1768. Ditto and Francis Bowler.
1769 to 1770. Ditto and Richard Mayo.
1771 to 1772. Ditto and Edmund Haynes.
1773. Charles Prince and ditto.
1774. Ditto and James Hugford.
1775 to 1776. Richard Moore and ditto.
   N.B.—Mr. Barrow nominated Richard Moore for Dr. Blair in 1776.
1777. Richard Moore and James Hugford.
1778 to 1779. Ditto and John May.
1780 to 1782. Francis Haynes and John Spurling.
1783. Ditto and William Durham.
1784. Ditto and Booker Derby.
1785. William Hart and ditto.
1786. Ditto and Robert Singer.
1787 to 1788. Robert Singer and Richard Shurley.
1789 to 1790. John Sheppard and William Osborn.
1791. Ditto and Thomas Wood.
1792 to 1793. William Haynes and Charles Powell.
1794. William Hart and ditto.
1795 to 1800. Ditto and John May.
1801. William Learner and ditto.
1802. James Haynes and ditto.
1803. Ditto and William Haynes.
1804. Richard Hart and ditto.

1805 to 1806. Richard Hart and John Philpot.
1807 to 1810. Thomas Maish and Henry Hickman.
1811. James Haynes and William Haynes.
1812. Stephen Pullin and ditto.
1813 to 1814. Ditto and Henry Hickman.
1815. George Stafford and William Giblet.
1816. Ditto and John Fulkes.
1817. Ditto and Stephen Pullin.
1818. Colonel Edward Parkinson and ditto.
1819 to 1820. James Holderness and Jas. Stevens.
1821. Timothy Colley Jenks, Esq., and Richard Hibbard.
1822. Ditto and Evan Evans.
1823. John Cook and ditto.
1824 to 1827. Ditto and Stephen Pullin.
1828 to 1829. Ditto and Joseph Reffell.
1830. Ditto and James Holderness.
1831 to 1832. Ditto and Henry Stevens.
1833. Ditto and Charles Williams, Esq.
1834 to 1842. Ditto and Stephen Pullin.
1843. Stephen Pullin, jun., and Francis Mallet Spong.
1844. Ditto and Thomas Ford.
1845. Ditto and J. Curtis.
1846-47-48. Ditto.
1849. Stephen Pullin and John Holderness.
1850-51-52. Ditto.
1853. Stephen Pullin, jun. and George Tupp.
1854. Stephen Pullin and Edward Tyrrell, Esq.
1855. Ditto.
1856. William Ashton, Esq. and Henry Pullin.
1857. George Tupp and Stephen Pullin.
1858. Henry Lamb and Stephen Pullin.
1859. Henry Lamb and R. L. Groom.
1860. Stephen Pullin, R. L. Groom, and Henry Lamb.
1861. William Stevens, John Williams, and Thomas Lawrence.

## PARISH REGISTERS OF HORTON.

The Registers, contained in five old books, commence in 1571 with Baptisms, written on vellum in a neat caligraphy, probably copied off temp. Jac. I. from older MSS., some of which have been lost since 1538, the date of the first parish registers on record by authority, p. 128.

### BAPTISMS.

1571. Joane, d. of William Puttock. Richard, son of George Edwards. Ambrose, of William Bromfield, Esq. Richard, of James Edwards.

1572. Garret, of William Bromfield, Esq. William, of Roger Hatton. Thomas, of Thomas Goughe.

1573. Susan, of George Edwards. Christopher, of Peter Marten; born at Mr. Essington's; rented Berkyn House. Sibil, of Richard Stanley. Elizabeth, of Robert Mascall. Edmund, of Edmund Drury, gentleman.
1574. Edward, of Thomas Gwynn, gentleman. Margaret, of John Haine.
1575. Mary, of John Wrastler. Jarmayne, d. of John Jarmayne. Catherine, of Richard Aprice.
1576. Edward, of John Boulstrode, 23rd August. Martha, of Henry Baldwin.
1577. Ann, of Richard Mele. William, of John Hollis. Agnes, of Hugh Plaighter.
1578. Margaret, of John Boulstrode.
1579. Edmund Lake.
1580. Dorothy, of Henry Baldwyn. Martha, of Thomas Langley. Margaret, of William Dickenson.
1581. Reynolds, of Thomas Lake. Agnes, of John Morer. Ambrose, of Roger Ambrose.
1582. — d. of William Darby, 4th June. William, of Robert Franklyn. Robert, of Edmund Bidle.
1583. Robert, of Robert Aprice. Robert Merrick, Parson of Horton.
1584. Thomas, of William Darby, 4th October. Dorothy, of Roger Leigh.
1585. John, of Jarmayne Haynes. Agnes, of Henry Osmond.
1587. Agnes, of William Lake.
1588. Andrew, of Richard Ward. p. 129. Judith, of Thos. Langley.
1589. Leonard, of Mr. John Chamberlayne.
1590. Margaret, of William Darby, 11th October. Grace, of Thomas Holman.
1591. George, of Thomas Hale. Dorothy of Thos. Langley. Robert, of Robert Taverner, 19th December. Richard, of John Lidgold, 13th February.
1592. Jane and Anna, of Richard Aleworth. Agnes, of William Peters, 10th April. Abigail, of William Farrars.
1593. Margaret, of Richard Ward.
1594. Robert, of Edmund Bidle.
1599. N.B.—There is a break here. Jone, of Thomas Holman. Alice, of Thomas Combes. William, of Marmaduke Aylward.
1600. Richard, of Ellis Winstowe. Edmund, of Jeffrey Dare. Agnes, of William Chenye. George, of Thomas Edwards. Edmund, of John Slocombe, 14th September.
1601. Mary, of William Wilcocks.
1602. William, of Thomas Cutt. Grace, of William Cheney. John, of John Herne.
1603. Edward, of Henry Cripps. William, of Thomas English. Helen, of William Stevens. Elizabeth, of Phil Rodyffe.
1604. John, of Henry Shorter. Susan, of Edward Piper. 11th October, Elizabeth, of Henry Bulstrode, Esq. Alice, of Mark Harrison.
1605. Anne, of Henry Atkyns. John of John Goodyeare. Christofer, of William Stokes.
1607. — d. of William Stiles.
1608. Son of Cutt Winselowe. 20th July, Edward, of Henry and Marie Bulstrode.
1609. Cicely, of Henry Bulstrode.
1610. Dorothy, of ditto.
1613. Margaret, of William Wenforth.
1614. Robert, of Thomas Astley.
1615. Thomas, of Thomas Benham. Denys, of Rowland Compton. Frances, of William Brackenbury.
1616. Thomas Pitt and Morris Fisher, Churchwardens. Edward, of Geo. Herne. Mary, of John and Mary Peters, 7th January.
1618. John, of John Ives.
1620. Sarah, of Richard Platt.
1621. Arthur, of Maurice Fisher. Judith, of Walter Strammel. William and Ann, twins of John Peters, 4th August.
1623. Elizabeth, of Thomas Peters. Grace, of John and Mary Peters.
1627. Elizabeth, of ditto. Susanna, of Thomas Peters.
1629. Samuel, of Thomas Bulstrode. Clement, of John Peters. 3rd December, Francis Boswell, Rector.
1630. Simon, of Thomas Bulstrode.
1634. Thomas, of Edmund Phipps.
1635. Mary, of Thomas Bulstrode.
1636. Mary, of Edward Bulstrode. Several of the Rector Goodall's family baptized.
1637. Thomas, of Thomas and Colibery Bulstrode. John Hawkins and Thomas Bowden, Churchwardens.

1640. Isaac, of Thomas and Coliberry Bulstrode. 11th August, Sarah, of Christopher and Thomazine Milton. Edward, of Richard West.
1641. Ursula, of John Peters, 7th Nov. Walter, of John Hemperley.
1642. Mary, of Anthony Chenies. Thomas, of George Goade. Elizabeth, of John Peters.
1646. Susan, of George Goade.
1647. Ann, of Francis Bowry.
1649. Sarah, Rebecca, Samuel, of George Goade.
1651. Mary and Rebecca, of Francis Bowry.
1652. Samuel, of Francis and Dinah Bowry.
1655. Dorothy, of John and Dorothy Boult.
1657. Ditto of ditto.
1658. Ditto, of Thomas and Dorothy Duncombe. Humphrey, of Mr. Robert Scawen and Katherine, 12th February. Elizabeth, of George and Mary Goade.
1659. John, of John and Joane Hall.
1660. Edward, of Edward and Ann Leone. William, of William and Catherine Taunton.
1661. Mary, of Thomas and Dorothy Burcombe. Mary, of George and Mary Goade.
1662. Leonard, of Robert and Elizabeth Peade.
1663. William, of John and Alice Hosier.
1664. Thomas, of Robert and Elizabeth Peade.
1665. John, of Aaron and Alice Sedgwick.
1666. Elizabeth, of George Goade. Lawrence, of Robert Peade. John, of John Stephens. Elinor, of Henry Ashton.
1667. Martha, of George Goade.
1669. Frances, of Ichabod Braybourn. Eda, of William Tillier and Jane.
1671. Ralph, of Ralph Beercroft.
1672. George, of George and Mary Holderness.
1675. Richard, of Richard Tudor. Mary, of George Holderness.
1676. Francis, of Francis Bowry.
1681. Lazarus, of George Holderness.
Here follow many of the names of Beechcroft, Stephens, West, Bezer, Dunt, Wicherly, Tillier, Haynes, Burcomb, Harwood.
1686. Dinah, of Samuel and Susan Bowry.
1688. Catherine, of Thomas and Margaret Bowry. Samuel, of Samuel and Susan Bowry.
1690. Edward, of Thomas and Margaret Bowry. Susanna, of Samuel Bowry.
1692. Francis, of Thomas and Margaret Bowry.
1693. Elizabeth, of William and Jane Bulpit. William, of Edward and Mary Scawen, 12th July.
1694. Henry, of Henry and Dorothy Tredway.
1696. Sarah, of ditto. John, of Thomas and Mary Bowry.
1699. John, of William and Lettice Tubbs. Samuel, of George Clanvill.
1701. Martha, of William Nanney and Mary. Rector of Horton, 15th August. William, of Thomas and Mary Bowry.
1703. John, of William and Elizabeth Virgoe, 12th May. Griffith and Scawen, twins of William and Mary Nanney.
1705. Francis, of William and Elizabeth Virgoe. Henry, of H. and Dorothy Tredway.
1706. Catherine, d. of William Cradock, Gent. and Elizabeth.
1708. Ann, of ditto. Edmund, of William and Elizabeth Virgoe.
1711. Francis of Edmund and Dorothy Bowry.
1713. Edmund, of ditto.
1715. Rowlson, of Thos. and Elizabeth Holderness.
1716. Jermin, of ditto.
1718. Frederick, of ditto.
1723. Edmund, of Edmund and Mary Holderness.
1724. Martha, of Thomas and Martha Virgoe. Katherine, of Robert and Elizabeth Nanney, 26th February.
1726. Thomas, of ditto.
1729. Thomas, of Thomas and Mary Virgo.
1733. John, of ditto.
1734. Mary Martha, of Mrs. Elizabeth Nanney, relict of Robert Nanney, clerk.
1741. William, of Thomas and Mary Virgo.
1747. Martha, of William and Margery Bullock.
1749. Sarah, of William and Sarah Pearson.
1750. Edith, of Lawrence and Elizabeth Cane.
1751. Francis, of Thomas and Mary Virgo.
1757. Richard, of Thomas and Sarah Bullock.
1759. William, of ditto.
1763. Richard, of Lawrence Cane.

Act of Parliament passed this Sessions, granting a stamp duty of 3d on Registry of Burials, Marriages, Births, and Christenings, commencing 2nd October, 1783; paupers exempt.

1787. William and Thomas, of William and Sarah Bullock.
1789. Ann, of ditto.
1792. Thomas, of ditto.  Mary, of ditto.
1793. Sarah, of ditto.
1794. William, of ditto,  Sarah, of ditto.
1802. James, of ditto.
1804. Robert, of William and Sarah Bullock.
1806. George, of ditto.
1808. Elizabeth, of Stephen and Jane Pullin.
1809. Mary, of ditto.
1811. Sally, of George and Sally Pitt.
1834. Albert William, of Joseph and Elizabeth Reffell.

## MARRIAGES.

1571. John Clarke and Anne Plaister.
1572. Robert Mascall and Agnes Wich.
1573. John Mather and Ann Stanley.
1575. Thomas Carpenter and Margery Langley.
1576. Nicolas Reeve and Catherine Haine.
1577. Edward Langley and Alice Gnott.
1579. John Owen and Catherine Edwards.
1581. William Darby and Prudence Cowper.
1582. Mich. Huggard and Elizabeth Brockhurst.
1583. William Puttocke and Mary Harris.
1591. Phil. Bourman and Elizabeth Langley.  John Edwards and Agnes Hearch.
1592. William Darby and Elizabeth Porter.
1593. John Kelye and Elizabeth Maschall.
1600. Nicholas Watts and Margaret Sandes.
1601. Reuben Wooldrent and Mary Salter.
1602. William Darby and Elizabeth Grove.
1604. Henry Browne and Jane Goodyeare.  John Page and Margaret Edwards.
1613. Robert Smith and Eliza Mumford.
1619. Roger Pitt and Catherine Haines.
1629. Edward Haynes and Dorothy Baldwin.
1630. Thomas Knight and Mary Bulstrode.
1632. Philip Smith and Cecil Bulstrode.  24th Sept., Edward Bulstrode and Mildred Brome.
1635. Thomas Newberye and Margaret Peeters.
1647. John Lipscomb and Hester Wrayt.
1661. Mr. James Stockdale and Mrs. Catherine Scawen, 9th February.
1663. Edmund Hearne and Dinah Bowry.
1666. John Stephens and Ann Fuller.  Edmund Webb and Frances Child.
1668. Edward Haines and Anne Bowry.
1669. Mr. George Calvert and Mrs. Joanna Meale, 11th Mary.
1671. George Holderness and Mary Ashley.
1676. John Hussey and Ann Scawen, 27th March.  Francis Bowry and Catherine Edwards.
1677. Solomon Stephens and Mary Butler.
1682. William Peacocke Power and Fenina Adderley.  John Fitzgerald, Earl of Kildare and Dame Mary O'Brien, 20th Sept.  Marquis of Thomond settled at Taplow by marriage with the Orkney family.
1689. John Wetherley and Mary Holderness.
1696. George Perkins and Dinah Hearne.
1699. Francis Blencowe and Elizabeth Beecroft.
1700. Francis Stanley of Twickenham, and Mary Finch of Stanwell, 29th April.
1704. John Salisbury and Dorothy Lewis.
1714. Ralph Beecroft and Joane Meale.
1715. William Chetwynd, Esq. and Mrs. Honora Baker, 19th June.
1716. Thomas Slater of Stanwell and Ann Merry.  John Roberts and Ruth Holderness.
1724. William Stannard and Hannah Basset.
1726. John Hounson and Margaret Holderness.
1735. Thomas Borret, Esq., and Mrs. Susanna Scawen of Carshalton, 16th September.
1738. Mr. Thomas Kinge and Mary Bowry.
1739. Mr. William Maund of Windsor, and Mrs. Elizabeth Randall of Eton, 26th July.
1743. William Gibbons and Mary Beecroft.
1747. Joseph Paine and Mary Stevens.
1748. Lawrence Cane and Edith Ayress, Banns.
1754. Thomas Dell of Datchet, and Mary, dau. of Mr. John Edwards, Rector of Horton.
1756. John Warder and Mary Bowry, Banns.
1762. John Stevens and Ruth Holderness.
1765. William Davis of Wraysbury, and Ann King.
1766. Richard West and Ann Cantrill.
1767. Charles Towsey and Susannah Pearson.
1769. Mr. James Pearson and Sarah Maxwell.

1771. Rev. Thomas Davis, of Fairford, Gloster, widower, and Ann Benham, widow, 2nd May. Thomas Gould, of Horton, and Susanna Cust, Banns.
1773. Thomas Perkins and Elizabeth Palmer, of Horton.
1775. John Pitt and Elizabeth Martin, Banns.
1777. Samuel Urling and Elizabeth Bowry.
1785. Thomas Buckland, of Wraysbury, and Ann Virgo, 15th August.
1786. Henry Peters and Jenny Guenint.
1788. John Peartin, of Wraysbury, and Mary Spurling.
1789. William Willis and Mary Green.
1793. William Holderness and Elizabeth West.
1795. Thos. Alman and Ann Tuck, of Wraysbury.
1807. Charles Toussaint, of London, widower, and Mary Ann Parsons, of Horton.

New Register by Act of Parliament for 1813, 52 George III.

1838. William Vernon Stevens and Ann Cook, p. 236.
1840. Charles Wise and Sarah FitzWater; latter an old name here since time of Henry VIII.
1850. James Salter and Elizabeth Miller.
1856. Roger Lee, clerk, and Ann Peto, d. of George Tupp, of the Cedars, 10th April.

## BURIALS.

1572. Jane Pultock, 9 November. Alice Edwards. Stephen Stephens.
1577. John Hailes, Barber Surgeon.
1579. John Boulstrode, 1st May.
1582. Agnes Haine.
1585. Mrs. Smith, from the Bridge.
1589. Mrs. Jane Higgins.
1590. John Lidgold. Elizabeth Edwards. Prudence Darby.
1591. Robert Taverner.
1592. Henry Cotterell. Mary, dau. of William Peters.
1593. Michael, son of Michael Goodyeare, 14th September. Dorret, son of Christopher Mele.
1595. William, son of William Garret, gentleman.
1600. John Sadler, of Colebroke. John Cheney.
1601. George Edwards, Sen., 31st December.
1602. Elizabeth, wife of William Darby.
1603. Michael Goodyeare. Martha, d. of Thomas Timothy, son of William Child.
1604. Henry, son of Henry Bulstrode, 29th Oct.
1606. Elizabeth Penistone.
1607. John Slocombe, 11th December.
1609. Richard, son of Ellis Winstowe. John Goodyeare, 9th April. Susanna, sister of Thomas Edwards.
1610. Mr. Marshal's mother.
1611. Mr. William Peters.
1612. James Edwards. Mr. Thomas Langley. John Edwards' wife.
1613. Ann, d. of Felix Wilson. John, son of ditto. William, son of Thomas Goade.
1615. John, son of Robert Balgrave. William Brackenbury.
1620. Catherine, wife of Roger Pitt, 27th Sept.
1621. Jeffry Dare.
1623. William Goodier, 25th May.
1624. Thomas Edwards.
1625. Elizabeth, widow of ditto.
1627. Elizabeth Darby.
1628. Edward Slocomb. Wife of William Peters.
1629. Dorothy Bulstrode.
1635. Wife of Edward Slocomb.
1636. Mary, d. of Edward and Mildred Brome.
1637. Sara uxor. Johannis Milton generosi, obiit 3rd April, and buried 6th, p. 240.
1638. Thomas, infant son of Sir John Trevor, Kt. Edward Loome, aged 50. George Edwards, husbandman, aged 40.
1639. Infant son of Christopher Milton, gentleman. Isaac, son of Edward and Mildred Bulstrode. Wife of Felix Wilson the younger, 16th November. Ann Buckingham, 12th March.
1640. Ann, wife of William Goade. John, of Thomas Pitt.
1643. Edward, of Edward Goodall.
1644. Widow of William Peters.
1653. Martha, of Anthony Cheney.
1658. Mr. Edmund Slocomb. Mr. John Peters. Alice Hall. William Goade.

1660. Elizabeth, wife of John Norland.
1661. Ursula, wife of Mr. Thomas Butler.
1662. John Norland, not buried, but put into the ground. Mrs. Ann Alsop. Ursula, d. of Mr. Thomas Butler. Dorothy, d. of Thos. Burcombe. Mr. John Turner.
1663. Francis Bowry. Richard, of Thomas Burcomb.
1664. Edwin Blunt, from London, 16th August. Edward Biddle, of Parnham Park, 27th December.
1666. Elizabeth, of George Goade, and Mary his wife. Martha, d. of Mr. William Clifton.
1667. Mr. Thomas Pitt, 29th June.
1668. Henry Goodall.
1669. Mr. Robert Scawen, Lord of the Manor, 15th March.
1670. Mrs. Slocombe, widow. Mr. Griffin, City of London. William Clifton, ditto.
1671. Mary Edwards, widow. Mr. William Goade. Mrs. Slocombe, wife of John Slocombe. George, son of George Holderness.
1672. William Peters. Mrs. Clifton, widow.
1674. Wife of John Norland. Mr. Joseph Henchman.
1675. Dorothy, wife of Thomas Burcomb.
1676. Mr. Humphrey Scawen, 5th June. Alice Goade, widow, of Colebroke.
1678. John Stephens. Burying in woollen began.
1679. Mr. Henry Scawen, 23rd May. Mr. Charles Peters, 3rd September. Some of the family of West.
1680. Mr. Edward Stradling. Elizabeth, d. of Mr. John Benar. Jane Virgoe, widow.
1681. Mr. Robert Meriton. Elizabeth, of Martin Call.
1682. Mr. William Scott. Elizabeth, wife of Mr. Robert Peade. Family of Wicherly, several of. Mrs. Maud Scott. Mrs. Blunt, widow, 19th March.
1684. Mr. Richard West, of Poyle. Geo. Goade. Mrs. Catherine Scawen, 12th August. Mr. Bates. John Haynes.
1686. Mr. Edmund Hearne. Mr. John West. William Fortescue. Priscilla, wife of John West.
1688. John, son of John West.
1689. John, son of Mr. John Style.

1690. Mrs. Mary Quarterman, widow. John Norland. John Virgoe.
1691. Mr. Edward Scawen, Lord of the Manor, 29th September. Mr. Robert Peade, Rector of Horton.
1692. Edward Bulstrode, Gent., 19th October. Phœbe, wife of Richard Tillier.
1693. Richard West, of Poyle. Joane Tillier, wid.
1694. Henry West, of Poyle.
1695. Since the tax for burials. Mrs. Mildred Bulstrode, widow, 26th August. Mr. John Scawen, Rector, 31st Aug. Samuel Bowry. Catherine Hearne, widow.
1696. George Child. Sarah Goodall, widow. Dr. William Goade, 4th Aug. Thomas Blunt, 8th August.
1697. Eliza Sedgwick. Catherine Haynes, widow.
1698. Thomas Brecknock, an old name in Wraysbury, temp. Henry VI. and Henry VII. Thomas Virgo. Dinah Hearne, widow.
1700. Catherine West, widow. Hannah Virgo.
1702. Agnes Tillier, of Langley. Hannah Cane.
1704. Griffith Nanney. John Haynes.
1705. Frances Nanney, 2nd May. John Wicherley. Roger West, painter in London.
1706. Dorothy Tredway.
1707. Mary Holderness. Ann West. Thomas Wycherley.
1708. Edmund, son of William Virgo. Ann Burcombe.
1709. Mary Goade.
1710. Francis Virgoe. Mr. Robert Scawen, 10th April. Colonel Francis Scawen, 17th Feb.
1711. William Virgoe. Thomas Bowry. Henry West.
1712. Ralph Beecroft.
1714. George Holderness. Giles Child, of Langley. Mrs. Elizabeth Slocombe. Solomon Stephens.
1715. Martha, wife of Jonathan Gibbons, of Wraysbury. Mr. William Child, of St. Martin's Fields. Mrs. Mary Bowry. Capt. John Beverley, died at the Bell Inn, Colnbrook.
1716. Frances, widow of John Haynes, of Wraysbury.
1717. Lieut. George Sherwood.
1718. Mary, wife of John Wycherley. Martha, wife of Thomas Child, a joiner in London.

Henry Child. Charles Brerewood's infant, 26th December. Martha, widow of Henry Child.
1720. Thomas Nightingale, of St. Martin's, Westminster. Mr. John Saltmarsh, Attorney.
1721. William Nanney, Rector of Horton, 27th August.
1722. Margaret Bowry.
1723. Catherine Nanney, 1st February.
1724. Martha Nanney, 18th April.
1725. Mary, d. of Sir Thomas Scawen, Kt., 19th August.
1727. Mary Bowry.
1729. William Tillier, of Colnbrook. Thomas, son of Thomas Holderness.
1730. Sir Thomas Scawen, Kt., 1st October.
1731. Mary Nanney, widow, 1st July.
1734. Robert Nanney, Rector of Horton, 3 April. Martha Bowry.
1736. William, son of Thomas Virgo.
1737. Martha, wife of ditto. Henry Tredway. Mrs. Mary, wife of Lewis Scawen, 20th September. Mary, wife of Wm. Bowry.
1738. Mary, wife of William Gibbon, paper-maker.
1739. Elizabeth Saltmarsh, widow. Mary, wife of Christopher Mele. William Bowry.
1740. Mr. John Nichols, Gent. Mrs. Selwin Leith, wife of Captain Leith. Mr. Lewis Scawen, 4th August. Thomas Haynes, from Wraysbury.
1741. Mary, widow of Mr. Lewis Scawen, 20th April.
1742. Thomas Lavender, paper-maker.
1743. John Burcomb, mercer. Mr. Edmund Biddle, from Richmond.
1746. Thomas Chely, paper-maker. Abraham, son of Lewis Scawen, 2nd December. Mr. West, paper-maker. Mary West, widow.
1747. Elizabeth Holderness. Widow Saltmarsh.
1748. Miss Susanna Scawen, 8th March.
1752. Mrs. Winifred, wife of Mr. Robert Scawen, 15th January. Miss Charlotte, d. of Mr. Robert Scawen, 20th July.
1753. Mary Virgo.
1754. Jane, d. of William Virgo. Thomas Virgoe, farmer. Mr. Thomas Biddle, apothecary.
1755. Mr. Thomas, son of Lewis Scawen, Esq., 18th February.
1756. Mr. Powel, a farmer. Lazarus Holderness. Francis Haynes, farmer.
1759. Mary Gibbons, widow.
1761. Mary, widow of William Burst, from Wraysbury.
1765. Mary, wife of John Tillier, from Drayton. John Virgo, from London.
1766. William Virgoe, farmer, Colnbrook. Dame Martha Scawen, 30th June.
1769. Francis Bowry, yeoman.
1770. Elizabeth, relict of Rev. William Nanney, Rector of Horton, 24th August.
1778. Mr. Robert Scawen, from Reigate, aged 69. 13th November.
1779. Francis Bowry, aged 60.
1780. Sarah Bullock, aged 63. Mary Virgo, widow, aged 66. John Virgo, aged 76. Sarah Pearson, widow, from Horley, aged 69.
1782. Henry Rayner, aged 70.
1783. An Act was passed granting Stamp Duties of 3d on Registers.
1787. Mary Nanney, aged 53, 4th August.
1789. William Stevens, aged 49.
1793. John Mayo, aged 26. William Smith, a poor man, aged 92.
1796. Jane Tupp, aged 59. Thos. Bullock, aged 80.
1798. Martha, d. of Lewis Scawen, Esq., aged 67, 27th January. Mary Bullock, aged 40.
1800. Henry Holderness, 82.
1802. Thomas Virgo, 73.
1804. Patience Holderness, 30.
1810. Francis Virgo, 59. John Virgo, 49.
1812. Sarah Bullock, 48.
1813. John Tupp, æt. 68. Richard Bullock.
1814. Mrs. Sarah Griffiths. Mrs. Bertha Way.
1815. Thomas Bullock.
1816. John Wagstaff.
1819. William Virgo, æt. 69.
1820. Mrs. Isabella Virgo, æt. 65.
1822. Jane Stevens, of Wraysbury, æt. 32.
1823. Derby Sullivan, of Colnbrook, æt. 40.
1826. Frances Harriet Elizabeth Derby, æt. 29. Sarah Hearne, æt. 82.
1830. Rebecca Burcombe, æt. 67.
1831. James Stevens.
1832. Elizabeth Derby, æt. 70.
1833. Elizabeth Pullin, æt. 62.
1834. Charles Reffell, æt. 18. Charles Reffell, æt. 34.

1835. Elizabeth Holderness, æt. 16. William Gould, labourer; an old name in Wraysbury. William Littlewood Stevens, æt. 9.
1836. Susanna Bullock, from Poyle, æt. 61.
1837. William Derby, of Gray's Inn, London.
1840. Joseph Holderness, æt. 56. William Stevens, æt. 74. Henry Bullock, Esq. from Poyle, æt. 76, buried 26th December.
1842. John Derby, Esq. æt. 82, 13th July.
1844. Elizabeth Caroline Derby, æt. 47. William Bullock, æt. 86, 27th October.
1845. Mary Ann Bullock, æt. 52.
1846. Stephen Edward Pullin, æt. 46. James Stephens, æt. 70.
1847. Mrs. Mary Stephens, æt. 60. Agnes Peters, from Windsor, æt. 25.
1848. Joseph Reffell, æt. 59. Francis Holderness, æt. 79.
1850. Martha Brown, æt. 73. John Hutton Stephens, æt. 32. Rev. William Brown, Rector, æt. 79. Henry Stephens, æt. 60.
1853. Martha Stephens, æt. 35. Rev. Thomas Tracey Coxwell, æt. 76.

As there have been persons of distinction and quality married and buried here, a brief recapitulation may not be out of place.

In 1571, Ambrose, son of William Bromefield, Esq. Garret, son of ditto, baptized 1752; probably of the family of Sir Edward Bromefield, Lord Mayor of London, 1636, whose issue were baronets.

Mr. Essington lived at Horton, and he may be of the same Gloster family to whom arms were granted in 1610; he either owned or leased Berkyn Manor.

The Drury family had a son, Edmund, baptized 1573, son of Edmund Drury. There was an intermarriage with Drury and Bulstrode, both of Hedgerly.

In 1574, the Welsh family of Gwyn, baptized 1574, Edward, son of Thomas Gwyn, Gent.

In 1640, Sarah, daughter of Christopher Milton, brother of John Milton the Poet, p. 238.

In 1660, William, son of William and Catherine Taunton, of the family in Somersetshire, from whom Sir William Elias Taunton, Knt. and Judge, who married Maria, a sister of Sir Jasper Atkinson, page 223.

In 1694, Henry, son of Henry Tredway, Gent. There are many entries of this name.

In 1706, Catherine, daughter of William Cradock, Gent. and Elizabeth. A Mary Cradock married 9th December, 1740, Gilbert Jodrell, Esq. page 23.

MARRIAGES.—In 1604, Henry Browne and Jane Goodyeare. 1619, Roger Pitt and Catherine Hayes. 1669, Mr. George Calvert and Mrs. Joanna Meale, of the family of Calvert, co. Herts. In 1682, John Fitzgerald, 18th Earl of Kildare, who died 1707, issueless, and Dame Mary O'Brien, daughter of Henry, son of the Earl of Thomond. In 1700, Francis Stanley, of Twickenham, and Mary Finch, of Stanwell. 15th June, 1715, William Richard Chetwynd, Esq. afterwards Viscount Chetwynd in 1767, married Honor, daughter of William Baker, Consul of Algiers, whose descendant, Richard, 6th Viscount, married Mary, daughter and heir of Robert Moss and Sophia, daughter of John Weyland, page 23. 1739, Mr. William Maunde, of Windsor, and Mrs. Elizabeth Randall, of Eton. 1754, Thomas Dell, of Datchet, and Mary, daughter of Mr. John Edwards, Rector of Horton. 1769, Mr. James Pearson (son of William Pearson) and Sarah Maxwell. 1771, Rev. Thomas Davis, of Fairford, co. Gloster, widower, and Ann Benham, widow. 1785, Thomas Buckland, of Wraysbury, and Ann Virgo, of Horton. 1856, Roger Lee, Clerk, and Ann Peto, daughter of Mr. George Tupp, of the Cedars, Horton.

BURIALS.—1572, Stephen Stephens, probably ancestor of that family now in Horton. 1579, John Boulstrode, Esq. 1589, Mrs. Jane Higgins. 1591, Robert Taverner, probably brother of

Richard Taverner, of Wood Eaton, Oxon, and of Essex. 1593, Michael, son of Michael Goodyeare, page 93. 1595, William, son of William Garret, Gent. 1604, Henry, son of Henry Boulstrode, Esq. 1612, Mr. Thomas Langley—see fine 1256. 1637, Sarah, wife of John Milton, Gent. 1638, Thomas, son of Sir John Trevor, knighted 1618, and died 1663, father of that Sir John who held the Great Seal in commission with two others in 1690. John, son of John Cooke, Gent. 1661, Ursula, wife of Mr. Thomas Buller. 1664, Edwin Blunt. 1666, Martha, daughter of Mr. William Clifton. 1667, Mr. Thomas Pitt. 1670, Mr. Griffin, of the city of London. 1671, Mr. William Goade, Physician, of Colnbrook. 1674, Mr. Joseph Henchman; in 1675, Dr. Humphrey Henchman, died Bishop of London. 1679, Mr. Timothy West. 1680, Mr. Edward Stradling; Mr. Stradling, Vicar of Iver, probably of the baronets of that name, married there, 3rd November, 1666, Margaret Salter. 1680, Elizabeth, daughter of John Benar. 1681, Mr. Robert Meriton. 1682, Mr. William Scott and William Meade Scott. 1684, Mr. Bates. 1690, Mrs. Mary Quatermaine, widow. 1691, Mr. Robert Peade, Rector. 1692, Edward Bulstrode, Esq. 1695, Mr. Mildred Bulstrode, page 22. 1696, Dr. William Goade, M.D. of Colnbrook. 1715, Mr. William Child, of St. Martins in the Fields—Captain John Beverley died at the Bell Inn, Colnbrook. 1717, Lieutenant George Sherwood. 1720, Mr. John Saltmarsh, Attorney. 1721, William Nanney, Rector; 1734, Robert Nanney intermarried with the Scawens. 1740, Mr. John Nichols, Gent.— Mrs. Selwin Leith, wife of Captain Leith. 1743, Mr. John Burcomb—Mr. Edmund Biddle, from Richmond.

## CONTINGENT MATTER.

In page 153, the subject of Railways has been mentioned, and we may remark that in Horton, as well as in Wraysbury, the village has been obviously ameliorated since their introduction, from the enhancement in the value of property, as well as convenience to the residents, some of whom avail themselves of this means of transit daily, and repair to the nearest station, to which we have adverted, page 79.

As the question of Railways is peculiarly interesting to the people of England (and such is their recognised utility that the most obscure and unimproving places on the Continent are seeing the stern necessity for laying them down, despite the *anathemas* once launched against them by those who hated any change which might rescue neglected humanity from the *slough of despond*), and we have reports as to their financial condition, I trust to be excused if I append here what may be read with greater curiosity when new improvement and augmentation shall have obliterated the remembrance of early attempts.

The total extent of railways now laid down in 1861 amounts to 10,433 miles, and the annual expense of maintaining in working order this immense tract, with its accessories, costs some 13 millions sterling, whilst the amount of capital invested reaches to the prodigious figure of 330 millions sterling. The report alleges that in 1860 the receipts were £27,750,000; but if from the receipts the expenditure be deducted, it will be seen that only £14,500,000 are left to constitute the *dividends* for the shareholders of the 330 millions. Large sums are expended in *compensations* "for moving accidents of flood and field;" and this very year 1861 some £181,000 have been appropriated for this contingency.

With respect to the passenger traffic, statistics shew that some $163\frac{1}{2}$ millions of persons have travelled by railway in the United Kingdom, the majority of passengers being *third* class; hence the returns published exhibit a steady improvement in the railway traffic, affording a correct index of the increasing commercial prosperity of the kingdom. Reflection and experience prove that it would be impossible to discover a solitary branch of industry, to point to a single industrial resource which has not received an *impetus* and does not in part owe its development to the facilities afforded for conveyance and transmission by the locomotive engine—this steam power being now recognised as one of the main sources of national greatness.

This generation begins to see, and another generation will realise in full, the good effects which this ceaseless inter-communion will have on society, and although we cannot hope to *purify* entirely a corrupt world, for 100,000 prisoners committed for serious offences are annually discharged from the criminal gaols, many ready and eager to prey again on society, yet we believe that steam as applicable to land and water will be the mysterious agency of enlightening mankind at large, and thereby reducing crime within a much more circumscribed area.

In various parts of this work the fact of this section of the county being partially divested of timber, and the *direful lopping* of beauteous boughs so much adopted has been noticed, we are glad to find in recent publications a vindication of *nature and ornament*, and proof adduced that trees are not *inimical* to agriculture, or birds so destructive in the main as is the *creed* of present agriculturists. Birds do almost as much good as evil by destroying insects, &c., and it is found that hail-storms and drought are the consequence of the *denudation* of lands by the extirpation of timber. Trees by attracting and absorbing electricity prevent the formation of hail, moderate the action of the winds, and temper the heat of summer. They attract clouds and facilitate the descent of rain; by means of their leaves they present a surface which may be said to be ten times more extensive than the soil on which they stand. When rain falls, the leaves receive and return it in such a manner as to prevent rapid evaporation; but if they are cleared away, the water which falls on the light soil of the hills is re-absorbed by the atmosphere. Thus wooded hills may be regarded as reservoirs that distil slowly their waters into the valleys. Rains percolate through the earth, and issue from the hills in the form of springs, which by this simple auxiliary can hardly ever be quite dried up.

Hail, drought, flood, *insect* visitations, epidemic of man and beast, and interruptions to industry, are traced to the *absence* of trees, and a benefit of the material class may be expected from the cultivation of trees even in towns. These are the inferences at which many modern naturalists have arrived; hence may we hope to see the vicinity and the villages of Horton and Wraysbury adorned at least with *natural* timber, although they be never

"Bosomed high in tufted trees."

# HISTORY OF COLNBROOK.

## DESCRIPTION OF THE TOWN.

**Colnbrook.** This part of the County of Bucks borders on Berks and Surrey, forming for Parliamentary ends the so-called Chiltern Hundreds, and the town under reference adjoins Middlesex, the northern portion of which is in that county, while the southern moiety is in Horton Parish. It is distant from the metropolis about 17 miles, is in the hundred of Spelthorne, by which the Western Railway passes three miles from the Slough Station, whilst the nearest station is at Wraysbury, made a little nearer by the removal of the old station to the site it now occupies at the Colne Bridge in that parish, where a platform has been set up, and by the filling up of the low parts towards the river, it will prevent an overflow, and secure a dry transit for person and for carriage.

There are many towns in several parishes, as Royston in Herts was in five parishes, in Herts and Cambridge, with two manors in the town, which were only in fee, for there were no demesnes or lands belonging to them—so this town might in reality be described under Iver, Langley Marsh, or Stanwell, or Horton, in which several parishes its population and houses are included. It consists of one principal street, continuous and sinuous, but rather narrow; and it is indeed surprising that the town has undergone so little change towards improvement, considering that it has been a corporate town with a very busy market centuries back, and that an immense traffic has been conducted through it, as a highway to Bath and Bristol, and the entire West of England, as well as to the Royal residence of Windsor.

Its name is not found in Domesday Book, but the place is of considerable antiquity, and is recognised in old deeds as *Viculus,* little town or street.

According to one Thomas of Reading (the rich clothier, temp. Edward I. about whom there are some fabulous histories, which shew that the clothing trade was eminent there) the name *Colnbrook* derives from one Thomas Cole, the Reading Clothier, who was murdered by the landlord of the inn here—probably the Ostrich—on his way to the metropolis, temp. Edward I. Such stories are traditional in most parishes where any legendary lore is preserved, and some like them better than the truth, as ladies are said to prefer romances to real history, or love courtship better than marriage.

However, the name is obviously deduced from the river Colne, to cross which from the remotest times bridges or ferries were in vogue. Indeed the spot is thought by some antiquaries to be the Pontes of the Itineraries, p. 3. The Colne, for a course of 14 miles, constitutes the eastern boundary of Bucks, separating it from Middlesex. The town is on four channels of this stream, over which there is a small bridge, entering at Colnbrook it quits the county at Maidenhead Bridge, and so westward travelled hundreds of coaches before the Railway superseded the traffic; novelty is ever rife in a world of variety, where one mutation treads on the vestige of another. This then new traffic of carriages interfered with horse or mule conveyance, when gangs of these useful sumpter quadrupeds were employed for inland communication, and preceded wains and coaches.

The muleteers and pack-horse conductors thought their long admitted usages were invaded when coaches were started, hence they cried out, invasion against *vested* interests. The same when canals were formed or rivers deepened for the transport of heavy commodities.

But as these innovations palpably improved traffic, the nerve and bone of a state, so have railways benefited every locality where they have been established. Still prejudice overlaps every consideration in some whom the *logic of facts* can scarce convince, yet do moments of crisis produce rather an increase of life and property than diminish them, and the culminating point of greatness is only obtained by patiently trying many things, and faithfully holding fast to that which is good, through ingenuity, labour, and patience—like religion, which has its foundation also in faith, and its roof in patience, says an old divine.

The length of Horton on the west side is about three-quarters of a mile from north to south. Diagonally from north-west to west is about two miles and a half. The eastern side is about a mile and three-quarters. South side one mile, according to the award map. The centre road through the parish is a mile and a quarter from Moor Farm Lane to its junction with Datchet parish. A gutter divides the parishes of Horton and Langley, and a brook separates Langley and Iver at the Bucks end of the town, near the Red Lion Inn, and the bounds are run once in some twenty years, I understand.

The town contains some 280 houses, and about 1400 souls. The buildings are of no great account on the Horton side—the opposite side boasts better edifices. Some in recesses are pretty good, but generally the buildings are of the cottage character, bearing an antique and dusky resemblance; and very few new houses have been built or are in process of erection. One house is the Colnbrook and Horton School, 1845. The Primitive Methodist Chapel, down a recess, a large red-bricked building, is seen through the pleasant avenue leading to Richings Park. Near this, at the end of Mill Street, is a very shattered building called the Malt House, once held by Mr. Ramsbottom, of Windsor.

There is a piece of land in Stanwell Parish which is said to belong to this section of Horton; the site is known as the Rookery, and it consists of four houses on the Middlesex side of the bridge. It is also known as King John's House, and tradition says that once a Charity School existed here for the teaching of eleven boys in the Latin dialect. The houses remain, but as the institution is gone into *thin air*, the inhabitants feed on sweet remembrance, and solace themselves that throughout England similar flagitious abuses have prevailed, and those who had the custody of these institutes for education have appropriated the funds—

> "And left the mansions so long tenantless,
> That growing ruinous the buildings fell,
> And left no memory of what they were."

There is a vague tradition about King John's House respecting the Rookery part of the locality; while this monarch's name seems to predominate in the vicinity, as at Place Farm, Wraysbury, (page 55). Another tradition exists as to a house in which Queen Elizabeth took refuge *what time* the *wheel* of her carriage came off, and the tenants of that house in memory keep the royal arms in a frame.

In the Acts and Monuments of Fox, the martyrologist, Queen Elizabeth is said to have slept one night at the George Inn, when brought a prisoner from Woodstock to Hampton Court in 1558, where Philip and Mary kept their Christmas with great solemnity, and peradventure some mishap befel the Royal conveyance on its emerging from the George, and this may be the foundation of the tradition, which sometimes embalms trivial as well as serious events.

Adjacent to King John's House is the old County Bridge, connecting Middlesex and Bucks, which was repaired in 1690. A charge was made 5th April, 1692, by one Isaac Redford concerning it, for the sum of £17. 9s 2d; and as he alleged that a balance of £4. 11s 5d was due to him which he could not recover, he sold the *communion plate* of the chapel to indemnify himself, consisting of a large silver cup, &c. There was however a dispute about the *validity* of the bill, and the claim was not allowed, but it is transmitted as a general belief that the *holy vessel* was not retrieved.

The bridge which spans the stream and unites the opposite shires is not very large or long, but under the pure fluid dashes glibly along. On the bridge are two stones, and thereon is a mark of a circle on either side of which are the figures 1777, two at top and two at the base—Langley Marsh parish—Stanwell parish.

At the Middlesex termination of the town is Mill Lane, by which there is an entrance to the new Church and to Richings Park under a very graceful avenue of lime and other deciduous trees, which reach some half mile in length. It is a private road. The juncture of this town at Stoke parish is about a mile and a half in distance.

At the end of Mill Street we find a flour mill, belonging to Mr. Mark Westaway, now of Hythe End, Wraysbury. It is supposed to have been a mill for generations, and was formerly in the tenure of Mr. Isaac Cane, who inhabited an old house, since demolished, near which was a starch house. The adjoining house, tenanted by Mr. Hickman, who has a farm adjacent, with very complete farm buildings, which he holds under Charles Meeking, Esq. of Richings Park, is an island, formed by the circuit round it of the Colne, which runs very boldly here, and may be about six feet deep.

There is a project for transmitting the Colne waters to the metropolis, under the superintendence of a company, which has been incorporated by Act of Parliament, to supply water in the west and south-western districts of London, including a population of 90,000 souls.

The proposed works are to commence at Staines, where engines will pump daily between two and three million gallons of water at high pressure, through a main extending along the road to a reservoir on Hanger Hill, near the station at Ealing, and about 18 feet above the high water mark of the Thames.

Here we may also add another project, that for establishing gasworks, should a suitable piece of ground be secured, for which end committees have been formed to treat for such a site, and shares are in the market, which will afford the investors a reasonable interest for their capital, and will meet the growing requirements of a thriving town.

At this end of the town a reading room has been established, open from ten to ten; and although this institution for reading and lectures is not at its height, it is hoped that its adoption will be appreciated, and that adequate funds will insure it a deserved success.

There are officers appointed for conducting all necessary arrangements. It numbers about 70 members, many of whom are mechanics, paying only 1d. a quarter. In the building is a large room with a gallery for strangers, and in it a discussion class meets, when questions of moral and social worth or popular interest are entertained, tending to improve the mind, give ardour to virtue, and confidence to truth. The world is in process of improvement, and the institution of lectures is among valuable helps to mental culture, with the aid of experiments and diagrams. This is the base on which art depends; sciences have their origin in industry; knowledge leads to skill, and that to lucrative occupations, which enable men to procure the staff of life. From this knowledge comes the rights of men, and the people must be the chief agents in accomplishing their redemption from ignorance and penury. As a member of the Royal Institution of Great Britain, I am pleased to add my testimony to the utility of lectures.

In these public rooms the casual gifts are distributed to the poor inhabitants of Langley and

Horton; many of the recipients are needy widows of good character, and in 1860 one received relief who had touched the patriarchal term of 97 years with unimpaired faculties. This case, with other instances of *longevity*,\* evince the salubrity of Colnbrook, and superintendence of "the angel of health."

At the dedication of the festival of St. Thomas's Day, the patron of the new church, after a full choral service at the church, large companies of communicants and church attendants assembled here to partake of refreshment, when carols and glees were sung by the choir of the church, and the going round of the "Loving Cup" completed the festivity.

Outside the town, in Middlesex, is Poyle House, where tan-pits once stood, and now converted into a handsome dwelling-house. It has passed from the possession of the Bullock family, who held also the Wraysbury Paper Mills, and is now the fee of George Paterson, Esq. (page 72).

The town of Colnbrook has the benefit of a fruitful nursery ground, rented by Mr. James Small, which comprised some 2½ acres of surface, with 4½ acres of nursery ground in Langley parish. The father of this respected parishioner, Mr. David Small, settled here in 1811, and here he died full of years and reputation in 1850. He is another proof of the industry and of that perseverance which keeps honour bright in his countrymen. He came from Fifeshire, in Scotland, and like his son was eminent for his ability in planting and rearing, and his choice horticultural productions.

The postal service is much improved in Colnbrook, what once was the general official letter office, is now a sub-office, since the establishment of the railroads. The delivery of letters and receipts amounts to about 80 daily.

In 1861 the enumerators announced 1312 as the population: there was an increase of a sixth. Langley, 499; Horton, 362; Stanwell, 141. Total, 1022. Stanwell population in 1861 is 1717, viz. 6 less than in 1851. Staines' census gives an increase of 182. Present number is 2577.

The rate is 1s in the pound, and the Union is at Slough. There are three overseers for Langley. One for Westmoor district, one for Huntsmore, and one for Colnbrook.

That cleanliness and love of pure water, which is now a national characteristic, is far from having been handed down to us as a relic of the good old times, and in bygone days Colnbrook was like most towns, with London also, anterior to the great fire in 1666, an ill-built, ill-drained, ill-ventilated, and evil-smelling metropolis, but now it is the purest of cities; and Colnbrook can also boast of its propriety and its abundance of the sweet element of water, so as to attract and merit the fashionable comments of sojourners and natives; they are a more healthy and longer-lived people than their ancestors were generations out of record.

## INNS OF COLNBROOK.

It is not impossible that the gift of a public inn, which was at Colnbrook, and conferred by Milo Crispin, of which hereafter, shews that the town was in some estimation, and from the dubious appellation of *Viculus* it assumed the significant appellative, Colnbrook, and this gave rise and justification to the establishment of large inns, which have been of peculiar notoriety here. Generally

---

\* Long life in England. It speaks well for the healthiness of England, that in the year 1859, for which the returns have been just published, the list of deaths included 25 men and 56 women who had attained what Dr. Farr calls "the natural life of 100 years." The oldest man in the obituary of the year died at Sunderland at 107. A woman in Wokingham district, Berks, 108. Two women in Monmouthshire and one in South Wales had reached the patriarchal age of 110. Of these centenarians eight were Londoners. There were seven persons in Somersetshire who were centenarians.

these places of public resort are made most comfortable, as well for attraction as profit, and Dr. Johnson thought an inn the house of bliss, as he deemed driving very rapidly in a post-chaise the *summum bonum* of locomotion.

In a tavern there is a general freedom from anxiety—in a private house no servants will attend with the alacrity which waiters do, who are incited by the prospect of an immediate reward in proportion as they please. The Doctor was wont to assert that a *tavern chair* was the throne of human felicity, and often quoted Shenstone's lines:—

> Whoe'er has travelled life's dull round,
> Whate'er his various tour has been,
> May sigh to think how oft he found,
> His *warmest* welcome at an inn.

The sad reputation of the Ostrich Inn in this small town leaves us to doubt if any who entered its doors experienced an oblivion of care or freedom from solicitude, for systematic *removal* of strangers, like to the enormities of Hare and Burke, of murder memory in 1829, prevailed here. Some proofs of which are found in a book difficult to be procured, written by one Thowe of Reading.

The house still remains on the Horton side of the town. It is of a very antique appearance, whitewashed, with a façade of some 80 or 100 feet in length, and is now divided into three houses; but it is not the principal inn in the town. Behind it are some 20 acres of field, which Rev. Arthur Hubbard recently sold to the Rayners, a family of some antiquity here.

Tradition, sometimes the channel of truth although disguised and garbled, avers that at one time, temp. Edward I., there were 13 bodies of murdered persons taken from this identical inn to be hurled into the Thames, one of which corpses slipped off the cart on a strip of land called Welly, now on the Horton side of the Fleet Ditch, which divides the parishes. Horton refused to bury the body, and Datchet buried it, and hence they claim a piece of land, and now receive rates for it. As the *conveyancers*, paid by the superintendants of the Ostrich Inn, were counting the corpses, they found only 12, and a Wraysbury fisherman, who had been laying eel-wheels, said, if you are so disconcerted about the loss, throw in one of yourselves, and that will complete the number. The conveyancers dismayed, shot some arrows at the fisherman, and one pierced and lodged in his boat, and in a brief space he walked with the arrow, using it as a stick, to Colnbrook. A little boy at the Ostrich claimed the arrow as belonging to his father, and this was the proximate cause of the discovery of the assassination, and the dissolution of the *fell* gang.

In 1516 King Henry VIII. with his suite and the Queen Catherine stopped at the Catherine-Wheel Inn here, of course the principal inn, of which more hereafter. In 1625 there was an inn here called the Talbot, in which house many died during the plague (page 250).

The Pelican was an inn of celebrity, and it still remains, and is on the Horton side. The White Hart once figured in this class of public conveniences, and Mr. John Ashton of this town has communicated to me that the Ballad of the Three Cooks of Colnbrook, which I have tried to see, but no copy is to be found, was composed here, and that it related to three apprentices who were engaged here in succession, viz. Sparks, Bedborough, and Tollit. The Angel Inn is cited as one of significance here in 1699.

The most important and most creditable inn is still the George, perhaps the oldest, and its situation was in the centre of the town, then on the north side, near which stood the chapel with a *market* house under it, which was eventually removed to the Horton side of Colnbrook; these together sadly obstructed the narrow gorge of road. Here it was that Queen Elizabeth slept as before observed, and where the magnates, proceeding to and from Windsor Castle, resorted.

This house of entertainment for travellers is said to derive its name from a statue of St. George carved in wood, which formerly stood in the porch of the parish church of Dursley, county Gloster, but it was surreptitiously removed by a clothier, and was carried in his waggon to Colnbrook on his passage to London, and this gave origin to the inn's name (see Rudder's Glostershire, p. 318), but neither date nor authority accompany the statement. The inn has a handsome appearance, with a long façade of some 80 feet, and is kept by Mr. Robert Irons, while of the opposite inn, the Checquers, his brother Thomas Irons is the host.

By deed 38 Elizabeth, 14th October, 1595, there was an Exchequer suit between William Higgins, who held land hereabouts, as well as at the George Inn, and Robert Cottys and John Bowser, against the visitors and travellers to Colnbrook. It is to be inferred that these inns were much frequented, and that it had been the custom to set benches, on which meat with other vendibles were ranged, against the walls of these inns (Shambles, scamel, scamnum). This disturbed the landlords and obstructed their business, so they petitioned to have the nuisance removed or abated in an action against the town.

In the recapitulation of the suit, the deed of Incorporation by King Henry VIII. was cited, 6th August, 30 Henry VIII. 1538, and the decision was that the practice should be discontinued on market or fair days. The names in the action appended are John Norreys, William Chirratt, and John Treaver, Clerk of Windsor.

There are certain deeds, 31 Elizabeth, 1588, between William Higgins, gentleman, and John Chamberlayn, relative to certain lands in Colnbrook, and by fine, Hilary 2 Jac. I. 1604, William Peters, gentleman, and George Higgins, gentleman, who sold the two inns in Colnbrook, similar allusions to lands in this town are made.

This inn, the George, once belonged to the Digby family, and a great stroke of business seems to have been transacted there, and many of the renters became rich by the tenure of it; perhaps the most distinguished was George Buckingham, whose son became an M.P., and wealth flowed to the family through the innholder. He was born in 1585, and he leased the George Inn for many years, and retired ultimately to Stanwell, and by his will proved 24th December, 1657, he states what property he had at Colnbrook, &c., which he leaves to his widow for life, and then to his son George. This worthy host of the inn must have been known to the Milton family who resided at Colnbrook previous to their removal to Horton, and probably were accommodated at his inn.

I have not traced the Buckinghams upwards; perhaps they were merely from the county, and so took their appellation. The distinguished member of the family was Owen, a salter and hemp merchant in Broad Street, London. He succeeded in business, became Sheriff of London in 1695, in which year he was knighted, 14th October, and subsequently on him was conferred the highest civic honour of Lord Mayor in 1704. He was soon raised to the rank of quality, and in 1708 he felt the genteel necessity of taking out a grant of arms. He did not enter his pedigree, but it is known that he married several times. He died in 1713, and left a son of the name of Owen, who bought Mousefield Hall, Berks, became M.P. for Reading, 1718, and Gentleman of the Privy Chamber to King George I. He does not appear to have signalised himself, and only living six years after his father, with his death in 1719 the male line became extinct, and his fortune chiefly devolved on a blood relation named Haistwell.

I find only one fine in 1694, by which Owen Buckingham buys land of John Slocomb in Colnbrook. An indenture with Christian Tendering exists, whereby George Buckingham buys property at Boreham, Essex, in 1627.

## PEDIGREE OF BUCKINGHAM.

Arms, granted 1708, O. Lion rampant G. debruised by a bend Az, charged with 3 bezants.

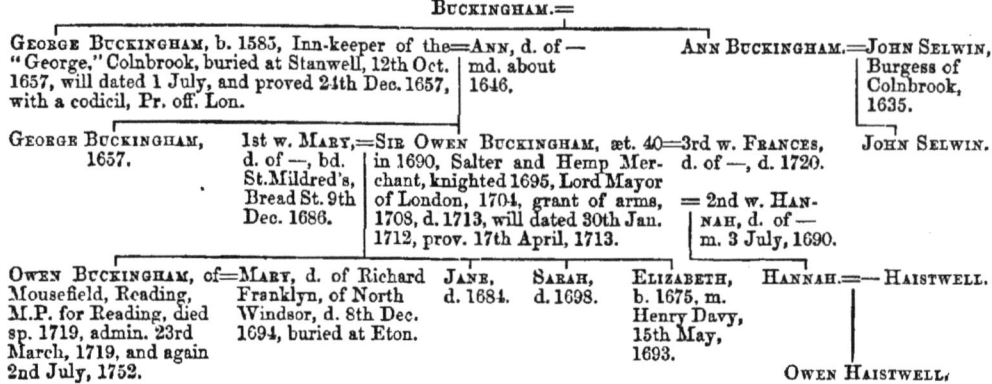

The care and good management of the innkeeper enabled the issue of Buckingham to rise to the rank of gentry, a fact which proves to us that travelling was becoming fashionable and frequent, especially to Windsor; but even in the days of the third George his travelling was circumscribed, and consisted merely in visits made to the castles and country seats of some of the principal of his nobility and gentry, and to periodical excursions to Weymouth, Brighton, &c. for he never ventured across the *ocean stream* to any part of the continent. Nor was this feat achieved before the days of George IV., who made a trip to Hanover. At the accession of William IV. in 1830 railroads had made but little progress in England and none abroad, and the common transit of steamers was as yet in embryo. But rail and steam, like printing, have changed the face of a mutable world, and now kings and queens and subjects are all transmitted from coast to coast, and roll along from town to town, which should improve the *status* of town and country inns and their holders, although it is rare for people of this class to retire with fortunes. The facilities of steam and rail have brought imperial and royal travelling into vogue, and it enables sovereigns to behold with their own eyes the improvements of other countries, and wisely improve their own, by recognising the fact that the prosperity of a people mainly arises from permitting them to make their *own laws*, and above all to *toleration* of religion—a principle imperative in a progressive age, and but for this England had still been a third or fourth-rate power. She rose with a bound from her shackles into a politically constitutional greatness, leaving Rome, then the hotbed of superstition and retrogradation, as the poet says, the Niobe of nations, " childless and crownless in her voiceless woe."

## PROPRIETORS IN COLNBROOK.

The recapitulation of the names of the twelve Burgesses under the second Charter of Incorporation in 1635, will announce to us who were the principal persons in this borough at that time, and what we want in names of those who were of position in the town, may be supplied from the parish registers, fines and recoveries. I will however advert to some names which may prove interesting to those who are curious about Colnbrook and its sojourners.

There was an influential family named Pitt, one of whom was a rich mercer here, when trade was superior to what it is now, and the town larger, houses better, and I presume the population larger also.

In 1635 Thomas Pitt, gentleman, is among the principal Burgesses, and he seems to be of the family who held Datchet Manor by patent, 1560. His son John Pitt was a London goldsmith, and his descendants settled in Colnbrook and Upton. He was a man of credit and renown in his time, so I will add his pedigree. In 1775 John Pitt married Elizabeth Martin Barns, after which the name disappears from the parish registers.

### PEDIGREE OF PITT.

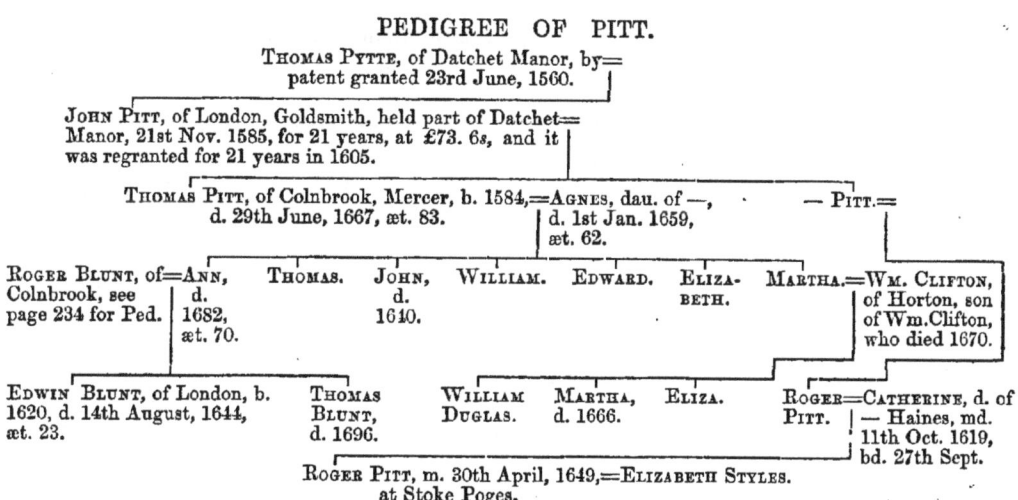

There was also a family of the name of Shorter, a branch of that of Staines, which became known to the world, had property here, and fulfilled the duties of Colnbrook town as functionaries, as appears in the Town Book, 1599, 1602, and in a deed of fine, 1613, in which Henry Shorter and Sir Robert Digby are introduced. Again a similar transaction as to purchase of property is found in 1634 between Robert (born 1594), son of Edmund Biddle and John Shorter, son of Henry Shorter. He was born 1604.

One of the descendants of the Staines members, Sir John Shorter, was in business in London as a Danish timber merchant, and 29th October, 1675, he was knighted, made Sheriff of London, and in 1687 he was made Lord Mayor of London by King James II. as a supposed *Papist*. To this city functionary, while proclaiming Bartholomew Fair according to annual custom under Newgate, the Ordinary offered a *cup of sack*, a beverage which retained its fame and name since the pot-valiant days of Sir John Falstaff, and which was always presented to the Mayor, but the horse on which he rode reared, and dislodging Sir John, he fell violently on the pavement. He was taken up, and was reported *dead*, however he was only insensible. He recovered sufficiently for the time being; he departed this world however during his mayoralty in 1688. This interposition of Providence has occurred to several mayors, and in our time a Lord Chancellor has died suddenly in office, viz. Lord Campbell in June, 1861; and this is generally thought to be without precedent, in the plenitude of power, whence arises a reflection on the vanity of ambition, for where and on what occasion could a trite morality receive a fresher point?

Sir John Shorter left a son of both names, who continued the timber business, and who bought an estate at Bybrook, Kent, whose eldest daughter and heir married in 1700 the famous statist Sir Robert Walpole, Prime Minister of England for so many years, and who to his credit preserved England from the scourge of war for nearly twenty years, a consummate politician, and although his memory is impeached for public corruption, in social life " He could win without art, and smile without a bribe."

The issue of this marriage was the celebrated Horace Walpole, in the evening of his days Earl of Orford, the author of many interesting and curious compositions, who at Strawberry Hill collected so many and valuable *pièces de vertù*, all which came to the hammer under the magic influence of Mr. George Robins, 25th April, 1842, after 24 days' sale. He was devoted to literature, being alternately a poet, historian, politician, antiquary and writer of dramas and romances. His Castle of Otranto was dramatised in 1782, when a passion for the marvellous prevailed, since become an epidemic. His letters too are models of social epistolary excellence.

Before giving the Shorter pedigree I may be excused for inserting here an anecdote of Mr. John Shorter. In 1489, 18th June, one John Shorter had a grant of office as *Launderer* of Clarendon Park, Wilts, on surrender of a grant made 25th September, 1 Henry VII. 1485, Close Rolls. The famous Lord Mohun, of intemperate memory, had been *twice* arraigned for murder, but on both occasions acquittals followed. He was engaged in a dispute with James Duke of Hamilton, and a duel ensued in Hyde Park, 15th November, 1712, wherein both combatants were slain. At Shredding's Green, Iver, in the house occupied by Lady Gambier, the Dowager Lady Mohun dwelt, widow of Lord Mohun.

In 1692 he had been indicted for the murder of Mountford the player, and in 1699 he and the Earl of Warwick were tried for the murder of Captain Richard Cooke. Mr. John Shorter, father of Lady Walpole, was walking down Norfolk Street, Strand, just before Mountford was stabbed, and Lord Mohun mistaking him for that unfortunate son of Thespis, came up, and embracing him, said, dear Mountford, but Mr. Shorter undeceived him, and walked home. He had scarcely reached his own house in Norfolk Street when he heard the noise and scuffle in the street which was occasioned by Mountford's murder. The exclamation of Lord Mohun was supposed to have been the *signal* for the assassins to attack their prey, and it was fortunate for Mr. Shorter that he was not their victim. The name of Shorter disappears from the Parish Books and Deeds after 1634.

## PEDIGREE OF SHORTER.

Arms granted 1687, S, Lion rampant, O crowned A between 3 battle axes of the last, handles of the second.

JOHN SHORTER, of Staines, Middlesex.=ELIZABETH, dau. of —.

JOHN SHORTER, of ditto.=SUSAN, d. of Richard Forbis or Forebank, of Surrey.

NICHOLAS SHORTER, bd. at Stoke Poges, 29 May, 1629.

HENRY, of Coln-=MARGARET, brook, bd. 25th d. of —
Oct. 1616.

SIR JOHN SHORTER, b. 1634, knighted=ISABELLA, d. of John Birkett, of Cumberland.
1675, Sheriff of London, 1675, Lord Mayor of London, 1688, d. 1688.

WILLIAM, 1621, of Colnbrook.

JOHN, 1626, of ditto.

JOHN, born 1614.

RICHARD, b. 1609.

JOHN SHORTER, of Bybrook, Kent,=ELIZABETH, d. of Sir Erasmus Phillips, of Picton Castle, Bart.
b. 1650, d. 19th Nov. 1734.

EDWARD TYRREL, of=JOANNA,=NATHANIEL WHETHAM, Colonel in Parliamentary Army.
St. Dunstan's. m. 12th Dec. 1632.

CATHERINE, d. and h. md.=SIR ROBERT WALPOLE, cr. Earl of Orford, d. 1745.
30th July, 1700, d. 1737.

CHARLOTTE, md. Lord Conway, (page 00.)

HORACE WALPOLE, Earl of Orford, d. sp. 1797, æt. 80.

## EARLY ACCOUNT OF COLNBROOK.

We have already noticed the fact that the name Colnbrook, a town in Bucks, is not to be found in Domesday Book, but Dugdale's Monasticon, Vol. I., says that Milo Crispin, who lived before and at the Conquest, while he dwelt in the Castle of Wallingford, near the time of his death received certain good offices from Faratius, Abbot of Abingdon, and did give in return to that Abbey a *public Inn*, and half a hide of land in Colebrook, on the road to London, and he sent Pipard his Steward, and Warine his Chaplain, to Abingdon, to lay the donative (a term signifying a benefice, and collated by the patron to one without presentation to the Ordinary, or induction by orders—but here a gift is meant) on the altar of St. Mary, in the presence of the Abbot and the whole convent.

But before the end of the year 1106 he had departed this life without issue, whereupon his own proper estate reverted to the Crown, while the Castle and the whole honour of Wallingford remained in right of her birth to Maude, his widow, styled *Matildis* Domina de Walengfort. She was a daughter of Robert D'Oiley, by the daughter and heir of Wigod, a powerful Saxon. She remarried one Brien Fitz-Count, and he betaking himself to a religious life, the King, Henry II., seized on the manor of Wallingford and its dependencies. These people occupied a prominent place in the early history of our island, so I shall affix a genealogy, as they held property in the county and vicinity, and in them Colnbrook was interested.

WIGOD, a powerful Saxon of Wallingford=

ROBERT D'OILEY, a General temp. William I.=ALDITH, daughter and sole heir.
He held 6 manors in Bucks, including Iver.
Died 1090.

MILO CRISPIN, Lord of Wallingford, held=MAUDE, daughter and heir, took=BRIEN FITZ-COUNT, became a
a manor in Bucks, and gave the donative    the veil or retired to a Con-    religious, and died sp.
relative to Colnbrook, d. 1106, sp.         vent.

After this date I do not find any record which adverts directly to this town by name, but in the excerpts of the Rolls, 3rd October, 7 Henry III. 1222, is an account of one Roger, son and heir of Hugh de Sancto Vedasto, who made a fine for 30 marks about the manor of Colebrok, but as the county of Bucks is not put in the deed, and this Colnbrook was never a manor, I presume it is meant for the shire of Devon.

The oldest appellation in the Fine deeds is Culbrok—Fine Mich. 3 Edward I. 1274, in which one Lucas de Baton of the City of London, holds a mill in this town, or near it.

In 1279 a family, by name Carliolo, buys certain messuages of one Guy of Culbrok and his wife, and in 1283 Henry, son of Guy. And this spelling it carries to the 16th century.

In 1334 and 1338 the same parties are found in the Fines, to the abstracts of which at the end of the work I refer the curious reader.

The fines entered for Colnbrook are not many, the purchases and sales being confined to Horton chiefly. In 1380 John Lambyn of *Colbrok* buys property of Thomas Herby, or Erby, of Colbrok, with a garden, &c., in Horton, and in 1386 one John Wytton and his wife make an investment of a messuage in this town, which had belonged to John Waryn and his wife. Close Rolls 18 Henry VI. 1438, John Erby grants to Laurence Colbroke and Isabel his wife, and heirs, &c., two tofts, two gardens, &c. called Salles Place, and a *pightel* in Colnbrook. All direct transfers relative to this date until 1582, cease. Some transactions, however, may be comprised in Horton deeds, where the Colnbrook property exchanged was inconsiderable, so I shall advert to some historical facts, derived from ancient chronicles.

In the history of the annals of Windsor, by Messrs. Tighe and Davis, occasional pieces of information relative to Colnbrook are found, extracted from the antique records of the locality. Fabyan's Chronicle says that in 1264 King Henry III. was at Windsor, and after the defeat of the Earl of Leicester at Evesham, county Worcester, the King came to Wyndesore with a great power, intending to destroy the City of London for the great ire and displeasure he had unto it. The citizens, to avert the royal anger, despatched eight of their number who had friends in the King's court with an instrument under the seal of the city, submitting their lives and goods to the King's mercy.

This deputation left London 6th October, and at Colnbrook they met Sir John Leybourne, one of the King's knights, who persuaded them to return to London. At a meeting of the citizens at Barking Church, on the following day, it was resolved to send the instrument of submission to the King by Sir Roger de Leybourne, who was earnestly entreated to be a mediator with King Henry for the citizens.

Again, in Froissart's Chronicles, Vol. I. ch. 24, is recorded an account of four ambassadors sent from Philip de Valois, King of France, styled Philip le Bel, to King Edward III. in 1337, to do him homage for the Duchy of Guienne, whose capital is Bordeaux, and they found the King at Windsor, who ordered them to return to London, and the translation says, " So they dyned in the Kynges chambre, and after they departed, and lay the same night at Colbroke, and the next day at London." The King of England was then to France in the relation of a *mesne* Lord who has tenants under him, but holds himself of a Lord Paramount.

It is not unlikely that the hotel chosen was the famous Ostrich Inn, which had been established at least as early as King Edward I., a place of frequent resort for visitors wending to and from the palace at Windsor.

The mission to Windsor was successful, yet Philip was prepared to compel homage by force of arms, and Edward, submitting to present necessity, went to Amiens and did homage to Philip, and in a formal deed acknowledged that he owed homage to France. Yet did this rankle in the breast of Edward, and it was the precursor movement of an invasion of France, and the fatal battle of Crecy in 1346, in which the King of Bohemia was slain, and his crest, with three ostrich feathers, was seized, which the Prince of Wales and his successors have adopted as a memorial.

The fall of Calais followed this event in 1347, and the recovery of Guienne. The English now peopled Calais, and the town was made the staple of wool, leather, tin and lead, the chief commodities of the kingdom, until it was recaptured in 1558 by the French.

Again in 1387, King Richard II. having determined to wage war against his uncles, the Dukes of York and Gloucester, the Duke of Ireland, as Lieutenant-General, headed the King's forces, and fixed his forces at Oxford. The Duke, to sound the Londoners, resolved to send thither Sir Nicholas Brembre (page 90), Sir Peter Goloufre, and Sir Michael de la Pole; these worthies, with only 30 horses, rode to Windsor and crossed the Thames at Staines, and dined at Shene (Richmond), and went to London, but finding no encouragement they reversed their steps to Windsor, and arrived at Oxford, where the Duke of Ireland and his army lay.

In the meantime, the Duke of Gloucester took the field against the Duke of Ireland, and marched from London and lodged at Brentford, and so to Colnbrook, their force increasing all the way. They followed the road to Reading, to gain a passage over the Thames, for the bridges of

Staines and Windsor had, by command of the Duke of Ireland, been broken down, by which they would have had a better and more level country for their march.

They met the forces of the Duke of Ireland and vanquished them, and on this the Duke fled to Holland, and the King assented to come to London.

In the Chronique de la traison et mort de Richart deux Roy d'Engleterre.—After the accession of King Henry IV. to the throne in 1399, plots were laid to destroy him and harass him during his reign. Among the rest, Lord Despenser, late Earl of Gloucester (page 29), Sir Thomas Blount, &c. On the first Sunday of the year the Duke of Exeter, Duke of Surrey, and the Earl of Salisbury met at Kingston, with 8000 archers and 300 lances of men at arms, the flower of all England, and on setting off for Kingston the Lords sent letters to Duke d'Aumarle, Earl of Rutland, son of the Duke of York, urging him not to fail to be at Colnbrook on the night of the *Kings*.

The Duke d'Aumarle was dining with his father, and he placed the indenture of their confederacy on the table, and the Duke asked what letter is that, when d'Aumarle handed the letter to his father, and when the Duke saw the six seals, he resolved to repair to Windsor to inform the King, Henry IV., of the conspiracy; but he was prevented by his son, who rode off and arrived at Windsor before his father, explained all to the King, and obtained pardon, and thus the conspiracy was quashed on the *day of the Kings*, the 6th day of the year 1389. At the hour of noon the King set out from London to encounter the Lords, his enemies, with only 50 lances and 6000 archers. In the meantime the Earl of Rutland, having left the King, went to Colnbrook, where the insurgent Lords were assembled, and pretended he was willing to live and die with them.

On the Monday night, 5th January, they entered the Castle of Windsor without opposition with about 500 horse, and searched the castle and the houses of the Canons in hope of finding him, " and purposed to have sclayn the Kyng and hise chyldren at Wyndesore, and thoo (they) that helde with them to be a *mommynge*. But as it fortuned the Kyng had warnynge, and anon he roode to London in gret haste, and made hym strong to ryde on his adversaries; and when they had espied that the Kyng was forth to London they token there wey to Surcetre (Cirencester) and made cryes be the wey." Froissart's Chronicles of London from 1189 to 1483.

When the Lords and their army had passed the two bridges of Maidenhead, four leagues beyond Colnbrook, the two vanguards of King Henry came in sight, and the Earl of Rutland cried out, They all flee. The affair ended in the capture of Cirencester, and the Earls of Kent and Salisbury were beheaded.

Among those who were engaged in this affair was Sir Bernard Brocas, whose landed possessions were in and about Windsor. The estate escheated to the Crown, but the King granted them to William Brocas, his son and heir, with the houses and lands in Windsor and Clewer, and the manors of Bray, Cookham, and Horton. Escheat, 1 Henry IV. 1399, p. 193.

The next piece of history disclosed in the annals of these ages that I have seen, is the following:—

The works of St. George's Chapel were terminated in the reign of King Henry VIII. On the 8th of this King's reign (1516), at the feast of the Order of the Garter, a subscription was opened and eventually a sum of £260 was raised, equal to £2030. Ashmole, in his Order of the Garter, describes a magnificent cavalcade on the eve of the feast of St. George, 11 Henry VIII. 1520.

On the 27th May, being Friday, the King removed from Richmond towards the Castle of Windsor, where the nobles, &c., were to meet the King, but owing to the *impurity* of the air, &c., with difficulty of securing lodgings, only a specific number of horses was to be used by each noble—every knight bachelor had 20 horses, and no other knight or noble to have above 16 horses, with their carriages and all; and the King, thus right nobly companyed, rode to Colnbrook, and at the sign of the Catherine Wheel the King took his courser, and his henchman richly apparelled followed, and also the King's horse of state led. *Gartier* King of Arms wore his coat of arms, with others giving attendance.

The Queen Catherine and the ladies and their *compaignies* stood in the field at the Town's End, beside the high ways towards Windsor, to see the King's company pass by, and then the Queen rode to the *fery* (Datchet) next way to the Castle. The King rode to Slow (Slough) and so to Eton College, where all of the College stood along in manner of procession, receiving his Grace (not then styled Majesty) after the custom.

The Datchet ferry as it was about 200 years ago, is still in plate engraving, before the bridge was built in 1706, by Queen Anne, in which year it belonged to Colonel Wheeler, who sold it to King William III. The bridge was rebuilt in 1770, but in 1795 it became impassable, and then George III. provided a ferry free, and this continued until a new bridge was opened in 1812, at the instance of John Richards, Esq., of Datchet.

History discloses nothing particular in regard to Colnbrook, which had its special exaltation in the two charters conferred on it by King Henry VIII., and had its consequent depression also in the charters abandonment, to be again raised by another endowment of a charter by King Charles I., as will be seen under the Corporation.

During the Stuart dynasty civil war inflamed the nation, when there were men and principles to die for. Church and King was a watchword dear to every royalist, so Cromwell and Religion was to the men of the Commonwealth, supported by the unspeakable *stamina* of a great and glorious cause.

The situation of the town, however, rendered it the scene of contending parties during the civil wars, which drew out the chivalry of the nation; and Echard, the Historian, remarks that this monarch, finding the two Houses of Parliament backward in sending their Committee, resolved to quicken them, and so he advanced from Reading with his whole army to Colnbrook.

A Committee of two Lords and three Commoners waited on his Majesty there, 11th November, 1643, Sir John Evelyn, the fourth Commissioner, being left behind as one unacceptable to the King, but whom the House had persisted in putting on their Committee.

The King received the address, which was in a strain less imperative than those which had preceded it, and returned an answer encouraging them to believe that he was disposed to a treaty.

In Whitelock's Memoirs he remarks, 2nd August, 1647, army quartered at Colnbrook and the King at Stoke Abbey, where he probably remained until he was removed to the palace at Oatlands.

This Stoke Abbey may mean the Hospital here, but probably the monarch resided at the Manor House. The lordship of the manor was then in Lord Purbeck to 1657, the year of his death—it passed to the family of Gayer, who retained it till 1724, when it was disposed of for some £12,000 to Edmund Halsey, Esq. who represented the town of Buckingham in Parliament in 1714. His daughter Ann was wife of Sir Richard Temple, who became Lord Viscount Cobham 1714, and after his death in 1749, his wife returned to Stoke and formed acquaintance with Gay the Poet. After her death in 1760 the house and manor was sold to Thomas, son of the famous William Penn, of Pennsylvania.

The King had resolved to retire to Reading, or at least to have staid at Colnbrook until he heard again from the Parliament, but Prince Rupert, (son of Elizabeth, sister of Charles I. and Frederick V. Count Palatine of the Rhine and King of Bohemia) whom his uncle, Charles I. had appointed General of the Horse, with some rashness, although somewhat with his Majesty's sanction, advanced the next morning to Hounslow with horse and dragoons, and there was involved in great danger of defeat, finding, as most warriors do, that victory is not always within grasp, and that actual warfare is a sharp and quick instructor.

Upon the 9th December, 1688, on the news that the Prince of Orange was advancing to Reading to prevent further desertions, the King's army, then quartered at Reading, was ordered to march nearer Colnbrook, but they returned to Reading.

I have not found the names of any persons of eminence who have resided in the borough of Colnbrook; but during the Long Parliament, when episcopacy was silenced, Dr. Henry King, Bishop of Chichester, lived in the house of Sir Richard Hobart, whose sister he married, at Langley, and doubtless was a frequent visitor in the town until he was replaced in his see at the Restoration.

He was highly esteemed in the neighbourhood. One, says a biographer, the epitome of all honours, virtues, and generous nobleness. He died in 1669. His grandfather, Philip King, was of Wornall, Bucks, and, to the credit of the family, in it there had been three bishops—London, Oxford, and Chichester.

I have reason to think, but without precise testimony, that some relationship existed between Dr. Henry King and John, son and heir of Sir George Gyll (page 100), whose will the Bishop proved in 1661 in the Prerogative Office. The testator earnestly entreats the Bishop "that he would be pleased to look upon his children with a favourable and gracious aspect, and that he would be pleased to take their concernments into his especial care."

It appears that the Hatton family were connected with Stoke, but they did not possess the manor. Lord Chancellor Hatton is referred to in Gray's "Long Story;" and he was famed temp. Elizabeth for his dancing propensities, despite the jeers of young and old, "when he had fifty winters o'er him;" but like courtiers he was obnoxious to the frowns and caprices of mutable masters, and he incurred the displeasure of the fickle Elizabeth. This reverse of royal countenance preyed on his too sensitive mind, and he died therefrom, says his biographer, in 1591, in the midday of life, aged 51. He held the manor of West Drayton for life, and Padbury, near Colnbrook, granted from the Crown for 21 years, and the estate of Perry Oaks, near Padbury, in 1587, the year he was appointed Chancellor of England. He died unmarried, but a nephew, Sir William Newport, assumed his patronymic, and became Lord Hatton. The title expired in 1762.

The antiquity and celebrity of Richings Park, where the nobility and sons of letters assembled, where the feast of reason and the flow of soul abounded, gave animation to Colnbrook; and as the entrance to the park is through the end of the town, it may not be irrelevant to advert to it and the possessors. Formerly it belonged to the Apsley family, and it descended to that of Bathurst, by them it was disposed of in 1739 to Algernon, son of Charles, sixth Duke of Somerset, commonly called the proud Duke, and hence took the name of Percy Lodge. Frances, Duchess of Somerset, held this estate in dower during her widowhood, and she gave celebrity to the spot by the classic elegance of her pen, as is shewn in an interesting volume of letters addressed from Richings in 1741. She describes several particulars relative to the domain and grounds, and noted that on the very spot where her greenhouse stood was the ancient chapel of St. Leonards; and also, that there and on an antique bench in the garden were exhibited many remains of the wit of her predecessor's visitors, comprising Addison, Pope, Prior, Congreve, Gay, the distinguished associates of Allen, Lord Bathurst, a wit and critic, who attained the patriarchal age of 91 the year he died, 1775.

Dr. Johnson says that the Duchess, when Countess of Stratford, was wont to invite poets to hear her lays and assist in her studies, and among them the famous Thomson was selected for that honour; but that the pleasures of the *table* so far exceeded those of *song*, that he neglected the aristocratic poetess and caroused only, and that he never received another *summons*. Yet was the Bard of Scotia not unmindful or ungrateful, for he dedicated to the Countess of Hertford his poem on Spring, beginning—

> O Hertford, fitted or to shine in courts,
> With unaffected grace, or walk the plain,
> With innocence and meditation joined
> In soft assemblage. Listen to my song,
> Which thy own season paints, when Nature all
> Is blooming and benevolent like Thee.

The Duchess here expired in 1754, when the estate came to her daughter Elizabeth, Countess of Northumberland, whose husband, in 1766, was created Duke of Northumberland and Earl Percy. In 1776 the Duke conveyed this estate to Sir John Coghill, and his widow sold it in 1786 to John Sullivan, Esq.

Soon after the conveyance, the old mansion, which had been put into a state of complete repair, was consumed by fire, and the present house was raised in a more elevated part of the park, which is however very flat, yet it is not destitute of ornamental landscape, and art has been made subsidiary to nature. As the estate came through the Apsleys to Bathursts, and they were by marriage connected with the Scawens (page 223), I subjoin a pedigree.

## PEDIGREE OF APSLEY AND BATHURST.

Arms of Apsley—Barry of Six, A and G, a Canton Erm.

Sir Allen Apsley, d. 1630, descended from Apsley of ditto, temp. Edward III. = Lucy, d. of Sir John St. John of Wilts.

Sir Allen Apsley = Frances, d. and heir of Peter Bowkay. = Barbara, m. Lieut.-Col George Hutchinson.

Sir Peter Apsley, d. 1691. = — d. of — Frances, d. 1696. = Sir Benjamin Bathurst, d. 1704.

Catherine, d. and h. = Allen, Lord Bathurst, d, 1775, æt. 91.

Henry, created Earl Bathurst, Lord Chancellor. = Tryphena, d. of Thomas Scawen, of Horton, p. 223.

As this neighbourhood has been famed for its timber, and the same reputation has continued, I will add here that elms were brought from the immediate vicinity of Eton, viz. from the Wyke, Boveney, Taplow, Maydenhythe, Horton, Langley, and Bottley's Grove, and alders from Ditton Park.

The timber was placed in the *Timbre-haw*, now called *Timbrells*, ready for use in 1440.

## CORPORATION OF COLNBROOK.

Formerly the words city and borough were equivalent, and there were 246 corporations aggregate in Great Britain.

It appears by the deed cited in the suit between William Higgins and Cottys and Bowser, in 1595, that mention is made of a licence of incorporation, 30 Henry VIII. 1538, but the town does not seem to have been duly incorporated till the 35 Henry VIII. 1544, seventh part of the patents. The preamble of the instrument states that it is a grant to the inhabitants of the towns of Langley Marsh and Colnbrook and their successors.

The King to all whom it concerns, greeting—Witnessed at Walden, 29th August, 1544, by writ of Privy Seal. Know ye that of our especial grace and of our certain knowledge and mere motion, and also on account of the intimate love which we bear and have towards our well-beloved subjects the inhabitants of our towns of Langley Mares and Colbrok, in our counties of Middlesex and Bucks, for the maintaining, building, and repairing of three bridges and our highways in these parishes, I have granted by these presents and do grant for us and our heirs as much as in us is to our aforesaid subjects, the men and inhabitants within our town of Colbrok, &c. that the said town shall be a town corporate of the inhabitants within the said town for ever, &c. and they may have a common seal for performing and transacting the affairs of the town, &c.

And further, that they may for ever have and hold *one* market in every week at our town of Colbrok, on every Tuesday; and two fairs or marts yearly, that is to say, on the eve of St. Mark the Evangelist, and to continue for two days, and the other on the eve of the Apostles Simon and St. Jude, to continue for two days, 5th April and 6th October.

The incorporation was instituted by the name of the bailiff and twelve burgesses.

It is much to be regretted that not a name of these burgesses of the first series is left. Nor is it known exactly how long the first corporation lasted, or for what reason it declined and died away. Some mismanagement, no doubt, for it is not in the *end* we propose, but in the choice of *means* that we deceive ourselves, and by turning things to their confounding contraries make confusion live.

The burgesses kept their own accounts and records, and it is certainly singular that not a soul has transmitted anything which bears relation to names, dates, or accounts of the two corporations that has come within the author's cognizance.

There was also a grant of a Court of Piepoudre during the fairs, and with the profits arising therefrom the inhabitants are to keep in repair the said bridges and highways, &c. This is one of the lowest courts of justice, and the origin of the term is "Curia pedis pulverizati," from the *dusty* feet of suitors, implying a summary court for the humble.

Coke says it is so called because justice is administered as quick as dust falls off the feet; and in 14 Edward IV. 1477, it took cognizance of all disputes within the precincts of the markets and fairs. The etymology may be found in pied puldreaux, pedlar in old French—petty dealer. Hence the court of such petty chapmen as resort to fairs and markets. It was chiefly established to rectify injuries and redress wrongs at fair times. Its judgment is not final, and from it appeals were made to higher judicature, but its chief virtue was to prevent delay and administer speedy justice. The Judge Greyhew mentioned in page 250, may be one of the superintendent judges of this court.

The Corporation had a seal, "Sigillum comune ad negocia ville de Colbroke," which was of silver, and it was sold at a public auction, but whether to satisfy a debt, as in the case of the Communion plate, or to satisfy cupidity, is not recorded; but it does appear rather blameable that a town to which incorporation had been *twice* granted, could not even find a depository for their annals, and a safe custody for the *paraphernalia* of office; and it is surprising to think how this town so full of traffic, and on the high road to Windsor and Bath and the West of England, could have declined so materially as to lose its properties of self-government and corporate rights with which it had been invested by royalty.

In 1653 there being no bailiff to receive the benefit of the markets and fairs, the causeways and bridges were much out of repair, and at the request of Mr. Andrew Meale and Mr. Thomas Pitt, who were two of the burgesses, Thomas Burcombe did receive the benefits of the markets and fairs for the years 1653 and 1654, and gave an account to the inhabitants of the town in the year 1655 of what he had received and disbursed, and then the Town, by reason there was no bailiff, chose chapel wardens as formerly. At the same time it was agreed that the limits, precincts, liberties, bounds and *metes* of the town should extend as they had been heretofore accustomed, beginning at a certain bridge called Mad Bridge, Stanwell, lying and being on the east side of the town of Colnbrook, on the King's highway, leading from London to Colnbrook, and from the said bridge to a certain other bridge called Gray Bridge, towards the south side of the town, and thence by a certain other brook or ditch called the Shire Ditch, on the north side of the said Mad Bridge.

After some suspension of the rights and jurisdiction of the town, a petition was made to King Charles I. to renew the Charter, but why they could not resuscitate themselves, unless the charter was abrogated by law or by the will of the sovereign, history has not furnished us with particulars. Suffice to say, that in the 11th year of King Charles I. 1635, it was again incorporated with extended privileges, and the Charter was signed at Canterbury, 8th October, 1635, by the name of Bailiffs, Burgesses, and Commonalty. The Bailiff, Capital Burgesses, &c. to be of the Council, and twelve burgesses are to be elected, and that David Salter, gentleman, be the first bailiff, and present bailiff until the first Friday in the month of September. In addition to a bailiff there was a Steward of the Town, learned in the law: the burgesses were also justices of the peace.

The names of the first twelve and only burgesses recorded are in the New Patent; had that not been so, even these names had been irrecoverable, the town having evinced neither pride nor care to transmit any of its transactions but what are found in the Town Book.

David Salter, gentleman, Andrew Meale, gentleman, Thomas Pitt, gentleman, John Child, Thomas Meale, Thomas Burcombe, John Selwyn, Edmund Slocombe, Stephen Mascall, John Burton, Henry Fuller, John Mudget, inhabitants of the town.

The seal although lost or rather sold, is not forgotten, and the impression is as follows:—

SIGILL: COMUNE: BURGI: DE: COLBROKE: IN: COM: BUCK. ET: MIDD.

The Arms were, A a mullet S. Crest, boar's head A armed and tusked O, langued G. Motto, In Domino Confido.

In Cole's MSS. Vol. XL. f. 42, is this letter, dated 1773.

"On the seal is a church, which the inhabitants told me was a true representation of the old chapel which was pulled down some years ago. They have a small market on Tuesday, and say they had tolls paid at their bridge formerly when the river was navigable, which has not been these many years.

"What I want to know is whether they were ever a Corporation, and if you can give me any further account of that place, it will much oblige. The seal is in the hands of Mr. Burcombe, a tradesman over against the George Inn, in whose family it has been ever since his grandfather's time."

Colnbrook and Fenny Stratford were the only market towns in the county held by charter, and were disused. A charter of fairs was established in the latter in 1609, but like Colnbrook it was discontinued during the civil wars, and although revived after the Restoration, the town suffered so much from the plague in 1665, that the market was never reopened. The inns upon which the inhabitants depended chiefly for support were shut up, and the road turned in another direction.

The plague of 1625 almost decimated Colnbrook (page 250), but it passed unscathed in 1665, and the dire effect of the civil wars caused the once chartered towns of Colnbrook and Fenny Stratford to dwindle into neglect and insignificance. If it was by mismanagement they fell, it was not so unfortunate to fall from a corporate state as a political one, such as we have seen in our times in the disfranchisement of St. Alban's and Sudbury, "where rank corruption mined all within."

These charters and corporations seem to have had affinity to garrisons, and were originally charged with the gates of the town when no military garrison was present. A soldier could enter any garrison town, and follow any employment without permission of the officers.

## MISCELLANEOUS MATTERS, WITH THE CIVIL GOVERNMENT OF THE TOWN.

With the consent of Mr. John Ashton, formerly Vestry Clerk of Horton and Stanwell, one of the oldest of the remaining families of Colnbrook, permission was given me to see the *Town Book*. There is a note in this book that it had belonged to Thomas Maish, a butcher of this town (there are several stones to this family in Horton churchyard), and that it cost him three guineas and a half to get it from the hands of Lawyer Round of Windsor. But being town property it was restored, and the valuable record of Colnbrook has been deposited in the town box since 1810, and has been in the custody of one of the Ashtons. Thomas Ashton was schoolmaster here for many years, and he died in 1834, a man of reputation and skill, one of those useful teachers of science who are the parents of the mind in the flexible age of youth.

This family came originally from Preston in Lancashire in 1650, and settled at Horton, and kept the inn, then called the Three Horses, now the Crown, and a descendant removed from Horton to Colnbrook in 1737.

To revert to the Book: it is an antique folio, bound in calf, in a dilapidated condition, with some leaves detached, and seeing how valuable it is, and the only depository of the town accounts and elections, &c., it is a pity a *crown* was not spent on its re-binding. The preciousness of the volume doubtless has been the cause why it has not recently left the custody of those who hold it, but MSS. of equal importance, parish registers, &c. are daily sent to the binder, and return better for the temporary transference.

The first date is 1612, beginning with the account of John Jeffrey and others, the chapel wardens, overseers and bridge wardens who were appointed annually. The first chapel wardens here cited were Roger Creker and Thomas Pytt, and the names of wardens, collectors and surveyors of the high roads, &c. are very well kept. In 1615 Henry Shorter and John Kelly were chapel wardens: in 1621 Mr. Shorter is collector for the poor of Horton, and after 1626 the name disappears (page 275).

Daniel Salter was warden in 1623, and in 1632 William Peters was warden, and rendered his accounts. From the year 1635 there is an *hiatus valde deflendus*, a lamentable gap of twenty long years. May be the civil commotions caused the want of entry or the loss by excision. A note is made of this fact " because the accounts should not be seen, which is false," adds the annotator.

In 1635 George Goade was warden; two members of this family had been physicians here (page 247). I subjoin a skeleton pedigree of Goade, as benefactors.

### PEDIGREE OF GOADE.

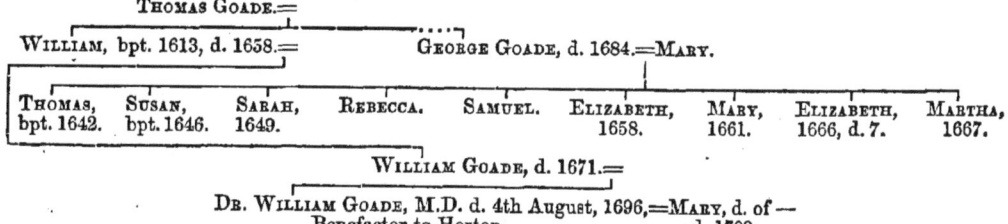

In 1654 Reginald Ludgold, John Burton and John Atlee gave in their summary of accounts, which averaged £50 yearly.

In 1655 the name of John Holderness appears, and he gives in his expenditure and collection in 1660. The last failure in the book is in 1770, and its entries terminate in 1821, after which new books have continued the entries until the present time.

The book gives no account of the mayors, which there seems to have been from an entry (page 250) of 30th July, 1626, when Thomas Head, Mayor of Colnbrook, died surfeited by drinking.

28th July, 1626-7, there is mention of *Judge Greyhew* of Colnbroke, probably judge of the Pie puldreaux Court.

It was the custom to read *Briefs* in the church, and these are noticed in the Town Book. The object of the reading these notices, similar to our Queen's Letters, was to obtain charities for foreign or domestic purposes, as a fire, a ransom from slavery in Africa, &c. The collections were *very small*, and in 1688 one amounted to only 9s 4d, and for the *prisoners* in Algiers 2s 10d; for a Horton fire, 22nd September, 1672, only a few shillings, so that what Sidney Smith remarked of a congregation after a charity sermon, that they were very fond of their *specie*, may be predicated here also.

The profits of the fairs were let out, and tolls for cattle and stalls, &c. realizing some £10 to £20. The present fairs are fixed 5th April and 16th October, and are held in a meadow near the town.

In another deed about the town it states that the limits, precincts, liberties and metes thereof shall extend as they have hitherto been accustomed. They shall begin at a certain bridge called Mad Bridge, in the parish of Stanwell, lying and being on the east side of the town of Colbroke, in the King's highway, leading from London to the said town of Colbroke, and from the said bridge unto a certain other bridge called Grey Bridge, in Stanwell parish, towards the south side of Colebroke town, and from there by a certain brook or ditch, commonly called Horton Allowance, in the parish of Horton, county Bucks, unto a certain house called the Spittle House, on the west side of Colebroke town, and thence by a certain other brook or ditch called the Shire Ditch, on the north side of Colebroke unto the said Mad Bridge.

It may not be out of place here to record the fact of the inhabitants of this town subscribing £17 towards the rebuilding of the town houses on the Horton side, and there was to be a reimbursement out of the rents, dated 30th January, 1667, John Holderness, George Richardson, and eight others contributing.

Inhabitants of *Langley* who subscribed towards the highway in 1699.

| £ | s. | d. | | £ | s. | d. | |
|---|---|---|---|---|---|---|---|
| 5 | 0 | 0 | John Slocombe. | 0 | 5 | 0 | John Banks. |
| 3 | 0 | 0 | Henry Goffe, Sen. | 0 | 5 | 0 | Mrs. Butler. |
| 2 | 0 | 0 | John Burcomb. | 0 | 10 | 0 | Mr. Tompson. |
| 1 | 0 | 0 | John Holderness. | 1 | 15 | 0 | John Guy. |
| 2 | 0 | 0 | William Guy. | 0 | 10 | 0 | Thomas Lewin. |
| 0 | 10 | 0 | Henry Woodnes. | 1 | 0 | 0 | William Darwill. |
| 1 | 0 | 0 | George Richardson. | 0 | 2 | 6 | Edward Holderness. |
| 0 | 10 | 0 | Edward Painter. | 0 | 5 | 0 | Thomas Ludgrove. |
| 1 | 0 | 0 | Henry Lane, Jun. | 0 | 5 | 0 | Aaron Sedgwick, Jun. |
| 1 | 0 | 0 | Henry Miller. | 0 | 7 | 6 | Benjamin Fellowes. |
| 0 | 7 | 6 | Henry Woodman. | 1 | 0 | 0 | Mrs. Fisher. |
| 0 | 5 | 0 | Richard Hippell. | 0 | 10 | 0 | Benjamin Thornton. |
| 0 | 15 | 0 | Richard Howe. | | | | |

*Horton Subscribers.*

| £ | s. | d. | | £ | s. | d. | |
|---|---|---|---|---|---|---|---|
| 0 | 15 | 0 | Samuel Hosey. | 0 | 10 | 0 | William Finch. |
| 0 | 8 | 0 | Thomas Amson. | 0 | 10 | 0 | William Russel. |
| 0 | 5 | 0 | William Dunt. | 1 | 0 | 0 | John Richardson. |
| 0 | 10 | 0 | Joseph Fulmer. | 2 | 0 | 0 | John Burcomb. |
| 1 | 5 | 0 | Thomas Rayner. | 1 | 10 | 0 | William Phillips. |

In 1700 the paving of the town was complete to the gates of John Wycherley, and the names of the subscribers are preserved:—

| £. | s. | d. | | £. | s. | d. | |
|---|---|---|---|---|---|---|---|
| 50 | 0 | 0 | King William III. | 5 | 7 | 6 | Sir Henry Seymour. |
| 10 | 0 | 0 | Thomas Lord Wharton.* | 3 | 1 | 6 | Sir William Scawen. |
| 25 | 17 | 6 | Sir Henry Seymour, Bart.† of Langley. Sir William Scawen, and other nobles and gentry. | 1 | 1 | 6 | Charles Moy. |
| | | | | 1 | 1 | 6 | Madame Houblon, wife of James Houblon, Esq. |
| | | | | 1 | 0 | 0 | Mr. Charles Daw. |
| 85 | 17 | 6 | | 1 | 0 | 0 | Samuel Starkey, Esq. |
| 14 | 3 | 0 | Two rates. | 0 | 10 | 0 | Mr. John West. |
| 3 | 0 | 0 | Coach and waggon masters. | 1 | 0 | 0 | Mr. William West. |
| 13 | 16 | 4 | Other monies. | 4 | 0 | 0 | Charles Chew, Esq. |
| | | | | 1 | 0 | 0 | Unknown gentleman. |
| £106 | 16 | 10 | | 2 | 17 | 6 | Langley side. |
| | | | | 5 | 15 | 0 | Horton side. |

In the Town Book there is a plan of Horton parish, according to the allotments in 1799, and this scheme was executed 23rd September, 1800, with the signatures appended—R. Davis, Thomas Wyatt, Joseph Pawsey, Thomas Williams, Esq., Lazarus Holderness. It is the same as in the award map in the parish of Horton, now preserved in the vestry-room of Horton Church.

As the Horton roads extend to Colnbrook, I will introduce here an abstract. There are 21 roads and paths, drifts and ways for footpaths, with supplementary swards for roads and streams. There are three public carriage roads and driftways, one public bridle road and footway, eight public footpaths, 12 private roads, and one private footpath.

There are three gravel and clay pits. There is also a poor and cottage allotment in Horton. To the allotment eight acres, glebe allotment not included.

The Lord of the Manor of Horton had 11 acres assigned to him, besides 10 acres especially as Lord of the Manor. Mr. Williams had 260 acres awarded to him as Lord.

Booker Derby, Esq. had four allotments, and a compensation was given to Mr. John Tupp for diverting the water-course.

All deeds enrolled and kept with the records in the office of the Clerk of the Peace for Bucks, dated 1st July, 47 George III. 1806. Acton Chaplin.

In 1699, the highway in this town was agreed to be paved from the bridge, near the Angell Inn, to the west end of the Ostrich Inn, towards the expense of which the following subscriptions were raised:—

---

* Thomas Wharton was fifth Baron. He was instrumental in accomplishing the Revolution, and was created, 1706, Viscount Winchendon of Bucks, &c. Subsequently he was raised to a marquisate. Dying in 1715 he was succeeded by his only son Philip, created 1718 Duke of Wharton. He became a follower of the Pretender, and died a *Capuchin* in a Spanish monastery in 1731. He was known as the frolic Duke, on whom Pope wrote some caustic lines in his first Epistle.

† Sir Henry Seymour (page 107) who subscribed was of Langley, and died unmarried 1714, when the Baronetcy expired, and was son of Henry Seymour, Esq. who followed the fortunes of King Charles I. and in 1666 resided at and then bought Langley Park, Bucks, in 1669, and got a grant from the King of the Manor of Langley under a reserved rent of £43. 8s 10d per annum. He built and endowed an almshouse at Langley for six poor people, and gave £400 to apprentice some boys. He died in 1686, æt. 74.

| £. | s. | d. | | £. | s. | d. | |
|---|---|---|---|---|---|---|---|
| 21 | 10 | 0 | Princess Anne of Denmark, afterwards Queen Anne. | 8 | 2 | 6 | Fifteen inhabitants of Langley. |
| 5 | 0 | 0 | Henry Lord Cavendish, son of William Duke of Devonshire. | 8 | 13 | 0 | Ten ditto of Horton. |
| 5 | 0 | 0 | Lord Cheney.* | 55 | 5 | 6 | Total. |
| 5 | 0 | 0 | Hon. Colonel Wharton, afterwards Duke of Wharton. | 53 | 9 | 0 | Disbursements. |
| 2 | 0 | 0 | Colonel Godfrey. | £1 | 16 | 6 | Balance. |

## ON THE CHAPEL AND CHAPELRIES.

Many parishes are divided into chapelries with boundaries as definite as those of the parent parish. This living is a perpetual curacy, in the archdeaconry of Buckingham, and now in the diocese of Oxford. The chapel is dedicated to St. Mary. The certified value is in the Liber Regis—Colnbrook Chapel, St. Mary, not in charge, clear annual value, £25. 15s.

It is thought that the curate may assume the title of rector. The gift either is or was in the College of Pembroke, Oxford, and its annual value is set at £103, and until lately the patrons were laymen.

The Rev. Charles Mackenzie, A.M. Vicar of St. Helens, London, and Master of Queen Elizabeth's Free Grammar School, St. Olave's, Southwark, was appointed to *the donative* of Colnbrook in 1834 by the trustees, with the consent of the Master and Fellows of Pembroke College, Oxon. Mr. G. A. Butler was the curate, and the incumbent in 1841 nominated Rev. Isaac Gosset to the curacy (p. 230). Previous to which Mr. William Brown, Rector of Horton, had been curate here from 1796 to 1830.

A commission was granted by the Bishop of Lincoln to the Bishop of Salisbury to consecrate the Chapel here, which was built in 1644, and stood in the centre of the town, adjacent to the George Inn, over the Market Place, a vast area capable of holding 40 loads of corn. It was removed in 1790, on being pronounced inadequate for the services of the town, and was rebuilt in Horton parish.

Why a proper church should not have been erected and supported in a twice-incorporated town with rich burgesses, &c. seems almost inexplicable, unless the fact of its being divided into so many parishes and dependencies be a solution. It had its donors at all times, and this arose from its not being supported by rates, and even the names and accounts of the parties endowing the Chapel are deficient for want of a *grateful record.*

There was a very old *Chauntry* here, which was served by Ankerwycke, it was endowed with lands, of which no vestiges remain, and which very likely were absorbed in the divisions just mentioned, or alienated at the Reformation. There is no record of the place in Domesday however, and the first chapel erected here is reported to have been built in 1344, 14 Edward III. in that part of the township of Colnbrook which is included in the parish of Langley Marsh, and it was afterwards twice rebuilt in the same parish. So that place, which was dignified by the appellation of a market town, was singularly situated in two dioceses, four different parishes, two counties, and two archdeaconries.

On the 9th February, 1540, King Henry VIII. granted the Park of Plaunt or New Park, in

---

* William Lord Cheney, M.P. for Bucks 1702, and Lord Lieutenant for ditto 1712, dying 1738, æt. 82, his honours became extinct.

Langley, and the advowson of the Chauntry in the Chapel of Colnbrook, to the then holders of the Park, to him and his heirs by knight's service. Rot. Parl. 32 Henry VIII.

It had been granted in 1523 to Henry Norris, Esq. (page 17), and ultimately it was in the tenure of Sir William Irby in 1743. (p. 78.)

The Chauntry was endowed in 1682 by George Townshend, Esq. with a moiety of the rents of certain London houses, and he directs by his will that the donative of this Chapel shall be conferred on an exhibitioner of Pembroke College, Oxon, who had been at Crypt School, Gloster. Mr. Townshend was of Lincoln's Inn, and he left certain rents in Long Acre for a lectureship, amounting to £101. 10s per annum.

Extracts of his will are in the Town Book, 4th December, 1682, and the will was republished in 1683.

There have been charities founded for education in Colnbrook, but neglect or appropriation have left only conjecture as to their whereabouts or value. (p. 268.)

It is the same in most parts of England, and complaints being made and long stifled, in 1816 an Education Committee, observing so many instances of malversation and negligence in managing trust property, recommended a Parliamentary Commission, which met in 1817. But many trustees pretended exemption from investigation by statute of Elizabeth. This however could not imply that the founders designed their trust to be abused. They who love peculation are interested in its concealment, hence it is but equitable that powers should be restored to the Legislature to adopt what is most expedient for general education—adult and infant education being of equal importance in the civil polity of the kingdom; and such institutions should be subject to public control, and be dealt with as public property, and all sums received and disbursed be in the accounts of those to whom the execution of the trust is confided.

I shall interpose here what has been preserved relative to gifts and charities:—

1622. Thomas Gasey gave to the town three tenements, the yearly profit to be employed for the good of the poorhouse dwellers for ever, after the decease of his mother, widow Whitlock, who had a life interest therein.

1623. Richard Goade gave three acres of land to the town. One acre yearly profit to be paid annually to the minister of the town for a sermon yearly, on Good Friday, in the Chapel; and the profits of the other two acres to be distributed on the said day, and in the chapel, to the poor and impotent of the town for ever.

1623. Bryan Chist gave by will to be distributed in the church to four poor people a 4d. loaf each, every Sabbath day.

1624. Edmund Jeffery, senr. gave a cloth for the reading desk, the first it ever had.

— David Salter gave a green cushion for the reading desk.

1625. Daniel Salter at his own proper cost built a Cripple house upon the Hermitage Green (and to this day it is there—the Golden Cross at the west side of the town), with a chimney of brick to it, allowing certain meat and drink, candles and coals for the lodging and relief of four poor cripples, &c. to stay all night; and also an allowance of bread and beef for four cripples as should be brought by passes through the town without staying there, and this gift to remain for ever, as it appears by the deed lying in the Chapel chest.

Memorandum.—That it is agreed by general consent that Ralph Flatcombe being the Chapel Clerk shall make the fire and buy the victuals, moved by Daniel Salter for the cripples, and so shall every Chapel Clerk hereafter; and he is allowed therefore 12d the quarter by the Chapel Wardens. Signed, Robert Binks, Minister, and 20 inhabitants.

1626. Edmund Jeffery, senr. replaced another cloth, his original one having been stolen. He also plaistered and white-washed the gallery.

1627. Sir John Kederminster, Knt. Lord of Langley Manor, re-edified the chapel with brick and hewn stone, which before was timbered and boarded, adorning it with a fair dial and glass windows, looking into the Market Place.

The widow of Sir John, who died 1632 (viz. Mary, daughter of Sir William Garrard, Knt. of Dorney, Bucks) provided a fair black cloth to the chapel, to be laid over corpses as they were conveyed to the grave, there being none in the memory of man. (p. 89.)

1628. Daniel Salter erected and otherwise beautified the north end of the chapel.

1629. Andrew Meale made a new pulpit, also a new dormer window (one in the roof of a house or above the entablature, or that part of the order of a column which is over the capital) on the north side against the pulpit.

1629. Robert Binks, Minister, floored and ceiled part of the chapel.

Thomas Burcomb put in new timbers under the dormer window.

John Child put in new timbers on the south side and aisle.

Thomas Pitt repaired the middle of the chapel and fitted up the gallery.

Edmund Slocomb put a mainpost to support the gallery, and divided it from the body of the chapel, and fitted up the gallery.

Reynold Ludgold repaired part of the chapel.

Robert Coe beautified the chapel.

1630. Lady Walter, at her own cost, did beautify and adorn with carving and gilding the south side of the chapel. Probably the widow of Sir John Walter, Chief Baron of Exchequer, who died in 1630, and whose son was created Baronet in 1641.

1630. William King put up the tablet in the middle of the chapel for the Ten Commandments.

Felix Wilson wainscotted part of the chapel, and put up the King's arms. He was a lawyer, and bought Place Farm, Wraysbury (page 58).

1630. Lady Ursula Salter beautified the south of the chancel. See pedigree, pages 43, 233.

1683. Mr. George Townshend, of Lincoln's Inn, left certain rents in Long Acre for a lectureship, amounting to £101. 10s per annum, see page 288.

1684. Henry Fuller, late of Westminster, grocer, gave towards the repairs of the chapel £50. £20 was paid by Mrs. Martha Fuller, of Clewer, Berks, mother of Mr. Henry Fuller; permitted £30 of the said £50 to be laid out in purchasing two acres of land in Meadfield, Langley Marsh, let to Robert Merry, of Ditton, for 30s per annum, on lease of 99 years, and certain trustees were appointed for receipt of rent, viz. Mr. John Slocomb, William Guy, Robert Bampton, John Burcomb, and John Guy.

The family of Meale was of some standing in the town, several purchases are recorded in the fines and benefactors also. So I put in a short pedigree here, as they were connected with the Higgins' family, considerable proprietors in this locality, and of some respectability.

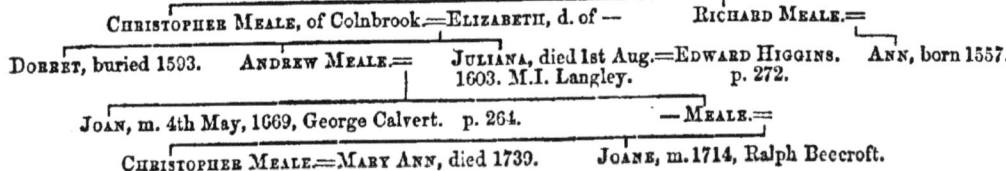

## THE CHURCH OF ST. THOMAS THE APOSTLE.

After the abolition or the abeyance of the Corporation, with its municipalities and rights, the property of the two markets and two fairs not supporting the dignity of the Corporation, it might seem that the maintenance of the Chapel had introduced to the Chapel Wardens a right to the exercise of municipal authority, arising no doubt from the seal of the Corporation having had an impression on it of the Chapel, which formerly stood over the market place. But as these Chapel Wardens had no power to levy a church rate for repairs, which had been within legality had this been a parish, and no supply being left to sustain the edifice, the then Chapel was rebuilt by Thomas Fennel of Colnbrook, which was consecrated by Dr. Prettyman, Bishop of Lincoln, 7th December, 1794, and which in 1834 declined into dilapidation again; but successive repairs has kept it from that neglect which had otherwise precipitated it into utter decay.

In 1840 a new gallery was added to the old church, and in 1842 further repairs were made. This was inadequate to the wants and the stirring increase of piety and zeal manifested in Colnbrook, when it was piously resolved to erect a church worthy of the time, occasion, and locality. Hence in 1848 the edifice dedicated to St. Thomas was begun, and soon finished, and on the 18th June, 1852, it was consecrated by the Bishop of Oxford. The expense of the building was £1521.

In it there are seats for 420 persons, and there are also two schools attached; the structure is of mediæval architecture. It is situated at the entrance to Richings Park, by Mill Lane, Colnbrook, and the acre on which the sacred edifice stands, comprising the cemetery, was purchased of John Augustus Sullivan, Esq., for £100 in 1847. To reach it the passenger goes under a very umbrageous avenue, which extends half a mile, passing a commodious house as residence for the Clergyman, who holds also five acres of glebe land adjacent to this Park, which is now the property of Charles Meeking, Esq., of the City of London, by recent purchase.

At the eastern end of the church is a stone infixed into the wall, on which are these words:—

"This stone of St. Thomas' Church, built by subscription, was laid for Jane Lady Montagu, by Colonel F. Clinton, 25th April, A.D. 1848. Charles Mackenzie, Incumbent. Benjamin Ferry, Architect. Thomas Taylor, Builder."

I shall content myself with giving a superficial description of the structure of the church. It is very light and elegant in its conception, composed of flint and stone outside.

It is open pewed within, with ribs appearing above roofwards, having a gallery on the west side. The communion table is covered with red velvet, on which is a cross in gold; over it at the east is a large and very elaborate stained glass window of three lights, representing various Biblical subjects.

The cemetery is circumscribed, and a wire fence surrounds it, which contains some tombstones indicative of pious devotion, as well from their inscriptions as their shapes.

In very antique characters on cruciform gravestones:—"Here rests the body of Euphemia Harriet Goldie, who fell asleep 26th February, 1860, aged 9 years."

"John Goldie, Esq., deceased 11th June, 1855, aged 88. Also, Elizabeth Georgina Goldie, deceased 23rd April 1849, aged 63."

"Sacred to the memory of Charles Rycroft, died 17th September, 1858, aged 50 years."

The Day and Sunday Schools are under the superintendence of Rev. Charles Dashwood Goldie, and the children constitute a good average. They have an annual entertainment at the commencement of each year.

The Ecclesiastical Commissioners, by an Order in Council, 13th June, 1853, united and consolidated contiguous portions in Iver, Langley Marsh, Horton, Stanwell and Poyle, for forming themselves into one Consolidated Chapelry for ecclesiastical purposes.

The Dissenters, nearly half the town and chiefly Baptists, have meeting houses here, supported mainly from other parishes. There are Congregational chapels at Poyle, and elsewhere in the vicinity, and last year, 1860, a 42nd anniversary was commemorated. In Colnbrook, near the centre on the Horton side, is a meeting house, on it "The Primitive Methodist Chapel. We preach Christ:" and on a stone below, "The foundation stone was laid by Rev. J. Fuller, 4th July, 1859."

The old Parish Registers of St. Thomas' are all lost, and the earliest extant date from the accession of King George III. 1760, The Chapel Wardens elected in 1761 were Thomas Cane and Abraham Grimsdal. The Registers record chiefly the names of the commonalty, very few yeomen, and no one of quality, hence extracts may not prove sufficiently interesting; the records are well preserved.

There are 190 church livings in Buckinghamshire, 28 Particular Baptists, and 121 Dissenting congregations.

As a copy of the Report of the Commissioners appointed to inquire into the state of popular education, for the purpose of obtaining an enumeration of *Dissenters'* schools, was issued in 1861, it may not be irrelevant to offer an abstract.

The returns from Day Schools include 363 from British, 146 from Baptist, 388 from Congregational, and 14 from undenominational schools. 934 schools furnished reports regarding accommodation. The total amount of accommodation is 110,935, viz. British, 46,375; Baptist, 15,449; Congregational, 48,671; unsectarian, 1040. Estimated increase since 1851 shews a total of 27,454, of which 8118 is British, 6510 Baptist, 12,826 Congregational.

As regards Sunday Schools: Baptist 1430 schools, 159,503 scholars, 23,635 teachers.

David Salter, in 1626, gave to the town four substantial ashen staves, tipped with brazen heads, piked with steel, coloured dark and painted with a scutcheon and a red cross on each of them; viz., two taller for the constables and two lower for the headboroughs.

An account of the Incorporation heads the old Town Book, and I add all the recoverable Chapel Wardens, which are dispersed in various places without the least regard to preservation or utility.

## NAMES OF THE CHAPEL WARDENS.

Chosen 28th April, by the common consent of the inhabitants.

1612. John Jeffery, Roger Creker, and Thomas Pytt, overseers for the poor of Langley.
1613. Roger Crockford and Ralphe Gatcombe.
1614. Stephen Mascoll and Henry Osmond.
1615. Henry Shorter and John Kelley.
William Goad and Gilbert Hedworth.
1616. Christopher Chapman and Jeffrey Dawe.
1617. Peter Chapman and Jeffrey Share.
1618. Christopher Meale and Thomas Fowler.
1619. Henry Rawson and John Mudgett.
1620. Thomas Meale and Richard Speed.
1621. Ralphe Ward and Thomas Pitt.
1622. Stephen Mascoll and Thomas Burcombe.
Gilbert Aldworth and Henry Shorter, Collectors for Horton.
1623. William Mascoll and Robert Cooe.
1624. Daniel Salter and Edmund Jeffery.
1625. Andrew Meale and John Mudgett.
1626. Thomas Meale and John Child.
1627. William Goade and Thomas Pitt.
1628. Ditto.
1629. David Salter and Edmund Jeffery.
1630. Thomas Swayne and John Graye.
1631. Edmund Slocomb and Frank Mascoll.
1632. William Peters and Robert Bedell.
1633. John Burton, Reginald Ludgold, and John Atlee.
1634. Ditto.
1635. George Goade and Thomas Porter.
A gap until 1655.

1655. Edmund Board and Henry Goffe.
1656. Edmund Kimber and Edward Chapman.
1657. George Fellow and William Englefield.
1658. Edmund Archer and William Francis.
1659. John Dunt and John Morris.
1660. John Holderness and Thomas Burcomb.
1661. Robert Biddle and William Guy.
1662. Andrew Meale and John Slocombe.
1663. George Fellow and Robert Staninat.
1664. John Holderness and William Englefield.
1665. Ditto.
1666. John Child and William Englefield.
1667. Ditto.
1668. William Guy and William Woodnut. William Lane and Thomas Richardson.
1669. William Mercer and James Squire.
1670. Moses Sedgwick and Robert Cox.
1671. George Fellow and John Fowdge.
1672. Samuel Goade and Roger Eldridge.
1673. Ditto.
1674. Blank.
1675. Ditto.
1676. William Mercer and James Squier.
1677. Thomas Biddle and William Stockley.
1678. Charles Boder and William Mercer.
1679. William Stockley.
1680. Ditto and Thomas Biddle.
1681. Ditto.
1682. Ditto and Isaac Redford.
1683. Ditto.
1684.
1685. Isaac Redford and William Stockley.
1686. Benjamin Fellowes.
1687. Ditto, John Burcomb and Thomas Biddle.
1688. John Burcomb.
1689. Thomas Burcomb.
1690. Ditto.
1691. Ditto.
1692. Ditto, Samuel Hosey and Isaac Redford.
1693. Ditto and ditto.
1694. Samuel Holderness and William Francis.
1695. Ditto.
1696. John Holderness and John Wicherley.
1697. Ditto.
1698. Ditto.
1699. Thomas Dew and William Phillips.
1700. William Phillips.
1701. John Wicherley and John Holderness.

1702. John Wicherley and John Holderness.
1703. Ditto.
1704. Benjamin Fellows and Samuel Hosey.
1705. Ditto.
1706. John Guy and John Burcomb.
1707. Richard How and William Finch.
1708. Ditto.
1709. Ditto and Joseph Fulmer.
1710. Ditto.
1711. Joseph Besouth and John Wells.
1712. Ditto.
1713. Ditto.
1714. Ditto.
1715. George Fellowes and Joseph Oburne.
1716. Ditto.
1717. Ditto.
1718. Ditto.
1719. Ditto and John Burcomb.
1720. Ditto.
1721. Ditto.
1722. Ditto.
1723. Ditto.
1724. Robert Hartwell and John Mason Onley.
1725. Ditto and Thomas Dee.
1726. Ditto.
1727. Ditto and ditto.
1728. Ditto and ditto.
1729. Ditto.
1730. Ditto.
1731.
1732. Thomas Dee and Joseph Rayner.
1733. Ditto.
1734. Ditto.
1735. Ditto.
1736. Ditto, in which year he, Thomas Dee, died; and William Dee and Joseph Rayner, and his accounts were made up by his widow, Ann Dee, who remarried with John Sexton.
1737.
1738.
    Interregnum.
1745. Thomas Fennell and Henry Smither.
1746. Samuel Besouth and Henry Smither.
1747. Ditto.
1748. Ditto and Richard Waring.
1749. Peter Wilson and ditto.
1750. Ditto and Thomas Webb.

1750. Thomas Fennell and Thomas Webb, Overseers of the Poor of Langley.
1751. Ditto.
1752. Thomas Fennell and Richard Hibbard, Surveyor of Highways.
1753. Thomas Fennell and Peter Wilson.
1754. Ditto.
1755. Henry Thompson and Thomas Rayner.
1756. Thomas Fennell and Thomas Webb.
1757. Thomas Fennell and Richard Warring.
1758. John Ashton and William Burcomb.
1759. Ditto and Thomas Cane.
1760. Abraham Grimsdall and Thomas Cane.
1761. Ditto and Thomas Ogilvy.
1762. Ditto.
1763 to 1770. Joel Hethering and John Maxwell. Here an unfortunate *vacuum* occurs of 70 years, and not a trace of who were Chapel Wardens until 1840.
1840. George Andrews and Samuel Oak.
1841. George Andrews and ditto.
1842. Ditto.
1843. James Laurence and Samuel Oak.
1844. Ditto.
1845. Ditto.
1846. Ditto.
1847. Joseph Bland, Gent. and James Laurence, Gent.
1848. Ditto, James Laurence, Gent., and George Paterson, Esq.
1849. Ditto.
1850. Ditto.
1851. Ditto.
1852. Henry Jones and James Small.
1853. Ditto.
1854. Ditto.
1855. Ditto and Frederick Westrup.
1856. Ditto.
1857. Ditto.
1858. Ditto and Vernon Hemmingway.
1859. Ditto.
1860. Henry Hickman and Henry Jones.
1861. Ditto.

Despite the neglected condition of the records of Colnbrook, we here recede further back than in the analogous Wardens of either Wraysbury or Horton—the difference is in the *quality* of the officers, the latter being more frequently composed of the class *Yeoman*, whom Fuller said, was a gentleman in *ore*, whom the next age may see *refined*, while the Colnbrook Wardens have been mainly composed of tradesmen, all doubtless of credit and renown.

## RAILWAY.

As the Railway, to which we have already adverted, p. 153-273—"Men's wings with which they make speed"—passes near Colnbrook, we advert to it again. The word Tram-way is said to be derived from Mr. Outram, father of Sir James Outram, and founder of the Butterley Iron Works, Herefordshire.

Just beyond Drayton the railway crosses the many-channelled Colne, which here divides Middlesex and Bucks,—

"Now as the Thames is great, so more transparent Colne
Feels with excessive joy her amorous bosom swoll'n."

And then it passes between farms and fields on the left, and low ground intersected by ditches and studded with ponds covered with duckweed, into a shallow cutting, emerging into the midst of cornfields and a wide expanse of pasture land, varied by irregular rows of tall branchless trees, with burly crowns of thick foliage.

Langley Station is 16 miles from London, and for a short distance beyond the line is skirted by brickfields, but they soon give place to open fields on both sides of the line, where cattle graze in profusion; and as the train thunders by the horses start and hastily retreat, the young colts become frolicksome, and give salutes with their heels.

About a mile on the right is the mansion at Langley Park, with its background of dark firs, "the Black Park." This introduces us to a district famous in English literature by the genius of Pope, Addison, Gay, Congreve, and Gray, p. 280.

Towering in the distance is regal Windsor, and near at hand the spot where Pope, in his youthful promise, wrote Windsor Forest; and away to the right is Stoke Poges, the scene of the "Elegy in a Country Churchyard." At Slough Station is the Windsor junction, just beyond which is Salt Hill, where until lately the Eton youths held their Montem, or the annual procession to the Hill, which custom began in the 18th century. It was discontinued in 1847. This was a scene of *jubilee* for the aspirants after college honours, and they revered the *Mons Sacer* of Eton like Epaminondas, who kissed his shield as the instrument of his glory and his labours. Here the youths innocently played the *Highwaymen*, and by virtue of *frolicksome artifice* extracting the *sterling* treasure, many deserve to have their names and feats recorded in that popular work, "Johnson's Lives of Highwaymen," who ventures and details biographical notices of these *minions of the moon*, from the days of Robin Hood and Sir John Falstaff to our own times—their genealogies and traditional stories are as manifold as the thefts of Mercury among the heathen—and the volume points the moral by graphic descriptions of their mournful exits from this ball of earth. Every exclusive pretension is a usurpation which encroaches on the claims or rights of others, hence the glory of the *Montem* passed away when it was no longer consonant with the feelings of the times.

The line quits Slough through a low cutting, and the traveller soon catches a glimpse of the square tower of Burnham Church, adjacent to the famous beeches, trees which have outlived the eagles, and like the Pyramids themselves doting with age, have forgotten the names of those who planted them, yet are still so dear to artists for the sylvan beauty of the scenery around, and such a favourite resort for the silken children of pleasure, who here, *sub Dio*, celebrate their pic-nic assemblages, after feasting the senses on the floricultural delights of Dropmore, the Adonis' gardens of the locality.

Hence in brief time, and with a moderate exercise of patience, we reach the next stations, which are at Maidenhead and Taplow; the latter was heretofore the residence of the present Earl of Orkney, and is now in the possession of the Grenfell family, descendants of Pascoe Grenfell, Esq., sometime connected with Wraysbury, page 73. Here the passenger crosses the Thames on a graceful stone bridge of some repute, constructed with curious flat arches, each 130 feet in span. The silver stream with its course is broken by green eyots, and from this engaging spot are discerned the towers of Bray Church, and the circumjacent heights—

> "Then hand in hand her Thames the forest softly brings
> To that supremest place of the great English Kings,
> The Garter's royal seat, from him who did advance
> That princely order first, our first that conquered France—
> The temple of St. George, whereat his honoured knights
> Upon his hallowed day observe their ancient rites—
> Where Eton is at hand to nurse that learned brood,
> To keep the Muses still near to the princely flood."
>
> *Drayton, 15th Song, Polyolbion.*

As the town of Eton and its College were connected with Ankerwycke, we have adverted to it, page 32; but it may not be uninteresting to know the numerical status of the school. We give the returns of Eton College for 1861, viz., 828, the highest number ever attained; so likewise in rank,

Eton never exhibited a more illustrious catalogue of nobility and gentry of the first eminence, united with the issue of nature's nobles, sons of science. Perhaps it would be politic to keep the school at its present average, unless its buildings and accommodations extended much beyond the existing area. Excess is worse than defect sometimes, and if the school should get beyond the reach of management it would lose golden opinion, which is the great pillar that upholds it, as well as other institutions of Great Britain.

## HORTON AND COLNBROOK FINES AND RECOVERIES.

The earliest fines do not reach beyond the time of King John, 1200; they are arranged in terms, Hilary, Easter, Trinity, Michaelmas.

5 John, 1203, Roll 93. Fine between William Prior of Merton, Surrey, and William de Wyndleshore, about an acre of land and a croft styled Rudding in West Horseley parish, Surrey. William Wyndleshore gave to the convent of St. Mary of Merton and the Canonesses, the lands which Geoffrey son of Okey hath in Horton, with all the waste thereto belonging; also 2 acres attached to the demesnes styled Buttes, with the closes and all the appurtenances (tota sequela sua) besides other property.

6 John, 1204, Easter term. Between Richard de Hakeburne and William Wendleshore, lands in Horton.

14 John, Roll 147, 1212. Between Hamond son of Henry Rex (the king) and William de Windleshore, a tenement and a virgate of land in Horton, and a mill and 3 acres of land.

15 John, 1213, —— son of Henry de Windleshore, lands and tenements in Horton.

7 Henry III. 1222, 3rd October. Excerpts of Rolls, Vol. I. p. 107, is an account of Roger, son and heir of Hugh de Sancto Vedasto, who made a fine for 30 marks about the manor of Colebrok, which belonged to Sancto Vedasto his father, deceased. The name of Henry de Colevil is cited in the deed. Given at Mugumi. N.B.—This deed does not specify Colebrok in Bucks, but the name only. It may be in Devonshire; both proper names are spelt the same way, and both are termed manors, p. 301. 1726.

8 Henry III. 1223, Easter. William de Wendleshore and Geoffrey de Mauriscis, lands here and in Wraysbury, &c.

9 Henry III. 1224, Trin. William de Gambrun and his wife v. Richard de Thorntagia and wife, lands in Horton.

16 Henry III. 1231, Mich. Thomas Abbot of Ruttlesdon, v. Walter de Horton, lands here.

25 Henry III. 1240, Hil. John fil. Regis v. Andrew, son of John of Horton, lands there.

39 Henry III. Mich. 1254. William, son of Theodulph and his wife, v. Walter de la Halle in Horton.

41 Henry III. Mich. 1256. Alice de Middleton v. Alexander, son of Richard de Langley, Horton.

45 Henry III. Easter, 1260, Roll 64. Between Eustace, Prior of Merton, Surrey, and Henry Maunsel and Joan his wife, about 13s 6d rents and appurtenants in Horton and Wexham.

46 Henry III. 1261, Roll 46. Between John, son of Walter de Horton and Richard de Oxeheye, whom Hugh, vicar of the Church of Wraysbury, calls to warrant, and to whom he is bail for two messuages, 2 virgates, 4 acres of land, 2 acres of meadow in Horton. N.B.—In the list of Wraysbury Rectors the name of Hugh does not occur; probably brother of Joan, wife of R. de Oxey, children of William Windsor, who died 1275, p. 106.

51 Henry III. 1266, Trin. Roll 92. Aunger de Chauncumbe and Joan his wife v. Ada de Maunsel, deforciant of lands in Horton and Langley.

3 Edward I. 1274, Mich. Lucas de Baton of the city of London, about a mill in Culbrok.

8 Edward I. 1279, Easter. Between William Karliolo and his wife v. Guy de Culbrok and his wife, about messuages there.

7 Edward I. 1278, Trin. Hugh, son of Hugh de Dychon and Alexander de Weyte and wife, lands, &c. Horton.

9 Edward I. 1280, Trin. Peter de Middleton and Robert de Middleton, messuage and lands, Horton.

12 Edward I. 1283, Trin. Henry, son of Guy de Culbrok, v. Guy de Culbrok, messuage, lands, tenements at Colnbrook.

13 Edward I. 1284, East. John de Scoteny and Nicholas de Crosier and wife, lands and tenements in Horton.

20 Edward I. 1291, Trin. John de Remenham and wife, v. John de la Halle, lands, &c. Horton and Wexham.

34 Edward I. 1305, Hil. Margaret, daughter of Edmund le Foghclere v. Edmund le Foghclere, Horton.

2 Edward II. 1328, Mich. John, son of Richard de Cadomo, v. William Thobiner de Wyselech, manor and advowson of Horton. Richard de Cadomo presents to the living of Horton in 1306. In 3 Henry III. 1218, fine was levied between Walter de Cadomo and Mary his wife, and Robert de Norfolk her son. She was daughter of Alexander Fitz Jorbauld.—Blomfield's Norfolk, Vol. X. p. 450.

4 Edward III. 1330, Mich. Richard de Cantelo of Horton, and his wife, v. Simon Russel and Stephen his brother, messuages, lands, rents, in Horton.

6 Edward III. 1332, Hil. Robert Pogys and his son Peter Pogys, v. Richard, son of Alexander of Datchet, messuages and lands in Mora (the marsh) at Datchet.

7 Edward III. 1333, Hil. John, son of Henry Christian, sen. v. Henry Christian of Horton, messuages and lands.

8 Edward III. 1334, East. William Karliolo and wife v. Guy de Colbrok and wife, lands, &c. in Colnbrook.

10 Edward III. 1335, Hil. William de Eyre of Langley, and wife, v. John de Taunton and wife, of London, messuages, lands, rents, &c. in 3 virgates, Horton and Langley.

11 Edward III. 1336, Trin. Thomas Prys and wife v. Peter de Middleton and wife, lands in Horton.

11 Edward III. 1337, Mich. Thomas, son of Richard Aunger, of Horton, v. Richard Aunger, messuages and lands there.

12 Edward III. 1338, Easter. Thomas Purchas (Purcha-cœur of Langley) v. Simon le Fullere of Yevely (Yeoveny, Middlesex) and wife, lands in Horton.

12 Edward III. 1338, Trin. Henry, son of Guy of Colbrok, v. Guy of ditto, mill and rent in Colnbrook.

12 Edward III. 1338, Easter. Imbertius de Scoteneye v. William Woodyat and wife, lands in Datchet.

12 Edward III. 1338, Easter. Robert Pogeys and Peter his son v. John de Bulstrode and wife, lands, &c. in Datchet.

39 Edward III. 1357, Mich. Sir Roger de Louthe, High Sheriff of Essex, 1358, and Robert Tame and wife, manor of Horton.

39 Edward III. 1365, Trin. John Louthe Turkeys, of Ditton, and William Brown of Horton, lands.

41 Edward III. 1367, Hil. William Seryth and his wife, of Horton, *v.* John atte Hall and wife, of Chetyndone, messuage and lands there.

41 Edward III. 1367, Hil. John Spelyng, Clerk, *v.* John atte Melve and wife, messuage and in Horton.

43 Edward III. 1369, Easter. John de Dratton and Henry Rabbe and ux., lands in Horton and Ditton.

44 Edward III. 1370. William Blakemore and William Brown and wife, Horton, messuages and lands.

47 Edward III. 1373. William Blacamore and wife *v.* Richard Fucour and wife, messuage and lands in Horton.

48 Edward III. 1374. Robert Heggeman de Kyngeston (Kingston) and others *v.* William le Thorpe and wife, of Langley, messuages in Horton.

3 Richard II. 1379, Trin. Robert Bathelye and wife *v.* John Creting and wife, lands in Horton and Iver.

4 Richard II. 1380, Easter. John Lambyn of Colbrok *v.* Thomas Herby of Colbrok, messuage, lands, garden, in Horton.

10 Richard II. 1386, Trin. John Wytton and wife *v.* John Waryn of Colbrok and wife, messuage there.

3 Henry IV. 1401, Mich. Richard Wyot and others *v.* Dionysia, widow of Richard Overton, messuage, lands, rents, Horton, probably related to John Wyot, collated to Horton Rectory, 1404.

11 Henry IV. 1409, Easter. Thomas Chaucer and others *v.* Robert Chichele, citizen and grocer of London, lands in Horton, see page 231.

9 Henry V. 1421, Hil. Richard Wyot and John Colesmore and others *v.* William Braveneye, messuage and lands in Langley and Horton.

6 Henry VI. 1427, Hil. Richard Wyot and others *v.* Thomas Say and Lawrence Dru and wife, about the manor of Horton and the advowson.

24 Henry VIII. 1532, Trin. William Sparry and William Wheler *v.* Reginald Dygby, Esq. and Ann his wife, advowson and manor of Horton, and property in Colebroke, Langley, Iver, and Wraysbury.

27 Henry VIII. 1535, Hil. John Wylliams, Esq. *v.* Simon Maynville, lands in Langley, Horton, Iver.

29 Henry VIII. 1537, Hil. Thomas Langley, Esq. *v.* Thomas Garleke, of Horton, yeoman. There are two deeds also relating to Brickhill, Bucks.

34 Henry VIII. 1544. Sir Andrew Wyndsor *v.* Reginald Digby, Esq., tenement, &c. in Horton.

6 Edward VI. 1553. Ralph Brome, Esq. and others *v.* Ann Digby, widow, deforciant of the manor of Horton, with appurtenants in Colebroke, &c. and advowson of the Church of Horton. This Ralph Brome married Alice, daughter of Reginald Digby, son of Sir Nicholas Brome, son of John Brome of Baddisley, Warwick.

3 Elizabeth, 1560. George Edwards *v.* Thomas Wyche, tenements in Langley Marsh and Horton. At the same time a fine between George Edwards and Henry Balnet, tenements in Langley Marsh, Horton and Wraysbury.

1563. James Mascall and Anthony Maxey, gentleman, tenements in Langley and Colnbroke.

1569. Edward Windsor, Esq. *v.* Ambrose Digby, Esq. senior, deed of recovery about certain rents and annates with George Digby in Horton, Colebroke and Langley.

1579. Francis Haynes and George Woodward, gentleman, tenements in Horton. George Woodward was nephew of Thomas Bulstrode, who died 1560, p. 215.

1588. Richard Tredway, Esq. and John Chamberlayne, Esq. manor of Stoke Poges. William Higgins, gentleman, and John Chamberlayne, tenements in Colnbrook.

1591. Edmund Rawson and Robert Mascall, tenement in Colnbrook. Ditto, fine with Thomas Heydon and Richard Mascall. George Croke, Esq. v. Edmund Bulstrode, Esq. Horton. Robert Cawcott and others v. James Haynes, tenement in Horton.

1594. William Peters and Sir Michael Blount, tenement in Horton. William Marsham and John Pennar, Esq. v. William Peters, 4 messuages, 4 gardens, 100 acres of land, 100 ditto, 4 ditto pasture, 4 wood, 10 briar, &c. 12s rent in Horton, Wraysbury, Iver, Stoke Poges, &c.

1595. Thomas Edwards and George Edwards, property in Horton.

1602. Sir William Bulstrode and Nicholas Georgye, gentleman, v. John Gyles, gentleman, and John Woodward, gentleman, 15 messuages, 10 cottages, 15 gardens, 500 acres arable, 80 open, 200 pasture, 300 wood, 40 briar, &c. Upton, Wexham, Iver, Datchet, Horton, &c.

2 James I. 1604. William Peters, gentleman, and George Higgins, gentleman (he held two inns at Colnbrook), tenements in Colnbrook, &c. John Bowser, gentleman, and Henry Bulstrode, tenements in Horton.

1605. Sir Michael Greene, Kt. v. Henry Rysley, gentleman, manor of Mansfield, recapitulating divers pieces in Iver, Langley, Horton. Vouchee, William Durwant. A Michael Greene was Yeoman of the Stirrup to Queen Elizabeth. Family of Risley descend from William Risley, temp. Henry VIII. The last, Paul Risley, died 1755, sp.

1606. Abigail Digby, widow, v. Robert Digby, tenements in Horton and Colnbrook.

1608. Thomas Woodward, gentleman, and Sir Michael Greene, Kt., Colnbrook.

1611. Sir John Jackson, Kt. v. Abigail Digby, Colnbrook.

1613. John Brocket, Esq. v. Edmund Salter, gentleman, Horton. Sir Thomas Cheney, Kt. v. Henry Cheney, Horton. Henry Shorter and Sir Robert Digby, Kt., Colnbrook.

1614. David Salter, gentleman, v. William Staunton, tenements in Horton.

1617. Henry Bulstrode, Esq. and Sir Richard Digby, defendant of the manor of Horton. Bartholomew Beale, gentleman, and William Robson, gentleman, v. Charles Docket, gentleman, and William Denys, Esq., manor of Wapeling and Cornwallis, Iver, Langley, Wraysbury, Colnbrook, Horton. Vouchee, Edmund Waller, Esq.

1618. Henry Rawson v. H. Bulstrode, Esq., Horton and Iver. Felix Wilson, gentleman, v. H. Bulstrode, manor of Horton, 14 acres waste, 4 cottages, 10 gardens, 300 acres of land, 50 ditto, 400 briar, with money rents in Horton, Langley, Wraysbury, &c. with advowson of Horton. Vouchee, Sir Robert Digby.

1620. Richard Hopkins v. John Hopkins, Horton.

1624. H. Bulstrode, Esq. v. George Edwards, Horton. Richard Smith v. Richard Newman, Horton. Felix Wilson, gentleman, and Joseph Lane v. H. Bulstrode, Esq., 1 messuage, 1 garden, 30 acres of land, &c. Horton, Wraysbury, Langley. Vouchee, George Cowardelow.

1627. John Thornton v. Thomas Hobbe, Horton.

1628. George Hatch v. John Goodyear, in Colnbrook.

1633. Henry Bulstrode, Esq. v. John Reeve, Horton. Henry Bulstrode, Esq. and Samuel Enderby, Horton. Philip Smyth, Esq. v. H. Bulstrode, Esq., one messuage, one garden, 12 acres arable, 25 pasture, Horton and Wraysbury.

1634. Robert Biddle v. John Shorter, Colnbrook.

1636. H. Bulstrode, Esq. and George Goade, Colnbrook. Edmund Bulstrode, Esq. and

Richard Edwards v. Edward Woodward, gentleman, 18 messuages, garden, 200 acres of land, 40 pasture, 60 pasture, Horton, Colnbrook, Wraysbury. Vouchee, Thomas Bulstrode, Esq.

1637. Michael Webb v. John Pitt, senior, Colnbrook.

1641. Robert Hall v. Thomas Bulstrode, Esq. in Horton. By another fine, the manor of Horton is sold to Robert Hall. Thomas Knight and H. Allen v. Robert Hall and Thomas Tredway, one messuage, 100 acres land, 20 waste, &c. Horton, &c. Vouchee, Thomas Bulstrode, Esq.

1645. Christopher Salter, Esq. v. John Peters, senior, gentleman, Colnbrook.

1646. Elizabeth Draper, widow, v. Thomas Bulstrode, Esq. in Horton.

1647. Thomas Knight, Esq. v. Thomas Bulstrode, Esq., in Horton.

1648. Anthony Cheney, Esq. v. John Abolee, in Colnbrook. William Fletcher v. Thomas Bulstrode, Esq. Horton. John Hall, gentleman, and Richard Price v. William Fletcher, Humfry Ford, Nicholas Bonfoy, 7 messuages and 40 pasture, 26 acres land, &c. Horton. Vouchee, Thomas Bulstrode, Esq.

1649. John Hemes v. Richard Reeve, Horton. Edward Porter v. John Peters, gentleman, Horton and Colnbrook. Francis Ridley, gentleman, v. Henry Rawson, Langley and Colnbrook. Francis Gillowe, gentleman, and Robert Hall, gentleman, v. Edmund Slocombe, Horton and Colnbrook. Vouchee, John Peters, junior. William Drier or Drey, gentleman, v. Francis Ridley, gentleman, 5 messuages, 2 mills, 6 gardens, 100 acres land, 20 waste, 30 pasture, in Langley and Colnbrook.

1650. Philip Seely, gentleman, v. Edward Goodwyn, gentleman, Langley, Colnbrook. Paul Day and Mariot his wife, vouchees. Daniel Coxe, gentleman, v. Thomas Bulstrode, Esq., Horton Manor and Church. Richard Ireland, gentleman, v. Henry Wyatt, gentleman, Colnbrook. Edward Goodall, gentleman, v. Thomas Bulstrode, Esq., Horton. Edward Goodyear v. —— Baye, Colnbrook.

1651. John Dutton and Edmund Slocombe v. Eleanor Price, 8 messuages, 8 gardens, Colnbrook, Horton. John Guy v. John Peters, gentleman, Colnbrook. John Haynes v. Francis Haynes, Horton.

1654. Thomas West and Richard Hall, Horton.

1655. Edward Morgan and Andrew Meale, Colnbrook.

1656. Thomas Wycherley v. Benjamin Hobbes, Colnbrook.

1657. Robert Childe, gentleman, v. John Goodyeare, Horton. Edward Slocomb and Charles Durdant, Horton.

1657. John Lee, gentleman (of Ankerwycke), and Ann, widow of Richard West, Horton. John Wadlow and Andrew Meale, gentleman, of Iver. John Wadlow and Henry Wyatt, Colnbrook. John Hosey v. Richard Smith, Colnbrook.

1658. John Salter and David Salter, Agmondesham. Edmund Slocombe v. Mary Hawkins, Langley Marsh.

1659. Thomas Hasel v. Leonard Bower, Langley Marsh. John Ladbroke v. Francis Ridley, gentleman, and others, and Chapman Meale, &c. Colnbrook.

1660. William Goddard v. Robert Wynch, Esq. proprietor, in Horton and Colnbrook.

1661. Clement Peters, gentleman, v. Oliver Pretty, Horton. Beatrice Guy, widow (John Guy) v. Robert Withey, Horton.

1662. William Guy v. Jos. Mone, Colnbrook.

1663. Thomas Chesterman, gentleman, v. Michael Sawyer, manor of Missenden, comprising many other places in Bucks, with Horton and Iver. Vouchee, Marmaduke Darell, Esq. Thomas West v. Robert Hall, Horton. Timothy West v. Thomas Bulstrode, Esq. Horton.

1664. James Seymour, senr. *v.* Richard Hall, Horton.

1666. John Durdant and George Cooke *v.* George Smith and William Peters, 3 messuages, 6 gardens, 160 acres arable, 15 meadow, 20 pasture, Burnham, Cippenham, Boveney, Dorney, Horton.

1667. Rose Seely *v.* Joseph Seeley, Colnbrook.

1668. Sir Purbeck Temple, Knt. *v.* John Haynes, Horton. Sir Purbeck was of Surrey and died 1695, sp. See page 71.

1669. John Duncomb, gentleman *v.* Thomas Bulstrode, Esq. Horton. Richard Dogget, gentleman *v.* John June ats. Hopkins, Horton.

1670. James Smyth *v.* Thomas Bulstrode, Esq. Hall, and others, Horton.

1671. Edward Horseman *v.* Thomas Bulstrode, Esq. Horton. Stephen Holland *v.* T. Southermond, Harris, and others, Colnbrook.

1672. Richard Parrey *v.* Ralph Ward, Chambers, and others, Colnbrook.

1673. John Paynter *v.* Thomas Berenger, Esq. Horton.

1674. James Seymour, senr. *v.* William Lane, Horton.

1675. George Hearne *v.* Edmund Hearne, 1 messuage, 4 gardens, 16 acres arable, 9 meadow, 9 pasture, Horton. Vouchee, Charles Peters, gentleman. Edward Hearne *v.* Charles Peters, gentleman, Horton. William Atlee *v.* Edward Hearne, Horton.

1677. Robert Bampton *v.* John Slocomb, 5 messuages, 10 gardens, 5 acres arable, 18 meadow, 8 pasture, in Horton and Wraysbury. Vouchee, Charles Peters, gentleman.

1679. William Hale *v.* John Slocombe, Horton. William Stockley *v.* Charles Salter, gentleman, Colnbrook. John Lee (Ankerwyke) *v.* Thomas Berenger, Esq. Colnbrook. Ditto, fine in Langley.

1680. Thomas Burcomb *v.* Guy Fisher, Colnbrook.

1681. Richard Burt *v.* John Tunstall, gent. Ashton, and others, Horton.

1682. John Slocombe *v.* John Goddard, Horton.

1683. Edward Camock *v.* H. Lewthall, Colnbrook. William Dunt *v.* William Herbert, Colnbrook.

1687. Thomas Hinton, gent. *v.* Thomas Childe, gent. the manor of Horton, with appurtenances, 6 messuages, 1 mill, 12 gardens, 160 acres arable, 24 meadow, 34 pasture, 6 acres of water course; 40s rent and frankpledge, Horton, Wraysbury, Colnbrook, Datchet, Upton, Iver, with the advowson of Horton Church. Vouchee, Edmund Swatkin, Esq. William Hale *v.* Abel Sorrel, Horton.

1688. Samuel Corbet, gent. *v.* William Hale, 2 messuages, 3 gardens, &c. Horton. Vouchee, Abel Daniel.

1689. Henry Guy, Esq. *v.* — Leigh, Knt. 4 messuages, 3 gardens, 50 acres arable, 20 meadow, 30 pasturage, Horton, Iver, Wraysbury.

1690. Francis Neale, gent. *v.* Samuel Bowry, the moiety of a messuage, 3 gardens, 10 acres arable, 127 meadow, 10 pasture, in Horton. Vouchee, Edmund Hearne. Ambrose Adkins *v.* John Slocombe, Horton. Samuel Bowry *v.* Dinah Hearne, widow, Horton.

1691. Sir Purbeck Temple, Knt. *v.* Edward Martin, Horton.

1692. Thomas Rowe, gent. *v.* John Scawen, Clerk, Horton.

1693. Ambrose Adkyns *v.* Henry Ashton, senr. — Hey and others, Horton. Aaron Sedgwick *v.* Edward Nicholas, Esq. Colnbrook.

1694. Owen Buckingham *v.* John Slocombe, Colnbrook. Jane Porter *v.* William Dunt, Colnbrook.

1695. John Duncombe v. John Slocombe, Colnbrook. Ambrose Adkyns v. John Slocombe, Horton. Samuel Leving, gent. v. Charles Meale, Hoskins and others, Colnbrook.

1696. Josias Darby v. John Hassell, gent. 2 messuages, 4 gardens, 26 acres arable, 7 meadow, 12 pasture, in Wraysbury and Horton. Vouchee, William Peake and Susan his wife, and Frances Fryar, widow.

1698. Thomas Rayner v. John Wycherley, jun. Colnbrook.

1699. Samuel Holderness v. William Johnson, West Blackwell, Horton.

1700. William Virgoe and William Darvell v. John Wycherley and wife, Colnbrook. Elizabeth Woodman, widow, v. John Madison, senr.—Taunton and wife, Colnbrook. Samuel Biddle, gentleman v. Thomas Robins, gentleman, the moiety of 1 messuage, 5 gardens, 7 acres arable, 9 meadow, in Horton. Vouchee, Edmund Hearne.

1701. Thomas Horsnaill, gentleman, v. George Levenlake, manor of Mansfield, appurtenants in Iver, Langley, Horton, Cheping Wycombe v. Richard Grive, gentleman.

1702. William Thompson v. Samuel Bazeley and wife, Colnbrook.

1703. John Mitcham v. Robert Briggs and wife, Horton.

1704. Henry Aldridge v. Thomas Mitcham, Horton.

1706. Robert Butler v. Robert Hopkins ats. Jane, Horton.

1707. John Tolen v. Benjamin Fellow, Colnbrook.

1709. Ellis Trippick v. John Hicks, — Fellows, &c. Horton.

1712. John Meres and Aaron Gibbs v. John Robinson, Horton.

1715. Robert Hoppert v. Edmund Bulpett, Roger Edridge, Horton.

1716. William Russell v. Richard Wormer, Horton. John Stevenson v. John Ashley, Horton.

1717. John Herbert v. Robert Beecroft, Colnbrook. Henry Bird v. Elizabeth Priddith and others, Colnbrook.

1718. William Wigginton v. Francis Sweeting, John Gisborne, Horton.

1720. George Fellowes, John Cooke, Charles Bowler, Joseph Ingram, property in Colnbrook.

1722. John Herbert v. Mark Beecroft and wife, Horton. Samuel Swenfen, gentleman, and William Cornish, gentleman, v. Sir Thomas Scawen, Knt. manor of Horton, Rectory House, and advowson of the church. Daniel Cock v. William Martin, Horton.

1723. John Hackshaw, Esq. v. John Marcham, John Style, Horton.

1725. John Gibbons, gentleman, v. William Noyes, senr. Horton. Emanuel Caton v. John Westall and wife, Colnbrook. Sir John Shelley, Bart. v. William Gascarth, gentleman, manor of Horton, 6 messuages, 130 acres of land, 50 meadows, 30 pastures, courts leet and baron, and frankpledge, Horton, Colnbrook, Langley, Datchet, Upton, Iver, with advowson of Horton. Vouchees, Sir Thomas Walkden and Thomas Walkden.

1726. Marshe Biddinson, gentleman, v. William Besley, gentleman, manor of Wordington and *Manor* of Colnbrook. Vouchee, Maurice Hunt, Esq. John Herbert v. Ralph Beecroft and wife moiety of property in Colnbrook. See p. 295. 7 Henry III. 1222, where Colnbrook is termed manor.

1727. Samuel Holderness v. Edward Borrett, gentleman, 4 gardens and 50 acres of land, Horton and Wraysbury. Vouchee, Stephen West.

1730. John Guy v. Samuel Foster, gentleman, Colnbrook and Langley Marsh. Vouchee, William Guy.

1731. William Gibbs v. Richard Perrott and his wife, Horton.

1734. Joseph Fulmer, junr. v. John Guy, Horton.

1735. Richard Brewer v. Michael Cooke, Horton.

1736. Lazarus Holderness *v.* Stephen West, Horton and Wraysbury.

1737. Daniel Foster *v.* Thomas Davies, William Thomas Smith and Richard Humber, Langley and Horton.

1739. John Virgo *v.* William Haynes, Horton.

1740. Christopher Blunt *v.* Morgan Slaughter and wife, Langley and Horton.

1741. Henry Bullock *v.* Stephen West, Colnbrook. Thomas Fennell *v.* William Galloway, Colnbrook. John Howell, Esq. *v.* Thomas Cater, gentleman, Langley and Horton. Vouchee, Hannah Langton, widow.

1742. Samuel Anderson *v.* Edward Anderson, Colnbrook. Thomas Bonfoy, Esq. *v.* Robert Palmer, gentleman, Iver, Langley Marsh, Colnbrook. Vouchee, Ann Williams, widow. John Tasker, junr. gentleman, *v.* Thomas Newsome, gentleman, moiety of 4 messuages, 4 gardens, 60 acres land, 20 meadow, 40 pasture, Horton. Vouchee, Francis Leigh, Esq.

1745. William Camden, gentleman, *v.* Charles Saltmarsh, 1 messuage, 1 toft, 2 gardens, about 40 acres of land, Horton and Wraysbury. Vouchee, Mary Binfield, widow.

1746. John Liming *v.* John Grove, Colnbrook.

1747. Charles Owen, gentleman, *v.* Thomas Powell, junr. Esq. and Harcourt Powell, Esq. Langley, Iver, Colnbrook.

1748. William Brookland, Esq. Elizabeth, widow of Lazarus Holderness, Philip Garden and wife, and Ann Holderness, Colnbrook, Langley, Horton. Richard Howell *v.* Joseph Child, Colnbrook.

1752. John Norton *v.* John Herbert and Mary his wife, Horton, Langley, Datchet. Duchess Dowager of Somerset *v.* Hugh Earl of Northumberland and Elizabeth his wife, lands in Iver, Langley, Colnbrook.

1753. Joseph Fullmar *v.* Joseph Fellowes and Grace his wife, Colnbrook. James Mills, Francis Tegg and Mary his wife *v.* John Bigg and Susan his wife, Colnbrook.

1754. William Markland, gentleman, *v.* Benjamin Chaplin and Ann his wife, Colnbrook.

1755. Thomas Haywood, Esq. *v.* Hugh Earl of Northumberland and Elizabeth his wife, Iver, Colnbrook. John Paterson, Esq. *v.* John Maxwell and Sarah his wife, and John Guy, Horton and Langley. Richard Blunt and Robert Wills *v.* John Patterson, Esq. and Richard Beale, gentleman, 10 messuages, 6 gardens, 40 acres of land, &c. Horton, Langley. Vouchee, John Guy.

1756. Samuel Tapscot, gentleman, *v.* Richard Hodgson and Ann his wife, Horton and Colnbrook. William Cobbett, gentleman, *v.* William Tyrrel, gentleman, Horton. Vouchee, Edward Hearne, gentleman.

1758. William Lucas, Esq. *v.* James Lucas, gentleman, Horton, Langley. Vouchee, Jocelyn Farrington, gentleman, who calls Hannah Farrington. John Turnhoe, gentleman, *v.* Holland Cookney, Esq. and Elizabeth his wife, Horton.

1759. Thomas Scawen, Esq. and James Scawen, Esq. are vouchees to some property in Boveney and Cippenham. Richard Standish *v.* Richard Hodgson and Ann his wife, Horton and Colnbrook. Algernon Percy, Esq. *v.* Hugh Earl of Northumberland and Elizabeth his wife, Iver, Langley, Colnbrook.

1769. Indenture between Neale William Townshend and John Barther, lands in Horton, 27th November. Ditto, John Barther, gentleman, *v.* William Townshend, gentleman, Horton. Vouchee, William Meale.

1778. Samuel Duplock, gentleman, *v.* Thomas Winckley, gentleman, the manor of Horton, 6 messuages, 1 dovehouse, 130 acres of land, 50 meadow, 30 pasture, 30 wood, Courts of Leet and

Baron, views of frankpledge, with appurtenants in Horton, Colnbrook and Langley, &c. with advowson of Horton Church. Vouchee, James Scawen, Esq.

1788. Leonard Housen, gentleman, *v*. Robert Woodgate, gentleman, Horton. Vouchee, Holland Cooksey and Elizabeth his wife, and Richard Cooksey.

1794. Cornthwaite Ommaney, Admiral, *v*. William Johnson, gentleman, the manor of Wraysbury, 10 messuages, 4 dovecots, 20 gardens, 300 acres of land, 100 meadow, 100 pasture, 50 wood, 200 furze heath, common of pasture, free fishing, liberty of foldage, Courts Leet and Baron, view of frankpledge in Wraysbury and Horton. Vouchee, John Simon Harcourt, Esq.

1803. Henry Hoyle Oddie, gentleman, *v*. John Foster, 1 messuage, 2 gardens, 12 acres of land, 8 meadow, 8 pasture, Horton and Wraysbury. Vouchee, Charles William Montagu, Earl of Dalkeith.

1830. Thomas Tilson *v*. Barry Parr Sequance, gentleman, 10 messuages, 6 gardens, 10 acres of land, 10 meadow, 10 pasture, &c. Horton and Langley Marsh. Vouchee, Richard Blunt Guy.

## PUBLIC RECORDS.

The public is much indebted to Mr. Abbot, Speaker of the House of Commons, subsequently Lord Colchester, for turning his attention to the state of the national records, and obtaining the appointment of the Royal Commissioners, who have effected the most careful preservation and accurate arrangement of these documents, and have made them more accessible to all who search their treasures. To Sir Francis Palgrave (one who did not overflow with zeal without knowledge or experience, at whose instance chiefly the *entire* deeds of the kingdom were deposited under *one* roof, now under the superintendence of Thomas Duffus Hardy, Esq.) perhaps, the greatest literary boon as a privilege that the public ever received is due, who obtained from Government the reasonable permission for all engaged in historical pursuits to search *gratuitously* the muniments of the realm which interest the public; but not the officials, who hitherto had with jealousy excluded the public, to whom these records belong, as far as investigations go—otherwise they were as good as if lodged under Mount Etna, or put into *flames*, as it is asserted at the time of the republic some modern *Goths* suggested. The public records of France were partially burnt at the period of the Revolution, and the same disaster took place at Edinburgh, so what by private conflagrations and public violence or corrosion, and the brush of time, some of the most precious documents, quite irreparable, have been lost to future inquiry.

The new Repository for national deeds, documents, &c. erected at the rear of Chancery Lane, is now completed, where most if not all these evidences of bygone times and deeds and acts are concentrated. Secured by all the safeguards that experience can suggest, defying *tempus edax rerum*, from the judicious adoption of all appliances conducive to preservation—and all at hand for diligence or curiosity, perhaps here is found one of the finest national collections in the world, in a muniment office worthy the records and the Empire—the Vatican of England.

---

P.S. During the progress of this work the restoration of WRAYSBURY CHURCH has been commenced, page 113. It is intended to increase the accommodation of the building by the addition of the south aisle, which for many years has been removed.

Some churches are constructed with a single aisle, but here the architecture evinces that an original aisle existed, although no parish records or tradition state when it disappeared.

The large portico attached to the south side is taken down, so that the new aisle is almost correspondent with the north aisle in symmetry—an exact parallel could not be accomplished. It extends over some 20 feet of the cemetery, and covers the vault of Mary Lee, who reposes therein with two of her relatives, viz. Simon and William Morse. The altar tomb surrounded with iron rails, noticed page 112, is entirely withdrawn; in the interior over this surface are arranged the new open pews. The reading desk is transferred to the south side corner; the pulpit remains. Some reduction in the size of the beautifully perforated oak-work Ankerwycke pew is effected, while the pews of the church are to be lowered to realise one uniform height and character. The interior roof of the chancel is to be restored, and the white plaister which surmounts the nave is also to be removed, that the ribs which ornament and support the building may be again displayed. The west portion of the church will be much improved from the access of light by re-opening a closed window. The organ loft will be disembarrassed of the *harmonium*, which will be conveyed to the body of the church, near the pulpit, and the new vestry-room will occupy the site, formerly an oratory, chantry, or Lady chapel. The late vestry-room has succumbed to its fate, as did its predecessor, formerly at the north-east of the church (p. 113), and both were gifts of the Gyll family (p. 134).

The good work of renovation began in October, 1861, and the first stone of the restored aisle was laid on the 9th November following; after an appropriate service, an elegant *dejeuner* was given at Ankerwycke House, by Cotterill Scholefield, Esq. to the supporters of the project. The expenses of this judicious restoration are estimated at about £1200, liberally raised, with equal spirit and zeal, by the Vicar, his friends, the gentry and inhabitants of the parish, aided by the Dean and Canons of Windsor.

Page 30. The intermediary Prioress of Ankerwycke between Letia and Alice de Stanford, in 1304, is Margery, who was Prioress, 53 Henry III. 1269.

Dugdale's Monasticon, Vol. IV. p. 231, original in Latin:—

To all the faithful in Christ to whom this present writing should come. Margery Prioress of Ankerwycke and of the same convent, health in the Lord. Let it be known that we of our common consent gave and granted and by this present paper do confirm to Adam of Shotton, Clerk, £1. 8s 10d of annual rent, with appurtenances in the City of London, to wit, a certain house in Aldrethesgate (Aldersgate) Street, which Robert Bokelere sometime held, in the parish of St. Agnes, 8th, and of a certain house in Distaff Lane, in the parish of St. Nicholas atte Coldabbey, which Walter Lightfot held, £0. 10s 10d; and of a certain house in Byllyngesgate, in the parish of St. Mary atte Hulle, which Martin de Garschirche holds, 6th; and of a certain house which John de Chikehall has now in Fisstrete (Fish Street), in the parish of St. Nicholas atte Coldabbey, 4th, to be received yearly through the hands of the said houses, at four distinct periods of the year, as our custom has been to receive these rents, to have and to hold of the said Adam, his heirs and assigns, of us and our successors, rendering to us and our successors one penny at Easter, in lieu of all secular demands, &c. For this donation, concession, and confirmation of the present writing and warrant the said Adam has given to us 18 marks of silver (£12.—in relative value about £120.)

In testimony of which we have appended our seal of the convent (p. 30), the witnesses being Hugh, son of Otho, the Constabulary of the Tower of London; Robert de Cornhall, Cornhill, or Cornhyll (Sheriff of London, 1258—1267, pp. 12, 208); Thomas (Adam Basing, Lord Mayor of London, 1251) de Basinges, then one of the Vicecõmes, Mayor or Sheriffs of London; John Adrian (Lord Mayor of London, 1270, p. 33); Walter Hervey (Sheriff, 1258, and Lord Mayor of London, 1272); Reginald of Suffolk; Bartholomew of Castell; and others.

Dated at Aunkerwike the day of March nearest after the Feast of the Conversion of St. Paul, (25th January) in the reign of King Henry, son of John, 54.—1269.

Page 33. At the end of the donations to Ankerwycke Priory are these witnesses—Roger le Bigod, Earl of Norfolk and Marshal of England; Hugh de Vere, Earl of Oxford; William de Valencia, our brother, (probably William Marshal, Earl of Pembroke, who married Elianor, sister of King Henry III. She died in a nunnery at Mortarges, in France;) Edmund de Lacy; John, son of Geffrey; Robert Walericus; William de Grey; Imbertus Pugeys (of Stoke Pogeys); Ralph de Bakep; William de Sancta Ermina; and others.

Given with our hand at Chester, XVI. day of August, of our reign 41, (Henry III.) 1256.

Petition in Parliament, page 28, of the poor nuns of Ankerwycke, temp. Edward III. Rot. Parl. II. 406, Num. 160. Dugdale's Monasticon, Vol. IV. p. 231:—

A n're Seigñr. le roi et a sun counseil monstrent ces poveres moneyns la p'ouresse et covent de Ankirkwyk, q̃ come la p'ouresse Alice, pdecessour ceste q'ore est, ensemblement ove le covent, purchaserunt a eux et a lour successurs a touz jours trente acres de trẽ vynt et nef acr. de pre, en la ville de Dachet, en le counte de Buckyngham issint q̃ eux furunt en possessiun de la dicte tere et pre et cel estat continuerunt pesiblement tut lour temps, taunt q̃ Sire Hugh le Despenser le pere a tort et saunz jugement, lour disseisi en le temps le roi q'ore est et cel tort continua taunt q̃ a sa mort saunz estre punyz, et lour chartres de lour purchaz p poer tollit de eux. De quei p̃nt remedie issint q̃ eux pensunt reaver la dite tere et pre, ensemblement ove restitucion de pfitz issaunz de la dite tere et pre q̃ amounte a c$^{li.}$

Responsio. Declare en qi mein la trẽ est.

# INDEX OF PERSONS.

Abbot, Mr. 303
Aberdeen, 146
Abolee, John, 298
Adderley, Fenina, 260
Adkin, Ann, 131
Adkins, Ambrose, 71, 75, 111, 158, 173, 300
" Mary, 111, 131, 173
" Samuel, 132, 173
" Joseph, 115, 129, 132, 135, 136
" Sarah, 132
" William, 173
Agar, 242
Albany, Robert, Duke of, 101, 191
" Pedigree of, 102
Albert, Prince, xii
Albemarle, Earl of, 52, 221, 223
Aldane, Charles and James, 87, 146
Aldridge, John, Mary, and Elizabeth, 73, 184
" Ann and Samuel, 75
" Henry, 98, 155, 301
" Dr. Robert, 301
" Dr. Thomas, 143
" Ambrose, 58, 155, 156, 157
" Thomas, 186
Aldworth, Gilbert, 291
" Richard, 82
" Thomas, 83
" Pedigree of, 82
Aleworth, Richard, Jane, and Anne, 258
Alexander, Lady Judith, 71
Allat, William, 138
" John, 158
Allen, Sarah, and Elizabeth, 184
" Henry, 298
Alman, Thomas, 261
Alsop, Catherine, 219
" Cavendish, 223
" Ann, 261
" Russel, 219
Altham, Sir Edward, 41
" John, and Joan, 61
Ambrose, Roger, 258
" William, 147
Ambroseden, Nicole de, 119
Amson, Thomas, 285
Amy, John, 107
Anagn, Silvester de, 106, 154
Ancren, rule, 26
Anderson, Mary Martin, 129
" Samuel and Edward, 301
Andrew, John, 75, 147
" Silvester, 174
Andrews, Henry, 181,
" George, 293
" Elizabeth, 208
Ankerwycke, Priory, 26
Anne, Princess, 287
Antoninus' Itinerary, 3
Aprice, Richard and Catherine, 258
Apsley, Lord, 223
" Pedigree of, 281
Archer, Thomas, 93, 143, 144, 155

Archer, Edmund, 292
" Ann, 93
Ardern, Sir Peter, 206
Armstrong, John, 95, 100
Arundell, William, 24
" Earl of, 11, 102, 238
Ashbrook, Pedigree of, 68, 91
Ashby, 160
" William, 85, 86, 148, 178, 180
" Robert, 85
" Thomas, 86, 137, 139, 167, 213
" Skidmore, 88, 136, 148, 169, 181
Ashe, Sir James and Sir Joseph, 102
Ashfield, John and Mary, 217
Ashurst, Sir Henry & Lady, 142, 146
Ashley, John, 301
" Mary, 260
" Richard, 218
" William de, 106
Ashmole, 278
Ashton, William, 229, 149, 257
" Thomas, 284
" John, 195, 249, 271, 283, 293
" Henry and Alinor, 259, 300
" Frances, 249
Aspland, Robert and Marcia, 100
Astley, Thomas and Robert, 258
" Richard, 218
Atkins, John, 164, 258
" William Martin, 236
" William, 147
" Henry, 258
Atkinson, Henry William, 223
" Sir Jasper, 3, 100, 223, 264
" Jane Laura, 3, 100, 223, 264
" Lady Louisa, 100
" Pedigree of, 223
Atkyns, W. M. 236
Atlee, William, 300
" John, 284, 291
Atterbury, Henry, 10
" Eliza, 132
Atwater, Bishop, 10
Aubenie, William de, 52
Aubrey, Sir John, 252
" Pedigree of, 229
Augusta, Princess, 136, 145
Aunger, Thomas and Richard, 296
Aylesbury, Earl of, 206
Aylet, Mr. 146
Aylward, William Marmaduke, 258
Ayress, Edith, 260
Ayscough, Francis, 158

Bachelor, Richard, 107
Bacon, John, Cordelia, Catherine, and Edmund, 95
" Anthony, 228
Baddlesmere, Giles, 6

Bailey, William and Susan, 121
Bainbridge, Thomas, 167
Baker, Ann, 183.
" William, 181, 183, 198, 264
" Honora, 260, 264
" John, 184, 185
" Alice, 93
" Bennet, 185
" Dorothy, 260
Baldwin, Henry and Martha, 258
Balgrave, Robert and John, 261
Ball, John, 56, 143
Ballinour, John and Catherine, 250
Balnet, Henry, 75, 156, 210, 232, 297
" John, 75, 147
" Joanna, 181
" Andrew, 182
Bampton, Robert, 158, 289, 300
Baltimore, Lord, 227
Banks, Sir Edward and Amelia, 77
" Dr. James, Dorothy, and Sophia, 230
" John, 88, 285
Bankworth, Robert, 157
Barantyne, William and Joan, 202
Barbaroux, Robert and Mary, 77, 132
" William, 77, 132, 184
Barker, William, 253
" Sir John, 95
" Robert, 63
" George, 63
" Ambrose, 218
Barlow, Thomas G. and James, 185
Barley, 8
Barne, George, 139
Barnes, Juliana, 194
" Ambrose, 217
Barney, Alexander, 182
Barrington, John and Fitzwilliam, 145, 177
Barrow, John, 109, 115, 136
" Elizabeth, 109
Barsett, John, 147
Barthen, John, 302
Barwick, Richard, 73
Basset, Hannah, 260
Batchelour, Mary, Richard, and Annie, 29
Batenor, Richard, 205
Bateman, Thomas & Elizabeth, 125
Bathebye, Robert, 296
Bathurst, Henry, 220, 223
" Tryphena and Frances, 220, 221
" Pedigree of, 280, 281
Baton, Lucas de, 276, 295
Batt, Elizabeth, John and Hannah, 130
Battaile, Thomas, 9
Baye, 299
Baytop, Thomas and Elizabeth, 100
Bazeley, Samuel, 300
Beale, Bartholomew, 157, 298

# INDEX.

Beale, Richard, 302
Beauchamp, Richard, 29, 82
„ Thomas, 176, 177
„ Mary, 177
„ Thomas, 146
„ Elizabeth de, 6
Beauclerk, Lord Charles, 47, 162
Beauly, Robert, 198
Beaumont, Lord, 68
Beaulieu, 69
Beckingham, Henry, 96, 144, 208
„ Thomas, 208
Bedborough, 271
Bedd, Richard, 157
Bedyll, or Bevill, Robert, 156, 291
Bedford, William, Duke of, 220, 223
Bedingfield, James, 181
Beecroft, Robert, Mark, and Ralph, 289, 301
„ Ralph, 200, 259, 260, 262, 289
„ Mary and Elizabeth, 260
Beighton, Thomas, 132, 184
Bel, Philip le, 277
Belitha, Edward and William, 76, 77, 158
Bell, Charles, 148, 178, 179, 181
Belson, James, 174
Benar, John, 262
Bengewyn, Thomas, 253
Benham, Thomas, 258
„ Ann, 261
Bennet, Thomas, 129, 250
„ Richard, 116, 129, 139, 198
„ Ann, 129
Berkyn, John, 235
Bernard, Ann, 147
Berenger, Thomas, 22, 89, 299
„ Elizabeth, 89
„ Richard, 22
Berry, Samuel, 183
Besley, William, 301
Besouth, Samuel, 292
Betham, Sir William, 216
Beverley, Capt. John, 262
Bevill, 59
Bezer, Mr. 259
Biddenson, Marshe, 301
Biddle, Thomas, 248, 249, 263, 292
„ Elizabeth, 248
„ Diana, 130
„ William, 130
„ Dr. William, 198
„ Samuel, 300
„ Mary, 130, 249
„ Edmund, 249, 258, 262, 274
„ Robert, 216, 248, 258, 274, 292, 298
Biddlesford, Walter de, 11
Bigg, John and Susan, 302
Bigod, Hugh de, 52
Billinghurst, John, 183
Binfield, Mary, 147, 158, 301
Binks, Robert, 288
Bird, Henry, 301
„ Edward and John, 183
Birket, John and Isabella, 275
Birks, Ann, 179
Bishop, Elizabeth, 198
„ Jane, 186
Bissel. John, 184

Board, Elizabeth and Timothea, 59
„ Edmund, 292
„ George, 59
Boddington, Timothy and Ann, 129
Bodle, Edward, 144, 150
Bohem, 229
„ Anthony and William, 229
Bohemia, King of, 27
Bohun, John, 205
Bolebec, Hugh de, 5, 11
„ Pedigree of, 6
Boleyn, Anne, 48, 102
Bonfoy, Nicholas, 298
„ Thomas, 301
Bond, Ann, 174
Bonner, Bishop, 38
Bonnel, James, 146
Bonnet, Richard, 138
„ Josua, 111
Bonyon, John, 182
Borrett, Thomas, 221, 260
„ Edward, 144, 158, 301
„ John, 221
Boston, Lord, 78, 145, 159
„ Pedigree of, 78
Boswell, Francis, 253, 258
Bothwell, Countess of, 191
Botter, John de, 154
Boult, Mary, 137, 177
„ Dorothy, 259
„ Stephen, 186
„ John, 259
Boulstrode, John, Dorothy and Mildred, 261
Boure, John, 210
Bouverie, Mr. 147
Bowden, Thomas, 256
„ Jane, 131
Bowdler, Samuel and Mary, 120
Bowes, Leonard, 299
„ John and Sarah, 86
Bowkey, Peter, 281
Bowler, Charles, 301
„ Francis, 259
Bowrie, Henry, 75
Bowry, Francis, 117, 132, 144, 157, 172, 247, 254, 262
„ Henry, 147
„ Edmund, 132, 158, 247, 256, 257
„ Thomas, 21, 22, 76, 132, 214, 172, 256, 259, 260
„ Dorothy, 76, 132
„ Catherine, 117, 232
„ John, 132
„ Dinah, 132, 172
„ Ann, 132
„ Samuel, 172, 254, 262, 300
„ Edward, 256
„ Margaret and Mary, 263
„ Martha and William, 263
Bowser, John, 156, 272, 297
„ Thomas, 210
„ Pedigree of, 234
Bowyer, Sir Henry, 43
„ William, 156
„ Sir Edmund, 102
Boyle, Peter, 106
Boyce, William and Henry Pytches, 77
Blacon, Richard, 107
Black, William, 107
Blair, John, 2, 197

Blair, Dr. Hugh, 220, 254
Blackwood, Thomas, 107
Blake, Admiral, 240
„ Kezia and Aaron, 131
„ John, 147
Blakemere, William, 296
Bland, John, 96
„ Joseph, 293
Blandy, Francis, 236
Blagrove, John, 145, 178, 136, 131
„ Family of, 24, 25, 47, 134
„ Pedigree of, 24
Blencowe, Francis, 260
Blount, Sir John, Sir Richard and Sir George, 58, 59
„ Pedigree of, 234
„ Sir Thomas, 278
„ Sir Michael, 156, 297
Blundell, Viscount, 71
Blunt, Edwin, 246
„ Robert and Richard, 302
„ Family of, 208, 222, 223
„ Pedigree of, 274
„ Christopher, 302
Brads, Moses, 256
Brackenbury, William, 258, 261
Bradshaw, Sarah, 242
„ John Augustus, 24, 179
Bradford, Theophilus and Lady, 186
Braisher, 163
Brambley, William, 131
Brandon, Gilbert, 250
Braveney, William, 297
Braybroke, Lord, 136, 145, 167
„ Pedigree of, 82
Braybourne, Francis and Ichabod, 259
Breadalbane, Marquis of, 69
Brecknock, David and Sibilla, 16, 57, 143
„ Pedigree of, 59
Brerewood, Charles, 263
„ Pedigree of, 227
Brembre, Sir Nicholas, 90, 203
Brewer, Richard, 301
Bridger, P.
Bridgewater, Earl of, 235
Briggs, Robert, 300
Brise, Colonel Ruggles, 21, 41
Brocas, Sir Bernard and William, 193, 278
„ John, 2, 193
Brocket, Edward, John and Ursula, 43, 233, 296, 211
Brockhurst, Elizabeth, 260
Brogden, Elizabeth, 71
Brook, Elizabeth, 249
Brooke, Captain William, 47, 147
„ James, 98, 122
„ Richard, 122
Brookland, William, 302
Brome, George, 144, 157, 218
„ Robert, 157
„ Sir Nicholas and Ralph, 209, 297
„ John and Alice, 98, 297
„ William and Mary, 98, 261
„ Mildred, 260
„ John and Mary, 101, 120
„ Sir William, 100
„ Pedigree of, 22
Bromefield, William, 253, 257, 264
„ Sir Edward, 264

INDEX.

Bromefield, Ambrose, 257
Brotherton, Thomas de, 155
Browne, J. B. G. 221
  „   John, 221
  „   John and Margaret, 220, 250, 251
  „   William and Henry, 158, 260
Brown, William, 255, 264, 244, 287
  „   Sir William and John, 41
Bruce, Robert, 191
  „   Pedigree of, 101
Brun, Walter, 32, 41
Brunsun, Elizabeth and Nanney, 175, 176
Brudenell, William, 217
  „   Edward, 206
  „   George, 69
  „   Pedigree of, 69, 206
Buat, John, 139
Buccleugh, Duke of, 69, 145, 146
  „   Duchess of, 137, 198
  „   Charles William, 159
  „   Pedigree of, 69
Buchan, Earl of, 191
Buckingham, Duke of, 44, 210
  „   Ann, 261
  „   George, 272
  „   Owen, 300
  „   Pedigree of, 273
Buckland, Thomas, 79, 84, 100, 130, 135, 146, 177, 178, 181, 198, 261
  „   Virgo, 79, 126, 130, 180, 181
  „   Elizabeth, 130
  „   Francis Virgo, 130
  „   Francis, 84, 136, 146, 148, 181
  „   William Thomas, 79, 92, 125, 146, 148
  „   Family of, 109, 130, 132, 181
Buller, Thomas and Ursula, 264
Bulkeley George, 229
Bullock, Jonathan, 78
  „   Pedigree of, 78
  „   Henry, 41, 72, 176, 198, 205, 248, 254
  „   John, 72, 176, 205
  „   Family of, 248, 259, 263, 264
Bulstrode, Edmund, 157, 215, 297, 298
  „   Henry, 18, 72, 141, 157, 183, 206, 214, 238, 253, 268, 298
  „   Thomas, 21, 157, 182, 213, 214, 215, 298
  „   Sir William, 210, 216, 297
  „   George, 156, 182, 214
  „   Edward, 182, 213, 215, 238, 144
  „   Richard, 155, 205, 206, 253
  „   John de, 296
  „   Robert, 206, 215
  „   William and Dame Matilda, 216
  „   Family of, and pedigree, 216, 217
Bunce, John and Martha, 129
Bunnin, Henry, 181

Bulpitt, Elizabeth, William and Jane, 259
  „   Edmund, 301
Burcomb, William, 248, 257, 293
  „   Thomas, 281, 282, 283, 289, 292
  „   John, 173, 248, 263, 285
  „   Family of, 248, 257, 262, 263
Burckhardt, 50
Burde, Edmund, 182
Burdens, Oliver de, 2
Burgis, John, 184
Burghersh, Sir John and Maude, 232
Burke, Sir Bernard, 216
Burle, William, 157
Burleigh, Lord, 58, 59
Burne, George, 146
Burnell, Robert de, 6, 10, 106, 143, 145
  „   Philip, 13
  „   Bishop of Bath and Wells, 13
  „   Pedigree of, 13
Burnett, Thomas and Mary, 185
  „   Gilbert, 184
Burt, Richard, 300
  „   Joseph, 177
  „   Family of, 129, 131
Burst, William, 263
Bury, Edgar, 41
Burton, John, 106, 283, 291
  „   Andrew, 156
Butiler, Thomas, 56
Butler, Richard, 181
  „   Mary, 260
  „   Thomas and Ursula, 262
  „   Robert, 110, 301
  „   Joanna, 110
  „   Family of, 285
Butterfield, Mrs. 221
Byde, William, 131

Cadamo, John, 253, 295
  „   Richard, 202, 253, 295
Caley, John, 131
Caldwell, Henry, 156
Call, Martin and Elizabeth, 262
Calthorp, John, 156
Calton, Nicholas, 253
Calvert, George, 260, 264, 289
Cambridge, Duke of, 55
Camden, William, 144, 158, 301
Came, Nicholas, 202
Camock, Edward, 300
Camoys, Lord, 59
  „   Ralph de, 59
  „   Pedigree of, 59
Campbell, Lord, 44, 274
  „   Sir Fred. 228
Campion, Thomas, 100
Cane, Isaac, 131, 262, 269
  „   Hannah, 262
  „   Lawrence, 260
  „   Ambrose, 135
  „   Family of, 132, 134, 135, 291, 293
Canon, George, 5, 31, 99, 188
Cantelo, Richard de, 296
Cantrell, 67
Cantrell, Ann, 260

Capel, General, 229
Capella, Martin de, 32
Cappe, Walter, 154
Cardigan, Earl of, 146, 149, 159, 200
  „   Lady, 138
  „   Pedigree of, 69, 206, 217
Carliolo, 276
Carpenter, Thomas, 260
Carleton, Sir Dudley, 94, 144, 145
  „   Pedigree of, 94, 95
Carter, Judge, 138
  „   George, 186
  „   Ralph, 87, 135, 143
  „   Richard, 146
  „   Pedigree of, 229
Canefield, Toby, 91
Catherine, Queen, 279
Cathcart, Sir John, 50
Caton, Emanuel, 303
Cavendish, Henry Lord, 287
Cawcott, Robert, 297
Cecil, Sir William, 58
Chamber, John, 253
Chamberlayn, Sir Thomas, 41
  „   John, 272, 297
  „   Family of, 210, 258
Champnes, Charles, 8, 103, 133, 162, 170
Chandler, William, 137, 172
  „   Ann, 131
Chandos, Marquis of, 148
Chantry, Robert, 184
  „   Thomas William, 107
Chapel, Richard, 106
Chaplin, Benjamin and Ann, 302
  „   Acton, 286
Chapman, William, 181
  „   Family of, 291, 292
Charles, Prince, 257
Charnock, Agnes, 37, 41
Chatelheraut, Duke of, 101
Chaucer, Thomas, Geoffry and Maude, 232
Chauncey, vii
Chauncumbe, Aunger de, and Joan, 202, 295
Cheal, 67
Cheeke, Sir John, 37, 59
  „   Mary, 59
Chelsea, Henry, 202
Cheley, Thomas, 263
Chenies, Anthony and Mary, 259
Cheney, Anthony, 261, 298
  „   John, 261
  „   Martha, 261
  „   Sir Thomas, 211
Chenye, William and Agnes, 119, 258
  „   Thomas, 119
Cheny, William, Lord, 287
Cheminant, Jemima, 236
Chester, Constable of, 52
Chesterfield, Earl of, 218
Cheshunt, Stephen de, 202, 253
Chesterman, Thomas, 299
Chetwynd, William, 260
  „   Lord, 264
Chew, Charles, 286
Chichele, Henry, Sir Robert and Thomas, 232
Chichester, Bishop of, 280

Child, Shadrach, 60, 61, 135
„ Family of, 67, 111, 129, 132, 247, 260, 262
„ Robert, 23, 131, 299
„ William, 101, 147
„ Joseph, 302
„ Geoffry, 211
„ Thomas, 173, 219, 300
„ Martha, 261
„ John, 280, 283, 291
Chippendale, John, 177
Chirrate, William, 272
Chist, Bryan, 288
Chitty, Rose, 131
Clopinden, Pedigree of, 217
Christian, John and Henry, 296
Church, William, 62
Churchill, 78
„ John, Duke of Marlborough, 206
Clanville, George and Samuel, 259
Clanwilliam, Earl of, 24, 112
Clare, Rich de, 203
„ Thomas, 3
„ Gilbert de, 29, 93
„ Earl of, 52
„ Countess of, 201
„ Matilda, 201
Clarendon, Sir Roger de, 102, 203
Clarke, William, 107, 110, 115
„ Thomas, Rebecca and Christopher, 173
„ Family of, 110, 242, 260, 264
Clarkson, Abner, 198
Clement, Thomas, 107
Cleveland, Duke of, 21
Clifford, William, 57, 136, 148, 155
Clifton, William, 274
„ Family of, 246
Cobbet, William, 257
Cobham, Richard, 66, 147
„ Lord, 279
Cochran, Mr. 221
Cock, Daniel, 301
„ Richard, 77
Codrington, William, 131
„ Col. Robert, 280, 291
Coghill, Sir John, 281
Coke, 282
Cokson, John, 106
Colborne, James, 242
Colbrok, Henry and Guy, 276, 296
„ Lawrence and Isabel, 276
Colebroke, Sir James, 229
Cole, 43, 283
Cole, J. K., 198, 267
Colesmore, John, 297
Colevill, Henry de, 295
Collins, James, 161
„ Robert, 158
Coleman, Edward, 76
Colchester, Lord, 303
Colson, Jukes, 139
Combes, William, 197
„ Thomas and Alice, 258
Compton, Denys and Rowland, 258
„ Sir William, 57
Confessor, Edward, 1, 3
Constable, Thomas, 176
Conway, Lord, 41, 60, 94, 275
„ Helegonway, 41
„ Dame Bridget, 60

Conyers, Pedigree of, 23
Cook, John, 222, 246, 250, 255
Cooke, Michael, 301
„ Sir Anthony and Mildred, 59
„ John, 182, 236, 237, 301
„ Ann, 254, 261
„ Richard, 275
„ George and Alice, 233, 299
Cookney, Holland, Richard, and Elizabeth, 302
Cooper, William, Daniel, and Mary, 110, 135 137, 143
„ Samuel Lovick and Frances, 236
Coore, H. J., 24
„ Pedigree of, 24
„ Frederick William, 131
Corbet, Nicholas and Margery, 6, 11
„ Family of, 300
Corderoy, John, 177
Cornhill, Ralph, 12, 208
„ Delicia, 208
Cornish, George, 148, 181, 187
„ Martha, 229,
„ William, 220, 301
„ Robert, 161
Cornwall, Robert, 58
„ Earl of, 261
„ Jacob, 188
Cotterell, Henry, 261
Cottington, Sir Francis Lord, 157
Cotton, Sir Robert, 53
Cottys, Robert, 272
Coventrie, Elias de, 143, 154
Coventry, Emily, 121, 132
„ Earl and Countess of, 77
Coverley, Sir Roger de, 55
Covert, William, 205
Cowardelow, Thomas, 212
„ George, 157, 298
Coward, Dr. William, 242
Cowderoy, John, 167
Cowper, 50
„ Prudence, 269
Cox, Thomas, 100
„ Daniel, 168, 214, 299
„ Ann, 181
„ Robert, 198, 202
„ John, 141
Coxwell, Rogers and Sir Henry, 234
„ R. Rogers, 254
„ Thomas Tracey, 242, 243, 249, 254, 264
Cradock, William, Catherine and Elizabeth, 259
„ Family of, 264
Cramavill, Robert de Constantin, 201
Crawford, Ann, 223
Crease, John, Frances and Sarah, 230
„ Ralph, 182
Creedy, William Rogers, 56
Creker, Roger, 284, 291
Crespigny, James de, 41
„ Sir Claude and Sir William, 78
„ Pedigree of, 78
Creting, John, 296
Crew, M. 198
Cricket, John, 47, 146
„ Charles Alexander, 47

Cripps, Reginald, 88
„ Richard, 88, 156, 213
„ Henry and Edward, 258
Crispin, Milo, 270
„ Pedigree of, 276
Croame, Mr. 183
Crockford, Roger, 291
Croft, Edward and Ann, 41, 42
„ Sir James, 31
Croke, Alexander and Frances, 18
„ John, 157, 218
„ Pedigree of, 217
„ Family of, 218
Cromwell, Oliver, 119, 248
Crosier, Nicholas de, 293
Crowder, John, 19, 111, 135, 141
„ William, 129, 131
„ Ann, 131
„ Family of, 19, 129, 132, 256
Currie, Wm. 190
„ Dr. 228

Dalkeith, Earl of, 159, 302
Dallian, James, 107, 129
„ Elizabeth, 129
Dalton, 146
„ Thomas, 180, 185
„ John and Mary, 176
„ Richard, 185
Dandridge, Frances, 185
Daniel, Abel, 300
„ John, 253
Dansy or d'Anesyn, Peter de, 13
Danvers, John, 16, 209, 253
Dare, Jeffrey, 258, 261
„ Edmund, 258
Darell, Marmaduke, 299
Darling, William and Elizabeth, 111
Darvell, William, 285, 300
Dartmouth, Earl of, 82
Darby, Josias, 158, 234, 300
„ Booker, 195, 198, 257
„ Cobbet, 188, 195
„ William, 260
„ Family of, 258, 261
Dashwood, Sir Francis, 75
„ George H. 148
Datchet, Alexander and Richard, 296
Davenport, Mrs. 142
David II. King, and Marjorie, 101
Davis, John, 131
„ Thomas, 261, 301
„ Henry, 117
Davies, R. 167, 286
„ Joseph, 136, 141, 163
„ William, 260
Davy, Henry, 273
D'aumarle, Duke of, 278
Daw, Charles, 286
Dawe, Jeffrey, 291
Dawes, John, 73
Day, Dr. William, 63
„ Paul and Mariot, 299
Dean, Thomas, 132
Deane, James, 163
Dee, Thomas, 292
Deerhurst, Viscount, 121
Delaford, William and Dorothy, 234
Delapole, Family of, 59
Dell, Thomas, 260, 264
Delawarr, Lord, 220, 223

# INDEX.

Delawarr, Family of, 205
Delaval, Gilbert, 52
Denham, 49
," Sir John, 50
," Francis, 146
Denny, Edward and Ann, 22
," Richard, 141
," William, 157
Denys, William, 298
Derby, Booker, 286
," William and John, 248
," Family of, 75, 246, 263
," Earl of, 239
Deschamps, John, 100
," Susanna, 185
," Family of, 121, 133
Despenser, Baron, 75, 143, 155, 278
," Hugh, 28, 145, 202
," Pedigree of, 29
Devonshire, Duke of, 287
Dew, Thomas, 292
Dicey, Edward, 220
Dickinson, William and Margaret, 258
Digby, Abigail and Robert, 157, 212, 274, 298
," Family of, 153, 156, 208, 297
," Reginald, 141
," Pedigree of, 209
Dinorben, Lord, 228
Dionysius, Cecilia, 154
Dipden, Thomas, 206
Dipple, Richard, 143
Ditchfield, Edward, 19, 60
Dixon, Thomas, 106
Docket, Charles, 157, 298
Dod, Richard, 58
Dodworth, Christopher, 218
Dogget, Richard, 299
Doiley, Robert, and Pedigree of, 276
Dolben, Sir Gilbert and Sir William, 183, 184
Dollond, John and Eliza, 236
Domby, William, 66
Domesday Book, 4
Dominique, Adam, 107
Domley, William, 35, 147
Dorchester, Lord, 94, 144, 145
Dorington, Sir John, Cordelia and Richard, 22, 157
," Pedigree of, 22
Dosset, Mary, John and Eliza, 129
Douglas, Earl of, 101
Downes, Walter & Margaret, 30, 71
Downham, Elizabeth, William and Edward, 109, 130, 164
Downshire, Marquis of, 70, 145, 146, 157, 176
," Marchioness of, 229
," Pedigree of, 71
Dowse, John and Lucy, 248
Drake, William and Rachel, 78, 86
," Thomas, 184
," Pedigree of, 78
Draper, Elizabeth, 213, 298
Dredge, Mr. 81
Drey, William, 299
Drokensfield, John, Claricia and Margaret, 202, 208
Dru, Robert, Richard and Lawrence, 204
Drummond, Lord, 101

Drury, Edmund, 258, 264
," Sir Robert, 206
Duck, Thomas and Esther, 173
Dugdale, vii.
Duncomb, John, 299, 300
," Thomas & Dorothy, 259
Dunn, Ralph, 159
Dunt, William, 285, 300
," John, 292
Dunton, William, 108
Duplock, Samuel, 222, 302
Durdant, Ralph, 182
," Family of, 181, 182
," Charles & John, 299, 233
Durham, William, 257
Durwant, William, 298
Duton, Isabel de, 14, 143
Dutton, John, 107, 299
Dychon, Hugh, 295
Dyer, Sir Swinnorton and Ann, 77
Dyneley, Edward, 218
Dyson, John, 168
," Thomas, 180
," Family of, 109
Dyve, Charles, 215

Easton, William, 131
Echard, Historian, 279
Echingham, Sir Thomas and Margaret, 64, 234
Edridge, Roger, 301
Edmead, William, 185
," Robert, 169
," John, 186
Ednam, John, 188
Edward III., 277
Edwards, Margaret, 260
," John, 254
," Thomas, 19, 35, 66, 147, 297
," Richard, 157, 218
," Family of, 232, 257, 258, 260, 297
," George, 156, 157, 210, 297
," Stephen, 87
," Catharine, 260
Egbert, King, 49
Egerton, Sir Thomas and Sir John, 235, 239
Elderton, John, 159
Elizabeth, Queen, 3, 268
Eldborough, Henry, 131
Eldridge, Roger, 292
," Bryan, 114
Ellesmere, Baron, 235
Ellis, Elias, 135
," Sir Henry, 4
Ellison, Rev. Mr. and George Thomas, 228
Ellys, Sir Richard, 75
Elphinstone, Lord, 102
Elwood, Thomas and John, 43, 241
Empson, Sir Richard, 182, 217
," Mary, 182
Enoe, Spencer and Ann, 250
Enderbie, Samuel, 156, 212
Enderby, Samuel, 298
England, Sir Richard, 54
English, William, 106, 258
," Thomas, 258
Englefield, Philip Philippa, 206, 217
," William, 292
Entwisle, Thomas, 206

Erby, Thomas and John, 276
Essex, Sir William, Thomas and Alice, 45, 100
Essington, Mr. 258, 264
Estwick, Peter, 186
Evans, Evan, 136, 257
," Mary and family of, 198, 245
," Ann, 131
," Henry, 218
Every, Sir Henry, 68, 91
Evelyn, William, 131
," Sir John, 279
," John, 45
Eyles, George, 107
Eyre, John de, 296
," Sir George, 218
," William, 6, 231
," Thomas, 232
," David, 181

Fabian, John, 156
Fairford, Lord, 70
Falstaff, Sir John, 274, 294
Fane, Sir Thomas, 82
Faratius, 276
Farmer, Richard, 250
Farnell, Henry and Elizabeth, 131, 181
Farnham, Nicholas de, 27, 32
Farr, Dr. 270
Farrars, William and Abigail, 258
Farrington, Jocelyn and Hannah, 302
Fawkes, Guy, 211
Feldoe, Charles, 158
Fellow, Benjamin, 301
," George, 292
," Family of, 247
Fellowes, Joseph and Grace, 302
," Benjamin, 285
Fenimore, Henry, 90
Fennell, Thomas, 292, 293
Fermour, Sir William, 212
Ferrall, Thomas, 301
Ferrers, Sir Humphrey, 82
," Catherine, 82
," Edward, 209, 211
," Pedigree of, 209
Ferry, Benjamin, 290
Fewaters, Juliana, Richard and William, 181
Field, Thomas and Alice, 250
Filse, Henry, 147
Finch, Mary, 260, 264
," Charles, 185
," William, 285, 292
Fisher, Morris, Martha and Susan, 250, 258
," Maurice, 256
," Guy, 300
," Mrs. 285
Fisse, Henry, 76
Fitz-Alan, Earl of Arundel, 102
Fitzcourt, Bryan, 276
Fitzgerald, Maurice, 29
," John, 260
," Mr. 221
," Keane, 168
," William Thomas, 48
Fitzgilbert, Richard and Robert, 93
Fitz-Lewis, 59
Fitzmaurice, John and Hamilton, 159

2 R

Fitz-Other, 5
" Walter, 200
Fitz-Rogers, John and family of, 234
" Coxwell, 234
Fitz-Robert, John, 52
Fitzwalter, Richard, 93, 143, 155
" Mr. 52
" Sarah. 261
Fitzwilliam, Sir William and Elizabeth, 206
Flatcombe, Ralph, 288
Flatt, Joseph, 216
Fleetwood, Charles, 239
" Sir George, 242
" Elizabeth, 131
" Thomas, 60
" Family of, 41, 42
Flemyng, Family of, 19, 100, 102, 110, 120
" Lady Lilias, 101
" Lord, 19
" Earl of Wigtoun, 146
" Pedigree of, 101
Flower, Pedigree of, 91
Fletcher, William, 213, 298
" James, 131
Fogelere, Margaret de and Edward, 295
Foote, R. G. 199, 200, 234
Foliot, Nicholas, 59
Folkes, William, 158
Forest, John, 253
Forbes, Richard, 275
Forde, William, 155
Ford, Humphry and Thomas, 257, 298
Forsyth, Dr. Alexander, 101
Fortescue, Sir Adrian, 59
Forth, Henry, 249
Fortibus, William de, 6
Foss, Mr. 11
Foster, Thomas, 242
" John, 159, 302
" Samuel and Daniel, 301
" Abraham and Mary, 223
Fournier, George, 185
Fowdge, John, 292
Fowler, Thomas, 291
Fowles, Mary Ann, 249
Fox, Mrs. 268
" George, 18, 241
Francis, William, 292
Franklyn, Richard, 273
Frankleyn, Walter, 32
Fray, Sir John, 5, 16, 143, 145
" Pedigree of, 16
Frazer, Sir Simon, 120, 121
Frear, R. John, 248
Frederick V. 279
Freville, George, 144, 145, 156
Frevylle, Baldwin de, 88
Friend, Maximilian & Susanna, 91
Fryer, Richard and Peter, 183
" Frances, 300
" Richard, 76, 96, 158
Frogley, 141
" Richard, 148
Froissart, 277
Frowyn, Richard, 143, 155
Fucour, Richard, 296
Fulk, John, 257
Fulkes, John, 249

Fuller, Ann, 260
" J., 291
" Henry and Martha, 283, 289
Fullere, Simon le, 296
Fulmer, Joseph, 285, 292, 301, 302
Fullywolle, Ralph and Lucy, 119
Fylce, John and Thomas, 181

Galloway, William, 301
Gambrun, William de, 295
Gamul, Sir Francis and Sydney, 227
Gardener, James Ballard, 229
Gardiner, Hamilton Gray, 190
Gardinière, Alicia de, 143, 155
Garleke, Thomas, 297
Garlick, 161
Garrard, Sir William, 289
" Mary, 89
Garret, William, 261, 264
" John, 108
Garth, George and Pedigree of, 95
Gaskarth, William, 220
Gasey, Thomas, 288
Gataker, Thomas, 252
Gatcombe, Ralph, 291
Gay, John, 320
" M. A., 198
Gayer, Family of, 279
Gaue, Ostibus de la, 154
Gaudon, John, 216
Gaunt, John of, 82, 191
" Joan, 82
Gaynsford, John, Alice and Catherine, 204, 205
" Pedigree of, 205
Genera, Ellen de, 11, 13
George III. 136, 137
Georgye, Nicholas de, 210, 207
Gerevend, William, 210
Gernandsworth, 217
Gernon, Robert de and William de, 3, 4, 28, 93, 143
" Pedigree of, 6
Gervan, Jeffrey de, 154
Geryng, Bartholomew, 253
Gestlingthorp, John de, 253
Gibbs, William and Aaron, 301
Gibbons, William and family of, 116, 117, 129, 131, 132, 174, 218, 260, 263, 301
" Sir John, 197, 205
" Sir William, 205
" Jonathan, 262
" Sarah, 129
" Henry, 76
" Grindling, 118
" Richard, 132
Giblet, William, 257
Gilbert, Richard and Pedigree of, 6
Giles, Henry, John and Martha, 130
Gill, John, 141
" Family of, 158
Gille, Dr. Alexander, 239
" Family of, 75, 210
" Bueth, 98, 99
Gillowe, Francis, 298
Gilman, Alice, 216
Gisborne, John, 301
Glascott, Elizabeth, 131
" George, 71
Glisson, Thomas, 209
Gnoll Company, 139

Gnott, Alice, 260
Gloster, Duke of, 277
" Robert de, 106
" Richard de, 14, 29, 104, 143
" Earl of, 52
Goade, George, 212, 259, 261, 262, 291, 298
" Family of, 129, 301
" William, 132, 247, 263, 291
" Dr. William, 262
" Samuel, 292
" Richard, 288
" Pedigree of, 284
Godden, Edward, 131, 248
" Mary, 248
Goddard, William, 299
" John, 300
Godfrey, Col., 287
Godman, Joan, 30
Godwin, John, 158, 181
Goffe, Henry, 285, 292
Goloufre, Sir Peter, 277
Golope, Elizabeth, 30
Goldie, Charles Dashwood and Euphemia, 290
Goldsbro, Family of, 230
Goodall, Edward, 213, 252, 258, 261, 299
" Sarah, 252
Goode, Robert, 121, 182
Goodman, John, 132, 135, 139
" Family of, 100, 129
Goodwyn, Edward, 299
Goodrich, Dr. Francis, 146
Goodyar, George and pedigree of, 24
Goodyeare, Michael and William, 156, 261
" Jacomina, 156
" John, 258, 298, 299
" Ralph, 144
" Jane, 149, 260
" Family of, 93, 299
Gordon, Charles, 180
" James, 148
" George, 190
Goring, John, 186
Gosset, Catherine, 229, 255
" Isaac, 287
" Pedigree of, 250, 230
Goughe, Thomas, 257
Gould, Edward and Alexander, 118, 144
" Thomas, 261
" Henry, 157
" Family of, 76, 130, 131
" Pedigree of, 75.
Gourney, William, Daniel and Susanna, 129
Grace, William, 78
Grantham, George and Elizabeth, 160, 163, 181
Grave, Georgina A. 185
" Walter, 143, 155
Graham, John and Lady Lilias, 102
Graves, William and Elizabeth, 130
" John, 221
Gray, Margaret Ann, 198
" Mr. 50
Greye, John, 291
Grayhew, Elizabeth and Judge, 250, 282
Greatorex, W. H. 149, 198

# INDEX.

Green, Mary, 261
" John, 22
" William, 147
Greenwood, Mr. 66
Greene, Sir Michael, 210, 298
Gregge, William, 156
Grenfell, Pascoe, 73, 145, 294
" William, 72, 73
Grenfield, Captain, 216
Grenville, Thos. 82
Gresham, Lady, 182
Grey, Lord, 82, 239
Griffin, James Lord, 82
" Sir Edward, 59
" Pedigree of, 82
" Family of, 216, 262
Griffith, Sarah, 263
Grimsdal, Abraham, 291, 293
Grimsthorp, William Lord of, 6
Grimshaw, 91
Grigby, Josua, 85, 86
Grive, Richard, 300
Groom, William, 65, 116, 135
" Mary, 111, 131
Grosvenor, Christiana, 227
" Richard, 227
Grove, Thomas de la, 206
" Richard and Martha, 111
" John, 135, 301
" William, 131, 136
" Weedon, 172, 173
" Lazarus, 58
" Elizabeth, 260
" Family of, 132
Guenint, Jenny, 261
Gundry, Henry, 180
Gurney, Bathsheba, 112
" Ann, 131
" Sir Richard, 214
Guy, Richard Blunt, 302
" Henry, 158
" William and John, 285, 292, 301
" Family of, 299
Gwatkin, Mr. 171
Gwyn, Thomas, 258, 264
" Edward, 258
Gyles, William, 182
" John, 210
Gyll, Pedigree of, 99, 100, 125
" Sir George, 45, 64, 88, 280
" Sir John, 3, 100, 280
" Sir Robert, 184
" Lady Harriet, 102
" Dr. Philip, 192
" Bueth, 98, 99
" Michael, 98
" George, 60, 205
" William, 145, 167, 176, 178, 179
" Brooke Hamilton, 113, 148, 184
" John, Dr. 124, 188
" Richard, 218
" Family of, 98, 99, 120, 136, 189
" Gordon, 22, 23, 24, 87, 145, 146, 148
Gynes, Robert de, 13

Hackshaw, John, 301
Hagthorne, Nathaniel, 95
Haine, Agnes, 261

Haine, Catherine, 274
" John, Margaret and Catherine, 258, 260
Haines, John, 213, 250
" Thomas & Sarah, 111, 131
Hailes, John, 261
Haistwell, Owen, 273
Hakeburne, Richard, 201, 231, 295
Halfacre, 147
Hale, George and Thomas, 258
" William, 300
" Dr. Richard, 144, 145, 157, 158
" Thomas, 156
" Family of, 60, 61
" Pedigree of, 62
Hall, Henry, 45, 62
" John and Robert, 157, 213, 234, 259, 298
" Joane, 144, 214, 259
" Family of, 62, 249, 293, 299
" Alice, 261
" Edward, 249
Halle, de la, John and Walter, 154, 261, 295
" atte John, 296
Halsey, Edmund, 279
Halys, Sir Roger, 102
Hamilton, Hans and James Earl of Clanboye, 40
" Lady Barbara and William, Duke of Chatelherault, 101, 275
Hamersley, Ralph, 144, 155
Hamerton, Thomas, Alice and Rachel, 130
Hammond, James, 164
Hamond, William, 131
Hampden, Sir John, 36, 41, 209, 216
" Family of, 192
" Pedigree of, 209
Hampton, William Fry, 158
" Ann, 131
Hanbury, Richard, 156, 233
" Thomas, 156
Hancock, Samuel, 77
Hancox, William, Mary and Nicholas, 222
Hand, William, 107
Handlo, John de, 11
Hardwick, Earl of, 94
" Eleanor, 181
Hardy, Thomas Duffus, 303.
Hare, Philip, 139, 146
Harewood, Earl of, 159
Harfield, Jane, 131
Hargrave, Christopher and Frances, 144, 159
Harman, Mr. 198
Harris, John, 129, 135, 147, 172
" Sir Arthur and Salter, 43
" William Philip and South, 148, 173, 181
" Family of, 88, 90, 131, 136, 145, 157, 250
Harrison, Mark and Alice, 258
" William, 106
" George, 158
" Robert, 198
Harcourt, Henry Duke of, 186
" Francis, 186
" George Simon, 23, 114, 127, 133, 136, 148

Harcourt, John S. Chandos, 133, 181
" Sir Philip, 23, 127, 144, 145
" Philip, 118, 135, 141, 176
" John, 137, 203
" Sir Robert, 205
" Family of, 44, 112, 113, 117, 130, 131, 132, 158, 159, 208
" Pedigree of, 45
Hart, William and Richard, 257
Hartfield, Earl of, 101
Harpesfield, William de, 202, 251, 253
Hartshorne, Archæolog. 11
Hartwell, Robert, 292
Harvey, Dr. Gabriel, 37
Hasel, Thomas, 299
Hassel, Robert Prouse, 77, 97, 121, 122, 148, 175
" Family of, 78, 129, 131, 123, 144, 183
" Pedigree of, 77
" John, 77, 97, 133, 158, 300
Hasson, Mr. 199
Hastings, Richard, 210
" Robert, 208
" Charles, 131
" Mary, 260
" Warren, 68
Hatche, Edmund and Ursula, 233.
" George, 236, 298
Hatton, Sir Christopher, 236
" Lord Chancellor, 257
" William Roger, 257
Haughton, Elizabeth, 242
Hawkins, John, 250, 256, 258
" Mary, 299
Haygarth, H. W. and W. 86
Hayner, Edward, 217, 245
" Francis, 198, 256, 297, 299
" William, 163, 179, 257, 301
" John, 76, 257
" Thomas, 245
Hayward, Thomas, 181
Haywood, Thomas, 302
" Sir Rowland, 212
Hazal, Edward, 245
Head, Thomas, 250, 284
Hearch, Agnes, 260
Heblethwayte, James, 156
Hedges, Sir Charles, 41, 230
" Pedigree and Family of, 230
Hedworth, Gilbert, 291
Heggeman de Kyngeston, 296
Hellen, John and William, 76, 147
Helmingham, Sir Arthur, 209
Helperley, Walter and John, 213, 259
Helpesly, Ralph, 76, 147
Hemes, John, 298
Hemingway, Vernon, 293
Hemson, Mr. 57
Henchman, Joseph, 262, 265
Hendeford, Thomas de, 52
Heneage, Michael and Thomas, 35, 210
Henesell, 114
Henniker, Lord, Major and John, 45, 113, 118, 181
Henry I., 2, 3, 11
" IV., 278

Herbert, William, 300
" James, 137
" Family of, 109, 169, 174, 301, 302
Herby, Thomas, 296
Hereford, Earl of, 52
" William de, 106
Herne, Edward and George, 258, 260, 302
" Edmund, 217, 262, 300
" William, 61, 147
" John, 258
" Pedigree of, 233
" Family of, 28, 186, 254, 260, 262, 299
Hertford, Countess of, 280
Herris, Sir Thomas, Pedigree of, 59
Hethering, Joel, 198, 293
Hewens, John, 181
Hewett, Mrs. 139
Hewlet, Charles, 109, 180, 181
" Martha, 169
Heydon, Henry and Mary, 250
" Anthony, 156
" Thomas, 297
Hoare, Charles Augustus, 193
Hobart, Richard, 280
Hobbes, Benjamin, 299
" Thomas, 298
Hoby, Sir Thomas, 206
" Sir Philip, 35, 57, 58, 144, 145
" Elizabeth, 119
" Pedigree of, 59
Hodenges, William and Ralph, 208
Hodges, Sir John, 205
Hodgson, Jane, 110
" Richard and Ann, 302
Hodleserg, Ralph, 201
" Gunnora, 208
Holbeche, Robert, 106
Holderness, James, John and Joseph, 196, 257, 264, 292
" George, 260
" William, 261
" Family of, 2, 46, 158, 259, 260, 262, 263, 264, 284, 285, 286, 300, 301, 302
Holbrok, Richard de, 4
Holcomb, Essex, William and Mary, 86, 184
" John, 73, 108
Holgate, William, 185
Holloway, Charles, 131, 141
" William, 132
Holland, John, 204
Hollis, John, 258
Holman, Grace, Thomas and Jone, 258
Holmes, John, 293
" Isaac, 131
" Thomas, 181
" Family, 117
" William Style, 132
Holt, Catherine and Edward, 89
Holte, Richard and Walter, 174, 182
Honeywood, Robert, 10, 155
Hood, Elizabeth, William, and Ellis, 111
Honson, Leonard, 302

Honson, John, 260
Hoppert, Robert, 301
Hopkins, Robert, 301
" John and George, 107, 126, 146
" Family of, 130, 131
" Richard Northey, 78
Horne, John, 182
" Randolph, 180, 185
Horseman, Giles, 158
Horsnail, Thomas, 300
Horton, Walter de, John and Andrew, 231, 295
" Family of, 201, 202
" Aunger de, 154
Hosey, John, 299
" Samuel, 289
Hosier, William John and Alice, 259
Houblon, Madame and James, 286
House, James and Susannah, 248
How, Richard, 285, 292
Howard, John H. 180
" Duke of Norfolk, 5, 6
" William, 248
" Pedigree of, 6, 7, 102
Howell, John, 301
" Richard, 302
Howthorne, Margaret, 63
Hibbard, Richard, 256, 257, 293
Hicks, John, 301
Hickman, Henry, 257, 293
" Mr. 222, 269
" Thomas and Dixie, 206, 208
Hieron, John, 256
Higgins, William, 209, 211, 234, 281, 297
" Jane, 261
" George, 211, 297
" Edward, 289
Highlord, John, 19
Hill, Arthur Lord Fairford, 70, 177
" John, 156
" Dorotty, 59
" Adam and Cordelia, 22
" Hudrell and Catherine, 230
Hilliard, Thomas, 216
Hilpe, John and Ann, 233
Hipkins, Richard, 183
Hippell, Richard, 285
Hiram, King of Tyre, 2
Horne, George, 190
Hubbard, Arthur, 197
Hudley, John, 186
Huggard, Michael, 260
Hugford, James, 222, 257
Hughes, Matthew, 73
" Edward and Margaret, 228
Humber, Richard, 301
Hungerford, Sir Robert, 191
" Lord, 192
Hunt, Maurice, 301
" Mary, 131
Hunter, Mr. 171
Huntercombe, Wm. de, 143, 154
Huntingfield, William de, 52
Huntingdon, Earl of, 204
Hurley, Richard, 157
Hurst, Thomas, 36
Husband, Richard and Beatrix, 232

Hussey, John, 219, 223, 260
" Ann, 219
Hutchinson, George, 281
Hutton, John, 97, 122, 132
" Pedigree of, 77
Hyde, Sir George, William and Dorothy, 82
" Leonard, 99
" Pedigree of, 82

Ibotson, William, 148
" Richard, 73, 134, 136
" Family of, 71, 73, 85, 112, 133, 160
Ikene, Richard, 9, 143
Ina, King, 197
Ingram, Joseph, 301
Ireland, Duke of, 277
" Richard, 299
Irons, Robert and Thomas, 272
Irby, Sir William, 288
" Pedigree of, 78
Isaac, Laurence, 157
Isherwood, George, 60
Ives, Jeremiah, 78
" John, 258

Jackson, Sir John, 209, 298
" Thomas, 180
Janaway, Mary, 186
Jannings, Peter, 250
Jarmyne, John, 258
Jeffries, Lord Chancellor, 215
Jeffrey, John, 156, 184, 291
" Edmund, 288
Jennings, —, 100, 139, 256
" William, 181
Jenks, Timothy Colly, 257
Jenyns, Roger and John Harvey, 175, 176
Jervis, Thomas, 131
Jocelyn, Ralph, 28
Jodrell, Major, 41
" Gilbert, 131, 139, 146, 264
" Pedigree of, 23
" Family of, 84, 218, 219
Jolliffe, Rev. William and Julia, 77
Johnson, Thomas, 41
" William, 24, 159, 300, 302
" Dr. 55, 215, 237, 280
" Samuel, 131
Jones, Richard, 135, 139, 198
" Henry, 293
Jorbauld, Alexander and Mary, 296
Jordan, Samuel, 65, 146, 148, 161
" Mary, 110
Jourdelay, John, 56, 143
" Thomas, 56
June, John, 299

Karkek, William, 38, 41
" Ralph, 41
Karliolo, William, 295
Keane, Mrs. 199
Keates, Joseph and Charlotte, 110
Keck, Arthur, 158
Kederminster, Edward, 144, 147
" Pedigree of, 89
" John, 88, 144, 156, 157
" Sir John, 157

# INDEX.

Keene, Mary, 17
Keith, Family of, 9
  „ George, 125
Kelly, John, 284, 291
Kelye, John, 260
Ken, William le and Ralph, 7, 12, 143
Kendall, Sir Edward and Elizabeth, 67
Kent, Duchess of, 68
Kerrett, Samuel, 142
Kildare, Earl of, 260, 264
Kimbell, Roger de, 253
Kimber, Edmund, 292
Kincaid, James, 100
King, Andrew, Sir Andrew, Ambrose and Pedigree of, 19, 44, 47, 95, 96, 144, 147, 157
  „ Daniel, 226
  „ Dr. Henry and Philip, 279, 280
  „ William, 89, 131, 289
  „ Ann, 260
  „ Mary, 137
  „ Colonel and George, 132
  „ John, 167
Kinge, Thomas, 260
Kingsbro', Lord, 146
Kingston, Duke of, 69
Kirkwall, Viscount, 159
Kirkman, Mr. 184
Kniffe, Richard, 155, 217
Knight, Thomas, 213, 218, 260, 298
Knox, Thomas, 228
Knyvett, Sir Thomas and Lord, 211
  „ Pedigree of, 212

Lacy, Roger de, 6
Ladell, William, 71, 136, 146, 148, 187
Ladbroke, John, 299
Laing, Family of, 249
Lake, Family of, 159, 253
  „ John, 25, 159
  „ Henry, 181, 285
  „ Joseph, 157, 212, 298
Lamb, Henry, 197, 257
Lamborde, —, 25
Lambyn, John, 276, 296 217
Lancaster, John and Edmund, 5, 6, 143
Landers, I. 142
Lane, William, 292, 299
Langdale, Alexander and Richard, 204
Langford, William, 155
Langley, Richard and Alexander, 231, 253, 298
  „ Elizabeth, 260
  „ Edward, 260
  „ Thomas, 253, 261, 297
  „ Judith and John de, 258
  „ William, 155, 217
  „ Margery, 260
Langton, Primate, 53
  „ Hannah, 301
Langridge, Thomas and Ursula, 100
Lanvaley, William de, 52
Lascelles, Edward, Duncan and Christian, 159, 201, 208
Laud, Archbishop, 91, 107

Lawrence, Thomas, 257
  „ James, 293
  „ John, 100, 122
  „ Elizabeth, 122, 189
Lavender, Thomas, 263
Lawson, Sir Gilfred, Sir Wilfred, and Emilia, 245
  „ Family of, 220
Leader, John and Judith, 72, 172, 173
Learner, William, 257
Le Bass, Charles, 45
Ledgold, Richard and William, 76, 147
Lee, Sir Robert and Sir Anthony, 225
  „ John, 19, 22, 44, 105, 112, 115, 205, 299
  „ Mary, 112
  „ Pedigree of, 23
  „ Roger, 261
  „ Family of, 227
Legg, Richard, 173
Legrande, —, 162
Leicester, Earl of, 38, 277
  „ Adam, 226
Leigh, Francis, 212, 301
  „ Edward, 158
  „ Ralph, 205
  „ Family of, 89, 158, 258
Leith, Captain Selwyn, 283
Leno, George, 103, 136, 178, 181
Leone, Edward and Ann, 259
Lethingburg, Nicholas, 253
Leverdake, George, 300
Leversedge, William, 173
Levery, Peter, 257
Levy, John, 158
Levyng, Samuel, 300
  „ Richard, 106
Lewin, Elizabeth, 131
  „ William, 139
  „ Robert, 132
  „ Thomas, 285
  „ Family of, 110, 129, 141
Lewington, Henry, Rose and Elizabeth, 129, 131, 132, 139
  „ William, 129
Lewis, Dorothy, 260
Lewthall, H., 300
Ley, Sir James, 94
Leybourne, Sir Roger and John, 277
Liber, Niger and Ruber, 4
Lidgold, John, 261, 258
  „ Richard, 258
Liming, James and Ann, 173
  „ John, 301
Lincoln, Bishop of, 114, 287, 290
Lingham, William, 236
Lipscomb, William, 131
  „ John, 260
  „ Doctor, 5, 8
Littlebury, Sir William, 99
Littlewood, John and Ann, 249
Lisle, Lord, 59
  „ Family of, 218
Livard, Thomas, 147
Livesay, Hugh, 106
Living, John and Ann, 156
Livingstone, Lord, 101
Lloyd, Richard, 62
  „ Catherine, 228

Lombe, Edward and Elizabeth, 23
London, John, 253
Long, Francis, 147, 172, 173
  „ Robert, 106
Lovel, 5
Lovelace, Henry, 59
  „ Low, 60, 82, 100
  „ Catherine, 60, 100
  „ Margaret, 157
  „ Sir Richard, 82
Lovegrove, John and Mary, 109, 130, 131, 132, 185
Louvaine, Godfrey de, 12
Lowndes, Pedigree of, 95
Lowe, Pedigree of, 95
Louthe, Roger de, 202, 253, 296
Lucas, George, 45
  „ William and James, 302
Ludgold, Abraham, 182, 183
  „ John, 186
  „ Reginald, 284, 289, 291
Ludgrove, Thomas, 285
Lybb, Richard, 76
Lyon, Sarah, 77
Lytton, Sir Robert, 207
Lyvelode, Ann, 64

Mabillon, 74
Maberley, Joseph, 185
Mackason, Robert, 71, 137, 177
  „ Mrs. 167, 169
  „ Family of, 160, 186
Mackenzie, Charles, 287
Macclesfield, Earl of, 215
Mackay, Mary, 174
Macneile, David, 190
Macreath, William, 146
Mackworth, Sir Herbert and Robert, 172
Madison, John, 300
Magna Charta, 4
Mainwaring, Dr. Edmund and Sir Randall, 226
Maish, Family of, 249, 283
  „ Thomas, 252
Malcolm, J. Wingfield, 78
Malet, William, 52
Malter, John, 193
Manders, 162
Manegdene, William and Hellen, 32
Manningham, Sir Oliver, 192
Mansfield, Thomas, 45
  „ Robert, 210
Marcham, John, 301
Marchford, Simon, 253
Marjoribanks, Edward, 190
Marlborough, Duke of and Amelia Sophia, 69, 77
Mareschall, William, 9, 52
Markland, William, 302
Marshall, Reginald and Richard, 156
Marsham, William, 156, 210, 297
Marten, Christopher and Peter, 258
Martin, William, 301
  „ Samuel, 155, 175
  „ Edward, 300
  „ Ann, 110
  „ Elizabeth, 261
Mascall, Richard and Elizabeth, 156
  „ William, 291

Mascall, James, 297
„ Stephen, 283, 291
„ Robert and Elizabeth, 167, 176, 258, 297
„ Robert, 260
Mascot, Frank, 291
Massington, James, John and Martha, 130
Masson, Mr. 194, 237
Mather, John, 260
Mathews, Christian, 111
„ Nathan, 137
„ Thomas and Martha, 58, 173
Mauduit, John and Margaret, 192
Maunde, William, 260, 264
Maunsell, Henry, John and Ada, 202, 295
Mauriscis, Geoffrey de, 14, 201, 231, 295
„ Christiana de, 1, 4, 7, 28, 143, 155
„ William de, 28
„ Family of, and Pedigree, 11
Maw, Captain R. S., 196
Maxey, Anthony, 253, 297
Maxwell, John and Sarah, 175, 293, 302
„ Joseph, 132
Mayhew, 228
Maynard, Sir William and Mary, 220, 223
„ Sir Henry, 156
Mayne, Simon and Colnbery, 218
Maynville, Sims, 297
Mayo, John, 263
„ Richard, 257
Mead, John, Earl of Clanwilliam, 45
„ John, 24
„ Sir Nathaniel and Martha, 223
Meale, William, 302
„ John, 173
„ Richard, 258
„ Andrew, 232, 289, 299
„ Sophia, 260
„ Christopher, 263
„ Thomas, 283
„ Family and Pedigree of, 258, 261, 289, 291, 300
Mede, Sir John, 102
Meeking, Charles, 269, 290
Meeres, Sir Thomas, 183
Melreth, Thomas, 155
Melve, John atte, 296
Melton, John de, 91, 106
Membyry, Mabilia de, 155
Mercer, William, 292
Meres, John, 301
„ Jones, 172
Meriton, Robert, 262
Merry, Robert, 289
Merton, John de. 155
Metcalf, Sir Thomas and Theophila, 91
Meux, Sir Henry, 41
„ Mrs. 139, 146
Michell, Nicholas, 256
Middleton, Peter de, 295, 296
„ Alice de, 204, 231, 295
„ Robert, 295

Milbourne, William, 110, 131
„ Martha, 110
Miller, Henry, 285
„ John, 182
„ Elizabeth, 261
Mills, S. Hugh, 137, 167, 175, 178, 302
Milton, John, 42, 244, 250
„ Sarah, 250, 259
„ Thomas, 42
„ Sir Christopher, 238, 259, 261, 264
Minshull, Randle and Elizabeth, 242
Mitcham, John, 300
„ Thomas, 301
Mitchell, William and Margaret, 142, 250
„ John, 66
Mocock, Joseph, 139
Mohun, Lord, 275
Mole, Henry, 131, 136
Moles, Elizabeth, 132
Moleyns, Sir William and Alianor, 191, 192
„ Family of, 192
„ Lord, 102
Molyneux, Admiral, 112
Mombezon, Roger de, 52
Moncriefe, Col. 230
Mone, Joseph, 299
Monnery, Josiah and Wilham, 83, 137, 167, 178
Monson, Sir James, 55
„ Sir John, 64
Montagu, John, Duke of, 138, 141, 146, 159
„ Charles William, 302
„ Edward and Mary Wortley, 69
„ Duchess of, 139, 145
„ Pedigree of, 69
Montfitchet, Richard de, 3, 154
„ Roger, 52
„ Sir Gilbert, 27
„ Robert, 101
„ Pedigree of, 3
Montford, Hugh, 217
Montrose, Earl of, 101
Moore, Thomas and Richard, 147, 257
„ Walter, 183
„ William, 109
More, John de la, 154
„ Elizabeth, 131
Morecock, Sarah, 131
„ Joseph and William, 186
Morer, John and Agnes, 258
Morgan, Walter, 157
„ Edward, 299
„ Robert, 179
Morse, George, 45
„ Simon, 131
„ Richard, 23, 44
Morrett, A. G. William, 132, 198
Morris, John, 181, 292
„ Charlotte, 87, 180
„ Gordon, S., 24
„ Joseph, 159
Mortlock, Roger, 184
Moss, Robert, 264
„ Family of, 264
Mounteagle, Lord, 211

Mountjoy, Lord, 208, 222, 234
Mountfort, Mr. 275
Mow, Thomas, 217
Mowbray, William de, 52
„ Lord, 102
Moy, Charles, 286
Mudgett, John, 283, 291
Mumford, Elizabeth, 260
Murimoth, Adam, 106
Murray, 121
„ Sir David, 101, 122
„ Sir John, 100
„ Family of, 102, 122
Mylsent, John, 205
Myngfield, Simon, 232
Mynne, Nicholas, 212

Nanney, Griffith, 262
„ William, 253, 259
„ Robert and Jeffrey, 223, 244, 254
„ Mary, 222, 254
Napton, Henry, 182
Neale, Francis, 300
Needham, John, 19
Neeld, Sir John, 1
Neketon, Ralph de, 56
Nelson, Thomas, 61, 156
Neville, Testa de, 3
„ Hugh de, 6
„ Elizabeth, 186
„ Sir Edward, 89
„ Montacute, Marquis of, 59
„ Seymour, 103, 107, 135, 148, 181
„ Agnes Mary, 112
„ Pedigree of, 82
New, John and Mary, 175
Newberye, Thomas and Mary, 233, 260
Newcastle, Duke of, 212
Newce, Ann, Samuel & Clement, 205
Newell, Joseph, 163
Newland, John, 183
Newman, John and Elizabeth, 137, 183
„ Thomas, 100
„ Richard, 298
Nicholas, Edward, 300
Nicholl, John, 37, 41, 263
„ Dr. Iltyd and Ann, 236
Nicholls, Edward and Mary, 83, 233
„ Humphry, 223
„ William, 174, 217, 233
„ Pedigree of, 83
„ Nichols, T. B., 118
Nickless, 43
Nightingale, Thomas, 263
Nixon, 122
Noble, Thomas, 59
Nomina, Villarum, 2
Norbury, Earl of, 147
Norfolk, Robert de and Mary, 296
„ Duke Muriel, 69, 212
„ Pedigree of, 7
Norman, Samuel, 146
Norreys, John, 272
„ Sir John, 6
„ Richard, 213
„ Pedigree of, 6
Norris, Sir Henry and Sir John, 35, 143, 144, 147, 288

North, George, 158
Northcroft, Thomas and Ann, 249
Northey, George, 144
Northland, Viscount, 228
Northumberland, Duke of, 35, 281
" Earl of, 302
Norton, 3
" John, 106, 175, 302
Norwode, Sir Roger de, 143
" Pedigree of, 7
Notte, John, 182
Nourse, Pedigree of, 23
Novell, John, 137
" Mary, 177
Noyes, William, 301

Oak, Samuel, 293
Obrien, Dame Mary, 260, 264
Oburne, Joseph, 292
Oder de Ponte, Thomas, 154
Oddie, Henry Hoyle, 159, 302
Offley, William and Margery, 182
Ogilvy, Thomas, 29
Okey, William and Jeffery, 201, 294
Ollerenshaw, or Wrench, 68, 219
Ommaney, Cornthwaite, 24, 159, 302
Onley, John Mason, 292
Opie, Barbara, 186
Oppenhoe, Alice de, 32
Orange, Prince of, 279
Originalia Rolls, 4
Orkney, Earl of, 78, 293
Orford, Earl of, 210, 275
Orleans, Duke of, 206
Ormond, Earl of, 203
Osborn, William, 257
Osgood, John, 213
Osman, William, 160
Osmond, Henry, 291, 258
" Agnes, 258
Other, Walter Fitz, 194
Oulton, 227
Outram, Sir James, 293
Overton, Richard and Dionysius, 204, 231, 297
Owen, Charles, 85, 302
" Sir David and Sir Henry, 205
" John, 260
" Pedigree of, 205
Oxenford, Thomas de, 90
Oxeheye, Richard de, 231
Oxey, Sir Richard, 108
Oxenbridge, John and Robert, 143, 144, 145
" John and Sir Goddard, 63
" Sir Thomas and Catherine, 205
" Pedigree of, 64
Oxford, Pedigree of, 7
" Countess of, 5

Packer, John, 137
" Joseph, 167
Padnore, Simon, 139
Page, John, 200
" William, 58
Paget, William, Lord, 45
Paine, John, 250

Paine, Joseph, 260
Painter, John, 111
" Edward, 285
" Mrs. 162
Palgrave, Sir Francis, 303
Pallavicini, Sir Toby, 88
Palmer, William, 236, 253
" Family of, 75, 109, 135, 159, 170, 186, 237, 261
" Richard, 107
" John, 136, 148, 159
" Robert, 155, 158, 301
" Roger and Thomas, 157, 159
Panxy, Mr. 221
Papworth, William de, 32
Paris, Mathew, 53, 194
" Thomas, 160
Parker, Sarah, 131
" Sir Henry, 86
" Sir Hyde, 66
" Sir William, 85
Parkes, James and Mary, 19, 144
Parkin, Pedigree of, 24
Parkins, Hugh, 47, 131, 145, 147, 179
Parkinson, Edward, 257
Parr, Thomas, 138
Parris, Thomas, 91, 169
Parrington, Richard, 148
Parry, Richard, 299
" Thomas, John, and Mary, 227
Parsons, Sir John, 35, 89
" Mary Ann, 261
Partington, Thomas, Richard, and Elizabeth, 129, 144, 159
Pasmore, Edward, 133, 136
Paterson, John, 302
" George, 270, 293
Patteshall, Martin de, 106
Paulet, George, and Sir William, 17, 38, 143, 209
" Pedigree of, 15
Pawsey, Joseph, 286
Paxton, Archibald, 100, 167, 185
" Harriet, 120
Paynter, John, 299
Peade, Leonard, Robert, and Elizabeth, 253, 259, 262
Peake, Sir John, 62
" William, 76, 158, 300
Pearce, Charles, 97
Pearson, William, 72, 73, 135, 141, 174, 184, 199, 256, 264
" Sarah, 259, 263
" James, 264
" Family of, 260, 185
Peartin, John, 261
Peecock, John, 167
Peeling, Ann, 173
Peland, John, 155
Pembroke, John, 129, 132
Pengree, George, 228
Penistone, Elizabeth. 261
Penn, Thomas and William, 18, 279
Pennar, William, 217
" John, 144, 210, 297
Pennington, Isaac, 18, 144, 145, 244
Penyman, George, 61, 158
Perci, Richard de, 52
Percival, Sarah, 132

Percy, Ingelram de, 6
" Algernon, 302
Perkins, Thomas and William, 147, 167, 261
" George, 260
" Francis, 173
" Ann, 142
" Edward, 248
" Family of, 175
Perrers, Richard and Alice, 203, 204, 208
Perrott, Richard, 301
Pert, Margaret, 30
Peryent, Sir John and Gertrude, 82, 160, 182
" Pedigree of, 95
Peters, John, 43, 75, 83, 147, 211, 213, 258, 259, 279, 298
" Charles, 254, 262
" Clement, 299
" Henry, 258, 261
" William, 144, 156, 210, 258, 272, 284, 291, 297
" Family of, 147, 186, 211, 233, 258, 259, 260, 261, 262, 264, 300
" Pedigree of, 233
Peto, Charles, 156
Pettus, Sir John and Sir Thomas, 214
Pettyward, Daniel, Roger, and Walter, 183, 184
Petworth, Richard, 253
Phelps, Richard, 247
Phipps, Thomas, Edward, and Elizabeth, 132, 258
Philip, King of France, 53, 102
Philibert, John, 32
Philipson, John, 89
Phillip, James, 107
" William, 285
Phillips, Edmund, 238
" John, 218
" Edward, 212
" Sir Erasmus, 275
" William, 292
" Elizabeth, 275
Philpot, John, 198, 257
Pickering, Sir Christopher, 212
Pierrepoint, Evelyn, 69
Piers, Walter, 253
Pigot, Francis and Joan, 217
" Michael, 100, 218
" Pedigree of, 218
Pinchon, Nicholas and John, 96, 158, 183
" William, 20, 96, 129
" Pedigree of, 21
Pinhorn, Sir John and Jane Price, 100
Pilgrim, William, 147
Pillessedisse, John, 32
Pinkeney, Henry de, 50
Pinner, John, 156
Pinnock, J. 66
" Henry, 135, 141, 172, 186
Pipard, 276
Piper, Edward and Susan, 258
Piscator, Salomon, 154
Pitt, Roger, 260
" John, 281, 298
" Thomas, 246, 255, 258, 260, 261, 282, 289, 291

Pitt, Pedigree of, 274
Plaighter, Hugh and Agnes, 258
Plaister, Ann, 260
Plaistow, Samuel, 110
Plaiz, Ralph de, and Richard, 5, 143
  ,, Pedigree of, 6
Plastrell, William, 232
Platt, Richard and Sarah, 258
Pleydell, Mr. 93
Plomer ats Laynham
  ,, Sir John, 16
Plumridge, John, Thomas and Martha, 248
Plunket, Richard, Sir Christopher, and Baron Dunsany, 12
Pocock, Mary, 109
Poges, Robert, Margaret, and Peter, 192, 205, 296
Pole, William de la, John, and Alice, 232
  ,, Michael, 277
Pollard, John, 56, 143
Pope, Thomas and Phœbe, 68
  ,, Richard, 155
  ,, the Poet, 49
  ,, the Pope Nicholas, 205
  ,, Dr. Robert, 179
  ,, Mary, 205
  ,, Samuel, 175
Portland, Duke of, 215
Portman, Sir Henry, 102
Porter, Thomas, 137, 177, 250, 291
  ,, Edward, 298
  ,, Elizabeth, 260
  ,, Jane, 300
Porteus, Juliana, 230
Potter, Thomas, 62
Poulter, Thomas, 148
Povery, John, 135
  ,, Elizabeth, 131
Pover, Christopher, 154
Powell, Mr. 227
  ,, John Harcourt, 85, 127, 137, 159, 179
  ,, Thomas and Harcourt, 45, 62, 130, 139, 145, 174, 176, 185, 302
  ,, Richard, 242
  ,, Charles, 257
  ,, Pedigree of, 86, 128
Power, William P. 260
Powncy, John, 21
Powndey, John, 158
Poyle, William de la, 204
  ,, Family of, 204
Prettie, Harris, 158
Prettyman, Dr. 290
Pretty, Oliver, 299
  ,, Thomas, 173
  ,, Elizabeth, 132, 173
Price, Joanna, 181
  ,, Eleanor, 299
  ,, Richard, 298
  ,, Martha, 131
Priddith, Elizabeth, 301
Pringle, James, 190
Pritty, Mr. 138
Proby, Charles and Agnes Mary, 82
Proctor, Sir Thomas B., William, and Sir William, 62
Prowse, Arms of, 121
  ,, Pedigree of, 77

Prunes, Walter, 144
Pryor, Felix, 114, 134, 147
Prys, Thomas, 296
Pullin, Stephen, 197, 246, 250, 257
  ,, James, 71, 126, 146, 148, 161
  ,, Family of, 130, 131, 196, 198, 250, 260, 264
Puttock, William, 257, 260
  ,, Jone, 257
  ,, Jane, 261
  ,, William and John, 76
Purbeck, Lord, 279
Purchas, Thomas, 296
Purefoy, John, 208
Pury, J. 253
Pynchon, John, 144, 145, 217, 232
  ,, William, Agnes, and Nicholas, 144
  ,, Pedigree of, 21
Pyne, History of Royal Residences, 2
Pytches, Sir Abraham and Dame Jane, 77, 121, 132, 181
Pytt, Thomas, 157, 284, 291
  ,, Pedigree of, 274

Raan, Walter de, 206
Rabbe, Walter, 56, 155
  ,, Henry, 206
Rainsford, Richard and Ann, 82
Ramsbottom, Mr. 268
Randall, William, 162
  ,, Elizabeth, 260, 264
Randell, Thomas, 131
Ramsgrove, Walter, 154
Ratcliff, John and Joane, 225, 227
Rawson, Henry, 292, 298
  ,, Edmund, 297
Rayner, Henry, 263
  ,, Thomas, 198, 285, 293, 300
  ,, Joseph, 292
Read, Thomas, 213, 218
Reading, Thomas of, 267
Rede, Lodowicke, 182
Redford, Isaac, 268, 292
Redvers, Baldwin, 6
Reed, Thomas, 175
Reeve, Richard, 75, 147, 298
  ,, William, 107
  ,, John, 212, 298
  ,, Nicholas, 260
Reeves, William, 198
  ,, Richard, 217
Reffell, Joseph, 165, 257
  ,, Family of, 196, 198, 250, 260, 264
Reid, Neville, 136, 145
Remenham, John de, Thomas, and Hugh, 56, 143, 154, 155, 231, 295
Repynton, Ambrose, 253
Reuter, Mr. 153
Rewys, Nicholas, 106
Reynell, Sir Thomas, 218
Rich, Sir Richard and Lord, 207, 212, 218
Richard, King of the Romans, 27
Richard II., 278
Richard, Thomas Lord Cramond, 214
  ,, Family of, 285, 292

Richardson, Mr. 236
  ,, John and Joyce, 173, 279
  ,, William and Marie Jane, 95, 121
Richmond, Duke of, 69
Riddlesford, Walter, 29
Ride, John, 148
Ridge, 91
Ridley, Francis, 255, 298, 299
Ringer, Thomas, 45, 85, 158
  ,, Pedigree of, 86
Rippon, Charles, 235
Roake, Thomas, 160
Robarts, Thomas, 254
Roberts, Thomas, 250, 251
  ,, John, 260
Robins, George, 275
  ,, Thomas, 77, 158, 300
Robinson, Mary, 68
  ,, Maurice, 158
  ,, Sir Thomas and William, 91
  ,, Thomas and Jane, 110
  ,, John, 301
Robson, William, 157, 298
Roche, Thomas de la, and Mariotte, 204
Rockley, John, 134
Rodyffe, Philip and Elizabeth, 258
Rodolph, George and Elizabeth, 71
Rodney, Sir George, 254
Roe, Thomas, 253
Rogers, Richard, 254
  ,, William and Ann, 249
    See Coxwell.
Rolfe, William, 147
  ,, Thomas, 135, 176
Rolls, John and Jessy, 45, 116
Rolt, Sir John, 41
Rooke, William and Saranmaria, 101, 120
  ,, Thomas, 210
Ros, Robert de, 52
Rose, Alexander, 225
Rosier, Rebecca, 131
  ,, Daniel, 135
Ross, Lord, 101
Rothwell, Elizeus, 253
Rotomage, Joan de, 30
Roumieu, Mr. 127, 131
Round, Mr. 284
Rous, George, 131
  ,, Thomas Bates, 139, 146
  ,, Nathaniel, 77
Rowden, Thomas, 258
Rowe, Thomas, 158, 222, 300
Rowland, John, 77, 97, 144
  ,, Pedigree of, 77
Roxburgh, Duke of, 68
Rudhall, Mary, 131
Rudstone, Robert, 147
Ruffo, Robert de, 201
Ruggles, Colonel Ruggles Brise, 21
  ,, Family of, 21, 41
Russel, Lord James and Tryphena, 220, 223
Russell, Thomas, 157
  ,, Simon and Stephen, 296
  ,, William, 285, 301
  ,, John, 111, 131, 141
  ,, Elizabeth, 111

Russell, Joseph, 173
Rupert, Prince, 42, 279
Rutland, Earl of, 278
Rutter, Leonard and John, 181
Rycroft, Charles, 290
Rysley, Henry and William, 210, 298

Sadler, Sir Seymour, 211
Sadleir, Sir Ralph, 39
  „  William and Margaret, 156
  „  Family of, 261
Salisbury, John, 260
  „  Bishop, 237
Saltmarsh, John, 263
  „  Charles, 144, 158, 301
Salter, Sir William, 41, 144, 147
  „  Christopher, 42
  „  Lady Ursula, 174, 289
  „  David, 241, 288, 291
  „  Mary, 260
  „  Daniel, 154, 284, 288
  „  Family of, 129, 156, 157, 211, 232, 261, 262, 283, 298, 300
  „  Pedigree of, 233
Sampson, Mr. 217
Sancto Vedasto, Roger and Hugh, 295
Sandes, Lord, 100
  „  Margaret, 260
Sanders, John, Simon, and Mary, 111, 176
  „  Thomas Cheadle and Harriet, 24, 93, 100, 121, 185
Sandford, William and Edward, 144, 157, 214
  „  John, 158
  „  Cordelia, 22
  „  Family of, 21, 22
Sandys, Colonel Martin, 100, 139, 144, 159, 176
  „  Pedigree of, 71
  „  Lord, 70, 100
  „  William Trumbull, 177
Sandwich, Earl of, 69
Sarney, John, 24, 45, 112
  „  Margaret Irene, 45, 131
Saunders, Simon, 178
  „  Mary, 177
  „  Joseph, 148
Saule, Nicholas and Alice, 223
Saumarez, John St. Vincent, 78
  „  Augusta Caroline, 78
Savan, Mrs. 142
Sawyer, Michael, 209
  „  Mark and James, 172
Say, Geffrey de, 6, 8, 52
  „  Beatrix, 6, 8
  „  Sir John, 16
  „  Thomas, 297
  „  Pedigree of, 16
Sayer, James and Martin, 117
Scalers, Richard de, 88
  „  Lord, 6
Scawen, Robert, 210, 218, 259
  „  Sir Thomas, 263, 281, 301, 302
  „  Tryphena, 281
  „  Francis, 244
  „  John, 300
  „  Pedigree of, 223

Scawen, Family of, 102, 219, 220, 222, 245, 253, 257, 260, 265, 286
Scholefield, Cotterill, 47, 54, 114, 131, 136, 148
Scoones, W. D., 103
Scotenye, Imbertius de, 296
  „  John de, 295
Scott, Henry James, 69
  „  William and Maud, 262
  „  Duke of Buccleugh, 69
  „  Sir Peter, 89
  „  Laurence William, 13, 41
  „  Pedigree of, 69
Scrimshaw, James, 107
Scrope, Lord, 102
Scudamore, Mr. 5
Scutz, Matthew, 254
Seames, John, 252
Seares, Edward, 157
Sedgwick, John, Ann, and Alice, 253
  „  Aaron, 285, 300
  „  Moses, 292
Seely, Philip, Josiah, and Rose, 299
Segrave, Lord, 102
Selwyn, John, 273, 283
Seryth, William, 296
Sequence, B. P. 302
Sewell, Mr. 75
Seymour, Sir Edward and Sir Henry, 107, 286
  „  James, 299
  „  Henry, 158
Sexton, James, 152, 163, 179, 181
  „  Henry, 222
  „  John, 292
Shakespeare, Alderman, 24
Shakerley, George, 131
Share, Geffrey, 291
Shareshall, John de, 106
Sharrow, John, William, and John, 95, 144, 214
  „  Family of, 18, 76, 96
  „  Pedigree of, 19
Sharington, William, 31
Sharpe, Robert, 207
Sheffield, Penelope and Sir Robert, 77, 121, 132
Sheldon, Joseph and Ralph, 183
  „  Gilbert, Archbishop of Canterbury, 183
  „  Sir Joseph, 183
Shelton, William, 80, 83, 134, 136, 145, 148
Shelley, Sir John and Catherine, 220, 223, 301
  „  Richard, 59
  „  the Poet, 59, 220
Shepperd, John, 198, 255
  „  A. H. 24
Sherbroke, Richard, 17
Sherland, Thomas, 43
Sheridan, R. B. and Frances, 68
Sherwood, Lieutenant George, 262
Shirley, R. 178, 198
Shobingdon, William and John, 205, 215
  „  Pedigree of, 215
Shobenangre, John de, 10, 143
Shorne, Sir John, 116

Shorter, Henry, 273, 284, 291
  „  Sir John, 186, 211, 258, 298
  „  Pedigree of, 275
Shortland, William, 256
Shuldham, Samuel, 24, 45, 46, 112, 118, 132, 146, 147
Shurley, Richard, 257
Shrewsbury, Earl of, 232
Shrub, Thomas, 147
Sills, William, Daniel and Ann, 66, 109, 135, 139, 160
  „  Richard, 66
  „  Joseph, 180
  „  Family of, 130, 131, 132
Simon, Sarah, 131
Sims, James, 138
  „  Family of, 110
Singer, Robert, 177, 247, 256, 257
Singleton, Charles and John, 183
  „  Margaret, 184
Skerne, Henry and Robert, 203
Skuller, Mary, 131
Skinner, Thomas, 186
  „  John H. 136
Slater, Thomas, 260
Slaughter, Morgan, 301
Slocock, Benjamin, 83, 130, 146, 148, 164, 169
Slocombe, Edmund, 283, 289, 291, 298, 292
  „  John, 61, 158, 232, 285, 300
  „  Family of, 258
  „  Pedigree of, 233
Small, David and James, 269, 293
Smart, William, 160
  „  John, 106
Smijth, Sir Thomas, 13, 37, 144, 145, 209
  „  Sir William, 58, 59, 78, 233
  „  Dame Bridget, 66
  „  George, 60
  „  Family of, 13, 100, 144, 233
  „  Pedigree of, 41
Smith, Robert and Philip, 218, 260, 298
  „  Diana and Vernon, 129
  „  Henry, 96
  „  George, 148
  „  Sarah, 131
  „  Ralph Colley, 171, 180, 185
  „  Family of, 111, 141, 176, 217, 298
Smither, Henry, 292
Smyth, Robert le, 10, 143
  „  Philip, 21, 212
  „  Thomas, 157
Snape, Thomas, 76, 147
Snowden, Mr. 198
  „  William, 250
Somerset, Duke of, 37, 215, 234, 288
  „  Duchess of, 302
Sorrell, John, 61, 62.
  „  Abel, 300
Southwell, Sir Robert, 183
  „  Francis, 82
  „  Family of, 57
  „  Pedigree of, 95
Sparks, Mr. 271

2 s

Sparry, William, 156, 208
Speed, Richard, 291
Spelyng, John, 296
Spencer, —, 50, 82
Spenser, Sir John and Alice, 239, 256
   ,, Isabella, 181
   ,, Family of, 82, 104
   ,, Pedigree of, 29
Spicer, John and Mary, 132
Spielman, Sir John, 73
Spigurnell, Henry, 202
Spiller, Sir Henry and Catherine, 218
Spilman, James and Julia, 229
   ,, Martha, 100
Spong, F. Mallet, 257
Springett, Guglielma, 18
Spurling, John, 257
   ,, Mary, 261
Squire, James, 292
St. Croix, William de, 96
St. Hilary, James, 201
St. John, Oliver, 64
Stacey, John and Margaret, 77
Stackpole, Baron, and Duke of, 97, 146
Stafford, Sir Humphrey, 16
   ,, George, 257
Stamford, Alice, 30
Standish, Richard, 302
Stanley, William, 253
   ,, Richard and Sibill, 258
   ,, Ann. 260
Stannard, William, 260
Stanney, Eliz. 173
Stanninat, Robert, 292
Stanny, Mr. 142
Stanton, Thomas, 137, 167
   ,, William, 250
Star Chamber, 4
Starkey, Samuel, 286
Staunton, William, 232
   ,, John de, 106
   ,, Adam, 4
Steele, E. 118
Steers, William, 183
Stennet, Dr. Joseph, 125
Stephens, John, 20
   ,, Matthew, 131
   ,, Family of, 60, 62, 110, 132, 158, 164, 176, 198, 240, 261, 263
Steppingley, Robert, 106
Sterling, Earl of, 71
Stevens, Willoughby, 186
   ,, William Vernon, 261
   ,, Mary, 132
   ,, Goldyne, 129, 132
   ,, Family of, 236, 257, 258
Stevenson, John, 301
Steward, Walter, and Pedigree, 102
Stewart, Lady Janet, 191, 201
   ,, Elizabeth, 102
Stigand. 194
Still, William, 75
Stockdale, James, John and Catherine, 219, 223, 260
   ,, Richard, 219
Stockley, Thomas, 131
Stockman, John, 182
Stockwood, Edward, 182

Stoke, William atte, 155
Stokes, William, 186, 258
   ,, Christopher, 251
   ,, H. 64
Stone, Ann, 131
   ,, Pedigree of, 95
   ,, Sir Richard, 95
Stonystrete, Giles, 154
Stonor, Walter, 143, 187
   ,, Family of, 16, 56, 57, 58, 119, 125, 153, 232
   ,, Pedigree of, 59
Stoughton, Mr. 96
Stracy, John and Margaret, 176, 184
Strachan, Andrew, 190
Strachy, William, 37
Stradbroke, Earl of, 206
Stradling, Edward, 262
   ,, Margaret, 233
Strammell, Walter and Judith, 258
Streatley, Richard, 131, 135, 139
Street, Ann, 186
   ,, Linwood, 131
Strike, Leonard, 148
Stroode, Henry, 50
Strongbow, Richard, 6
Stukeley, Dr. 90
Sturges, William, 130, 131
Style, John, 262, 301
   ,, Anthony, 147
   ,, Robert, 37, 38, 79, 135, 156, 183
   ,, Family of, 66, 110, 117, 129, 130, 157, 158, 186, 258
Styles, Simon, 27
Suffolk, Earl of, 212
   ,, Duke of, 232
Sullivan, Derby, 363
   ,, John A. 290
Sutherland, Duke of, 69
Sutton, Mr. 43
Sybel, John, 69
Sydenham, John, 102
Symonds, William and Joan, 182
Swain, Thomas, 137, 247
Swatkin, Edward, 219, 300
Swayne, Thomas, 291
Sweeting, Francis, 301
Swenfen, Samuel, 220, 301

Tame, Robert, 202, 296
Tanner, Thomas, 57, 170, 181, 187
   ,, Elizabeth, 137, 176
   ,, Jone, 187
Tanner's Notitia, 30
Tappin, Sarah, 111, 112
Tapscot, Samuel, 302
Tash, Hatton and George, 139, 158
Tasker, John, 301
Tatton, William, 91
Taunton, John de, 296
   ,, Sir William, William and Catherine, 259, 264
Taverner, Robert, 258, 261, 264
   ,, Richard, 264
Taylor, William, 131, 136
   ,, James, 167
   ,, George, 108, 130, 254
   ,, Henry, 146
   ,, Samuel, 110
   ,, John, 36, 236, 196

Taylor, Richard, 186
   ,, Family of, 90, 110, 130, 137, 148, 167, 250, 290
Tegg, Francis and Mary, 302
Telford, David, 190
Temple, Robert, 107
   ,, Sir Purbeck, 71, 299, 300
   ,, Sir Richard, 279
   ,, Sir Thomas, 71
Tendering, Christian, 272
   ,, William and Dorothy, 82
   ,, Sir William and Alice, 6, 102
Terry, William, 147
Thackeray, Dr. George, 68
Thanes, 3
Theed, John, 193
Theodulph, William, 295
Thessiger, Frederick, 87
Thomas, Charlotte and Mary, 131
   ,, Family of, 111, 100
Thomond, Marquis of, 260, 264
Thompson, Henry, 293
   ,, Mr. 68
   ,, William, 300
   ,, Robert, 170
   ,, James, 280
   ,, Elizabeth, 247
Thomson, William, 180
Thoresby, Thomas, 212
Thorntagia, Richard, 295
Thornton, Benjamin, 285
   ,, John, 298
Thowe, Mr. 271
Throgmorton, George, 209
Throsby, John, 159
Thurbin, William, 137, 178, 198
Thurley, family of, 249
Tillier, William, 259, 263
   ,, Agnes, 262
   ,, James, 173
   ,, Family of, 130, 259
Tilson, Thomas, 302
Tingledon, John and Charles, 205
Tipper, Samuel, 245
Tippet, Mr. 196, 198
Tolen, John, 80
Tollit, 271
Tollemache, J. R. 206
Tompson, Mr. 285
Topham, John and Richard, 20, 96, 144, 158
Torkington, Peter and Bridget, 205
Torrington, —, 67
Toussaint, Charles, 261
Tower, Christopher, 61, 69, 144, 159
   ,, Thomas, 144, 172, 174, 176
   ,, Family and pedigree of, 62, 137, 138
Townshend, Cornelius, 46, 139, 146
   ,, Isaac and Charles, 46
   ,, Neale William, 302
   ,, George, 288, 289
Towsey, William A., Charles and Susanna, 73, 177, 260
Towte, John, Juliana and Alice, 181
Tracy, Sir Humphrey, 212
   ,, Henry, 16
Trash, George and Elizabeth, 111
Treaver, John, 172

# INDEX.

Tredway, Henry, 210, 259, 263, 264
" Thomas, 213, 298
" Dorothy, 259, 262
" Richard, 210
Trenchard, Ann, 223
Trevilian, Hugh and Jane, 100
Trevor, Sir John, 261, 263
Trippick, Mary, 186
" Ellis, 117, 132, 172, 173, 301
Trotman, Shadrach, 131, 137, 177
" Sarah, 111
Trotter, John, 41
Trout or Tout, James, 84
" William, 257
Trumball, Dr. William, 19, 61, 70, 139, 144, 145, 157, 159
" Pedigree of, 71
Trumper, George, 198
Tubbs, Family of, 259
Tubb, Sarah, 170, 180, 181
Tuck, Ann. 261
" Mr. 160
Tucking, William, 156
Tucker, Jeffrey, 142
" John, 138, 181
Tudor, Richard, 259
Tulloch, Francis and Thomas, 97
Tunnell, Henry, 180
Tunstall, John, 300
Tupp, John, 198, 244, 263
" George, 195, 198, 257, 261
Tupper, Geoffrey, 157
Turkeys, T. L. 296
Turboe, John, 302
Turner, John, 262
Turpin, Richard, 229
Turton, William, 158
Tyrel, William, 302
" Ann, 131
" Sir Charles, 102
Tyrrell, Edward, 149, 198, 257, 275
" Captain, 216
" Family of, 196
" Pedigree of, 236

Unton, Sir Alex. 218
Upenon, Walter de, 201
Urwin, Gilbert and Mary, 83, 172, 173
" George, 184
" Pedigree of, 233

Val, Hugh de la, 6
Valois, Philip de, 277
Vandernan, Fretwell, 107, 116, 139, 143
Vandeput, Peter, 41
Vane, Sir Henry, 21
Vansittart, Mr. 55
" Augustus, 78
Vedasto, Hugh de, 276
Vere, Robert de, 52
" Jeffrey, John Earl of Oxford, 45
" Family of, 5, 143
Verney, Mary, 156
" Sir Edmund, 157
Vernon, John. 144
Verry, Samuel and John, 137, 177
Verwins, Mr. 146

Very, Richard, 110, 135
Vesci, Eustace de, 52
Veysey, John, 106
Vicar, Richard and Frances, 250
Virgo, William, 147, 259, 300
" Jane, 262
" John and Elizabeth, 259
" John, Frances and Anne, 248
" Family of, 174, 248, 256, 262, 263, 301

Wade, Richard, 148
Wadham, John and Florence, 102
" Nicholas, 102
Wadlow, John, 292
Wagstaff, John and Sarah, 245, 255, 265
Walden, John de, 9, 154
" Family of, 143, 186
" Pedigree of, 9
Waldegrave, Sir Thomas, 16
Waleden, Richard and Humphry, 204
" Pedigree of, 9
Walengfort, Motildis de, 276
Waleys, John, 239
Walford, John, 142
Walger, Henry and Ursula, 156
Walkden, Sir Thomas, 301
Walker, George, 137
" Richard, 135
" Sir Thomas, 220
Wall, Robert and Sarah, 227
Waller, Edmund, 89, 206, 298
" Sir William, 23, 45
" Family of, 50
Walley, Thomas, 159
Walpole, Sir Robert, 274
" Horace, 94, 275
" Lady, 275
Walshe, William, 66, 144, 145, 156
" Walter, 57, 119, 144
" Family of, 58, 119
" Pedigree of, 59
Walter, Lady and Sir John, 287
" Edmund, 157
" Thomas, 109
" The Steward, 102
Walthowe, Peter, 107
Walworth, Sir William, 89
Wapshot, Thomas, 172
" Reginald de, 172
" Nicholas, 186
Warburton, Dr. 240
Ward, Sarah, 125
" Richard, 258
" Ralph, 299
Warde, Ralph, 29, 129
" Andrew, 129, 144, 258
" John, 260
Wardock, John, 155
Warle, Ingeland de, 106
Warne, William, 61
Warner, pedigree of, 23
Warnett, John and Joane, 205
Warren, George, 157
" Richard, 232
" Earl of, 7
Waryng, 77, 293
" Richard, 292
Warwick, Earl of, 82, 275

Washington, Laurence, 157
Water, Henry, 143
Watkinson, William and Mary, 223
Watson, Edward Temple, 196, 198
Watts, Nicholas, 260
Way, Dr. Thomas, 101
" Bertha, 263
Waynough, Joseph, 158
Wears, William, 160
Webb, Richard, 133
" Edmund, 260
" Eliza, 31
" Michael, 268
Webber, William and Thomazina, 238, 242
Webster, Mr. 248
" Thomas, 183
Weincham, Henry, 154
Weir, James, 190
Wenforth, William and Margaret, 258
Wenard, 59
Wendleshire, William de, 295
Wentworth, Lord, 59
Werndley, John C. 107
Wessel, Leonard and Martha, 223
" Abraham, 219
West, Thomas, 181, 299
" Richard and Ann, 198, 260, 299
" J. W. 230
" Captain William, 216
" Elizabeth, 261
" Family of, 20, 21, 108, 109, 129, 158, 230, 259, 262, 286, 300
Westall, John, 301
Westaway, Mark, 112, 116, 148, 269
Westbury, Dr. William, 16, 235
Westen, Humphry, 186
Weston, Ann, 147
" Richard, 106
Westminster, Abbot of, 2
Westmoreland, Earl of, 23, 29, 82
Westrop, Frederick, 293
Wexford, 154
Wexham, Thomas, 147
Weye, Alexander, 295
Weyland, John, 23, 41, 102, 186
" William, 62
" Cecily, 102
" Pedigree of, 23
Weymouth, Lord, 68
Wharton, Thomas Lord, 286
" Colonel, 287
Wheate, Sir Thomas, 75
Wheatley, General, 228
Wheler, William, 208, 297
" Sir Edmund and Alice, 208, 233
Whetham, Nathaniel, 275
Whethill, Pedigree of, 205
Whethanstead, Geoffrey, 202, 253
" John, 253
Whitaker, John, 198
White, John Jervis, 42, 131
" Mary, 131
" Henry, 182
" Francis, 159
" Joseph, 85
Whistler, John and Thomas, 95, 144

Whitechurch, Deborah, 75
Whiteing, William, 183
Whitehead, Gilbert, 115
,,  Paul, 77
Whitelock, Bulstrode, 218
,,  Sir James, 218
Whitfield, Robert, 137, 168
Whitlock, Sir James, 218, 279
Whitmarsh, William, 131, 135, 137, 168
,,  Ann, 131
Whitmore, William, 83
Whittington, 225
Whitwall, John, 107
Whitwell, William, and John Griffin, 82
,,  Pedigree of, 82
Whyttlebye, Alberic, 202
Wich, Agnes, 260
Wicherley, John, 262, 292
Wickham, Edward, 253
Widwick, Richard, 217
Wigginton, William, 301
Wigley, William, 185
Wigtoun, Earl of, 102, 120, 122, 131, 146
,,  Pedigree of, 102
Wildman, Thomas, 147
Wilcox, William, 258
Wilford, Philippa, 38, 89
,,  John, 41, 209
Wilfred, Bishop, 2
Wilken, T., 228
,,  Michael, 132, 111, 135
,,  Family of, 130
Wilkins, Henry Field, 181
Wilkinson, John, 159
Willesden, Walter de, 201
,,  John and Ann, 122
William III. King, 279, 286
Williams, Ann, 301
,,  Thomas, 70, 146, 180, 198, 222, 286
,,  Colonel, 136, 164, 196, 234
,,  Pedigree of, 228
,,  Eusebius, 186
,,  Charles, 257
Williamson, Harriet Frances, 198
Willingham, Sarah, 246
Willis, John, 25, 131, 142
,,  Solomon, 186
Wilmot, Nathaniel and William, 87, 135, 137, 167, 178
,,  Elizabeth, 131
,,  Alice, 132
,,  Family of, 107, 110, 127
Wilson, Peter, 292, 293
,,  John, 261
,,  Felix, 58, 144, 147, 157, 212, 261, 289, 298
Wiltshire, Mary, 132
Willey, Sir Richard and Matilda, 67

Willey, Milo and John, 67
Wills, Robert and Ann, 131, 302
Winch, Ann and John, 105, 141, 172, 174
,,  Family of, 110
Winchester, Earl of, 143
Winckworth, Job, 160
Winchley, Thomas, 222, 302
Windham, William and Mary, 186
,,  Pedigree of, 7
Winder, Edward, 131, 177
Windleshore, Hugh de, William de, and Ralph, 143, 144, 251, 254
,,  Pedigree of, 208
Windsor, Thomas, 156
,,  Edward, 297
,,  Family of, 31, 35, 82, 106, 201, 202, 203, 204,
,,  Pedigree of, 209
,,  Andrew, Lord, 82, 147
,,  Charles, 186
,,  George, 155
Wingfield, R., 198
Wingrove, David and Mary, 109, 132, 135, 185
,,  William, 186
Winselowe, Cutt, 258
Winson, William, 173
Winstowe, Ellis and Richard, 258
Winter, John, 159
Winterton, Earl of, 100
,,  Countess of, 121
Wise, Charles, 261
,,  Elizabeth, 131
Wiseman, John, 62
Withers, John, 250
,,  Richard, 110
Witherston, James, 186
Wix, John, 183
Wolket, John, 186
Wood, Richard, 181
,,  Adam at, 253
,,  Joan, 182
,,  Anthony, 94
,,  Thomas, 257
,,  Colderton, 229
,,  Ann, 131
,,  Family of, 182
,,  Alan, Abigail and Andrew, 41
Woodcock, Catherine, 242
Woodford, John, 147
,,  Sarah, 132
Woodgate, Robert, 302
Woodman, Henry, 285
Woodnes, Henry, 285
Woodnut, William, 292
Woodrofe, Timothy, 45, 112, 118
Woodward, George, 156, 216, 297
,,  John, 210, 218, 297
,,  Thomas, 236, 298
,,  Edward, 63, 64, 144, 157, 213
,,  Elizabeth, 300

Woodyat, William, 296
Woolrent, Reuben, 260
Woolley, John Paul, 185
Worcester, Earl of, 82
,,  Alice, 30
Wormer, Richard, 301
Worseley, Otwell, Ralph and Sir James, 205, 210
Worthington, James, 253
Wotton, Mr. 39
Wrastler, John and Mary, 258
Wrayt, Hester, 260
Wrench, Henry, 68, 219
Wright, Thomas and Ann, 100, 122, 132, 133
Wyat, Richard and Sarah, 184, 186
,,  Thomas, 167, 286
,,  John, 253
,,  Henry, 299
Wyche, Thomas and Agnes, 156, 232
Wycherley, Thomas, 299
,,  Alexander, 248
,,  John, 300
Wyckham, William de, 2
Wyeth, John and William, 174
Wylde, Diana, 236
Wylly, Sir Richard and Matilda, 14, 143
Wyllyams, John, 232, 297
Wymarke, Edward, 31
Wynch, Thomas, 248
,,  Mary, 132
,,  Robert, 299
Wyndham, John, 41
,,  Pedigree of, 7, 102
Wyndleshore, William, 294
Wyndsor, Sir William, Thomas and Sir Myles, 207
,,  Lord, 1
,,  Pedigree of, 208
,,  Sir Andrew, 297
Wynferthing, Richard de and Hugh de, 10, 143
Wynn, Sir Edwin, 139, 146, 147
,,  Sir W. W. 131
Wyot, Richard, 204, 231, 297
,,  John and Thomas, 155, 204, 231, 297
Wyrardesbyr, Ralph de, 143, 154
,,  Alexander, 143
Wyse, Robert le, 106
Wyselech, William and Thobinar de, 295
Wytton, John, 276, 297

Yeates, William, Elizabeth and Frances, 248
Yardley, Sir William and Amelia, 149, 228, 229
Yarway, Robert, 61
York, Edmund Duke of, 253
Young, Sir Charles George, 236
,,  Sir William, 148

FINIS.

PRINTED BY G. NORMAN, MAIDEN LANE, COVENT GARDEN, LONDON.

# ADDITIONS AND CORRECTIONS.

Page 7. In the pedigree after Thomas de Vere, eighth Earl of Oxford, who died 1371, add, his son Robert, ninth Earl, created Marquis of Dublin, 1386, and Duke of Ireland, ob. 1392, sp. And in page 278, the Duke of Ireland could secure personal safety only by abandoning his sword, gauntlets, and armour, and swimming the Isis. In the pursuit his Grace's chariot fell into the hands of his foes, and a discovery was made of letters from the King (Richard II.), requesting his presence in London, and that his Majesty would live or die for him.

The Duke was attainted by Parliament. He effected an escape to the Continent, and his end was accidental death whilst hunting a wild boar, at Louvaine, in Belgium, in 1392, sp. Like the Duke of Buckingham, temp. Car. II. who finished his sad end in 1687, at an obscure inn in Yorkshire, reduced to the utmost misery—even more famous for his vices than his misfortunes—so died Robert de Vere Duke of Ireland, in penury, his property having been confiscated, and his honours extinguished by attainder.

Page 21. Wife of William Pyncheon, who died 1592, was Rose, daught of Thomas Reading, of Pinner, Middlesex.

Page 38, line 20. 1549 for 1849.

Page 41. Helegonway was daughter of Lord Conway by his first wife.

Page 43. Ursula Brockett died 1649.

Page 66, lines 31-32. Styles should be Sills.

Page 69. John, second Duke of Montagu, son of Ralph, son of Edward, Lord Montagu, by Ann, daughter of Sir Ralph Winwood, whose son Richard Winwood bought the Manor of Ditton.

Page 85. Harcourt Powell married, 1760. See page 128.

Page 93, line 27. 1565 for 1665; and in line 37, 1564 for 1654.

Page 95. Children of Sir Dudley Carleton and Ann Lucy: Eliz. ux. Sir Giles Vanbrugh; Mary, ux. Edward Pearce; and Lucy, a daughter.

Page 96. Richard Topham died, 1729. His sister, Arabella, wife of Mr. Justice Reeve died, 1731. She was a benefactress to Windsor.

Page 98. See MSS. of the late Sir Thomas Barrett Lennard, Bart. for the family of Gille, collected by Thomas, 15th Lord Dacre. The arms of Gille—Chequé, A and G; the seal a griffin eating a lizard.

Gille of the Barony of Gille's Land, Cumberland, an aboriginal of Albion. Bueth Gille in possession when the Conqueror William drove him out to banishment, and gave his lands to Hubert, a follower. Gille Bueth, his son, claimed the lands, and was barbarously murdered by Robert, son of Hubert, who took the name of De Vaux-Vallis, which is a synonyme for Gille. To expiate this murder he founded Lanercost Abbey, in Cumberland. On a stone on the inside of the east wall of the Priory is inscribed—Robertus de Vallibus, filius Huberti Domini de Gilles-land—Fundator Prioratus de Lanercost, A.D. 1116.

From this Gille Bueth proceeded the Gilles of the North, branches of which descended to Lincolnshire, temp. King John, and Cambridgeshire, where they were found as householders 1278. From Richard Gille of Shelfordparva, 1278, descended John Gille and his brother Richard Gille, who appear in a fine about Buckland, Herts, in 1483. See pedigree. This family returned to Little Shelford, and the last piece of property was sold there in 1662 by Charles, grandson of Sir George Gyll, Knt. p. 64.

Page 153, line 1. 7—not 17 miles.

Page 205. In the pedigree of Whethill, Mary Elizabeth and Bridget are sisters of George Gyll, and not children of Robert Whethill, and in the same pedigree Sir David Owen should be natural son of Sir Owen Tudor, grandfather of King Henry VII.

Page 219, line 20. 1699 should be 1669.

Page 223. Martha Scawen married Edward Diccy, not Dicas.

Page 233. The public records do not exactly verify the pedigree of Peters. Some of the children were by the first marriage of William Peters. Sir Edmund Wheeler was son of Humphry Wheeler, of co. Worcester; and Richard Hanbury, of Datchet, goldsmith, by his second wife, was ancestor of Lord Sudeley, of Toddington, co. Gloucester.

Page 235, line 21. Afterwards this Manor of Berkyn was in the tenure of Essington, page 258-264.

Page 236. Thomas Wood, not Woodward.

14 DE 61

Lightning Source UK Ltd.
Milton Keynes UK
UKHW031815230419
341498UK00006B/637/P